Sport and Social Order: Contributions to the Sociology of Sport

Foreword

The nature of this work is perhaps best indicated by its subtitle, "Contributions to the Sociology of Sport." The volume is neither an anthology nor a general textbook. It is a handbook comprised of a set of original contributions. Thus the aim of this volume is not to reprint a collection of classic studies nor to outline the current state of sport sociology per se, but rather to examine critically in a sport context a number of significant problems raised and largely informed by several substantive areas of general sociology. A historical note about the origins of the series of which this volume is a part may further explain its purpose and scope.

My initial idea for the "Social Significance of Sport Series" was to develop a set of research monographs on substantive topics related to sport studies (i.e., the history, philosophy, psychology, and sociology of sport). It was my intent to recruit as authors young scholars who had just completed an original Ph.D. dissertation and ask them to prepare an advanced topic text based on the theoretical and methodological thrust of their doctoral work. Needless to say, when I conceived of this idea seven years ago, the specialty areas within physical education and the social sciences were not so developed as to justify such a specialized series.

Accordingly, attention was first turned to publishing a set of books which would serve as upper-level undergraduate texts for students taking coursework in the major areas of sport studies. To date, the following textbooks have been published in the Series: Harold J. VanderZwaag, *Toward a Philosophy of Sport* (1972); John F. Rooney, Jr., *A Geography of American Sport* (1974); John R. Betts, *America's Sporting Heritage: 1850–1950* (1974); Ellen W. Gerber, Jan Felshin, Pearl Berlin, and Waneen Wyrick, *The American Woman in Sport* (1974). While these books well serve the undergraduate population in sport studies, there has yet to appear a book designed for the graduate student population of any given area of sport studies.

Thus, the present volume is written to meet the needs of the increasing number of graduate students wishing to pursue in depth particular topics within the rapidly developing area known as the sociology of sport. The exponential growth of interest in the sociology of sport in the past two decades has created a need for a source book more focused than the general collection of readings and at the same time more advanced than the typical undergraduate textbook. This handbook attempts to fulfill this need through the combination of twelve contributed chapters. In essence, the majority of the chapters of this volume constitute either analytical reviews or micro-research monographs on substantive issues within sport sociology and thus suitably reflect the initial conception of the "Social Significance of Sport Series."

In view of the close correspondence between the content of this handbook and my initial idea for the Series, I felt compelled to serve as coeditor. However, Donald W. Ball in his capacity as senior editor provided equal guidance in the development of this volume.

Both of use were especially successful in soliciting the work of several young, outstanding social scientists actively engaged in the study of one or more of the social dimensions of sport. The several authors represent a balance of Americans and Canadians, physical educators and sociologists, theorists and empiricists (and for good measure, an Australian and an Englishman, and a geographer and a kinesiologist). In point of fact, most authors are hybrids of these bipolar dimensions as evidenced by their place of residence, location of their doctoral institution, joint academic appointments, journals of publication, and blend of theoretical and empirical emphases in their writing.

As there are relatively few individuals devoting the majority of their teaching and research to the sociology of sport, the emphasis in the development of this book was on the person rather than the problem. That is to say, the editors elected to select active workers in the field and give them a relatively free rein in the construction of their chapter, rather than to create a tight conceptual framework and restrict the contributors to a rigid table of contents. Thus each contributor was given a broad area of focus and a general page limit, and then left to develop matters in his own idiosyncratic manner.

On the one hand, it may be conceded that the preceding editorial procedures resulted in important omissions as not all areas within the sociology of sport are covered. Moreover, areas that are dealt with herein are not covered with equal thoroughness. On the other hand, the dozen contributions represent a good cross-section of current substantive concerns, reflect a variety of theoretical viewpoints, illustrate a range of methodological perspectives, and depict numerous research techniques. In short, although coverage is not complete, it strains toward the comprehensive.

In conclusion, I note that I once defined a sport sociologist as an individual who appears to be playing while working as he studies those who ostensibly work by playing. Although I am not anxious for readers of this handbook to accept my proffered definition of a sport sociologist, I do hope that most will readily grasp the notion that studying sport is often as much fun as playing sport and upon occasion just as serious as well.

Amherst, Massachusetts   John W. Loy
January 1975   *Consulting Editor*

John W. Loy

Birth Place: Dodge City, Kansas

Age: 36

Birth Order: One younger brother

Formal Education:

B.S., Lewis and Clark College, Oregon	1961
M.A., University of Iowa	1963
Ph.D., University of Wisconsin	1967

Present Position:

Professor, Departments of Sport Studies and Sociology, University of Massachusetts, Amherst

Professional Responsibilities:

Teaching lower- and upper-level undergraduate, and beginning and advanced graduate courses on the Sociology of Sport.

Scholarly Interests:

The study of sport and social differentiation, sport and formal organization; the construction of theories of agonetic behavior.

Professional Accomplishments:

Coeditor of *Sport, Culture and Society.* Coauthor of *Physical Education: An Interdisciplinary Approach.* Articles published in the *American Sociological Review, Black Sports, International Journal of Sport Psychology, International Review of Sport Sociology, Journal of Psychology,* and *Quest.*

Hobbies:

Collecting sporting books, prints, and stamps.

Sport Activities:

Avid but awkward racquetball and tennis player. Armchair football player and trackman.

Most Recent Books Read:

Jay Acton	*The Forgettables*
John LeCarré	*Tinker, Tailor, Soldier, Spy*
Lewis S. Feuer	*Einstein and the Generations of Science*
Clifford Geertz	*The Interpretation of Cultures*

Contents

Chapter 5   Sport and Politics   185
Brian M. Petrie

Chapter 6   Sport Consumption and the Economics of Consumerism   239
Barry D. McPherson

Chapter 7   Sport and Collective Violence   277
Michael D. Smith

PART III   THE OCCUPATIONAL ORGANIZATION OF SPORT

Chapter 8   Occupational Subcultures in the Work World of Sport   333
Alan G. Ingham

Part I
The Sociological
Analysis of Sport

Chapter 1
Sociology of Sport: an Overview

Eldon E. Snyder and Elmer Spreitzer
Department of Sociology
Bowling Green State University
(Bowling Green, Ohio)

Eldon E. Snyder

Birth Place: Anthony, Kansas

Age: 44

Birth Order: Oldest, two brothers, one sister

Formal Education:

A.B., Southwestern College, Winfield, Kansas	1952
M.S., Kansas University, Lawrence, Kansas	1956
Ed.D., Kansas University, Lawrence, Kansas	1962

Present Position:

Professor, Department of Sociology, Bowling Green State University

Professional Responsibilities:

Currently teaching courses in Introduction to Sociology, Sociology of Sport, Sociology of Education.

Scholarly Interests:

Sociology of sport, leisure–work, youth, socialization, aging.

Professional Accomplishments:

Coeditor of *Studies in Sociology.*

Articles published in more than 15 journals, some of which are: *Educational Leadership, International Journal of Sport Psychology, International Review of Sport Sociology, Journal of Gerontology, Journal of Marriage and Family, Journal of Secondary Education, Pacific Sociological Review, Physical Education, Rural Sociology, Sociology of Education, Sociological Quarterly, Sociology and Social Research, Youth and Society.*

Hobbies:

Gardening, traveling, reading.

Sport Activities:

Varsity tennis in college, former basketball official, competitive handball.

Most Recent Books Read:

Allen Ballard	*The Education of Black Folk*
Sam Keen and Anne Valley Fox	*Telling Your Story*
Keith W. Prichard and Thomas H. Buxton	*Concepts and Theories in Sociology of Education*

Elmer Spreitzer

Birth Place: Cleveland, Ohio

Age: 38

Birth Order: Youngest, three brothers, two sisters

Formal Education:

B.S., John Carroll University, Ohio	1962
M.A., Case Western Reserve University, Ohio	1964
Ph.D., Ohio State University	1968

Present Position:

Associate Professor of Sociology and Associate Dean of the Graduate School, Bowling Green State University

Professional Responsibilities:

Currently teaching courses in research methodology, statistics, and medical sociology.

Scholarly Interests:

Work and leisure, medical sociology, higher education.

Professional Accomplishments:

Articles published in *Journal of Rehabilitation, American Sociologist, Journal of Health and Social Behavior, Sociological Focus, Youth and Society, Sociology and Social Research, Pacific Sociological Review, Sociological Quarterly, Sociology of Education, Phylon, Journal of Marriage and the Family, Research Quarterly, Psychological Reports, Journal of Gerontology, International Journal of Sport Psychology, Journal of Leisure Behavior.*

Hobbies:

Gardening, travel.

Sport Activities:

Jogging, spectator at most any sport.

Most Recent Books Read:

David Halberstam	*The Best and the Brightest*
Michael Novak	*Ascent of the Mountain*
	Flight of the Dove

INTRODUCTION

Sport is a pervasive institution in our society, yet the sociology of sport is not a major specialty within the discipline of sociology. The present overview sketches some strengths and weaknesses in this subfield and its potential for generating and testing theoretical frameworks. The analysis includes research on sport from the following perspectives: inter-institutional relationships, social stratification, small groups, and social psychology. In recent years, the sociology of sport has become more sophisticated in terms of the research questions posed, research design, quantitative analysis, and cross-cultural comparisons. As one dimension of leisure, sports represents a serious topic for scholarly research to round out a comprehensive view of the human person as a social being.

Rationale

The sociology of sports has yet to become a widely practiced specialty within the discipline, and some might question whether it should ever become one. Given the proliferation of specializations within sociology, it might be asked to what end is such elaboration of descriptive content ordained? In other words, does a discipline grow by spinning off more and more content areas, or does it develop through the creation of paradigms that are generic in nature? The "hard" sciences did not develop by continually carving out new content areas; rather, they developed through the creation of theoretical frameworks that transcend specific content. Why, then, should we legitimate an area such as the sociology of sport by instituting journals and convention sessions on that topic, textbooks and courses, and state-of-the-field essays? We suggest that sport as a substantive topic has as much claim to the sociologist's attention as the more traditional specialties of the family, religion, political, and industrial sociology.

Sports and games are cultural universals and basic institutions in so-

From *The Sociology Quarterly*, Vol. 5, No. 4, Fall, 1974. Reprinted by permission.

cieties, albeit somewhat more epiphenomenal and "higher" in the super-structure than most other institutions. Basically, we argue that a sociologist studies sport for the same reasons as any other phenomenon—for intrinsic interest and to impose sociological frameworks as a means of constructing and refining concepts, propositions, and theories drawn from the larger discipline.[1] However, a scholar's claim on institutional and societal resources to pursue one's intrinsic interests does not carry much weight these days. Thus we suggest that the sociology of sport is of value to the larger discipline primarily in terms of its capacity to serve as a fertile testing ground for the generating and testing of theoretical frameworks.

Sport and Leisure

One might argue that the sociology of sport is a species of the sociology of leisure. Clearly, sport could be subsumed under leisure studies as simply another way in which people spend their discretionary time. Since both the sociology of leisure and sport focus on the noninstrumental facets of social life, they probably will merge eventually into a more generic specialization such as the sociology of expressive behavior. Presently, however, the two content specialties are very distinct in the sense of having their own associations, conventions, professional registers, journals, and sessions within the conventions of general sociology. Given the separate evolution of the two specialties of leisure and sport, the present analysis focuses solely on sport.[2]

The phenomenon of sport represents one of the most pervasive social institutions in the United States. Sports permeate all levels of social reality from the societal down to the social psychological levels. The salience of sport can be documented in terms of news coverage, financial expenditures, number of participants and spectators, hours consumed, and time samplings of conversations. Given the salience of sport as a social institution, a sociology of sport has emerged that attempts to go beyond the descriptive level by providing theoretically informed analyses and explanations of sports activity.

One might speculate as to why sport is a recent entry to the substantive specialties within sociology. If, in fact, sociology is a residual field that assimilates topics unclaimed by more established fields, why is it that sport (also, leisure and recreation) was not an early part of the sociological package? One answer to this question lies in the increased salience of these spheres as concomitants of economic development and affluence. Another explanation may be that sport previously was viewed as primarily physical, rather than social, interaction and thus devoid of sociological significance. Still another explanation may be that the world of sport is often perceived as illusionary, fantasy, and a sphere apart from the "real" world (Huizinga, 1955). Perhaps North Americans are uneasy with play and this ambivalence may explain the relative lack of interest in sport on the part of sociologists (Stone, 1971: 48). Similarly, Dunning (1967) argues that sociologists who have defined play and sport in terms of fantasy and who are thus ambivalent about seriously studying the topic, may be reflecting a Protestant Ethic orientation toward work and leisure. In fact, an element of snobbery is probably involved: "The serious analysis of popular sport is construed to be beneath the dignity of many academics" (Stone, 1971: 62). In response to such sentiments, Dunning (1971: 37) emphasizes that "sports and games are 'real' in the sense they are observable, whether directly through overt behavior of people or indirectly through the reports which players and spectators give of what they think and feel while playing and 'spectating.' " There is increasing realization that sport as an institution permeates and articulates with other institutions. Consequently, a substantial literature is developing in the sociology of sport, some of which is cumulative, and much of which goes beyond description toward explanation.[3] Disciplines other than sociology contribute to this literature; physical educators are particularly visible in this specialty. Moreover, some prominent physical educators researching in this area are, in effect, sociologists, either through formal or informal training.

DEFINITION OF SPORT

The meaning of sport, like time, is self-evident until one is asked to define it. There is little disagreement in classifying physical activities such as basketball, football, handball, tennis, and track as sports. Hunting, fishing, and camping are often considered sports, but do they contain the same elements as, say, football and basketball? Can mountain climbing, bridge, and poker be classified as sports? Edwards (1973) presents a typology to clarify the concepts of play, recreation, contest, game, and sport. He arrays these activities on a continuum in the order presented above with play and sport as the polar activities. As one moves from play toward sport the following occurs:

> Activity becomes less subject to individual prerogative, with spontaneity severely diminished.

> Formal rules and structural role and position relationships and responsibilities within the activity assume predominance.

> Separation from the rigors and pressures of daily life becomes less prevalent.

Individual liability and responsibility for the quality and character of his behavior during the course of the activity is heightened.

The relevance of the outcome of the activity and the individual's role in it extends to groups and collectivities that do not participate directly in the act.

Goals become diverse, complex, and more related to values emanating from outside of the context of the activity.

The activity consumes a greater proportion of the individual's time and attention due to the need for preparation and the degree of seriousness involved in the act.

The emphasis upon physical and mental extension beyond the limits of refreshment or interest in the act assumes increasing dominance.*

Loy (1968: 1) defines sport as "a game occurrence, as an institutionalized game, as a social institution and as a social situation or social system." Luschen (1967: 127; 1970: 6; 1972: 119) defines sport as an institutionalized type of competitive, physical activity located on a continuum between play and work. Sport contains intrinsic and extrinsic rewards; but the more it is rewarded extrinsically (including socially), the more it tends to become work in the sense of being instrumental rather than consummatory.

Attempts to define sport are admittedly imprecise. Sport may be defined in terms of the participants' motivation or by the nature of the activity itself. Sport is a playful activity for some participants, while others participate in the context of work or an occupation. Moreover, the boundaries of sport as an activity blend into the more general sphere of recreation and leisure. In the present paper, we shall not attempt to carve out any boundaries for the topic; rather, we delineate the specialty in operational terms of what sociologists actually do with the content of sport. We attempt to synthesize and interpret the work done in this area while organizing the literature in terms of the unit of analysis. We begin by analyzing sociological research concerning sport at the macro level.

SOCIETAL PERSPECTIVES

One research tradition within the sociology of sport focuses on the relationship between sport and the larger society. The analysis involves the

---

* Harry Edwards, *Sociology of Sport*. (Homeward, Illinois: Dorsey Press, 1973.) Reprinted by permission.

following basic questions (Luschen, 1970: 8): What is the nature of sport as a social institution, and how does it relate to other institutions? What is the structure and function of sport, and what social values does it promote?

Social Functions of Sports

This macro level of analysis is probably the most well-developed area in the sociology of sport. Sport as a microcosm of society is a *leitmotiv* that permeates much of the literature. Particular emphasis involves the social values, beliefs, and ideologies that are expressed and transmitted through the institutional configuration of sports. This theme is discussed by Boyle (1963) in *Sport: Mirror of American Life* which analyzes sport as a mirror of society involving elements of social life such as stratification, race relations, commerce, automotive design, clothing styles, concepts of law, language, and ethical values. In this context, a recent study by Snyder (1972*a*) classifies slogans placed in dressing rooms by high school coaches into motifs that are used to transmit beliefs, values, and norms to athletes. These slogans emphasize the development of qualities such as mental and physical fitness, aggressiveness, competitiveness, perseverance, self-discipline, and subordination of self to the group. Many of these characteristics are supported by values inherent in the Protestant Ethic. In this sense, sport is a "value receptacle" for dominant social values (Edwards, 1973: 355). Furthermore, cross-cultural data concerning sports and games show that they tend to be representative of a particular society's values and norms (Roberts and Sutton-Smith, 1962), as well as its structural arrangements (Ball, 1972*a*, 1974).

Numerous researchers have documented this interrelationship between sport and society by analyzing specific sports. Riesman and Denny (1954) describe how rugby changed to become the game of football that was congruent with the American ethos. Similarly, cultural themes in major league baseball reflect American values of specialization, division of labor, individual success, and the importance of teamwork (Voigt, 1971; Haerle, 1973 and Chapter 10 of this volume).

The prevalence of writing on the social functions of sport is found in several disciplines—sociology, history, philosophy, and physical education. Methodologically, this literature relies much on historical accounts, autobiographies, content analysis, and other qualitative techniques, although quantitative techniques are increasingly used (e.g. Loy and McElvogue, 1970). These studies explicitly or implicitly embrace the theoretical posture of functionalism. In this regard the study of sports provides ample evidence of pattern maintenance, tension management, integration, and systemic linkages with other social institutions.

Many observers have pointed to the safety-valve function that sport serves for society. On a structural level of analysis, a vulgar Marxism is sometimes invoked in viewing sports as an opiate and as producing unreality, mystification, and false consciousness (cf. Edwards, 1973, especially Chapters 4 and 8). Similarly, many scholars have commented on the psychodynamic function of sports. Gerth and Hills (1954: 63), for example, suggest that "Many mass audience situations, with their 'vicarious' enjoyments, serve psychologically the unintended function of channeling and releasing otherwise unplaceable emotions. Thus, great values of aggression are 'cathartically' released by crowds of spectators cheering their favorite stars of sport—and jeering the umpire."

Sport and Political Ideology

In related context several empirical studies have attempted to document political concomitants of participation in sports (see Petrie, Chapter 5 of this volume). For example, several surveys have found that athletes tend to be more conservative, conventional, and conformist than their nonathletic counterparts (Phillips and Schafer, 1970; Rehberg and Cohen, 1971; Schafer, 1971; and Scott, 1971). According to these observers, sport has a "conservatizing" effect on youth through its emphasis on hard work, persistence, diligence, and individual control over social mobility. Clearly, the transmission of societal values is an important function of schools anywhere. Schafer (1971) suggests, however, that the value mystique surrounding high school sports may be dysfunctional in the sense of producing conformist, authoritarian, cheerful robots who lack the autonomy and inner direction to accept innovation, contrasting value systems, and alternative life-styles. This provocative hypothesis is worthy of testing with a longitudinal design.

Although the above observations are intuitively persuasive, Petrie (1973) reports no significant political differences between athletes and nonathletes among Canadian college students in Ontario. Perhaps there are subcultural differences between the intercollegiate athletic programs in Canada and the United States that would account for his findings. Many questions in this area await further research. If sport promotes a conservative ideology, how pervasive is its influence, and what is the *process* by which it has this effect? Additionally, how much transfer effect is there into adult life, if any? And, if sport induces a particular type of politico-economic mentality, are the consequences primarily for athletes, or are other segments of the population likewise affected?

Sport and the Economy

Economic, commercial, and occupational facets of sport have also been analyzed (see McPherson, Chapter 6 of this volume). Furst (1971: 165) attributes the rise of commercialism in sports to the increasing number of people "with time, money, and energy to engage in and embrace the world of sports." Kenyon (1972) cites the changes in North American society toward mass consumption and professionalism as having ramifications within sport. The economic aspects of sport are evident in the conflicts in several cities over the securing of professional sports franchises and the location of new stadiums and arenas; this is because of the multiplier effect of restaurants, hotels, parking lots, theatres, bars, etc. The fact that general scheduling of television programs is partly determined by the timing of prominent sports events, and vice versa, bespeaks the economic salience of sports in the United States and Canada.

Sport and Religion

The articulation of sport with the religious institution is also of interest. As the ancient Olympic games were grand festivals with much religious and political significance, contemporary sports events can be seen as America's "civil religion" (Rogers, 1972: 393). Athletic events often open with prayer as well as the national anthem, teams frequently have a chaplain, and many teams have prayer sessions prior to the contest. In a survey of high school basketball coaches and players, Snyder (1972a: 91) found that the majority of the teams sampled invoke prayer before or during games. Football coaches generally welcome reinforcement from the religious sector. "Louisiana State University's coach . . . credits a [Billy] Graham campus crusade in the Fall of 1970 with helping his football team win a victory over Auburn University. Dallas Cowboy's head football coach. . . presided over a Billy Graham Crusade For Christ held on the Cowboy's home field, the Cotton Bowl, in 1971" (Edwards, 1973: 124). Rogers (1972: 394) suggests that "sports are rapidly becoming the dominant ritualistic expression of the reification of established religion in America." In this context, a number of writers have suggested that religion and sports interact to reinforce the status quo and to reaffirm the conventional wisdom.

Sport and the Schools

Similarly, the linkage between sport and the educational institution has been explored by sociologists. The United States and Canada differ from most nations in that amateur athletes are almost totally dominated by high schools and colleges; comparatively little is carried on in North America, especially the United States, under the aegis of clubs or governments. The incorporation of amateur athletics into educational institutions has had important consequences. As early as 1929 the Lynds noted the position of honor attributed to athletics and the low esteem accorded to academic pursuits in the high school status hierarchy of *Middletown*. Waller (1932) viewed the high school as a social organism and suggested that interscholastic athletics were justified because they promoted the competitive spirit, acted as a means of social control and system integration, and prepared students for adult life. The various sports themselves constitute status hierarchies in schools and colleges; generally there is more interest in football and basketball than all other sports and extracurricular activities combined (Hollingshead, 1949: 193; Gordon, 1957; Coleman, 1961). These studies provide quantitative and qualitative documentation of the value orientations among youth and the relative importance of sports in the spectrum of high school activities. A cumulative research tradition in the sociology of sport focuses on the academic, psychological, and social concomitants of participation in interscholastic athletics. The studies in this area are discussed below in the section on social psychological aspects.

Sport and Social Problems

It is interesting to note that although conflict has long been defined as an essential element of sport, a functional model is nevertheless inherent in most social scientific research on sport. In other words, the ways in which sport facilitates social integration and equilibrium have been of more interest than the social conflict over scarce resources in the world of sport. The paradox of viewing explicit, structured conflict in the world of sport through the lens of an equilibrium framework is indicative of a root orientation toward harmony that spilled over from the larger discipline. It is curious that contemporary research on sport is almost completely devoid of attention to current structural conflicts in the world of sport—exemption from anti-trust laws, interleague raiding of players, player drafts, the reserve clause, league expansions and mergers, strikes, and working conditions. That professional athletes themselves have not been unaware of economic antagonism in sport is evidenced by the players' ready reception of competing leagues, strikes, formation of players' associations (unions), and use of the judicial system for redress of economic grievances.

It is only in the last five years that the back regions and infrastructure of organized sports have been brought to light, and most of this writing appears in semi-popular outlets such as the *Intellectual Digest, Psychology Today,* and the *New York Times Sunday Magazine*. Serious observers in this tradition (Edwards, 1969, 1973; and Scott, 1971) argue that the youth movement of the late 1960s has had reverberations in the world of sport. Perceived injustices in the sports establishment have come under blistering attack. One segment of this "revolution" involves the black athlete and traces its roots to the civil rights movement. The threatened boycott of the XIX Olympiad and the clenched-fist demonstration by black sprinters from the United States on the victory stand exemplify this reaction. Another facet of the conflict trend centers around objections by athletes to the imposition of a monolithic life-style by their coaches and managers (short hair, clean shaven, etc.). More recently, women's liberation has appeared in the world of sports. Women seek more equitable distribution of the resources and rewards, as well as emancipation from arbitrary sex role definitions regarding appropriate physical activities.

In sum, we argue that sport contains many of the sources of conflict inherent in the larger society. The contours of conflict in the world of sport are evident in bold relief as compared to the veiled manipulation of power in society at large. Therefore, the arena of sports represents a potentially rich area for the testing of generic theoretic frameworks concerning conflict:

> It seems not unreasonable to suggest that football and other, similar sports can serve as a kind of 'natural laboratory' for studying the dynamics of group conflicts in a more detached manner than has often proved possible in the past with respect, for example, to the study of union-management conflict, class, international and other types of groups conflicts where the strength of the involvements on one side or the other has acted as a hindrance to the achievement of full objectivity (Dunning, 1971: 43).

STRATIFICATION ASPECTS

When one considers the pervasiveness of social stratification, it is not surprising that processes of social differentiation operate within the world of sport (see Gruneau, Chapter 4 of this volume). As early as the turn of the century, social scientists noted the patterning of leisure behavior along social class lines. Veblen (1899) suggested that a new era was emerging in which leisure for the few was yielding to leisure for the masses. Sports as a species of leisure is no exception to the pattern of differential participation across class lines.

Luschen (1969), for example, found a positive relationship between socioeconomic status and sports involvement in Germany. Differences by class have also been reported in the preference, meaning, and salience of sports (Stone, 1969; Luschen, 1972). However, when Kenyon (1966) studied patterns of indirect and direct involvement in sports among adults in Wisconsin, he found no consistent relationship between social status and the degree of sports participation. Burdge (1966) analyzed involvement in sports according to level of occupation; he found that both active participation and spectatorship were more common at the higher occupational levels.

Although the above research documents the expected variations in sports activities by social class, recent research indicates additional complexity. Thus, recent data collected in the Midwest using a refined measure of sports involvement found a positive relationship between socioeconomic status and *cognitive* involvement (knowledge about sports), but no consistent relationship was observed on the *behavioral* and *affective* (meaning of sport) dimensions of involvement (Snyder and Spreitzer, 1973a). This study suggests that sports involvement tends to cut across social categories. Sport is so much a part of the cultural air (through mass media and conversation) that one cannot be totally insulated from its influence.

Sport and Social Mobility

Within the sociology of sport, athletic achievement is frequently cited as an avenue for social mobility, particularly for minority groups, and there is a sufficient number of superstar celebrities to sustain this perception. Clearly, such cases are a tiny fraction of professional athletes; however, there are other ways in which sport can facilitate social mobility. Loy (1969) suggests that participation in athletics can stimulate higher levels of educational aspirations in order to extend one's athletic career, and, thus, indirectly result in higher educational achievement and the acquisition of secular skills that are functional in the nonathletic sphere. Young people who excel in athletics frequently receive educational and occupational sponsorship by influential persons which gives them leverage in the larger world. In this connection, a recent study shows that high school athletes rank their coach second only to parents in terms of influencing their educational and occupational plans (Snyder, 1972b). Moreover, coaches often gratuitously advise their players on educational and occupational matters. In addition, ever since the English gentleman proclaimed that the Battle of Waterloo was won on the playing field of Eton, it has been argued that participation in sports generates character traits which transfer to other areas of life. (There is limited evidence for this contention; we shall analyze the pertinent studies below in the section on social psychological aspects of sport.)

There are contrasting research findings to those above which suggest, however, that sport may also have a negative effect on the social mobility of participants. Spady (1970) interprets his findings as showing that athletic involvement is sometimes counterproductive in the sense of raising educational aspirations without providing the necessary cognitive skills for educational achievement. With respect to blacks, sports may function as a magnet attracting youth to one specialized channel of mobility which tends to cut down the number of other mobility options perceived as available. Edwards (1973: 201–202) argues that the success of black athletes tends to have the boomerang effect of attracting black youth away from other avenues for mobility. Of course, the actual number of individuals of any race who achieve eminence in sports is very small.[4]

Most of the literature concerning sports and social mobility is conjectural, anecdotal, or at best descriptive. It is an area ripe for systematic research particularly with longitudinal designs. The studies cited herein are based on cross-sectional data, and thus the inferences drawn are tentative and exploratory. Recently some interesting research has emerged concerning the career patterns and mobility processes of athletic coaches (Loy and Sage, 1972; Snyder, 1972c). This line of research contributes to the literature on the sociology of occupations (see Part III of this volume).

Sport and Race

Sociologists have focused considerable attention on race as a dimension of stratification within sport. Since coaches are likely to recruit and play the most capable athletes regardless of race in order to enhance their own reputation as successful (winning) coaches, sport is often seen as a sphere of pure achievement and racial integration. Several studies question this assumption. Rosenblatt (1967) analyzed the batting averages of baseball players from 1953 to 1965 and concluded that discrimination is not directed at the superior black player; rather, he saw discrimination being directed at black players of the journeyman level. Pascal and Rapping (1970) extended this line of research and concluded that black pitchers must be superior to white pitchers in order to play in the big leagues. Yetman and Eitzen (1971, 1972) reached a similar conclusion from their findings that black players are disproportionately distributed in starting (star) roles. Johnson and Marple (1973) provide evidence to suggest that journeyman black players are dropped from professional basketball faster than comparable whites, a fact that would have serious economic consequences; this is because pension plans are based on number of years played.

There are several explanations for the apparent discrimination against medium-grade black players. One interpretation is that some coaches are prejudiced against blacks, but they must recruit the best minority players to remain competitive; yet they informally use a quota system to limit the number of blacks on the team. Thus, black players are more likely to be on the starting team (Yetman and Eitzen, 1972). Brower (1973: 27) reports two reasons cited by owners of professional football teams for preferring white players: ". . . white players are desirable because white fans identify with them more readily than blacks, and most paying customers are white"; and "there are fewer problems with whites since blacks today have chips on their shoulders."

Another form of apparent discrimination in sports involves the practice of "stacking," by which black athletes are assigned only to certain positions on the team and excluded from others (Edwards, 1973: 205). In an interesting, theoretically informed study based on propositions derived from Grusky's (1963a: 346) theory of the structure of formal organizations and Blalock's (1962) theory of occupational discrimination, Loy and McElvogue (1970: 7) hypothesized: "There will be less discrimination where performance of independent tasks are largely involved, because such do not have to be coordinated with the activities of other persons, and therefore do not hinder the performance of others, nor require a great deal of skill in interpersonal relations." Loy and McElvogue found support in the data for their hypothesis that blacks are less likely to occupy central positions on professional baseball and football teams. Extending the Loy and McElvogue model to Canadian professional football, Ball (1973) showed its applicability in that context as well. However, an alternative model based upon task-importance was shown to be a more powerful predictor of "stacking" by nationality, i.e., American as contrasted to Canadian players.

The above studies are interesting contributions to the sociology of minority group relations. The work by Loy and McElvogue (1970) in this area is noteworthy since it synthesizes two theoretical frameworks from the larger discipline—Grusky's (1963a) propositions on the formal structure of organizations and Blalock's (1962) propositions on racial discrimination. Such research efforts illustrate fruitful reciprocity between the sociology of sport and the larger discipline.

Sport and the Sexes

Current research also focuses on discrimination in sport with respect to females. A woman actively involved in sports is likely to have her "femininity" called into question (Harris, 1973: 15). Traditional sex role definitions either do not legitimate athletic pursuits for females or they narrowly define the range of appropriate physical activities (Griffin, 1973; Harris, 1971, 1973; Hart, 1972). In this regard, women are clearly at a disadvantage in terms of opportunities and resources available for physical expression of the self in the form of sport.

Metheny (1965) has traced the historical antecedents of the feminine image and the degree of acceptance for females in competitive sports. It is generally considered inappropriate for women to engage in sports where there is bodily contact, throwing of heavy objects, aggressive face-to-face competition, and long distance running or jumping.

A recent survey study by the authors of this chapter asked respondents: "In your opinion, would participation in any of the following sports enhance a woman's feminine qualities?" The frequency distribution of affirmative responses was as follows: swimming, 67 percent; tennis, 57 percent; gymnastics, 54 percent; softball, 14 percent; basketball, 14 percent; and track and field, 13 percent.[5] The impression of the women's liberation movement on female involvement in sport represents a topic for additional research. It is a research topic that can feed back to the larger discipline in areas such as socialization, sex roles, and social movements.

SMALL GROUP PERSPECTIVES

The sociology of sport is a natural testing ground for theoretical frameworks in areas such as small group processes, collective behavior, personal influence, leadership, morale, and socialization. In sport the roles are clearly defined; performance measures are comparatively straightforward; and the contamination involved with artificiality and obtrusiveness of the investigator is less problematic than most areas of sociological research. Nevertheless, the sociology of sport includes relatively few experimental or even field studies. Sport teams represent an *in vivo* laboratory for the study of communication networks, cooperation, competition, conflict, division of labor, leadership, prestige, cohesion, and other structural properties of small groups.

Several small group studies have focused on the effect of interpersonal relations among team members on team performance. One of the first studies in this area (Fiedler, 1954) analyzed the relationship between team effectiveness and the personal perceptions that team members have of one another. His findings suggest that winning teams are characterized by players who prefer to relate to one another in a task-oriented manner as contrasted with affective relations. Klein and Christiansen (1969), on the other hand, found a positive relationship between cohesiveness (interpersonal attractiveness) and performance of basketball teams. Their study also suggests that focused leadership (consensus concerning the peer leader) is conducive to team success. Heinicke and Bales (1953) likewise found an association between focused leadership and achieving task-oriented group goals. In a recent study, Eitzen (1973) found that homogeneity in background characteristics of team members was positively related to team success. The relationship was interpreted in terms of heterogeneity increasing the likelihood of cliques within the team which reduce cohesion and ultimately cause poor team performance.

Other studies, however, fail to replicate the findings of a relationship between cohesion and team success (Fiedler, 1960; Lenk, 1969; Martens and Peterson, 1971). Nevertheless, these studies indicate the fruitfulness of research on sport teams using small group theoretical frameworks. The ambiguity of the findings shows the need for additional research to clarify our understanding of team structural characteristics, cohesiveness, and conflict according to the type of sport. For example, the role relations among a rowing crew (Lenk, 1969) require a synchronization of effort with each member performing a similar task, whereas most team sports involve individualization, specialization, and division of labor. Clearly, the dependent variable of team success is a practical measure and approaches an applied market research orientation. However, we suggest that theoretically informed propositions that are derived from this type of research ultimately are generalizable to intergroup relations in general.

The utility of a sport context to test sociological propositions is illustrated in a further extension of Grusky's (1963a) concept of organizational centrality to the study of professional baseball team managers. Grusky analyzed differential recruitment of baseball players into managerial positions in terms of the centrality of the player's position. He found support for the hypothesis that centrality of position (i.e., infielders, catcher) is associated with higher rates of recruitment into managerial positions. Loy and Sage (1968) extended the centrality framework to explain the emergence of informal leaders on baseball teams. They found support for Grusky's hypothesis: infielders and catchers were more likely to be chosen as team captains, best liked, and perceived as highly valuable members of the team.

Grusky (1963b) also studied managerial succession (firing the manager) and team performance in major league baseball. He found that changing managers was negatively associated with team performance; however, he rejected the intuitive notion that managers are fired because of the team's poor performance. Rather, he suggested that the causal direction is two-way since managerial succession can also produce poor team performance. In a stimulating exchange, Gamson and Scotch (1964: 70) argue that "the effect of the field manager on team performance is relatively unimportant." They suggest that Grusky's findings should be interpreted in terms of ritual scapegoating. Grusky's (1964) response included a specification of the relationship in terms of "inside" successors to the managerial position being less disruptive than "outside" successors (cf., Gouldner, 1954). Eitzen and Yetman (1971) also used Grusky's propositions concerning managerial succession in their study of coaching changes and performance of college basketball teams. They found support for Grusky's hypothesis, but basically concluded that in the long run teams with poor performance records are likely to improve their records with or without a coaching change.

SOCIAL PSYCHOLOGICAL ASPECTS

When viewed from the standpoint of a collectivity, socialization refers to the process of transmitting social values and norms to the individual members. Viewed from the perspective of the individual, socialization refers to the resulting changes that occur within the individual. Numerous observers have pointed to the potential of sport as an agency for socialization.[6] The theoretical rationale for examining socialization within the world of sport is implicit in the classic works of symbolic interaction (Cooley, 1922; Mead, 1934) where play and games are analyzed as models of, as well as part of, the socialization process. More recently, psychologists have analyzed games and sport in the context of socialization (Piaget, 1962; Erickson, 1965; and Sutton-Smith, 1971). Ingham, Loy, and Berryman (1973: 243) observe that "the processes involved in the social construction of life-worlds are also in evidence in the social construction of play-worlds. Similarly, the processes by which we come to know the life-world are the processes by which we come to know the play-world."

Sport and Socialization

Basically, it is suggested that the athlete undergoes a socialization process when interacting with coaches and fellow athletes in the subculture of sport (Phillips and Schafer, 1970; Ingham, Chapter 8 of this volume). If this line of reasoning is extended, one would expect the potency of the socialization process to vary according to the individual's degree of involvement in sport. Kenyon (1969) provides a theoretical discussion of this process, and Snyder (1972b) provides empirical support for the hypothesis of differential consequences according to degree of sport involvement. In the latter study, interestingly, the interaction patterns between the coach and outstanding athletes were markedly different from the coach's relations with marginal players.

Kenyon (1969: 81) proposes that the socialization consequences of sports involvement be considered from a temporal perspective—particularly in terms of the stages of becoming involved, being involved, and becoming uninvolved. He suggests that research from this perspective could be informed by role theory and reference group frameworks. An intriguing study would be to trace the social psychological dynamics that trigger changes in the individual's progression from one stage of involvement to another.[7] In a similar vein, Page (1969: 20) suggests the possibility of an identity crisis emerging after a successful athlete has completed his/her active playing days. A study of prominent soccer players in Yugoslavia reveals some negative psychological concomitants of the players' disengagement from athletic careers (Mihovilovic, 1968). The study indicates the importance of gradual withdrawal from the active role, especially when the athletic role is the individual's major identity anchor. Taking on the role of coach, referee, or similar official has been one way in which the transition process is softened for former athletes (Snyder, 1972d).

Sport and Personality

Perhaps the topic that has received the most cumulative, quantitative research in the sociology of sport concerns the social psychological consequences of active participation in athletics by youth. A series of studies focus on the question of whether athletes differ from nonathletes on personality dimensions such as extraversion, conformity, conventionality, aspirations, conservatism and rigidity (Schendel, 1965; Schafer and Armer, 1968; Phillips and Schafer, 1970). Several recent studies report a positive relationship between participation in interscholastic athletics and academic performance and aspirations among high school boys (for review, see Spreitzer and Pugh, 1973). Rehberg and Schafer (1968) report that participation in sports has the most effect on boys least disposed to attend college by raising their educational expectations to attend college. We alluded above to the possible two-edged sword effect of sports serving as a channel for mobility while also raising levels of aspiration without providing the instrumental skills (Spady, 1970). Similar studies on college level athletes yield inconsistent findings (Pilapil et al., 1970; Sage, 1967; and Spady, 1970). Additional research at the college level would seem indicated.

A relatively unexplored area is the social psychology of consciousness states, intrinsic satisfactions, body perceptions, and affective concomitants of sport. Some journalistic reports argue that commercialized sports desensitize, exploit, and manipulate players to achieve the ultimate goal of winning and profits (Meggyesy, 1971; Hoch, 1972; Shaw, 1972). On the other hand, several studies point to positive affective consequences of sport involvement (Layman, 1968, 1972). There is empirical evidence to suggest, for example, that sports participation is associated with life satisfaction (Washburne, 1941; Snyder and Spreitzer, 1973b). This finding is consistent with many studies documenting a positive relationship between social participation and psychological well-being (Wilson, 1967). Further explanation may rest with the intrinsic satisfaction that flows from involvement in sport. Dunning (1967: 148) reasons that sport participation generates a "tension-excitement" that forms a pleasurable contrast to routinized aspects of everyday life (also see Ball, 1972b).

A pertinent study by Snyder and Kivlin (1974) studied the self-perceptions of outstanding female athletes with the expectation that female athletes would evince low scores on measures of psychological well-being and body image on the basis of role conflict. The findings did not support the hypothesis, and the authors concluded that the intrinsic satisfaction flowing from sports participation tended to counteract any negative impact from sex role stereotyping. Additional research is needed on this topic.

The "athletic revolution" described above involves protests against authoritarian practices within sport, particularly among coaches (Scott, 1971). A popular explanation is that the coaching profession either attracts persons with an authoritarian personality or, alternatively, coaches are socialized into this personality type. This explanation ignores the structural interpretation of authoritarian behavior developed in recent years.[8] In the latter context, Edwards (1973) reasons that the coach is *fully responsible* for the team's victories and defeats; yet he has *limited control* in determining the outcomes. Under these circumstances, then, Edwards (1973: 139) points out that coaches insist upon "running a tight ship" and, consequently, a democratic leadership style would not enable the coach to maintain compliance under the tense conditions of a match where unquestioning obedience is required. Edwards' analysis of the coach's role argues that the authoritarian aspects of coaching behavior are structurally induced. Although the behavior of athletic coaches is not a particularly significant problem, it is a context in which the interpenetration of social structure and the personality is readily apparent.

CONCLUSION

Basically we have argued that sport is a social institution which interfaces with, and reflects, many dimensions of social life. Despite the pervasiveness of sport in society, the sociological study of sport is still not completely legitimated within the larger discipline. We suggest that research in this area will enter the mainstream when it reaches the level of theoretical and methodological self-consciousness characteristic of the better works in the larger discipline. In other words, it is vain to argue in the abstract that the world of sport is worthy of social scientific study. A more fruitful approach to legitimacy for a new specialty is simply for the practitioners in that area to produce research that will be interesting to social scientists at large. Research that is of interest only to persons who are already intrinsically interested in sports will necessarily be of dubious value from a social scientific perspective.

In analyzing the sociology of sport, we were struck by the "loyalty" of the scholars in this area. That is, many of the researchers in the specialty publish regularly in the area over the years. This is apparent because of the fact that most of the literature in this specialty is contained in comparatively few outlets. Moreover, judging from the congregation of the scholars in the sociology of sport at conventions, there is a strong affinity among social scientists in this specialty. There is always a danger that a given specialty will become too insulated from the larger discipline; this is particularly a problem with the sociology of sport because of the multidisciplinary composition of the specialty.

Our argument is based on the assumption that a strong identification with, and immersion in, the larger discipline is necessary to keep the taproot of the sociological imagination alive. The most enduring contributions to the sociology of sport are likely to come from research efforts informed by intellectual concerns derived from the larger discipline.

We venture to predict that the field will continue to be strengthened by increased theoretical and methodological sophistication. The present state of development reveals less barefooted empiricism and more theoretically informed hypothesis testing. The research designs and interpretations of data show increasing sensitivity to alternative explanations and spurious relationships.[9] We observe a greater use of multivariate statistical techniques, but, most importantly, the sociological imagination is increasingly evident by research that is going beyond the surface manifestations of sport to pose generic theoretical questions stemming from the larger discipline. Consequently, we conclude that the sociology of sport is shedding its *lumpen* heritage and is gaining respectability. Sociologists in general can look forward to some interesting contributions from this fledgling subfield in the years to come.

NOTES

1. The term sociology of sport is simply a shorthand expression referring to "social scientific research in the area of sports."

2. For an overview of the sociology of leisure as an academic specialty, see Rolf Meyerson, "The Sociology of Leisure in the United States: Introduction and Bibliography, 1945–1965." *Journal of Leisure Research*, **1** (Winter): 53–68.

3. See Luschen (1968) for an extensive bibliography on the sociology of sports.

4. A newsletter dated June 21, 1973 from the U.S. Department of Labor reports "that about 400,000 young men played on high school baseball teams in 1970, another 25,000 were on college teams, and about 3,000 were in the minor leagues. However, only about 100 rookies made the 24 squads in the major leagues that year."

5. See Snyder and Spreitzer (1973a) for a description of the research procedures of this survey.

6. It is interesting to observe in this context that totalitarian governments invariably place a high priority on sport activities for youth.

7. Arthur Miller (1958) poignantly illustrates this type of process in his literary masterpiece, *Death of a Salesman* (1958).

8. See Killian (1952), Lohman and Reitzes (1952), Kohn and Williams (1956), Reitzes (1959), and Yinger (1965).

9. Parenthetically, we have found that research from the sociology of sport, particularly the analysis of the commonly held assumptions, are helpful and vivid aids in *teaching* general sociology and research methodology courses.

REFERENCES

Ball, Donald W.
1972a "The Scaling of Gaming: Skill, Strategy, and Chance." *Pacific Sociological Review*, **15** (July): 273–294.
1972b "What The Action Is: A Cross-Cultural Approach." *Journal for the Theory of Social Behavior*, **2** (October): 122–143.
1973 "Ascription and Position: A Comparative Analysis of 'Stacking' in Professional Football." *Canadian Review of Sociology and Anthropology*, **10** (May): 97–113.
1974 "Control *versus* Complexity: Continuities in the Scaling of Gaming." *Pacific Sociological Review*, **17** (April): 167–184.

Blalock, H.
1962 "Occupational Discrimination: Some Theoretical Propositions." *Social Problems*, **9** (Winter): 240–247.

Boyle, R.
1963 *Sport: Mirror of American Life.* Boston: Little, Brown.

Brower, J.
1973 "Whitey's Sport." *Human Behavior*, **2** (November): 22–27.

Burdge, R.
1966 "Levels of Occupational Prestige and Leisure Activity." *Journal of Leisure Research*, **1** (Summer): 262–274.

Coleman, J.
1961 *The Adolescent Society.* New York: Free Press.

Cooley, C.
1922   *Human Nature and the Social Order.* New York: Scribner's.

Dunning, Eric
1967   "Notes on Some Conceptual and Theoretical Problems in the Sociology of Sports." *International Review of Sport Sociology,* **2**: 143–153.

1971   "Some Conceptual Dilemmas in the Sociology of Sport." In *Magglinger Symposium, Sociology of Sport,* pp. 34–37. Basel, Switzerland: Birkhauser Verlag.

Edwards, Harry
1969   *The Revolt of the Black Athlete.* New York: The Free Press.

1973   *Sociology of Sport.* Homewood, Illinois: Dorsey Press.

Eitzen, S.
1973   "The Effect of Group Structure on the Success of Athletic Teams." *International Review of Sport Sociology,* **8**: 7–17.

Eitzen, S., and N. Yetman
1971   "Managerial Change and Organizational Effectiveness." Paper presented at the Ohio Valley Sociological Society, Cleveland, Ohio.

Erickson, E.
1965   *Childhood and Society.* New York: W. W. Norton Company.

Fiedler, Fred
1954   "Assumed Similarity Measures As Predictors of Team Effectiveness." *Journal of Abnormal Social Psychology,* **49** (July): 381–388.

1960   "The Leader's Psychological Distance and Group Effectiveness." In *Group Dynamics,* D. Cartwright and D. Zander (eds.), pp. 526–606. Evanston: Northwestern.

Furst, R. T.
1971   "Social Change and the Commercialization of Professional Sports." *International Review of Sport Sociology,* **6**: 153–173.

Gamson, W., and N. Scotch
1964   "Scapegoating in Baseball." *American Journal of Sociology,* **70** (July): 69–72.

Gerth, H., and C. W. Mills
1954   *Character and Social Structure.* New York: Harcourt, Brace and World.

Gordon, C.
1957   *The Social System of the High School.* New York: The Free Press.

Gouldner, A.
1954   *Patterns of Industrial Bureaucracy.* Glencoe, Illinois: The Free Press.

Griffin, P.
1973   "What's A Nice Girl Like You Doing in a Profession Like This?" *Quest,* **19** (January): 96–101.

Grusky, O.
1963a "The Effects of Formal Structure on Managerial Recruitment: A Study of Baseball Organization." *Sociometry,* **26** (September): 345–353.

1963*b* "Managerial Succession and Organizational Effectiveness." *American Journal of Sociology,* **69** (July): 21–31.

1964 "Reply to Gamson and Scotch." *American Journal of Sociology,* **70** (July): 72–76.

Haerle, R.

1973 "Heroes, Success Themes, and Basic Cultural Values in Baseball Autobiographies: 1900–1970." Paper presented at the Third National Meeting of the Popular Culture Association, Indianapolis, Indiana.

Harris, D.

1971 "The Sportswoman in Our Society." In *Women in Sports,* D. Harris (ed.), pp. 1–4. Washington, D. C.: American Association for Health and Physical Education, and Recreation.

1973 "Dimensions of Physical Activity." In *Women and Sport: A National Research Conference,* D. Harris (ed.), pp. 3–15. University Park: The Pennsylvania State University.

Hart, M. Marie

1972 "On Being Female in Sport." In *Sport in the Socio-Cultural Process,* M. Hart (ed.), pp. 291–302. Dubuque, Iowa: Wm. C. Brown, Company.

Heinicke, C., and R. Bales

1953 "Developmental Trends in the Structure of Groups." *Sociometry,* **16** (February): 7–38.

Hoch, P.

1972 *Rip Off The Big Game.* Garden City, New York: Doubleday and Company.

Hollingshead, A.

1949 *Elmtown's Youth.* New York: John Wiley and Sons.

Huizinga, J.

1955 *Homo Ludens: A Study of the Play Element in Culture.* Boston: Beacon Press.

Ingham, A., J. Loy, and J. Berryman

1973 "Socialization, Dialects, and Sport." In *Women and Sport: A National Research Conference,* D. Harris (ed.), pp. 235–276. University Park: The Pennsylvania State University.

Johnson, N., and D. Marple

1973 "Racial Discrimination in Professional Basketball: An Empirical Test." Paper presented at the North Central Sociological Association Meetings, Cincinnati, Ohio.

Kenyon, Gerald S.

1966 "The Significance of Physical Activity as a Function of Age, Sex, Education, and Socio-Economic Status of Northern United States Adults." *International Review of Sport Sociology,* **1**: 41–57.

1969 "Sport Involvement: A Conceptual Go and Some Consequences Thereof." In *Aspects of Contemporary Sport Sociology,* G. S. Kenyon (ed.), pp. 77–87. Chicago: The Athletic Institute.

1972 "Sport and Society: At Odds or in Concert." In *Athletics in America*, A. Flath (ed.), pp. 33–41. Corvallis, Oregon: Oregon State University Press.

Killian, L.
1952 "The Effects of Southern White Workers on Race Relations in Northern Plants." *American Sociological Review*, **17** (June): 327–331.

Klein, Michael, and G. Christiansen
1969 "Group Composition, Group Structure, and Group Effectiveness of Basketball Teams. In *Sport, Culture and Society*, John W. Loy, Jr. and Gerald S. Kenyon (eds.), pp. 397–408. London: Macmillan Company.

Kohn, M., and R. Williams, Jr.
1956 "Situational Patterning in Intergroup Relations." *American Sociological Review*, **21** (April): 164–174.

Layman, E.
1968 "The Role of Play and Sport in Healthy Emotional Development: A Reappraisal." In *Contemporary Psychology of Sport: Proceedings of the Second International Congress of Sport Psychology*, G. S. Kenyon and T. M. Grogg (eds.), pp. 249–257. Chicago: The Athletic Institute.
1972 "The Contribution of Play and Sports to Emotional Health." In *Psychological Aspects of Physical Education and Sport*, J. E. Kane (ed.), pp. 163–185. London: Routledge and Kegan Paul.

Lenk, Hans
1969 "Top Performance Despite Internal Conflict: An Antithesis to a Functional Proposition." In *Sport, Culture and Society*, John W. Loy, Jr. and Gerald S. Kenyon (eds.), pp. 392–397. London: Macmillan Company.

Lohman, J., and D. Reitzes
1952 "Note on Race Relations in Mass Society." *The American Journal of Sociology*, **53** (November): 240–246.

Loy, J.
1968 "The Nature of Sport: A Definitional Effort." *Quest*, **10** (May): 1–15.
1969 "The Study of Sport and Social Mobility." In *Aspects of Contemporary Sport Sociology*, G. S. Kenyon (ed.), pp. 101–119. Chicago: The Athletic Institute.

Loy, J., and J. McElvogue
1970 "Racial Segregation in American Sport." *International Review of Sport Sociology*, **5**: 5–24.

Loy, J., and J. Sage
1968 "The Effects of Formal Structure on Organizational Leadership: An Investigation of Interscholastic Baseball Teams." Paper presented at Second International Congress of Sport Psychology, Washington, D. C.
1972 "Social Origins, Academic Achievement, Athletic Achievement, and Career Mobility Patterns of College Coaches." Paper presented at the American Sociological Association, New Orleans, Louisiana.

Luschen, G.
1967 "The Interdependence of Sport and Culture." *International Review of Sport Sociology,* **2**: 127–141.
1968 *The Sociology of Sport.* Paris: Mouton and Company.
1969 "Social Stratification and Social Mobility Among Young Sportsmen." In *Sport, Culture and Society,* John W. Loy, Jr. and Gerald S. Kenyon (eds.), pp. 258–276. London: Macmillan Company.
1970 "Sociology of Sport and the Cross-Cultural Analysis of Sport and Games." In *The Cross-Cultural Analysis of Sport and Games,* Gunther Luschen (ed.), pp. 6–13. Champaign, Illinois: Stipes Publishing Company.
1972 "On Sociology of Sport—General Orientation and Its Trends in the Literature." In *The Scientific View of Sport,* Ommo Grupe et al. (eds.), pp. 119–154. Heidelberg: Springer-Verlag Berlin.

Lynd, R., and Helen Lynd
1929 *Middletown.* New York: Harcourt, Brace and Company.

Martens, Rainer, and J. A. Peterson
1971 "Group Cohesiveness as a Determinant of Success and Member Satisfaction in Team Performance." *International Review of Sport Sociology,* **6**: 49–61.

Mead, G.
1934 *Mind, Self, and Society.* Chicago: University of Chicago Press.

Meggyesy, D.
1971 *Out of Their League.* New York: Paperback Library.

Metheny, Eleanor
1965 "Symbolic Forms of Movement: The Female Image in Sports." In *Connotations of Movement in Sport and Dance,* E. Metheny (ed.), pp. 43–56. Dubuque, Iowa: Wm. C. Brown Company.

Meyersohn, Rolf
1969 "The Sociology of Leisure in the United States: Introduction and Bibliography, 1945–1965." *Journal of Leisure Research,* **1** (Winter): 53–68.

Mihovilovic, M.
1968 "The Status of Former Sportsmen." *International Review of Sport Sociology,* **3**: 73–96.

Miller, Arthur
1958 *Death of a Salesman.* New York: Viking Press.

Page, Charles
1969 "Symposium Summary, with Reflections upon the Sociology of Sport as a Research Field." In *Aspects of Contemporary Sport Sociology,* G. S. Kenyon (ed.), pp. 189–202. Chicago: The Athletic Institute.

Pascal, A., and L. Rapping
1970 *Racial Discrimination in Organized Baseball.* Santa Monica, California: Rand Corporation.

Petrie, B.
1973   "The Political Attitudes of Canadian University Students: A Comparison
        Between Athletes and Nonathletes." Paper presented at the National Con-
        vention of the American Association of Health, Physical Education, and
        Recreation, Minneapolis, Minnesota.

Phillips, John C., and W. E. Schafer
1970   "The Athletic Subculture: A Preliminary Study." Paper presented at the
        American Sociological Association.

Piaget, J.
1962   *Play, Dreams and Imitation in Childhood.* New York: W. W. Norton
        Company.

Pilapil, B., J. Stecklein, and H. Liu
1970   *Intercollegiate Athletics and Academic Progress: A Comparison of Aca-
        demic Characteristics of Athletes and Nonathletes at the University of
        Minnesota.* Minneapolis: Bureau of Institutional Research.

Rehberg, Richard, and M. Cohen
1971   "Political Attitudes and Participation in Extra-Curricular Activities with
        Special Emphasis on Interscholastic Athletics." Paper presented at the
        Conference on Sport and Social Deviancy, SUNY, Brockport, New York.

Rehberg, Richard, and W. E. Schafer
1968   "Participation in Interscholastic Athletics and College Expectation." *Amer-
        ican Journal of Sociology,* **73** (May): 732–740.

Reitzes, D.
1959   "Institutional Structure and Race Relations." *Phylon* (Spring): 48–66.

Riesman, D., and R. Denny
1954   "Football in America." In *Individualism Reconsidered,* D. Riesman (ed).,
        pp. 242–257. Glencoe, Ill.: The Free Press.

Roberts, J. M., and Brian Sutton-Smith
1962   "Child Training and Games Involvement." *Ethnology,* **1** (April): 166–185.

Rogers, Cornish
1972   "Sports, Religion and Politics: The Renewal of an Alliance." *The Chris-
        tian Century,* **89** (April 5): 392–394.

Rosenblatt, A.
1967   "Negroes in Baseball: The Failure of Success." *Trans-action,* **4** (Septem-
        ber): 51–53.

Sage, J.
1967   "Adolescent Values and the Non-participating College Athlete." Paper
        presented at the Southern Section, California Health, Physical Education
        and Recreation Conference, San Fernando Valley State College.

Schafer, W. E.
1971   "Sport, Socialization and the School: Toward Maturity or Enculturation?"
        Paper presented at the Third International Symposium on the Sociology
        of Sport, Waterloo, Ontario.

Schafer, W. E., and M. Armer
1968 "Athletes Are Not Inferior Students." *Trans-Action*, **5** (November): 21–26, 61–62.

Schendel, J.
1965 "Psychological Differences between Athletes ₃nd Nonparticipants at Three Educational Levels." *Research Quarterly*, **36** (March): 52–67.

Scott, J.
1971 *The Athletic Revolution*. New York: The Free Press.

Shaw, G.
1972 *Meat On the Hoof*. New York: Dell Publishing Company.

Snyder, E.
1972a "Athletic Dressingroom Slogans as Folklore: A Means of Socialization." *International Review of Sport Sociology*, **7**: 89–102.

1972b "Athletes' Careers: The Role of the Coach in the Athletes' Future Educational Attainment." Paper presented at the Scientific Congress in conjunction with XXth Olympic Games, Munich.

1972c "High School Athletes and Their Coaches: Educational Plans and Advice." *Sociology of Education*, **45** (Summer): 313–325.

1972d "Social Characteristics and Motivations of Basketball Officials and Aspects of Sports Involvement." *The Ohio High School Athlete*, **32** (November): 66–67, 83.

Snyder, E., and J. Kivlin
1974 "Women Athletes and Aspects of Psychological Well-Being and Body Image." Paper read at the Popular Culture Association, Milwaukee.

Snyder, E., and E. Spreitzer
1973a "Family Influence and Involvement in Sports." *Research Quarterly*, **44** (October): 249–255.

1973b "Involvement in Sports and Psychological Well-Being." Paper read at the Third World Congress of the International Society of Sports Psychology, Madrid.

Spady, W.
1970 "Lament for the Letterman: Effects of Peer Status and Extra-Curricular Activities on Goals and Achievement. *American Journal of Sociology*, **75** (January): 680–702.

Spreitzer, E. and M. Pugh
1973 "Interscholastic Athletics and Educational Expectations." *Sociology of Education*, **46** (Spring): 171–182.

Stone, G.
1969 "Some Meanings of American Sport: An Extended View." In *Aspects of Contemporary Sport Sociology*, G. S. Kenyon (ed.), pp. 5–16. Chicago: The Athletic Institute.

1971 "American Sports: Play and Display." In *Sport: Readings from a Sociological Perspective*, Eric Dunning (ed.), pp. 47–65. London: Frank Cass and Company.

Sutton-Smith, Brian
1971 "A Developmental Approach to Play, Games and Sports." Paper presented at the Second World Symposium on the History of Sport and Physical Education, Bannf, Alberta, Canada.

U.S. Department of Labor, Bureau of Labor Statistics
1973 "Careers in Professional Sports." *Occupational Outlook Quarterly,* **17** (Summer): 2–5.

Veblen, T.
1899 *Theory of the Leisure Class.* New York: Random House.

Voigt, D.
1971 *America's Leisure Revolution.* Reading, Pennsylvania: Albright College Book Store.

Waller, W.
1932 *The Sociology of Teaching.* New York: John Wiley and Sons.

Washburne, J. N.
1941 "Factors Related to the Social Adjustment of College Girls." *Journal of Social Psychology,* **13** (May): 281–289.

Wilson, W.
1967 "Correlates of Avowed Happiness." *Psychological Bulletin,* **67** (April): 294–306.

Yetman, N., and S. Eitzen
1971 "Black Athletes on Intercollegiate Basketball Teams: An Empirical Test of Discrimination." Paper presented at the American Sociological Association, Denver, Colorado.
1972 "Black Americans in Sports: Unequal Opportunity for Equal Ability." *Civil Rights Digest,* **5** (August): 21–34.

Yinger, J. M.
1965 *Toward A Field Theory of Behavior.* New York: McGraw-Hill Co.

Chapter 2
A Note on Method in the Sociological Study of Sport

Donald W. Ball
Department of Sociology
University of Victoria
(Victoria, Canada)

Donald W. Ball

Birth Place: San Francisco, California

Age: 40

Birth Order: Only child

Formal Education:

B.A., History, University of California in Santa Barbara 1960

M.S., Polical Science, University of Oregon   1962

M.A., Sociology, University of California in
Los Angeles   1966

Ph.D., Sociology, University of California in
Los Angeles   1969

Present Position:

Associate Professor and Chairman, Department of Sociology, University of Victoria

Professional Responsibilities:

Sociology of Families and Households, Sociology of Sport.

Scholarly Interests:

Sport and social organization, cross-cultural analyses.

Professional Accomplishments:

Microecology: The Sociology of Intimate Space.

Recent works appear in Truzzi, *Humanities as Sociology;* Scott and Douglas, *Theoretical Perspectives on Deviance;* Mizruchi, *The Substance of Sociology: Codes, Conduct, Consequences;* Skolnick and Skolnick, *Intimacy, The Family, and Society,* and many others.

Articles published in *Social Forces, Sociological Analysis, Canadian Review of Sociology and Anthropology, The Sociological Quarterly, Trans-Action, Social Problems, International Journal of Comparative Sociology, Pacific Sociological Review, Journal Work and Occupations,* and others.

Papers, lectures, and addresses presented at many American and Canadian conferences, colleges, symposiums.

Hobbies:

Good conversation, trashy novels.

Sport Activities:

Participant: tennis, surfing.

Spectator: baseball, football, rodeos.

Most Recent Books Read:

P. Roth   *The Great American Novel*

C. Levis-Strauss   *The Elementary Structures of Kinship*

INTRODUCTION

As the contributors to this volume make clear, there is no special sociology for the study of sport. Sport is a social institution, a social process, a structured social activity—just as are more traditional topics of sociological investigation such as family and kinship arrangements, the polity, the economic sector, to name only a few.

Many, if not most sociological analyses of sport have focused on sport per se, thus contributing to the sociology *of* sport. However, the ultimate goal of sociological considerations of sport is to develop sociology *through* sport, by drawing upon examinations of sport which contribute more generally to our understanding of the social world beyond the confines of the sporting life.

It follows, then, that there is no special methodology associated with the sociological analysis of sport. Indeed there is no special method peculiar to any of the substantive areas which divide up the sociological domain. Participant observation—where the investigator is a part of the social world studied, questionnaires and interviews, experiments—the manipulation and control of variables *a la* the laboratory procedures of the natural sciences, and secondary research—the employment of already existing data; these are all strategies for sociological investigations—of social phenomena, of which sport is only one order.

Although there is no unique methodology associated with the sociology of sport, Loy and Seagrave (1974) have reviewed the traditional methods of sociological inquiry, their characteristics, and the sport-based research employing them. Because of its scope, completeness, and thoroughness, the reader seeking an overview of sociological methodology with particular reference to the literature in the sociology of sport is referred to the Loy and Seagrave overview.

THE VIRTUES OF SPORT FOR SOCIOLOGICAL STUDY

To say that there is no special method for the sociological investigation of sport is *not* to say that there are not particular characteristics which make sport an especially useful substantive area within which to do sociological analysis.

The following will make note of three of these virtues: (1) sport and the study of organizations, (2) the public record of sport, and the precision of measurement of sport activities, and (3) opportunities for comparative, cross-cultural analyses via sport.

Sport and the Study of Organizations

The study of structured organizations, often called formal organizations, has long been a major sociological preoccupation, following the pioneering turn-of-the-century work of Max Weber (see Gerth and Mills, 1946: 196–244). Etzioni (1964: 3) defines organizations as social units, groups of persons, purposefully constructed or structured so as to pursue specific or limited goals. By limited goals Etzioni means to differentiate between such global and undefinable (if attainable) quests as "the pursuit of happiness" as contrasted to the more specific shorter work-week of the trade union or the restrictions on imports sought by a trade association. In sport a similar contrast would exist between the ephemeral of the "athletic revolution" proposed by Jack Scott (1971) and the more pragmatic aims regarding salaries, pensions, and the option clause sought by the National Professional Football Players Association.

Further specification of the concept of structured organizations is given by Caplow (1964: 1–3), who defines them as social systems [which persist over time] and which have:

1. *An unequivocal identity*, i.e., an organizational name, recognized by members as well as many nonmembers.

2. *An exact roster of members*, such that members and nonmembers can be specified and differentiated. We would add to this a roster of positions or statuses within the organization—what Caplow calls a table of organization, the familiar linked boxes of the organization chart.

3. *A program of activity*, i.e., a set of definite goals, either extensive or brief, *and* a division of labor and plans for their achievement.

4. *Procedures for replacing members*, so that new members may be recruited and vacancies filled; and, further, that existing members may be transferred from one position to another within the division of labor.

These characteristics define a number of commonly found organizations. The well-known typology of Blau and Scott (1962: 45–57) identifies four categories: *business concerns; service organizations,* those whose prime beneficiary is the public with which it has contacts; *commonweal organizations,* service organizations with over-arching clienteles, the public-at-large, e.g., fire departments, the federal government's Department of Health, Education, and Welfare; and *multi-benefit associations,* where organization members are the prime beneficiaries, for instance, professional associations and religious sects.

And it is precisely those entities most unequivocally categorized by the Blau and Scott typology which have most frequently been the targets of the sociological analysis of organizations: corporations, social service agencies, the military, voluntary associations and the like. It is interesting to note the way sport organizations cross-cut the typology: professional sport teams obviously take on some, if not all of the attributes of a business concern; sport as entertainment becomes for spectators a service organization; as sources of community and even national identification, teams function as commonweal organizations; and for participants, certainly amateurs and to a lesser extent professionals, sport organizations (save with the possible exception of administrators) operate as mutual-benefit associations.

What makes sports, especially team sports, most useful as subjects of organizational analyses are their *structural characteristics* or, more particularly, the characteristics of size, normative codification, and positional interrelationships.

Size. Two aspects of size make sport teams particularly amenable to a sociological-organizational perspective. The first of these is their relative "smallness" as compared to most other organizations; the second is that constant team or roster size aids in the comparative analysis of different organizations of the same type.

In general, and *ceteris paribus,* we can state that the smaller the organization, the more completely the totality of its complexity can be apprehended. This is not to say that smallness guarantees total knowledge (whether this is ever possible is a philosophical issue), but that in probabilistic terms the investigator can come closer.

Thus, if the student of organizations is interested in questions concerning the effect of ascribed characteristics such as race or nativity/nationality on the achieved positioning of organizational members, he is more likely to get such information on a higher proportion of the members of a small organization than a large one. In part this is due to the higher probability of centralized sources of information or data; in part it is also due to the greater "manageability" of such data. Both Loy and McElvogue (1970) and Ball (1973) have shown the utility of drawing upon professional football and baseball leagues *qua* organizations to examine this type of problem.

The other valuable size aspect of teams is the constant size of their rosters. For interscholastic, intercollegiate, professional, and virtually all amateur team sports, roster size is set by the league or association of which the team is a member. This constant size greatly facilitates comparative analyses within leagues and between leagues with comparable restrictions. By way of contrast, we can imagine the sociologist interested in the study of organizations whose units of analysis are post office branches: ranging in size from the one-person counter in the back of the general store to the multi-leveled organizations constituting post offices in urban settings.

More importantly, since organizations may be defined by their division of labor—their constituent positions, as well as their membership rosters—the number of organizations of a constant size for comparative purposes is expanded to almost incredibly large numbers. Irrespective of level of play, all baseball teams have nine positions, basketball five, ad infinitum. This fact gives the organizational analyst a powerful tool: whether Little League or World Series champions, 10-year-olds or veteran professionals, size (and organizational structure) remains constant, thus allowing the investigator the opportunity to examine the impact of non-size (or nonstructural) variables on organizational activity and performance.

Normative Codification. By definition, all social activities are rule-bound, regulated by norms of conduct which give rise to expectations and obligations, rights and duties, which are shared (usually) by performers and their audience alike. In most arenas of social life, however, these rules are not codified: law being a significant exception. More often than not, these rules rest upon custom, tradition, hearsay, or the mutual negotiations of social actors and/or groups.

Sport provides another significant exception. It begins, exists, and terminates its very life—episodes of its life would be more correct—by its *rulebooks*. There are few if any areas of social life, including organizations, where outcomes are as clearly defined as the result of normative constraints as is sport. Sport is, in effect, a closed system: although rules may be modified or changed, this does not occur through the give-and-take, by mutual lines of activity modifying the game, but externally and not during the game, e.g., by rules committees of leagues, national and international bodies and the like.

As a result, by looking at sport as organization, the analyst has before him an organization whose goal-related activities are (a) codified, and (b) virtually free of subtle, member-negotiated change, while experiencing major changes only during nonplaying periods.

Positional Interrelationships. The rules of sport also, to an extent rarely found in other organizational contexts, spell out the interrelationships between organizational positions and their occupants. Thus, the rights, duties, obligations, and tasks specific to sport positions vis-a-vis other positions are specified by the rules of the game. Thus, Loy and McElvogue (1970) are able to identify baseball positions as proactive (initiators of organizational interaction) or reactive (recipients of others' proactivity). Similarly, Ball (1973) is able to differentiate football positions as primary, i.e., goal-related, or supportive, those which assist the primary positions to attain goals.

The Public and Precise Record of Sport

There are few activities which are as assiduously recorded and publicly recorded as sport. Additionally, much of this public information involves a highly precise and quantitative mode of measurement. Scores, team standings, batting averages, percentage of passes completed are just a few: some measuring league phenomena, some team performance, and others those of individual actors in the drama of sport.

Books such as the *Baseball Register* and *Football Register*, both published annually by the Sporting News of St. Louis, are, for a price of less than ten dollars, virtual data banks for the sociologist interested in the study of work, occupations, organizations, and the like. These two volumes (and we do not wish to imply that they are the only viable sources of sociologically relevant sport data—we use them as examples) provide complete "work histories" on all active players in the National Football League or baseball's major leagues for a given year.

Thus, data are available on a player's age, birthplace, educational background, team affiliation(s) over his professional career and the like. Further, there is data on each player's year-by-year performance: position and games played, all-star recognition, as well as performance statistics specific to each sport and/or position within it.

These data can be employed to investigate a variety of substantive questions in sociology. For example: what is the relationship between performance, e.g., batting average, passes completed, and occupational mobility—both vertically, as from major to minor league and vice versa, and horizontally, from team to team at the same league level. Such questions invite and await sociological scrutiny. Relatedly, what accounts for the variation, if any, in rates of turnover by position in teams or leagues looked at as work organizations. One study, employing the *Football Register* as a data bank (Ball, 1974a) finds that the visibility, the ease of accurate evaluation of performance at a position, related to such turnover. The less visible the performance (e.g., interior linemen), the lower the turnover; the higher the visibility (e.g., quarterbacks, kickers), the greater the turnover. It was also found that salaries and turnover were directly related to one another. As visibility turnover rates went up, so too did the average salary for that position. In effect, risky jobs with low security of tenure were associated with compensatory financial rewards.

There are a variety of other sources of similar data ranging from publications by various sports organizations; special interest magazines, such as *Skating* (for data on international figure skating); through newspapers, and the raw data such as box-scores compiled by teams and individual participants themselves. We would emphasize that the special virtue for sociology is their low cost and ready availability, the precision of measurement they offer, and their particular utility as regards sociological investigations of organizations, work and occupations, and social stratification and mobility.

Comparative and Cross-Cultural Analyses

One of the major goals of sociology, and also anthropology, is to develop general propositions about social systems. One class of such systems is societies themselves: typically nation-states for the sociologists, while historically anthropologists have looked to tribal societies for their data (although this division of labor is by no means universally observed or accepted). As sport is a worldwide activity it provides an excellent arena for comparative and cross-cultural studies.[1] World championships, the Olympic Games, the playing of the same sport in many nations, e.g., track and field, soccer, all provide opportunities for comparative analyses. In effect, the basic question to be asked is this: can we account for variations in national sport performances by reference to variations in the nonsport characteristics of these nations? What structural variables, for instance, account for differential performances by national Olympic teams? How, in other words, is sport related to broader patterns of the social organization of nation-states?

If one is willing to treat games, especially those involving physical skill as at least nascent sport, then there is abundant data available on these activities in tribal societies, including information which classifies and codes societies on the basis of the types of games found within them. The major source of this material is the *Ethnographic Atlas* (Murdock, 1967) which also contains a variety of coded nongame information.

Based upon the original definitions of games developed by Roberts and his associates (Roberts, et al., 1959), the *Atlas* codes societies as to whether they have games of physical skill, games of strategy, games of chance, combinations of these, or no games at all.[2] For further precision these codes can be converted into ordinal scales (Ball, 1972a, 1974b).

Other information in the *Atlas* codes the societies on variables relating to kinship, stratification, technology, and so on. Thus, it is possible to examine relationships between gaming and other features of sociocultural organization in tribal societies. It is also possible to take coded information from other samples, overlap the sample with that in the *Atlas*, and examine the shared cases in the two samples to explore other questions not possible with the *Atlas* alone.

Finally, Textor's *Cross-Cultural Summary* (1967) cross-tabulates some 400 variables, including those relating to games, and prints out cross-tabulation tables for all significant relationships. The *Summary* includes variables on social organization, religion, medicine, and a large range of social and cultural practices. This *Summary* is an excellent source for pursuing hunches about variable relationships, but because of sampling problems must be augmented by further research should promising relationships be found between any two variables (Ball, 1972b).

OVERVIEW

The above has looked at three methodological aspects of the sociological examination of sport. We have seen that team sport is, because of its structural characteristics, especially amenable as a laboratory for the study of formal organizations. We have also noted the public and precise nature of much sport data and thus its utility as sociological data, particularly for studies of organizations, work and occupations, and stratification and social mobility. Finally, given the international and probably universal distribution of sport (and games), we have noted the possibilities for comparative and cross-cultural analyses which they provide.

But to reiterate an earlier theme: there is no special methodology for the sociological study of sport. What exists, though, are some special opportunities to use sport data as particularly appropriate to substantive issues which transcend mere sport itself.

NOTES

1. We use comparative to refer to comparisons between and among two or more nation-states (although comparisons of other units can and are made by "comparative sociologists"), and cross-cultural to refer to the same mode of analysis when the units are tribal societies. Ideally, both modes of analysis employ some kind of counting of the units and the distribution of their relevant characteristics, i.e., quantification.

2. Of the over 850 societies included in the *Atlas*, 399 are reported on the game variable. Of these, 25 are coded as having no games at all, although this coding is of dubious accuracy and probably reflects the disinterest in the subject on the part of the original observer(s) of the society upon whose report the codes are based.

REFERENCES

Ball, Donald W.
1972a "The Scaling of Gaming: Skill, Strategy, and Chance." *Pacific Sociological Review*, **15** (July): 277–294.
1972b "What the Action Is: A Cross-Cultural Approach." *Journal for the Theory of Social Behaviour*, **2** (October): 121–143.
1973 "Ascription and Position: A Comparative Analysis of 'Stacking' in Professional Football." *Canadian Review of Sociology and Anthropology*, **10** (May): 97–113.
1974a "Replacement Process in Work Organizations: Task Evaluation and the Case of Professional Football." *Sociology of Work and Occupations*, **1** (May): 197–217.
1974b "Control *versus* Complexity: Continuities in the Scaling of Gaming." *Pacific Sociological Review*, **17** (April): 167–184.

Blau, Peter M., and Richard Scott
1962 *Formal Organizations*. San Francisco: Chandler.

Caplow, Theodore
1964 *Principles of Organization*. New York: Harcourt, Brace and World.

Etzioni, Amatai
1964 *Complex Organizations*. Englewood Cliffs, N.J.: Prentice-Hall.

Gerth, Hans, and C. Wright Mills (eds.)
1964 *On Max Weber: Essays in Sociological Theory*. New York: Oxford University Press.

Loy, John W., and Joseph F. McElvogue
1970 "Racial Segregation in American Sport." *International Review of Sport Sociology*, **5**: 5–24.

Loy, John W., and Jeffrey O. Seagrave
1974   "Research Methodology in the Sociology of Sport." In *Exercise and Sport Sciences Reviews*, J. Wilmore (ed.). Vol. II. New York: Academic Press: 289–333.

Murdock, George Peter
1967   *Ethnographic Atlas*. Pittsburgh: University of Pittsburgh Press.

Roberts, John M., Malcolm J. Arth, and Robert R. Bush
1959   "Games in Culture." *American Anthropologist*, **61** (August): 597–605.

Scott, Jack
1971   *The Athletic Revolution*. New York: Free Press.

Textor, Robert B.
1967   *A Cross-Cultural Summary*. New Haven: HRAF Press.

Part II
The Social Organization
of Sport

Chapter 3
Sports from a
Geographic Perspective

John F. Rooney, Jr.
Department of Geography
Oklahoma State University
Stillwater, Oklahoma

John F. Rooney, Jr.

Birth Place: Detroit, Michigan

Age: 34

Birth Order: Oldest, one brother, two sisters

Formal Education:

B.S., Illinois State University	1961
M.S., Illinois State University	1962
Ph.D., Clark University, Worcester, Massachusetts	1965

Present Position:

Professor and Head, Department of Geography, Oklahoma State University

Professional Responsibilities:

Administration of the teaching, research, and extension functions of the geography department.

Teaching a course on the Geography of Sport, and the Geography of the United States. Seminar on Regional Analysis.

Scholarly Interests:

Geography of sport: spatial reorganization of sport, athletic recruitment.

Social geography of the United States: leisure pursuits, diet and drinking variations, religious regions.

Professional Accomplishments:

A Geography of American Sport: From Cabin Creek to Anaheim. Coauthor of *A Geography of the United States* (in press).

Journal publications in the *Geographical Review, Annals of the Association of American Geographers, Professional Geographer, The American City, Journal of Leisure Research, Pro.*

Grants over $250,000 from Department of Interior Office of Water Resources Research for studies on water-oriented recreation. Member of the Association of American Geographers Committee on Recreation, Tourism, and Sport.

Hobbies:

Travel.

Sport Activities:

Participant: golf, handball.

Spectator: football, basketball, baseball.

INTRODUCTION

Where are the hotbeds of American football and basketball? What is the direction and magnitude of the major migratory streams of college-bound American athletes? and how and why have they developed? Where has ice hockey been adopted during the past decade? What has been the pattern of lacrosse diffusion and where is it apt to catch on next? How could the geographical organization of professional football and basketball be changed to maximize rivalries and to deliver live sport to a greater percentage of the American public? Why has wrestling failed to diffuse throughout Oklahoma and to surrounding state high schools despite a half century of wrestling leadership and supremacy at Oklahoma State University? What can be done to lessen the inequality of access to participation in high school sport which characterizes the United States? Why has women's sport been most popular in rural America? Should the new football and baseball stadium be located downtown or in the suburbs?

These are a few of the topics, and the kinds of questions about them, which fall under the broad cloak of sport geography. Since geography is concerned with the character of place, locational analysis and human behavior, sport represents rich grist for its bustling mill. Geographic analysis can help to create a better understanding of sport's significance to society and can aid in promoting an awareness of the changing role of sport over time; its origins, spread and modifications.

There is a geography of every game and a sports geography of every area.[1] This can be demonstrated by a rather simple conceptual framework designed to highlight the various elements involved in the geographic analysis of sport (Fig. 1). The framework is divided into two sections. One section focuses on a given sport; the other on a given area.

The Topical Approach to Sport

Beginning with the left or topical side of the framework, which deals with a selected sport, we start with the premise that all sports must originate *somewhere, sometime*. In many instances it is extremely difficult to iden-

A CONCEPTUAL FRAMEWORK
FOR THE GEOGRAPHIC ANALYSIS OF SPORT

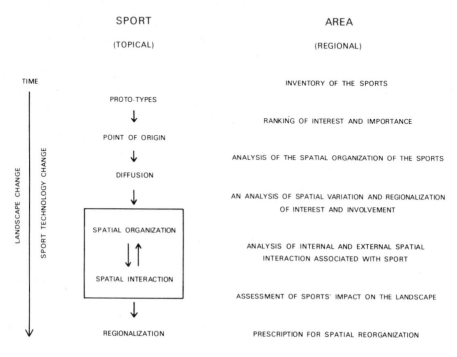

Figure 1

tify precisely the place where a sport begins. Most sports, American football, baseball and basketball not excepted, started under rather obscure
circumstances. Although we are told that each began at a certain place on
a certain day we can be sure that a great deal of experimentation preceded
the actual events. They were not invented, but were usually the product
of an evolutionary process. Therefore, it is important to identify a prototype era in a development of sport. A great deal of work has been devoted
to the discussion of certain sports prototypes as engaged in by the Egyp-
tians, the Greeks, and the pre-Columbian peoples of North America. And
there is undoubtedly a strong link between our present day sports and the
types of activities in which these people engaged. There are also a number of children's games like rounders and one-o'-cat which helped to spawn
modern sport.

After settling on the point or area of origin of any game, we can trace its movement outward from the source area. The diffusion of a game is related to the other games that were available at the time of its development. It is also related to the extent to which the competing game or games are socially and spatially entrenched. For example, a brand new game like basketball, within its first few years of existence, had little difficulty attracting players from all over the United States. It was diffused, in part, via the YMCAs and immediately caught on in the high schools and colleges. There simply was no game like basketball and, as such, it quickly filled a vacuum for indoor winter participation. On the other hand, the professional version of rugby, "Rugby League," has long been confined to three counties in the English midlands. Attempts to spread "Rugby League" throughout England have been stifled by a strong amateur rugby organization (a competing force which has functioned like a hulking mountain barrier), despite the existence of "League" fans in all parts of Great Britain. There are many other examples (national boundaries are probably the most significant) in the realm of sport which demonstrate the role of existing games or organizations relative to the spread of new ones.

After a sport has diffused, and a number of teams have been assembled, it undergoes a process of spatial organization. The type of spatial organization is related to the level of interest in the sport, available modes of transportation, and the geographical distribution of capital. Existing facilities also play a part in the emergence of the spatial organization, and the ensuing interaction. Once a league, conference or similar form of government is established there is immediate spatial interaction, and connectivity develops between the places involved. The positioning of the teams which compete with one another controls the nature of the interaction. For example, during the early days of the National Football League, most of the members were located in Ohio, Illinois, and Indiana. Hence, the early rivalries were basically local in nature. As the years passed the League relocated in the nation's largest cities. But the most intense rivalries were maintained between teams in the same geographical area, i.e., Los Angeles–San Francisco, Chicago–Green Bay, New York–Philadelphia.

The present spatial organization of sport is a product of a long range and complex decision-making process. It is hierarchical in nature, ranging from the professional leagues to those designed for schoolboy and schoolgirl competition. The stated objective for the organization of sport for young people is to promote mass participation. Professional sport is geared to market the product as entertainment for the spectator. Thus, it follows that the participatory activities are arranged to serve small group markets, and are found almost everywhere that there are enough people to field a team. The spectator-oriented activities include the big time college scene and the major professional sports. As indicated in the case of professional football, they tend to be more geographically concentrated than the participant-based activities. And since their survival is highly dependent on gate receipts, they generally have gravitated to city locations where a profit is likely.

The distribution of big time sport coincides with the theoretical framework which is referred to as central place theory.[2] Central place theory is based on the assumption that settlements exist to serve the needs of their surrounding territory, referred to as the sphere of influence or hinterland. Very small places exist to serve local needs and offer only a few basic services: groceries, fuel, a place to get lubricated, and a place to go to church. There is a hierarchy of community sizes with larger centers offering a greater variety of services to larger areas. In the case of sport, certain activities such as little league teams, high school football, basketball and baseball teams, bowling facilities, and so on are available in relatively small places. Minor league, professional, and major collegiate sports are often found in medium-sized towns, whereas major league sport is a service traditionally provided in the "major league" cities.[3]

When a sport has become established and has spread throughout an area a regionalization process becomes evident.[4] Some areas adopt the sport to a greater extent than others. They devote more time to playing, talking and writing about it, and tend to produce a greater number of high quality performers. In the case of the American games football, basketball and baseball, there are certain sections of the country which excel in each. Basketball dominates in Indiana, Kentucky, and Illinois and in a number of cities along the East Coast. Football is the major sport in certain parts of Pennsylvania and Ohio, throughout Texas, Oklahoma, and a large segment of the Southeast. Baseball is associated with California and the South.

Another form of sports region involves a central focus such as a baseball or a football team. The center or core of the region is the location of the team's home field and, to a lesser extent, the city in which the home field is located. Loyalties to the team normally decrease in intensity as one moves outward from the home field location. This area which identifies with a given team can be called the fan region. There are as many fan regions as there are teams. Some are small and embrace only a few people, while others affiliated with the professional teams include millions of followers. Fan regions tend to overlap and as a result cover almost all of the territory in any country.

A sport originates and diffuses, develops a spatial organization, stimulates interaction, and finally becomes regionalized. In some cases the evolution drags on for hundreds of years; in others it is a very short process. Regardless of the time span, the chain of events stimulates a landscape change, in the form of new facilities which affect surrounding land use, and in the form of transportation changes necessary to move people to and from the events. There is a begging need for an investigation of land use related to sport. There are also many unanswered questions concerning the placement of new facilities and recreational areas devoted to sport. Many controversies are currently raging relative to *where* a new stadium should or should not be, and, in most instances, in the absence of any type of scientific assessment of the alternatives.

The process that a sport goes through prior to regionalization is related to technological advances. These technological advances are both independent of the sport, such as those involving transportation and communications, and directly related to the sport, such as those involving equipment and playing fields. An examination of any sport is sufficient to surmise the tremendous impact that technology can have. A look at the equipment located in the Baseball Hall of Fame in Cooperstown suggests that great changes have taken place. The size and nature of the gloves, the bats, the balls, and even the stadiums themselves have changed significantly. Recently, artificial playing surfaces have altered the very nature of the game. Golf, football, basketball, track and field, and most of the other sports have undergone similar structural change as a result of advancing technology.

The Regional Approach to Sport

The right side of the conceptual framework begins with the identification of an area or national unit. This type of analysis represents the regional approach. A regional geography of any area may center on a single phenomenon such as sport, manufacturing, religion, architecture, transportation, or agriculture or it can be devoted to a combination of topics. A geography of England would deal with the economic, social and physical aspects of that country. It would also examine the country's external relations, its land use and settlement patterns.

The type of analysis suggested by the conceptual framework represents a concentration on one social element, sport. In analyzing sport from a regional point of view, the first step is the identification of the sports played in the region. After the inventory some ranking of the importance of the various sporting activities, including an historical treatment of the role of sport within the territory, would be required. The remaining elements of the framework, with the exception of that dealing with spatial reorganization, are very similar to those discussed earlier. The only difference is that we are beginning with a preconceived *area* as opposed to a selected sport. Spatial organization, spatial variation, interaction, and landscape impact all would be considered. Spatial reorganization could be recommended after making an assessment of the existing spatial organization. If the present organization does not afford an equitable delivery of sports services to the area's population then reorganization would be advised.

AMERICAN SPORT

Perhaps the best way to illustrate the myriad elements of the geography of sport is to concentrate on the sports geography of the United States. Most of my previous work has been devoted to American sports, particularly football, baseball, and basketball.[5] However, we have assembled a great deal of data on a variety of games played in the United States, which in many cases illustrate strong regional concentrations.[6] Thus, by focusing on the geography of American sports the broad realm of sports geography can be illustrated. The games with which nations identify are in part related to their climatic environment. In the beginning, most games were very seasonal in nature. Summer was associated with cricket in England and baseball in America. Soccer and football were played in the cooler seasons, and when it was too cold people moved indoors for such things as basketball in the United States and hockey in Canada. For this reason nations have tended to embrace two or more sports which could be deemed as having national interest.

In America, baseball, basketball, and football form our trilogy of national games. Their seasonality is more difficult to identify than it once was but they are still somewhat confined by climatic considerations. There are many more national and regional sports played in America. They include golf, track and field, horse and automobile racing, boxing, wrestling, swimming, bowling, tennis, and ice hockey. Winter activities such as curling, skiing, skating, and sledding are more spatially concentrated and, in some cases, more popular within their regions than the "national" games. Rodeo, polo, lacrosse, handball, racquetball, badminton, and squash are games played by many, but which receive scant attention from the media. More individualistic-oriented sports such as hunting, fishing, hiking, and climbing based on the idea of competition between man and his natural environment are also spatially patterned.

Spatial Organization

The geographic organization of American sport is now in a period as tumultuous as has existed since the early days of professional baseball, when new teams came and departed like relief pitchers at a Sunday doubleheader. After a steady state for over 50 years, relocation in baseball began in 1953 with Boston moving to Milwaukee, followed by the transcontinental treks by the Brooklyn Dodgers and the New York Giants. The expansionary express pulled out of the station in 1960 with the addition of the California Angels and the Minnesota Twins, and has been picking up steam ever since. Note the following statistics: major league baseball has grown from 16 to 24 teams; the number of professional football teams has more than tripled with the establishment of two new leagues; professional basketball has ballooned from 8 to 27 quintets; and professional hockey has increased almost fivefold. All this growth is translated into new "major league" cities, new league alignments (some of them spatially ridiculous), and extreme dislocation of fan-team relationships. Since the express shows no sign of abating in its lust for new passengers, it would seem that now is the time for a planned approach toward expansion. But first let us examine the road that led to the present dilemma.

American sport has been geographically organized to promote both competition and participation. At the professional and major college level, it has been set up so as to operate profitably. Conversely, the participatory activities are essentially ubiquitous, with teams located wherever there are enough people to warrant them. Hence, as the number of athletes is thinned out moving up the competitive ladder, i.e., grade school to high school, to college, to minor leagues, and finally into the major professional leagues, the number of teams is also drastically reduced.

The spatial organization of American sport has evolved somewhat haphazardly. During the early period of professional baseball, the location of the franchises changed almost annually. Similar situations existed in football and basketball, and was also common in a number of other sports. The initial growth era of any professional sport generally finds the locations of teams in what might be termed a state of *spatial flux*. During this embryonic stage, the precise location of the teams is related to the availability of capital and the whereabouts of individuals interested in sponsoring teams. Baseball's early days, prior to the advent of the railroad and other modern means of transportation, saw teams confined to the most populous section of the United States, the Eastern seaboard. As the railroad opened up the West, teams were able to move there and compete in the same league with those in the East. By 1900 major league baseball had migrated to most of the large cities within the Northeastern quadrant of the United States and minor league baseball was being sponsored everywhere.

Baseball developed primarily as a professional sport in contrast to football and basketball. The latter sports were initially played at the amateur level in the high schools and colleges. With the development of big time collegiate sport, America began on a path which was to separate it from most other countries in the world. Collegiate sport, first football and later basketball, became as important as professional baseball to many average American sports fans. Professional basketball and football became established as profit-making ventures, only after acceptance at the collegiate level. For a long time professional football and basketball occupied a secondary role to the college game, and in some areas they still do.

To understand the spatial organization of American sport one must first comprehend the unique nature of the collegiate-professional relationship. This can be examined by observing the locations of the scholarship subsidized collegiate programs and the professional franchises (Fig. 2). We must keep in mind that decisions to have big time collegiate programs and to establish professional teams were made at different times. The most important period for the development of collegiate sport was between 1890 and 1930. The glory days of professional football and basketball came much later.

Location of most of the big time colleges is a function of the political organization of the United States. Traditionally the states have placed a premium on establishing and nurturing state universities. Most states have at least one major public institution and a significant number have groups of schools located so as to serve their various regional markets. Virtually all the states, regardless of population or location, have elected to support big time athletic programs in at least one of their institutions. Added to this are a number of randomly located private universities which are also engaging in big time sport.

Most of the colleges have elected to join some type of athletic conference. The conference generally facilitates competition between universities located in the same region. At last count there were 149 athletic conferences in the United States. These included (depending on one's bias) somewhere between 9 and 20 major conferences (Fig. 3). There has been some tendency to put greater emphasis on football in those areas which are removed from immediate access to professional competition. The mania for the college game seems to be strongest in places like Lincoln, Austin, South Bend, Fayetteville, Norman, Columbus, and Tuscaloosa, where the collegiate game is taking the place of professional football as an entertainment medium.

With the role of big time collegiate and professional sport being so intermingled, it is probably unfair to separate them for this type of analysis. For we cannot understand the present distribution of professional franchises without studying their collegiate counterparts. The extreme pressures for excellence in collegiate sports are undoubtedly the result of the geographical concentration of professional opportunities within certain sections of the United States. Excellence is demanded whether it be from

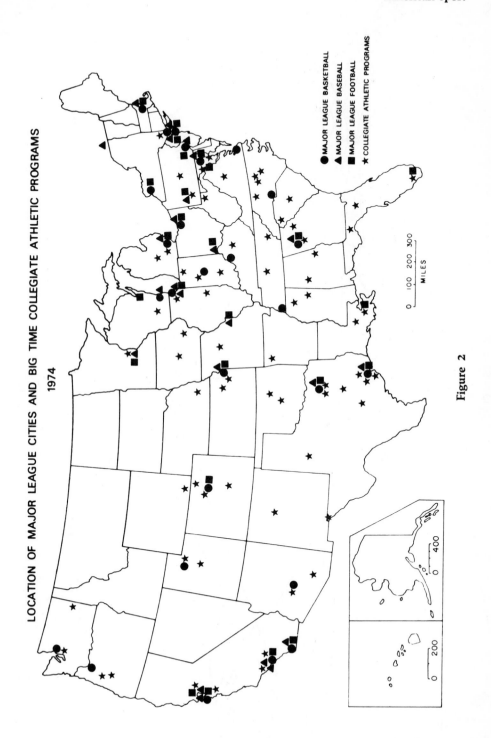

LOCATION OF MAJOR LEAGUE CITIES AND BIG TIME COLLEGIATE ATHLETIC PROGRAMS

1974

● MAJOR LEAGUE BASKETBALL
▲ MAJOR LEAGUE BASEBALL
■ MAJOR LEAGUE FOOTBALL
★ COLLEGIATE ATHLETIC PROGRAMS

0 100 200 300
MILES

0 400

0 200

Figure 2

CHICAGO WHITE SOX MOVEMENT

1974 SEASON

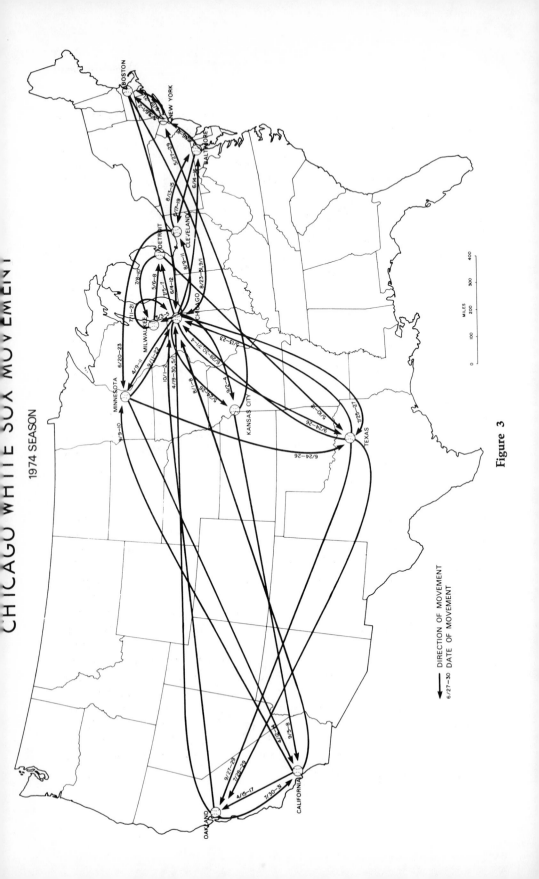

DIRECTION OF MOVEMENT
6/27—30 DATE OF MOVEMENT

Figure 3

professionals or the so-called amateurs. It is therefore possible, that the financial crisis which plagues so many college athletic departments is a direct result of the paucity of professional teams. With more professional teams, the need for "semiprofessional" collegiate sport would be reduced. Admittedly, the period of de-emphasis would be lengthy and would be stubbornly resisted, but it could happen.

Why have the professionals been so slow in expanding their numbers? We must first remember that the location of professional sport franchises, as well as their numbers, is primarily governed by profit motivation and an assumed knowledge of consumer preference. Most professional teams are businesses first and entertainment second. For this reason their location corresponds closely to the distribution of the largest population concentrations (Fig. 2). Those who control professional sport have been consistently unwilling to gamble on expansion. As a consequence of this attitude, most of the recent expansion has come from outside the establishment: witness the American Football League, the World Football League, the World Hockey League, the American Basketball Association, and the newly proposed World Baseball Association. These groups were organized by adventurous capitalists willing to gamble on expansion, and, in most cases, they have succeeded. However, during the first 50 years of this century, when collegiate football and basketball were expanding, the professional games were floundering. So, as professional football and basketball really began the big push, the college sports continued along the same path that already had been worn. As professional sport grew, more and more money was also funneled into the collegiate athletic coffers. The result was a greater regional exposure to professional sport and continued growth of big time college football and basketball. Today most sections of the country have access to either professional or collegiate sport and, in some cases, to both. Collegiate sport, particularly football, seems to thrive as a business enterprise in those areas which are removed from professional teams.

The spatial organization of sport contains a variety of *periodic* market traits. Major league stadia are geared to the movements of teams to and from their "home" locations. Professional teams may be regarded as mobile receptors moving about over a money emission field and drawing down on the money resource base (Fig. 3). The Professional Golf Tour represents another form of periodic market in that players lacking a home turf peddle their services along a circuit that leads from one town to another over the course of a year, followed by a similar trek in ensuing years (Fig. 4). The regional franchise, as exemplified by several professional basketball teams and a number of collegiate football teams, is still another form of periodic market organization.

PROFESSIONAL GOLF ASSOCIATION TOUR

1974

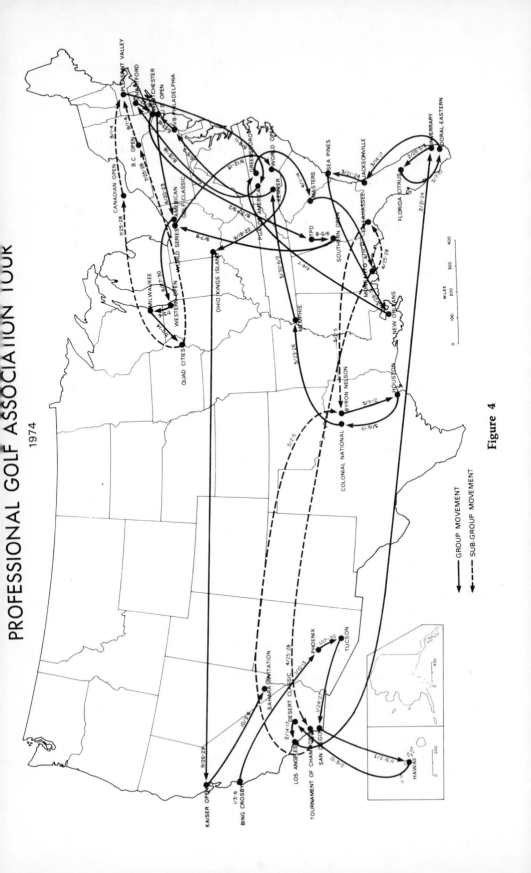

GROUP MOVEMENT

SUB-GROUP MOVEMENT

Figure 4

The Case for Spatial Reorganization

There is increasing evidence that American professional sport has re-entered a state of extreme spatial flux. Major league baseball, the "national game" during the first half of this century, was geographically entrenched from 1902 to 1953. On the other hand, professional basketball and football, second-rate challengers for the American sports dollar, were jumping from town to town in search of permanent fan support. As football grew in popularity during the 1950's and 1960's the locations of teams became relatively stable. Basketball, though, has never reached a geographically stable position.

The baseball establishment finally agreed to expand its membership beginning with the 1960 season, and has since grown by 50 percent. The short-lived football stability was rocked by an outside force, the maverick American Football League. Ten new teams were created overnight, accompanied by internal expansion by the existing National Football League. As a result the number of professional football teams has increased by over 100 percent. Basketball, too, was caught up in the expansionary spiral, with the number of teams tripling in less than ten years. Professional hockey has followed a similar pattern. The periodic market sports—golf, tennis, and bowling—have also boarded the expansion express.

This great growth period has not been without its problems. Many of the new franchises were located in marginal market areas and failed due to meager fan support. In some cases the expansion teams were so weak that even the New York Mets's "Support-Your-Local-Loser" syndrome could not keep them going. The placement of many of the new franchises was based strictly on the availability of capital, as opposed to a market research analysis. Because of this, many franchises located in cities which already identified with competitive teams, in areas which were not particularly interested in the sport involved, or in centers with relatively small population bases. It is unlikely that the failures could have been totally avoided but a more carefully planned approach to expansion and team location may have substantially reduced the problem.

Since it is obvious that the expansionary winds are not abating (the new World Football League being a case in point), perhaps a rational approach to team location can still be employed. Utilizing a location/allocation computer program called LAP, the expansion of professional franchises to a total of 52 and finally to a total of 104 has been simulated. The locations are based primarily on the distribution of population but also take into account the geographic organization of television market areas. At this stage the model assumes equal interest levels in all sports over the national population surface. Income and recreational tastes and opportunities are also held constant. These assumptions can be relaxed in selecting sites for different types of sports franchises. For example, based on what we know about football and basketball preferences, Texas could be assigned more football teams, while Kentucky might support an additional basketball entry.

The cities of New York, Chicago, and Los Angeles have been removed from the analyses and automatically assigned franchises. The 52-team scheme allocates four teams to the New York city region and two each to Chicago and Los Angeles. At the 104-team level New York was automatically assigned eight, with Los Angeles and Chicago receiving four each. After these three cities were removed from consideration, the United States was first divided into eleven areas of equal population. Successive computer runs then identified two teams from each area, then four teams, and finally eight. The first run based on two teams from each area, plus the New York, Chicago, and Los Angeles contingents, simulated the current 26-team National Football League (Fig. 5). In many instances the existing team locations were identical to those selected by the computer allocation program. However, it was demonstrated that the South, Southwest, and Northwestern sections of the United States are currently under-represented, and that a number of the present teams were not optimally located to maximize their potential audiences. For example, relative to the actual distribution of the American population the Kansas City franchise should be located in Tulsa. The Tulsa representative would dominate the television market areas of Kansas City, Oklahoma City, Little Rock, Shreveport, Springfield, Joplin, Fort Smith, and Ardmore-Ada.

The 52-team set-up would provide approximately one team per four million people (Fig. 6). Since the population is concentrated primarily in the Eastern half of the nation the teams are there too. Relatively speaking, the Southeast would have considerably more exposure than it presently does. However, the Rocky Mountain and Plains areas would remain as a professional sports void. Even with one hundred and four teams, it is impossible to justify professional sport in certain sections of the country (Fig. 7). There would simply be a greater concentration throughout the heavily populated Northeast, within the South, and also in Texas and Oklahoma. The Pacific Coast and the Southern Rocky Mountain area would also be well-represented.

Both of the theoretical expansion proposals would allow regional competition to flourish. Professional sport could be organized so as to maximize the natural place-to-place rivalries which stem from a combination of local pride and first hand knowledge of nearby places. The fierce crosstown rivalries of the past could be reincarnated. A New York metropolitan league could stand by itself and New England and upper New York state

OPTIMAL VS. ACTUAL LOCATION OF PROFESSIONAL SPORTS FRANCHISES
BASED ON POPULATION DISTRIBUTION
1974

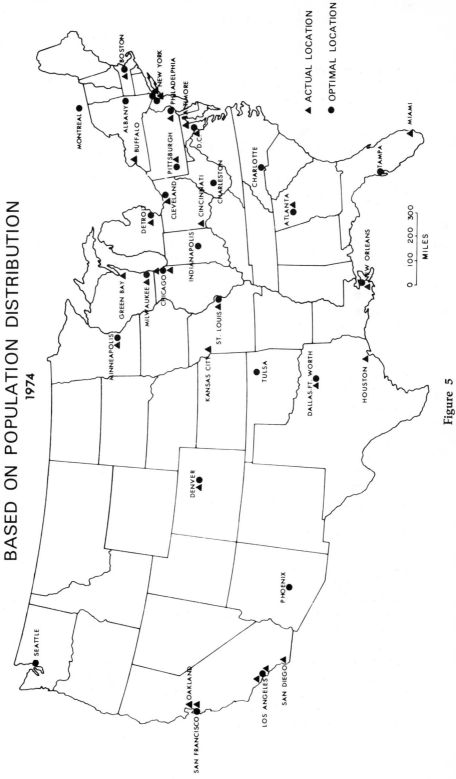

▲ ACTUAL LOCATION

● OPTIMAL LOCATION

Figure 5

A THEORETICAL MARKET-ORIENTED EXPANSION
OF PROFESSIONAL SPORTS FRANCHISES

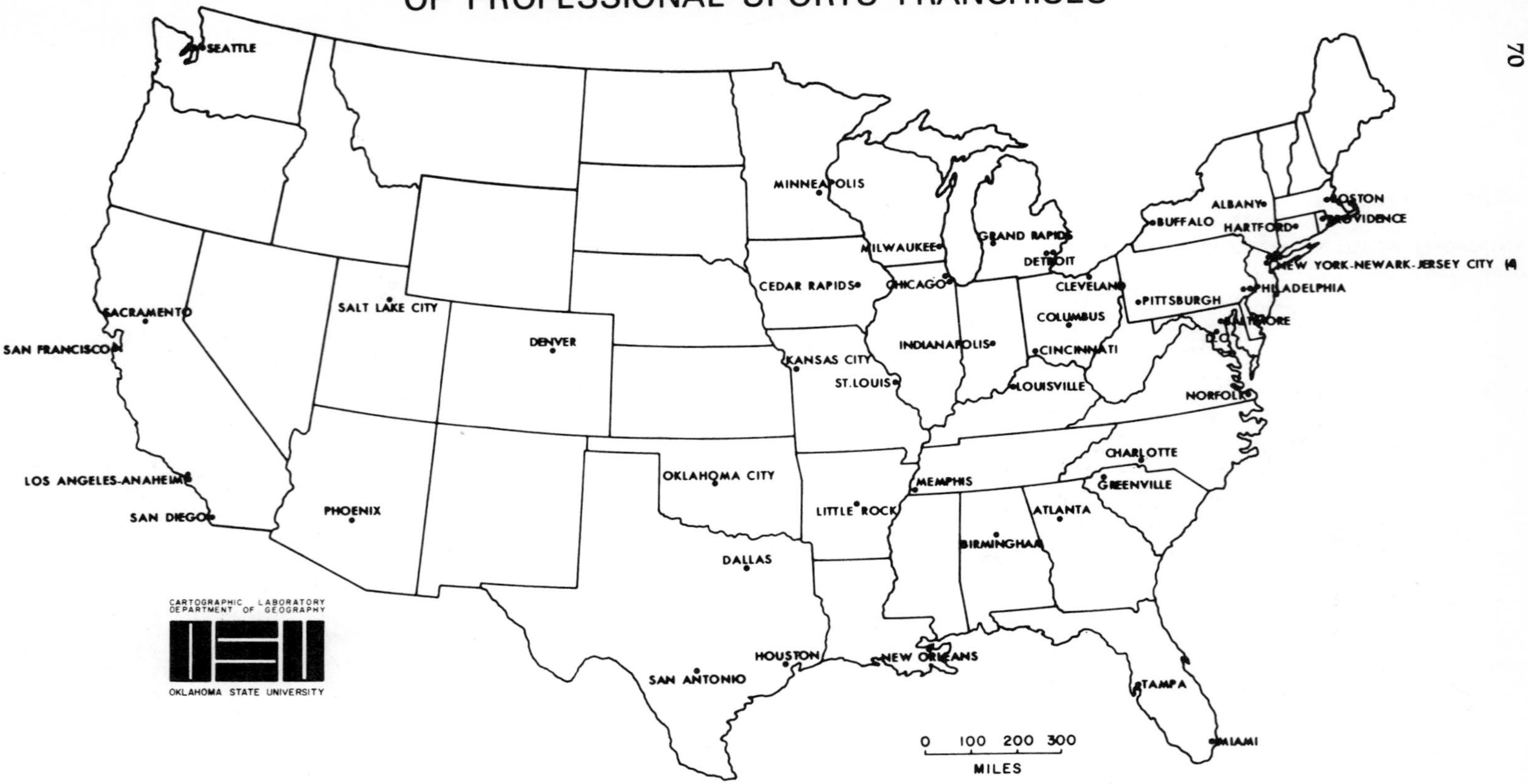

FRANCHISE LOCATIONS ARE BASED ON T.V. MARKET AREAS.

EACH FRANCHISE SERVES ONE OR MORE T.V. MARKET AREAS.

0   100 200 300

MILES

CARTOGRAPHIC LABORATORY
DEPARTMENT OF GEOGRAPHY

OKLAHOMA STATE UNIVERSITY

Figure 6

A THEORETICAL MARKET-ORIENTED EXPANSION
OF PROFESSIONAL SPORTS FRANCHISES

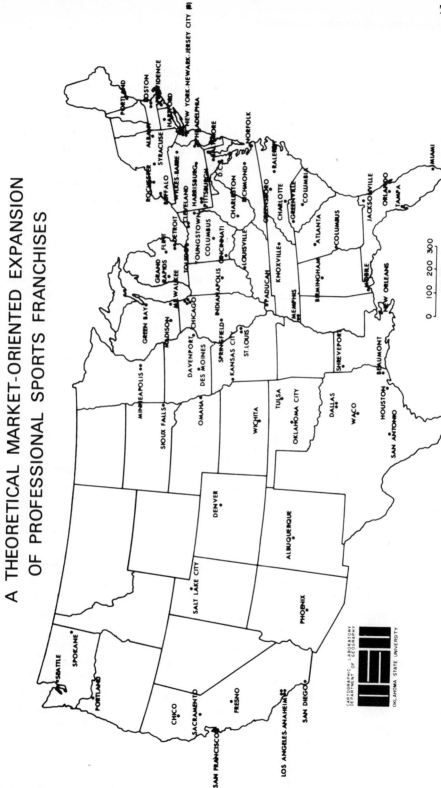

FRANCHISE LOCATIONS ARE BASED ON T.V. MARKET AREAS.

EACH FRANCHISE SERVES ONE OR MORE T.V. MARKET AREAS.

could comprise another. Conferences in the South, Oklahoma and Texas, the Pacific Coast, the Midwest and Mideast could all be realities, and, with reasonable control of television broadcasting, might mark the rebirth of a spectator sport era that, according to Kahn, was destroyed by the greed of the baseball owners during the early 1950's. Speaking of the period in which the Giants and Dodgers televised all home games Kahn states: "You have to go out to see your team. You have to buy a ticket. Now, with every home game visible free in black and white, a man could sit home, catch three innings, and should the game turn one sided, switch to Milton Berle or Jackie Gleason." [7]

If indeed such a geographical reorganization did result in a renewed spectator involvement, it would reverberate throughout collegiate athletic circles. This would be particularly true in the case of football, where many of the new franchises would be located in or very near the present hotbeds of the collegiate gridiron spectacle. But perhaps if the proposed reorganization could be accomplished gradually it would put amateur sport in a more realistic and defensible framework. Additionally, it would provide a much greater opportunity for collegians and even high school graduates to earn a living as sports professionals. It would also result in a much more equitable delivery of sports services to the American public.

Sports Regions

There is a staggering number of sports regions throughout America. Certain areas function as centers of football or basketball mania. Others are highly involved with baseball, or such sports as lacrosse, auto racing, soccer, or curling. Much more could be written about the regions if we had better data on such things as participation, the generation of quality athletes, press and other media coverage, money devoted to sports facilities and programs, and, perhaps most importantly, the conversation time devoted to sport.

In attempting to identify sports regions, it was determined that the most accessible and reliable data are associated with the origins of athletes. Football, basketball, baseball, golf, bowling, and several other sports have been regionalized on this basis. The following maps tell much of the regional story where these sports are concerned.

The data on player origin are based on two samples of athletes. The first sample was assembled during the years 1961–67 and contained 136 university division football teams and 161 university division basketball teams.[8] There were 14,500 football players and approximately 4,200 basketball players in the sample. A second data set was assembled for the 1971–72 football and basketball seasons and contained all the university division teams plus a 50 percent sample of all colleges and universities from each state. The second sample contained over 24,000 players.

In assessing regional concentrations of football and basketball players the data can be viewed from both a total numbers and per capita standpoint. In the regional identification process it is vital to examine the *relative* producing capacities of various places in order to compensate for variations in population. Per capita transformation of the data was based on the 1960 and 1970 population of the United States, and the individual states, counties, and metropolitan areas.

The per capita data transformation, utilized to assemble each of the following maps, can be demonstrated by the 1961–67 football sample. Based on a 1960 U.S. population of nearly 180 million the 14,500 football players represented roughly one person in 12,500. A ratio of one player per 12,500 people constitutes the national average of football player production. Hence, if a state or county is supplying players at a rate of 1 per 25,000 total population, it would be operating at only 50 percent of the national norm. A ratio of 1 per 6,250 would amount to twice the production characteristic of the nation as a whole. Normal output of 1 per 12,500 can be represented as an index value of 1.00. And by using this simple formula:

$$\text{Index value} = \frac{\text{Number of players}}{\text{population}} \div \frac{1}{12,500}$$

we can establish an index for any area, which can be used for all kinds of comparative purposes.

Let us now turn our attention to several different types of sport distributions and see what kinds of regions can be identified. The origin of major college and university football players is first depicted on a total output basis (Fig. 8).[9] The symbols represent player production for each county in the United States. A rapid perusal of the map leads one to the immediate conclusion that the cities are producing the bulk of the nation's football talent. However, some urban areas are sending forth many more players than others; Los Angeles, Chicago, Pittsburgh and Cleveland are prominent examples. Many of the smaller towns particularly in the Southeast and throughout the Southern Plains are also notable producers. It is also apparent from the map that several sections of the country are producing very few players. The problem with this type of map is that it is extremely difficult to regionalize with any authority or confidence.

The map displaying per capita production of college football players, however, makes the identification of regions much easier (Fig. 9). Here we can see that most of the cities which stood out on the total output map are producing football players at the national average rate or considerably

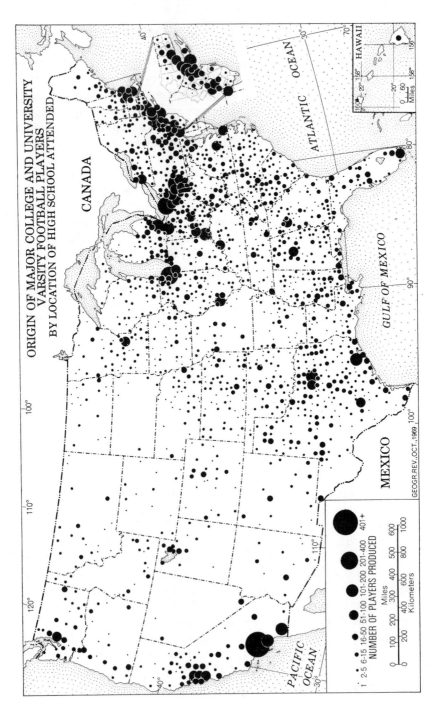

Figure 8

The Per Capita Production of Major College & University Varsity Football Players* by Counties

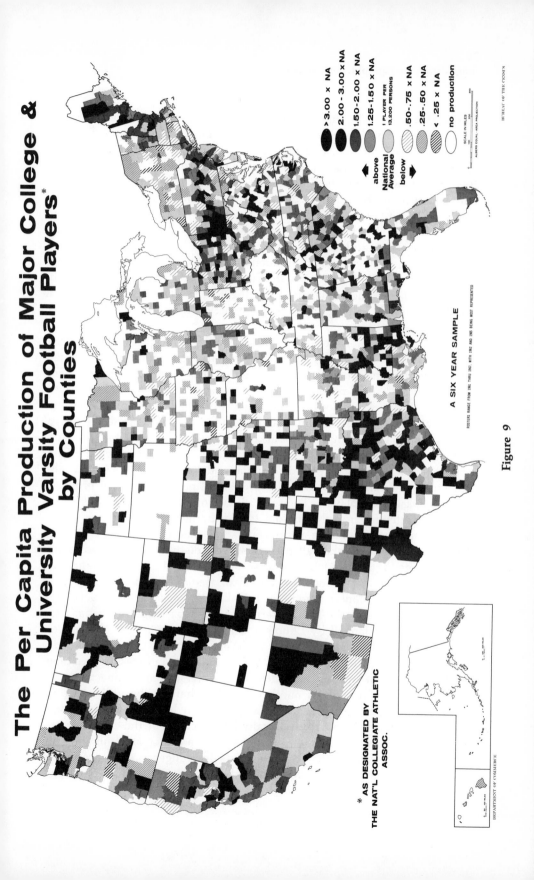

* AS DESIGNATED BY THE NAT'L COLLEGIATE ATHLETIC ASSOC.

> 3.00 × NA
2.00 - 3.00 × NA
1.50 - 2.00 × NA
1.25 - 1.50 × NA

1 PLAYER PER 13,200 PERSONS

.50 - .75 × NA
.25 - .50 × NA
< .25 × NA
no production

above
National
Average
below

SCALE IN MILES
ALBERS EQUAL-AREA PROJECTION

A SIX YEAR SAMPLE

ROSTERS RANGE FROM 1961 THRU 1967, WITH 1962 AND 1965 BEING MOST REPRESENTED

BUREAU OF THE CENSUS

DEPARTMENT OF COMMERCE

Figure 9

below that rate. The high production regions, Western Pennsylvania, Eastern Ohio, Southern Mississippi, four sections of Texas, the East Bay area near San Francisco, and the Wasatch Valley of Utah are strikingly visible. Each of them has two to four times the quantity of athletes that their population warrants. Conversely Southern Missouri, Northern Arkansas, much of Kentucky, Southern Illinois, and Southern Indiana are sending forth a very small number of players. In addition there are numerous sections of the Great Plains and Rocky Mountain west which produced only a few gridiron stalwarts.

After identifying the high production and low production regions, they can be analyzed in detail to isolate those variables which account for the level of success. The explanation for the football fever, or lack of it, is both elusive and challenging, as is its impact on the society and culture of the area.

The source regions of quality basketball players are very different than those for football (Fig. 10). The primary production region centers on Illinois, Indiana, and Kentucky. Together these states are breeding college bound basketball players at a rate in excess of twice the national average. The "IllInKy" region extends eastward along the Ohio River into Southern Ohio, West Virginia, and includes the Pittsburgh district of Pennsylvania. Other important basketball regions are in Utah, Western Oregon, and Washington, D.C. The "city game" flourishes along the Eastern seaboard in New York, Philadelphia, and Washington, D.C. and also in Detroit and Chicago. During the 1961–1967 period the South produced very few basketball players. The same situation was true of the North Central belt stretching from Minnesota to Northern New England.

We can also regionalize at the state scale. Based on the 1971–72 sample of football and basketball players several distinct groupings of states emerge (Figs. 11 and 12). In the case of football, Texas, Louisiana, and Mississippi represent a Southern region of tremendous player output. In the north, Idaho, Montana, and North Dakota are operating at a very high rate. Ohio dominates the Midwestern scene. For basketball Indiana, Kentucky, and Ohio flanked by Illinois and Pennsylvania are far above average. Utah and Idaho stand out in the West as do the Dakotas. The city production is paced by Washington, D.C. with a rate in excess of five times the national norm, and is also evident in New Jersey and Connecticut.

Participation in sport is another variable that can be utilized in the regionalization process. Take for example tenpin bowling, a sport dominated by adults and popular in virtually every section of the United States. Although the bowling alley is considered to be a center of community social activity, we can see that bowling is much stronger in some areas than in others (Fig. 13). As an indoor sport, bowling attracts many more par-

The Per Capita Production of Major College & University Varsity Basketball Players* By Counties

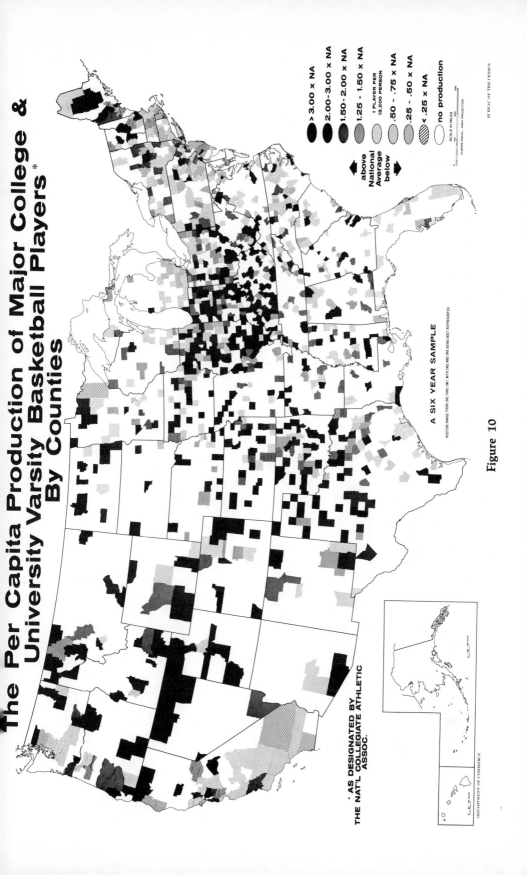

> 3.00 x NA

2.00-3.00 x NA

1.50-2.00 x NA

1.25 - 1.50 x NA

above National Average / below

1 PLAYER PER 13,200 PERSON

.50 - .75 x NA

.25 - .50 x NA

< .25 x NA

no production

SCALE IN MILES

ALBERS EQUAL AREA PROJECTION

BUREAU OF THE CENSUS

A SIX YEAR SAMPLE

ROSTERS RANGE FROM 1961 THRU 1967, WITH 1962 AND 1965 BEING NOT REPRESENTED

* AS DESIGNATED BY THE NAT'L COLLEGIATE ATHLETIC ASSOC.

DEPARTMENT OF COMMERCE

Figure 10

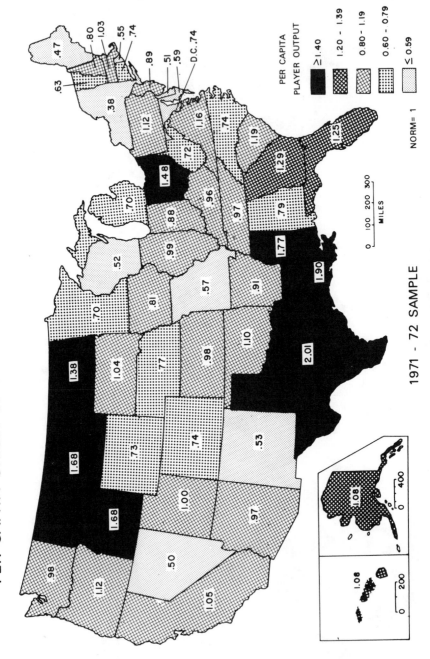

PER CAPITA ORIGIN OF MAJOR COLLEGE FOOTBALL PLAYERS

1971 - 72 SAMPLE

Figure 11

PER CAPITA
PLAYER OUTPUT

≥ 1.40
1.20 - 1.39
0.80 - 1.19
0.60 - 0.79
≤ 0.59

NORM = 1

PER CAPITA ORIGIN OF MAJOR COLLEGE BASKETBALL PLAYERS

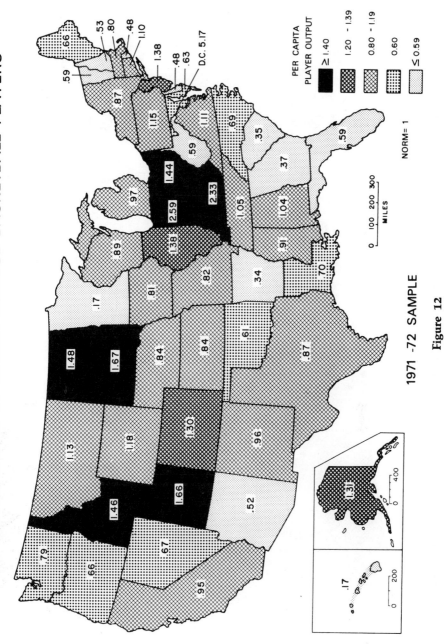

PER CAPITA
PLAYER OUTPUT

≥ 1.40

1.20 – 1.39

0.80 – 1.19

0.60

≤ 0.59

NORM = 1

100 200 300
MILES

1971 -72 SAMPLE

Figure 12

400

200

MALE PER CAPITA PARTICIPATION IN BOWLING AS MEASURED BY
MEMBERSHIP IN THE AMERICAN BOWLING CONGRESS

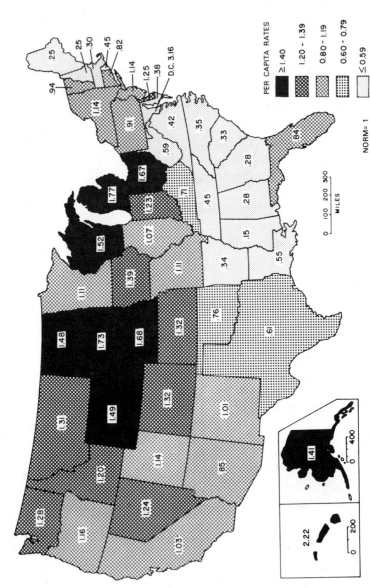

PER CAPITA RATES

≥ 1.40

1.20 - 1.39

0.80 - 1.19

0.60 - 0.79

≤ 0.59

NORM = 1

SOURCE: BASED ON DATA FROM THE AMERICAN BOWLING CONGRESS, 1969-70.

Figure 13

ticipants in the North than it does in the South. It is especially strong in the Great Lakes area with Michigan, Wisconsin, and Ohio exceeding the national average by over 50 percent. It is also very important throughout the Northern Plains and most of the Midwest. New York has more bowlers than any other state but has a per capita rank of only 15 percent above the national average. With the exception of Florida, all the Southern states are far below average and Mississippi has a per capita rate of only 15 percent the national norm. Hawaii is surprisingly above average and, from a per capita standpoint, leads the nation. Apparently the sport has followed a migratory diffusion process westward to California and eventually to the Pacific Islands. The lack of participation in eastern New England appears to be the result of the substitution of duck and candlepin bowling in place of tenpin bowling.

We can also examine high school and collegiate sport on the basis of participation. Soccer is a good example and the high school and college samples have much in common (Figs. 14 and 15). Soccer is definitely a regional sport. It thrives in the Northeast and in the St. Louis area and has begun to diffuse to the West Coast. The greatest amount of participation is concentrated in New England, New York, Pennsylvania, Maryland, and Missouri. The college game has spread to a greater degree than the high school sport. This is evidenced by the number of universities now fielding teams throughout the Midwest and Western sections of the country. Like other social phenomena, the game has been very slow in gaining support in the South.

Events focusing on horse shows also demonstrate pronounced regional variation. Much of what has become part of the standard American horse show was imported from Great Britain. We would therefore expect a higher level of attraction to this type of endeavor in those areas which were dominated by the English Colonials. And based on the residence of approved American horse show judges and stewards, New England, Virginia and Kentucky reinforce this notion (Fig. 16). Commitment to this type of recreation has leaped across the midsection of the country to the West Coast with a little enthusiasm generated along the way in the states of Colorado and Arizona. Overall involvement with horses is not nearly as important in the South as one might imagine, and is particularly low in the Mississippi Delta region.

A look at one of the specialty breeds, the American quarter horse, presents us with quite a different picture of regional interest (Fig. 17). The quarter horse which was bred by the American cowboy for work purposes, and which is still used in that way, dominates in the animal grazing country of the West. It has also developed a considerable following in states like Iowa, Illinois, and Indiana, but seems to have little following else-

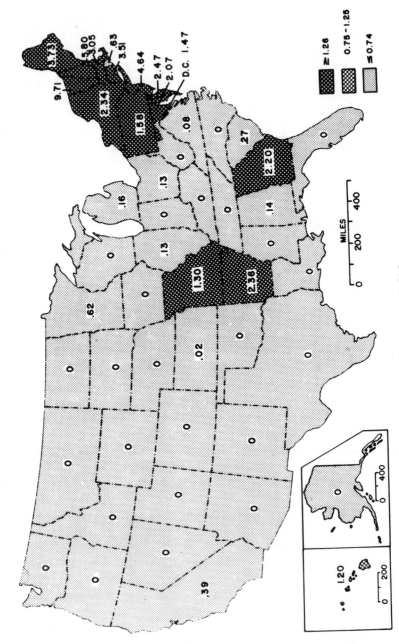

PER CAPITA PARTICIPATION IN HIGH SCHOOL SOCCER - 1971 - 72

AVERAGE PARTICIPATION = 1 PER 202 PEOPLE IN THE 14-17 AGE GROUP

Figure 14

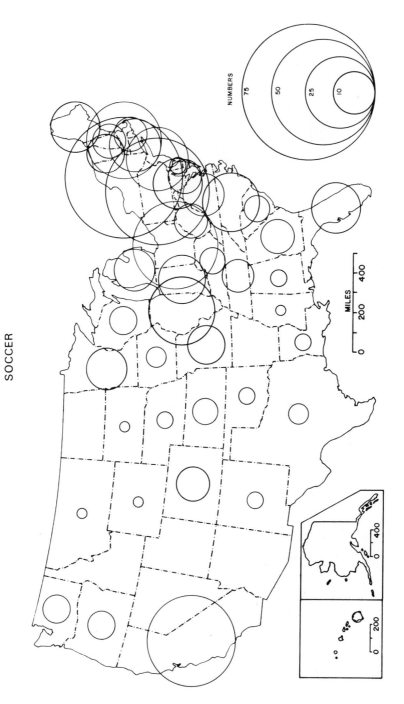

NUMBER OF COLLEGES AND UNIVERSITIES SPONSERING INTERCOLLEGIATE COMPETITION 1970 - 71

SOCCER

NUMBERS

Figure 15

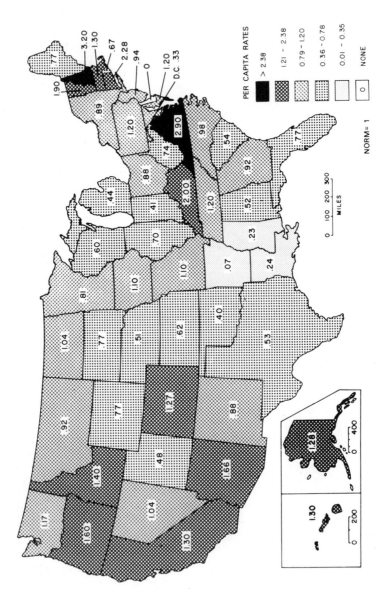

PER CAPITA INVOLVEMENT IN THE AMERICAN HORSE SHOWS ASSOCIATION AS MEASURED BY THE RESIDENCE OF APPROVED JUDGES AND STEWARDS

SOURCE: BASED ON DATA FROM THE AMERICAN HORSE SHOWS ASSOCIATION RULE BOOK, 1972.

Figure 16

PER CAPITA INVOLVEMENT IN THE AMERICAN QUARTER HORSE ASSOCIATION AS MEASURED BY THE RESIDENCE OF APPROVED JUDGES AND STEWARDS

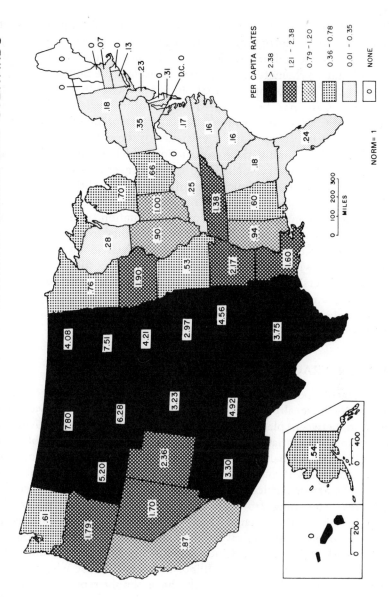

Figure 17

SOURCE: BASED ON DATA FROM THE AMERICAN QUARTER HORSE ASSOCIATION, 1972.

where. This speedy horse, like most other specialty breeds, tends to be most popular in those areas where it was originally utilized as a working animal.

Still another form of sports region can be identified by the facilities devoted to it. In his intriguing article "Carolina Thunder: A Geography of Southern Stock Car Racing," Richard Pillsbury focuses on the location of facilities and the hometowns of drivers to isolate the Southern stock car region (Fig. 18).[10] He points out that stock car racing first became established in the Carolinas before spreading to other regions. The cultural hearth of NASCAR Grand National Racing still dominates that sport.

It is difficult to account for the existence of the various types of sports regions. There is a multivariate explanation which seems to differ from place to place. The Pennsylvania–Ohio football fever appears to be related to a group of economic, ethnic, demographic, and political variables, in combination with a strong game-oriented tradition. Texas football thrives under a sharply contrasting socioeconomic situation, and a much more amenable natural environment. There are still other explanations for the Illinois, Indiana, Kentucky basketball scene. Some regions are dominated by a single sport while others embrace a medley of sporting activities. The amount and diversity of participation in any area appears to be related to the income and priority which that area accords to education. A state like Minnesota provides extensive sports opportunities for participation while Mississippi supports programs for only a few.

SPATIAL INTERACTION

The medium of sport affords the opportunity for considerable spatial interaction. We have already referred to the development of rivalries and competition between places. The communications network provides another example of spatial interaction. Networks have been established to beam football, basketball, and baseball games, as well as numerous other sports, to audiences throughout the United States. The football and baseball networks are of particular interest. Who gets which game? Television market areas stemming from advertising now govern the geographical transmission of sporting events. Thus, the Kansas City games are received in an area surrounding that city. The Kansas City network overlaps the Dallas network in Oklahoma. Chicago Bears and St. Louis Cardinals football games also overlap in central Illinois. This is the case where all teams are concerned. The television networks have simply replaced, or in some cases complimented, the radio networks which were laid out during an earlier period.

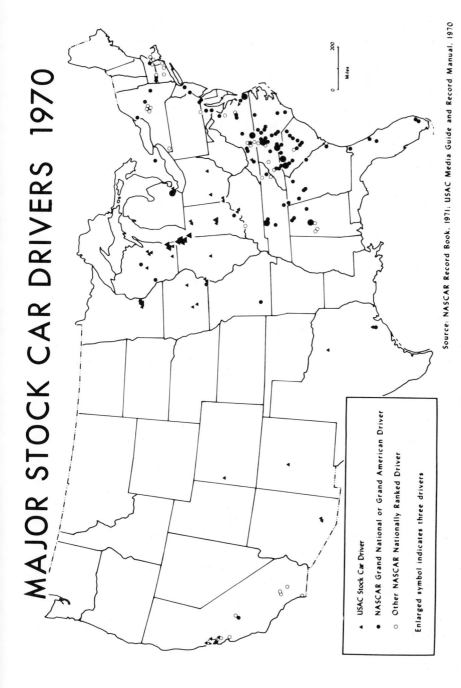

MAJOR STOCK CAR DRIVERS 1970

Source: NASCAR Record Book, 1971; USAC Media Guide and Record Manual, 1970

Figure 18

▲ USAC Stock Car Driver

● NASCAR Grand National or Grand American Driver

○ Other NASCAR Nationally Ranked Driver

Enlarged symbol indicates three drivers

Athletic Recruitment

Another form of spatial interaction stems from the recruitment of collegiate athletes from the high schools and junior colleges throughout the United States. The pattern of movement can be portrayed as a spatial model. It involves the spatial arrangement of athletic production and consumption, individual spatial decision-making on the part of the athletes and the recruiters, and group decision-making on the part of university officials, governing boards, and the general populace. The pattern of recruiting has been greatly influenced in recent years, particularly since 1950, by the strong desire of geographically remote universities to gain national exposure through the medium of athletics. As a result, numerous recruiting forces (in this case, geographical points) have been added, and have served to make the "recruiting game" a much more spatially complex business.

A spatial model of recruiting can be set up as follows. One major element of the model involves the geography of production. It has been demonstrated that athletic production varies considerably from place to place. Some areas are producing many more athletes than others. This is due to a discontinuous distribution of populations, spatial variation in the emphasis placed on different sports, variation in social-economic character, climatic variations, and so on. Thus, recruiters are confronted with identifying the locations of collegiate prospects, selecting those people on which to concentrate, and luring them to the desired playing location, a place that in most instances is removed from the athlete's home location. The second important element of the model involves the spatial arrangement of playing opportunities, or the points of consumption. This might best be referred to as the *market*. And the market has even less resemblance than the production function to the distribution of population (Tables 1 and 2).

To further complicate the model, there is a hierarchy of markets for the potential athletes. The major athletic schools constitute one segment of the market and should realistically be divided into at least two groups. These can be based on athletic budgets which are highly correlated with the successful pursuit of national honors. In addition to the big time market, there exists the scholarship-subsidized state college group, the small state colleges, and a wide range of private institutions. Most of the latter group are operating on a very limited athletic budget. The effect of the distance between the production regions and the market varies considerably at different levels within the hierarchy. The really big name universities are much better at overcoming the *friction of distance* than are the small state colleges. Hence, the better financed schools have the potential to recruit from all the lucrative production regions, while the small state and private colleges are usually confined to their immediate locales.

The recruiting pattern of a single university or regional grouping of universities should reflect, therefore, their location relative to the location of available athletes. If they are situated within or near a region of high productivity, most of their recruiting should be local; if not, it should be spatially linked with the closest source region or regions.

A spatial model of athletic recruiting cannot stop with the analysis of production and consumption fields. For many athletes, it is no longer a direct move between their high school site and the site of the college which they select. A growing number are making an intermediate stop at a junior college. Many of these two-year schools now serve as "farm clubs" to the major universities. Junior college locations then must also be considered in any realistic model, because they provide intervening opportunities within the consumption field.

Other variables which demand inclusion are the geographical experiences of recruiters and coaches as well as their reputation, the distribution and interest of alumni, and the strength of the attachment that athletes from various sections of the country have for their "place" or local area. The geography of recruiting at any given college will reflect the geographical experience of its coaches and the strength of their contacts with other areas. For example, the recruitment of Ohio or New York athletes to a university in the Rocky Mountain region may simply mean that the coaches have experience and influence in those states. Another nearby university may concentrate on California and Illinois for similar reasons. Recruiters also possess a given set of perceptions in regard to *where* the best athletes come from. These perceptions are related to their own place experience and, to some extent, reflect their place-pride. A recruiter who is strongly attached to his state or culture region will seldom leave that region for recruitment purposes. In the same vein, an athlete who is strongly attached to his area will be reluctant to select a school outside his perceived cultural region.

Alumni play a large, but difficult to measure, role in the "recruiting game." They donate funds which enable the university to overcome the impediments created by distance. Their distribution is also a significant factor. A dispersed group is likely to be more effective than one which is agglomerated almost exclusively within the "home" region. The Notre Dame and the Armed Forces Academy alumni have access to the chief production fields. The Notre Dame radio network reaches all sections of the United States and has yielded a great impact through the years. It provides an excellent example of alumni influence.

TABLE 1
PER CAPITA EMPHASIS ON COLLEGIATE FOOTBALL BY STATES (1970)

State	Number of major colleges	Index of emphasis (Average=1.00)	Total colleges	Index of emphasis (Average=1.00)
Alabama	2	.81	11	.99
Arkansas	1	.74	12	1.92
Alaska	0	.00	0	.00
Arizona	3	3.05	4	.70
California	10	.84	40	.62
Colorado	3	2.26	10	1.39
Connecticut	2	1.04	9	.91
Delaware	1	2.97	2	1.11
District of Columbia	1	1.73	6	2.46
Florida	3	.80	8	.36
Georgia	2	.67	7	.50
Hawaii	1	.38	2	.79
Idaho	3	5.97	5	2.17
Illinois	3	.39	24	.66
Indiana	3	.85	19	1.12
Iowa	2	.96	22	2.40
Kansas	3	1.82	19	2.59
Kentucky	2	.87	9	.86
Louisiana	2	.81	11	.93
Maine	1	1.37	5	1.55
Maryland	2	.85	6	.47
Massachusetts	5	1.29	16	.86
Michigan	3	.51	20	.69

State				
Minnesota	1	.39	21	1.70
Mississippi	3	1.82	9	1.25
Missouri	1	.31	15	.99
Montana	2	3.92	8	3.56
Nebraska	1	.94	14	2.90
Nevada	0	00	2	1.25
New Hampshire	2	4.36	4	1.69
New Mexico	2	2.78	5	1.52
New Jersey	2	.44	10	.43
New York	6	.47	34	.57
North Carolina	6	1.74	20	1.21
North Dakota	2	4.17	7	3.53
Ohio	9	1.23	36	1.04
Oklahoma	3	1.71	13	1.56
Oregon	2	1.50	11	1.62
Pennsylvania	6	.70	49	1.28
Rhode Island	2	3.08	2	.64
South Carolina	4	2.22	8	.95
South Dakota	0	.00	12	5.52
Texas	10	1.38	29	.80
Tennessee	3	1.11	17	1.37
Utah	4	5.94	6	1.75
Vermont	1	3.39	2	1.36
Virginia	5	1.67	16	1.06
Washington	2	.93	9	.81
West Virginia	2	1.42	13	2.29
Wisconsin	1	.34	20	1.40
Wyoming	1	4.01	1	.94

TABLE 2
PER CAPITA EMPHASIS ON COLLEGIATE BASKETBALL BY STATES (1970)

States	Number of major colleges	Index of emphasis (Average=1.00)	Total colleges	Index of emphasis (Average=1.00)
Alabama	2	.95	19	1.10
Arkansas	1	.63	15	1.55
Alaska	0	.00	2	1.33
Arizona	3	2.58	5	.56
California	11	.78	57	.57
Colorado	3	1.92	12	1.07
Connecticut	2	1.32	15	.99
Delaware	0	.00	3	1.07
District of Columbia	2	2.95	9	2.38
Florida	3	.68	19	.57
Georgia	2	.57	17	.73
Hawaii	0	.00	3	1.93
Idaho	1	1.68	6	1.69
Illinois	6	.67	44	.79
Indiana	4	.96	33	1.26
Iowa	2	.81	26	1.83
Kansas	3	1.54	20	1.77
Kentucky	6	2.21	19	1.18
Louisiana	3	1.03	16	.88
Maine	1	1.15	14	2.80
Maryland	2	.72	13	.66
Massachusetts	5	1.09	35	1.22

Michigan	4	.57	31	.69
Minnesota	1	.32	24	1.26
Mississippi	3	1.54	13	1.17
Missouri	2	.52	26	1.10
Montana	1	1.63	9	2.59
Nebraska	2	1.59	16	2.15
Nevada	0	.00	2	.83
New Hampshire	2	3.65	9	2.44
New Mexico	2	2.34	7	1.36
New Jersey	3	.55	19	.53
New York	12	.80	77	.84
North Carolina	5	1.23	33	1.29
North Dakota	1	1.77	8	2.60
Ohio	9	1.04	46	.86
Oklahoma	4	1.92	18	1.40
Oregon	3	1.90	15	1.43
Pennsylvania	7	.69	65	1.10
Rhode Island	3	3.88	6	1.26
South Carolina	4	1.88	14	1.09
South Dakota	0	.00	12	3.55
Texas	10	1.17	42	.75
Tennessee	3	.94	33	1.67
Utah	4	5.06	6	1.13
Vermont	1	2.82	9	4.00
Virginia	5	1.41	25	1.07
Washington	3	1.18	14	.82
West Virginia	2	1.20	16	1.83
Wisconsin	2	.56	24	1.08
Wyoming	1	3.44	1	.62

The model must finally take into account the athletes themselves. For, after all, it is they who make the decisions which transfer them from the production to the consumption fields. Each athlete is influenced by the extent and nature of local playing opportunities and his own degree of place-pride. His decision is affected by many things over which he has little or no control: the distribution of various alumni; recruiters; his own perceptions, and those of his family and friends. The end result is a spatially complex, yet reasonably predictable, athletic migration pattern.

Interregional Migration

The geographical interaction stimulated by athletic recruiting can be analyzed in several ways. The major flows are apparent when we subdivide the United States into nine football and ten basketball production and consumption sectors (Figs. 19 and 20). The most important football export regions are Pennsylvania–Ohio, California, the Midwest and the Northeast. Distance and the geographical variations in football emphasis, as well as the regional variations in the production of players, account in large measure for the migratory patterns. Similar forces are at work in the world of collegiate basketball, where Illinois, Indiana, and Kentucky replace Pennsylvania–Ohio as the chief exporters.

The migratory behavior of college athletes can also be examined at the interstate level. Using the 1971–72 sample of major college football and basketball players referred to in the discussion of sport regions, all interstate movements of ten or more football players and five or more basketball players have been plotted (Figs. 21 and 22). In the case of football, geographical interaction is extremely pronounced. Athletes are moving primarily from the populous industrial states, which contain a relatively limited number of big time football schools, to the more sparsely settled states which sponsor many more teams than their population warrants (Table 3).

There is also a great deal of interaction between the surplus states. Pennsylvania is interacting with New York, Ohio, and Indiana; Ohio is interacting with Michigan, Kentucky, West Virginia, New York, Indiana, and Illinois. In addition, there are athletes from Pennsylvania–Ohio making long treks to the Great Plains and even to the Southwest. The South is interacting on a very small scale with states outside the region. The Southern states, however, tend to trade players with one another. For example, Georgia is sending players to Alabama, Tennessee, Florida, and the Carolinas.

The degree of interaction is much less in the Central and Western United States, where most of the states supply their own needs or recruit token numbers from a variety of sources. California is a leading supplier

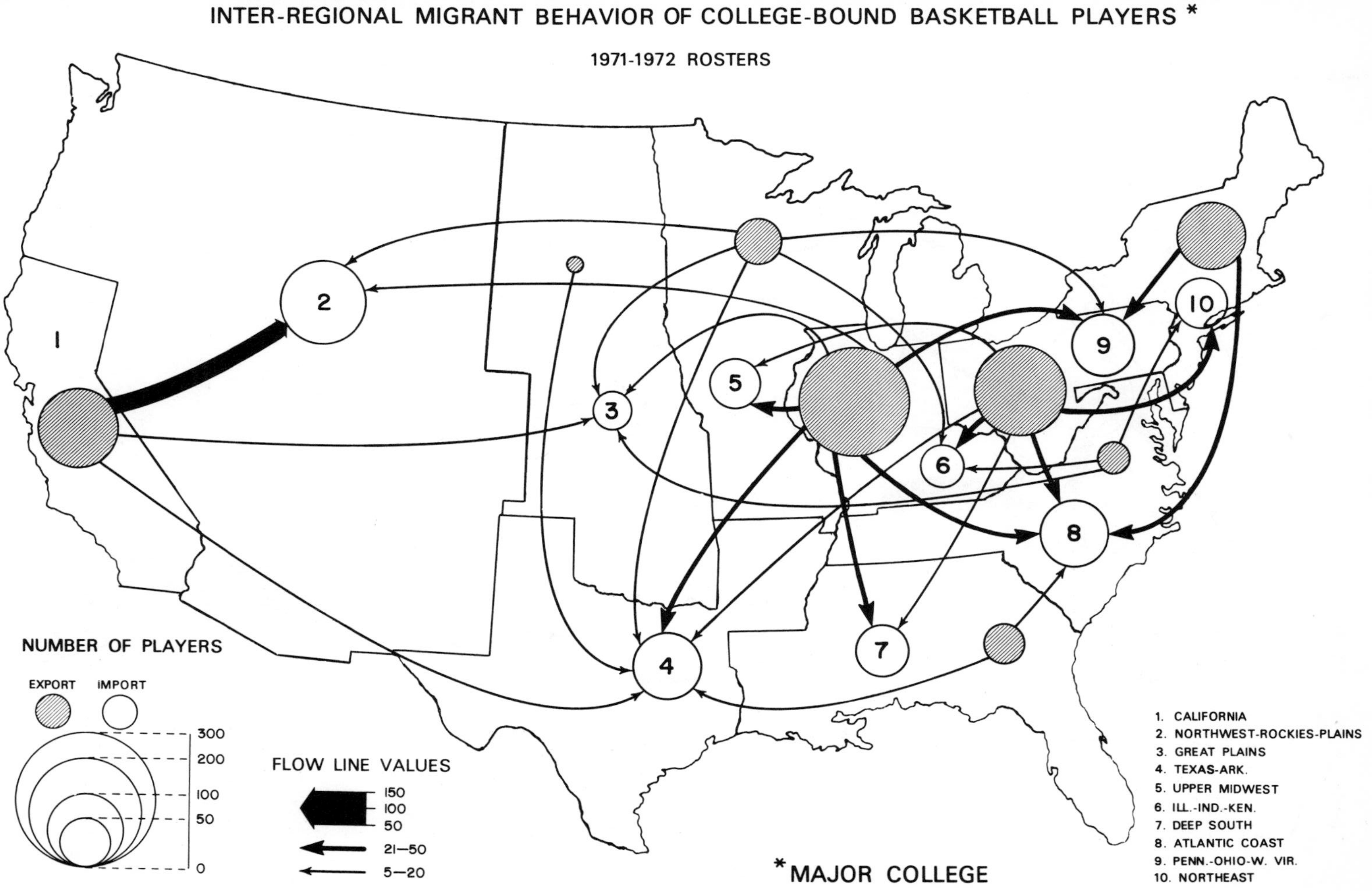

INTER-REGIONAL MIGRANT BEHAVIOR OF COLLEGE-BOUND BASKETBALL PLAYERS *

1971-1972 ROSTERS

1. CALIFORNIA
2. NORTHWEST-ROCKIES-PLAINS
3. GREAT PLAINS
4. TEXAS-ARK.
5. UPPER MIDWEST
6. ILL.-IND.-KEN.
7. DEEP SOUTH
8. ATLANTIC COAST
9. PENN.-OHIO-W. VIR.
10. NORTHEAST

*MAJOR COLLEGE

Figure 19

FLOW LINE VALUES

150
100
50
21—50
5—20

NUMBER OF PLAYERS

EXPORT   IMPORT

300
200
100
50
0

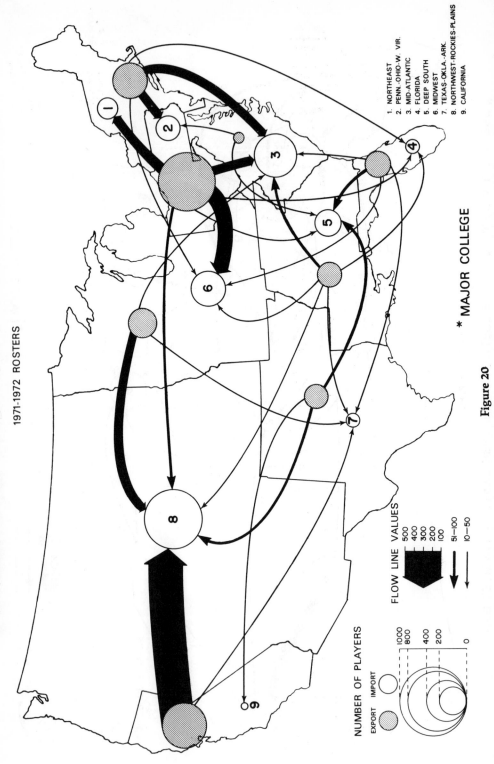

INTER-REGIONAL MIGRANT BEHAVIOR OF COLLEGE-BOUND FOOTBALL PLAYERS*

1971-1972 ROSTERS

1. NORTHEAST
2. PENN.-OHIO-W. VIR.
3. MID-ATLANTIC
4. FLORIDA
5. DEEP SOUTH
6. MIDWEST
7. TEXAS-OKLA.-ARK.
8. NORTHWEST-ROCKIES-PLAINS
9. CALIFORNIA

* MAJOR COLLEGE

FLOW LINE VALUES

500
400
300
200
100

51—100

10—50

NUMBER OF PLAYERS

EXPORT   IMPORT

1000
800

400

200

0

Figure 20

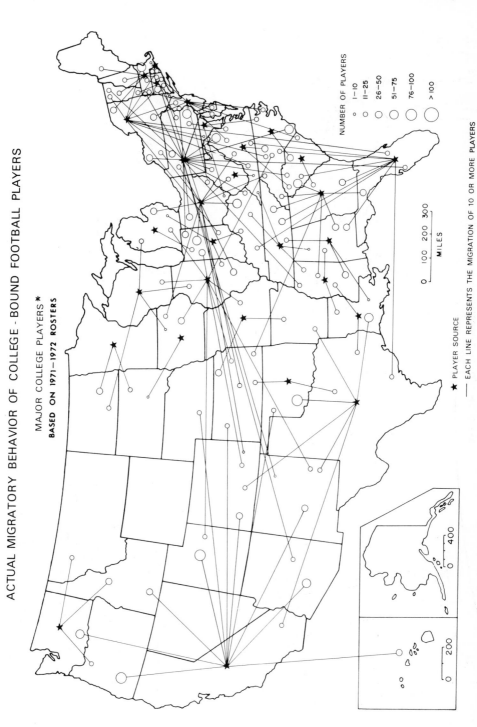

ACTUAL MIGRATORY BEHAVIOR OF COLLEGE - BOUND FOOTBALL PLAYERS

MAJOR COLLEGE PLAYERS *

BASED ON 1971-1972 ROSTERS

NUMBER OF PLAYERS

1-10
11-25
26-50
51-75
76-100
>100

0   100 200 300
MILES

★ PLAYER SOURCE

— EACH LINE REPRESENTS THE MIGRATION OF 10 OR MORE PLAYERS

* AS DESIGNATED BY THE NCAA AND NAIA
AND INCLUDING A 100% SAMPLE FROM EACH STATE

0   200

0   400

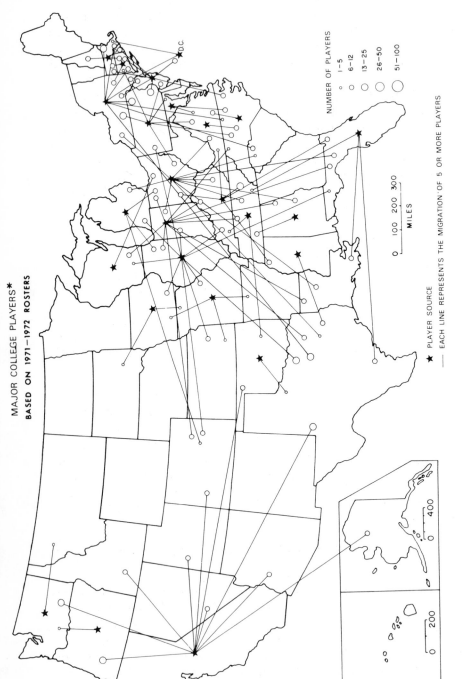

ACTUAL MIGRATORY BEHAVIOR

MAJOR COLLEGE PLAYERS*

BASED ON 1971–1972 ROSTERS

NUMBER OF PLAYERS

1–5
6–12
13–25
26–50
51–100

0   100 200 300

MILES

★ PLAYER SOURCE

—— EACH LINE REPRESENTS THE MIGRATION OF 5 OR MORE PLAYERS

0   200

0   400

* AS DESIGNATED BY THE NCAA AND NAIA
AND INCLUDING A 100% SAMPLE FROM EACH STATE

Figure 22

to its immediate neighbors. It is also sending football talent as far east as Oklahoma, Kansas, and Nebraska. In summary, there is a tremendous amount of movement between adjacent states. There is also a major flow from the most populous states such as California, Pennsylvania, Ohio, and Illinois to those both within their immediate regions and outside of them.

The interstate basketball migration is not as great as that which characterizes football (Fig. 22). The direction of flow is different, primarily as a result of the South's inability to grow its own talent. Major Midwestern suppliers, Illinois, Indiana, and Ohio, are shipping substantial numbers to the South and also westward to the Plains states, as well as trading players with one another. Pennsylvania, New York, and New Jersey are filling the needs of the East Coast states and New England. In the West, California functions in much the same way as it does for football (Table 4).

This great athletic stampede contributes in large measure to the financial crisis which grips collegiate sports today. The cost of recruiting a football or a basketball team, or, for that matter, any type of team, has been increasing at a blistering pace during the past few years. To be successful a recruiter must get the best prospects in his own area plus a number of players from other parts of the country.

But these challenges and the problems that beset collegiate athletic recruitment are by no means new. The following quotations from the Carnegie Foundation Study of American Collegiate Athletics (done in 1929) is indicative:

> Intercollege athletics are highly competitive. Every college or university longs for a winning team in its group. The coach is on the alert to bring the most promising athletes in the secondary schools to his college team. A system of recruiting and subsidizing has grown up, under which boys are offered pecuniary and other inducements to enter a particular college. The system is demoralizing and corrupt, alike for the boy who takes the money and for the agent who arranges it, and for the whole group of college and secondary school boys who know about it.[11]

Referring to the role of collegiate alumni, the Carnegie Commission had this to say:

> In a matter of competitive athletics the college alumnus has, in the main, played a sorry role. It is one thing for the old grad to go back and coach the boys of his college as at Oxford or Cambridge, where there are no professional coaches and no game receipts. It is quite another thing for an American college graduate to pay money to high school boys either directly or indirectly in order to enlist their services

TABLE 3
ACTUAL MIGRATIONS, MAJOR COLLEGE FOOTBALL PLAYERS
Based on 1971-72 Rosters

				No. of Players
From	Alabama	To	Louisiana	10
From	Alabama	To	Mississippi	31
From	Alabama	To	Tennessee	23
From	California	To	Arizona	65
From	California	To	Colorado	45
From	California	To	Hawaii	30
From	California	To	Idaho	44
From	California	To	Kansas	14
From	California	To	Nebraska	12
From	California	To	New Mexico	34
From	California	To	Oklahoma	15
From	California	To	Oregon	82
From	California	To	Utah	90
From	California	To	Washington	59
From	Connecticut	To	Massachusetts	16
From	Connecticut	To	New York	10
From	Connecticut	To	Pennsylvania	17
From	Connecticut	To	Vermont	18
From	Florida	To	Alabama	29
From	Florida	To	Georgia	28
From	Florida	To	Kentucky	21
From	Florida	To	North Carolina	15
From	Florida	To	South Carolina	23
From	Florida	To	Tennessee	30
From	Florida	To	Texas	18
From	Florida	To	Virginia	12
From	Georgia	To	Alabama	28
From	Georgia	To	Florida	37
From	Georgia	To	Kansas	13
From	Georgia	To	Mississippi	14
From	Georgia	To	North Carolina	16
From	Georgia	To	South Carolina	52
From	Georgia	To	Tennessee	28
From	Illinois	To	Colorado	15
From	Illinois	To	Indiana	45
From	Illinois	To	Iowa	43

TABLE 3 (CON'T)

				No. of Players
From	Illinois	To	Kansas	21
From	Illinois	To	Michigan	22
From	Illinois	To	Missouri	16
From	Illinois	To	New Mexico	12
From	Illinois	To	North Carolina	13
From	Illinois	To	Utah	14
From	Illinois	To	Wisconsin	18
From	Indiana	To	Illinois	19
From	Indiana	To	Kentucky	16
From	Indiana	To	Michigan	10
From	Iowa	To	South Dakota	10
From	Louisiana	To	Mississippi	21
From	Louisiana	To	Texas	14
From	Maryland	To	North Carolina	18
From	Maryland	To	Ohio	10
From	Maryland	To	Pennsylvania	16
From	Maryland	To	Virginia	20
From	Massachusetts	To	Connecticut	20
From	Massachusetts	To	Maine	17
From	Massachusetts	To	New Hampshire	18
From	Massachusetts	To	New York	31
From	Massachusetts	To	Rhode Island	12
From	Massachusetts	To	Vermont	15
From	Michigan	To	Indiana	12
From	Minnesota	To	North Dakota	45
From	Minnesota	To	South Dakota	15
From	Mississippi	To	Alabama	12
From	Mississippi	To	Louisiana	23
From	Missouri	To	Arkansas	13
From	Missouri	To	Kansas	32
From	New Jersey	To	Connecticut	13
From	New Jersey	To	Delaware	18
From	New Jersey	To	Maryland	16
From	New Jersey	To	Massachusetts	23
From	New Jersey	To	New York	46
From	New Jersey	To	North Carolina	18

TABLE 3 (CON'T)

				No. of Players
From	New Jersey	To	Ohio	16
From	New Jersey	To	Pennsylvania	72
From	New Jersey	To	South Carolina	13
From	New Jersey	To	Virginia	22
From	New York	To	Connecticut	32
From	New York	To	Florida	11
From	New York	To	Indiana	14
From	New York	To	Maryland	10
From	New York	To	Massachusetts	52
From	New York	To	New Jersey	12
From	New York	To	North Carolina	22
From	New York	To	Pennsylvania	43
From	New York	To	Rhode Island	21
From	New York	To	Vermont	20
From	New York	To	Virginia	15
From	North Carolina	To	South Carolina	29
From	Ohio	To	Colorado	10
From	Ohio	To	Connecticut	14
From	Ohio	To	Illinois	30
From	Ohio	To	Indiana	65
From	Ohio	To	Iowa	16
From	Ohio	To	Kansas	21
From	Ohio	To	Kentucky	79
From	Ohio	To	Michigan	50
From	Ohio	To	New York	17
From	Ohio	To	North Carolina	13
From	Ohio	To	Pennsylvania	16
From	Ohio	To	Virginia	15
From	Ohio	To	West Virginia	23
From	Oklahoma	To	Kansas	21
From	Oklahoma	To	Texas	13
From	Pennsylvania	To	Arizona	16
From	Pennsylvania	To	Connecticut	12
From	Pennsylvania	To	Delaware	17
From	Pennsylvania	To	Florida	14
From	Pennsylvania	To	Indiana	38

TABLE 3 (CON'T)

				No. of Players
From	Pennsylvania	To	Kentucky	21
From	Pennsylvania	To	Maryland	27
From	Pennsylvania	To	Massachusetts	11
From	Pennsylvania	To	Mississippi	11
From	Pennsylvania	To	New Hampshire	12
From	Pennsylvania	To	New Jersey	22
From	Pennsylvania	To	New Mexico	10
From	Pennsylvania	To	New York	37
From	Pennsylvania	To	North Carolina	51
From	Pennsylvania	To	Ohio	32
From	Pennsylvania	To	South Carolina	12
From	Pennsylvania	To	Virginia	67
From	Pennsylvania	To	West Virginia	16
From	Rhode Island	To	Massachusetts	10
From	South Carolina	To	Georgia	12
From	Tennessee	To	Alabama	10
From	Tennessee	To	Kentucky	20
From	Tennessee	To	Mississippi	14
From	Tennessee	To	Virginia	10
From	Texas	To	Arkansas	21
From	Texas	To	California	14
From	Texas	To	Colorado	20
From	Texas	To	Louisiana	75
From	Texas	To	New Mexico	25
From	Texas	To	Oklahoma	85
From	Virginia	To	North Carolina	50
From	Virginia	To	South Carolina	16
From	Washington	To	Idaho	31
From	Washington	To	Montana	24
From	Washington	To	Oregon	25
From	West Virginia	To	Virginia	10
From	Wisconsin	To	Illinois	16
From	Wisconsin	To	Iowa	10
From	Wisconsin	To	Michigan	11
From	Wisconsin	To	North Dakota	12

TABLE 4
ACTUAL MIGRATIONS, MAJOR COLLEGE BASKETBALL PLAYERS
Based on 1971-72 Rosters

				No. of Players
From	Alabama	To	Tennessee	12
From	California	To	Alaska	7
From	California	To	Arizona	12
From	California	To	Colorado	8
From	California	To	Idaho	11
From	California	To	Nevada	6
From	California	To	Oklahoma	8
From	California	To	Oregon	21
From	California	To	Texas	14
From	California	To	Utah	12
From	California	To	Washington	16
From	Connecticut	To	Massachusetts	8
From	Connecticut	To	New York	7
From	District of Columbia	To	Massachusetts	5
From	District of Columbia	To	New York	7
From	Florida	To	Louisiana	6
From	Florida	To	Tennessee	5
From	Florida	To	Texas	6
From	Illinois	To	Colorado	7
From	Illinois	To	Florida	5
From	Illinois	To	Indiana	8
From	Illinois	To	Iowa	10
From	Illinois	To	Kansas	6
From	Illinois	To	Kentucky	9
From	Illinois	To	Michigan	9
From	Illinois	To	Missouri	9
From	Illinois	To	Pennsylvania	8
From	Illinois	To	Texas	18
From	Illinois	To	Wisconsin	5
From	Indiana	To	Alabama	7
From	Indiana	To	Colorado	12
From	Indiana	To	Florida	8
From	Indiana	To	Illinois	7
From	Indiana	To	Kentucky	8
From	Indiana	To	Louisiana	8

TABLE 4 (CON'T)

			No. of Players
From Indiana	To	North Carolina	5
From Indiana	To	Ohio	9
From Indiana	To	Tennessee	11
From Indiana	To	Texas	12
From Indiana	To	Wisconsin	6
From Iowa	To	Missouri	5
From Iowa	To	South Dakota	5
From Kentucky	To	Florida	6
From Kentucky	To	Mississippi	6
From Kentucky	To	Ohio	6
From Kentucky	To	Tennessee	16
From Kentucky	To	Virginia	5
From Maryland	To	North Carolina	7
From Maryland	To	Virginia	5
From Massachusetts	To	Connecticut	6
From Massachusetts	To	New Hampshire	9
From Massachusetts	To	Rhode Island	5
From Michigan	To	Colorado	5
From Michigan	To	Illinois	6
From Michigan	To	Ohio	9
From Mississippi	To	Texas	6
From Missouri	To	Arkansas	5
From Missouri	To	Iowa	5
From Missouri	To	Kansas	5
From New Jersey	To	Connecticut	6
From New Jersey	To	District of Columbia	6
From New Jersey	To	Massachusetts	10
From New Jersey	To	New York	12
From New Jersey	To	North Carolina	8
From New Jersey	To	Pennsylvania	24
From New Jersey	To	Rhode Island	8
From New York	To	Connecticut	11
From New York	To	Massachusetts	17
From New York	To	New Jersey	10
From New York	To	North Carolina	5

TABLE 4 (CON'T)

				No. of Players
From	New York	To	Pennsylvania	17
From	New York	To	Rhode Island	6
From	New York	To	South Carolina	6
From	New York	To	Texas	13
From	New York	To	Virginia	7
From	North Carolina	To	Virginia	6
From	Ohio	To	Alabama	7
From	Ohio	To	Florida	7
From	Ohio	To	Indiana	12
From	Ohio	To	Kentucky	12
From	Ohio	To	Louisiana	6
From	Ohio	To	Michigan	6
From	Ohio	To	New York	8
From	Ohio	To	South Carolina	5
From	Ohio	To	Tennessee	12
From	Ohio	To	Texas	5
From	Ohio	To	Virginia	8
From	Oklahoma	To	Texas	5
From	Oregon	To	Washington	5
From	Pennsylvania	To	Connecticut	5
From	Pennsylvania	To	Maryland	5
From	Pennsylvania	To	New Jersey	12
From	Pennsylvania	To	New York	16
From	Pennsylvania	To	North Carolina	10
From	Pennsylvania	To	Ohio	7
From	Pennsylvania	To	Virginia	7
From	Tennessee	To	Kentucky	5
From	Tennessee	To	Oklahoma	5
From	Virginia	To	North Carolina	6
From	Washington	To	Montana	5
From	Wisconsin	To	Ohio	7

for a college team. The process is not only unsportsman-like, it is immoral to the last degree.[12]

Present day costs of maintaining a major collegiate athletic program are startling. Take for example the University of Tennessee, one of the nation's perennial football powers. The situation there is probably typical of the member schools in our major athletic conferences. The 1973 football budget at the University of Tennessee was as follows:[13]

Salaries	Athletic Scholar-ships	Recruiting	Travel	Equip-ment	Bowl Game Expenses
$250,176	$260,301	$105,456	$59,681	$62,973	$299,467

The admitted recruiting costs of the University of Tennessee represent only a small part of the total dollar outlay. Realistically, a substantial portion of the salary, scholarship, travel money is utilized for recruiting. There is no way to tell how much additional recruiting funds come from alumni input at Tennessee or at any other big time university.

Each major college has developed a sophisticated recruiting plan. The recruiting territory is first identified and then parceled out to the various members of the coaching staff, under the jurisdiction of the recruiting coordinator. Each coach is responsible for obtaining game films and other material on prospects from his area. He is also responsible for making personal contacts with the coaches and the prospects in whom the university is most interested. Many days are spent in each segment of the recruiting territory in the attempt to sign the best 30 football prospects. A typical university may offer over 100 scholarships to enlist 30 players. That means that time spent with many high school boys is wasted by coaches, faculty advisors, coed athletic supporters, and even university presidents.

The frustrations of the recruiting game are inescapably obvious. It is these frustrations and the extreme pressure to win that have resulted in wholesale abuses of the NCAA regulations. Examples of recent charges compiled against Southwestern Louisiana University follow: recruitment of one blue-chip prospect with a promise of a full scholarship, $450 a month, free clothing, free air travel for himself and his parents, free laundry, free transportation to the campus for registration, and a substitute to take his scholastic aptitude test; erroneous certification of academic eligibility; free long-distance telephone privileges; free air transportation home for a number of players; purchase of poker chips in a gambling casino for two players on the same trip.[14] Even the established football powers like Oklahoma and basketball stalwarts like North Carolina State have been caught operating outside NCAA regulations.

The results of this highly competitive recruiting game are very evident from the maps (Figs. 21 and 22). There is a geographical solution to the current recruiting mess—namely, a reduction in the amount of movement from players' homes to the universities of their choice. By utilizing a computer program called TRANSUB, which allocates players to their own state first and then proceeds to minimize the distance which they travel to school, it is possible to distribute athletic talent in a far less costly manner. The computer allocation program which has been fed the actual data on the supply and demand points is based on two assumptions. The first requires that a state consume as many of its own products as its universities demand. The second requires that any excess is then distributed to adjacent states in such a way as to minimize the travel of each potential player and in so doing to minimize aggregate distance for the total pool of recruits. The program is based on the 1971–72 athletic production data, and the location, by state, of all major universities in football and basketball.

The geographical changes in recruiting under this system are dramatic (Figs. 23 and 24). The degree of interstate movement has been cut by approximately 80 percent. Pennsylvania which actually sends 10 or more football players to 17 *different* states is an excellent case in point. Under the optimization system the state of Pennsylvania would consume all of the players that its major universities demanded and then send forth large supplies to South Carolina, West Virginia, Tennessee, and Kentucky. After local demands had been met, New York products would move to Michigan, Vermont, New Hampshire, Maine, Massachusetts, and Rhode Island. The Illinois footballers would go West to Kansas, Colorado, Nebraska, and Wyoming. Only California would operate in essentially the same way as it does now.

The basketball case is not as complicated as football because there are only about one-third as many players in the sample. The optimization procedure would change the directional flow of the recruits. Illinois would supply states to the West; Indiana and Ohio, to the South and Southwest; and New York, to the East. California would continue to disperse its exports to the far West. Interstate flows in the South and in the Atlantic Coast region would be halted. Southeastern Conference and Atlantic Coast Conference schools would utilize their own talent first and then import from the Midwest and New Jersey. The Washington, D.C. surplus would be directed South instead of North.

What would be the benefits and drawbacks to such a recruiting plan for collegiate football and basketball? It must be remembered that the optimization process is based on real data. These data include the locations of all universities attempting to field big time football and basketball teams, and the location of all high school athletes who were recruited to the

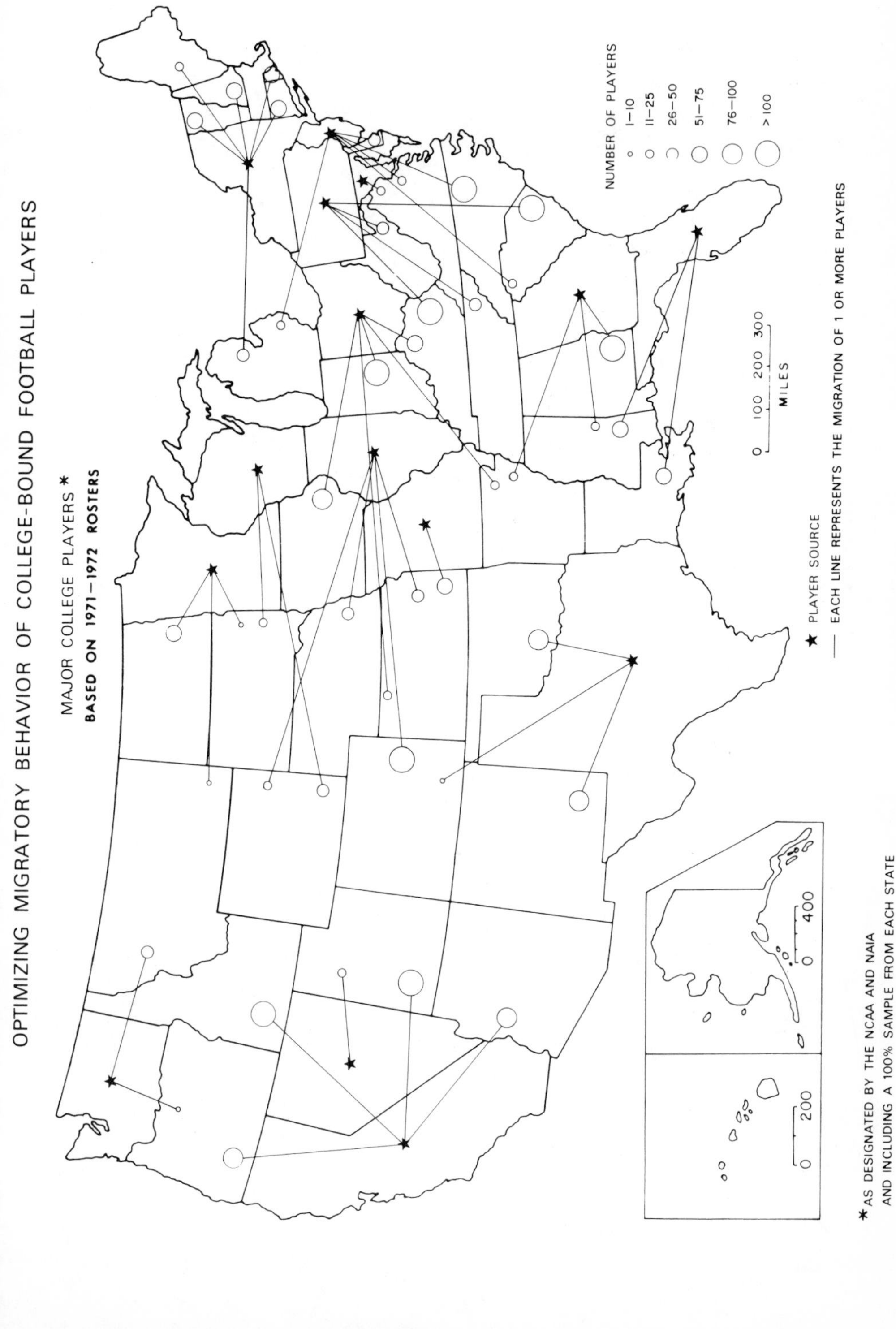

OPTIMIZING MIGRATORY BEHAVIOR OF COLLEGE-BOUND FOOTBALL PLAYERS

MAJOR COLLEGE PLAYERS *

BASED ON 1971—1972 ROSTERS

NUMBER OF PLAYERS

1—10
11—25
26—50
51—75
76—100
>100

0   100   200   300
MILES

★ PLAYER SOURCE

— EACH LINE REPRESENTS THE MIGRATION OF 1 OR MORE PLAYERS

200   400

*AS DESIGNATED BY THE NCAA AND NAIA
AND INCLUDING A 100% SAMPLE FROM EACH STATE

Figure 23

OPTIMIZING MIGRATORY BEHAVIOR OF COLLEGE-BOUND BASKETBALL PLAYERS

MAJOR COLLEGE PLAYERS*
BASED ON 1971-1972 ROSTERS

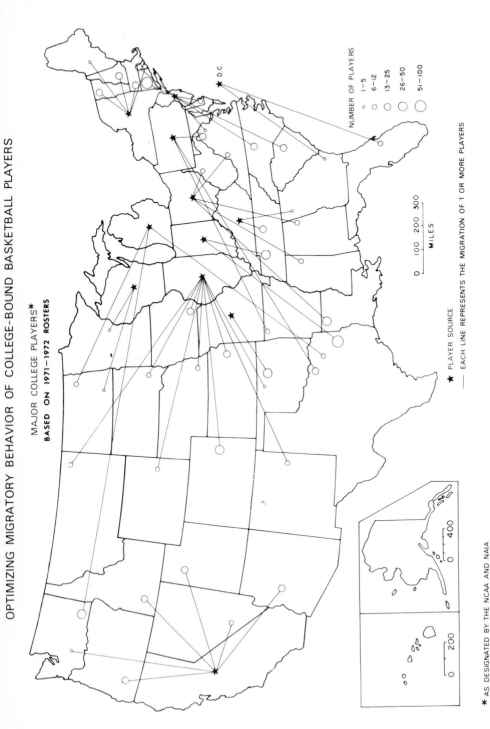

NUMBER OF PLAYERS

○ 1-5
○ 6-12
○ 13-25
○ 26-50
○ 51-100

0 100 200 300
MILES

★ PLAYER SOURCE
— EACH LINE REPRESENTS THE MIGRATION OF 1 OR MORE PLAYERS

0   200

0   400

* AS DESIGNATED BY THE NCAA AND NAIA
AND INCLUDING A 100% SAMPLE FROM EACH STATE

Figure 24

major institutions during the 1968–1972 time period. One obvious benefit is that the competition for the best high school players would be substantially curtailed and therefore the costs of obtaining these players would also be cut. Essentially, competition would be among institutions in each state for high school boys in their state. For those states with a shortage of high school talent, the competition would go beyond the state boundaries and include the other states designated as their suppliers. If such a plan were adopted the distance traveled by each athlete would be substantially reduced. Therefore, the cost of recruiting the athletes—primarily the expenditures of athletic department recruiting teams—would also be cut.

The drawbacks to this type of geographical solution would fall primarily upon the athletes; their freedom of choice would be severely restricted, for presently any person with collegiate athletic potential can select from any school in the nation. This freedom in addition to the mounting emphasis on winning has caused the funding problem that now exists. Under the proposed plan an athlete would be assigned to his home state or to a nearby state. There would also be an unequal degree of freedom in university selection from state to state, depending upon productivity. Athletes living in deficit states would have fewer choices than those residing in surplus states. For example, a California resident could normally select from universities in five to seven states, while a South Carolina resident would have to choose between staying home or going to Georgia.

This type of inpingment is intolerable in a society as free as ours. However, some type of compromise plan could be worked out so as to allow a certain amount of migration and at the same time restrict the total freedom that now exists. One possibility would be the establishment of a percentage formula. This would allow schools in a given state to recruit somewhere between 10 and 30 percent of their athletes from outside the designated recruiting territory. The percentage could be set on the basis of current and past recruiting behavior. States which have had to rely on foreign products for a long period of time could still do so, but to a lesser extent than at present. Those which are recruiting primarily at home would not be as affected by any rule change.

Another plausible variation of the optimization plan could be based on the creation of recruiting districts. Boundaries could be drawn so as to group a surplus state with one or more deficit states. Percentages of in-state and out-of-state recruits could then be set up for each state in the district. The surplus state might be required to procure 80 percent of its athletes locally whereas deficit states might be assigned values ranging from 50 to 80 percent.

Sport and the Landscape

The American sports landscape has never been thoroughly examined. Numerous urban centers have completed land use and planning studies, which include a recreational and sports component, but no summary of sport-related land use has ever been made. We know that most communities, even the very small ones, have constructed such sports facilities as football fields with bleachers or fixed seating, baseball diamonds, gymnasiums, golf courses, and tennis courts. And we know that cities are likely to have facilities for professional sport and myriad forms of recreational activities. We have some idea as to how these facilities affect surrounding land use and traffic flow.

A few examples serve to illustrate the general impact of sport. Its effect on the landscape is perhaps most dramatized by the recent stadium construction within the cores of American cities. St. Louis, Atlanta, Oakland, and Pittsburgh are exemplary. The resurgence of downtown St. Louis has been stimulated by the construction of Busch Stadium, the home of the St. Louis professional teams. Ramshackle tenements and marginal business establishments have been replaced by the stadium, parking structures, stores, and restaurants. The success of the Gateway Arch and Spanish Pavilion have also been influenced by the stadium location, not to mention the impact of three million fans who flock to the downtown area each year. The Houston Astrodome has produced many land-use alterations, and is now the center of a vast entertainment complex in that city. Oakland and Atlanta have experienced immeasurable economic and social benefits from major league sports. Considerable building activity has occurred in both places in response to stadium and coliseum construction. And there are many possibilities for future developments both within and around our central cities.

Should professional sport expand significantly in coming years, there will be a need for many new stadia and arenas. Where these will be put is a central geographic question. And in order to make the best decisions, we will need a much better understanding of the sports land-use situation than we presently have.

SOME CONCLUDING THOUGHTS

The geographic investigation of sport is a relatively new development. Its emergence, however, as a serious subdiscipline is necessary for the solution of numerous problems which confront the realm of sport. I believe that segments of the challenge issued in my book, *The Geography of American Sport: From Cabin Creek to Anaheim*, bear repeating here.

The geography of sport is a broad and exciting subject. The geographic analysis of sport offers great potential for the fuller understanding of society at the local, national, and world scales. It can also provide answers of prescriptive value. For example, where and how should amateur sport be expanded? How will given sports be received in different areas? Where are new professional franchises apt to succeed? How can the geographic organization of sport be altered at the high school, collegiate, and professional level to provide equal opportunity for participants and spectators alike?

We also need to know much more concerning the place of sport in total leisure behavior. Would the American population like to spend more of its leisure time on sport, if the opportunity was available? And given a constant amount of leisure time what kind of trade-offs would occur as a result of increases in sports participation? If city kids had the same accessibility to participation as small-town kids, which of their present leisure activities would decline? Before decisions are made in regard to the increased provision of both schoolboy and professional opportunities we must answer this question.

In-depth studies on all sports, particularly with a world perspective, are vitally needed. A hard look at the Olympic games is also in order, for the 1972 Olympics seemed to reflect the best and the worst of the people-place tie which makes sport such a geographical phenomenon. Country first, athlete second seemed to be the rule of the day, thus making the Olympics an excellent laboratory for geographical investigation.

We need to know more about minority groups in sport. Why do some sections of the country emphasize women's athletics while others ignore them completely? Where are blacks being given the greatest opportunity? What role do the black colleges play in collegiate sport?

There is much to be done if we are to attain the vast potential inherent in the geographic study of sport.

NOTES

1. For a comprehensive examination of the relationship between sport and geography, see: John F. Rooney, Jr., (1974) *A Geography of American Sport: From Cabin Creek to Anaheim*. Reading, Massachusetts: Addison-Wesley.

2. For a detailed discussion of the central place concept, see: Walter Cristaller, (1966) *Central Places in Southern Germany*. New Jersey: Prentice Hall.

3. The term "major league city" generally connotes a place with a large variety of services and complex urban functions. On the other hand, the term "bush league town" indicates a place which lacks key urban amenities.

4. James McDonald (1972) eloquently addresses the subject of spatial regionalization in his book *A Geography of Regions,* Dubuque, Iowa: Wm. C. Brown Company, Publishers.

5. John F. Rooney, Jr., (1974) *A Geography of American Sport: From Cabin Creek to Anaheim,* Reading, Massachusetts: Addison-Wesley. John F. Rooney, Jr., "Up From the Mines and Out From the Prairies." *The Geographical Review,* Vol. LIX, No. 4, 1969, 471–492. "A Geographical Analysis of Football Player Production in Oklahoma and Texas." *Proceedings of the Oklahoma Academy of Science,* Vol. 50, 1970.

6. Randy Thaman, "A Geography of Rugby," paper presented at the Annual Meeting of the Association of American Geographers, Atlanta, April, 1973; Ronald C. Pearson, "Football Recruiting in Texas: A Spatial Analysis," master's thesis, Oklahoma State University, 1972; George H. Sage and John W. Loy, "Career Mobility Patterns of College Coaches: Geographical Implications of College Coaches," paper presented at the Annual Meeting of the Association of American Geographers, Atlanta, April, 1973; Douglas McDonald, "Geographic Variation in Athletic Production: Axiomatic or Accidental," master's thesis, Department of Geography, Southern Illinois University, Carbondale, 1969; Mark M. Miller, "A Spatial Analysis of Golf Facility Development in the United States, 1931–1970," master's thesis, Oklahoma State University, 1972.

7. Roger Kahn, "Why Football?" *New York Times Magazine,* October 7, 1973, 22.

8. The six-year sample was based on two mutually exclusive roster samples taken between 1961 and 1967 for each team. Teams were selected on the basis of the National Collegiate Athletic Association major college ratings. Several college-division teams (whose recruiting budgets are smaller than those of schools rated "major" by the N.C.A.A.) were included in the sample in cases where their schedules and performances against major college teams seemed to justify it. It is assumed that differences in player ability tend to cancel each other out when such a large sample is used. Differences in the areal distribution of professional and college player origin suggest a slight underrepresentation in the South and an overrepresentation in the Northeast.

9. For a detailed examination of football, basketball, baseball, and other kinds of sport regions, see J. F. Rooney, Jr., (1974) *A Geography of American Sport: From Cabin Creek to Anaheim,* Reading, Massachusetts: Addison-Wesley.

10. Richard Pillsbury, "Carolina Thunder: A Geography of Southern Stock Car Racing." *Journal of Geography,* Vol. 73, January, 1974, 39–47.

11. Carnegie Foundation Study of American Collegiate Athletics, New York, Carnegie Foundation, 1929.

12. Ibid.

13. Richard Starnes, "Tennessee, with a $3 Million Sports Budget, Keyed to Winning." *The Chronicle of Higher Education*, October 9, 1973, 3.

14. Richard Starnes, "Abuses Frequent as Colleges Vie for Blue Chip Athletes." *The Chronicle of Higher Education*, October 23, 1973, 3.

Chapter 4
Sport, Social Differentiation and Social Inequality

Richard S. Gruneau
Departments of Sociology and Physical Education
Queens University
(Kingston, Ontario, Canada)

Richard S. Gruneau

Birth Place: Toronto, Ontario Canada

Age: 27

Birth Order: Oldest, one sister, one brother

Formal Education:

B.A., Honors Degree, Sociology and Geography,
University of Guelph, Ontario   1970

M.A., Sociology and Anthropology, University of
Calgary, Alberta   1972

Ph.D., Sociology, University of Massachusetts
(expected in April 1975)

Present Position:

Assistant Professor, Department of Sociology and Physical
Education, Queen's University

Professional Responsibilities:

Teaching courses in Introductory Sociology, Social Stratification and the Sociology of Sport.

Scholarly Interests:

Research: Leadership, class, and power in Canadian sport.
Areas of professional interest: Social inequality, political
sociology; sociology of sport, leisure and popular culture;
social theory.

Professional Accomplishments:

Papers presented at major American and Canadian social
science conferences.

Articles published in *Social Science* and *International
Review of Sport Sociology.*

Currently at work on book about the social dimensions
of Canadian sport.

Hobbies:

Cooking and science fiction.

Sport Activities:

Active participation maintained in skiing, waterskiing, and
a variety of competitive sports.

Enjoy watching most spectator sports.

Former Canadian record-holder in swimming; past Canadian National Water Ski Champion; occasionally waterski
on newly developed professional tour.

Most Recent Books Read:

I. Asimov	*The Early Asimov*
Robert Presthus	*Elite Accommodation in Canadian Politics*
K. Marx (D. McLellan, ed.)	*Marx's Grundrisse*

INTRODUCTION

All human societies are characterized by basic divisions that can readily be observed between their members. Some of these variations like race, or sex, are biological, while others such as occupational distinctions or gradations in prestige and power, are primarily social products. In both cases, many of the differences provide the foundations for discrete social positioning and the creation of specific roles in the patterned organization of human affairs. The analysis of such positions and roles in the context of biologically inherited and socially created variability is generally referred to by sociologists as the study of social differentiation.[1]

Like all areas of social life, sport has been greatly influenced by the institutionalized divisions and inequalities that serve to differentiate societies. The impact of widespread social distinctions between classes, between ethnic and racial groups, and between the sexes for example, has been consistently reflected in the changing scope and definition of the sporting enterprise. In turn, the manifestations of such divisions in sport have often suggested numerous implications for the organization of human choices and social relationships at the broadest societal level.

Yet, while it has been generally recognized that such reciprocal implications exist, there has been little popular or scholarly agreement over the nature of the complex interrelationships of sport to various forms of social differentiation. The powers of tradition and ideology, which have continually obscured the line between fact and rhetoric in the social consciousness, have found their expression in a great diversity of competing perspectives each linking explanatory theory to a certain amount of normative appraisal. The extent to which a consensus of these views is factually

My thanks to Lee Wetherall, Peter Stephenson, Alan Ingham, Charles Page, Jim Curtis, Jim McKay, and Brian Milton whose criticisms and suggestions proved instrumental in the creation of this chapter.

possible may be a somewhat debatable question, as I will suggest later in this discussion. Nonetheless, a growing number of sociologists, physical educators and popular writers are making important contributions toward a better understanding of the way in which certain facets of social life interact with the structure, values and organization of sport in the Western industrial societies. Such works by no means amount to any sort of comprehensive theory of sport and social differentiation. But they do provide a welcome body of empirical data, and a more or less systematic inventory of the outstanding problems and competing explanatory ideas that underlie the justification, criticism and even the supposed "understanding" of the relationship of sport to various social divisions and their manner of organization.

There is some credibility in suggesting that the majority of the data, and many of the problems of social differentiation research in sport settings, focus specifically on the existence of social inequality. This does not mean that inequality and differentiation should be thought of as synonymous concepts. Inequality exists as a specific aspect of biological and social differentiation, whereas, as Ralf Dahrendorf has stressed (1969: 27), "the notion of differentiation itself does not imply any rank or value among the differentiated elements." Thus, the invidious comparison of social and biological characteristics, and the institutionalization of defined differences into structured social inequality includes an *evaluative component* that is not distinctly present in the categorically inclusive meaning of social differentiation as an analytic concept. However, assessments of such invidious distinctions provide so much of the data of human experience that most social theorists have emphasized the problem of inequality in their writings, and in some cases have even claimed that inequality is a logical and inevitable consequence of differentiation.[2] To be sure, this latter contention is highly problematic, and attempts at such causal theorizing do not inform the inquiry at hand. At the same time, inequality is treated throughout this discussion as the centrally important aspect of the differentiation of contemporary social structures.

The range of social differentiation in the Western industrial societies has included four main variants of inequality. The *first* variant has to do with the historical inheritance of three general categories of stratification: traditional *class inequality*, where class has been defined by lineage and "estate"; *racial and ethnic inequality*, where elite ethnic and racial groups have appropriated desirable positions and social roles and have designated out-groups for less preferred ones (often by political domination or slavery); and *gender inequality*, where males have displayed greater access to positions and privileges. All three of these manifestations of inequality can be traced back to the earliest stages of social organization. The *second* variant contributing to the scope of social inequality has been the great increase in the functional division of labor provided by the industrialization of the Western societies (Mann, 1973). In countries already differentiated in an asymmetric manner, this has meant the development of complex structured inequality based on market position and reflected in occupational and educational attainment. Closely related to this has been a *third* variant—the "success" of modern capitalism, and the intimately associated spread of a rational utilitarian philosophy. Here, as Marx indicated, the exploding *quantitative* differences between individual roles and positions were given a distinctly *qualitative* aspect as bourgeoisie and proletariat emerged as significant forces to replace the traditional class inequalities of the "ancien-regime." [3] Finally, the *fourth* variant stems from the fact that the capitalist polarization stimulated the growth of socialism which has sought to eliminate all forms of inequality through the establishment of a classless and egalitarian society.

Today's "post-industrial" societies, as they are sometimes called, contain residues of all four of these historical variants of differentiation and inequality. For most of the twentieth century, the latter three, those constituting the parameters of the "class-labor issue," have been emphasized by sociologists and political thinkers. To paraphrase Daniel Bell (1972), the conflict between classes has very often been thought of as the axis around which all major social divisions of society have rotated. But, at the same time, the ubiquity and persistent strength of those amorphous "communities" that Max Weber called "status groups"—ethnic, religious, and even racial—has continually been demonstrated. These aspects of social differentiation may or may not be circumscribed by class position, but often the loyalties and emotional identification involved with them have rivalled and surpassed those of class, and frequently the divisions have cut across class lines.

This fact, plus continuing changes in the social conditions of the so-called "post-industrial" societies, have led some critics (cf., Nisbet, 1968) to suggest that the whole problem of class inequality is essentially a dead issue. Others, like Dennis Wrong (1972), have gone on to claim that the continuing emphasis on class analysis in sociology may be concealing other more significant areas of inequality. The rise of a bureaucratic state, for example, may make traditional interpretations of class inequality obsolete as government authorities can overtly and effectively change the class structure and the system of rewards and privileges that are most essential for social status (cf., Ossowski, 1963; Habermas, 1971). Paradoxically though, as Weber so greatly feared, the growth of a bureaucratic structure itself seems less the harbinger of the end of inequality than the purveyor of new forms of social distinction (cf., Aron, 1950). The controllers of the "means of administration" may be the new upper classes of the "post-industrial" societies.

Notwithstanding the persistence of debates concerning the relationship of social class to all forms of social inequality, most people—whether they are studying the so-called "positive functions" of inequality, or are concerned with how inequality disrupts societies and makes them less satisfying than they might otherwise be—tend to recognize the importance of economic and political variables in its development and sustenance. However, the question often is whether these dimensions overshadow and consume other aspects of differentiation and inequality, or whether such status group differences as race or ethnicity stand relatively autonomous and independent. In either case, it cannot be emphasized enough that the defining characteristics of social inequality are awash in a confusing background of historical residues, competing theory and rapid social change. This realization must be extended to any discussion and review of social differentiation, inequality and sport. Despite the often-mentioned separateness and "nonseriousness" (cf., Huizinga, 1955) of sport's "ludic" elements, the broadest contours of the institution itself are closely tied to the material foundations of social life and to the ideological differences of conflicting interest groups.

In this chapter, I attempt to articulate some of the key aspects of these relationships, centering around problematical interpretations of class structure and their implications for sport, and, to a lesser degree, around the differential exposure of major "status groups," to the sporting world.[4] First, I present a general introduction to early studies of sport and inequality, the rise of critical philosophies and some suggested relationships between competitive sport and ideology. Second, the focus is on divergent theoretical interpretations of sport and class inequality, and, finally, some of the results of recent research into class, racial, ethnic, and sexual dimensions of inequality are explored.

SPORT, SOCIAL INEQUALITY, AND IDEOLOGY: INTRODUCTION AND OVERVIEW

Early Studies and the Rise of Critical Philosophies

Inequalities in wealth, privilege and power, as specific characteristics of social differentiation, have been prominent and near universal features of human societies. But while the general issue of social inequality has always attracted the speculative comments of social thinkers and philosophers, it has been only recently that sociologists in any number have begun to express a serious interest in the relationship of sport to its contributing dimensions. As might be expected, the few exceptions to this tradition have primarily dealt with those inequalities associated with social class. The comparative exposure of racial and ethnic groups to sport and specific forms of physical activity has largely been ignored as a sociological question until the last twenty years, and, although Herbert Spencer in 1882 lamented the fact that women were largely excluded from sport,[5] his concern was far from characteristic of the general feeling of the time.

Max Weber's few comments on the importance of sport and games in maintaining "traditional domination" in European and Japanese feudal societies, typified the concern of late nineteenth and early twentieth-century theorists with class inequality. Weber suggested that sporting activities played an important function in helping to create and sustain a system of ranks having a general ethos that helped to "bar the door to all forms of utilitarian rationality" (Bendix, 1962: 364). Yet Weber, like the few others writing in the "classical" tradition whose works touched on sports and games, only referred to such items tangentially in his broader discussions of stratification and the class antagonisms of society.

Probably the first well known attempt to focus on the relationship of sport to societally structured class and status inequalities was Thorstein Veblen's satirically insightful book *The Theory of the Leisure Class*. Writing in 1899, Veblen was reacting to an America that he saw beset with the ills of capitalist acquisitiveness and the blatant "predatory temperament" of those who were located at the "upper end of the pecuniary scale." These "pecuniary" but nonproductive groups could be termed the "leisure class."

Veblen's "theory" is relatively straightforward. Throughout history, as predatory warlords seized the property and women of an enemy, the very fact of their ownership became honorific in that it revealed their prowess and asserted their superior strength. In the ensuing struggle for existence this aspect of predatory culture never died out, but was supported by "pecuniary emulation." To own property was to possess honor and set up invidious distinctions between individuals and groups. Set in this background (and contributing to it), manual labor became associated in men's minds with weakness and inferiority. Productive work was, as Veblen suggested, "unworthy of man in his best estate." Thus, the "dignified" individual abstained from work through the conspicuous display of leisure tastes and pastimes. Since sports and conspicuous leisure were "not only a waste of time, but also a waste of money" (Veblen, 1953: 256), they put one's wealth on display and this became their essential value—so much so, that the desire to impress observers with expensive and wasteful activities became elevated to a social need. Of course, mere idleness on the part of the leisure class was not enough to generate status,

> it had to be the idleness of expensive discomfort, of noble vice, and costly entertainment. It had, in short, to be conspicuous consumption: the obvious waste of valuable goods as a means of gaining respectability (Mills, 1953: xiii).

Sport, with the values, pomp, and display that surrounded it provided the ultimate consumptive enterprise and therefore was to be considered central in the lives of predatory individuals.

In many ways, Veblen's often quoted contentions maintain a certain credibility today despite the fact that sport, as we know it now in the industrial societies, is a far more complex and highly variable phenomenon than that which is described in *The Theory of the Leisure Class*. As the product of a particular historical era, and given to a distinctly American frame of reference, Veblen's analysis and its predictive capacities should be guided by certain reservations. First, he tended to confuse the sport of the aristocratic classes with that of the bourgeoisie, and he largely ignored the existential impact that self-actualizing leisure probably had on the "industrious" (to use his term) classes. Moreover, it may have been unrealistic to downgrade the extent to which the "industrious" classes themselves were influenced by "pecuniary emulation" . . . but even more importantly, "conspicuous consumption" has probably been a more significant factor in the status overcompensation of the rising middle classes than that of the settled American high bourgeoisie or the young American aristocracy. One need only look at the status gaming that can go on at the local ski hill today to see how the middle classes have gone on to appropriate many aspects of the conspicuously consumptive lifestyle.

A second reservation over the continuing relevance of Veblen's arguments has to do with the fact that sport was and is, not only functional display, but as Gregory Stone (1973) says, both "play and dis-play"; and in some cases it is even *work*. As sport has become professionalized and rationalized,[6] it has taken on a set of productive characteristics that are ideologically more compatible with the Puritan work ethic so characteristic of the rhetoric of North American life and western utilitarian philosophy, than with the functional nonproductivity associated with Veblen's leisured classes. But, at the same time, sport has at least partially maintained its "ludic" foundations (cf., Stone, 1973; Ingham and Loy, 1972) no matter how intimately these have become entwined with our work. The "dialectic" (to use a much overworked term) between work and leisure pastimes is, according to many analysts of popular culture and leisure,[7] a central aspect of life in the modern industrial societies.

A final reservation has to do with the almost cavalier treatment of the relationship of *status* to *power* as a factor in Veblen's arguments. Veblen saw the "leisure class," with its strange combination of bourgeois and aristocratic traits, as a functionless and comic parasite—an anachronistic caricature of the seigneurial regime of feudal Europe set in an American context. Accordingly, while he mocked the "kept classes" he did not see the seriousness of a possible "power elite" (Mills, 1953: xvii)—that is, in his disdain for their frivolity and barbarian temperament he underplayed the objective and symbolic aspects (which would include sport) of their corporate control and "ideological hegemony."[8] "In fact," says Mills (1953: xvii), "Veblen explicitly believed that 'they (the leisure class) are not in the full sense an organic part of the industrial community.'" As a result, he never fully explored the complexity of the relationships of sport participation, and control of the sporting enterprise, to class inequality and political order. Nonetheless, partial aspects of Veblen's theory remain as important characteristics of modern sport; especially in their suggestion of an asymmetrical relationship between hierarchially arranged classes, demonstrated both in and through the structure and values of the sporting world.

Veblen's largely utilitarian critique of the leisure class was in part, reflective of the broader currents of social criticism directed toward the social inequalities of feudal and early industrial societies. For most of human history, the widespread differences in such things as wealth and privilege have very often been defended as a "natural" and unalterable state of affairs, usually associated with a certain organic mysticism, or related to powerful religious and political doctrines that could justify the established order. To be sure, there has usually been some sort of opposition that has deplored such inequalities and the attitudes supporting them, but it has only been in more modern times that the legitimacy of inequality reflected in the ranking of classes, strata, and personal or biological characteristics, has been challenged by clearly articulated philosophy and theory. In the last three centuries two such critical perspectives have had the greatest impact on conceptions of inequality.

The first perspective centers on the crosscurrents of democratic feeling and the criticism of utility lodged against the aristocratic classes of feudal Europe by the bourgeoisie of the eighteenth and nineteenth centuries. The rising middle classes exerted a demand for "usefulness" and polemicized against the feudal norms and ascriptive claims of the old regimes "in which the rights of men were held to be derived from and limited by their estate, class, birth or lineage" (Gouldner, 1970: 62). This demand for usefulness was an attempt to modify the bases on which public rewards and opportunities were allocated.

> Utility took on a meaning in a specific context involving a particular set of social relations, where it was used initially to legitimate the claims and social identity of the middle class. In this regard, the standard of utility entailed a claim that rewards should be allocated not on the basis of birth or inherited social identity, but on the basis of talent and energy manifested in individual achievement.*

Thus, the thrust of bourgeois democratic sentiment and the institution of capitalism brought on a greater degree of "equality of opportunity" through the extensions of what T. H. Marshall (1950) refers to as "civil" and "political" rights—but, these failed to completely eradicate the ascriptive foundations of class and status inequality and in fact, institutionalized new forms of social distinction based on the equation of personal worth to exchange value and position in the market. Accordingly, the second critical perspective on inequality arose in reaction to the first, and was given its most powerful expression in the writings of certain nineteenth and twentieth century scholars like Karl Marx who came to despise the capitalist industrial complex of the bourgeoisie, the new hierarchy of wealth and power that it augered, and the Benthemite utilitarian philosophy that was its *raison d'etre*.[9] Marxist theory, however, placed no less a value on social utility than did the bourgeoisie (cf., Gouldner, 1970: 108); where it differed as a criticism of inequality was in its belief that people's claims to gratification were ultimately rooted in basic "species-needs" rather than in a utility conceived in terms of rational consequence and exchange value. Much of Marx's anti-utilitarianism, then, is a reaction not so much to the concept of "usefulness" as it is to the idea of exploitative rationality. Utility was necessarily "ends" oriented and often lent itself to the development of "reciprocal exploitation as the general relationship of individuals to one another" (Marx, 1964: 162).[10] Therefore, as Gouldner concludes:

> What Marx rejects in Benthemite utilitarianism is precisely its instrumental calculation and expedience; what Marx wishes is a *noncalculating, moral* utilitarianism, where men feel a genuine obligation to be useful to a decent society.*

Both of these critical philosophies—bourgeois rational utilitarianism, and Marxist moral utilitarianism—have had a major impact on the contemporary social consciousness; and it has been the debates between those

---

* Alvin Gouldner, *The Coming Crisis of Western Sociology.* (New York: Basic Books, 1970), p. 63. Reprinted by permission.

expressing a nostalgia for the ascriptive solidarity of an ancien regime; the defenders of bourgeois rationality; and the marshalled forces of those who seek true "equality" in a classless society that have helped to provide for the development of often antithetical positions from which to view the nature, problems, and functions of inequality in all institutions—including the institution of sport.

Competitive Sport and Competing Ideology

In many ways, sport can provide important insights into the workings and functions of differentiation and inequality in human affairs. Its myths are popular ones that reflect cultural traditions, and in turn, through the amplification such traditions get through their expression in the sporting ethos, they are reinforced. Additionally, the variability in organizational structure and emphasis that can be found in sport often corresponds to a similar variability in the organization of groups and cultures. For example, as professional and as rationalized as today's competitive sport is, it still contains important and persistent residues of ascriptive privilege (epitomized by the "amateur" concept and the whole "Olympic" movement) and at the same time, it can, under certain circumstances, have a phenomenological meaning for individuals that is far from rationally utilitarian. But, in its most common "agonetic" or competitive forms, sport essentially remains a stark embodiment of the principle of inequality. As Clifford Geertz (1972) has suggested in his study of the Balinese cockfight—the "angle" of understanding social life that you get when you study sport is usually "stratificatory." This seems true primarily because "hierarchy," as a concept, is a cornerstone of the sporting ethos. Any emphasis or outcome wherein winning is at all valued is a basic statement of a distributive relationship. The winner presumably shows his or her excellence, and:

> From the fact that honour is derived from a concept of excellence it is inevitable that the process of honouring creates hierarchical distinctions. The order of ranks that it sets up determines the image of the right life (Speier, 1969: 41).

This is not to imply that the loser is totally without honor if the contest as a whole is held in high esteem, or even in play, if the contest is "not serious." Rather, I am suggesting that the ideological foundations of organized competitive sport are characteristically *meritocratic* rather than *egalitarian*.

At the risk of again digressing from a specific discussion of sport, this last elliptical comment should be clarified. Frank Parkin has argued that inequalities associated with class or status differentiation are founded upon "two interlocking, but conceptually distinct, social processes" (Parkin, 1970: 13). One has to do with the allocation of rewards attaching to different "positions" or social roles in societies, and the other has to do with the process of "recruitment to these positions" or roles.[11] All of the Western industrial societies exhibit *both* of these aspects of inequality, but, set in the context of the ideological conflicts I have described above, social theorists and political reformers have tended to distinguish between them and evaluate them differently. The *egalitarian* critique of inequality seems an important ideological component of moral utilitarianism. It focuses its objection on the widespread differences of reward that accrue to different positions and social roles. Neo-Marxists and other egalitarian reformers ask: On what moral grounds is it legitimate to give greater economic and social benefits to one group of people over another, when all men and women have equal social needs and family responsibilities and all, theoretically, should contribute to the social good? Moreover, it is argued that inequality of all types and most major problems today are primarily social products anchored to an easily defined class structure. These inequalities are seen as "created and maintained by the institution of property and inheritance, of political and military power, and supported by particular beliefs and doctrines, even though they are never entirely resistant to the ambitions of outstanding individuals" (Bottomore, 1970: 130).

The *meritocratic* critique of inequality is far more rationally utilitarian and in tune with the mainstream values of the modern capitalist societies. It is less concerned with inequalities of reward accruing to different positions and roles "than about the process of recruitment" to these positions and roles (Parkin, 1970: 13). From this perspective, the existence of hierarchy and inequality is non-problematic (indeed, some view it as necessary, cf., Davis and Moore, 1945) as long as the system is "open" and allows ample opportunity to "compete" for positions and rewards. An open system is necessary so that the most qualified—the most useful—persons in a society will come to occupy the most important positions. It is in this way that meritocratic critics of social inequality suggest that the effective "functioning" of the system will be best served.

On the surface, the suggestion that there is an ideological compatibility between the ethos of competitive sport and the meritocratic value system of the capitalist industrial classes, seems to contradict the descriptions of sport posited by Max Weber and Thorstein Veblen. Each of these sociologists saw sport as running contrary to rational utility. However, neither Weber nor Veblen was writing about the rationalized outcome-oriented forms of physical activity that pass for organized competitive sport today. That is, in the case of feudal societies, or with Veblen's "leisure class," forms of sporting activity tended to be morally tied to ascriptive contingencies. In the sense that sport was either "nonproductive," or functioned to aid in the development of "young gentlemen," its extreme meritocratic elements were held in check by more powerful forces. Thus, while modern Olympic founder Pierre de Coubertin often spoke of sport as "the democracy of ability," the "democracy" he referred to was essentially limited to a highly selective group of "amateur" sports*men*, and in this context, achievement was equally weighted with aristocratic conceptions of character development and sportsmanship (cf., Mallea, 1972).

These ascriptive foundations of sport in feudal and early industrial societies have been well documented (Brailsford, 1969; Mallea, 1972). Despite its combination of "elite" *and* "folk" origins (cf., Page, 1973), the contours of the sporting world *at the organizational level* were generally conditioned by their intimate association with the privileged classes and elite ethnic and racial groups. According to John Mallea, aristocratic groups in Victorian England formed the first sports governing bodies, and the impact of "the Victorian legacy" was felt throughout the Western societies, it ingrained a distinctive aristocratic bias to the earliest organization and administration of sport (cf., Metcalfe, 1972, Eggleston, 1969; Denney, 1969). This bias manifested itself in certain formal rules of class, racial and sexual exclusion—(early rules of the AAU, for example, stated that anyone who was "by trade or employment for wages a mechanic, artisan or laborer" was ineligible to enter its competitions)—but the bias was given its general expression in simple conditions of scarcity. In all but a few sports, most people had neither the time, money nor opportunity to compete in an organized fashion, and when they were involved, it was often through the "vulgarity" of professionalism.

Sport has had a definite and enduring ascriptive heritage, yet in many ways, the history of modern competitive sport in the Western societies has been a history of its association with the changing social conditions of the capitalist-industrial complex, and with the increasing values placed on achievement, performance, and the equality of opportunity. In the United States, objective developments in technology, changing religious attitudes, the presence of military sports, and the rise of industrial leisure programs were all important in broadening the exposure of sport to diverse groups in the population (Betts, 1969; Berryman and Ingham, 1972). However, in an ideological sense, with the increasing professionalization and rationalization of the American social structure, achievement, success, and the *outcome* of sporting events all became sufficiently important to challenge the utility and the desirability of differentiation by class, race, or ethnicity. Indirectly then, the meritocratic emphasis of the "competitive" ethos has supplied both an implied criticism of closed recruitment, and an objective democratizing force (cf., Page, 1973: 27).

Jürgen Habermas (1972: 44) has suggested that the rationalization of sport has occurred to the extent that today's competitive sport "is in fact, show business—professionals on one side, consumers on the other," with the exceptions of a few amateurs as "private remnants" outside the professional organization and the market. While Habermas may be guilty of overstatement here, there at least seems to be some credibility in assuming that the meritocratic emphasis of the sporting ethos today often symbolizes the ideological manifestations of the modern capitalist infrastructure. This structure may have functioned to eliminate some of the traditional ascriptive foundations of sport, but at the same time, it may have simply replaced one form of asymmetric differentiation with another. On this basis, in the eyes of many egalitarian critics of inequality, the desire that sport should be "open" to all for participation and *achievement* is only a criticism of inequality in a bourgeois liberal sense. For many radical thinkers, "equality of opportunity" and "equality" are not always synonymous. The first emphasizes the desirability of an open base of recruitment, and the second emphasizes the eradication of widespread differences in reward that accrue to different positions or social roles in societies (e.g., in sport, between winner and loser and between athlete and nonathlete and between other aspects of differentiation and these roles). In other words, the former presupposes the opportunity to rise to a higher level in a stratified society, and the latter implies the termination of entrenched distinctions of privilege.

Recent egalitarian criticisms of sport are far more radical than their meritocratic counterparts, in that they challenge the whole concept of rationalized competition and suggest that the popularity of sport aids in the "ideological hegemony" of ruling groups. This hegemonic process operates at two levels: (a) a social psychological level wherein sport involvement is seen to inculcate a belief in inequality through meritocracy; and (b) an institutional level, wherein the apolitical mythology of sport's "ludic" foundations ostensibly eliminates the exposure of athletes to any radical political framework.[12]

By virtue of their different critical foci, liberal and radical theorists have tended to view sport in an antithetical fashion. The implications of these often rhetorical alternatives have created growing levels of anxiety for many people both inside and outside the world of sport. Such anxieties can hardly be understood simply as "personal troubles"; they are far better thought of as important "public issues" (cf., Mills 1970: 14–15). In this sense, these ideological aspects of modern sport represent the broader philosophical and political clash between rational utilitarian and meritocratic conceptions of modern democracy, and the egalitarian moral philosophy of democratic socialism; they provide the normative context for understanding sport, differentiation and inequality.[13]

DIVERGENT THEORETICAL INTERPRETATIONS OF CLASS INEQUALITY

Differential Images of Class Structure and Sport

The images of class structure and power relations that are especially compatible with liberal and radical criticisms allow for considerably divergent interpretations of the possible relationships of sport to forms of social differentiation and related inequalities. A number of contrasting stereotypes readily come to mind: sport as an area where ability and achievement count most, *or* an area marked by rampant sexist and generally bigoted practices; a means of providing access to material wealth and material symbols, *or* merely a means of displaying the prerogatives of wealth and privilege; a largely autonomous distributive system in its own right whose subcultural manifestations cut across class, racial and ethnic group lines, *or* a function of the economic system and accompanying values; a necessary alternative from the dull routine of our overly regulated lives, *or* an opiate and agency that keeps the working classes in an advanced state of false consciousness.

All of these stereotypes have some basis in fact, but, as Page (1973: 3) has suggested after a similar but more general set of comparisons, each considered independently is probably a "distortion." Nonetheless, the interpretive polarities described here are typical of competing understandings of the socio-historical relationship of sport to the variety of "class" definitions and images of society (both with respect to what "is" and what "ought" to be) that are offered up in the popular and scholarly literature. The majority of these differences can be summarized under two headings: (a) differences in *"distributive"* characteristics, and (b) differences in *"relational"* attributes. The first set of differences refers to the variety of underlying objective and symbolic factors that contribute to *structured* social ranking and inequality;[14] that is, those factors such as income, wealth, occupation, skill, prestige or social esteem. The second set of differences refers to the ways "in which individuals differentiated by these criteria are related to each other within a system of groups and categories" (Béteille, 1969: 13); either through a relationship of asymmetrical dependence (exploitative), mutual dependence (functionally related), no dependence, or some combination of these.

As I have stressed throughout this chapter, basic differences in distributive emphasis and relational assumptions are often set in the background of conflicting ideological positions. Sport is no more immune to rhetorical conflicts than any other area of social life. Popular (and scholarly) impressions of sport often align with popular conceptions (and condemnations) of class inequality and with competing understanding of its supposed causes and functions.

Two somewhat antagonistic views of the relationship of sport to class inequality have probably had the greatest impact on the social consciousness: *first*, Marxist and "class" conflict interpretations, and *second*, status continuum and functional approaches. Taken as a whole, an inventory and discussion of the problems of synthesizing these theoretical perspectives should outline a set of basic concepts that are especially useful in understanding the complex and changing relationships of sport to "class" and "stratification" in the Western industrial societies.[15]

Marxist and Class Conflict Interpretations of Sport

The thrust of Marxist theory can be outlined in the following assumptions:

1. In every society beyond the most primitive, two categories of people may be distinguished; (a) a ruling class and (b) one or more subject classes.

2. The dominant position of the ruling class is to be explained by its possession of the major instruments of economic production, but its political dominance is consolidated by the hold which it establishes over military force and the production of ideas.

3. There is a perpetual conflict between the ruling class and the subject class or classes; and the nature and course of such conflict is influenced primarily by the development of productive forces, i.e., by changes in technology.

4. The lines of class conflict are most sharply drawn in the modern capitalistic societies, because in such societies the divergence of economic interests appears most clearly, unobscured by any personal bonds such as those of feudal society, . . .

5. The class struggle within capitalist society will end with the victory of the working class, and this victory will be followed by the construction of a classless society. [Note: Until this occurs it is suggested that all men should work toward this end.]*

It is important to realize in understanding these assumptions that classes in the orthodox Marxist sense have a certain solidarity based on an awareness of mutality of interest. A class (especially the bourgeoisie) exists not only "in itself," but also "for itself"—it is "real" in the sense that it is

---

* T. B. Bottomore, *Elites and Society*. (C. A. Watts, London, 1964), pp. 24–25. Reprinted by permission of the Publishers.

not merely some statistical category that is arbitrarily constructed. Furthermore Marx did not claim that the proletariat were fully conscious of their position at the time of his writing. Rather, he predicted that "class consciousness" and accompanying "class conflict" was a direction of future change.

Marx was reacting to the widespread differences in rewards that characterized the early industrial societies, but he was also advocating a sound theoretical framework on which to anchor his criticisms. Marxist "theory" is less a descriptive statement of the *distributive* aspects of inequality than it is a critical assessment of its *relational* forms and the impact of these on social change and human life chances. Failure to recognize this has led to some key misconceptions about Marxist class analysis.

First, Marx did not claim that his image of classes was "perfect" or even the most accurate description of how capitalistic societies were *empirically stratified*. But he did suggest that his mode of analysis had utility in illuminating the structural basis of the conditions of human life and also the future course that class inequality would take (cf., Stolzman and Gamberg, 1973: 108).

Second, Marx's classic division of capitalist owners (bourgeoisie) and wage earners (proletariat) as the two classes that circumscribed all other forms of life did not deny the existence of other attendant nonclass forms of stratification (racial, sexual, religious, etc.). What this distinction did assume "is that the social relationship between the two major classes created and recreated by capitalism constitutes *the proper focus* for an understanding of the structure and dynamics of industrial capitalistic society" [emphasis mine] (Stolzman and Gamberg, 1973: 121).

Finally, Marx did not claim that the material level of the working class would arbitrarily decline with the development of capitalism. He did in fact point out that the worker would partake of some of the fruits of surplus that would be realized in the economic improvements of his living conditions. Yet, however affluent the worker could become he would still be selling his labor in the cause of buttressing a social world which guaranteed his subjugation. Additionally, when all factors are considered, Marx suggested in *Wage Labour and Capital*, the material level of living of the working class would decline *relative* to that of the bourgeoisie either by remaining stationary while the latter rose, or by developing at a slower pace (Bottomore, 1966: 22).

In summary, Marxist theory, guided by its *morally* utilitarian and egalitarian philosophical foundations offers, in one package, a description of Western industrial capitalistic societies, a criticism of class inequality in these societies, and a prescription for action within them. Today, in our understanding of sport and class inequality many aspects of the Marxist legacy continue to find their expression in the polemics of some popular writers (cf., Hoch, 1972) but for the most part, sophisticated class analyses in the Marxist tradition are virtually nonexistent in North American sport sociology. I would suspect that there are three related reasons for this: (a) the ideological compatibility of sport's meritocratic foundations with the moral order of the North American societies has discouraged "egalitarian" criticisms of sport-related inequalities, (b) as the theoretical and philosophical foundations of socialism, Marxist class analysis has been held in some disrepute in the ostensibly "classless" American and Canadian democracies, and (c) much of the sociological thought in North America is cast in the mold of the natural sciences, and therefore scholars have tended to dismiss the normative and analytic combination of elements constituting the *praxis* of Marxism as ideology rather than social science.[16]

By far, the greatest proportion of sport studies coming out of the Marxist tradition have come from European observers. Sport has drawn some attention from those "critical theorists" associated with the Frankfurt Institute for Social Research,[17] and it has been heavily criticized by communist-affiliated journalists and political economists in France, Germany, and Italy (cf., Rigauer, 1969; Böhme et al., 1971; Marcuse, 1969; Brohm, 1972; Laguillaumie, 1972). From this "critical" and "class conflict" oriented perspective, the nature, functions, and internal structure of sport are viewed as being conditioned by its relationship to the ruling class and economic infrastructure of societies (Laguillaumie, 1972: 32–33; Brohm, 1972). "Hierarchy" and "centralization" are emphasized as key aspects of sport, and its essential unity is reinforced by the fact that it has a universal language—the record—which allows people of all cultures to compete according to the same criteria. Pierre Laguillaumie claims that the record is to sport what money is to political economy: an abstract means of comparison and trade (Laguillaumie, 1972).

In this context, sport supposedly recreates the class structure by serving in the hegemony of the ruling classes. It supposedly inculcates a bourgeois ideology and also defines its limits as somehow transcendentally apolitical. Thus, to sum up the fundamental aspects of the relationship of class inequality to sport as analysts in the Marxist tradition have seen them:

1. Sport must be understood in the broader context of the material conditions of the capitalist societies.

2. Sport is intimately associated with classes that exist on the basis of widespread differences in wealth and power.

3. All competitive sport reflects bourgeois ideology; it is rationally utilitarian, meritocratic, and mobility oriented and contains a belief in linear progress. Accordingly, it is control-oriented and helps to maintain a "false consciousness."

4. Sport is "alienating" to professional athletes caught up formally in the productive process.

5. A truly egalitarian, self-actualizing sport can be achieved only in a society having democratic control over societal economic life: a classless and egalitarian society where "competitive sport" in a rational sense is nonexistent.

On the surface, the propositions listed above provide a polemical, yet powerful interpretation of the relationship of sport to class inequality and the structural organization of the Western societies. There can be no denying that the ideological foundations of modern competitive sport are often rationally utilitarian and meritocratic, or that critical thinking is hardly encouraged in an institutional arena that defines character in terms of "control of temper, acceptance of authority, obedience to rules, self-discipline, subjugation of self for the good of the organization and cooperation" (Radford, 1973: 10). Moreover, with respect to the objective position of sport, there is considerable evidence suggesting that professional sports are imposing conglomerates of economic and political power, and that rationalized "amateur sport" is increasingly becoming controlled by the state. Finally, while opposition to these power blocs in sport has been at a minimum (for the "Good of The Game" as Curt Flood (1970) sarcastically put it), there seems to be a developing tendency on the part of some athletes and fans to become possessed by an issue-oriented collective consciousness.

Despite the seeming credibility of partial aspects of the class exploitation and conflict approach, there are several caveats that should be introduced regarding its applicability to more general forms of inequality. To begin, the relationship of the control and administration of sport to modern societal class structures has rarely been studied in anything other than a superficial fashion.[18] Thus, one can only *infer* its class constitution from general studies of societal class and power structures, and here, the class conflict approach has been criticized by a variety of theorists as being either incomplete or factually incorrect. Many of these criticisms are particularly challenging, especially when the focus reveals the desire to understand empirically the hierarchical arrangement of distributive systems rather than an attempt to view the structural *causes* of class inequality, their relationship to the dominant institutional structure, and to macro-sociological questions of social change.

Neither history nor a variety of empirical studies has provided the whole-hearted support for Marx's dichotomic views on class. Anthony Giddens (1973) has argued that class exploitation and some conflict may be demonstrable facts in the Western societies, but that this has resulted more from contradictions between the feudal and capitalist modes of production than from within the contradictions of capitalism itself. Other theorists (cf., Bell, 1972) have suggested that in the "post-industrial societies" widespread changes in the productive process have not allowed for the disappearance of the middle classes; but by far the most damaging criticisms of the limitations of class conceptions born out of Marxist theory have had to do with the recognition of prestige and power as important ranking determinants in their own right, and with the recognition that increasing class conflict and class consciousness *have failed to materialize in anywhere near the frequency predicted by Marx*. This large scale absence of class consciousness has seemed most evident in the failures of the working class to mobilize effectively. It has seemed less evident in the case of bourgeois power holders, and the extent to which monolithic and pluralistic trends have existed in this realm has been the subject of considerable debate.[19] Yet, despite the existence of such debates, when given the desire to understand all aspects of what Lenski (1966) called the "dynamics of distributive systems," it has been only logical to concede that "class," in the dichotomous and pervasive sense originally meant by Marx, may be more an analytical artifact than an accurate description of reality.[20]

This is not meant to suggest that there is no credibility in an image of the Western industrial societies as settings where social relationships are seen to be dominated by classes whose interests are in conflict. What is being suggested is that social divisions coming out of the productive process, property ownership and prestige variables, are more complex than a dichotomized system of inequality. Nonetheless, while modern "conflict" theorists like Heberle (1959) or Dahrendorf (1959) have recognized some of the empirical problems surrounding the two class approach, and the existence of prestige and power as *sometimes* independent contributions to social ranking, they have argued forcefully for the retention of two assumptions borne out of the Marxist tradition: (a) the significance of economic contingencies in the all-important designation of power holders and their subordinates, and (b) the "reality" of classes as conflict groups which have identifiable goals and interests. Here, although classes may be roughly defined with vaguely demonstrable boundaries; although they may be limited to a certain degree of contextual or institutional anchorage and may be better represented by power differentials shown between major economic interest groups than by two great classes facing each other; they still are assumed to be the dominant aspect of inequality in the Western societies and, therefore, are seen to affect the nature and functions of all institutions.

All of the "class conflict" interpretations that I have just been describing owe some debt to Marx. Accordingly, their focus is on power, productive forces, and labor, and on an egalitarian criticism of the rewards associated with different positions. But, while the modern capitalist societies do lend themselves to analysis in this fashion, they are not completely the products of capitalist contradictions. As I have suggested earlier, they have a history, and part of that history has been the legacy of a certain degree of traditional class inequality where class position has been defined as much by lineage, family prestige, and estate, than by productive factors. Such residues die hard.

The remnants of the traditional ascriptive foundations of sport do not fit simply into an explanatory framework based on restricted conceptions of *bourgeois* and proletarian economic classes in conflict. An historical analysis of the development of sport in the Western industrial societies indicates not just the growth of mass sport as a rationalized activity dominated by corporate power, but also a sometimes independent mix of the business standard with the restricted amateurism of an ancien régime, and with the growing impact of the politically motivated bureaucrat.

The degree to which traditional propertied elites, bureaucrats and bourgeois power holders have merged to form a modern ruling class may be a problematic question for the Marxist viewpoint. But the intertwining of these dimensions at least suggests that "status," in a nonproductive sense, continues to be an important distributive characteristic of the Western industrial societies. While neo-Marxist class theorists have continued to argue that such status factors are essentially conditioned by property and the productive process, a great number of their critics have argued that such interpretations underplay the existence and the independence of prestige variables. There is, albeit in a sometimes limited sense, power in "honor" and excellence, and this factor serves to complicate a purely economic and conflict-oriented interpretation of modern class structures.

These types of complications are responsible for a view wherein classes are simply "all divided up." A multiplicity of fine status gradations is seen to exist both inside classes (defined in economic terms) and between them. In his critical description of this perspective, Bottomore (1966: 25) conceives of intermediate status positions connecting or being interposed between discrete class groups as these make up the reward system. *In the extreme case,* this is assumed to be true to the extent that classes as discrete groups are pictured as not really existing at all. The structure of class inequality is represented as a continuum of status positions along which there are no "breaks" which set off distinct groups. *In a more moderate case,* discrete class or status groups are seen as very real, but only in "semicrystalized form with somewhat indistinct and highly permeable boundaries" (Gordon, 1963: 247). *In a more traditional case,* the ranked status positions coalesce into "class-like" groups that are sharply delineated and face each other with a maximum degree of group identification (cf., Gordon, 1963: 247).

Without doubt, views on sport are severely affected by these alternatives. The last alternative, however, is not all that incompatible with the assumptions of radical conflict theorists. The addition of a "prestige" dimension in defining the dynamics of distributive systems does in fact lend power to the "realistic" position. Classes, or even discrete status groups, are seen to exist and still may have what MacIver called a "corporate class consciousness." In this light, sport still can be described in terms of its problematical relationship to conflicting groups, although the nature of the groups involved might change on the basis of the prestige criteria being considered as the primary distributive dimensions. The class system then becomes complicated to the extent that we now have to take into consideration such things as the prestige value of sport involvement and excellence, its potential as a mobility mechanism in both long and short range terms, the degree to which prestige in sport itself is translated above and beyond economic factors, and as well, how that prestige may be differentially defined in alternative settings and still contribute to an individual's class position. The key point here is that the distributive characteristics of class, whether defined in purely economic terms or in broader prestige terms, can easily be interpreted from the perspective of social conflict. When classes are defined as "real," relational assumptions of exploitation and conflict generally allow for a particular style of interpretation: one that views sport as an institution in an exploitive class system and questions its relationship to the widespread differences in reward that accrue to different positions in that system. But this image of class structure is not the only image that one finds in the sociological literature.

An entirely different understanding of sport and class inequality is achieved when "prestige" is treated as a distributive characteristic that surpasses, or becomes equated with, the contingencies of economic and political power; when the reward structure is viewed as a linked hierarchy of status positions; and when inequality itself is not viewed as being pathological. The focus on prestige has led many theorists to abandon the idea of "class inequality" and emphasize instead the complex stratification of social systems and the processes that supposedly allow for highly qualified individuals in society to achieve the highest positions. Sport is sometimes analyzed as one of these processes.

Status Continua and Functional Approaches to Sport and Social Stratification

When "classes" are no longer thought of as "real" groups (the "extreme case" referred to above), one also eliminates the potential and probable existence of class conflict (Aron, 1969).[21] A "nominalistic" conception of class structure suggests a definite hierarchy based on multiple status positions that are better thought of as providing "strata" than "classes." This image of structured inequality has been described as "a ladder with closely adjacent rungs which individuals may climb or descend according to their capabilities" (Bottomore, 1966: 26). Each person has a status that is defined less by objective criteria like income or education than by the esteem of others. Thus, while some "competitive class feeling" might exist, "class consciousness" is a near impossibility.

A distributive emphasis on subjective prestige and esteem often implies a relational focus on social order and on the mutual dependence of status positions, rather than on the asymmetrical dependence and conflict that can exist between "conscious" classes. At least conceptually, one can presume that if there is to be stability in the status order (when described in these terms) there has to be a minimal level of consensus as to the amount of prestige associated with specific positions and activities. Consensus as to the structure of the status hierarchy implies that the overall society is "integrated" to the extent that such a widespread agreement can be achieved. This systematic aspect and the nature of integration are characteristic of a view of inequality that sociologists have come to know as "functionalism."

The functional interpretation of social differentiation and inequality is based on the idea that all societies *must* effect a division of labor that guarantees that the most important positions of authority come to be filled by the "most qualified persons" (Davis and More, 1945). In other words, societies exhibit a "need" for a generally acceptable hierarchy of rewards. The social ranking system that comes to exist ostensibly conforms to that need, and functions to ensure optimal individual placement for systemic efficiency. Parsons (1966) poses four functional imperatives that should be met in order to guarantee that cultural role prescriptions are filled. These are adaptation, pattern-maintenance, goal-attainment, and integration; and each of these, in its association with a particular subsystemic element in the society, is responsible for the level of consensus that is the Parsonian backbone of social order.

As stated above, it has often been suggested that sport functions in accordance to the above "imperatives" (cf., Lueschen, 1970: 93). That is, it is depicted as functioning to satisfy the needs of societies, and closely aligning with that certain amount of "institutionalized inequality" that uncritical functionalists presume to be characteristic of all social structures. The manner in which this occurs is summed up by the following functional assumptions:

1. Competitive sport reflects a set of values held to be important by the society. Therefore, recruitment into sport serves an integrative function.

2. Sport functions to make the stratification of a society more explicit. (Social systems stress a "need" for a hierarchy of rewards that is related to a search for status under conditions of scarcity. Status is usually gained by a variety of means, including possessions and performance, both of which may be readily reflected in sport involvement. These reflections operate at two levels. Performance in sport may be a means of generating status at one level, but at another level, participation in sport, or in a specific sport, may function as a display of status. Thus, sport and specific sports may function as symbols of stratification in society and along the way provide arenas for the learning of important social roles.)

3. Sport functions as a mobility mechanism in the Western industrial societies. ("Performance," as such, is a transitory and impermanent means of moving up the hierarchy of rewards, but high performance in sport may allow entrance into positions based on more durable criteria such as the possession of valuable material goods and the control of nonmaterial values.)

Criticisms of the extremes to which some sociologists have pushed "functional analysis" have been clearly stated and restated to the degree that it has become "de rigeur" to preface any discussion of either social differentiation, social inequality or general sociological theory with at least a moderate denunciation of functionalist orthodoxy.[22] The foundations of this "orthodoxy" rest in the assumption that inequality in societies is inevitable and necessary and is supported by a high level of consensus over the status associated with different positions. If one accepts these assumptions, then the concern of analysts should not be over the comparative values of "equality" or "inequality," but rather over the processes by which a society motivates actors into the assumption of specific social roles. For instance, in any uncritical functional analysis of sport, the values of sport or values in sport would be considered nonproblematic. The analyst would be concerned with the observation and articulation of the relationship of sport to the "effective functioning" of the system in question. Critics of this approach have suggested that it is conservative and teleological.

The logical position of "functional" causation with respect to social phenomena is contentious at best (cf., Buckley, 1968), and when taken in its extreme formulations, the assumption that societies are purposeful goal-oriented systems seeking the fulfillment of a set of necessary "imperatives" seems to have profound ideological consequences. Collectivities are not thinking beings, and to assume that they attempt to ensure that their most important positions are filled by the most qualified persons is tantamount to suggesting that the existing system of rewards and privileges in a society is beyond criticism. Perhaps, as Page (1969: xii) has suggested, the idea that social stability and systemic efficiency requires a certain amount of institutionalized inequality is more realistically explained as a reflection of power in the upper strata. The "needs" of those who occupy the command posts of the institutional hierarchies can hardly be equated with some abstract imputed needs of the society. Moreover, following Tumin's argument (1953), even from a functional perspective, it seems doubtful whether all inequality serves positive functions for the society. Inherited wealth and privilege when structured into the framework of inequality often serve as barriers to the mobilization and recruitment of many potentially qualified societal members.

One of the most critical problems associated with an orthodox functional interpretation of sport and social stratification arises out of conflicts due to differences in context and level of analysis. That is, to assume "societal needs" is to suggest an holistic interpretation of inequality and to emphasize the functional interdependence of parts. Holistic (or systemic) functionalism tends to lack an ability to provide a specific frame of reference other than that wherein spheres of status must be viewed in light of the "functional requirements" of the system as a whole.[23] In reality, questions must be placed in a comparative context; what is functional for one group in society is not necessarily functional for other groups, or even for the society as a whole. We get an excellent example of this from Pooley's discussion of ethnic soccer clubs in Milwaukee (Pooley, 1972). Is sport, as Lueschen suggests, an integrative mechanism? Pooley's data suggest otherwise. The involvement of minority groups in situation-specific sporting activities inhibits their assimilation into the mainstream of the national belief and value system in spite of the supposed "pattern-maintaining" aspects of sport's achievement orientation. But, while the clubs may be dysfunctional from a topside perspective, they are functional for the maintenance of the micro system of the ethnic community.

It has generally been recognized that criticisms of the type that have just been mentioned have damaged the credibility of the orthodox functional position. However, not all "functional" assumptions have been entirely discredited. Often there do seem to be at least constraints toward minimal consensual value levels, as well as possible asymmetric differentiation that can exist as a natural function of roles.

Additionally, depending on the frame of reference, social phenomena can be viewed as having consequences that are "functional" or beneficial for certain groups. In this latter sense, both class conflict and functional-consensus interpretations of differentiation and inequality often share in the language of orthodox functional analysis (Dahrendorf, 1959; Cohen, 1968). For instance, the critics of functionalism are primarily interested in explaining (and denouncing) how class systems (especially the ruling classes) "function" to maintain themselves: "Their conception is one of a set of interacting and mutually reinforcing processes" (Cohen, 1968: 61). Thus, it is not unusual in the sociological literature to find surprisingly functional assertions being used to damn the conservative bias of "functionalist orthodoxy." Sport sociology offers no exception. For example, Paul Hoch's (1972) polemical statement of the relationship of sport to monopoly capitalism is in some ways more compatible with Parson's work than with Marx's or Gramsci's.[24] Sport is depicted as functioning (very effectively) in accordance to the needs-desires of the "ruling class" (who generally represent the system). It functions as "an opiate"—it functions to "mould the modern militarist"—it functions to inculcate a bourgeois and "elitist" mentality. All of these functions aid in the continuance of the dominant institutional structure.

Perhaps ironically then, there is some credibility in assuming that the evaluation of sport as a shameless integrative device is equally compatible with basic Durkheimian and Marxist thought even though these interpretations of social inequality are highly divergent. Put most simply, from one perspective the supposed integrative power of sport is pictured as being "bad"; from the other perspective it is assumed to be a "good" and perhaps "necessary" thing. In both cases, it is assumed to exist, and these conflicting views seem to underline the fact that any theory of "class" or "stratification" has to be critically analyzed in both its substantive and ideological forms.

There does in fact seem to be considerable substantive justification for the efficacy of certain restricted functional assertions in sport, although these are probably better thought of as important functional *consequences* rather than systematic *functions* themselves. A variety of scholars have demonstrated how sport functions to integrate individuals into the mainstream values of the capitalist societies (cf., Webb, 1969; Lueschen, 1970). We also have evidence that in many settings sport has functioned to make all aspects of the stratification of communities more explicit (Baltzell, 1958; Veblen, 1953); that sports and games have functioned to provide a learning arena for important social roles (Loy and Ingham, 1972); and that they have aided in the development of the "self" (Mead, 1934; Piaget, 1962). Finally, sport has also seemed to provide for some measure of mobility in the Western societies (cf., Loy, 1972; Lueschen, 1969; Page, 1973) although the relative degree of this mobility, or its permanence, has seldom been explored in anything other than a facile and superficial manner.[25]

It is important to realize that while all of the above "empirical" manifestations of the ostensibly "functional" relationship of sport to class differentiation and inequality can be seen to exist, none of them necessarily reflects the existence of systemic "needs" or of a rigid and immutable consensus. Also, these manifestations should not be interpreted as universals. The integrative power of sport can just as easily be interpreted as "dysfunctional" for the underprivileged in societies, and the few documented cases of mobility through sport do not suggest the extent to which this is a general trend.

It has been suggested in this discussion that analysts holding a variety of contradictory perspectives often utilize the language of functional analysis without sharing in the basic suppositions of the orthodox functional framework. It should also be pointed out that major functional assumptions have not been strictly limited to the image of class structure as a status continuum. In settings where a rigidly defined class structure has been cemented by personal bonds and religious beliefs such as feudal society, the emphasis on consensus and "organic" unity has stimulated functional interpretations. However, the period of functional legitimacy in American sociology exactly coincides with (and is partially related to) that period when scholars were preoccupied with "status hierarchies and status seeking" in "traditional small town America" instead of macrosociological interpretations of the "contours of economic and political power"[26] (Page, 1969: xvii).

Thus the emphasis for understanding differentiation and inequality has often been on consensus, mobility, and the processes by which individuals achieve this mobility, and the basic criticism of inequality has been meritocratic.[27] When images of "class" structure are circumscribed by these assumptions, the prevailing interpretation of the relationship of sport to differentiation and inequality has been a positive one, or at least sport has been viewed as an essentially benign social institution. Table 1

Table 1

A comparative summary of the dominant distributive and relational characteristics of divergent views of social class

	Dominant distributive characteristics		Dominant relational attributes	
	Class conflict	Functional-consensus	Class conflict	Functional-consensus
Image of class structure				
1. Classes as real groups	market position and property ownership	lineage and "estate"	asymmetric dependence (exploitative)	mutual dependence (functionally related)
2. Status continuum (nominalistic approach)	X* (compatible only in the sense of slight interstatus friction)	interpersonal prestige and esteem	X* (possibly some element of non-egalitarian classlessness)	mutual dependence
Implications for sport				
1. Classes as real groups	contours of sport shaped by productive process (highest market position guarantees access to participation, control and administration)	sport as a functionally important display of prestige related to lineage and "estate" (bars door to rationality)	sport as ideologically hegemonic (leads to false consciousness on the part of the underclasses)	sport as valuably integrative (aids in learning positionally associated social roles and beliefs)
2. Status continuum (nominalistic approach)	X*	sport as a display of prestige *and* as a generator of prestige (fundamentally meritocratic)	X*	

* X signifies theoretical and empirical improbabilities.

presents a summary and description of status continuum and functional interpretations of sport and social stratification. These are compared with the class conflict approaches discussed previously.

Prospects and Problems of Theoretical Synthesis

Most recent writings pertaining to the class systems of the Western industrial societies have tended to be "synthetic," reflecting among other things what Charles Page (1969: lviii) calls a "confrontation and in some degree a reconciliation of aspects of functionalist and Marxist orientations." Given the complexity of our modern sociopolitical systems it seems rather obvious that the relational characteristics of class inequality almost always involve conflict and functional attributes, and that there can be both classes and "stratification" related to the multiple dimensions of economics, prestige, and politico-community power. Max Weber (1958) saw class and status inequality as coexisting in the modern societies with "their relative importance fluctuating with changes in technology and economic conditions" (Bottomore, 1966: 26), and a great many more sociologists have emphasized the importance of a multidimensional approach to understanding differentiation and inequality (cf., Runciman, 1969; Gordon, 1963).

The most common view of modern multidimensional theorists is that individuals do not necessarily occupy a single position in the reward structure, but can occupy several positions; that inequality is not related to a singular distributive source but is related to several sources; and that both conflict *and* consensus characterize social relationships (often centered around the consistency or lack of consistency associated with ranks on the different dimensions). An individual may be a highly skilled athlete yet be comparatively uneducated; he may make a high income but nonetheless be black and be discriminated against; and finally he may feel some anxiety over the "status" inconsistencies that permeate his life.

Possibly, this multidimensional approach is the most fruitful means of fully understanding the relationship of sport to social differentiation and inequality in the Western societies. The problem, however, remains as to which distributive dimension and which "relational" focus (if any) *dominates* in today's postindustrial societies, and to what extent any of these are structured into a set of institutional arrangements which guarantees a degree of social continuity in the reward positions of specific groups.

Max Weber's position was to recognize the importance of status groups and "political parties" in the study of inequality, but to make classes (the structured forms of inequality based on market position) his centrally important concern. Yet many self-professed neo-Weberians paradoxically have chosen to expand the concept of multidimensionality to the point where its "synthetic" properties become lost in an uncomfortable compatibility with status continua interpretations of inequality and stratification. In many extreme cases, the exaggerated flexibility of the multidimensional approach is difficult to reconcile with the notion of enduring systems of structured inequality—thus leading to a synthesis that is somewhat illusory. As Frank Parkin argues:

> To plot each person's position on a variety of different dimensions tends to produce statistical categories of those who have a similar 'status profile'; but it does not identify the type of *social collectivities* or *classes* which have traditionally been the subject matter of stratification. Such an approach tends to obscure the systematic nature of inequality and the fact that it is grounded in the material order in a fairly identifiable fashion.* [my emphasis]

It is possible to discern two distinct and usually overlapping approaches to multidimensionality. The first is a synthetic combination of divergent images of class and status structures, and of alternative distributive and relational characteristics of *structured* inequality. A synthesis is forged primarily on the basis of an analytic separation of institutional spheres and levels of analysis. The analyst may recognize class conflict at one level in one institutional sphere, but also he may assume the existence of nominalistic systems of mutual dependence in other settings.[28] In the second approach to multidimensionality, the sociologist tends to emphasize the distribution of honor through the assignment of a more or less equal weight to all forms of status evaluation. It is this second type of multidimensionality that Parkin so forcefully argues against, but there are problematical elements in both cases.

In the first, the analytic separation of institutional spheres and levels of analysis can be too easily mistaken for, or become confused with, a denial of their empirical interrelationships. Thus when Dahrendorf (1959) tried to disassociate the economic and institutional spheres of the modern industrial societies he came under a great deal of criticism (cf., Bottomore, 1966; Bell, 1972).

In the second case it seems that the near equal weighting of dimensions is somewhat improper. The relegation of market factors to a minor status concern seems to bear little empirical relationship to the importance of the market in the reward structure. It is, in fact, marketable expertise and the occupational order that constitute the backbone of the system of

---

* Frank Parkin, *Class Inequality and Political Order.* (London: Paladin Books, 1972), p. 17. Reprinted by permission.

rewards in the modern industrial societies. Other sources of economic and symbolic advantage or disadvantage certainly coexist and contribute to the positions of individuals in the market place, but these sources of advantage and disadvantage *generally* seem to be secondary to those deriving from the division of labor, property ownership, and the productive process.[29]

Even in recent multidimensional approaches there is a continual difficulty in achieving any sort of consensus over the relative importance of alternative distributive and relational characteristics of structured and unstructured inequality in different societal settings. Which of the often competing foci provides the most coherent understanding of sport—both as a distributive system in its own right and as a factor related to other distributive systems? The question itself is not strictly an empirical one, and more than likely the final answer is *perspectival*. What I am suggesting is that the answers—perhaps even the questions themselves—are anchored to a combination of historical understanding, factual evidence, personal belief and world view, and especially to the kinds of problems in which you are interested. In the words of Stanislaw Ossowski:

> Different conceptual categories correspond to different problems. . . . Depending on the kind of problem in which one is interested, one can interpret the same society in terms of a dichotomic scheme, of a scheme of gradation, or of a functional scheme; or alternately, one can apply the same scheme to it in a different manner, for example, by introducing different criteria of gradation or of functional divisions.*

The relationships of sport to inequalities in "status" or to different "status groups" are important, and some may choose to focus on them. At the same time, this does not preclude the fact that many status inequalities may be directly limited to market position and the productive process. Others, then, may choose to view status differences in the context of broader political and market factors. But what is prone to happen with factual evidence in either case is that it often seems compatible with more than one problematic focus and theoretical interpretation. To borrow an example that will be discussed in the next section: for some people, there is probably as much evidence suggesting that modern sport is an effectively "democratized" institution in the Western industrial societies as there is in suggesting that it essentially remains the prerogative of the privileged. My own feeling will be made fairly clear on this issue a little later, but it is crucial to realize that the data do not speak for themselves; they have to

---

* Stanislav Ossowski, *Class Structure in the Social Consciousness.* (New York: The Free Press, 1963), p. 176. Reprinted by permission.

be interpreted. When they are viewed from different perspectives you sometimes get different answers (cf., Connolly, 1973; Sallach, 1973).

Earlier, it was suggested that all interpretations of sport, social differentiation and social inequality contained *normative* and *analytic* elements, and that the major criticisms of inequality have easily defined ideological foundations. Following this assumption, it might be argued that the extent to which many of the interpretive divergences that occur between conflicting perspectives can be reconciled in *purely analytic* syntheses is questionable. Class theory, for instance, in the extreme forms given it by Marx, allows for a "qualitatively different test of thought than that provided for in a model of social discourse fashioned after the natural sciences" (Birnbaum, 1969: 17). As observed previously, it offers both a description of a society and a related prescription for action within it.

Thus, an empirical synthesis of propositions from class conflict and functional-consensus approaches to sport, differentiation and inequality is not tantamount to a synthesis of the positions in their entirety, because in many ways their normative and ideological underpinnings are inherently hostile to one another and are based on different assumptions.

> Because of its characteristic assumptions, each perspective gives highest priority to a particular set of questions which the other tends to treat as less fundamental or self-explanatory. And when those immersed in one perspective do turn to the highest priority questions of the other they tend to redefine them in subtle ways and anticipate answers which are compatible with assumptions already accepted.*

It is not relevant for present purposes to provide an extended discussion of the difficulties of theoretical synthesis; it will perhaps suffice to state that the study of differentiation and inequality, in its broadest sense, *is not strictly an empirical field. It is an historical interpretive one as well.* Each major perspective on inequality consists of an alternative problematic focus and a combination of normative and analytic elements. While it may be possible to synthesize some of the analytic elements, you cannot synthesize the full meaning that each position has for its practitioners. The analytic synthesis of functional-consensus and class conflict approaches (cf., Lenski, 1966) has proven to be a useful corrective to orthodox Marxist dogmatism and to the equally dogmatic orthodoxy of holistic functionalism, but as Gouldner (1970) and Sallach (1973) have argued, the majority of the syntheses that have occurred have been far more compatible with

---

* William Connolly, "Theoretical Self-Consciousness," *Polity*, Vol. VI, no. 1, (Fall, 1973), p. 17. Reprinted by permission.

the liberal tradition of "administrative sociology" than with the union of thought and action that constitutes the *praxis* of radical criticism. As such, analytical syntheses themselves often reflect a dogma of their own—the dogma of empirical analytic science. In the sense that purely empirical-analytic syntheses essentially seek to ignore important normative questions and ideological positions, they may themselves be as ideologically bound to the preservation of the basic structure of the existing system of rewards as a critical interpretation is to its alteration (cf., Mills, 1970).

The study of differentiation and inequality is an important responsibility of social science, and as sport continues to increase in importance with respect to modern reward structures, some of that responsibility must be shared by sport sociologists. Yet, to understand social theory, it is necessary to consider personally the ideological implications that often gird it and to realize their relationship to one's own "domain assumptions." It is only through an attempt at understanding and comprehending alternative systems of knowledge, however, that one's own tacit views become more explicit (cf., Connolly, 1973; Feyarabend, 1967). For instance, and notwithstanding the recognition of certain "functional" attributes of sport, the assumption that runs throughout this chapter is that the array of social and symbolic elements that make up our conceptions of social inequalities are rooted in the material order, take on an existential quality, and in turn react upon this order (cf., Parkin, 1972: 26).

To talk in terms of the relationships of the objective and symbolic manifestations of structured inequality to sport, demands not just an objective description of the socioeconomic characteristics of sports participants but also a discussion of the nature of the institutional and political arrangements which underlie how sport "fits" into the distribution of advantages. In other words, the study of sport, social differentiation, and social inequality should be concerned *both* with an objective description of the structure and ideological characteristics of sport and with the relationship of this structure and ideology to the social mechanisms by which the dominant classes, strata and major "status groups" in societies seek to preserve their rewards and privileges vis-à-vis their positional subordinates.

To summarize the prospects of theoretically synthesizing diverse interpretations of sport, differentiation, and inequality, it seems that decisions as to what problems are seen as relevant or as to what elements constitute the dominating distributive and relational characteristics of modern sport essentially remain personal ones. But these decisions should be informed by evidence, and more importantly, they should include the ability to recognize the empirical limitations of specific theories and their normative assumptions and to interpret them correctly.

EQUALITY AND THE EQUALIZATION OF OPPORTUNITY IN MODERN SPORT

On the Democratization of Sport

Three aspects of the historical legacy of preindustrial sport continue to find their expression in widely supported assumptions and beliefs in today's Western industrial societies: (a) the legacy of the "folk" or "elite" heritage of particular sports, (b) the legacy of racial and ethnic groups that have traditionally been associated with certain athletic activities, and (c) the "Victorian legacy" of major "amateur" organizational structures. Images of such things in the minority-group participant in boxing, ski instructors named Hans or Stein, the necessarily wealthy in polo or equestrian events, and the elitism of the amateur code, had their origins in the development of sport within the class and power structures of the Western industrial societies, and all continue to have some impact on modern life and the social consciousness. However, as observed earlier in this chapter, the objective and subjective manifestations of capitalist industrialism and bourgeois democratic feeling seem to have initiated an erosion of many of the rigidities of sport's traditionally ascriptive particularisms. This overall process of "leveling" out the class bias and exclusionary nature of a variety of sport-related aspects of social life has been called the "democratization" of sport (cf., Page, 1969; 1973).

Regrettably, few scholars have dealt with the concept of "democratization" in any detail, and when they have dealt with it, its limits, theoretical importance, and sociopolitical implications have rarely been mentioned. For instance, the fact that the decline of exclusionism in sport has been closely related to its rationalization and professionalization has significant implications. As Page (1973: 27) argues, the democratization of sport goes

> hand in hand with the replacement of personalistic and sentimental considerations by the rational calculation of modern business enterprises and the consequent employment of athletic laborers on the basis of performance skills and potential irrespective of their social credentials. This sketchy depiction of an important trend should not obscure persistent non-rational elements in professional sport: traditionalism; cronyism; sentiment-based decision making; ethnic, racial, and sexual discrimination and so on. But these elements, understandably stressed by the muckrakers of sport, have been, and continue to be, substantially weakened by the rational calculation of big business.*

---

* Charles H. Page, "The World of Sport and Its Study." In *Sport and Society*, John Talamini and Charles H. Page (eds.). Boston: Little, Brown (1972). Reprinted by permission.

Thus, one might suggest that while some of the more traditional ascriptive biases seem to be disappearing in modern sport, they may be doing so only in exchange for the asymmetric differentiation that Marx described as being characteristic of capitalistic industrialism. In this sense, democratization itself may hardly be truly "democratic," but may be differentially felt in the separate spheres of the bourgeois industrialist and manual laborer. Moreover, the downward extension of middle-class athletic pastimes with utilitarian and rationalistic emphases and restrictions on the availability of political meaning available in participation may have an ultimately hegemonic effect on lower class life.

An additional aspect of the democratization of sport that comes specifically out of the leveling forces of capitalism has to do with the accessibility of formal leadership positions to the underclasses. Are, in fact, the highest positions "open," or are they restricted to the upper classes and to high-ranking status groups? Following Gramsci's (1971) arguments, if sport can be considered as an "ideological institution" (and I have tried to show earlier that the competitive ethos has ideological implications), and if there appears to be an essentially monolithic and closed group controlling the institution, then the status of the "sport as ideological hegemony" thesis is further enhanced (cf., Sallach, 1974). Few studies have examined democratization at this organizational level, and it may be particularly misleading to infer from studies of athletes or sports consumers that some measure of organizational democratization is occurring. When Page (1973: 26) claims that "the misleading nature of prestige grading of sports, sportsmen and their followers is attested to by the democratization of almost all major sports in recent years," he is not talking about the controllers or owners of the means of athletic production but of the producers of themselves. The implications of a broadening base of athletic recruitment, of increased opportunities for minority groups or for women do not necessarily provide indices for assessing the extent to which institutional leadership has been opened up or is becoming truly meritocratic.[30]

Some sport analysts have extended their interpretations of the democratization thesis far beyond the restricted version that is briefly described above. The supposed overall democratization of sport is often seen in the background of recent changes in societal reward structures that have allowed for the extension of sport to almost all sections of the populations of the Western industrial societies. In this setting, the equalization of opportunities in sport ostensibly corresponds with the shift in structured forms of differentiation from traditional or bourgeois class inequality to a "mass" and essentially middle class situation characterized by status hierarchies and congeries of strategic elites; and from social inequalities based on property ownership and control of the productive process, to meritocracies based far more on personal achievement. Sport in these supposedly "post-industrial" spheres of social organization is depicted as a highly democratized institution that is an important product of mass consumption and is of increasing interest to national governmental bureaucracies. Commenting on the American experience, Stone (1973: 67) argues:

> As our social organization has shifted from a system of estates, through a system of production and classes, to an arrangement of consumption and masses, play and sport have always been affected by the cleavages and processes built into such organizational patterns.

Stone then goes on to suggest that "the leisure class that inspired the irony of Veblen has become a leisure mass" (Stone, 1973: 75).

The extent to which Stone's foregoing suggestion is an accurate reflection of the current status of sport in the reward systems of the Western industrial societies, or even specifically in the United States, is a somewhat debatable question. The legacy of traditional class privilege and inequalities stemming directly from the productive process at least continue to find their expression in what Reuel Denney (1969) has called "standards" for participation; and Stone himself recognized that the intertwining of traditional ascriptive criteria, bourgeois rationality, contemporary standards of mass consumption, and the existence of complex status systems, suggest the extent to which modern sport is "fraught with anomalies." However, in spite of these anomalies, many people feel that the dominant characteristic of modern sport is its "massification." In the passages that follow, some of the limits and preconditions of this "massification" are explored with specific references to the findings of specific studies of sport, social differentiation and inequality, and with hypothetical parameters of "industrial" and supposedly "post-industrial" stages of socioeconomic organization.

Industrialization and the Decline of Ascriptive Privilege

Any discussion of the extremes and limits of the equalization of opportunity to participate in sports and in their control and administration is very much dependent on an historical awareness of the changing distributive and relational characteristics of structured inequality and of their theoretical (and ideological) relevance. Particularly important is the understanding that even the most radical changes in economic and social organization are seldom as ubiquitous as they seem. The inevitable danger of ideal-typing lies in the all too frequent relegation of nonemergent or hypothetically declining social conditions to a marginal status that may overlook their continuing importance.

Social structures do not magically become transformed from feudal or semifeudal economic and political arrangements into rationally utilitarian settings characterized by a basic division between capital and labor; nor are they instantly transformed from highly "industrial" stages to potentially "post-industrial" ones. "We must bear in mind," Marx argued in the *Grundrisse*, "that new productive forces and new relationships of production do not evolve from nothing, nor from the air of the womb of the self-positing idea; they evolve inside, and in opposition to, an already present stage in the development and (*sic*) inherited, traditional property relationships" (Marx, 1973: 90). The negation of traditional propertied elites by capital and wage-labor does not occur in any sort of instant fashion. "Landed property," ascriptive privilege, and the industrial bourgeoisie together reflect a totality at given stages of socioeconomic organization, but the point is that the "democratization" of sport is better thought of as a gradual process than an apocalyptic antithesis.

As I have suggested throughout this chapter, two key aspects of the development of the capitalist industrial complex and the ascendency of the bourgeoisie had implications for the democratization of sport: (a) the competitive and meritocratic elements of the sporting ethos began to replace more traditional aspects of sports and games, and (b) the rationalistic forces that helped to spur the beginnings of professional sport, consumerism and the sports industry, began to reduce the barriers of economic scarcity which had made participation in some forms of sport impossible for many groups. It should be emphasized however, that the key aspect of the democratization of sport associated with early capitalist industrialism was the growing accessibility of the traditionally "elite" pastimes to the increasingly privileged industrial bourgeoisie.

To use an American example, Alan Sack (1973) has hypothesized that Yale's continual domination of Harvard during Walter Camp's coaching era was explicable because of the differential meaning of football for each campus.

> At Harvard, just as among the British Aristocracy, sport was viewed as an essential aspect of a well-bred gentleman's education. At Yale, on the other hand, football functioned to reinforce the values of America's rising business class" (Sack, 1973: 32).

The broader recruiting practices and the comparative "over" emphasis on developing the most highly skilled football players enabled Yale to maintain an athletic supremacy over their supposedly more "aristocratic" rivals. Conversely, from the perspective of the "proper" Bostonians, such an overt emphasis on competition and victory as ends in themselves was hardly the province of young "gentlemen." However, as Sack points out, by the turn of the century, the rationalistic exigencies of the ascending American industrial bourgeoisie even began to influence the conceptions held at Harvard of sport.

Sack's interesting discussion should not be interpreted as showing how the conditions were set for a wholesale democratization of America's elite academies of higher learning. On the contrary, Berryman and Loy (1972) have shown that even today most athletes at Ivy League universities continue to have private school backgrounds and comparatively high socioeconomic levels.[31] What Sack's example does suggest is the influence of rationality within certain categorically restricted limits.

Even in the most rationally utilitarian settings, the meritorcratic foundations of competitive sport have been restricted by traditional, and often irrational, factors. A belief in meritocracy in order to maximize productive output is frequently confined within specified limits of class, race, ethnicity, and gender. Illustrations of this last point are legion. For example, despite a desire for recruiting the best possible players for team "success," for many years American professional baseball excluded talented blacks because of the infamous color ban.[32] In a similar vein, but in the amateur context, the rationalization and democratization of sports in the Ivy League only seems to have occurred within certain limits of "propriety." At present there is little reason to believe that this will change unless categorically restricted meritocratic values become stronger and more universal or until there is some sort of radical reconstruction of existing systems of rewards and privileges.

Paradoxically, the substantial democratization of sport that has occurred among the bourgeois classes of the Western industrial societies has often served to reinforce certain class distinctions rather than to symbolize their demise. According to John Mallea (1972), the encroachment of the bourgeoisie into the traditional athletic domains of propertied elites in the early phases of capitalist industrialism partially increased their exclusionary nature. The field sports (equestrian events, or the hounds, for example) and conservative elite clubs became the last bastions of the courtly manner and were vigorously defended against bourgeois accessibility (cf., Baltzell, 1958). In a similar fashion wealthy bourgeoisie themselves maintained public distance from lower status wage earners and manual laborers by similar club involvement, even though, in many cases, the same activities were being made accessible to people of lower socioeconomic standing. Where such activities were made widely available, "style" and type of involvement seemed to become the modern indices of public distance. A private membership in an exclusive golf course and club hardly displays the same class or status implications as mere access to a crowded public course.[33]

Baltzell (1958) and Lueschen (1969) have stressed how club organization is a direct inhibitor of the complete "democratization" of sport, even in the rationalized environment of capitalist social structures. In Baltzell's discussion, the mid-twentieth century urban and suburban American clubs readily suggested the extent to which status distinctions maintained themselves between the existing American bourgeoisie and old family elites, and *between* these groups and the lower classes.

> Below the level of such patrician strongholds as the Somerset, Knicker-bocker, or Philadelphia Clubs, a hierarchy of lesser clubs follows a fairly uniform pattern from city to city. First, there are the union leagues in Philadelphia (the oldest), New York and Chicago. These strongholds of Republican respectability are more indicative of elite than upper-class status. At approximately the same social level as the union leagues, although perhaps attracting a professional rather than business membership, there are university clubs in most large cities. Finally, there are the athletic clubs. These are of two sorts and must not be confused. In each city the racquet club is favored by the more fashionable young bloods with an athletic turn of mind who pride themselves on "keeping in shape." The various "Athletic Clubs" such as the New York A. C., the Chicago A. C., or the Penn. A. C. in Phila-delphia mark the lowest fringes of clubdom in most cities.*

Ironically, even the "lowest fringes" of clubdom did not specifically recruit their members from unskilled labor occupations, the poor, or marginal status groups.

Notwithstanding the gradual development of industrial sports leagues and religiously oriented organizations like the YWCA and YMCA during the first half of the twentieth century, the participation of the under-classes remained greatly limited to those sports like boxing or wrestling that had comparatively humble or "folk" origins. As Weinberg and Arond (1969) suggested in their study of the occupational culture of American boxers, the position of boxing in the reward structure has always been compara-tively depressed. Participants have come almost exclusively from the lower classes and from severely disadvantaged status groups. Furthermore, in the professional realm, despite some financial success, upward mobility has generally been limited and temporally restricted. Careers have often been far more characterized by a short spurt of economic success followed by an inevitable drop in status and accompanied by frequent emotional and financial difficulties than by any enduring "embourgeoisement" or objec-tive change in living conditions.[34]

---

* E. Digby Baltzell, *Philadelphia Gentlemen*. (New York: The Free Press, 1958), p. 339). Reprinted by permission.

The problematical career contingencies of many professional boxers underlines at least one of the limits of the democratization that arose out of the *initial* confrontation between ascriptive factors and bourgeois rationality. More specifically, these limits can be stated in the following manner. *First,* while some general "recreational" democratization often occurred among the disadvantaged classes and status groups, the locus of the democratization of organized athletics could be found in the bourgeois classes. *Second,* the capitalistic era initiated a bifurcation of sport into "amateur" and "professional" spheres each clearly related to their socioeconomic heritage. *Finally,* while the professionalization of sport has initiated a more meritocratic pattern of recruitment which included large sections of the underclasses. The putative "disreputability" of professionalism has given indications of enduring well into the twentieth century, and at the same time, sport-related manifestations of upward mobility have mostly been temporally limited, especially for members of minority groups.

In summary, it seems that the relationship between the preliminary directions of increased opportunity in sport in the capitalist societies is relatively clear. While expanding the accessibility of sport to diverse groups in societies, the industrial democratization process has nonetheless institutionalized its own forms of distinction. Industrial sport may in fact have provided some measure of individual equality of opportunity but it seems to have had only slight impact on the problem of *equality* itself both in and outside the sporting world.

"Post-industrialism" and Mass Sport

The major differences between ideal-typical conceptions of industrial capitalist and supposedly "post-industrial" (and thereby post-capitalist) societies can be summed up as follows: (a) a post-industrial society is characterized by an expansion of middle-class service industries at the expense of the significance of the industrial core, (b) the emphasis in post-industrial societies is on "mass" education and industries based on an accumulation of research knowledge as marketable expertise, and (c) a post-industrial society is characterized by a leveling wherein the essential particularisms related to traditional inherited inequalities, and the productive process, have been resolved in new systems of bureaucratic organization.[35] While there can be little doubt that all of these dimensions of post-industrialism reflect important *trends* in the capitalist societies, the extent to which they actually imply a new and radical stage of socioeconomic organization is far from self-evident. As Robert Heilbroner (1973) has suggested, it may be premature to assume that objective changes in the life conditions of manual laborers coupled with their symbolic "embourgeoisement" have entirely eliminated the dramatis personae of the Marxian drama. That is:

> the organizational character of industrial capitalism, with its hierarchies, bureaucracies, and above all its trend toward concentration, seems likely to continue in the post-industrial society (Heilbroner, 1973: 169).

On the other hand, with the marked increase in levels of education; in "tertiary" sectoral labor force growth; and with the development of fundamentally "egalitarian" social rights of citizenship, it is clear that we are getting some distance from simplistic understandings of the distributive and relational characteristics of structured inequality in ideal-typical settings of industrial capitalism. Unfortunately, the complexity of the relationship of sport to social differentiation and social inequality in these complex settings is all too often subsumed under the shorthand (but misleading) expression "mass sport."

As stated at the outset of this section, a commonly expressed conception is that traditional estate, bourgeois class, and status related barriers and relational conflicts have largely disappeared in a "melting pot of mass consumption, mass recreation and entertainment" (Zuzanek, 1972: 22). That this is an overly simplified and, in many cases, erroneous conception has been alluded to already. However, notwithstanding the staggering development of "mass" sport as an almost ubiquitous area of accelerated importance, recent studies of the social origins and labor status of athletes in a variety of countries graphically display the existence of continuing particularisms and inequalities in the modern sporting world. For example, the existence of marked particularisms in the American sporting scene of the seemingly "post-industrial" 60s and 70s has been commented on by several scholars (cf., Loy 1969; Stone, 1957, 1969; Webb, 1969; Petrie, 1973; Berryman and Ingham, 1972; Kenyon, 1966), and at the same time, the continuity of the differential involvement of classes and status groups, in sport and in specific sports, has been observed in many of the other capitalist nations (Collins, 1972; Gruneau, 1972, 1972(a); Lueschen, 1969; Sugawara, 1972).

It might be argued with some success that the limits of the "democratization" of sport in all of these settings are defined by the varying contours of industrialism and post-industrialism. That is, in countries where an aristocratic tradition has been and continues to be strongly felt, the universality and democratization of certain institutions will be restricted by the power of the traditional class legacy. This follows Giddens' (1973) argument that was referred to earlier, wherein the conflicts and inequalities in certain societies are still more rooted to the "dialectic" between bourgeoisie and traditional landed property than the contradictions of capitalism itself. On the other hand, the democratization of sport in the United States, the model post-industrial and thereby "post-capitalist" country, may show a far more democratized and "mass" pattern of recruitment. However, the extent to which the massification of sport in the United States has transcended alternative forms and meanings for manual laborers or for the poor, and essentially middle- and upper-class individuals is still somewhat dubious.

If specific studies of American amateur athletes do not directly answer the questions posed above, they do nonetheless underline some of the limits of the democratization of modern sport. Persisting relationships between class, race and ethnicity continue to exist, not only with regard to formal particularisms in organized competitive sports, but with respect to leisure athletic pastimes and to related involvement in voluntary associations.[36] Moreover, despite the ubiquity of sport consumption,[37] involvement in organized competitive activities continues to be greatly related to class and status group position. As Harry Webb argues (1969: 123), athletes in general (and specifically amateur athletes) do not come from disadvantaged homes. When compared to all U.S. families, Webb found that few of the athletes in his sample of Michigan State scholarship athletes came from families occupying the bottom fifth of the income range. In a study of U.C.L.A. athletic award holders, Loy (1969, 1972) found that athletes came from even higher levels. The lowest mean occupational score of athletes' fathers on the Duncan Status Index was 43 (cf., Duncan, 1961) and in spite of Loy's preference for calling this level "lower-lower," an examination of Duncan's scale suggests that a score of 43 hardly indicates a thoroughly impoverished family background. For the most part however, if there is a segment of the reward structure that is overrepresented in studies of American college athletes, it is the middle classes. This does in some ways align with a key aspect of "post-industrialism" but it hardly corroborates the massification thesis in its entirety, and partially suggests my earlier hypothesis of the categorically restricted democratization that is a prime function of the early stages of bourgeois rationality.

Moving the discussion to other settings, it can often be found that "amateur" athletes are recruited from even higher socioeconomic levels. For instance, in Table 2 the occupational backgrounds of samples of male amateur athletes in Canada, Germany, and Britain suggest the degree to which amateur athletics in these countries continue to be overrepresented in high ranking professional and managerial occupations and underrepresented in blue-collar (especially unskilled labor) occupations.

Table 2

Occupational characteristics of male athletes from British, Canadian, and German sport studies (in percent)*

Occupational category	Occupations of British Olympic male athletes (Collins, 1972) n = 184	Occupations of fathers of Canada Games male athletes (Gruneau, 1972) n = 509	Occupations of fathers of young German sportsmen (Lueschen, 1969) n = 1474
Professional and managerial	29	21(8)	10(5)
Clerical and finance	50	33(29)	52(39)
Manual labor	21	32(63)	38(52)
Other	—	13(—)	0(5)
Total	100%	99% †	100%

* National averages for labor force listed in parentheses when given by original author.
† Does not add up to 100 percent due to rounding.

What is particularly interesting about the breakdown presented in Table 2 is the similarity between the occupational characteristics of Collins' (1972) sample of 184 British male Olympic athletes, and my own (Gruneau, 1972) sample of 509 male athletes from the 1971 Canada Winter games.[38] In both of these samples of relatively highly skilled amateur athletes, professional and high status occupations are strikingly overrepresented. Focusing on a different group, Lueschen (1969) sampled over 1400 male members of German sporting clubs. Presumably this did not make for any "built-in" controls for level of athletic achievement. The fact that the drive for high achievement is often thought to be an essentially bourgeois phenomenon, and that the pressures of amateurism in Canada and Britain continue to allow for some economic discrimination related to the accessibility of the time, facilities, and coaching needed to reach higher status levels, may explain the upward skew of the British and Canadian data. However, even with this achievement variable missing Lueschen's data nonetheless demonstrate the existence of noticeable class distinctions among young German sportsmen.

The comparative overrepresentation of athletic males in professional and middle-ranking white-collar occupations in the Canadian and German samples referred to above becomes exaggerated in the case of female competitors (see Table 3). The fact of discrimination in women's sport is well-known. However, it is less well-known that it often has a class base. That is, in both the German and Canadian samples, female competitors came from much higher occupational levels than their male counterparts. As Lueschen suggests, in the face of overall inequality by gender, "there appears to be a rather strong barrier for girls from the lower class" (Lueschen, 1969: 263).

Table 3

Differences between occupational statuses of fathers of male and female athletes in Canadian and German sport studies (in percent)

Occupational category	Occupation of fathers of Canada Games athletes (Gruneau, 1972)		Occupation of fathers of German sports people (Lueschen, 1969)	
	Male (n = 509)	Female (n = 368)	Male (n = 1474)	Female (n = 405)
Professional and managerial	21	30	10	14
Clerical and finance	33	35	52	72
Manual labor	32	25	38	14
Other	13	10	—	—
Total	99% *	100%	100%	100%

* Does not add up to 100 percent due to rounding.

Marked social differentiation by class and by gender in "mass" sport also seems accompanied by overall racial and ethnic particularisms. The situation of American blacks, and their underrepresentation in many amateur sports, has been so thoroughly documented that it need not be repeated here (cf., McPherson, 1974; Edwards, 1973). However, the persistence of ethnic particularisms in the "mass" sport of other western capitalistic societies is far less often referred to. In Canada, for example, Landry et al. (1972) have commented on the marked underrepresentation of Francophones on Canadian international sports teams since 1900, and it has also been demonstrated that Francophones were greatly underrepresented at the 1971 Canadian Winter Games (cf., Gruneau, 1972).[38] I suspect the point here is that in pluralistic societies, despite the exigencies of democratization of sport, many groups have been proportionally left out of the sporting world. Whether this is benignly explained as minority group socialization, or by human nature or class preference, or whether these elements are depicted as anchored to exploitative systems of asymmetrical dependence depends greatly on our understanding of the relationships of the groups in question to societal reward structures.

One problem with viewing the general socioeconomic characteristics of any group of athletes has to do with the fact that critical subsample variations become submerged in the aggregate. "Sport," per se, is so wide a category that to assess its relationship to differentiation and inequality without examining specific sport differences can be misleading and tends to neglect the "folk" and "elite" traditions of specific activities. Thus in Table 4 it is possible to observe marked differences in the occupational status of the fathers of competitors in the different sports that were contested at the 1971 Canada Winter Games.

An incredible 72 percent of the fathers of synchronized swimmers and 61 percent of the fathers of male badminton players came from families where the father was involved in some sort of professional, managerial, or finance activity. In contrast are weightlifters and boxers who come from much lower socioeconomic levels. However, if these data are compared with national averages, it can be seen that in all but four cases, Canadian Games athletes are overrepresented in the highest occupational categories, and except for two cases substantially underrepresented in unskilled labor categories. Despite relative overall differences in socioeconomic association, there is some consistency between the ordering listed in Table 4 and the rank-ordering of sport groups found in other studies and generally documented in the literature (cf., Loy, 1969; Lueschen, 1969). Notably those sports that seem to emphasize physical toughness, physical strength, or combat usually ranked much lower than those which are associated with what some scholars have confusingly called "physical skill" (cf., Roberts and Sutton-Smith, 1969) or which presumably require an expensive venue.

One final comment on these Canadian data has to do with the fact that the indications of some proportional representation by diverse class groupings in all sports are truly evident. However, if these at all can be construed as the results of democratization, then the nature of democratization in the Canadian setting seems to be working from the bottom up. That is, those sports that seem associated with the lowest levels have more middle and upper level participants than upper level sports have lower level participants. Like many areas of Canadian society, ascriptive traditions in sport continue to assert themselves despite Canada's accelerated industrial development. Both Stone (1957, 1969) and Loy (1969, 1972) have reported approximately similar rankings in studies of American sport. In 1957 Stone asked a sample of Minneapolis adults about their sport preferences, and

Table 4

Sport Group (male and female) by fathers' occupational level (percent) for 1971 Canada games athletes*

Sport group	Subsample size (n)		Professional, managerial, and finance		Clerical and skilled labor		Unskilled labor	
	Male	Female	Male	Female	Male	Female	Male	Female
Synchronized swimming	—	42	—	72	—	22	—	2
Badminton	18	26	61	49	23	23	6	—
Alpine skiing	30	32	36	59	46	10	7	—
Gymnastics	20	26	40	54	35	35	20	—
Speed skating	25	27	48	36	32	55	12	—
Figure skating	25	21	32	52	52	34	8	14
Volleyball	17	60	40	38	30	42	20	12
Basketball	14	53	40	38	46	26	7	17
Nordic skiing	29	12	41	32	31	34	3	17
Table tennis	14	21	65	10	12	67	6	19
Curling	27	37	30	30	67	49	—	16
Fencing	10	11	20	36	30	27	10	9
Hockey	84	—	22	—	50	—	18	—
Wrestling	43	—	21	—	24	—	33	—
Judo	25	—	16	—	32	—	28	—
Weightlifting	36	—	9	—	50	—	28	—
Boxing	28	—	4	—	35	—	36	—
National averages (%) Canadian male labor force			17%		52%		31%	

* Cf., Gruneau, 1972.

aligned these preferences with "status" position in approximately the following manner:

upper stratum	hockey	
	golf	
	tennis	
	football	baseball
middle stratum	basketball	(all strata)
	bowling	
	hunting	
lower stratum	boxing	
	wrestling	

The position of "individual" sports at both ends of the socioeconomic scale and the typically low ranking of boxing and wrestling is highly compatible with the Canadian data presented above and with Webb's study of Michigan State athletes. Somewhat similar patterns are not only described by Loy in Table 5, but they also partially characterize the sport-class differences found in Lueschen's study of German sportsmen (see Table 6).

What all of these studies of athletes essentially do is put defining limitations on our conceptions of mass sport. Despite the pervasive "middle classness" of post-industrial contingencies, it is evident not only that class, racial, ethnic, and sexual particularisms continue to exist, but that there is a somewhat enduring consistency between the rank orderings of certain physical activities on the basis of the classes and status groups from which they draw their membership. This seems true both in a variety of societal contexts and with respect to differentially selected sample groups.

The final aspect of this discussion of post-industrialism and mass sport concerns the professional and bureaucratic spheres of sport's organizational structures.[39] In a post-industrial setting one could expect not only the proliferation of professional franchises, sport related industries, and the increasing association of sport with the state bureaucracies, but one would also expect that the organizing principles of these expanding bureaucratic structures would be far more meritocratic than their Victorian counterparts, or the categorically restricted pseudomeritocracies of capitalist industrialism.

However, just as the massification extremes of the democratization thesis must be understood within certain limits, so must an understanding of the meritocratic aspects of sport's proliferating organizational structures be conditioned by certain caveats. Most important is the recognition of substantial changes in sport policy within the last five years. Governments

Table 5

Mean occupational status scores of fathers of former athletes in 20 collegiate sports (Duncan Socioeconomic Status Index)*

Sport	Number	Status score	Category
Wrestling	27	43	Lower-lower
Boxing	12	47	Upper-lower
Football	192	48	
Baseball	89	49	
Soccer	32	51	Lower-middle
Rifle team	12	51	
Rugby	16	52	
Handball	6	53	
Track	119	53	
Team managers	34	55	Upper-middle
Volleyball	3	55	
Basketball	91	57	
Gymnastics	33	58	
Fencing	5	60	Lower-upper
Crew	64	62	
Ice hockey	9	62	
Cricket	17	63	
Swimming	78	64	
Tennis	50	64	
Golf	19	74	Upper-upper

* From J. W. Loy, "The Study of Sport and Social Mobility" in *Contemporary Aspects of Sport Sociology*, G. Kenyon (ed.). (Chicago: The Athletic Institute, 1969.)

are actively seeking to broaden the base of athletic recruitment, salaries between black and white professional sports players finally seem to be levelling off, the "embourgeoisement" of the professional athlete is becoming enhanced by the push for player pension plans and better contracts, and women's sports, especially in the United States, seem, in W. W. Rostow's words, about to "take off." Yet none of these aspects of modern sport are thoroughly convincing in their suggestion that somehow sport has become either a full blown area for the equality of opportunity, or any more egalitarian than in the past. Government programs seem rooted to no less rationally utilitarian motives than professional sports; the development of women's sport has been somewhat contingent on the sudden recognition that there is a bullish market in women's athletics; and the key managerial positions in the professional leagues do not show a great

Table 6

Sport group by social class for German sports people (in percent)*

Sport	Number of cases	Lower-class	Lower middle-class	Middle middle-class	Upper middle-class
Soccer	470	53	29	12	5
Wrestling, weight-lifting	35	51	26	14	9
Field handball	158	54	41	19	6
Badminton	33	27	46	24	3
Gymnastics (with apparatus	279	31	39	23	7
Table tennis	73	23	44	24	8
Canoeing	34	21	41	38	
Gymnastics	44	16	43	41	
Riding	33	18	49	15	18
Swimming	143	17	41	31	11
Track and Field	231	19	40	24	17
Rowing	57	12	47	26	14
Skiing	72	11	33	20	36
Field hockey	34	3	26	53	18
Tennis	101	2	27	28	42

* Adapted from G. Lueschen, "Social Statification and Social Mobility Among Young Sportsmen," in *Sport, Culture and Society*, John W. Loy and Gerald S. Kenyon (eds.). (Toronto: Macmillan, 1969.)

degree of openness to marginal status groups of any type. If it is only now that we are beginning to get black quarterbacks in professional football; presumably it will be a while longer before we get black ownership.

Mobility through sport for both the lowest classes and status groups may in fact stop at the comfortable level of middle class athlete. In this sense, the structure of rewards is not so much a ladder on which individuals may continue to climb but rather a tree wherein a specified limb spells the absolute extent of upward travel. Wiley (1967) refers to this concept as a "mobility trap" and it may have considerable relevance in assessing the meritocratic potential of post-industrial sport. As Roy (1974) points out in his study of the National Hockey League, despite the prominence of several near-legendary Francophone hockey players, few Francophones have found their way into managerial positions, and they remain heavily underrepresented in hockey's organizational framework. All of this seems to run somewhat contrary to the meritocratic foundations of both sport and post-industrialism, yet, as Heilbroner has stressed, the narrow concentration of restricted capital continues on in the West.

SUMMARY AND CONCLUDING COMMENTS

In this chapter I have attempted a review of some of the basic literature weighing on an understanding of sport, social differentiation and social inequality in the modern capitalist societies. In presenting this review, three distinct areas were judged to be central: (a) the relationship of the sporting ethos to ideology and theory, (b) the relationship of divergent theoretical interpretations of class inequality to an understanding of sport, and (c) the relationship of specific empirical studies of modern sport to general interpretations of socioeconomic organization. The current status of modern sport with respect to social differentiation and social inequality is highly complex. It seems not only to vary by societal context but also by its association with "amateur" and "professional" spheres. The most viable theoretical framework for the analysis of modern sport, social differentiation and social inequality must take such factors into consideration.

In an empirical sense, the widespread changes in the status of the underclasses, in the broadening base of athletic recruitment, and in post-industrial changes in relational attributes between classes and status groups seem problematic for Marxist class theorists. At the same time, such analysts must face the difficult problem of defining the existence of a ruling class from within the often antagonistic spheres of traditional elites, corporate bourgeois, and political bureaucrats. However, nominalistic stratification theorists have no less a problem with the fact that the aforementioned groups tend to represent a privileged and somewhat exclusive collection of individuals; that marked inequalities continue to exist that can be firmly tied to socioeconomic factors; and that some degree of exploitative asymmetric differentiation seems an enduring factor of modern life.

In an ideological sense, it can be argued that meritocratic and egalitarian critics of social inequality share essentially irreconcilable views. Meritocratic critics of sport in the class and status structures of the Western industrial societies argue that inside the institution itself, athletic achievement and recruitment into managerial or bureaucratic positions should reflect the ability of individuals rather than be based on less rational and often exclusionary criteria. Furthermore, the problematical expansion of the base of athletic recruitment is viewed as being not only a valuable end in itself, but also a combination index and symbol of an overall growth of equality of opportunity in the social order. By this standard, meritocratic critics can only feel distressed at the categorically restricted democratization that has characterized modern sport. Yet, the accelerated importance of sport, and the expanding emphasis of its merito-cratic elements can only be examined from this perspective with consid-erable optimism.

Conversely, the increasing institutionalization of the competitive ethos of so much organized sporting activity can only be seen by egalitarians as a disturbingly powerful challenge to the principal of equality. Egalitarians generally suggest two things: first, that an overall "equality of opportun-ity" is difficult to achieve because of class- and status-related barriers to necessary expertise (cf., Bottomore, 1970); second, that in meritocracies, "inequalities of result create privileges that vitiate the equality of oppor-tunity and thereby render inequitable the results that have in fact emerged and will continue to emerge" (Spitz, 1974: 78). Thus it is argued that as long as the critical focus remains on problems of recruitment rather than fundamental reevaluations of positional status, structured inequality and some measure of exploitation will continue to exist. Notwithstanding the fact that specific individuals may ascend to elite positions, a great percent-age of the population will nonetheless be substantially underprivileged. George Orwell (1950: 173) has expressed thoughts related to these later statements:

> A ruling group is a ruling group as long as it can nominate its succes-sors . . . *who* wields power is not important provided that the hierarchi-cal structure remains the same.

Finally the balance between playful and egalitarian competition and centralized, outcome-oriented forms of physical activity and their adminis-tration may be a barometer for the direction that future inequality is tak-ing. Somewhat ironically however, the fact that the high levels of athletic expertise that are the most enjoyable to watch are closely associated with an accelerated importance of rationalized competition and accompanying nonegalitarianism poses an interesting dilemma for even the most radical and egalitarian critics of inequality.

NOTES

1. This definitional statement is a composite drawn from several sources. For background reading on the nature of social differentiation see Svalastoga, 1965; Dahrendorf, 1969; Mayer and Buckley, 1969.

2. See especially, Dahrendorf's discussion (1969) of the works of Gustav Schmoller and others who developed theories of class formation out of the division of labor. This theoretical position has also been partially adopted

by "functional" theorists of stratification (cf., Davis and Moore, 1945). However, as Tumin (1967:v) has stated; "In fact there are at least four major processes at work in the operation of any system of stratification—differentiation, ranking, evaluation, and rewards. . . ." The last three of these processes are the foundations of inequality.

3. This is not to imply that these traditional forces died out, only that in many cases they become secondary to the class formations derived directly from the productive process. In reality the hypothetical "balance" between these forces and residues is a question for studies of social differentiation and social inequality.

4. Throughout this chapter I have deliberately underplayed and, in some cases, omitted specific references to the various subspecializations that have surrounded differential status groups. Moreover, I have tried to avoid, where possible, a strictly reportorial approach to existing literature. Much of the literature that is of direct relevance to this chapter has been reviewed in several other sources (cf., Edwards, 1973; Lueschen, 1968). Accordingly, I have been guided by a desire to integrate conceptual material directly from the general field of sociological theory with a discussion of macrosociological issues relating to social differentiation, social inequality and sport. Thus, this chapter does not go into any detail on such topical area of social differentiation research as the black athlete or women in sport. Readers who are especially interested in the specifics of these areas should consult McPherson, 1974(a), 1974(b); Edwards, 1970, 1973; and Gerber et al., 1974.

5. See the selection by Herbert Spencer, "The Dynamics of Exclusion" in Talamini and Page (1973: 274–277).

6. While the term rationalization can have a variety of meanings (cf., Mannheim, 1960; Gerth and Mills, 1958), my usage of it throughout this chapter has primarily been influenced by the interpretations of its meaning and significance that can be found in the writings of Karl Marx and Max Weber. In a general sense, "rationality" refers simply to a "disenchantment" or demystification of the world. Logic and reason, other than ideational factors, underlie its development. In an applied economic sense, it becomes the driving force of utilitarian productive process and, in a bureaucratic sense, it refers particularly to "rational efficiency, continuity of operation, speed, precision, and calculation of results" (Gerth and Mills, 1958: 49).

7. For example, see Stanley Parker's *The Future of Work and Leisure* (1972).

8. Where a dominant class in a society is able to reinforce its superior position through the successful extension of its influence to the ideological arena, this process is called "ideological hegemony" (cf., Sallach, 1974a, 1974b; Gramsci, 1971).

9. This reference is, of course, to the prominent utilitarian theorist Jeremy Benthem, whom Marx once labelled as that "insipid, pedantic, leather-tongued oracle of the commonplace bourgeoisie intelligence of the nineteenth century" (Marx, quoted in Gouldner, 1970: 190).

10. Consult Marx and Engels (1970: 109–114). It should be noted that Marx suspected that the thrust of rationality, as it becomes experienced in fundamentally utilitarian relationships, was essentially "irrational." The "dialectical" relationship between rational technological advances of the productive process and the contradictory "fetters of private property, private profit, and unmanaged market competition" (Gerth and Mills, 1958: 49) characterized an "anarchy" of production. True rationality for Marx, unlike Weber, was tied to moral contingencies. Despite its rationalistic foundations, the utilitarian revolution of the bourgeoisie could only be eliminated by the eradication of the "irrational" elements of capitalist industrialism—both in the sense of traditional feudal ties and of bourgeois private property.

11. I have relied heavily here on Parkin's discussion of these differences in *Class Inequality and Political Order* (1972). However, in some cases his comments have been slightly modified to suit my own analytical biases.

12. These two levels approximate Sallach's (1974b) distinction between two major approaches to the hegemony problematic. While Sallach stresses the primacy of an "institutional" approach to an understanding of hegemony his arguments do not seem so convincing that an "inculcation" interpretation should be entirely abandoned.

13. The fact that many Eastern communist countries continue to participate in highly competitive and rationalized forms of sporting activity at the same time that they are damning the essence of bourgeois sport is a paradox that has not been lost on many Western communists. Thus, Jean-Marie Brohm (1972) has argued that the intense involvement of Eastern socialist countries in competitive organized athletics runs completely contrary to the egalitarian principles of democratic socialism.

14. Inequalities tend to become "structured" by virtue of the tendency of those occupying relatively privileged positions to ensure that their own progeny are recruited into similar situations. Quoting Parkin (1972: 14): "The ability of well-placed families to confer advantages on their younger members thus encourages a fairly high degree of social self-recruitment within privileged strata from one generation to the next. Partly as a result of this there often develops a pattern of social and cultural differentiation which, in turn, reinforces the system of occupational recruitment and so crystallizes the class structure through time." (From Frank Parkin, *Class Inequality and Political Order*, London: Paladin Books, 1972).

15. I differentiate here between class and stratification in an effort to underline the problems of terminology that accrue as a result of theoretical differences. Class, while most often used synonymously with the term stratification, does not in the writings of many analysts automatically refer to the same principles. This distinction is a central one in the analysis at hand. For further elaboration see Aron's "Two Definitions of Class" (1969); Centers (1949); and Ossowski (1963).

16. "The concept of praxis in Marxism refers to the activity of man which aims at transforming the world as well as aiding in his own self development" (Jarousek, 1972: 279). More specifically praxis might be defined as "the dual process of (1) constructing the meanings of situations and actions, and (2) acting on the basis of those meanings" (Sallach, 1973: 135).

17. Probably the best description and analysis of the "Frankfurt School" can be found in Martin Jay's book *The Dialectical Imagination* (1973).

18. In this statement I am not only referring to the organizational hierarchies of professional sports, but also to the bureaucratic hierarchies of government departments designed specifically to stimulate athletic development.

19. While "monolithic" power theorists like Mills (1956) and Hunter (1953) do not interpret Marx literally, they do tend to maintain that members of ruling groups act in concert when it serves their self-interest. The power elite in any setting ensures a uni-directional flow of power and decision from "authorities" down to average citizens and potential partisans. Criticism of the monolithic approach has been severe; see Rose, 1967 (especially pages 1 through 39) and Gordon, 1963: they epitomize the American position. Also see Porter, 1966 and 1970, and Bottomore, 1966, for reactions regarding other settings.

20. This particular statement is an exaggeration and does not quite do justice to Marx's position. Marx did not ignore what he called the "mass of the nation ... standing between the proletariat and bourgeoisie" (Marx, 1951: 137). It was Marx the revolutionary and Marx the dramatist of history who developed a dichotomic conception of classes in capitalist societies. Marx, the sociologist was compelled to recognize the existence of important "intermediate" classes as these existed both throughout history and in his own era (cf., Ossowski, 1963: 75). However, as this sociological aspect necessarily became compromised in Marx's more political writings, the pervasive asymmetric and dichotomous conceptions of bourgeoisie and proletariat became the bulwark of the Marxian legacy.

21. This does not mean to imply, however, that in situations characterized by what Ossowski (1963) called "nonegalitarian classlessness," measures of interstatus friction will be absent.

22. Interesting and provocative discussions of functionalism are not uncommon in sociological literature but one of the more informed criticisms can be found in Cohen, 1968. Walter Buckley's short piece on homeostatic, equilibrium and processual systems is another of my favorites. (Cf., Buckley, 1967; R. Blain, 1970; and Max Black, 1961.) The functional issue in the field of "social stratification" is best addressed by reviewing the Davis and Moore versus Tumin, Wrong and Buckley series. These are excellently reviewed in Gordon's *Class in American Sociology* (1963) as well as in Page's "Introduction Thirty Years Later" (1969). (Cf., Davis and Moore, 1945; Tumin, 1953, 1963; Buckley, 1958; Moore, 1963.)

23. This inability (more specific to systemic functionalism, than functional analysis generally) is often not so much a problem of the perspective than it is a problem of those who utilize it. For a sympathetic review of the flexibilities of functional analysis, cf., Merton's essay, "Manifest and Latent Functions" (1967).

24. The similarity lies in the compatibility of the thoroughly endorsed "inculcation" approach to ideological hegemony with the assumption of consensual value levels among the underclasses. As Michael Mann (1970) has argued, compliance to political order on the part of the underclasses is based on a *lack* of consensus and a lack of internal consistency that prevents that class from translating its experiences into any sort of political framework—*not* from the robot like internalization of bourgeois ideology. Mann's contentions seem well founded, but we should not overlook the importance of bourgeois contingencies in contributing to the lack of working class consensus that he describes.

25. Specific studies of sport and social mobility have been especially flawed by methodological shortcomings. For instance, Lueschen (1969) simply asks a sample of young German sportsmen what occupations they aspire to (a crude mobility index indeed), and Loy's ambitious study of UCLA athletes could not really discern the extent to which sport involvement or college degree contributed to upward movement in the reward structure. Even in the often-cited case of college scholarships allowing for mobility, or in the learning of a desire to achieve which alternately results in payoffs in the educational sector, answers to the mobility question have been far from satisfactory. A lack of socioeconomic and status group controls may in fact have some relevance for the somewhat positive findings of some scholars (cf., Schafer, 1968; Schafer and Armer, 1968; Schafer and Rehberg, 1970). Moreover, the inevitable problems of spurious causation and post hoc ergo propter hoc reasoning continue to obfuscate the problem.

26. Understandings of sport are tied up with culturally accepted definitions of the class structure. The American emphasis on "status" and on "mobility" stems from a particular world view and set of social conditions that Lenski (1966: 62) says have no "counterpart in most societies." Many European scholars label the exaggerated endorsement of this world view (and its extension into other settings) as the ultimate example of American ethnocentrism. However, as Béteille (1969: 11) notes . . . "no doubt the European preoccupation with class consciousness and class conflict appears equally bizarre to many American observers."

27. This is not meant to contradict the assertion made earlier that functional interpretations tend to legitimate inequality. Rather, I am suggesting that many functional theorists would view the existence of "irrational" barriers to the widest possible recruitment of individuals as "dysfunctional" for systemic maintenance.

28. This particular "synthetic" approach to an understanding of sport, differentiation and inequality is detailed in Gruneau (1975). However, my position

on some of these issues has shifted slightly since that particular essay was originally written.

29. Regardless of their theoretical orientations, most scholars have come to recognize the importance of the occupational order in studies of inequality. It combines both *objective* (income, education) and, in the case of related prestige scales, *subjective* measures of social position.

30. Nor do such studies pose, in any problematic form, a definite egalitarian critique of this leadership and the possible vested interests leadership figures may have with respect to sport policy.

31. See also Eggleston's (1969) description of the continuing exclusivity of "Oxbridge Blues."

32. Yet, blacks were not being restricted from all aspects of baseball; they did in fact develop their own leagues. Nonetheless, in the successful "major" leagues, blacks were absent until after Jackie Robinson's entrance in the late forties. See Peterson's (1970) accounts of life in the black leagues.

33. See Kaplan's arguments on this point in *Leisure in America* (1960), also Berryman and Ingham (1972).

34. Scoville's (1971) discussion of professional athletes in the labor force suggests that this mobility pattern has not been restricted solely to athletes from marginal status groups. After the peak earning years of 25 to 35 the average salaries of all players without college degrees descends to a rate far lower than the median income for comparable noncollege members of the American labor force. In the case of players with college degrees, the inflated peak earning rate drops to a level approximately compatible with comparative college educated members of the labor force.

35. A great amount of literature now deals with post-industrial society. See Daniel Bell (1971; 1972; 1973); the article by Robert Heilbroner cited above; and Brezezinski's *Between Two Ages* (1970).

36. On leisure, see Curtis and Milton, 1973; Boston, 1968; Zuzanek, 1972; White, 1955; Thomas, 1956; Emmett, 1971; Bishop and Ikeda, 1970. For a review of the voluntary association literature, see Tomeh (1974).

37. See McPherson's discussion in this volume.

38. These particular socioeconomic data come out of a larger analysis conducted by R. E. DuWors and the author (cf., DuWors and Gruneau, 1972).

39. While opinions as to the fulfillment of Marx's predictions about the fate of the "middle classes" depend greatly on how these are defined in today's societies, in contexts where professional and technical occupations numerically outweigh labor one presumably has to adapt the orthodox Marxist viewpoint to new conditions. Thus, several Marxist-oriented analysts speak of the white-collar or professional "specialist" as the "New Working Class" in Western industrial societies. By abstracting their arguments, and considering the proliferation of professional semi-professional, and high level "ama-

teur" sports teams, it may be somewhat realistic *from this perspective* to fit the "jock" into this category. The first Marxist attempt to seek a theoretical formulation that could be modified to these new problems was Mallet's *La Nouvelle Classe Ouvriere* (1963) (although Veblen did in fact make a similar "new proletariat" type of distinction between the class of engineers and the class of finance capitalists or managers, cf., *Theory of Business Enterprise*). Mallet separates the psychological spheres of production and consumption by noting the possibility that the worker may cease to regard his occupational role as soon as he leaves the work site. But, when in the actual productive context, even professionals might be described as belonging to the "New Working Class." Even though well paid, the skills of many professionals are inevitably broken down, compartmentalized, massproduced and routinized to the extent that they are reduced to the role of highly trained drones without any degree of self-expression and self-direction (cf., Mallet, 1963; Gorz, 1967; and Gintis, 1970). One wonders, however, the extent to which the "New Working Class" is not just a statistical or imaginary group created by those who perhaps too readily accept the decline of manual labor as a social force. The reality of this "class" and its supposed levels of alienation seems problematic: they do not tend to identify with the "exploited" in dichotomic terms and futhermore, their psychological reactions and motivations seem more generally rooted to the immediate problems of lifestyle and their work situation than to more abstract notions of class position. Faulkner notes in his study of studio musicians that many types of occupations cannot be conveniently fitted into the alienated artist framework without "flattening the contours of occupational problems and their impact on inner experience" (Faulkner, 1971: 179). Moreover this "proletarianization" of middle and upper level occupational groupings seems to run completely contrary to the advantaged positions that these groups hold in the reward structure (cf., Parkin, 1972).

REFERENCES

Aron, Raymond
1969   "Two Definitions of Class." In *Social Inequality*, André Béteille (ed.). Baltimore: Penguin Books.
1950   "Social Structure and the Ruling Class." *British Journal of Sociology*, **1** (March); **2** (June).

Baltzell, E. Digby
1958   *Philadelphia Gentlemen*. New York: Free Press.

Bell, Daniel
1971   "The Postindustrial Society: The Evolution of an Idea." *Survey* (Spring).
1972   "Labour in the Post-Industrial Society." *Dissent* (Winter).
1973   *The Coming of Post-Industrial Society*. New York: Basic Books.

Bendix, R.
1962 *Max Weber: An Intellectual Portrait.* Garden City, New York: Anchor Books, Doubleday.

Berryman, Jack, and Alan Ingham
1972 "The Embourgeoisement of Sport in America." Paper presented at the 1972 annual meetings of the American Sociological Association. New Orleans, Louisiana (August).

Berryman, Jack, and John W. Loy
1971 "The Democratization of Sports in the Ivy League. . . ." Paper presented at the Third International Symposium on the Sociology of Sport, Waterloo, Ontario, Canada. August 22–28.

Béteille, André
1969 *Social Inequality.* Baltimore: Penguin Books.

Betts, John
1969 "The Technological Revolution and the Rise of Sport." In *Sport, Culture and Society.* J. W. Loy and Gerald S. Kenyon (eds.), Toronto: Macmillan, 145–166.

Birnbaum, Norman
1969 "The Crisis in Marxist Sociology." In *Recent Sociology,* Vol. 1, Hans Peter Dreitzel (ed.), London: Macmillan Co.

Bishop, Doyle W., and Masuru Ikeda
1970 "Status and Role Factors in the Leisure Behaviour of Different Occupations." *Sociology and Social Research,* (January, Vol. 54, No. 2: 190–209).

Black, Max
1961 *The Social Theories of Talcott Parsons.* Englewood: Prentice-Hall.

Blain, Robert R.
1970 "A Critique of Parson's Four Functional Paradigm." *The Sociological Quarterly,* 157–168.

Böhme, J. O., J. Gadow, S. Guldenpfennig, J. Jensen, R. Pfister
1971 *Sport im Spätkapitalismus.* Frankfurt.

Boston, R.
1968 "What Leisure?" *New Society,* (December 26).

Bottomore, T. B.
1966 *Classes in Modern Society.* New York: Vintage Books.
1970 *Elites and Society.* Middlesex: Penguin Books.

Brailsford, Dennis
1969 *Sport and Society: Elizabeth to Anne.* Toronto: University of Toronto Press.

Brohm, Jean-Marie
1972 "Sociologie politique du sport." In *Sport, Culture, et Répression.* Paris: petite maspero.

Brzezinski, Zbigniew
1970   *Between Two Ages: America's Role in the Technotronic Era.* New York: Viking.

Buckley, Walter
1958   "Social Stratification and the Functional Theory of Social Differentiation." *American Sociological Review*, Vol. 23, No. 4, (August).
1967   *Sociology and Modern Systems Theory.* Englewood Cliffs: Prentice-Hall.

Centers, Richard
1949   *The Psychology of Social Classes.* Princeton: Princeton University Press.

Cohen, Percy
1968   *Modern Social Theory.* London: Heinemann Books.

Connolly, William E.
1973   "Theoretical Self-Consciousness." *Polity*, Vol. VI, No. 1, (Fall).

Curtis, James, and Brian Milton
1973   "Social Status and the 'Sedentary Society': National Data on Leisure-Time Physical and Sport Activities in Canada." Paper presented at the Southern Sociological Society Annual Meeting, Atlanta (April).

Dahrendorf, Ralf
1959   *Class and Class Conflict in Industrial Society.* Stanford: Standford University Press.
1969   "On the Origin of Inequality Among Men." In *Social Inequality*, André Béteille (ed.). Baltimore: Penguin Books.

Davis, Kingsley, and Wilbert Moore
1945   "Some Principles of Stratification." *American Sociological Review*, Vol. 10, No. 2, (April).

Denney, Reuel
1969   "The Spectatorial Forms." In *Sport, Culture and Society*, John Loy and Gerald Kenyon (eds.). Toronto: Macmillan, 337–347.

Duncan, Otis Dudley
1961   "A Socio-economic Index for all Occupations." In *Occupations and Social Status*, Albert J. Reiss (ed.). New York: The Free Press.

DuWors, Richard E., and Richard S. Gruneau
1972   "Facts Toward a Foundation for Canadian Programmes in Amateur Sports." Research Report presented to the Canadian Fitness and Amateur Sport Directorate, Ottawa, Ontario, (April).

Edwards, Harry
1973   *The Sociology of Sport.* Homewood: The Dorsey Press.
1970   *The Revolt of the Black Athlete.* New York: The Free Press.

Eggleston, John
1969   "Secondary Schools and Oxbridge Blues." In *Sport, Culture and Society*, J. W. Loy and Gerald S. Kenyon (eds.). Toronto: Macmillan, 277–287.

Emmett, Isabel
1971   *Youth and Leisure in an Urban Sprawl.* Manchester: Manchester University Press.

Faulkner, Robert
1971   *Hollywood Studio Musician.* Chicago: Aldine-Atherton.

Feyarabend, P. K.
1968   "How to be a Good Empiricist—A Plea for Tolerance in Matters Epistemological." In *The Philosophy of Science,* P. H. Nidditch (ed.). New York: Oxford University Press.

Flood, Curt
1970   *The Way It Is.* New York: Trident Press.

Geertz, Clifford
1972   "Deep Play: Notes on the Balinese Cockfight." *Daedalus* (Winter).

Gerber, Ellen, Jan Felshin, Pearl Berlin and Waneen Wyrick
1974   *The American Woman In Sport.* Reading: Addison-Wesley.

Gerth, H. H., and C. Wright Mills
1958   *From Max Weber: Essays in Sociology.* New York: Oxford University Press.

Giddens, Anthony
1973   *The Class Structure of the Advanced Societies.* London: Hutchinson Books.

Gintis, Herbert
1970   "The New Working Class and Revolutionary Youth." *Continuum* (Spring-Summer).

Gordon, Milton
1963   *Social Class in American Sociology.* New York: McGraw-Hill.

Gorz, Andre
1967   *Strategy for Labor.* Boston: Beacon Press.

Gouldner, Alvin
1970   *The Coming Crisis of Western Sociology.* New York: Basic Books.

Gramsci, Antonio
1971   *Prison Notebooks.* New York: International Publishers.

Gruneau, Richard S.
1975   "Social Inequality, Images of Class Structure and Sport: A Critical Review." *International Review of Sport Sociology,* forthcoming.
1972   "A Socioeconomic Analysis of the Competitors at the 1971 Canada Winter Games." M.A. thesis, U. of Calgary.
1972   "Sport and Class Concepts in Twentieth Century Canada." Paper presented at the 1972 annual meetings of the American Sociological Association, New Orleans, Louisiana (August 28–31).

Habermas, Jürgen
1971   *Knowledge and Human Interest.* Boston: Beacon Press.

1972   "Sociologische Notizen zum Verhaltnis Von Arbeit und Freizeit" quoted in *The Scientific View of Sport*, Ommo Grupe, Dietrich Kurz and Johannes Marcus Teipel (eds.). Berlin: Springer Verlag.

Heberle, Rudolf
1959   "Recovery of Class Theory." *Pacific Sociological Review*, **II**, (Spring).

Heilbroner, Robert L.
1973   "Economic Problems of a 'Postindustrial' Society." *Dissent* (Spring).

Hoch, Paul
1972   *Rip Off The Big Game.* New York: Doubleday.

Huizinga, Johan
1955   *Homo Ludens.* Boston: Beacon Press.

Hunter, Floyd
1953   *Community Power Structure.* Chapel Hill: University of North Carolina Press.

Ingham, Alan G., and John W. Loy
1972   "The Social System of Sport: A Humanistic Perspective." *Quest* XIX (Fall).

Janousek, Jaromir
1972   "On the Marxian Concept of Praxis." In *The Context of Social Psychology: A Critical Assessment*, Joachim Israel and Henri Tajfel (eds.). New York: Academic Press, 279–294.

Jay, Martin
1973   *The Dialectical Imagination.* Boston: Little, Brown.

Kaplan, Max
1960   *Leisure in America.* New York: Wiley.

Kenyon, Gerald S.
1966   "The Significance of Physical Activity as a Function of Age, Sex, Education and Socio-Economic Status of Northern United States Adults." *Int. Review of Sport Sociology*, **1**: 41–54.

Laguillaumie, Pierre
1972   "Pour une critique fondamentale due sport." *Sport, Culture et Répression.* Paris: petite maspero.

Landry, Fernand, Roger Boileau, Claude St.-Denis, Ives Trempe and Carol Turgeon.
1971   "Les Canadiens-francais et les grands jeux Internationaux." Presented at the Third International Symposium on the Sociology of Sport, Waterloo, Ontario (August 22–28).

Lenski, Gerhard
1966   *Power and Privilege.* New York: McGraw-Hill.

Loy, John W.
1969   "The Study of Sport and Social Mobility." In *Aspects of Contemporary Sport Sociology*, G. S. Kenyon (ed.). Chicago: The Athletic Institute, 101–119.

Loy, John W., and Alan G. Ingham
1972 "Play Games and Sport in the Psychosociological Development of Children and Youth." In *Physical Activity: Human Growth and Development*, G. Lawrence Rarick (ed.). New York: Academic Press.

Lueschen, Guenther
1968 "The Sociology of Sport: A Trend Report and Bibliography." *Current Sociology*, Vol. 15.
1969 "Social Stratification and Social Mobility Among Young Sportsmen." In *Sport, Culture and Society*, John W. Loy and Gerald S. Kenyon (eds.). Toronto: Macmillan, 258–276.
1970 "The Interdependence of Sport and Culture." *The Cross-Cultural Analysis of Sports and Games*. G. Lueschen (ed.). Champagne: Stipes Publishing.

Mallea, John
1972 "Class and Sport: The Victorian Legacy." Paper presented at the 1972 annual meetings of the American Sociological Association, New Orleans, Louisiana (August 28–31).

Mallet, Serge
1963 *La Nouvelle Classe Ouvrière*. Paris: Le Seuil.

Mann, Michael
1970 "The Social Cohesion of Liberal Democracy." *American Sociological Review* **35** (June).
1973 "Sleight of Class." *New Society* **6** (December).

Mannheim, Karl
1960 "Types of Rationality and Organized Insecurity." In *Images of Man*, C. Wright Mills (ed.). New York: George Braziller Inc.

Marcuse, Herbert
1955 *Eros and Civilization*. New York: Vintage Books.

Marshall, T. H.
1950 *Citizenship and Social Class*. London: Cambridge Press.

Marx, Karl
1973 "Wage-Labour, Capital and Landed Property." In *Marx's Grundrisse*, David McLellan (ed.). London: Paladin Books.
1964 "The Ideology of Capitalism." In *Karl Marx: Selected Writings in Sociology and Social Philosophy*, J. B. Bottomore and Maximilien Rubel (eds.). New York: McGraw-Hill.

Marx, Karl, and Friedrich Engels
1951 *Selected Works in Two Volumes*. Moscow: Foreign Languages Publishing House.
1970 *The German Ideology*, C. J. Arthur (ed.). New York: International Publishers.

Mayer, Kurt B., and Walter Buckley
1969 *Class and Society*. New York: Random House Inc.

McPherson, Barry D.

1974a "The Black Athlete: An Overview and Analysis." *Proceedings of the Conference on Sport and Social Deviancy,* forthcoming.

1974b "Minority Group Involvement in Sport: The Black Athlete." In *Exercise and Sport Sciences Reviews,* Vol. II, J. Wilmore (ed.). New York: Academic Press.

Mead, G. H.

1934 *Mind, Self and Society.* Chicago: University of Chicago Press.

Merton, Robert K.

1967 *On Theoretical Sociology.* New York: Free Press.

Metcalfe, Alan

1972 "Sports and Class Concepts in Nineteenth Century Canada." Paper presented at the 1972 annual meetings of the American Sociological Association, New Orleans, Louisiana (August 28–31).

Mills, C. Wright

1970 *The Sociological Imagination.* Middlesex: Penguin Books.

1956 *The Power Elite.* New York: Oxford University Press.

1953 "Introduction to the Mentor Edition." In *The Theory of the Leisure Class,* Thorstein Veblen. New York: Mentor Books.

Moore, Wilbert

1963 "But Some Are More Equal Than Others." *American Sociological Review,* Vol. 28, No. 1 (February).

Nisbet, Robert

1959 "The Decline and Fall of Social Class" *Pacific Sociological Review,* 2 (Spring).

Orwell, George

1950 *1984.* New York: Signet Classics.

Ossowski, Stanislav

1963 *Class Structure in the Social Consciousness.* New York: The Free Press.

Page, Charles H.

1969 *Class and American Sociology.* New York: Schocken Paperbacks.

1973 "The World of Sport and Its Study." In *Sport and Society,* John Talamini and Charles H. Page (eds.). Boston: Little Brown, 3–39.

Parker, Stanley

1972 *The Future of Work and Leisure.* London: Paladin Books.

Parkin, Frank

1972 *Class Inequality and Political Order.* London: Paladin Books.

Parsons, Talcott

1966 *Societies.* Englewood Cliffs: Prentice-Hall.

Peterson, Robert

1970 *Only the Ball Was White.* Englewood Cliffs: Prentice-Hall.

Piaget, Jean
1962   *Play, Dreams and Imitation in Childhood*. New York: W. W. Norton & Co.

Pooley, John
1968   "Ethnic Soccer Clubs in Milwaukee: A Study in Assimilation." M.Sc. thesis, Department of Physical Education, University of Wisconsin.

Porter, John
1970   "Research Biography." *Macro Sociology: Research and Theory*, James S. Coleman, Amitai Etzioni and John Porter (eds.). Boston: Allyn and Bacon.
1966   *The Vertical Mosaic*. Toronto: University of Toronto Press.

Radford, E. Howard
1973   An address by the Secretary Treasurer of the Organizing Committee for the XXIst OLYMPIAD to the Ontario Recreation Society. Toronto (January 25).

Rigauer, Bero
1969   *Sport und Arbeit*. Frankfurt: Suhrkamp.

Roberts, John M., and Brian Sutton-Smith
1969   "Child Training and Game Involvement." In *Sport, Culture and Society*, John W. Loy and Gerald S. Kenyon (eds.). Toronto: Macmillan, 116–136.

Rose, Arnold
1967   *The Power Structure*. New York: Oxford University Press.

Roy, Gilles
1974   "Centrality and Mobility: The Case of the National Hockey League." M.Sc. thesis, Department of Kinesiology, University of Waterloo.

Runciman, W. G.
1969   "The Three Dimensions of Social Inequality." In *Social Inequality*, André Béteille (ed.). Baltimore: Penguin Books.

Sack, Allen L.
1973   "Yale 29-Harvard 4: The Professionalization of College Football." *Quest* XIX, (Winter).

Sallach, David
1974a   "Class Domination and Ideological Hegemony." *Sociological Quarterly*, forthcoming.
1974b   "The Meaning of Hegemony." *Australian Left Review* (Winter).
1973   "Critical Theory and Critical Sociology: The Second Synthesis." *Sociological Inquiry*, Vol. 43, No. 2.

Schafer, Walter
1968   "Athletic Success and Social Mobility." Paper presented at the National Convention of the American Association for Health, Physical Education and Recreation, St. Louis, Missouri (March 30).

Schafer, Walter E., and J. Armer
1968   "Athletes are Not Inferior Students." *Trans-Action*, 6 (November).

Schafer, Walter E., and Richard A. Rehberg
1970   "Athletic Participation, College Aspirations and College Encouragement."
       Pacific Sociological Review: **13** (Summer).

Scoville, J. G.
1971   "Labour Aspects of Professional Sport." Paper presented at the Brookings
       Conference on Government and Sport (December).

Speier, Hans
1969   "Honour and Social Structure." In *Social Order and the Risks of War.*
       Boston: M.I.T. Press.

Spitz, David
1974   "A Grammar of Equality." *Dissent* (Winter).

Stolzman, James, and Herbert Gamberg
1973–
1974   "Marxist Class Analysis Versus Stratification Analysis As General Ap-
       proaches to Social Inequality." *Berkeley Journal of Sociology,* Vol. 18.

Stone, Gregory P.
1973   "American Sport: Play and Display." In *Sport and Society,* John Talamini
       and Charles H. Page (eds.). Boston: Little, Brown, 65–85.
1957   "Some Meanings of American Sport." Proceedings of the 60th Annual
       College Physical Education Association Meetings, Columbus, Ohio.
1969   "Some Meanings of American Sport: An Extended View." *Contemporary
       Aspects of Sport Sociology,* Gerald S. Kenyon (ed.). Chicago: The Athletic
       Institute, 5–16.

Sugawara, Ray
1972   "The Study of Top Sportsmen in Japan." *International Review of Sport
       Sociology,* **7**: 45–68.

Svalastoga, Kaare
1965   *Social Differentiation.* New York: D. McKay Co.

Thomas, Lawrence
1956   "Leisure Pursuits by Socioeconomic Strata." *Journal of Educational Soci-
       ology,* Vol. **29**, (May).

Tomeh, Aida K.
1973   "Formal Voluntary Organizations: Participation, Correlates and Interrela-
       tionships." *Sociological Inquiry,* Vol. 43, No. 3–4.

Tumin, Melvin
1953   "Some Principles of Stratification: A Critical Analysis." *American Soci-
       ological Review,* Vol. 18, No. 4, (August).
1967   *Social Stratification: The Forms and Functions of Inequality.* Englewood
       Cliffs: Prentice-Hall.
1963   "On Equality." *American Sociological Review,* Vol. 27, No. 1, (February).

Veblen, Thorstein
1953   *The Theory of the Leisure Class.* New York: Mentor Books.

Webb, Harry
1969   "Professionalization of Attitudes Toward Play Among Adolescents." In
        Aspects of Contemporary Sport Sociology, Gerald S. Kenyon (ed.). Chi-
        cago: The Athletic Institute, 161–178.

Weber, Max
1958   "Class, Status, Party." *From Max Weber: Essays in Sociology*, H. H.
        Garth and C. Wright Mills (ed.). New York: Oxford University Press.

Weinberg, S. Kirkson, and Henry Arond
1969   "The Occupational Culture of the Boxer." In *Sport, Culture and Society*,
        John W. Loy and Gerald S. Kenyon (eds.). Toronto: Macmillan, 439–452.

White, Clyde, R.
1955   "Social Class Differences in the Use of Leisure." *American Journal of So-
        ciology*, Vol. **61**, (September).

Wiley, Norbert F.
1967   "The Ethnic Mobility Trap and Stratification Theory." In *The Study of
        Society*. New York: Random House.

Wrong, Dennis H.
1972   "Social Inequality Without Stratification." *Readings in Introductory So-
        ciology*. Dennis H. Wrong and Harry L. Gracey (eds.), New York: Mac-
        millan.
1972   "How Important is Social Class?" *Dissent*, (Winter).

Zuzanek, Jiri
1972   "Leisure, Life Styles and Stratification (Comments on Future Trends of
        Leisure and Stratification)." Mimeo: The University of Western Ontario.

Chapter 5
Sport and Politics

Brian M. Petrie
Faculty of Physical Education
University of Western Ontario
(London, Ontario, Canada)

Brian M. Petrie

Birth Place: Forbes, N.S.W., Australia

Age: 39

Birth Order: One older brother, one younger brother

Formal Education:

Diploma of Physical Education, Sydney Teachers' College, Australia	1954
B.P.E., University of Alberta, Canada	1965
M.A., Physical Education, University of Alberta, Canada	1967
M.A., Sociology, Michigan State University	1968
Ph.D., Michigan State University	1970

Present Position:

Associate Professor, Faculty of Physical Education, University of Western Ontario, London, Canada

Professional Responsibilities:

Undergraduate: Sociology of Leisure

Graduate: Sociology of Sport

Scholarly Interests:

Social differentiation in sport; economic and political socialization through sport.

Professional Accomplishments:

Coauthor of book of proceedings on conference dealing with the regulation of snowmobiles and all-terrain vehicles.

Author of several chapters and articles in anthologies.

Published articles in *International Review of Sport Sociology, Research Quarterly, CAHPER Journal,* and others.

Hobbies:

Photography and travel.

Sport Activities:

Downhill skiing and off-shore sailing.

Most Recent Books Read:

Kurt Vonnegut	*Breakfast of Champions*
Kurt Vonnegut	*Player Piano*

INTRODUCTION

There has been a long tradition attached to the belief that sport is essentially an apolitical institution. Indeed, the intrusion of political considerations into sport was, and, to a large extent, still is, regarded as likely to have negative consequences. The result has been a surprising lack of interest in investigating the dimensions of involvement of one of the major institutions of society, the polity, into the milieu of sport. This neglect becomes more astonishing when one considers the degree of public interest in spectator sports and the consequent economic strength of the athletic entertainment industry. Few institutions with large-scale popular support and economic significance have been able to maintain a level of insulation from the incursions of political considerations.

Several historical and social philosophical analyses of the association of politics to sport have raised a number of issues meritorious of research evaluation. Mandell (1971) and Holmes (1971) wrote of the 1936 Olympic Games held in Berlin and revealed the dangers inherent in the intrusion of excessive levels of nationalism and political propaganda into athletic pageants. Natan (1969) and Lund (1972) revealed the hypocrisy implicit in the repeated assertions made by representatives of the Olympic Movement that "countries show that they are unaware of one of our most important principles, namely that sport is completely free of politics" (Natan, 1969: 204).

There have been few claims that sport and economic concerns should not be mixed in international competition, and where the prospect of economic disaster has been raised the International Olympic Committee has shown its readiness to respond to political considerations. In 1956 the international crisis precipitated by the combined effects of the Hungarian Revolution and the Suez Crisis led several nations to withdraw their teams from competition in protest. Natan contended that the Games were not cancelled because to do so would have led to huge financial losses (Natan, 1969: 205). In 1968 and 1972, the International Olympic Committee bowed to the pressure and threats of withdrawal of the socialist and Third World countries and excluded South Africa from the Games. Withdrawal of up to 30 teams from competition and negative publicity could have had severe economic consequences for the Games in question. In each case, economic considerations led the I.O.C. to compromise its position and adjust to political realities.

Lund was concerned with the belief that continued competition against communist countries was indefensible on ethical grounds. He advocated elimination of such nations from Olympic competition and bolstered his arguments with examples of political intrusions by representatives of the Soviet Union into the business meetings of international sports-governing bodies (Lund, 1972).

These studies have had little impact on the public consciousness that remains committed to the idea that sport is separate from the reality of life. The acceptance of this belief has been maintained in the generally accepted definitions of the component elements of physical activity. Both Huizinga (1955) and Caillois (1962) regarded play as separate and distinct from real life. Huizinga even proposed that, in beginning to play, one stepped into a temporary state with a separate reality or disposition of its own (1955: 8). Various authors have drawn upon these ideas and incorporated the separate reality concept into their definitions of games and sport. This continued academic substantiation of the public awareness has sustained the belief that sport has, and should continue to have, little association with the major elements of human existence.

If one defines the boundaries of the field of competition as the fringes of the real world, and the blast of the referee's whistle as a time out for a break during which reality intrudes, then it is not difficult to maintain the belief that sport is separate. Sport may be regarded as such only if it can be demonstrated to exist predominantly for the resolution of satisfactions intrinsic to the participants. Only then could the claim be legitimately made that sport is truly divorced from the considerations of the real world. However, it is clear that acceptance of such a view of sport is utopian in essence and that social change directed to such an end product would have limited possibilities of success.

Sport is an element of social reality, strongly anchored to the political-economic system in which it is placed, that has significance far beyond the trivial. It provides a means of underlining and exhibiting the major elements of the ideological base of the power structure of society.

It is the purpose of this chapter to explore the linkages between the two institutions from the critical perspective that has begun to challenge the traditional theoretical approaches of sociology. Within this framework, the emphasis is upon social organization and the analysis of social change.

Each element of social structure and social life is continually subjected to examination, evaluation, and redefinition, with culture and character being determined by the prevailing structure and organization of society. Through this dialectic process, change is brought about, at least in the United States, through the confrontation politics of groups provided with differential levels of power in society (Reynolds and Henslin, 1973: 1–17).

It is obvious that the institution of sport has recently seen considerable conflict generated by particular interest groups over the responses that should be made to a variety of social pressures. This conflict has been clearly evident to the public through publicity generated by the mass media, although such publicity was subordinate to the focus of the press and television upon the wider conflict in the educational sector. Nevertheless, tension and conflict were present and widely publicized by the various interest groups in order to draw implications about the state of the major institutions of society.

As well as being a focus for social confrontation by various interest groups, sport has attracted many supporters in the upper levels of the power structure who see it as an arena for the demonstration of positive socialization experiences and, especially for spectators, a means for draining potentially harmful levels of frustration and aggression. When an institution such as sport is evaluated in terms of its capacity for social control, and large scale involvement is supported by the power elite as having a potential for collective catharsis, then it is possible to contend that large masses of the population are being diverted from consideration of relevant social issues through their involvement in the entertainment and glamor of the world of sport.

In the evaluation of the relationship between sport and politics, emphasis should be placed upon the utilization of sport for its instrumental significance in reinforcing particular political ideologies derived from alternative approaches to economic organization. From such an approach, the meanings bound up in the term "political" must be regarded as having a considerable degree of overlap with the domains of economic concern. Support for this linkage at the theoretical level was provided by McKee who recognized that

> ... the economy has now been subject to *politicization,* and the differentiation of the economy from the polity in classical liberal theory is no longer as much a fact of life as it once was (1969: 433).

In addition, Shaw and Wright (1967: 301–302) recognized the difficulty in separating the component values and ideological constructs of the two institutions as a prior necessity for attitude scale construction.

Analysis of the association between sport and politics must, in view of the events of the 1960s and early 1970s, revolve around three basic dimensions: the use of sport by political figures, community identification and nationalism in sport, and the conflict between conservatives and radicals over the relevancy of the institution of sport in society.

The *first* dimension is concerned with the apparently increasing tendency for individual politicians to secure a beneficial and "saleable" image through an attachment to sports participation and to attract the interest of spectators to themselves and their policies.

The *second* dimension is related to the tendency to employ competition against outsiders in order to develop social integration within school and community groups, or to transfer aggressive nationalism from direct conflict on the battlefield to symbolic conflict between the representatives of rival political-economic systems at major international sporting events.

Finally, the dimension of political ideological confrontation must be considered, especially in relation to the disputes between conservatives and radicals over the social significance of sport. The political conservatives regard sport as important in illustrating the verities of the American Dream and in producing individuals who exhibit the most desired characteristics of American youth. By definition, they resist change in the institution of sport and decry attempts to modify its practices to reflect current and possibly transient social trends.

The political radicals believe sport serves as an opiate for the masses of spectators and a diversion from the development of an effective political consciousness. They believe that considerable change is necessary in the institution of sport to enhance the potentialities of the individual participants; to provide for increased individual power and autonomy in an environment freed of excessive competition; and to ensure racial and ethnic equality. In this view, if the institution does not change, then it is likely to become redundant.

In summary, then, this chapter will analyze the linkages between the institutions of polity and sport from the theoretical perspectives of critical sociology. The discussion will center upon the use of sport by political figures, the substantiation of community and national superiority through sporting success, and the conflict between groups representing opposing ideologies in relation to the societal significance of sport.

THE USE OF SPORT BY POLITICAL FIGURES

On an individual basis, much of the political attachment to sport appears related to the twofold desire of the politican to: (a) secure a media image as a virile individual capable of withstanding the physical pressures of office, and (b) mold the political consciousness of spectator groups. Political figures appear to regard as desirable being portrayed as having a high level of intellectual capacity, a strong moral stance, and a readily demonstrated degree of physical vitality. Traditionally, vitality has been substantiated through the provision of evidence of past or present athletic participation, even though such participation may have been minor. By demonstrating intellectual, moral, and physical strength, however, a candidate hopes to assure the public that he will be able to withstand all pressures following his election without impairment.

Spectators of sporting events constitute a social group which merits political interest, and just as any ethnic, religious, or special interest group, they can expect individual politicians to make personal appearances in an effort to win identification and support. Supporters of professional sport are an extremely large group and this element of size leads to a continuing level of interest rarely provided by politicians between elections. For the same reasons, sports which attract a high level of spectator support become the focus of political interest on broader issues related to support of government positions and maintenance of the national identity.

The Media Image of the Virile Politician

There is little empirical basis for acceptance of the view that the attachment of a virile image to a political candidate through publicity about his involvement in sport can actually be translated into endorsements in the voting booth. Regardless of this fact, it appears to be a media necessity to include in the biographies and photographic coverage of a candidate some reference to athletic history and portrayal of the individual in the act of a sport- or game-related activity. The tactic is so common that it would appear to be politically dangerous for a candidate to run for office and take a basically anti-physical stance in the development of his image.

One notable exception, however, was the campaign of Pierre Salinger for a U.S. Senate seat in 1966. Salinger, the former Press Secretary of President Kennedy, attempted to portray himself as a sporting anti-hero. He released information that while serving in the Navy during World War II,

> he had managed to knock himself out during a boxing contest by hitting his own jaw with a right-hand swing. In the election, as in the ring, Salinger lost again—to George Murphy, the film star.*

---

* P. Goodhart and C. Chataway, *War Without Weapons* (London: W. H. Allen, 1968), p. 103. Reprinted by permission.

The fact remains, though, that this aspect of image making has become a pervasive part of the American political reality. Its influence is most visible in the various campaigns leading to the election of the president and vice-president, and in the continuing publicity provided to the incumbents of these offices following election. Accordingly, discussion of this dimension will be limited to the publicity surrounding such elections and political figures.

Although many bases behind the development of association between participation in sport and electoral support may be proposed, one has had a relatively longstanding influence. Here, it is recognized that the requirements of exercise of the role of president of the United States places a heavy burden on the physical well-being of the incumbent. It would appear, then, that each candidate should demonstrate his capacity to withstand such strain prior to his acceptance as a legitimate aspirant for the office.

Schlesinger quotes a 1908 statement of Woodrow Wilson, that,

> Men of ordinary physique and discretion cannot be Presidents and live, if the strain be not somehow relieved. We shall be obliged always to be picking our chief magistrate from among wise and prudent athletes —a small class (Schlesinger, 1973: 45).

It is ironic that Wilson did not fulfill this image and was himself unable to withstand the physical demands of the task of the Presidency.

In referring to athletics as a source of potential presidential candidates, Wilson must have been referring to those members of Veblen's Leisure Class who made use of sport as a modern survival of the need to demonstrate prowess and exploit. Veblen, of course, identified the Leisure Class as a group which favored as desirable activities for the exercise of conspicuous leisure, those associated with government, war, religious observance, and sport (Veblen, 1953: 44). Certainly, it is difficult to imagine athletes drawn from the middle and lower classes fitting Wilson's rather aristocratic conception of the presidency.

Drawing upon recent presidents and vice-presidents as examples, it can readily be seen that participation in sport, and its significance as a demonstration of physical stamina and virility, has become a desirable element of the life style of the incumbent, both prior to and during his term of office. It should be noted, however, that the association with sport is not always positive. There have been some examples of a backlash effect operating in response to attempts to please all groups simultaneously. Both the apparent positive and negative effects will be considered here.

Although there were earlier examples, most notably with the image of Theodore Roosevelt, the publicity campaigns supportive of Franklin Roosevelt present an interesting example of the extent to which media personnel attempt to portray a particular impression. President Roosevelt had been particularly active in the early stages of his political life but had contracted poliomyelitis and, as a result, lost most of his capacity for mobility at the age of 39. Cooke (1973), in the book written to supplement his successful television series on the history of the United States, noted that there was a tacit agreement among photographers to show Roosevelt only in static poses. The President was never portrayed being carried from automobiles or in the act of movement. To have done so would have dramatically depicted the extent of his physical disability. As a result, most of the photographic record shows Roosevelt behind a lectern or desk, gesturing in a style indicative of strength and vitality.

Maintenance of such an image of strength was essential with Roosevelt, whose presidency began with an economic crisis and continued through most of World War II. If the public had attached an impression of weakness to the President, his capacity to successfully pursue his policies to bring the United States out of the Depression, and later to deal with the problems of the war, would have been diminished.

Harry Truman did not, in retrospect, appear to radiate an impression of physical vitality. One feature of his life style and apparent attempts at impression management may be seen in the tradition of the President's daily walks. Considerable publicity was generated about the difficulty reporters had in keeping up with Truman's pace.

President Eisenhower's passion for golf, while initially supported, later became a political liability. In the later years of his presidency, his highly publicized involvement in the game led to claims that he was neglecting his political responsibilities. Satirical comment and cartoons contributed to the impression that the administration had lost its effectiveness. The consequent politically detrimental image attached to golf led John Kennedy to suppress reference to his own ability and accomplishments in the sport during the 1960 presidential campaign (Goodhart and Chataway, 1968: 104).

The mystique of the Kennedy family was very much bound up with the youthful, aggressive, and competitive participation in a wide variety of sports. Kennedy attached a positive political impression to the concept of vigor, and his personal style exemplified his own ideals. Kennedy showed to politicians who were to follow him that the construction of an image of virility through active involvement in sport could have a powerful impression upon the electorate. In addition, the wartime heroism attached to his life-saving swim from the wreckage of the torpedo boat he commanded provided substantiation of his physical prowess.

Johnson apparently miscued in his approach to sport. Merchant reported that Johnson had regarded one of his major political blunders to have occurred in 1967 when he neglected to take a foreign official to a football game on the grounds that it showed the violent side of American life. Many may have agreed with his caution, but adverse publicity in his home state of Texas and from sports columnists across the country brought home to Johnson the realization that he had antagonized a highly vocal group of male spectators who were critical of such an insult to their sport (Merchant, 1971: 22).

President Johnson's attempts at developing the virility image were negligible in comparison with Kennedy's, but he did develop and extend the traditional association of presidents with spectator sports. Although the opening day of the baseball season has had a long tradition of attendance by the chief executive, Johnson became the first president to attend a professional football game, even though this came during the same year as his crucial gaffe (Merchant, 1971: 25).

The Nixon Administration used an attachment to sport in a variety of ways. The President's college involvement was widely publicized, even though his contribution to the football team was minimal. Nixon preferred a vicarious form of participation through a form which led him to be regarded as a super-spectator. This association developed through support of college football teams and widely publicized additions to the play books of favored coaches prior to crucial games.

Athletes in all types of sport received congratulatory telephone calls from President Nixon immediately following successful competitions. This feature of presidential style became prevalent for a time, but was reduced during the second term of office. The tactic had definite advantages in that it provided a level of personal attachment to a proven winner or winning team, and also indicated a continuing level of interest on the part of the President in matters of relevance to dedicated supporters of sport. On many occasions, Nixon cultivated the impression of knowledgeability of sport and the records of sporting personalities, and it is obvious that such a high level of interest is regarded as flattering by those associated with the athletic institution.

In addition, the Nixon Administration made continual, and eventually overplayed, use of the sporting analogy in political explanation. This rather simplistic device had the advantage of explaining complex political decisions in terminology readily understood by the mass of the population. Nixon, of course, was not the first president to see the political advantages that could develop from the use of such a device. There has been a tradition attached to oversimplification in political explanation, and various presidents, including Johnson and Kennedy, have resorted to the vocabulary of sport for assistance. However, the information releases of the Nixon Administration developed the game-of-football–game-of-life analogy to an extreme. There were continual references to "game plans," "cheap shots," and "running the same play again" as well as naming of military operations to reflect a sporting content, such as Operation Linebacker (a euphemism for the saturation bombing of Hanoi over Christmas of 1972).

Ultimately, both sides in the political debate over the Vietnam War drew imagined lessons from the small stock of militaristic terms utilized in the game of football. Accordingly, there was an attempt by social critics to employ the sporting analogy against the Nixon Administration. They attempted to label football, which employs terms such as "field general," "suicide squad," "blitz," and "shotgun formation," as a logical creation of a hyper-aggressive, excessively competitive and militaristic society. Indeed, there was considerable concern among members of the political opposition that the Nation's quarterback might be tempted to "throw the long bomb" to end the war.

Despite the popularity of this linkage between football and militarism, the association must be regarded as more glamorous than real. Merchant disposed of the issue by indicating that the continued utilization of the analogy by political figures had given football an undeservedly bad name.

> Political football has evolved from a shopworn phrase to a disquieting attempt to take over the game by politicians and super-patriots . . . (but) like the single wing and the double wing, and even the shotgun formation, the right wing's influence too shall pass (Merchant, 1971: 23).

The superficiality of such sport metaphors as explicators of political activity should not be provided with more attention, then, than is deserved.

An additional device employed by President Nixon was to use his involvement with sport as a means of trivializing the activities of his opponents. He was able to demonstrate a well publicized indifference to anti-administration political demonstrations in Washington by indicating that he had watched a sporting event on television rather than take note of the protests.

At the vice-presidential level, little success was achieved in the attempt to portrary Agnew as a sporting figure, and after several highly embarrassing moments in golf and tennis matches, he retreated to less publicized involvement. The Vice-president hit several spectators who were in close proximity to the tee with successive drives during a nationally televised golf tournament, and, during a friendly game of doubles, hit his tennis partner with his service. This latter event, which was the subject of some hilarity at the time, especially when the partner returned to the court wearing a hard hat, also received national TV news coverage.

Following Agnew's resignation the media gave considerable attention to the sporting history and continued active involvement of Gerald Ford. Certainly his football career at the University of Michigan and his association with skiing were not regarded as detrimental to his image as an acceptable vice-president, although it would be a mistake to believe that such participation was as important as assumptions regarding his political honesty following the Agnew scandal. Since his promotion to the presidency of the United States following Nixon's resignation, the mass media have continued to emphasize Ford's athletic background, stress his current participation in "active" sports, and continually photograph him in sport situations and/or athletic poses.

The feature of theoretical, as distinct from passing, interest is the belief that political support can be generated from an association with sport at the active or vicarious level of involvement, and that such an expression of interest in the physically demanding world of sport can demonstrate a politician's capacity to cope with the pressures of the physically exhausting world of politics.

Considering the prevalence of this belief, it is surprising that so few athletes have been able to translate that favorable association into successful endeavours to secure political office. Goodhart and Chataway (1968: 101–103) discussed the attempts of a variety of international sporting figures who generally failed to secure the support of a political electorate.

Most major candidates feel that it is necessary to attract the endorsement and active campaigning assistance of professional athletes as well as other "stars" of the entertainment industry. News magazines tabulate the names of athletes who endorse rival presidential candidates, while television and media photographic coverage of motorcades have frequently shown athletes in protective roles in the candidate's cars. The high level athlete, then, because of his stronger commitment to sport rather than to politics, is welcomed to participate in a supportive role that will reflect positively upon the candidate. The candidate or political figure, of course, must provide his stronger level of commitment to politics, and to concentrate too heavily on his image as a sportsman could have detrimental effects on ultimate success.

The association of individual politicians with sport has additional benefits. There is, of course, the benefit of being identified with "winners." On the assumption that successful people have a natural bond and tend to cluster together, politicians attach themselves to the champions of the sporting world. In this way, the aura of success may be transferred to the politician in his own effort to be a winner.

The use of superlatives in describing athletes helps to encourage political figures to attach themselves to sportsmen. When an athlete is defined as a "winner" and awarded the accolade as World's Fastest Human, World Champion, or Player of the Year, he becomes an attractive figure for individuals who seek to identify themselves with a "super human."

In addition, the social stereotype of the athlete incorporates the idea that such individuals are worthy role models for children by virtue of the possession of a high level of morality. Admittedly, this image was built up on the sporting literature of the Frank Merriwell genre, but the "unreal ideal" still has its supporters (Boyle, 1963: 241–271). By contrast, the political institution has considerable difficulty in maintaining its image of morality. The portrayal of a political figure in the company of an athlete who is regarded as a desirable model of adult behavior, and the implied willingness of the athlete to encourage such an association, includes the politician in the halo of respectability.

In each of these examples, little evidence substantiates the implicit beliefs and assumptions. Indeed, it could be argued that all individuals directly involved are aware of the shallowness of the association. If this is so, then it is obvious that a considerable degree of cynical exploitation of the public is associated with the attempts to magnify the characteristics of both athletes and politicians in order to secure a desirable media image and public support.

The continuing flood of publicity on the physical characteristics and sporting capacities of political candidates clearly indicates that politicians remain convinced of the necessity of such publicity in the substantiation of their claims for electoral support.

Molding the Political Consciousness of Spectators

Within the context of the second dimension of the use of sport by political figures, it is obvious that there is a mass of individuals, all potential voters, who can become conscious or subconscious recipients of political messages and images while involved as spectators. Here, it is not only possible for an individual politician to develop a positive or negative personal image with such audiences, but it is also possible to use the events themselves as foci of patriotic and policy statements. Attention should be drawn to the use of patriotic symbols and anthems, militaristic half-time performances, and the broadcasting of government policy statements in official programs and television presentations.

The fact that spectators at a sporting event are a relatively captive audience and that television will focus upon a celebrity who is willing to attend the event in person, leads many political figures to curry favor with these groups with some frequency. Not only are politicians willing to attend and secure such recognition, but even papier mache figures of candidates have been paraded during half-time shows in order to secure attention prior to national elections.

The intrusion of politics into the arena of sport can have unintended consequences, but generally, it appears as though politicians believe the effort to be worthwhile.

Image making through attendance at sporting events is a somewhat recent phenomenon with most sports. The exception is, of course, baseball which attracted the interest of President Lincoln who took his son to see a game in Washington in 1862 (Voigt, 1966: 11–12). By 1894 the official opening day of the baseball season in Washington had become an event supported by the social elite and major figures in the political, judicial, and diplomatic circles (Voigt, 1966: 282).

Present-day campaign managers would be delighted to associate a candidate with a major international sporting event such as the Olympic Games. It should be noted, then, that in 1932 Herbert Hoover indicated that the time commitments of the presidential campaign did not allow him to pause from his political tasks to officially open the Olympic Games held in that year in Los Angeles (Goodhart and Chataway, 1968: 15–16).

President Johnson, as indicated earlier, gained favor by becoming the first incumbent to attend a professional football game, but aroused the anger of many supporters of sport by refusing to invite a visiting dignitary to see such a spectacle. In retrospect, Johnson's involvement with spectator groups would appear to have had mixed results.

President Nixon, by contrast, appeared to have been able to maintain good relations with spectators and representatives of the sporting media throughout his political career. During his tenure as vice-president surprise was registered when Nixon visited the locker room of the New York Giants and greeted the players by their first names (Merchant, 1971: 26). Personal visits and telephone calls to the locker rooms of successful teams became an element of the Nixon style during his presidency.

One error Nixon made in his association with spectators occurred in 1969 when he proclaimed the University of Texas Longhorns as the top college football team of the nation. The supporters of Pennsylvania State University were angered as they believed that their team had the better credentials for that honor.

Presidents and members of the Cabinet have officially thrown out the first pitch of the baseball season for many years, and the event has usually been regarded as a light-hearted though well-publicized tradition. In 1971, however, the Secretary of Defense, Melvin Laird, made use of the occasion to include a strong endorsement of the Administration's Vietnam policies as part of the ceremony.

Politicians at all levels appear to approach the sporting crowd in much the same way as they approach ethnic and regional groups. Spectators constitute one more group to be shown that someone in politics has concern for and knowledge of their interests. As such, one might expect an acceleration of interest immediately prior to elections, but the numbers of people involved and the need for continued contact frequently leads incumbents to make appearances at major events regardless of the proximity of the next election. The attendance of governors at bowl games in support of their state's representatives must be evaluated from this perspective: support of the elements of state pride has positive electoral consquences in the expectations of such figures.

In addition to the individually perceived advantages of attempting to win the votes of members of the spectator group, advantages of a more general nature are believed to be secured within the context of sport. One such feature of generalized political significance is the employment of the instruments of the national identity within the pageantry of sport. In recent years, for instance, the flag-raising ceremony and the singing of the anthem prior to play became the focus of political controversy.

Much of the concern over the use of national symbols at sporting events dated from the events of 1968 which culminated in the creation of the Olympic Project for Human Rights. This movement developed as a means of publicizing the grievances of black athletes and their concerns over generalized racism in society.

The demonstration and closed fist salutes of Tommie Smith and John Carlos on the victory stand following the 200 meter sprint race led to their expulsion from the U.S. Olympic team and their departure from Mexico. The media protest and the drastic response of the U.S. Olympic Committee polarized many of the remaining black athletes of the team into making other forms of protest at the Games (Edwards, 1969: 102–105).

It is interesting to note the different response of the media to the nationally supportive gesture of George Foreman and the subtle political protest of Vera Caslavska. Both gestures reintroduced political content to the victory celebrations but were applauded by the American media. Foreman, following his victory in the heavyweight boxing final, waved a small American flag as he acknowledged the applause of the crowd. Caslavska, a Czechoslovakian gymnast, turned her head to one side in an apparently deliberate gesture while the anthem of the Soviet Union was played. In view of the recency of the Soviet invasion of Czechoslovakia to end the "liberalization" experiment, Caslavska's action, though supported in the media, was as much a direct political protest as that of Smith and Carlos.

Following the Mexico Olympics, groups of black spectators and athletes staged frequent demonstrations at college sporting events by refusing to stand for the anthem, or raising their clenched fists in the gesture of Smith and Carlos.

At the 1972 Olympic Games, the flag bearer for the United States team, Olga Connolly, was believed to be planning to break a longstanding national tradition and dip the flag in salute to the representatives of the host country. Although this action did not transpire, considerable hostility was expressed at the time, indicating the significance which many have come to attach to the display of national symbols in association with sport.

There was a further protest of black athletes at Munich in continuation of the theme of Mexico City. Vince Matthews and Wayne Collett stood together on the victory stand and exhibited a casual disregard for the anthem as a protest against racism in American sport and society. For this action, both were banned for life from Olympic competition by the International Olympic Committee (Edwards, 1973: 109–110). A further example of the protective response to a perceived disregard for national symbols was illustrated when Dave Wottle won the 800 meter race. Wottle continually wore a golf hat during his races and inadvertently failed to remove his cap for the national anthem during the victory ceremony. The television commentators drew attention to this fact and interviewed Wottle later to determine whether there was political meaning in his action.

The debate over the flag and anthem ceremonies of the Olympic Games became associated with the larger concern over nationalism and the intrusion of politically inspired violence following the murder of many members of the Israeli Olympic Team at Munich. This movement to reduce the amount of nationalistic pageantry in sports also became evident in the United States in the early part of 1973, when athletes were jeered at the Nassau Coliseum for not standing at attention for the playing of the national anthem at the beginning of the Knights of Columbus track meet. The failure of the athletes to interrupt warm-up routines was believed to show disrespect. The issue developed into a major debate following the announcement by the organizers of the Olympic Invitational track meet that the anthem would not be played at Madison Square Garden as part of the program. Statements of protest by Mayor Lindsay and members of City Council, management officials of the Madison Square Garden, veterans' groups, and members of the public quickly forced a reversal of the decision (Anderson, 1973: S3).

At the time of the controversy at Madison Square Garden, the *New York Times* interviewed various athletes to determine their attitudes toward the flag ceremony at sports events. Responses were mixed, with support being provided for both perspectives (*New York Times*, 1973: S1,3). The amount of press coverage for the flag debate indicated that there was doubt as to the necessity of having patriotic ritual presented in conjunction with sport. Anderson asserts that patriotism is not the issue: the main reason for continuing the ceremony being habit. Most spectators seem to respond as if to a conditioned reflex, standing up when the music starts and sitting down at the conclusion.

> If they were watching the event on TV, it never occurred to them to stir from their easy chairs. Nor did many patriotic emotions stir within them. In sports, the anthem has evolved into more of a signal than anything else. Hey, the game's about to start (Anderson, 1973: S3).

Any attempt at change, however, is likely to be heatedly contested by the super-patriots (or extreme conservatives) who believe that an attempt to eliminate the ritual is automatically a negation of the national identity. Political figures, rather than risk the antagonism of these super-patriots, may be expected to vigorously defend the practice, and, as the City Council of New York indicated, react quickly to provide some measure of legal enforcement.

Although little change may be expected in the use of patriotic symbols at national and dual-nation meets within the United States in the near future, the International Olympic Committee has shown its awareness of the problem. The past president of the I.O.C., Avery Brundage, said in 1960 that,

> I propose to ask the International Olympic Committee to examine the desirability of eliminating the use of national flags and hymns . . . Contestants in the Olympic Games should come simple [*sic*] as sportsmen and not as representatives of a country (Brundage, 1969: 102).

To date, no change in the practice has been announced, but the Olympic Games may be the first international event to attempt to minimize the degree of nationalistic pageantry present in its competitions.

In addition to the continuing use of patriotic symbolism, the last years of the Vietnam war were accompanied by direct military involvement at sports events, as well as the intrusion of displays in support of the war during half-time shows. The most familiar of the military gestures was to have the jet fighters flying past during half-time shows, with one aircraft peeling away from the formation while directly over the stadium. This action was employed to symbolize the fact that the prisoners of war had not been released from Vietnam, and deliberate attempts were made to keep their status in the public mind.

In an article deploring the mixture of politics with sport, Padwe commented on the jet fighter displays:

> ... the prisoner issue in the Vietnam war is a politically sensitive area. The government's use of the fighter formation was political exploitation at its best—or worst—depending on your politics (Padwe, 1971: 35).

In addition, half-time shows have been used as occasions for the induction of groups of young men into the armed forces. At times, these events have been televised as part of the national distribution of the sporting event. On another occasion, the induction of two members of the Louisiana State football team into the Army during practice for the 1971 Sun Bowl received wide publicity (*Philadelphia Inquirer*, 1971: 44).

Professional baseball seasons have been opened in Washington by a variety of political figures. More recently, the Secretary of Defense, a wounded Vietnam veteran, and a Green Beret who had been a prisoner of war in Vietnam, have made the traditional first pitch of the season. An event which was previously lighthearted became an occasion for speechmaking in support of government policy.

It is clear, however, that the intrusion of militaristic displays and policy statements at athletic events must only present viewpoints supportive of administration policy. In 1970 the students of the State University of New York at Buffalo planned a "Let's give peace a chance" half-time show featuring its 100 member marching band. Despite the fact that the ABC network usually televises the half-time show at college football games, no part of the antiestablishment performance which focussed on war, racism, and pollution, was aired. The network stated that its refusal to televise was justified as the program was a political demonstration (Deeb, 1971: 25).

Bowl games usually feature some patriotic content, with the Orange Bowl and the Liberty Bowl programs being the more extreme examples of the genre in recent years. When the University of Michigan was chosen to represent the Big Ten Conference at the 1971 Rose Bowl, its band requested the opportunity to present a four minute "peace segment" as part of the half-time performance. Among other things, the band planned to release black balloons and play "Taps." After considerable publicity and controversy, the Rose Bowl committee endorsed its original decision to refuse permission for the intrusion of such content (Padwe, 1971: 35).

It is evident, then, that some forms of political expression are permissible within the context of televised sporting performances. Such statements must be consistent with the evaluation made by organizers and television executives of what constitutes official government policy. The relationship between sport, especially televised sport, and political and social control mechanisms becomes clear when such inconsistencies occur. Such instances also point to the high level of significance placed upon television as a medium for the dissemination of socially "correct" viewpoints and the depiction of images supportive of prevailing ideologies in spheres outside the milieu of sport.

The responses made by major figures in the sports industry to the 1973–74 energy crisis were mainly in terms of minor rescheduling of games to reduce some of the need for stadium illumination. Some early statements indicated that athletic events would not be affected because the power used at the stadia would not be equal to that employed cumulatively by the masses of spectators if they stayed home. Such reasoning did not take into account the basic cost of heating empty homes, or the fact that in many cases lighting would be needed by baby-sitters, people of the same household who did not attend games, or for minimal lighting needed to discourage burglars.

Television, and particularly televised sporting events with a perceived cathartic effect, felt sport was too important as a social therapeutic to be greatly influenced by the rationing of power in response to an energy crisis. An exchange of views in a Cleveland newspaper was concerned with the wastage of power for

> stadium lighting, "before, during and after" a professional baseball game played in Cleveland during the daytime. The paper's response came from staff writer Dennis Lustig who commented, "The lights are needed for the color cameras, and television goes on energy crisis or not" (*I.S.S.S. Newsletter*, 1973: 2).

Sport, then, appears to be looming as the new opiate of the masses. The combined impact of sport and television has major significance in the maintenance of social harmony, keeping potentially troubled people at home vicariously participating in the exciting performances that divert attention from the evaluation of the causes and consequences of inflation, energy shortage, and political alienation upon the society of the near future. This feature of modern life is obviously political in its significance and, as a consequence, one should not expect the sports-television entertainment connection to be affected to any significant degree by energy cutbacks.

The final area of discussion of the potential for spectator manipulation for political ends may be treated with brevity. It is obvious that public service advertising related to government policy is a frequently utilized component of the television coverage of sporting events, and that such advertising also appears in the official programs purchased at stadia by spectators.

One example of this trend has been the widespread use of athletic figures to caution against the use of drugs. Although such advertisements might have some impact on impressionable children, their effectiveness with other age groups must be questioned. The basis for this belief may be seen in the impact of the publicity given to the large scale utilization of a variety of drugs to assist athletic performances. The hypocrisy attendant upon the use of athletes as role models for the denial of drug use does not become the responsibility of the individual athletes involved, but of those who wish to maintain the fiction that the athletic world remains largely resistant to modern social reality. The athlete should not be regarded as one who is automatically free of fault: a living talisman for adulation and emulation. The role is obviously too difficult for many to fulfill and the continued casting of athletes in the Frank Merriwell mold in order to sell political ideas is a disservice to both institutions.

A further example of the use of individuals with "star quality" to sell ideas was evident during the 1973–74 energy crisis. Television personalities and athletes were involved as narrators of public service advertisements exhorting the public to refrain from the excessive use of power. Again, there appeared to be an element of hypocrisy present as both segments of the entertainment industry utilize a considerable amount of electrical power for illumination and the significance of both for public diversion indicates that neither television nor sports would follow the advice being given to any major extent.

In summary, there would appear to be considerable support in both the mass media and the actions of campaign personnel for the proposition that political figures, either directly or through the manipulation of spectator attitudes, make considerable use of the institution of sport for the achievement of personal or ideological ends. Political candidates have found it to their advantage to develop some personal attachment at the active or vicarious level with sport. For presidential candidates it has almost become a necessity for the prospective chief magistrate, as well as his running mate, to proclaim some attachment to the active life. For the most part this trend appears explicable in terms of the necessity for the candidate to demonstrate his capacity to withstand the physical pressures of the office. Once such an image has been established, the candidate must keep it to the forefront of the public awareness as a major, nonissue-related feature with positive electoral benefit.

The spectator group, whether in attendance at the stadium or watching the event on television, constitutes a social group worthy of the attention of political figures on other dimensions. As an identifiable group, spectators can be courted by politicians who wish to seek the support of various sub-

units of society. Seeking to leave no such ethnic, regional, or special interest group out in the political cold, candidates support local teams and gain
some favor through being introduced to the spectators.

The spectator group also becomes a readily available mass of voters to
serve as recipients for a variety of politically oriented messages disseminated through published programs, half-time shows, and policy advertising
on television. It was not the purpose of this analysis to regard the intrusion
of such attempts to mold the political consciousness of spectators as having negative consequences to the institution of sport. The basic premise
was that sport and politics are linked, and to criticize this linkage on idealistic grounds is essentially unrealistic. Criticism can legitimately be directed to the fact that most of the attempts to use sport to influence political sentiment violate the fairness doctrine that is a regulating tenet of the
broadcast media. The majority of the material disseminated is either in
direct support of administration policies or regulated in keeping with the
perceived acceptability of the content to the executive branch of government. There is little provision for equal time to be given for the expression
of views at variance with establishment positions. This was clearly evident in the refusal to televise anti-war half-time shows while providing a
forum for Cabinet members to give supportive addresses while the nation
was polarized on the issue.

It is evident, however, that the association between politics and sport
can be highly variable in its consequences. The politician may not be able
to convince a substantial group of the body politic to support his image
package, or he may inadvertently antagonize the group he was attempting
to court. The spectators and viewers may also be unaware or unresponsive
to the other forms of attempted influence. Accordingly, the elements of
linkage between politics and sport illustrated above must be regarded as
of somewhat lesser significance than those which follow, even though
many of those features have entered into the public consciousness through
media glamorization.

POLITICS, COMMUNITY REPRESENTATION, AND NATIONALISM

An area of considerable concern in the institution of sport has been the
developing awareness that nationalism has evolved from a rather mild version of support for the athletic representatives of one's own country, into
what Goodhart and Chataway proclaim to be "war without weapons"
(1968).

To focus upon the international aspects of this program would be somewhat shortsighted, for although national systems openly proclaim victory

in major sporting events to be a triumph for their particular economic order, similar problems appear at the community level and exacerbate tensions between neighboring groups.

Community-level Conflict

Coleman focussed upon the role of the school athletics program as a means for developing community identification in his analysis of the adolescent subculture of high schools of the Midwest. His analysis of the function of competition was illustrative of the scope of the problem regardless of the level of analysis. Although the overall flavor of Coleman's study was somewhat negative towards athletics, he did indicate that such programs were important as means to motivate students and generate a strong positive identification of the majority of the students toward the school. Without interscholastic athletics programs,

> the school would be lifeless for the student, deficient in collective goals. With athletics, it is possible for all students to identify with their school through their teams. Not only schools but whole communities depend upon the collective enthusiasm generated by their local high school athletic teams (Coleman, 1961: 33).

The athlete in the school team, then, is placed in a position of having to: (a) concern himself with his own high level competition and attempt to demonstrate his superiority over his rivals for a place on the status hierarchy of his chosen sport, and (b) submerge some of his individuality to the dominance of a given social institution (school, university, municipality, etc.) so that he can act as its chosen representative in a manner which will bring credit to all its members.

Under the American system, there developed a need for someone in the adult community to assist the athletes in the performance of these dual responsibilities. The coach came to assume considerable importance in the fulfilment of community aspiration for the demonstration of regional and national potency.

Hollingshead believed that athletic teams had come to be regarded as the collective representation of the entire school by the majority of the members of the community. It was regarded as essential that the school board hire a coach who could consistently produce winning teams.

> The Board pays the maximum salary to the coach, and it expects him to "deliver the goods." A coach knows his "success" is determined wholly by the number of games he wins—particularly in basketball and football (Hollingshead, 1949: 193).

It is interesting to note that the coach's task in this study was primarily to provide teams which brought credit to the community through their successes over neighboring communities. Apart from the New York Mets teams of the 1960s, only a rare community wants to identify with losers. The primary task of the coach is not related to the maximization of personal enjoyment for his athletes or for development of the educational potential of athletics; it has been seen purely in developing and sustaining a vicarious feeling of regional superiority.

A recent development in community representative sport has been an extension of the logic to regard the team as the personal representatives of the coach himself.

> If a coach has good grooming habits and looks like a male, only rationalization and compromise would permit him to be represented (by his player's) sloppiness and abnormality ... A coach should see each individual, and the team as a unit, as a personal representative (Simpson, 1973: 76–77).

It would probably be best to regard the development of such an attitude by coaches as an aberration, with the longstanding community focus of representation being the feature of greater theoretical significance. An explanation of the creation of the in-group feeling may be seen in the analysis of the differential effects of various types of competition upon the development of group goals and cohesion.

Deutsch (1953) determined that problem solving was better in groups which were compared on performance with other groups, and when the available rewards were distributed relative to those other groups. This form of competition had more positive consequences in terms of achievement, within-group feelings of members towards one another, and group unity. The phenomenon resulted from the fact that superior performances of individuals benefited the group as a whole, rather than becoming the focus for competition for scarce rewards among the individual participants.

In extending Deutsch's study to the analysis of the effects of interscholastic athletics programs, Coleman indicated that competition with outgroups could generate a "we" feeling not only within the school, but in the larger community from which the students were drawn. Competition with other groups seemed to have the capacity to develop a strong group goal orientation.

> ... there will be support first from other team members, then from other nonparticipating students, and finally from persons in the community. That is, if the school's winning gives the community pride in itself and its school, they will encourage its efforts (Coleman, 1959: 348).

Continued success maintains and enhances this team support which derives from community pride in the performances of its representatives relative to other schools and their supporting communities.

In an amplification of this explanation of the need to encourage in-group cohesion through sport, Webb drew attention to a trucking company of Benton Harbor, Michigan, which decorated its rigs with the successes and team performances of the school basketball team. The trucks constituted mobile reinforcers of Benton Harbor's claim of athletic superiority over other cities in the Midwest (Webb, 1968: 21).

Community representation through sport functions, not only at the high school level, but also with considerable influence at the college and university level as well. Traditional athletic powers, such as the Universities of Alabama, Texas, Michigan, Oklahoma, Nebraska, and Southern California, have become the focus of identification, not only of their local communities, but also of their respective states.

Indeed, the University of Notre Dame, with its succession of strong football teams, has become the focus of in-group feeling for many of the members of the Roman Catholic faith throughout the nation. Successes are celebrated and the weekly national ratings are eagerly awaited to see whether the team has been voted "Number One." There is so much support for the football teams of this university, that many allege that the ratings are generally inflated out of justice to'the team's actual position relative to the other contenders.

Whenever teams compete for the scarce resource, winning, and the avoidance of the frustration of failure, there is a high potential for inter-group conflict. When such a situation is exaggerated by the development of a long standing rivalry and an attachment of regional chauvinism and antagonistic stereotypes to the competition, the probability of conflict is increased. The most favorable conditions for the development of strong group identification and for the formation of in-group and out-group feelings occur in the two-opponent situation (Heinila, 1970).

Traditional rivalries in interscholastic and intercollegiate sport have frequently led to violent outbursts between spectators and players following perceived instances of unsportsmanlike conflict or the completion of the game with a result that is not satisfactory to the more vociferous group of supporters. When there is too much action (whether financial or symbolic) riding on the result of an athletic contest, in-group–out-group tensions over the outcome can magnify to reinforce the tendency to seek evidence of community superiority through physical combat among the spectators.

Such community identification does not necessarily have to be based upon neighborhood linkages to lead to intergroup conflict. The reentry of

Notre Dame University into postseason bowl competitions amplified the development of a religious identification. The unofficial alumni of Notre Dame have shown a readiness to attach a strong personal significance to the team's record. Such a strong Catholic orientation led to a Protestant counter-orientation which was clearly evident in the reactions of spectators at the first two bowl appearances of Notre Dame against Texas. Irresponsible comment during the various events prior to the game developed the potential for considerable religious conflict over the competition, and players came to perceive the game as something larger than a contest between two university football teams.

Ethnic conflicts brought to the New World by immigrants are also likely to be acted out on the playing fields. Pooley (1972) demonstrated the considerable attachment of ethnic sentiment, often to the detriment of assimilation, among soccer teams in the Milwaukee area. Spectator violence, again illustrative of the in-group–out-group tensions evident in sport, has frequently been associated with soccer competitions in the United States and Canada. Although it would be incorrect to regard the development of community identification as being automatically injurious to the athletic institution and to social harmony, there is obviously a propensity for such feelings to become exaggerated.

When tensions are artificially developed towards the end of the season by the sporting press, or when unreasonable expectations are generated within the media about the possibilities for success of the local team, feelings are aroused within the community to artificially encourage their paid attendance at the event. The level of economic complicity between the media and the management of the teams exacerbates the in-group–out-group tensions among spectators and between communities. The greater the level of tension, the greater the inability to perceive the referee's decisions as balanced and just; the greater the likelihood to perceive aggressive play as a deliberate attempt to maim star players; and the greater the likelihood that resolution of the contest will be followed by a spectator invasion of the field and random vandalism along streets leading away from the stadium.

Such forms of aggressive identification expressed within a country are rarely the focus of attempts to reduce the degree of group identification with athletic teams. There have, of course, been isolated instances of official concern when violence becomes a regular feature of spectator behavior. The response of the riot between spectators and players at an interscholastic event in Washington, D.C. (White, 1970), and analysis of general problems with spectators throughout the U.S. by Calisch (1954) and others, motivated the American Association for Health, Physical Education, and Recreation to prepare a report on the control of such behavior (JOHPER,

1969). Such efforts at exposure and resolution have not been matched by large-scale nationwide action and leadership such as that exerted by President Theodore Roosevelt at the beginning of the century to reduce the violence in college football.

Nation States

The tensions evident in response to community identification become magnified in the competitions between nations. The issue of nationalism, with its consequent attachment to the political institution, and the potential for conflict has been the focus of major concern. Sporting competition can become an arena for the demonstration of the superiority of a given political-economic system (capitalism versus communism; Third World versus the developed countries; etc.), or, as was demonstrated at the Munich Olympics in 1972, a highly publicized event where an act of terrorism for a political cause can have immediate international television coverage and propaganda potential.

The significance of international competition as a means of demonstrating physical, national, and economic potency has not been lost on many of the governments of the nations of the world. Elaborate state-financed and state-controlled agencies have been created in an attempt to maximize the probability of winning medals and cups at the major international competitions. In some cases, these efforts are disguised as ways to motivate mass participation in sport and physical recreation, but generally the justification is simply to provide the support that will allow athletes to develop their skills and defeat as many of the representatives of other countries as possible. In such success, national pride and superiority may be generated and substantiated.

The Olympic Games, and more recently, the World University Games, have become the focus of a considerable degree of nationalistic display and political intrusion. It is reasonable to assume that as a sporting event begins to draw support from the majority of the nations, that event will become the focus of political attention. Amateur or quasi-amateur competitions probably manifest this situation even more than professional competitions, but, as the World Cup Soccer championship has shown, even warfare between neighboring countries can erupt over sport. The conflict which developed during the El Salvador and Honduras regional finals in June 1970, although limited in scope, became known as the Soccer War after spectator riots at all three of the games caused a disruption of diplomatic relations and several bombing raids between the two countries (Lever, 1969).

The impact of an unexpected loss at the highest levels of international competition can have disastrous consequences upon the national psyche.

Local newspaper coverage of the loss of the Italian World Cup soccer team to the North Korean team of 1966 attributed the defeat to the

> decadence of Italian football and to the general decadence of Italian life itself (Goodhart and Chataway, 1968: 98).

The fall from prominence in ice hockey was regarded as a great blow to the Canadian pride and identity. When a professional all-star team played the best team from the Soviet Union in an eight game series in 1972, the Canadians were confident that they would have little difficulty with their opponents. Early losses by Canada left the series tied prior to the final game. Throughout Canada, and presumably throughout the Soviet Union as well, many workers and students clustered around television sets to watch the final game. Canada won to great national rejoicing, but the narrowness of the victory did little to restore the self-perception of Canadians that their hockey players were the best in the world.

The recent emergence of the People's Republic of China into relatively open international competition has brought even the sport of table tennis into the political arena. After overtures of friendship were extended to the United States team by the Chinese table tennis players, the U.S. team was invited to tour China. This "ping pong" diplomacy escalated into large-scale diplomatic contact and was followed by moves toward restoration of normal relations between the two countries.

Goodhart and Chataway devoted a considerable proportion of their book to the discussion of the intrusion of politics into the Olympic Games. Although some degree of nationalism was present in all of the preceding Games, it was not until the Berlin Olympics of 1936 that nationalism, generated for blatantly political reasons by the host country, became a significant problem. Since that time, most countries have relished the opportunity to celebrate sporting success and to ensure such success through government assistance. Few of the countries represented can hope to compete with the two major powers in terms of intellectual, technological, or aesthetic achievement, but in sport the smaller countries can still hope to excel and defeat the representatives of the U.S. or the U.S.S.R. A small measure of success can reduce a level of inferiority and provide a measure of glory and prestige to a minor country (Goodhart and Chataway, 1968: 149–50).

In view of the significance of international sport in general, and the Olympic Games in particular, it was inevitable that some nations would utilize sport

> as if it were an extension of their foreign policy. When the miniaturized symbolic conflict on the sports field is watched by millions with

more attention than the real clash of interest between nations, it becomes almost impossible to insulate sport from politics (Goodhart and Chataway, 1968: 128).

When nations compete with each other to secure, not only medals, but proof of their country's virility through the successful performances of its youth, more is encompassed in the term "virility" than would appear. Obviously, many nations have particular climatic, geographic and resource advantages that can maximize the probability that their athletes will be successful. In addition, the agricultural productivity of the country could provide a nutritional advantage to its citizens relative to others. Of greater significance are the structural variations between nations and the development of ideological competition between differing forms of political-economic organization (Ball, 1972).

A nation's political and economic superiority is frequently perceived to be at stake when its chosen athletes engage in symbolic conflict against others. Although it was common for military dictatorships to utilize sporting victories to demonstrate their claims of superior ethnic or "racial" status, the entrance of the Soviet Union into Olympic competition in 1952 brought the two major powers into direct rivalry.

Propaganda advantages were seen in success on the unofficial point score at the Games, and although it was possible to award "victory" to the United States or to the Soviet Union depending on the system used to award points for places and medals secured, the Soviet media proclaimed that the

> outstanding success was natural. This is the natural consequence of the great attention and care of the Party and the government for the physical development of the Soviet people. This is still another victory of our Soviet system (*Sovetskii Sport*, 1952).

Although Baron de Coubertin, the revivor of the Olympic Games, believed that they would lead to the development of positive political relationships between the nations represented, it has been common practice for the leaders of the movement to deny that there is any form of political intrusion into the competitions. Indeed, it appears to be apparent that the Arab guerrilla attack on the Israeli quarters in the Olympic Village at Munich is regarded as an aberration that will be swept aside by the continuing peaceful thrust of the Olympic Movement. The organizers of the 1976 Games in Montreal, however, are taking precautions to deal with similar events. It is obvious that the world media focus upon the Olympics will continue to secure the attention of politically oriented groups who are attracted by the potential for instant exposure of their cause.

In view of the increased manifestation of nationalism at the Olympic Games, it would appear timely to consider proposals advanced by the spokesmen of the "athletic revolution" to correct the situation (Scott, 1969). This group would prefer to see the elimination of the national anthem and flag ceremonies at the victory celebrations for the successful athletes. Instead, it should be possible to play an Olympic anthem or fanfare to honor the individuals and their efforts, rather than the countries where they were born. In addition, it is proposed that all athletes wear similar uniforms while competing, or, in the interests of following the performance of a favored athlete, different colors could be employed for uniforms which would be devoid of national symbols. There has even been a suggestion that a return to the nudity characteristic of the Ancient Olympics would be a way to resolve the national identification problem. Granted, such a suggestion is difficult to take seriously, but it should be recognized that even at the Ancient Olympics, nude athletes and all, local and community identification, as well as nationalism, became a problem.

To allow all qualified athletes to attend (rather than be barred for professionalism, political reasons, or the limitation of team size per event), regional and hemispheric elimination contests for all who met the standards could be held prior to the Games. In these ways, it could be possible to alter the focus of the Olympic Games (and similar events) from competition between national teams to competition between individuals, and to reduce the degree of politicization of the Olympics (Scott, 1969: 44–45). Such changes could not be expected to eliminate totally the intrusion of milder forms of nationalism from the Games, but the wider political use of the events as a competition between rival economic systems and power blocs would be difficult to sustain.

In summary, the development of in-group–out-group feelings in representative sport serves an administratively desirable function in directing individual excellence to the service of the collective. The benefits which accrue from this practice have been shown to enhance group achievement, social cohesion, and friendship patterns among the members of the group from which teams are drawn.

Once chauvinism develops and an opponent is perceived as an enemy rather than as the essential other half of the competition, negative stereotypes develop and the potential for conflict derived from community identification is heightened. The administrative enhancement of this practice has political overtones at the lower levels in view of the role of the neighborhood solidarity effect in reducing the potential for alienation within the collective. Individuals become socially anchored to their community through the shared in-group feelings that are heightened by the successes of the local sporting representatives.

At the international level, the development of in-group feelings, ethnocentrism, and negative stereotypes have potential for social control at a wider level, and direct political intrusion into sport on this basis leads to athletic competition becoming an arena for the comparative evaluation of the efficacy of rival political-economic systems. In this form of competition, sport itself is the loser.

Political-ideological Disputes over Sport

The period from 1960 to 1970 was characterized by a heightened political awareness among university and high school students. Commencing with support for the black minority in its drive for equal opportunity, the politicization of students led to the development of antagonistic positions relative to the power structure. The major issues concerned America's place in the world community, racism, the Vietnam War, the personal moral question of adherence to the draft laws, opposition to restrictive drug laws, and traditional student problems with institutional authority.

In the early press for attention to these larger problems, the acceptability of athletics in the educational institutions was not a subject of awareness or interest. Late in the 1960s, however, various academic units were identified as supportive of establishment positions on the major issues, and these units became a focus of hostility. Military studies programs available through R.O.T.C. were immediately subject to the attention of activists. The physical and verbal harassment of parades, demands for the removal of such programs from campuses, and the attempted burning of classrooms and office buildings, were some of the varied approaches used to express disapproval.

At about the same time, counter-demonstrations became a relatively frequent form of expression in reaction to the disruptive tactics of the campus protest movement. The underground media and the supporters of the counterculture directed their attention to the identification of these counter-demonstrators, and the "jocks" were singled out as offenders.

While it would be grossly unfair to label athletes as the only counter-demonstrators who physically attacked members of the radical protest movement on campus, it is undeniable that on several occasions athletes were identified as being involved. This recognition, and acceptance of the generalization that athletes were strong supporters of the campus and the political establishments, made athletics programs a focus of critical attention.

In 1968, Babbidge warned that intercollegiate athletic programs, because of the perceived association with the establishment and its values, and the gap between philosophy and delivery, would become a prime target for activist criticism, protest, and disruption (Babbidge, 1971: 30).

The issues advanced in the debate over athletics revolved around the question of whether such programs "belonged" in the academic community, or, more deeply, whether the experiences secured within athletics had positive or negative social consequences. The supporters of athletic programs generally couched their defense in the terminology of the conservative political ideology; emphasizing tradition, the need for authority in a permissive society, resistance to drastic social change, and the role of athletics in the fulfilment of the American Dream for the participants. The detractors evaluated athletics programs from the radical ideological perspective. The radical orientation was based on the ideological positions of the New Left, with additional infusions from the Youth Underground (hippies, yippies, etc.).

The conservative position holds that sport is a social integrator: blending athletes into the mainstream of society. The radical position held that sport created maladjusted, inadequately socialized individuals out of tune with the tempo of the times. The feature of interest in the debate between these groups was the fact that both sides drew their conclusions from essentially the same data, but interpreted it in consistency with their own value orientations.

Evaluating this data, or interpreting the substantial body of sport related myth, it was possible for former California State Superintendent of Schools Max Rafferty to state that:

Interscholastic sports, rising surprisingly and increasingly above their age-old status as mere games, serve today as the staunch custodians of these treasured concepts out of our great past (Rafferty, 1971: 21).

Employing the same material it was possible to indicate that the athletes faced problems of acceptance within their own peer group.

The athlete has been identified as being excessively oriented to the defense of the status quo, as being an establishment man, and to be an unquestioning supporter of conservative or reactionary political positions. To be a "Jock" on many campuses, is to be regarded as being deviantly out of step with the new politics, the new humanism, and the youth culture (Petrie, 1971b: 3).

The major areas utilized by both groups in the demonstration of their points during the late 1960s and the early 1970s were as follow.

1. the relative primacy of personal orientations consistent with those of the economy and polity,
2. the differential acceptance of authority,
3. the differential levels of respect for civil and individual rights, and
4. differences in the personality structures of athletes and nonathletes.

Personal Orientations Toward the Economy and Polity

One of the major concerns of the New Left, and more especially among members of the Youth Underground, has been an awareness that the advent of the post-industrial society in North America has left the majority of the population unable to adjust to the new contingencies.

> Point is, we can't conduct the present, any part of it, with the techniques of the nineteenth century. The Industrial Revolution is over & we lost . . . (Anderson, 1971: 226).

There is an awareness of the problems and promises of affluence and increased leisure, and recognition of the fact that industrialization and cybernation may magnify the development of a variety of social pathologies among individuals employed in certain work environments. Of these social pathologies, the central concern is with alienation: the separation of the individual from the fruits of his labor and the consequent development of conflict, misery, and revolt (Bottomore, 1969: 74–77).

Regardless of the political orientations of the students concerned, there is a belief that the thrust of automation is having a significant effect upon the structure of the work force and is creating social problems with respect to unemployment, displacement, and occupational redundancy. The radical perspective supports the view that an adequate response to these problems would be a reduction of the tremendous emphasis upon achievement and its importance in the generation of social status, and the elimination of individualistic competition.

While supporting the view that achievement and competition are excessively emphasized in modern society, the Youth Underground took this awareness one step further. This group looked to the replacement of work as the major social force by a new social necessity based upon individual self-realization and autonomy in leisure. Neville, who attempted to delineate the major ideological positions of the international counterculture, indicated that the predominant attitude of the youth underground towards work was to regard it as redundant (Neville, 1971: 207).

Much of the antagonism of the radical groups towards athletics was motivated by the belief that the participants in such programs were active, and frequently aggressive, supporters of conservative positions. But on a somewhat deeper level, there was a recognition that the value system of the institution of sport was consistent with the least desirable values of the economy and polity.

> Organized sport isn't play ... it's a ritualized, legitimized narcotic; hard work, competitive, corrupt. Ever seen an Olympic contestant smile? (Neville, 1971: 223).

Considering the fact that the stress upon achievement orientations was at the core of the intellectual rejection of athletic programs among members of the New Left and Youth Underground, what evidence is available to indicate the strength of such values among members of the athletic subculture?

In a study of student attitudes and value structures towards features of significance in the milieu of play, Webb surveyed a group of over 1200 children drawn from grades 3 to 12 in a major school system in Michigan. He determined that achievement orientations were progressively more important with increasing age and that the transition into high school marked the beginning of a surge in preference of such evaluative criteria in the play situation. Differences were evident in the sample on the basis of sex, and these effects were explained in terms of the fact that the socialization experience emphasizes the schooling of males for long term involvement in the occupational sector, where achievement and success are crucial components in the evaluation of efficiency (Webb, 1969). An extension of this study at the university level indicated the continued significance of achievement orientations in the environment of play, but it was obvious that both males and females were less committed to such evaluative criteria than had been the case among high school students (Petrie, 1971a).

Although both the Webb and Petrie studies looked at the student populations without controlling for athletic participation, several studies have been completed which looked for differences between athletes and nonathletes on achievement orientations. Mantel and VanderVelden determined that,

> ... the professionalization of attitudes toward play among preadolescent boys is directly related to participation in organized sport. Specifically, participants in organized sport regard skill or victory as the most important factor in play while nonparticipants emphasize fairness (1971: 5).

Although the Mantel and VanderVelden study employed a rather small sample, an analysis of similar hypotheses in a Canadian setting provided considerable support for their findings. Sampling students in grades 8, 9,

10, and 12, it was found that (a) the males gave higher endorsement for the achievement components of the Professionalization Scale, (b) the professionalization of attitude toward play increased among the males as they progressed through school, and (c) those respondents who had the greater degree of involvement in interscholastic and community representative athletic programs gave significantly higher endorsements for the achievement evaluative criteria and were, accordingly, placed higher on a Professionalization Scale than nonathletes (Maloney and Petrie, 1972: 188–193; see Webb, 1969, for a description of this scale).

On the basis of the evidence, it is possible to agree with Webb's conclusions in relation to the effect of the development of work-oriented values in the play situation. He felt that to continue to insist that play contributes to the development of desirable but non-specific social development characteristics

> is to ignore its structural and value similarities to the economic structure dominating our institutional network, and the substantial contribution that participation in the play arena thus makes to committed and effective participation in that wider system (Webb, 1969: 178).

The development of such values in the sporting group does not appear to be regarded as dysfunctional in the social settings of the school and university by teachers and students adhering to either conventional liberal and conservative ideological stances. These individuals would regard the progressive development of support for the values of success and the attainment of high levels of skill as evidence of the effectiveness of athletics programs in providing socialization experiences relevant to the career goals of students.

Some criticism, however, could be directed towards the fact that athletics, with its greater capacity for substantiation of achievement values of direct occupational significance, provides such experiences to a very small proportion of the student group. The high selectivity factor prevalent in athletics could be regarded as working against the potential that exists for occupational socialization.

Both sides in the ideological debate over athletics could find support for their positions from the evidence presented. Athletics does develop a high respect for the value of achievement, and, depending upon one's outlook and perspectives on the future, this could be regarded as having positive or negative consequences for the participants.

Progressing beyond the investigation of value orientations related to the economy, it is clear that there is a considerable body of literature indicating that members of the athletic subculture are conservative in their political viewpoints. The institution of sport has many linkages with the polity: the crucial difference between them being the fact that although both are concerned with the dissemination and reinforcement of values, the political institution is also concerned with value implementation. The institution of sport, then, being responsible only for value dissemination, can hold closely to the positions of social ideals rather than practice. Here, inflexibility is desirable if the purity of the ideal is to be maintained. It is this inflexibility that leads to accusations that the institution of sport consistently operates within the political framework of conservatism (Edwards, 1973: 91).

In the schools, athletics programs serve as a means of enculturation, guiding young people

> into the mainstream of American life through the overt and covert teaching of "appropriate" attudes, values, norms, and behavior patterns. As a result, school sports tend to exert more of a conservatizing and integrating influence in the society than an innovative or progressive influence (Schafer, 1971: 6).

Apart from the basic influence of the institutions of sport and education in developing an acceptance of organizationally established standards of behavior, members of the faculty also exert an influence that has consequences for political socialization. Chief among the faculty in the provision of influence among the athletes are coaches, and there is some recognition that the individuals occupying such positions are politically and socially conservative. The media evidence in support of this belief is considerable, with the disputes over the development of innovation in dress and hair styles being an example of inflexibility in response to change.

Of greater significance is the body of empirical evidence relating to the political ideologies of coaches. Such evidence has been developed through the use of standardized personality inventories and an established measure of political ideology. Following the development of a profile of the personality structure of college coaches, Ogilvie and Tutko indicated that one of the features that gave them concern was the

> inflexibility and rigidity in terms of utilization of new learning. Though they were a reasonably bright sample of men, there seemed to be a personality trait of extreme conservatism that would tend to limit their use of new information or different thinking in terms of dealing with new problems (1970: 24).

It should be noted, however, that the characteristics of the sample from which this interpretation is drawn has not been made public.

Sage utilized the Polyphasic Values Inventory to analyze the political orientations of a random sample of college coaches and determined that on 14 of the 20 items, coaches were significantly more conservative than college students. Although the study provided little support for the notion that coaches were extreme in their conservatism, there was one area of potential conflict arising from the discrepancy in orientations between the two groups. The P.V.I. does not measure authoritarianism directly, but the coaches consistently placed higher emphasis on those dimensions related to obedience to authority and acceptance of established standards of conduct (Sage, 1972).

There is a substantial body of literature to support the view that university students are essentially liberal in their political beliefs, but little information is available on such viewpoints among athletes. In a study conducted in New York State, high school athletes were found to be more conservative than nonathletes on three dimensions: acceptance of authority, traditionalism with regard to their view of American society, and acceptance of the draft as a legal obligation rather than as a moral decision (Rehberg and Cohen, 1971: 14).

On the West Coast, college athletes were also found to be more conservative than nonathletes. In addition, the athletes were (a) less interested and more inclined to be passive in response to politics, (b) more tolerant of violations of civil liberties, and (c) more likely to support repressive responses to campus unrest (Norton, 1971).

However, in a similar study in Canada it was found that athletes and nonathletes were predominantly liberal in their political ideologies. Differences between the American and Canadian data on political attitudes may be accounted for in the fact that the athletic environments in the universities are dissimilar. Only one Canadian institution provides grants-in-aid for student-athletes. Without the financial tie to a particular athletic department the athlete is more likely to associate with members of the student population, and, as a result, the potential for strong subcultural influence in the athletic setting is minimized (Petrie, 1973).

In summary, athletes have been shown to relate strongly to particular value orientations of the economy and polity. They provide strong support for achievement orientations, and, as one might expect, indicate that the drive for success and the refinement of skill is significant. Athletes and coaches have been found to be basically conservative in their political viewpoints. These features of the value orientations of athletes place them at variance with the positions of the radical activists, but it should also be noted that on all these characteristics, athletes hold to different value perspectives than those held by the generalized student population, at least in the United States, though not, perhaps, in Canada.

Acceptance of Authority

One of the traditional areas of dispute between students and faculty has been in the differential assessment of the degree of coercive power that should be available to the teachers and administrators. In the campus movement of the 1960s considerable stress was placed upon the idea that the individual was responsible for his own moral decisions and that the humanistic-existential doctrine was incompatible with the notion of infallible authority held by faculty.

Within athletics, however, a much greater hold was exerted over individual athletes, who often either made the choice to remain in sport and voluntarily conform to the authority of the coach or convinced themselves that no choice was available but to accept such authority.

The impression held by many coaches is consistent with that of Rafferty:

> There are two great national institutions which simply cannot tolerate either internal dissension or external interference: our armed forces, and our interscholastic sports program. Both are of necessity benevolent dictatorships because by their very nature they cannot be otherwise (1971: 14).

Rafferty did not effectively indicate what were the features within the institution of sport which made it, by nature, dictatorial. The theme of his article was couched in consistency with the conservative position that athletics was one of the few areas where it was possible to exert a level of authority to counter the permissiveness that was believed to be the basic cause of student disturbances. Permissiveness is a major theme in the conservative criticism of the changing society, and forecasts are made of drastic consequences for the American system if authority and discipline are not re-established in the education of youth.

High school coaches have generally been successful in maintaining their authority, and athletes appear to accept the differential power relationship as correct. Certainly, those individuals of athletic talent who adhere to the idea that democratic ideals should be applied in all settings would be selected out of further participation unless an exceptionally high level of skill were present. The athlete who questioned authority, however, regardless of his ability level, would be defined as a "problem athlete" and this label would have consequences for continued participation. The more likely response of individuals who reject the authority model prevalent in sport would be refusal to continue involvement. Those athletes who remain would be committed to the belief that traditional authority was desirable in the administrative style of the coach, or would make a psychic trade-off in order to continue participation. In either case, the athlete would be expected to exhibit a basically conservative stance with respect to authority.

Research support is provided for this assumption at the high school level in the studies of Schafer (1971), Phillips and Schafer (1970), and Rehberg and Cohen (1971). In each of these studies, athletes were higher in their endorsement of those dimensions of conservatism related to acceptance of authority and the necessity of strict control by the coach, acceptance of the social norms and traditions of the school, and support for stringent school rules. The coaching preference for an authoritarian interaction style apparently operated as a self-fulfilling prophecy through selectivity on the part of the coach and athletes, and the manifestation of some degree of existential "bad faith" among those who believe no voluntaristic choice existed.

Little research substantiation is available at the university level, although the media indicated some counter-reactions to the dominant control of the coaches and athletic departments at various institutions. The black athletes were more inclined to be the leaders in the initiation of activism in the mid-1960s. Activism among white athletes to humanize their environment was slower to start, but became a significant force by 1970 following the creation of "jock liberation" and the beginning of the "athletic revolution."

In the beginning period of the radical protest movement, there was some justification in the allegation that athletes in the universities were dominated by generally authoritarian coaches and athletic administrators. But, by the time that the attention of the activists was directed against athletic programs, there was equal justification to accept the view that athletes were beginning to move in a direction worthy of radical support. Unfortunately, the earlier characterization was used to accept negative stereotypes until the protest movement itself became reduced in scope.

Respect for Civil and Individual Rights

One of the central tenets of the campus protest movement was that the civil and individual rights of the relatively powerless and dispossessed members of society had to be forceably brought to the attention of an allegedly complacent bureaucracy. The expectations brought about by political rhetoric had not been translated into practical terms and student leaders directed their attention to assisting in the restoration of such rights to ethnic, racial, and economically powerless minorities. In the face of such activity, the awareness that groups within the university were submissive to the denial of various rights was an anathema to be erased or changed in conformity with the prevailing social ideals.

Considerable attention has been directed to the allegation that sport, as it is presently constituted, is dehumanizing (Scott, 1969, 1971). Well-publicized departures from professional athletics motivated by the perception of such conditions brought the issue to the awareness of the general public (Meggyesy, 1971; Sauer and Scott, 1971).

Part of this complaint stems from the tendency to regard the athletes as objects having utility in providing for the successes that can be translated into some form of social or financial profit for the group in control of that sporting situation. Thus, we have sporting success regarded (a) as a means for securing individual prestige for the coaches and institutional prestige for the school or college, (b) as a means for developing a level of positive identification among the nonathletic members of the institution, (c) as a means of allowing socially acceptable and controlled release of tensions and anxieties, and (d) as a way to achieve personal and institutional financial gain. In each of these cases, the athlete is evaluated in terms of his instrumental efficiency in attaining these goals.

Associated with this feature of dehumanization has been the disregard by members of the coaching fraternity for the individual rights of the players. This disregard was expressed in the form of restrictive dress, behavior, and dating codes that acted against any move toward conformity with the prevailing trends of the youth culture. The response to nonconformity to traditional athletic images was frequently expressed by the coach in terms of an accusation that the athlete who desired such expression had a latent tendency towards radicalism and was, accordingly, suspect.

Additionally, tolerance for the development of individualized training schedules and the expression of the need for democratic interaction styles within sports have not been readily accepted as desirable modifications by coaches.

> In an age where students are making strong requests for recognition of their individuality, their right of self expression, and their personal involvement in the school, it is incongruous for sport to drag its feet by holding to antiquated traditions and crew-cut stereotypes (Melnick, 1969: 33).

A small sample study by Puretz indicated that, at the college level, differences were evident in the attitudes of athletes and nonathletes towards the expression of individual rights in the athletic situation. His interpretation suggested that athletes value their personal rights and the rights of others to a lower degree than was the case among nonathletes (1969). Apart from this one study of limited scope, the literature to provide empirical substantiation of the diminished regard for individual rights in the athletic subculture is lacking. The main support for the proposition is derived from anecdotal material that has been published by retired athletes or from analyses by individuals who maintain a close association with university athletics programs and the "athletic revolution."

The unfortunate feature is that it has not been demonstrated that authoritarianism and the denial of the rights of athletes is a necessary concomitant of successful coaching. Some experimentation is being done with innovative coaching techniques in various high schools and small colleges but no significant change in the view of the coach as an authority figure with considerable control over the sporting, social, and educational lives of athletes has been manifest to this time.

It is apparent that the mood of the athlete has changed since the initial thrust of the protest movement against athletics. Activist protest from outside the institution has largely ceased to be a factor, but the athletes themselves are continuing the move towards the establishment of their own codes of behavior, and are resisting forms of influence that do not have direct application to performance. Until recently, however, athletes appeared willing to be less concerned with coaching intrusion into individual concerns as a price to be paid for continued participation.

Personality Structures of Athletes and Nonathletes

Considerable attention has been directed towards the determination of the various dimensions of personality which differentiate athletes from nonathletes. The aim of such research was to locate the particular factors which must be present or emphasized if an individual is to become a superior performer. In the pursuit of significant differences, few paused to reflect on the trilogy of associated problems. These problems relate to the awareness that (a) personality inventories are subject to the ideological influence of the researcher: if a researcher is testing on behalf of a particular coach, his work may be subconsciously influenced by the expectations of that individual; (b) the precision of measurement achieved in personality testing is of insufficient predictive power to justify their use in making any of the major decisions in coaching; (c) there is a tendency to regard the differences between athletes and nonathletes as being automatically positive. There has been little consideration of the fact that the end product of the socialization experience in the athletic subculture may bear characteristics that impede the capacity for adjustment into the wider society.

No attempt will be made to summarize the body of literature generated from the studies of the athletic personality, although the results are consistent with the information presented here. Of interest in the present context is the recent work of Ogilvie and Tutko which brought the question of social development through sport into focus. These authors collated the results generated from over 15,000 applications of their Athletic Motivation Inventory (other than its size, nothing else is known about the parameters of this sample) and provided support for the view that the long-standing belief in the social and character development potential of athletic participation should perhaps be discarded.

Those athletes who have survived the high attrition rate consistent with the philosophy of elitist participation could be characterized as bearing all or the majority of the following personality traits: (a) a high need for achievement and a tendency to set high but realistic goals for themselves and others; (b) a high level of personal organization, respect for authority, and dominance; (c) a high level of trust, psychological endurance, and ability to express aggression; and (d) low resting levels of anxiety, low interest in receiving support and concern from others, low need to take care of others, and a low affiliation need (Ogilvie and Tutko, 1971: 61).

The personality profile expressed here does not appear to bear much relationship with the features provided with positive reinforcement within the youth culture. In this group, at least as far as the idealistic positions would indicate, there is low emphasis upon achievement secured at the cost of others, a questioning of authority and of those who seek dominance, and a high willingness to provide cooperation and assistance to others (Reich, 1971).

In view of the fact that athletes are significantly higher on personality dimensions regarded with disfavor by the youth culture, it is clear that the athletic group emphasizes characteristics which work against their possible integration with their student peers.

The somewhat depersonalized personality structure of the athlete, as evidenced in the work of the personality researchers, does not provide one with confidence that the athlete will be able to relate to the prevailing trends within his own peer-oriented society (assuming its untested homogeneity actually does exist).

It is obvious, however, that in recent years numbers of athletes have exhibited characteristics consistent with the new humanism. If this trend continues, then the personality data and interpretation concerning athletics will be re-evaluated in terms of the cultural shift which developed in the 1960s.

Following the explosive period of the sixties, which culminated in the shootings of students at Kent State and Jackson State Universities in 1970, a period of relative calm developed that led many to believe that students had rejected further participation in the political arena. With this change, the pressure upon the athletic establishment was greatly reduced, but it is obvious that the athletes themselves have begun to question the more restrictive elements of their environment.

Various reasons may be advanced to explain the withdrawal of student involvement from activism against the political and educational establishments. The main explanation, however, may be found in the withdrawal of the traditionally liberal middle mass of students from support of radical causes. With their immediate goals solved by the ending of United States involvement in the Vietnam War, and the elimination of the draft, masses of students retreated to the classic liberal position of "slightly left of center." When this group of politically committed students was added to the group of alienated intellectuals and those who had remained apolitical throughout, it was apparent that a new coalition had emerged. This coalition of the disenchanted, alienated, and uninvolved is the new majority which appears reluctant to provide support for extreme groups at either end of the political continuum. The radical activists could not expect to see any major thrust against athletics and R.O.T.C. becoming a reality, and they adjusted their goals to more central concerns.

The fact that the majority of students had not entirely rejected political involvement was seen in the involvement of youth in the 1972 presidential campaign. Disenchantment over the Watergate Issue may reduce such participation in future elections and add to the numbers of the alienated intellectuals and disenchanted. One result of the activism of the sixties, however, was the development of awareness among the athletes. Admittedly, there were athletes at many institutions who supported the student movement from its beginnings, but these were generally isolated cases involving few athletes at any given campus.

Black athletes had been associated with their own militant groups in attempting to secure equality and redress of various educational grievances, but, again, their numbers were small even though their cause predated other concerns of the New Left. The black athletes did generate the first really successful movement in the sixties to attract national media coverage for activities utilizing athletic competitions as the focus for the illustration of social problems. This was, of course, the work of Harry Edwards together with black athletes of San Jose State College.

There were gestures towards activism among black athletes towards sport in general, and the Olympic Games in particular, from as early as 1960. Dick Gregory, the black comedian who has been noted for civil rights activism, attempted to organize a boycott of the United States–Soviet Union track meet of 1963, but he failed to secure sufficient support from among the black athletes. Gregory also tried to organize a boycott of the

1964 Olympic Games, but again failed to attract enough interest. The first successful boycott saw New Orleans rejected as the host city for the 1965 American Football League East–West All-Star game over charges of racism, but the Olympic Games remained the focus for the demonstration of discontent (Edwards, 1969: 38–51).

The relative success of the Olympic Committee for Human Rights in its actions to secure world-wide publicity at the 1968 Olympic Games in Mexico City identified some athletes, albeit a black minority, as involved in activities worthy of support by white activists. Black Power salutes were employed by blacks and whites during the playing of the national anthem at college football and basketball games in the 1968–1969 academic year, while many students wore black armbands to further proclaim their support. It was apparent, however, that the black athletes reserved their support, for the most part, for activities closely associated with the alleviation of racism and generally avoided joining other demonstrations.

Early activism of white athletes was identified with support of conservative positions in university demonstrations. Frequent references in the media attributed the propensity for counter-demonstrations to members of intercollegiate teams, athletically oriented fraternities, and "jocks" at various universities. Scott (1971: 112) mentioned the athletes who operated under the direction of the crew coach to attack demonstrators at Columbia University in 1968, while *Time* (1970: 65) reported the same coach's involvement in leading a police raid during the same disturbances. *Time* identified the counter-demonstrators who attempted to break up the black student occupation of Straight Hall at Cornell University as members of Delta Upsilon fraternity (*Time*, 1969: 37), while white intercollegiate athletes were accused of several counter-demonstrations at Michigan State University in 1968.

The propensity to regard "jocks" as counter-demonstrators became widespread, but documentation of involvement by athletes in such groups is not generally available. Certainly, Kunen (1970: 24, 60) did not restrict the term to athletes when he wrote of the Columbia demonstrations. In his analysis of the Kent State tragedy, Michener provided information in the labeling of "jocks" and "Greeks" in the various campus disputes, but indicated that the football players, at least, had not been involved in the counter-demonstration at the Music and Speech Building a year prior to the shootings, even though the allegation was widely reported (Michener, 1971: 170).

Intercollegiate athletes were frequently labeled as being involved in vigilante activity in support of conservative positions, and the stereotype may have been damaging to the integration of the athletes in the university communities. It should be emphasized that there was little solid evidence to support the contention that such involvement led them to be regarded as deviant by more than the hard core activists of the New Left.

By 1970, however, an opposite trend was in evidence. Intercollegiate athletes, particularly at the University of California at Berkeley, began to develop their own coalitions and join in the wider student movement against the war. Over 150 athletes and members of staff attended a protest meeting and subsequently released a statement rejecting the proposition that athletics was essentially apolitical. They further agreed to

> ... condemn United States activity in Southeast Asia and call for a unilateral withdrawal of all United States forces in Southeast Asia. Furthermore, we call for a reconstruction of American universities as centers against the war.*

Scott documented responses by intercollegiate athletes to the Cambodian invasion at various other universities. The statement released by athletes of the Ivy League Colleges prior to the 1970 Heptagonal Track and Field meet was so strong that the Army and Navy teams withdrew from the competition. Eighty-five football players at Columbia University signed a petition calling for a national student strike, while members of five teams voted to cancel their competitions. Elsewhere, individual athletes became involved at sit-ins and protest demonstrations against the war. The publicity given to athletic activism led one administration spokesman to comment, "Once we heard that the athletes and pom-pom girls had joined the demonstrators, we knew we were in trouble." (Quoted in Scott, 1971: 110–113).

Following the disengagement from Vietnam, and the elimination of the draft, the athletes, as with the majority of students, withdrew from activism and the support of general student movements. The continued reports of the involvement of athletes in confrontation with coaches and administrators indicate that the "athletic revolution" has continued its thrust in opposition to specific features within the immediate athletic environment. What is now in question is the opportunity for self-fulfillment through sport and the establishment of equality of opportunity within sport. Black and white athletes are working to secure recognition and control over the potentially dehumanizing features of professional and semiprofessional participation where economic rather than human considerations appear to predominate.

---

* Jack Scott, *The Athletic Revolution* (New York: The Free Press, © 1971), p. 110. Reprinted by permission.

Forced by the challenges and stereotypes of the competing ideologies in the universities to evaluate their positions vis-a-vis political issues, the athletes eventually appeared to move in the direction of active or passive support of the New Left. The prospect for the future would be for continued agitation to take place to improve the degree of power available to athletes within their own environment, with isolated activism, at least in the northern arc of the United States, with respect to political issues of wider relevance.

CONCLUSION

Continued acceptance of the belief that sport is an apolitical institution has been shown to be erroneous. On a variety of dimensions, a close relationship has been shown to exist between the supporting institution of sport and the master institution of the polity. The dimensions analyzed were:

1. The use of personal and vicarious involvement in sport as a means for the substantiation of a positive and politically rewarding image for political figures. This dimension was treated in terms of the personal use of such involvement by individual politicians, and in terms of the intrusion of political messages and national symbolism into the milieu of sport so that spectators might be persuaded to follow positions supportive of particular parties or politicians.

2. The use of sport as a means for the development of community cohesiveness and national identity. Community identification can be substantiated through the provision of wide publicity for the successes of the local high school, university, or professional teams. This effect, when magnified to include all members of a given national system, becomes nationalism. The response of the identifying public is essentially the same regardless of the unit of analysis: a locality, state, region, or nation is led to believe that pride, potency, and political-economic superiority are at stake in the athletic competitions against outsiders. The promotion of such associations has clear political implications in terms of the maintenance of a community or national identity, and the belief that system superiority in one area of competition has a carry-over significance into areas beyond the purely physical and aesthetic.

3. The use of sport as a field of competition between political ideologies over the relevance of large scale, elitist athletic programs in schools and universities. In this discussion, the conflicting approaches of the 1960s saw sport as either a major force for social integration, or as an institution providing a socialization experience at inordinate public and social cost,

that had negative consequences for the participants in terms of peer acceptability.

In this section, the discussion was limited to sport in the educational environments, as professional athletes—being members of a particular work force—had usually chosen to follow courses of action consistent with the maintenance of image, or passed responsibility for change to players' associations, specialists in player management within the legal profession, or collective bargaining on an ad hoc basis.

The institution of sport has transcended its earlier basis as an environment for the establishment of excellence in physical performance with benefits intrinsic to the individual and extraneous to the "real world." Sport is a highly publicized milieu for the demonstration of characteristics that have instrumental significance to the substantiation of the prevailing political-economic ideology. This propensity for system support incorporates a potential for social control and brings the institution of sport clearly into focus as an element in the political arena. A symbiotic relationship between the dominant political institution and the supporting institution of sport provides personal, group, and national benefits for the more powerful members of both structures, and, to the extent that the instrumental significance of sport maintains dominance, the athletes and their performances will remain of long term significance only to themselves, the afficianados, and the collectors of sports trivia.

The current agitation among athletes is to secure a greater level of control of their environment, and recognition that the pursuit of excellence is sufficient justification in itself for sport. Attempts to magnify the attachment of politically important instrumental values to sport denigrates athletic effort and reduces the phenomenological significance of self-substantiation through physical excellence.

REFERENCES

Anderson, C.
1971   Cited by R. Neville. *Playpower*. London: Paladin. 226.
1973   Sports Editorial. *New York Times*. (January 21): p. S3.

Babbidge, H.
1971   "Athletics and the American Dream." In *The Athletic Revolution*, J. Scott. New York: The Free Press. 23–34.

Ball, D. W.
1972   "Olympic Games Competition: Structural Correlates of National Success." *International Journal of Comparative Sociology*, **13** (3–4): 186–200.

Bottomore, T. B.
1969   *Critics of Society.* New York: Vintage Books.

Boyle, R. H.
1963   *Sport-Mirror of American Life.* Boston: Little, Brown and Company.

Brundage, A.
1969   Cited by J. Scott. *Athletics for Athletes.* Oakland, California: An Other Ways Book. 102.

Caillois, R.
1962   *Man, Play, and Games.* London: Thames and Hudson.

Calisch, R.
1954   "Spectator Problems in Secondary School Athletics." *Research Quarterly,* **25**: 261–268.

Coleman, J. S.
1959   "Academic Achievement and the Structure of Competition." *Harvard Educational Review,* **29** (4) (Fall): 330–335.
1961   "Athletics in High School." *The Annals of the American Academy of Political and Social Science,* Monograph 338 (November): 33–43.

Cooke, A.
1973   *Alistair Cooke's America.* New York: Random House. Cited in Books Feature. *Time.* (December 3): 96.

Deeb, G.
1971   Sports Editorial. *Variety.* (July 7): 25.

Deutsch, M.
1953   "The Effects of Cooperation and Competition upon Group Process." In *Group Dynamics,* D. Cartwright and A. Zander (eds.). Evanston, Illinois: Row Peterson. 319–353.

Edwards, H.
1969   *The Revolt of the Black Athlete.* New York: The Free Press.
1973   *Sociology of Sport.* Homewood, Illinois: The Dorsey Press.

Goodhart, P., and C. Chataway
1968   *War Without Weapons.* London: W. H. Allen.

Heinila, K.
1970   "Notes on the Inter-group Conflicts in International Sport." In *The Cross-Cultural Analysis of Sport and Games,* G. Luschen (ed.). Champaign, Illinois: Stipes Publishing Company. 174–182.

Hollingshead, A. B.
1949   *Elmtown's Youth.* New York: John Wiley and Sons, Inc.

Holmes, J.
1971   *Olympiad 1936.* New York: Ballantine Books Inc.

Huizinga, J.
1955   *Homo Ludens.* Boston: Beacon Press.

I.S.S.S. Newsletter
1973   Sports Feature (December): 2.

JOHPER
1969   "Crowd Control at Athletic Events." *Journal of Health, Physical Educa-
        tion, and Recreation,* **40** (4): 27–31.

Kunen, J. S.
1970   *The Strawberry Statement: Notes of a College Revolutionary.* New York:
        Avon Books.

Lever, J.
1969   "Soccer: Opium of the Brazilian People." *Trans-Action,* **7** (2): 36–43.

Lund, A.
1972   "Sports and Politics." In *Sport in the Socio-Cultural Process,* M. M. Hart
        (ed.). Dubuque, Iowa: Wm. C. Brown Company Publishers. 482–485.

Maloney, T. L., and B. M. Petrie
1972   "Professionalization of Attitude toward Play among Canadian School Pu-
        pils as a Function of Sex, Grade, and Athletic Participation." *Journal of
        Leisure Research,* **4** (Summer): 184–195.

Mandell, R. D.
1971   *The Nazi Olympics.* New York: The Macmillan Company.

Mantel, R. C., and L. VanderVelden
1971   "The Relationship between the Professionalization of Attitude toward
        Play of Preadolescent Boys and Participation in Organized Sport." Paper
        presented: Third International Symposium on the Sociology of Sport. Wa-
        terloo, Canada (August).

McKee, J. B.
1969   *Introduction to Sociology.* New York: Holt, Rinehart and Winston, Inc.

Meggyesy, D.
1971   *Out of Their League.* New York: Paperback Library.

Melnick, M. J.
1969   "Footballs and Flower Power." *Journal of Health, Physical Education, and
        Recreation,* **40** (8) (October): 32–33.

Merchant, L.
1971   *. . . And Every Day You Take Another Bite.* Garden City, New York:
        Doubleday and Company, Inc.

Michener, J. A.
1971   *Kent State: What Happened and Why.* New York: Random House.

Natan, A.
1969   "Sport and Politics." In *Sport, Culture, and Society,* J. W. Loy, Jr. and
        G. S. Kenyon (eds.). Toronto: Collier-Macmillan, Ltd. 203–210.

Neville, R.
1971   *Playpower.* London: Paladin.

New York Times
1973   Sports Feature. (January 21): p. S1,3.

Norton, D. J.
1971   "A Comparison of Political Attitudes and Political Participation of Athletes and Non-Athletes." M. A. Thesis. University of Oregon.

Ogilvie, B. C., and T. A. Tutko
1970   *Problem Athletes and How to Handle Them.* London: Pelham Books.
1971   "Sport: If You Want to Build Character, Try Something Else." *Psychology Today,* **5** (5) (October): 60–63.

Padwe, S.
1971   Sports Editorial. *Philadelphia Inquirer.* (December 14): 35.

Petrie, B. M.
1971a   "Achievement Orientations in Adolescent Attitudes toward Play." *International Review of Sport Sociology,* **6**: 89–101.
1971b   "The Athletic Group as an Emerging Deviant Subculture." Paper presented: Conference on Sport and Social Deviancy. State University College at Brockport, New York (December 9–11).
1973   "The Political Attitudes of Canadian University Students: A Comparison between Athletes and Non-Athletes." Paper presented: National Convention of A.A.H.P.E.R. Minneapolis, Minnesota (April).

Philadelphia Inquirer
1971   Sports Feature. (December 17): 44.

Phillips, J. C., and W. E. Schafer
1970   "The Athletic Subculture: A Preliminary Study." Paper presented: Annual Meetings of the American Sociological Association. Washington, D.C. (August).

Pooley, J. C.
1972   "Ethnic Soccer Clubs in Milwaukee: A Study in Assimilation." In *Sport in the Socio-Cultural Process,* M. M. Hart (ed.). Dubuque, Iowa: Wm. C. Brown Company Publishers. 328–345.

Puretz, D.
1969   "Athletics and the Development of Values." Paper presented: National Convention of A.A.H.P.E.R. Boston, Massachusetts. (April).

Rafferty, M.
1971   "Interscholastic Athletics: The Gathering Storm." In *The Athletic Revolution,* J. Scott (ed.). New York: The Free Press. 13–22.

Rehberg, R. A., and M. Cohen
1971   "Political Attitudes and Participation in Extra-Curricular Activities with Special Emphasis on Interscholastic Athletics." Paper presented: Conference on Sport and Social Deviancy. State University College at Brockport, New York (December).

Reich, C. A.
1971   *The Greening of America.* New York: Bantam Books.

Reynolds, A. R., and J. M. Henslin
1973   *American Society: A Critical Analysis.* New York: David McKay Company, Inc.

·Sage, G.
1972   "Value Orientations of American College Coaches Compared to those of Male College Students and Businessmen." Paper presented: 75th Annual Meetings of National College Physical Education Association for Men. New Orleans, Louisiana (January).

Sauer, G., and J. Scott
1971   "Interview by Jack Scott with George Sauer on the Reasons for Sauer's Retirement from Professional Football While at the Height of His Career." Research Paper: Department of Physical Education. California State College, Hayward, California.

Schafer, W. E.
1971   "Sport, Socialization and the School." Paper presented: Third International Symposium on the Sociology of Sport. Waterloo, Canada (August 22–28).

Schlesinger, A. M.
1973   "The Runaway Presidency." *The Atlantic,* **232** (5): 43–55.

Scott, J.
1969   *Athletics for Athletes.* Oakland, California: An Other Ways Book.
1971   *The Athletic Revolution.* New York: The Free Press.

Shaw, M. E., and J. M. Wright
1967   *Scales for the Measurement of Attitudes.* New York: McGraw-Hill Book Company.

Simpson, T.
1973   *Intellectual Digest,* **4** (3) (November): 76–77.

Sovetskii Sport
1952   Sports Feature. July 31. Cited by H. W. Morton. *Soviet Sport.* New York: Collier Books (1963). 35.

Time
1969   Education Feature. (May 2): 37.
1970   Sports Feature. (November 23): 65.

Veblen, T.
1953   *The Theory of the Leisure Class.* New York: Mentor Books.

Voigt, D. Q.
1966   *American Baseball: From Gentleman's Sport to the Commissioner System.* Norman, Oklahoma: University of Oklahoma Press.

Webb, H.
1968   "Social backgrounds of M.S.U. Athletes." Research paper: Department of Sociology. Michigan State University.

1969   "Professionalization of Attitudes toward Play among Adolescents." In
       Aspects of Contemporary Sport Sociology, G. S. Kenyon (ed.). Chicago:
       The Athletic Institute. 161–178.

White, C. M. D.
1970   "An Analysis of Hostile Outbursts in Spectator Sports." Ph.D. Disserta-
       tion, Dept. of Physical Education. University of Illinois. Champaign,
       Illinois.

Chapter 6
Sport Consumption and the Economics of Consumerism

Barry D. McPherson
Departments of Kinesiology and Sociology
University of Waterloo
(Waterloo, Ontario, Canada)

Barry D. McPherson

Birth Place: Toronto, Ontario, Canada

Age: 33

Birth Order: Younger sister

Formal Education:

B.A., University of Western Ontario	1964
M.A., University of Western Ontario	1965
Ph.D., University of Wisconsin	1972

Present Position:

Associate Professor and Graduate Officer, Department of Kinesiology, University of Waterloo, Waterloo, Ontario, also, cross-appointment with Department of Sociology.

Professional Responsibilities:

Undergraduate: Sociology of Sport, Research Design, Sociology of Aging and Leisure.

Graduate: Sociology of Sport

Scholarly Interests:

Socialization into sport: cross national analyses.

Sport as a social problem, specifically minor hockey in Canada.

Preretirement life-styles and aging.

Professional Accomplishments:

Articles published in *The Journal of Sports Medicine and Physical Fitness, Research Quarterly, International Review of Sport Sociology, Sportwissenshaft, Canadian Review of Sociology and Anthropology.*

Hobbies:

Departmental administration and committee work.

Sport Activities:

Participant: tennis, squash, hockey, sailing.

Spectator: tennis, hockey, football.

Lifetime Won-Lost-Tied record against J. W. Loy in tennis is 99–0–0.

Most Recent Books Read:

Light: recent articles by J. W. Loy.

Intellectual: recent articles by D. W. Ball.

INTRODUCTION

Among the plethora of possible leisure roles an individual might occupy, the role of sport consumer is one of the most pervasive in North America. For example, over 10 million spectators (one million are season ticket subscribers) attend regular season professional football games, while approximately 31 million attend games in the two major baseball leagues. Nor is the phenomena restricted to actual attendance at a sport event. For example, approximately 15 percent (over 900 hours) of all programs produced by the three major television networks are sport telecasts, for which the estimated number of viewers (primarily male adults and teenagers) ranges between one and 65 million depending on the day, time and event (Nielsen, 1972).

Although statistics are not readily available to indicate how many people listen to sport events on the radio, read about sport in newspapers and sport journals,[1] or talk about sport both at and away from work, there is little doubt that sport consumption is a pervasive element in contemporary life styles. In fact, it is quite likely that the consumption of sport preoccupies a greater proportion of our ever-increasing leisure time than does active participation in sport. As both a cause and a consequence of this behavioral pattern, there has been in recent years an expansion of professional sport organizations into new urban areas, an increase in the number of sport leagues and sport journals, and an increasing number of sport telecasts (an increase of 65 percent from 1960 to 1972) produced by the major television networks.

Despite the fact that many are playing the role of sport consumer, there have been few attempts to examine such facets of the phenomenon as the function of spectator sports, the motivation of sport fans, and how spectators behave in a collective situation. Therefore, the first section of this chapter reviews the literature concerned with the demographic characteristics of sport consumption; the causes, functions and effects of sport consumption; and how individuals are socialized into the role of sport consumer.

As a result of the increasing number who are willing to consume sport, a concomitant development has been the attempt by entrepreneurs to maximize the opportunity for the masses to consume, thereby generating either direct profits from sport, or tax advantages for other enterprises they control. While it is difficult to identify a cause-effect relationship between the willingness to consume by the masses and the promotion of sport for profit by entrepreneurs, there is little doubt that mass consumption and economics are inexorably interrelated at the present time.

In the second section, the economics of sport from the perspective of the consumer, the media, the entrepreneur, the community, and the laborer (i.e., athlete) are discussed.

THE CONSUMPTION OF SPORT

Introduction

Sport consumption in North America is not a recent phenomenon. For example, Voigt (1971: 34–37) noted that spectator sports were popular as early as 1860, while Betts (1953) described the impact that urbanization and the technological revolution had on the rise of sport, especially commercialized spectator sport. However, it is only in recent years that the age of high mass consumption (Rostow, 1971) has been attained. Discussed in the following sections are (a) the current degree of consumption, (b) the functions, causes and effects of consumption, and (c) the process whereby individuals become socialized into the role of sport consumer.

Degree of Consumption

The data describing the number who consume sport are vast and this section could consume the entire chapter. However, since statistics become obsolete as this chapter is being read, they are presented only to serve as a baseline to indicate the degree of sport consumption in the early 1970's. The consumption of sport can be either direct or indirect (Kenyon, 1969). In the direct form, the individual attends a live sport event and is part of the spectacle, whereas, the indirect form involves consuming sport via television or radio; via books, magazines or newspapers; or, by discussing sport with others.

Degree of Direct Sport Consumption

Direct sport consumption appears to vary by sex, age, season, and sport. In the following, statistics first from empirical studies are presented; these are then followed by those released by sport organizations. Kenyon (1966) reported that only a small minority of adults actually attend sport events, and that the attendance varies by season. For example, he found that 29 percent of the men and 21 percent of the women attended events once per month or more often in the summer; 26 percent of the men and 15 percent of the women attended once per month or more often in the fall; while only 12 percent of the males and 12 percent of the females attended sport events once per month or more often in the winter.

In a cross-national study of adolescents, Kenyon (1968) found that two-thirds of the adolescents studied consumed sport directly once per month or more. Again, there was lower direct consumption in the winter compared to the summer and fall, and by females compared to males. Similar trends were noted by McPherson (1972) from a sample of urban-dwelling Canadian adolescents. In fact, only 4.8 percent of the males and 4.3 percent of the females reported that they never attended a sport event in a given year.

A study by Lowe and Harrold (1972) indicated that among college students direct attendance is declining. They found that the percentage of students purchasing season tickets for events dropped from 51 percent in 1962 to 13.8 percent in 1971. Thus, while direct attendance by adolescents in the high school system appears to be high (Kenyon, 1968; McPherson, 1972), there is a declining involvement after the high school years, even among college students (Lowe and Harrold, 1972). This results in relatively few adults consuming sport directly.

Despite the small percentages, the actual number who attend sport events is quite high compared to attendance at other forms of mass consumption. For example, in 1972, approximately 60 million North Americans spent more than $300 million for tickets to watch 95 major sport teams (Toronto Globe and Mail, October 2, 1973: 34). More specifically, over 17 million attended professional baseball games, over 13.5 million attended professional football games, while approximately two million attended golf tournaments. Similar statistics are readily available from all organized sport leagues or associations. In addition to interest in attending regular season games, there is an even greater interest in special events such as the Super Bowl (80,000 plus), the World Series (350,000 plus), the Olympics, the Michigan–Ohio State football game (100,000), and the Bobby Riggs–Billy Jean King tennis match. For the most part, this direct attendance at professional sport events is restricted to the higher-income residents of large urban centers. Unfortunately, statistics are not readily available to indicate how many attend sport events below the college and professional level.

Degree of Indirect Sport Consumption

Although most consumption tends to be indirect, the data are less accurate since they are based on estimates rather than tickets sold or number of admissions. Therefore, the following statistics could be overinflated or underinflated because of sampling errors. As in the previous section, the results from empirical studies are presented first, followd by a brief presentation of statistics released by the media or survey agencies.

In his study of adults in a midwestern state, Kenyon (1966) found that over 50 percent of the sample listened to sport on the radio or watched it on television at least once a week. Again, there were sex differences, as 79 percent of the men and 59 percent of the women reported that they consumed sport at least once per week. In the cross-national study with adolescents, Kenyon (1968) found that four to five hours per week of watching sport on television was not unusual. As with direct consumption, males were more involved than females. It was also noted that 75 percent of the males and 50 percent of the females read the sport pages in the newspaper at least once per week.

In a more recent study (McPherson, 1972) of Canadian adolescents, it was found that the type of indirect consumption varied by sex (Table 1).

Table 1

Type of Indirect Consumption By Sex For Male and Female Adolescents*

Type of consumption	At least once per week		Never	
	Males	Females	Males	Females
Television	64.3	40.4	1.3	1.4
Radio	21.7	19.1	29.9	36.9
Reading	57.4	34.0	12.1	12.1
Talking	69.3	47.6	1.9	0.7

* From McPherson, 1972.

More specifically, consuming sport on television and talking about sport appeared to be the most frequent form of indirect consumption for both sexes. Lowe and Harrold (1972) also indicated that there was considerably more indirect than direct consumption. They reported that almost 80 percent of the college students watched sport on television at least occasionally, 50 percent read a sport magazine occasionally, while 40 percent read the sport page in the campus newspaper.

In the studies cited above most indirect consumption occurred via television. In view of this it is not surprising that detailed statistics are recorded concerning the consumption habits of North American viewers by both the networks and by independent rating services. Again, since statistics become dated, the following are presented only to indicate variations by sport and season. The most popular viewing times are Saturday and Sunday afternoons and between 7:30 p.m. and 11:00 p.m. each weekday. However, even when special events (e.g., Olympics) are telecast early on a weekday morning or after midnight during the week, it is not unusual to find that four to five million consume the event. In recent years it has been estimated that over 100 million watch the entire World Series, that an average of five million view a regular season National Basketball Association game, that 7.5 million consumed each Olympic telecast from Munich, that 60 million viewed the Riggs–King tennis match, and that over 80 million consume the Super Bowl each year. In fact, whereas 64 million viewed Super Bowl V, three weeks later at the same time only 55 million watched the launch of the Apollo 14 spacecraft. In short, sport consumption via television is a pervasive facet of contemporary lifestyles.

In addition to television, the growth of specialized sport magazines and sport journals has increased the opportunity to consume sport. Thus, not only are there daily, weekly, biweekly, and monthly newspapers or magazines which report news about all sports, but also many specialized publications covering such sports as yachting, skiing, tennis, auto racing, snowmobiling, fishing, and roller derby. In fact, one of the indicators that a new sport has become institutionalized is the appearance of a periodical which describes the rules, outcomes, personalities, strategies, and techniques of the sport; and advertises the fashions, equipment, and accessories necessary for playing or consuming the sport. In summary, North Americans are insatiable sport consumers, especially via television, publications and discussion.

Background Factors Influencing the Rate of Consumption

Before an individual can participate in or consume sport, an opportunity set must be created. For the sport consumer, the opportunity to directly attend a sport event is facilitated by the length of sport schedules and by the amount of overlap between sport seasons. For example, the elapsed time from preseason games until the final championship game in 1968–69 was 173 days for professional football, 214 days for basketball, 226 days for baseball, and 239 days for hockey (*The New York Times*, April 13, 1969: 45). As the number of teams and games increases each year due to expansion the seasons become longer and the overlap between sports increases to the point that there are very few weeks in the year when at least three of the major sports are not being offered to the consumer. For those who consume indirectly there are daily newspapers and either live or delayed sport telecasts every weekend of the year. The opportunity to consume is also influenced by the economic situation of the consumer in that the admission to events ranges from no cost for some amateur events to as high as $100 per ticket for championship boxing matches. As indicated earlier, there do appear to be sex differences in the type of sport which is consumed directly or indirectly. A report by Nielsen (1971) indicated that the 1970–71 average for sport consumption via television was 5.8 million male adults, 3.4 million female adults, and 2.6 million non-adults (i.e., under 18 years of age) per broadcast. The rate of consumption by females tends to be higher for special events (e.g., Super Bowl, World Series) than for regularly scheduled contests.

Marital status may also be related to sport consumption in that those who are single may have higher rates of direct consumption than the married because there are fewer constraints as to how and where they spend their incomes. Similarly, the married may be more involved in indirect consumption since it is a home-centered activity. Finally, it might be hypothesized that more single women than married women would consume sport directly since the dating patterns of high school and college students often include attendance at sporting events. To date, however, there are no data to support the hypotheses concerning marital differences.

Another background factor which influences consumption is age. Nielsen (1971) noted that males under 35 years are the highest consumers, followed in order by those over 50 years and those 35–49 years of age. The decrease in television consumption across all sports for males between 35 and 49 years of age may possibly occur because of career and family commitments. The increase in the later years may be accounted for by those who need to fill time as they approach or enter retirement.

Education and occupation also influence the pattern of consumption. Kenyon (1966) found that those from the lower socioeconomic strata did not attend sport events as frequently as others, but that there was no relationship between socioeconomic background and the indirect consumption of sport. Similar results for adolescents were reported by McPherson (1972). Thus, it appears that while direct consumption may be related to socioeconomic background, indirect consumption is not.

A final factor which may influence the degree of direct attendance, at least for college students, is proximity to the arena or stadium. Lowe and Harrold (1972) found that a large proportion of those who purchased the all-sport season ticket lived in fraternity or sorority homes, university residence halls, or homes which were within walking distance of the campus. This, of course, may reflect a general desire to live close to the campus action, sport being but one type of leisure activity. Thus, it appears that background factors may influence whether individuals consume sport initially, and whether they are direct or indirect consumers at different stages in the life cycle. However, such factors as age, sex, and socioeconomic background are considerably less influential for sport consumption than for sport participation.

In summary, this section has indicated that the rate of sport consumption is high in North America, and that in all likelihood the number of consumers is increasing exponentially as new sports appear on television, as new franchises enter communities, and as technological advances enable sport to be telecast live from any locale in the world.

Sport Consumption: Functions, Causes, and Effects

The phenomenon of sport consumption has been considered from a number of different perspectives in recent years. Most frequently the reports have been descriptive statistical presentations which indicate the number of people who attend or view specific sport events. It is interesting to observe that the sport fan as an entity has been virtually ignored, whereas spectators or consumers as a collective entity have received considerable attention. Nevertheless, three definitions of a sport fan have been suggested. Loy (1968) described the fan as an individual who has both a high personal investment in and a high personal commitment to a given sport. Spinrad (1970: 1) described the fan as a person who thinks, talks about, and is oriented toward sport even when he is not actually observing, reading about, or listening to an account of a specific sport event. More recently, Voigt (1971: 20–40) indicated that Caillois' (1965) mimicry classification is represented in America by the dedicated fan who identifies strongly with a team or star performer.

A number of scholars have been interested in the function of spectator sports. As early as 1929, Brill (1929) stated that vicarious spectator sport meets an important need in providing for the exercise of man's aggressive combative instincts. Similarly, Gerth and Mills (1954: 63) reported that many mass audience situations, with their "vicarious" enjoyments, serve psychologically the unintended function of channeling and releasing otherwise unplaceable emotions. Thus, great amounts of aggression are "cathartically" released by crowds of spectators cheering their favorite stars of sport and jeering the umpire. Some studies, however, have found that observers are likely to be more aggressive after viewing violence than before (Bandura and Walters, 1963; Berkowitz, 1969; Dollard et al., 1939; Goldstein and Arms, 1971). As a result of the equivocal findings, it appears that the reaction to a sport contest may be sport or person specific.

More recently, it has been suggested that sport consumption serves a number of social functions. Beisser (1967: 124–141), in a discussion of the spectator, suggested that sport consumption is a socially sanctioned mode of behavior wherein an individual can share something in common, on an equal basis, with others in the community. He noted that this is not possible in other spheres of an anonymous society. In addition, Beisser indicated that sport spectating, as opposed to sport participation, enables both males and females to play the role at any stage of the life cycle. Similarly, Gross (1961: 2–8), Dunning (1969: 21), and Voigt (1971: 27) suggested that sport consumption may assist in the process of social integration. More specifically, Dunning (1969: 21) indicated that spectator sport serves as a medium through which individuals can identify with wider social groupings. Voigt (1971: 27) suggested that:

> Attendance at a scarce and expensive spectacle like the World Series helps to validate one's social worth in a society that demands ceaseless validation of one's status claims by means of elegant consumership . . . and . . . the game fosters surrogate kinship experiences or at least, along with other spectator sports, the game functions as a social ice-breaker and as a launching pad for other forms of social interaction.*

Similarly, Stone, as cited by Boyle (1963: 65), noted that consumption of sport is a necessary food for conversation and provides mutual accessibility to anonymous members of the mass society.

In an examination of the quest for excitement in unexciting societies, Elias and Dunning (1970) stated that:

> The quest for excitement . . . in our leisure activities is complementary to the control and restraint of excitement in our ordinary life . . . the mimetic sphere provides a specific type of pleasurable excitement . . . which does not disturb and endanger the relative orderliness of social life . . . the mimetic sphere offers . . . refreshment of the soul . . . it is excitement which we seek voluntarily . . . it is socially and personally without danger and can have a cathartic effect.†

Zurcher and Meadow (1967) viewed sport as a legitimate opportunity for release of repressed tension and for the expression of frustration created by cultural institutions. Finally, in the most comprehensive impressionistic analysis to date, Spinrad (1970) suggested six functions of spectator sport. These included the following.

---

* D. Q. Voigt, *America's Leisure Revolution*, D. Q. Voigt (ed.). (Reading, Pennsylvania: Albright College Book Store, 1971), p. 27. Reprinted by permission.

† N. Elias and E. Dunning, "The Quest for Excitement in Unexciting Societies," in *The Cross-Cultural Analysis of Sport and Games*, G. Lüschen (ed.). (Champaign, Illinois: Stipes Publishing Co., 1970), pp. 32–41. Reprinted by permission.

1. serving as a mechanism of vicarious combat,
2. providing psychic gratifications through identification with sport heroes and the local community,
3. enabling the individual to participate in a subcultural folklore through the accumulation of knowledge about the history and strategy of a particular sport,
4. enabling the individual to accumulate a set of statistics and thereby retain his interest in the subject,
5. stimulating rational dialogues about players or teams,
6. playing at mock administration by running a team and employing appropriate strategy.

Kaelin (1968), in a discussion of violence in American sport, stated that the value of violence to the spectator is not in its expression per se, but in its control toward the achievement of a contested end. He added that where violence may be sufficient to generate interest in an activity, its control is necessary to sustain continued interest in its expression.

Closely related to the functions of spectator sport are the factors causing such vast numbers of people to consume sport. Again, only impressionistic works have considered this problem. Stone (1955: 83–100) studied the phenomenon of spectatorship and noted that with the massification of sport spectators began to outnumber participants, with the result that the spectator encouraged the spectacular, or in Stone's term, the "display." Rousseau (1958) believed that spectator sport began when the idea of the self-made man began to decay. Goffman (1967: 197) observed that individuals can experience a certain kind of excitement "by consuming valued products, by enjoying costly and modish entertainment, by spending time in luxurious settings, and by mingling with prestigeful persons. This brief descriptive passage certainly suggests one possible reason for the incidence of sport consumption in the 1970's.

Dunning (1969: 10, 13) suggested that a quest by people for pleasurable excitement and a need to "lose themselves," and thereby fuse their identity with that of others in the crowd, were factors causing the rise of sport consumption. In addition, he suggested that one of the motives for consuming soccer in Britain may be a desire to compensate for the fact that one's own work offers few opportunities for the expression of physical skill, hence one vicariously experiences the high level of skill displayed by the athletes. He further stated that:

Ability in sport is almost universally regarded as a desirable "masculine" trait in our society. Men who lack this ability may derive some vicarious satisfaction and compensation for their own "lack of manliness" through identifying with successful sportsmen.*

From a philosophical perspective, Weiss (1969) indicated that a basic cause of spectator sport is the pleasure derived from viewing excellence in an activity that the individual may have attempted at some time. Thus, through observation, identification occurs. Stone (1955: 85), indicating that sport provides a continuity of one's personal life and in the events of the world, suggested that:

> Team loyalties formed in adolescence and maintained through adulthood may serve to remind one, in a nostalgic way, that there are areas of comfortable stability in life—that some things have permanence amid the harassing interruptions and discontinuous transitions of daily experience.†

An empirical study by Lowe and Harrold (1972) examined the factors which attract college students to sport events. First they found that those who participated in sport were more likely to purchase the all-sport ticket (rather than a ticket for one sport or one event). In fact, they noted that 61 percent of the students who purchased an all-event ticket also participated in sport, usually at the recreational or intramural level. Lowe and Harrold (1972) also asked all students to rank the factors which were important in influencing their attendance at a specific game. The following were their responses in rank order: (a) the popularity of the sport in the particular social system (i.e., campus); (b) the record of the team; (c) the presence of a superstar; (d) the cost of tickets; (e) the location of the facility; (f) the number of parking and traffic problems to be encountered; (g) the availability of good seats; and, (h) the amount of promotion the event has received. Thus, the most important factors influencing attendance appears to be the presence of a popular sport in a specific subculture and a winning team, preferably with a superstar.

A survey by Harris (1972), based on a probability sample of all households in the United States, sought to determine the motivating factors behind the appeal of professional football. They interviewed 1,614 sport fans 18 years of age and over and found that football was the favorite sport in both cities and towns in every region of the country. When asked what it is about football that appeals to them, 43 percent indicated it was en-

---

* E. Dunning, "Some Conceptual Dilemmas in the Sociology of Sport." Paper presented at the International Workshop on Sociology of Sport, Macolin, Switzerland, September 1969. Reprinted by permission.

† Excerpt from "American Sports: Play and Display," by Gregory P. Stone, copyright © 1955 by Chicago Review. Reprinted by permission.

tertaining and enjoyable; 33 percent reported that it was relaxing and recreational; nine percent liked the excitement and thrills; seven percent indicated that it drew the family together; six percent stated that they watched it because it gave them something to talk about with friends; while another six percent felt that it gave them an outlet (i.e., catharsis) for tensions and pressures. When asked whether they watched football on television alone or with others, 25 percent reported that they watched it alone, 34 percent watched it with one other person, while 18 percent watched it with two or more friends or relatives.

Turning to a discussion of the *effects* of spectator consumption, it will be noted that a number of empirical studies have considered various facets of this problem. Hastorf and Cantril (1954) studied the reactions of spectators to an aggressive Dartmouth–Princeton football game in order to illustrate the readiness of individuals to take sides and express partisanship. They found that this readiness influenced their perceptions of the game, and concluded that people behave according to the expectations which they bring to the situation. In a study of the interaction between two social institutions, the family and national sport, Zurcher and Meadow (1967) speculated that the emotional participation of the baseball spectator in the game is distant and safe. Thus, such vocal statements as "murder the bum" or "kill the umpire" do not have enough of a personal referent to arouse guilt or anxiety. In short, vocal outbursts are a safety valve. In a similar discussion, Elias and Dunning (1970) noted that mimetic excitement can transform itself into nonmimetic excitement wherein men are liable to lose control over themselves and to become a threat, both to themselves and to others.

As an indication of the potential harmful effects of sport consumption, four studies are cited.[2] Lever (1969), in a paper designed to study the soccer player in a society that exhibits sports enthusiasm to an excessive degree, cited a number of incidents related to soccer matches. First, she noted that El Salvador severed diplomatic relations in 1968 with Honduras after the World Cup regional finals were interrupted by riots between the fans of the two countries. Second, she cited a study by the fans of the two countries. Third, she cited a study by Teixeira that indicated the tremendous influence of soccer on an individual's lifestyle. She reported (Lever, 1969: 3) that:

> In the weeks that the Corintheans (the most popular team in Sao Paulo) won, production rose 12.3 percent. In the weeks in which they lost, the number of accidents at work increased by 15.3 percent.

In a theoretical paper, Ingham and Nixon (1970) presented qualitative data which tested two hypotheses generated to explain one facet of soccer fan behavior, namely, the destruction of trains in Britain. They provided tentative support for the hypotheses that the amount of damage or number of arrests following a game was directly related to the ranking of the offender's team, and to their team losing the game. Heinila (1966), in a discussion of intergroup conflict in international sport, hypothesized that the number of enthusiasts and identifiers increases when international competition occurs. This increase in numbers leads to a high in-group identification, or ethnocentrism, which heightens the potential for intergroup conflict. Lang (1970), in a paper based on documentary material, suggested four types of riotous outbursts in sport. Each type was characterized by the predominance of a particular response pattern. These included the response:

1. where a fanatic public extends its support through some form of violent protest against a decision or act viewed as damaging to the player or team it follows,

2. where an acquisitive audience acts collectively in a form of anomic protest against a decision or act it defines as unfair or potentially damaging to themselves.

3. where the crowd seizes an opportunity to indulge individual whims or appetites, resulting, purposefully or accidentally, in destructive behavior, and,

4. where a polarized audience uses the occasion to continue a conflict that has roots outside the sport arena.*

Finally, Dunning (1969), citing the regular fights between the Protestant supporters of Glasgow Rangers, and the Catholic supporters of Glasgow Celtics, stated that such incidents are caused by the fact that the teams involved are representatives of national ethnic or religious groups between which there is a high, pre-existing level of tension.

Three recent field studies have considered the effects of viewing sport events on the aggressive responses of male spectators. Kingsmore (1970) found that spectators at a professional wrestling match displayed significantly less extrapunitive aggression after viewing the event, and that there was a significant precontest to postcontest decrease in their self-reported aggression. The subjects who viewed the professional basketball game showed no change in aggressiveness. In a similar study, Turner (1970)

---

* G. E. Lang, "Riotous Outbursts in Sports Events," a paper presented at the 7th World Congress of International Sociological Association, Varna, Bulgaria (1970). Reprinted by permission.

compared the effects of viewing a college football, basketball, and wrestling contest on the aggressive responses of male spectators. He found that the football and basketball games significantly increased the subject's frequency of aggression from pretest to posttest sessions, whereas, for the three groups, the intensity of aggression did not change. Most recently, Goldstein and Arms (1971) found that while hostility increased after observing a football game, it did not increase after viewing a gymnastic meet.

In concluding this section, four general articles related to consumption are noted. Kleinman (1960) investigated the factors that influence the behavior of high school basketball crowds. He found that the coach and the administration were primarily responsible for the behavior demonstrated at home games. Specifically, the coach was found to be the source of poor sportsmanship if he had a high level of aspiration, if he demonstrated mobility by a readiness to change jobs, and if his level of activity during a game was high. Similarly, the administration was a factor if it did not accept responsibility for procedures at home games; if it did not have an accurate or realistic perception of the role of athletics in the total school program; and if it failed to create a structure which established limits on what constituted acceptable behavior within the school during sporting events.

In a study of vocational school pupils in Germany, Bloss (1970) found a positive relationship (a) between those who are spectators and those who participate, (b) between those who attend games in person and those who use the media to consume sport, and (c) between playing and watching the same sport. Similarly, in a study of Canadian students, Buhrmann and Jarvis (1971) found a positive relationship between athletic participation and attendance at athletic events as a spectator. Finally, Schafer (1969) suggested four consequences of involvement in interscholastic athletics for adolescent fans. These included:

1. a stronger identification with other facets of the school's program,

2. through identification with athletes, more than usual achievement values and behavior,

3. less deviancy in their social behavior in and out of school,

4. a positive effect of participation on school grades.

Socialization into the Role of Sport Consumer

Although there are many social roles inherent in the sport system (cf., Kenyon, 1969), the role of sport consumer is increasingly being learned and enacted by all ages. As with any social role, the earlier it is learned the more likely the role will remain a part of one's life style. While not much is known about how one learns to play this role, some recent efforts have been directed toward this problem.

Although it is not possible at the present time to delineate all of the role expectancies associated with the role of sport consumer, some preliminary attempts have been made. Kenyon (1969: 79) conceptualized the sport consumer as a spectator, viewer, listener, or reader. An additional parameter was noted by Page (1969: 21) in his statement that "spectatorship involves more than merely watching. It involves a great deal of cognitive activity on the part of spectators. It involves knowledge, an increasing knowledge. It involves expertise." Most recently, McPherson (1972) noted that an individual who plays this role may be expected to:

1. invest varying amounts of time and money in various forms of direct and indirect secondary sport involvement,

2. have varying degrees of knowledge concerning sport performers, sport statistics, and sport strategies,

3. have an affective (emotive) involvement with one or more individuals or groups in the sport system,

4. experience, and either internalize or verbalize feelings and mood states while consuming a sport event,

5. employ sport as a major topic of conversation with peers and strangers,

6. arrange their leisure time life-style around professional and amateur sport events.

The process by which this role is learned has been discussed and investigated in recent years. In the earliest attempt to study socialization into sport, Stone (1957) found that the formation of loyalty to a team occurs prior to the formation of a loyalty to a specific player. He also noted that men form these loyalties at an earlier age than women, and that there are class differences as to when these loyalties are initiated. In a paper primarily designed to introduce and test the utility of path analysis for sport sociologists, Kenyon (1970) investigated the causal factors influencing college students to consume major league baseball and the 1964 Summer Olympic games. Although most of the variance in the two models remained unexplained, this initial attempt indicated that the most influential factors leading to baseball consumption (in order of importance) were: sport aptitude, general sport interest in high school, involvement by same-sex peers in sport consumption, and secondary involvement in baseball during high school. The most important factors accounting for consumption of the Mexico Olympic Games included secondary involvement in the previous Olympic Games, and familiarity with the athletes who participated in the Tokyo Olympics.

It would appear that in comparing the baseball with the Olympic data, some differences emerge. For example, general sport interest in high school appears to contribute to secondary involvement in baseball in college, but not to one's later interest in the Olympic Games.

In short, the factors which generate interest in one form of sport, may not be the same factors which generate interest in other forms. Thus, as in primary sport role socialization, it may be necessary to account for considerable sport differences. Moreover, enactment of secondary sport roles as a young adult may not be very heavily dependent upon enactment as an adolescent. For example, being interested in baseball during high school is only weakly related to being interested in baseball in college.

Kelly (1970), in a secondary analysis of some factors hypothesized to be important in the sport socialization of male adolescents in Canada, the United States, and England, found that frequency of attendance at sport events was directly related to family size and indirectly related to age. He also noted that frequency at attendance at winter sport events was positively associated with social class background for Canadian and American adolescents, but negatively associated for British youth.

In a study conducted at the University of Wisconsin (Kenyon and McPherson, 1973), 96 college sophomores and juniors were interviewed to determine the factors accounting for socialization into the role of sport consumer. Although considerable unexplained variance remained, it was found that the major factor accounting for the learning of the role was primary sport involvement, that is, the more the individuals enacted primary sport roles, the greater their interest in other facets of sport, and therefore the greater their consumption of sport.

In an examination of the sport consumer in a small midwestern community, Toyama, (1971) investigated the influence of the mass media on the learning of sport language—specifically, football terminology. She found that 65 percent of her sample spent more than three hours per week consuming sport on television, and, of these, 36 percent spent five hours or more. It was not surprising, then, to find that 65 percent of the sample reported that they learned football terms by watching television. In addition, another 16 percent learned the terms while actually playing the game. Thus, it appears that the mass media, especially television, is an important agent in cognitive sport socialization.

The most recent study to examine the process whereby individuals are socialized into the role of sport consumer was carried out by McPherson (1972). The data for this study were collected by administering a questionnaire to 157 male and 141 female adolescents. It was found that the degree of sport consumer role socialization was positively related to: the number of significant others who consume sport; the frequency of sport consumption by significant others; the amount of interaction with significant others who consume sport; the number of sanctions received from significant others in the family who think about sport; the importance of sport in the parent's hierarchy of leisure-time pursuits; the amount of primary sport involvement by the respondent; and the presence of an opportunity set to engage in sport as a participant.

At the system level sex differences in terms of the relative importance of particular social systems in influencing an individual to learn the role of sport consumer were found. For example, for male adolescents, in order of importance: the peer group, family, and school were the most supportive social systems in learning this role. For females, the peer group, and community were the supportive social systems. That is, the general community was relatively unimportant for the males while the school was unimportant for the female cohort.

The important factors within each social system were identified by means of path analysis. Within the *family system* the most important contributing factors to consumer role socialization were: a value climate which considered sport participation and sport consumption to be a worthwhile leisure time pursuit; a high frequency of interaction with parents and older siblings concerning sport; plus, for males, a high degree of intellectual involvement in sport by family significant others; and, for females, the availability of mass media sources which produce sport, and frequent sport consumption by significant others. For the *peer system* the most important factors were frequent interaction with peers concerning sport, and frequent consumption of sport by the peers. Regarding the *school system*, the most influential factors were high frequency of interaction with school personnel concerning sport and a high degree of primary involvement in elementary and high school sport by the respondent. Finally, within the *community system*, the most important factors leading to consumer role socialization were found to be a high frequency of interaction concerning sport with nonfamily adult significant others (e.g., neighbors, coaches, relatives), plus, for males, positive sanctions from nonfamily significant others for consuming sport, and for females, an opportunity set which enabled them to participate in sport during childhood and adolescence. In short, the process whereby one becomes a sport consumer appears to be a complex phenomenon in that it is sport specific and varies by sex.

THE ECONOMICS OF SPORT CONSUMERISM

Introduction

With the arrival of the age of high mass consumption (Rostow, 1971), it is not surprising that the consumption of sport should also increase. Concomitant with this increased consumption, there has been an increased expenditure of money by spectators to consume sport and by local governments, team owners, and the media, to produce sport. As a result of this exchange, sport has had a profound influence on the economy and has become a source of income for athletes, coaches, officials, writers, television and radio broadcasters, concession operators, manufacturers, and many others who directly or indirectly produce sporting events. For example, the manufacture of sporting goods is a billion dollar industry (Snyder, 1972: 438–442) while clothing manufacturers have found a lucrative market in manufacturing practical, attractive attire to be worn while playing or consuming sport. Similarly, building contractors and architects have become wealthy by building (at a cost of up to $700.00 per seat) or remodeling stadia, games sites, or ski resorts. For example, the recently constructed stadium and arena in Kansas City cost $71 million and $18 million respectively (*Sports Illustrated*, 40, February 4, 1974: 11).

Concomitant with this increasing interdependence between the propensity to consume sport and the economy, the following sections indicate that sport is heavily imbedded in the bureaucratic facets of mass-consuming society and that sport is truly an economic phenomenon. Moreover, as Schecter (1969) noted, winning, losing, and playing the game, may all count far less than counting the money. In the sections that follow the economics of sport consumerism will be considered from the perspective of the consumer, the media, the entrepreneur, the local and federal governments, and the athlete.

The Consumer

The income necessary to operate sport organizations is derived from ticket sales, television and radio network rights, concessions and parking. According to Noll (1971), ticket prices for baseball average $3.10; for football, $6.80; for basketball, $4.17; and for hockey, $4.00. More specifically, Noll reported that the revenue from tickets varies from $1 million to 4.5 million in hockey, all of which goes to the home team. In all cases these averages have increased annually since 1971. In addition to the admission price, spectators must often pay for parking and usually make a purchase at concession stands (40 cents by the average fan per game: Noll, 1971). These two expenditures alone have led to the growth of million dollar enterprises, with most of the profits being retained by the owners or agents to whom they sublet the contract. As reported earlier, over 16.5 million attend professional baseball games each year, while over 10 million pay admission to professional football games. In addition to the money paid for admissions, parking, and refreshments, sport consumers wager as much as an estimated $15 billion a year on sport events (*Time*, January 14, 1974: 47). While none of this money accrues to owners or athletes, it is but another example of the investment consumers are willing to make in organized sport.

The Media

Televised sport has become an integral facet of contemporary life-styles now that over 95 percent of the homes in North America have a television set. Each year television networks in the United States produce over 1,200 hours of sport, or approximately 15 percent of all programs (Neilsen, 1971). Not only does this medium provide the consumer with low-cost entertainment, but it also provides sport organizations with a sizeable and predictable revenue; and it provides sponsors with a known audience at which to direct their promotional efforts. With respect to this latter situation, broadcast media serve as middlemen by collecting revenues from sponsors, deducting their expenses, retaining a profit, and returning the remainder to sport leagues or individual sport teams. In effect, the process works in reverse as the media buys the right to broadcast games from sport organizations, and then sells advertising time slots to sponsors willing to pay the price.

The selling of broadcasting rights is therefore an increasingly important source of revenue for organized sport. In major league baseball, for instance, the range of regular season rights-payments in 1971 was $800,000 to $2.2 million, and for football the range was $1.7 to $1.9 million (Horowitz, 1971). The rights for the 1974 Super Bowl were sold to CBS for $2.75 million which in turn made an estimated $1.2 million in profit by selling commercial time at a rate of $240,000 per minute (Lalli, 1974). The wide interclub differences are accounted for largely by the number of telecasts and the size of the broadcast market. Most recently, the American Broadcasting Corporation won the bid to televise the 1976 Olympic Games, in the United States only, by offering to pay $25 million for the rights. Additional revenue will be derived by the Canadian Olympic Committee from the sale of European and Canadian rights. Because the sale of broadcast rights has become a major source of revenue, sport organizations have become heavily dependent on them and franchises have been shifted primarily to take advantage of a more lucrative television market. In fact,

Horowitz (1971) noted that not a single major league baseball team would have earned a profit in either 1952 or 1970 if broadcast receipts were not available as revenue. Although many have argued that gate receipts would increase if games were not broadcast on television or radio this has proved difficult to verify. Furthermore, sport may be dependent on the media as an interest-generating source to promote attendance at the events.

Horowitz (1971) outlined some of the factors influencing the amount of revenue generated for local and national rights. He reported that the size of local rights was influenced by the philosophy of the owner (e.g., non-profit-oriented teams such as the Boston Red Sox and Chicago Cubs demand lower revenues); the size of the potential viewing population; the amount of interest by fans in the team; the past performance and future prospects of the team; the extent to which there are competitive broadcasts (i.e., from other teams in the city); the extent of the coverage; whether the club is offered a long-term contract (usually by one sponsor); and the bargaining skill of those involved.

In most cases, network television rights far outweigh local rights in importance. The size of national rights is influenced by a sponsor's interest in gaining a monopoly for the league and thereby utilizing an attractive game, either regionally or nationally, to promote its products. Thus, the price the sponsor will pay is greater. From the perspective of the team, each club receives an equal share of the revenue through collective bargaining so that the economic power in the league is more equitably distributed. As a result of this policy, the most successful and powerful teams have lost power. Finally, the size of the national rights continues to increase because of the insatiable demand for sport telecasts on holidays, "prime-time" telecasts, and football double-headers, all of which generate greater revenue for the owners (Horowitz, 1971).

In summary, the local and national sale of television and radio rights benefit both the sport organizations and the sponsors. The rights enable the financially weak and less successful teams to survive and, because the network agreements are frequently long-term, the league gains some financial stability since revenues are independent of team performance. Furthermore, the rights have been instrumental in the promotion and formation of new leagues and the expansion of established leagues, often into smaller cities. For the sponsors, the economic advantage of securing rights is that they gain a monopoly of the audience to which they can direct their advertising. Since the composition of this audience is well known they thereby insure a greater likelihood of reaching the "right" clientele. It is no accident that breweries, gasoline refineries, insurance companies, automobile[3] and cigarette manufacturers are the major sponsors of sport telecasts. In order to gain this right a sponsor would normally pay between

$32,000 and $75,000 for one commercial minute, depending on the time and event. However, the cost per reaching a household ($0.00521) is relatively low since the average audience size for all sport broadcasts is approximately 5,380,000 (Horowitz, 1971). Horowitz also noted that the practice of selling rights has implications for the public in that fewer competitive broadcasts are available and they have fewer viewing choices because of local blackouts.

The Entrepreneur

With few exceptions, the owner of a professional sport organization is an entrepreneur whose ultimate goal is to maximize profits either directly from the sport franchise, or indirectly by using financial losses in the sport domain as a tax deduction for other interests. Although a large amount of capital is required to purchase a franchise, profits are realized by those who have been owners for a number of years. For example, in 1910 the Montreal Canadian Hockey Club was purchased for $7,500. Eleven years later it was sold for $11,000 and in 1935, it was sold again for $165,000. This same organization was purchased in 1957 for an estimated $2.7 million and in 1971, 58 percent of the shares were sold for an estimated $15 million (Kidd and Macfarlane, 1972: 120). This latter exchange represents a 14-year profit of $13.5 million plus annual dividends approaching three million dollars. It is not only the major owners who have profited from professional sport, but also those who purchased stock in this industry. Kidd and Macfarlane (1972: 120–121) reported that 100 shares of Maple Leaf Garden Stock purchased at $100 in 1936 and would be worth $18,750 today.

In this era of team and league expansion, original owners are reaping vast profits by new franchises. For example, an original franchise in the World Hockey Association cost $25,000, yet three years later the cost increased to $200,000. Thus, those who paid out $25,000 now share $200,000 each time a new team is admitted to the league. Yet, this is still a bargain in that the latest National Hockey League franchise cost $6 million. Furthermore, when the New York Islanders entered the league in 1972 they were required to pay an additional $4 million to compensate their cross-town rivals, The New York Rangers. These prices are again modest compared to the minimum entry fee into the National Football League, which is $15 million. This sum is divided equally among the existing teams and is intended to pay for the thirty to forty players received from existing teams. In effect, this means that a second string tackle making $20,000 a year is suddenly worth $400,000 (*Sports Illustrated*, 37, October 23,

1972: 83). (More will be said about the effect of expansion on the players in the next section.)

The amount of profits realized by a professional sport organization is difficult to identify or substantiate. Most of the evidence is based on a combination of ticket prices, attendance, concessions, broadcast revenues, salaries paid, and rental payments. To date, the only comprehensive analysis of team profits has been completed by Noll (1971) in a report given at the Brookings Conference on professional sport. He estimated that total revenues (broadcast rights, total sales) probably range from $2 million to $6.5 million per team. From this revenue, he indicated that basketball and baseball teams realize an annual profit of approximately $200,000 and $500,000 respectively, while professional hockey and football teams may accumulate almost one million dollars per team each year.

In an attempt to determine the factors which influence team profits Noll (1971) employed regression analyses for baseball attendance between 1969 and 1971. He found that the most important factors included winning a pennant, the presence of superstars, the demand for tickets, and the population of the community. More specifically, he noted that winning a pennant has an influence up to two years later if the team stays close to the top of the league standings. He suggested that league attendance is higher, and, so too, profits, if several teams alternate in winning league championships.

With respect to the presence of superstars in baseball, Noll predicted that in a city of 3.5 million, a superstar may add 90,000 fans per season. Finally, an examination of community size indicated that to draw one million fans per year, an average team would have to be located in a metropolitan area of at least two million residents. Similarly, a last-place team would have to be in one of the five largest urban areas to draw one million spectators.

In his conclusion, Noll (1971) stated that, based on the financial data gathered for his study, after-tax profits total about $56 million for all teams in professional baseball, basketball, hockey, and football. Furthermore, he reported that in cities where the demand for sport is great, team profits are between 25 and 50 percent of revenue. Thus, he concluded that most teams could cut ticket prices in half and still realize a profit, that the larger cities could support more sport franchises, and that all sports could expand to smaller cities if gate and broadcast revenues were shared as they are in football.

To this point it has been seen that professional sport is a profitable enterprise. On the surface this appears surprising if one examines the revenue-expense breakdown. It appears that revenue is generated from the sale of tickets and broadcast rights. On the other hand, the major expenses include salaries, travel costs, rental of facilities, equipment, and publicity. If these revenues and expenses were balances, most teams would find it difficult to show a profit. However, a detailed study by Okner (1971) revealed that professional sport organizations receive subsidies from local and federal governments in the form of tax concessions and low rentals of stadiums.

At the local level, Okner (1971) found that of the 77 different stadiums being used by professional sport teams, 54 were publicly owned. Thus, the public actually owns more than 70 percent of all professional sport facilities and rents the facility to the owners, often at a rate below that which a similar nonsport facility would cost. In this way the owners are able to improve their financial position. Okner cites the following reasons as to why communities give this rental break to sport organizations:

1. to enhance the prestige of the community and thereby stimulate economic activity in non-sport enterprises,
2. to generate employment, consumer sales and tax collections from sporting events,
3. to provide recreational opportunities for community residents,
4. to improve the moral of the citizens.

In addition to direct subsidies at the local level there are also indirect subsidies in the form of reduced taxes. For example, Okner (1971) estimated that for 44 of the 54 publicly owned facilities, the property taxes foregone amounted to about $9 million to $12 million. Thus, while the community loses this tax, the subsidy assists in keeping admission prices lower, provides the athletes with higher salaries, and enables the owners to increase their profits.

Professional sport organizations also receive subsidies at the federal level in the form of tax breaks and tax exemptions. In the late 1960s and early 1970s the construction of most new sport facilities was financed by stadium or arena construction bonds which were tax exempt. Okner indicated that if the interest on stadium construction bonds were taxable, federal government revenues would be increased by about $10.2 million annually. Furthermore, he noted that interest on these bonds is usually exempt from state and local taxes, thereby resulting in a further loss of revenue to government agencies. In addition to tax exemptions or construction bonds, the income derived from the sale of players, franchises, or equipment is not taxed as capital gain. Furthermore, team owners are permitted to account for depreciation in player contracts, equipment and facilities when filing tax returns.

By way of summary, Okner estimated that the subsidies to professional sport owners approximately $40 million per year, of which $18 million (45 percent) resulted from publicly owned facilities that are rented at less than full cost and from local property taxes foregone. The remaining $22 million (55 percent) was secured via tax provisions. Further, based on the findings of this study, Okner (1971) concluded that, because of subsidies, needed public services are not undertaken; that the benefits from publicly owned facilities do not accrue to the poor; that the major benefactors of subsidies are the owners; that owners realize profits because they can depreciate player contracts for accounting and tax purposes; that league expansions produce millions in capital gains for existing franchises, yet are not taxed as such; and, that the subsidies have the effect of raising net profits before depreciation from 17 to 30 percent of gross revenue.

In short, professional sport owners are engaged in a profitable enterprise, especially if they are the original owners of a franchise, and do very little to pass the benefits of these subsidies on to the consumer via lower admission prices, or to athletes via higher salaries.

A final factor hypothesized to contribute to team profits is the legislative regulations which enable team owners to monopolize the pool of labor in the marketplace. In order to maximize attendance and interest, uncertainty of outcome must be managed. This can be realized by promoting equality of competition between teams so that one or two teams do not become consistent winners. Jones (1969: 45) indicated that the major element promoting uncertainty is that the players and therefore the clubs "have adopted a system of what could be called cooperative 'handicapping,' the object of which is to try to ensure that individual clubs do not accumulate all the best players and so destroy interclub competition." As a result, team owners have adopted contractual arrangements whereby they agree "to hire only certain prospective players, and not others; to divide the market for prospective players so that only one team negotiates with any one player; and to prohibit competitive bidding for players once they have contracted to play with any one team" (Canes, 1971) in a given league.

These regulations are variously known as the "reserve clause," the "reserve system," the "free agent draft," and the "player draft." While these regulations are designed to distribute playing talent equally among the teams in a league, there is little evidence to support the belief that they do (Canes, 1971). For example, such practices as trading future draft choices for present excess talent helps the rich get richer (e.g., Montreal Canadiens), while the formation of a new league (e.g., WHA, ABA, AFL) generates competition for services and higher salaries to players, thereby decreasing profits. It is not surprising then that owners are ready to merge leagues as soon as a new league threatens to become a viable entity. In a series of papers, El-Hodiri and Quirk (1971, 1972) concluded on the basis of their economic model of professional sport leagues that equalization of playing strengths is generally not consistent with profit maximization by teams. They argued that the initiation of rules to prohibit the sale of player contracts among teams could guarantee convergence over time to equal playing strength.

To summarize, this section has indicated that the large profits derived by team owners is the result of the sale of tickets and television rights, combined with favorable rental agreements and tax provisions provided by local and federal regulations. Furthermore, despite the annual profits, ticket prices continue to increase, thereby generating greater revenues and greater profits.

The Laborer

Although the occupational organization of sport is discussed elsewhere in this volume, this section briefly discusses the economic effects of consumerism for contemporary professional athletes. Until recently the salaries paid to professional athletes were relatively low considering the profits maximized by the owners. This situation held because there was no competition for their services (i.e., a second league), there was little intraleague movement because of the "reserve clause" and "waiver rule" (only in football was it possible to "play out one's option"); because television revenues were small; and because player associations were nonexistent. Nevertheless, although underpaid in comparison to present salaries, at certain stages in their career the salaries of athletes exceeded other males of comparable age and education in the civilian labor force.

Using 1960 Census data, Scoville (1971) found that the average income of active male athletes was higher than for all males in the labor force, and peaked at least a decade ahead of the whole group. He also noted that between 1950 and 1960 the median income of male athletes rose 131 percent compared with 77 percent for the rest of the male labor force. During this same period personal consumption expenditures on spectator sports rose 31 percent. In the late 1960s and early 1970s the average salary in football ranged from $18,600 to $31,300; in baseball from $12,007 to $29,470; and in basketball from $30,000 to $83,000. Scoville found significantly lower salaries in the newer and less-established franchises since many of the employees were castoffs or unproven draftees. Furthermore, employing a regression analysis, he noted that the age of the franchise and the won-loss percentage were the principal factors influencing the salary levels for a football team.

More recently, as a result of competition for services because of expansion and increased television revenues, salaries have risen. That is, the law of supply and demand is now closer to being totally functional in professional sport since there are relatively few highly qualified employees available for the over 95 professional teams representing most professional sports. Eagleson (*The Globe and Mail,* October 2, 1973: 34) reported that the average salary of hockey players has increased from about $30,000 in 1971 to $55,000 in 1973; that those in basketball have risen from an average of $12,000 to $85,000 since the ABA–NBA player war began; and that the average salary in football has dropped from $40,000 to $30,000 since the merger of the two rival leagues.

At the upper end of the wage scale, there are now athletes in the four major professional team sports and in golf, tennis, and boxing whose salary or earnings exceed $200,000 per year (Pietschmann, 1973).

Not only are athletes accuruing larger salaries, but those who are highly successful or who exhibit some element of charisma are able to generate endorsements far exceeding their salary. For example, it has been estimated that while Pelé earns $218,000 per year playing soccer, he earns over $250,000 per year on promotions and outside investments. Similarly, Bobby Orr Enterprises includes a $300,000 summer hockey camp, a car wash, apartment projects, stocks, a farm, and a condominium (Kidd and Macfarlane, 1972: 128). In summary, professional athletes, especially the stars, are extremely well-paid laborers at the present time.

Despite the high salaries, a recurrent theme throughout sport has been that blacks are discriminated against with respect to salary (Ball, 1974). An article in *Time* (April 6, 1970; 79) reported that black athletes, at least those who are highly successful, do not lag behind in salary. They noted that in the 1970 season four of the six baseball players earning over $100,000 were black. An empirical study by Pascal and Rapping (1972) also supports this finding. They found that contrary to popular belief there was no salary discrimination (1968–1969), regardless of position, against black baseball players who had achieved major league status. This conclusion was based on a linear regression model in which the player's salary for the coming season was regressed on his expected ability (based on lifetime batting average, batting average for the previous year, and number of years of experience in the major leagues) and the alternative salary that the player could earn outside baseball. In addition, they reported that, on the average, black salaries were higher than white salaries in the major leagues. They suggested that this occurs for two reasons: (1) major league executives tend to pay players as a function of their demonstrated ability, and (2) baseball may restrict major league opportunities to those blacks who are superior to their white counterparts. Thus, they noted "that there seems to occur equal pay for equal work but unequal opportunity for equal ability" (Pascal and Rapping, 1972: 149).

Scully (1971) also examined this question. Employing the salary data from the Pascal and Rapping study, he found that blacks earn more, position by position, than whites. However, he also noted that whites earn significantly more than blacks for improving their hitting performance, while blacks gain larger salary increments over their playing careers than do white players. He indicated that the salary differentials favoring blacks are due to the "equal pay for superior performance" theme. Thus, based on regression analyses, he stated that to earn $30,000 black outfielders must out-perform whites by about 65 points in their slugging average. In summary, by holding performance levels constant, Scully found that there was salary discrimination against blacks since they earn less for equivalent performance. A more recent study by Mogull (1973), based on 96 questionnaires returned by professional football players, found no significant differences in salaries between blacks and whites among either rookies or veterans.

Similar to contemporary white athletes, the black athlete seeks to pursue entrepreneurial gains while he is an active player and can capitalize on his achieved prestige from the role of professional athlete. Two additional sources of income include a bonus for signing the initial contract with a team, and remuneration received for endorsing or promoting commercial products. Again it has been claimed that access to these benefits is highly dependent on the race of the athlete. For example, Boyle (1963: 129–30) reported that black major league baseball players complained about the lack of commercial endorsements, and about receiving lower bonuses than whites when they signed their initial contract.

It has been additionally charged that only the few black athletes who are potential "stars," and who therefore are highly visible, will receive a bonus comparable to that which a white player might receive. Pascal and Rapping (1972: 135–36) found that the difference in the percent of whites and blacks who received large bonuses was substantial and statistically significant prior to 1958 in professional baseball. However, this difference decreased so that by 1965–1967 it was almost totally eliminated. They interpreted the initial differential to be the result of "a combination of information lag and monopolistic practice rather than bigotry per se" (Pascal and Rapping, 1972: 137). This study should be replicated for other professional sports.

Similarly, it has been argued that only a minority of black athletes are associated with commercial product endorsements, and that those offers they do receive are less lucrative than those received by their white teammates. For example, Pascal and Rapping (1972: 148), citing the equal Employment Opportunity Commission report of 1968, reported that black athletes appeared in only five percent of 351 television commercials associated with New York sport events in the fall of 1966. In a similar analysis, Yetman and Eitzen (1972) found that of the starting players on one professional football team in 1971, eight of eleven whites and only two of thirteen blacks appeared in advertising and media program slots. They hypothesized that this difference may be related to the fact that blacks are relegated to nonglamor positions. For example, for the 17 professional football teams which returned data to the investigators in 1971, 75 percent of all advertising opportunities (television, radio, newspapers) were given to football players who occupied glamorous positions.

A final impact of the rise of consumerism on the players' affluence has been the growth of player associations which demand fringe benefits for the sport employees. For example, expense money during spring training and removal expenses when traded, are now part of professional baseball contracts, while pension plans have been initiated, such that a 15-year veteran in the NFL receives an annual pension of $13,020 at age 55. However, very few athletes are employed in a league for more than five years and thus postcareer opportunities must be available for ex-athletes who enter the civilian labor force in their thirties or forties. Recognizing that many have failed to make the transfer, a group of ex-professional athletes recently instituted an organization entitled the United Athletes Coalition of America (UACA) to help ex-athletes initiate a second career.

To summarize, this final section has indicated that while player salaries and benefits have increased greatly, the employees of professional sport organizations still consider themselves underpaid if they are part of a cartel where competition for their services is restricted by contractual arrangements. Furthermore, only the established "stars" or those with unique charisma derive the benefits of outside endorsements. Finally, within the labor force a number of ex-athletes are attempting to create organizations and conditions whereby the former professional athlete can be resocialized into a second career.

SUMMARY AND CONCLUSIONS

In this chapter the phenomenon of sport consumption has been examined as a social problem. More specifically, this review of literature has considered the degree of direct and indirect consumption; the background factors influencing consumption; the functions, causes and effects of consumption; the process whereby individuals become socialized into the role of sport consumer; and the economics of consumerism from the perspective of the consumer, the media, the entrepreneur, and the athlete.

In conclusion, the evidence indicates that the rate of sport consumption is increasing at such a rate that the phenomenon merits considerable further study, especially at the explanatory rather than the descriptive level.

NOTES

1. In February, 1973 the weekly circulation for *Sports Illustrated* was 2,250,000 and its annual advertising revenue $72.2 million.

2. For a more detailed discussion and exploration see the following chapter by M. Smith.

3. Lalli (1974) reported that the Ford Motor Company annually spends $10 million for advertising during professional football games.

REFERENCES

Ball, D. W.
1974   "Replacement in Work Organizations: Task Evaluation and the Case of Professional Football." *Sociology of Work and Occupations,* **1**: in press.

Bandura, A., and R. H. Walters
1963   *Social Learning and Personality Development.* New York: Holt, Rinehart and Winston, Inc.

Beisser, A.
1967   "Membership in The Tribe." In *The Madness in Sports,* A. Beisser (ed.). New York: Meredith Publishing Company. 124–141.

Berkowitz, L.
1969   "The Frustration-Aggression Hypothesis Revisited." In *Roots of Aggression,* L. Berkowitz (ed.), New York: Atherton Press. 1–29.

Betts, J. R.
1953   "The Technological Revolution and the Rise of Sport, 1850–1900." *Mississippi Valley Historical Review,* **40**: 231–256.

Bloss, H.
1970   "Sport and Vocational School Pupils." *International Review of Sport Sociology,* **5**: 25–58.

Boyle, R. H.
1963   *Sport-Mirror of American Life.* Boston: Little, Brown and Company.

Brill, A. A.
1929   "The Why of the Fan." *North American Review,* **228** (October): 429–434.

Buhrmann, H. G., and M. S. Jarvis
1971   "Athletics and Status: An Examination of the Relationship between Ath-

letic Participation and Various Status Measures of High School Girls."
*Journal of the Canadian Association of Health, Physical Education, and
Recreation*, **37** (January-February): 14–17.

Caillois, R.
1965   "The Structure and Classifications of Games." *Diogenes*, **12**: 62–75.

Canes, M. E.
1971   "Public Policy Towards Professional Team Sport." Paper presented at the
        Brookings Conference on Government and Sport. Washington, D. C. De-
        cember 6–7.

Charnofsky, H.
1973   "Ballplayers, Occupational Image, and the Maximization of Profit." In
        Varieties of Work Experience, P. Stewart and M. Cantor (eds.). Cam-
        bridge: Schenckman.

Dollard, J.
1939   "Culture, Society, Impulse, and Socialization." *American Journal of So-
        ciology*, **45** (July): 50–63.

Dunning, E.
1969   "Some Conceptual Dilemmas In The Sociology of Sport." Paper presented
        at the International Workshop on Sociology of Sport, Macolin, Switzer-
        land (September).

El-Hodiri, M., and J. Quirk
1971   "An Economic Model of A Professional Sports League." *Journal of Politi-
        cal Economy*, **79** (November-December): 1302–1319.
1972   "On The Economic Theory of A Professional Sports League." Social Sci-
        ence Working Paper Number 1 (January), California Institute of Tech-
        nology, Pasadena, California.

Elias, N., and E. Dunning
1970   "The Quest for Excitement in Unexciting Societies." In *The Cross-Cul-
        tural Analysis of Sport and Games*, G. Lüschen (ed.). Champaign, Illinois:
        Stipes Publishing Co. 31–51.

Gerth, H. H., and C. W. Mills
1954   *Character and Social Structure.* London: Routledge and K. Paul.

Goffman, E.
1967   *Interaction Ritual.* Garden City, New York: Doubleday and Co., Inc.

Goldstein, J. H., and R. L. Arms
1971   "Effects of Observing Athletic Contests on Hostility." *Sociometry*, **34**:
        83–90.

Gross, E.
1961   "A Functional Approach to Leisure Analysis." *Social Problems*, **9** (Sum-
        mer): 2–8.

Harris, Lou
1972   "A Survey of the Reactions and Opinions of Professional Football Fans."
        Study Number 2153 (January).

Hastorf, A. H., and H. Cantril
1954 "They Saw A Game: A Case Study." *Journal of Abnormal and Social Psychology*, **44**: 129–134.

Heinila, K.
1966 "Notes on the Inter-Group Conflicts in International Sport." *International Review of Sport Sociology*, **1**: 31–40.

Horowitz, I.
1971 "Professional Sports Broadcasting and the Promotion of Sequential Oligopoly." Presented at the Brookings Conference on Government and Sport. Washington, D.C. December 6–7.

Ingham, A. G., and H. Nixon
1970 "Riots on the Rails—An Axiomatic Approach to Collective Behavior." Paper presented at the 74th Annual Conference of the National College Physical Education Association for Men, Portland, Oregon. December 29.

Jones, J. C. H.
1969 "The Economics of the National Hockey League." *Canadian Journal of Economics*, II (February): 1–20.

Kaelan, E. F.
1968 "The Well-Played Game: Notes Toward An Aesthetics of Sport." *Quest*, **10** (May): 16–28.

Kelly, C.
1970 "Socialization into Sport among Male Adolescents from Canada, England and the United States." Master of Science Thesis, Department of Physical Education, University of Wisconsin.

Kenyon, G. S.
1966 "The Significance of Physical Activity as a Function of Age, Sex, Education and Socio-Economic Status of Northern United States Adults." *International Review of Sport Sociology*, **1**: 41–54.

1968 "Values Held for Physical Activity by Selected Urban Secondary School Students in Canada, Australia, England and the United States." Report of U.S. Office of Education, Contract S-276. Washington: Educational Resources Information Center.

Kenyon, G. S., and B. D. McPherson
1973 "Becoming Involved in Physical Activity and Sport: A Process of Socialization." Chapter 12 in *Physical Activity: Human Growth and Development*, G. L. Rarick (ed.). New York: Academic Press.

Kidd, B., and J. Macfarlane
1972 *The Death of Hockey*. Toronto: New Press.

Kingsmore, J. M.
1970 "The Effect of a Professional Wrestling and a Professional Basketball Contest upon the Aggressive Tendencies of Spectators." In *Contemporary Psychology of Sport*, G. S. Kenyon (ed.). Chicago: The Athletic Institute. 311–315.

Kleinman, S.
1960   "A Study to Determine the Factors that Influence the Behavior of Sports Crowds." Ph.D. Dissertation, Department of Physical Education, The Ohio State University.

Lalli, F.
1974   "And Now For the Pre-Game Scores." *Rolling Stone*, **155**, February 28: 40–41.

Lang, G. E.
1970   "Riotous Outbursts in Sports Events." Paper presented at the Seventh World Congress of the International Sociological Association, Varna, Bulgaria (September).

Lever, J.
1969   "Soccer: Opium of the Masses." *Trans-Action, 7* (December): 36–43.

Lowe, B., and R. D. Harrold
1972   "The Student as Sport Consumer." Paper presented at the 75th Annual Meeting of the National College Physical Education for Men, New Orleans (January).

Loy, J. W.
1968   "The Nature of Sport: A Definitional Effort." *Quest,* **10** (May: 1–15).

McMurtry, J.
1972   "Economics of International Sport." *McLean's Magazine* (January).

McPherson, B. D.
1972   "Socialization into the Role of Sport Consumer: A Theory and Causal Model." Ph.D. Dissertation, University of Wisconsin.

Mogull, R.
1973   "Football Salaries and Race: Some Empirical Evidence." *Industrial Relations,* **12** (February): 109–112.

Nielsen, A. C.
1971   *A Look At Sports.* Chicago: Media Research Division, A. C. Nielsen Company.
1972   *A Look At Sports.* Chicago: Media Research Division, A. C. Nielsen Company.

Noll, R. G.
1971   "Attendance, Prices and Profits in Professional Sports." Presented at the Brookings Conference on Government and Sport. Washington, D.C. December 6–7.

Okner, B. A.
1971   "Direct and Indirect Subsidies To Professional Sports." Paper presented at the Brookings Conference on Government and Sport. Washington, D.C. December 6–7.

Page, C. H.
1969   "Reaction to Stone Presentation." In *Aspects of Contemporary Sport Sociology,* G. S. Kenyon (ed.). Chicago: The Athletic Institute. 17–27.

Pascal, A. H., and L. A. Rapping
1972 "The Economics of Racial Discrimination in Organized Baseball." In *Racial Discrimination In Economic Life*, A. H. Pascal (ed.). Lexington, Massachusetts: D. C. Heath and Company. 119–156.

Pietschmann, R. J.
1973 "Salaries In Professional Sports." *Mainliner* (December): 18.

Rostow, W. W.
1971 *The Stages of Economic Growth*. London: Cambridge University Press.

Rousseau, E. L.
1958 "Great American Ritual: Watching Games." *Nation*, October 4: 188–191.

Schafer, W.
1969 "Some Social Sources and Consequences of Interscholastic Athletics: The Case of Participation and Delinquency." In *Aspects of Contemporary Sport Sociology*, G. S. Kenyon (ed.). Chicago: The Athletic Institute. 29–44.

Schecter, L.
1969 *The Jocks*. New York: Paperback Library.

Scoville, J. G.
1971 "Labour Aspects of Professional Sport." Paper presented at the Brookings Conference on Government and Sport. Washington, D.C. December 6–7.

Scully, G. W.
1971 "The Economics of Discrimination in Professional Sports: The Case of Baseball." Paper presented at the Brookings Conference on Government and Sport. Washington, D.C. December 6–7.

Snyder, R.
1972 "The Sporting Goods Market at the Threshold of the Seventies." In *Sport In The Socio-Cultural Process*, M. Hart (ed.). Dubuque, Iowa: W. C. Brown Company. 438-442.

Spinrad, W.
1970 "Functions of Spectator Sports." Paper presented at the Seventh World Congress of the International Sociological Association, Varna, Bulgaria (September).

Stone, G. P.
1955 "American Sports—Play and Dis-Play." *Chicago Review*, 9 (Fall): 83–100.
1957 "Some Meanings of American Sport." Proceedings of the National College Physical Education Association for Men, 60: 6–29.

Toyama, J. S.
1971 "The Language of Sport: A Study of the Knowledge of Sport Terminology as a Function of Exposure to the Mass Media." Master of Arts Thesis, Department of Physical Education, University of Wisconsin.

Voigt, D. Q.
1971 "America's Leisure Revolution." In *America's Leisure Revolution*, D. Q. Voigt (ed.). Reading, Pennsylvania: Albright College Book Store. 20–40.

Weiss, P.

1969   *Sport: A Philosophic Inquiry.* Carbondale, Illinois: Southern Illinois Press.

Yetman, N. R., and D. S. Eitzen

1971   "Black Athletes on Intercollegiate Basketball Teams: An Empirical Test of Discrimination." In *Majority and Minority: The Dynamics of Racial and Ethnic Relations*, N. R. Yetman (ed). Boston: Allyn and Bacon. 509–517.

Zurcher, L. A., and A. Meadow

1967   "On Bullfights and Baseball: An Example of Interaction in Social Institutions." *Journal of Comparative Sociology*, **8**: 99–117.

Chapter 7
Sport and Collective Violence

Michael D. Smith
Departments of Physical Education and Sociology
York University
(Downsview, Ontario, Canada)

Michael D. Smith

Birth Place: Kingston, Ontario, Canada

Age: 36

Birth Order: Oldest, one brother, one sister

Formal Education:

B.A., University of Toronto	1960
B.P.E., McMaster University, Ontario	1965
M.S., University of Wisconsin	1967
Ph.D., University of Wisconsin	1972

Present Position:

Assistant Professor, Departments of Physical Education and Sociology, York University

Professional Responsibilities:

Currently teaching courses in Sociology of Sport, Introduction to Sociology, Outdoor Education Programme

Scholarly Interests:

Determinants of individual and collective violence in sport and in other spheres, occupational careers of pro athletes.

Professional Accomplishments:

Articles published (or forthcoming) in *International Review of Sport Sociology, Canadian Review of Sociology and Anthropology.*

Contributed articles in several books of readings on Sport and Society.

Report on the Effects of Hockey Violence for the Government of Ontario Commission on Violence in Amateur Hockey, May, 1974.

Hobbies:

Reading, building things, playing with my children. ← ooh err

Sport Activities:

Participant: squash, bicycle riding, canoe tripping.

Spectator: hockey, football.

Played on University of Toronto Varsity Football Team, 1959.

Most Recent Books Read:

Light:

Louis Nizer	*The Implosion Conspiracy*

Intellectual:

Marion Starkey	*The Devil in Massachusetts*
Herman Hesse	*The Glass Bead Game*

INTRODUCTION

Collective behavior has traditionally referred, in the broadest sense, to those actions of collectivities that are spontaneous, volatile, and transitory in contrast to behavior that is conventional, routine, and predictable. The concept has encompassed such diverse phenomena as fad, fashion, rumor, mania, stampede, panic, lynching, riot, revolution, propaganda, public opinion, and social and religious movements of all sorts. Although social scientists have often disagreed on definitions and boundaries of the field, and although increasingly the similarities rather than the dissimilarities of collective and institutional behavior have been emphasized, most contemporary writers acknowledge that the former involves at least a ". . . partial derailment of social interaction from its normatively structured course" (Lang and Lang, 1968: 556).

Perhaps more than any other area of sociology or social psychology collective behavior suffers from a dearth of carefully constructed empirical research. One reason for this is the resistance of many of its forms to the measurement techniques commonly employed by social scientists. Another is the strong emotional reactions and ideological commitments aroused by its more dramatic variants such as crowd outbursts. These sentiments, needless to say, hamper objective analysis.

It is not surprising, then, that nineteenth century notions about "mob psychology" linger and that some writers continue to describe collective episodes as if they were the "work of mysterious forces" (Smelser, 1962: 1). Nor is it surprising that American social scientists, who tend to espouse "liberal-to-left" social and political philosophies (Marx, 1972), sometimes overrationalize the motives and conduct of those caught up in collective behavior.

Despite these problems, more sophisticated theories, grounded in reliable empirical data, increasingly are undermining some of the staple notions propagated by earlier thinkers. Lang and Lang (1968: 564) propose a blueprint for research in the area.

The special mystique with which the crowd has so often been invested
—that of a pathological force compelling men to act contrary to their
usual behavior—must finally be put to rest and be replaced by a sociological analysis. The main task for such analysis is to find links between the specific content of the impulses, fears, grievances, and demands that characterize the participants in any crowd episode and the
conditions under which the crowd comes to form and the goals it pur-
sues. The conceptualization of crowd episodes in terms of collective
processes emphasizes the relationship of such apparently irrational
outbursts to inadequacies and strains in the social structure. Crowd behavior needs to be studied as collective problem solving activity within
the larger context of social and organizational breakdown and change.*

In short, the Langs underscore the importance of examining both the social structural conditions from whence collective behavior arises as well as
its dynamics. It is the latter that preoccupied most investigators until the
1960's.

Overview

Although the concept of collective behavior covers a wide spectrum of
meanings, this chapter is concerned mainly with violence in one type of
collectivity: the crowd. In the first section, the present state of research in
the field is discussed. In the second, conceptions of the crowd are put into
historical perspective. Third, an overview of mainstreams in collective behavior theory is presented. And fourth, an examination is undertaken of
the social structural determinants, dynamics, and consequences of collective violence in sport.

RESEARCH ON CROWD BEHAVIOR: NOTES ON THEORY
AND METHOD

Comments on the sad state of research on collective behavior often preface
works on the subject. Despite great strides forward in recent years, such
indictments are sound for several reasons. First, much of what passes for
theory is *not* in any rigorous sense of the word. And second, knowledge
concerning collective processes per se is more speculative than scientific.
These issues are dealt with below, together with a discussion of the merits
of continuous archival materials as sources of data on crowd behavior.

---

* K. Lang and G. Lang, "Collective Behavior," in *International Encyclopedia of
the Social Sciences*, D. L. Sills (ed.). (New York: Macmillan, 1968) **2**; 564. Reprinted by permission.

Collective Behavior Theory

Blumer's (1957: 128) statement of more than a decade ago decrying the "... crude descriptive level of knowledge and the relative lack of theory" in the literature on collective behavior is still pertinent. Part of the problem lies in the loose usage of the concept "theory." "Theory" is often misused to describe typologies and taxonomies (which abound in the study of collectivities). Such classificatory schemes are useful, of course, in indicating the boundaries of a field, providing a perspective from which to view it, indicating key variables, and suggesting how the variables should be treated empirically (Loy, 1971). Classifications, moreover, are an essential element of theory construction. But they are not sociological theory which, strictly speaking, consists of "... lawlike propositions about society that can be supported by evidence" (Zetterberg, 1965: 22).[1] Smelser's "value-added theory" of collective behavior, for instance (generally recognized to be the most systematic, comprehensive, and useful treatment of the field), is more taxonomy than theory. Like earlier "theorists," Smelser appears to have approached the subject as "a formidable problem of definition and classification" (Currie and Skolnick, 1972: 63). What is more, to come under the heading of theory requires that there be specification of the best possible explanation of the relationship of one phenomenon to another and that this explanation is testable and, hence, refutable (Abel, 1970). The breadth and lack of precision of Smelser's scheme may prohibit refutation (Manning, 1970).

A second difficulty lies in the plausible ex post facto interpretations which predominate in research on crowd behavior and which sometimes pass as theory. After-the-fact explanations, unfortunately, sometimes violate the nature of the empirical world; for instance, meanings imposed upon observations by scientists may not be congruent with the meanings for the actors. A related but more subtle problem arises when investigators, questionnaires in hand, seem inclined to accept uncritically the legitimations of crowd members for their own behavior after it has occurred (e.g., that it was politically motivated), thereby leaving the researcher open to the danger of converting the "ideology of the participants into a theory for the investigator" (Smelser, 1972b: 80).

This is not to say that meanings people impute to their own behavior should be discounted. To the contrary, the actor's definition of the situation is what impels his actions, and it is this definition that should be under study. It is to say that uncritical acceptance of the explanations of the participants is problematic, especially in the context of an emotion-charged, media-saturated event such as a riot.

W. I. Thomas pointed out long ago that there is a rivalry between the actor's spontaneous "definition of the situation" and the one society has provided for him. Further, it is possible to view the actor's legitimation as a consequence of his behavior rather than a cause of it. Individuals sometimes make decisions randomly, on a nonlogical basis, and then find themselves having to acquire a supportive rationale (if only on a subliminal level) which affirms the wisdom of their decisions (Hornbach, 1970). As Berger (1963: 23) astutely observes: "... the first wisdom of sociology is this—things are not as they seem ... social reality turns out to have several layers of meaning."

A third problem stems from the traditional hiatus between ad hoc middle range theories of collective behavior and general sociological theory, a situation caused in part by the failure of the former to break away from "special explanations" (Weller and Quarantelli, 1973: 666). More specifically, they argue (1973: 673) that the sociological study of collective behavior, despite recent advances, still is

> identified or conceptualized in terms that can most clearly be seen as properties of individuals, not collectivities. ... Thus, collective behavior is assumed to be described and explained adequately by accounting for how a single individual in a given situation could pursue the course of action observed of the collectivity as a whole.[*]

They suggest alternatively a fully social level conceptual framework which may prove fruitful in the development of theory in the area.

A major cause, then, of the underdevelopment of collective behavior theory is that a "dominant theoretical paradigm has not been achieved" (Manning, 1973: 285). But in addition, insofar as theory ought to be grounded in data, part of the problem lies in the nearly insurmountable difficulties peculiar to research in this area.[2]

Research on Collective Processes

Most research on collective violence focuses either on conditions preceding the behavior or on the results of the behavior, but seldom on actual crowd process (Berk, 1972). It is relatively easy to collect information on conditions antecedent to a riot because most of the measuring techniques commonly used by sociologists are applicable. For example, demographic characteristics of the population of rioters can be determined (Lieberson and Silverman, 1965). Similarly, the results of a collective episode are easily ascertained since "crowds usually leave plenty of data in their wake" (Berk, 1972: 113); thus, the Kerner Commission (1968) was able to de-

---

[*] J. M. Weller and E. L. Quarantelli, "Neglected Characteristics of Collective Behavior," *American Journal of Sociology* 79 (1973: 665–685). Reprinted by permission of The University of Chicago Press.

termine the extent of property damage, number of people involved, etc., in the 1967 urban riots in the United States.

The actual process of crowd behavior, in contrast, is extremely difficult to study for several reasons (Berk, 1972): First, the time and place of collective outbursts are unpredictable making it difficult for interested observers to be on the scene. When, on occasion, trained observers are present, the risk of personal injury tends to persuade many to make their observations from a distance. Events, moreover, usually occur quickly and over a wide geographical area, and many events may occur at once. Second, participants in the crowd are unlikely to stop what they are doing to cooperate with the investigator. Third, the accounts of crowd members who are interviewed, during or following the disorder, are especially vulnerable to conscious or unconscious distortion since members often have "very salient vested interests in the interpretation of the phenomenon" (Berk, 1972: 113). (The dramatic nature of crowd outbreaks, of course, excites strong emotions which add to any distortion.) Fourth, experimental control is almost impossible to achieve. Fifth, it is hard to sample from populations of collective episodes.

These difficulties, together with the fact that crowd processes per se leave few traces, force the student of collective dynamics to rely on journalistic accounts and on reconstructions based on these accounts, and to interpolate from related research. For all these reasons, the crowd provides a poor prototype for collective behavior in general; nevertheless, it has often been used as such with the result that mistaken notions of the crowd have led to several erroneous stereotypes about the entire spectrum of collective phenomena (Couch, 1968).

Despite the lack of data on process, some investigators insist on concentrating their analyses on it. Such analyses sometimes ". . . more closely resemble a projective test than an examination of collective behavior . . . descriptions of crowds often take on an other-worldly flavor because we have little data with which to anchor crowds to this world" (Berk, 1972: 114). In short, researchers extrapolate forward from data antecedent to crowd behavior and backward from the visible results of it, and speculate on the intervening processes. Berk's injunction that "students of crowd behavior should . . . wherever possible seek the original data, and not interpretations of that data" is well-founded but difficult to put into practice. It is not hard to see, then, why the state of data collection and theory on collective processes remains relatively undeveloped.

Nonreactive Research: A Rationale for the Use of the "Running Record"

Investigators of collective violence appear more and more to be turning for data to continuous archival materials such as the daily newspaper.[3] As

Webb et al. (1966: 75) note: "The variety, texture, and scope of this enormous data pool have been neglected for too long." Since a sizeable portion of the meager amount of research on sport crowd violence is based on newspaper reports, it is important to examine the advantages and pitfalls inherent in using this information in social scientific research.

The advantages of using what Webb and his colleagues call the "running record" are several: It offers a massive source of data for many areas of research. In most cases, it is readily available and inexpensive to obtain. It is easy to sample, and population restrictions associated with it often can be ascertained and controlled by reference to known population characteristics such as contained in census materials. The problem of "selective survival" usually is minimal. There is low risk of "reactive measurement error": the respondent and interviewer contaminants always present in the standard tools of social science, the interview and the questionnaire. Most important, perhaps, is the potential for historical analysis contained in the "running record," analysis ". . . in which one may test a hypothesis by subjecting it to the rigor of evaluation in multiple settings and at multiple times" (Webb et al., 1966: 87).[4]

Many problems, on the other hand, confront the researcher who generates his data from the newspaper or other continuous archival sources. One class of problems is that of "selective deposit": fluctuations in the amount of reportage of events. It has been observed, for example, that the frequency of riots at a given point in time affects the probability that riots occurring shortly after will be reported (Lieberson and Silverman, 1965). Regional biases in coverage may occur: In a study of political violence in the United States, 1818–1968, in which data were obtained chiefly from the *New York Times*, Levy (1969) notes that "mild riots" in the New York and mid-Atlantic region were more likely to be reported than equally severe riots elsewhere. Similarly, there is a regional bias in Smith's (1973*b*) study of sport crowd violence during the decade 1963–1973. The problem of "selective deposit," then, hampers accurate statement of a sample's representativeness.

Another type of difficulty is the contamination of comparisons over time by changes in the size, circulation, and character of the "running record," and by shifts in population characteristics. First, the larger the newspaper and the wider its circulation, the greater the probability that a given event will be reported. In addition, most newspapers take ideological stances which may affect both volume and tone of reportage on a given subject. Changing social conditions, such as the climate of interethnic relations, may affect the way information is presented. Second, changes in the composition of a critical group—say, journalists—may introduce distortions to time-series comparisons. These kinds of contaminants, although usually controllable, pose major difficulties in research covering extended periods of time.

Perhaps the most obvious difficulty in the use of continuous archival material is distortion and incompleteness in reporting. Newspaper stories of riots and other dramatic happenings are prone to exaggeration: "scare" headlines unsupported by mild stories that follow (Kerner, 1968: 364); and maximization of number of participants, injuries, deaths, etc. (Levy, 1969). These inaccuracies, however, are probably not as rampant as some would have it. The Kerner Commission (1968: 364) checked the reliability of 3,779 newspaper articles on 1967 racial disorders by interviewing media people, police, and ghetto residents, and by cross-checking facts against other newspapers and newsmagazines. It concluded that the articles, on the whole, were ". . . calm, factual, and restrained." Another possible source of distortion stems from faulty information released to the press: During the 1967 disturbances in the United States, officials, usually inexperienced in dealing with civil disorder, tended to give overestimates of the magnitude of the disturbances (Kerner, 1968: 364). A final problem is the brevity of some accounts. This, fortunately, can be alleviated by turning to other sources; Lieberson and Silverman (1965) supplemented *New York Times* reports of riots with information from local newspapers.

It is important not to overstate the case for the "running record." The Webb et al. monograph, among other things, is a plea for multiple operationism. Webb and his colleagues note correctly that no social science research method is without bias, but they lament especially the overdependence upon a single fallible method, namely, the interview and the questionnaire. They argue that interviews, questionnaires, and any other means of acquiring data must be supplemented by methods which test the same hypotheses but which have *different* methodological weaknesses. They state that

> Once a proposition has been confirmed by two or more independent measurement processes, the uncertainty of its interpretation is greatly reduced. The most persuasive evidence comes through a triangulation of measurement processes. If a proposition can survive the onslaught of a series of imperfect measures, with all their irrelevant error, confidence should be placed in it.*

In summary, theory and research in collective behavior are underdeveloped relative to other substantive areas of sociology. This seems due

---

* E. Webb et al., *Unobtrusive Measures: Nonreactive Research in the Social Sciences* (Chicago: Rand McNally, 1966), p. 3. Reprinted by permission.

mainly to special difficulties in obtaining reliable empirical data. Research on the crowd, moreover, has carried from the start a heavy load of value-judgements; the effect of these on crowd theories is considered next.

COLLECTIVE VIOLENCE IN HISTORY: THE INFLUENCE OF SOCIAL AND POLITICAL PHILOSOPHIES ON THE STUDY OF THE CROWD

The exotic and often threatening nature of crowd behavior has attracted the attention of social observers at least since the time of Aristotle (Bell, 1956). It was the French Revolution, however—particularly the violent activities of the "sans culottes"—that planted an enduring fear of the crowd in the minds of the European middle and upper classes, a fear which, in turn, stimulated the development by nineteenth century conservative thinkers of the field initially known as "crowd psychology" (Allport, 1954; Mazlish, 1970).

Nineteenth century theories of the crowd carried an uncommonly heavy freight of value judgements—a characteristic that did not disappear during the adoption of the field by American sociologists in the twentieth century. But in this process, many of the European concepts underwent a subtle transformation in which they were rendered compatible with the social and political milieu of America. To ignore the historicist flavor of crowd theories is to run the risk of failing to recognize and confront the preconceptions present-day social scientists bring to their work. E. G. Boring (1963: 5) states this position succinctly:

> The best fact is one that is set in a context, that is known in relation to other facts, that is perceived in part in the context of its past, that comes into understanding as an event which acquires significance because it belongs in a continuous dynamic sequence.

The European Perspective

Precursors of formal theories of crowd behavior are found in the writings of late eighteenth and early nineteenth century conservatives, such as Burke, Bonald, and de Maistre; writers who were directly opposed to the rationalistic and individualistic conception of man held by Locke, Voltaire, Bentham, and other philosophers of the Enlightenment. The former group foresaw in the weakening of traditional social ties that accompanied the decline of divine-right monarchy, aristocracy, and the Church in the aftermath of the Revolution ". . . the creation of a mass of alienated and isolated individual atoms, an easy mark for the demagogue offering political panaceas for salvation in this world" (Bramson, 1961: 15). These "individual atoms" were, in short, potential crowd-men.

Several studies on the crowd appeared in Europe at the turn of the century. Although seeming to come from nowhere, they were usually inspired by sentiments of the sort expressed above and appear to have been aimed at "discrediting not only the lower orders, with their claims for increased political power through the general franchise, but also in some cases the whole liberal scheme of parliamentarianism" (Bramson, 1961: 53). The chief writers in this mold were the Frenchmen Gustave Le Bon (1960) and Gabriel Tarde (1901), and the Italian Scipio Sighele (1901). The main thrust of their arguments was against the rationalistic aspect of the liberal faith which was attacked by undermining the concept of individual consciousness. The crowd-man was not conscious of his acts.[5]

Although Le Bon, Sighele, and Tarde wrote about the same time, history has accorded Le Bon the credit for popularizing the study of crowd behavior. His book, *La Foule,* first published in 1895 and translated into English the following year, established an excessively negative and psychological image of the crowd which some claim (Currie and Skolnick, 1972) persists to this day. Like many of his contemporaries, Le Bon was preoccupied with discovering the "eternal laws" of human behavior, one of which was "the futility of rationality" in societal affairs: An idea did not prevail because it was true, but because psychological mechanisms like "mental contagion," having nothing to do with reason, caused ideas to penetrate into the unconscious where they became the basis for action. It was through "mental contagion" (which he compared vaguely to hypnotism) that seemingly rational individuals were transformed in the crowd into brutes. By the same process crowd members became aware of a unanimity which led to intolerance, feelings of invincible power, and a sense of irresponsibility. The crowd, furthermore, was characterized by emotionality: Its conduct was sudden, extreme, intense, simple, and changeable (Le Bon, 1895; 1960; Stoetzel, 1968).

Le Bon's career had three overlapping phases: anthropology and archeology, experimental and theoretical natural science, and social psychology.[6] Much of what he learned in his first two phases he transposed to his analysis of the crowd. Ever concerned with establishing hierarchies, he established, for example, a list of "inferior beings" based on psychological criteria, which he claimed in some cases to confirm on anatomical grounds (variations in brain size). This curious list of "inferior beings" included animals, the insane, socialists, women, children, the Latin "races," degenerates, primitives, the crowd, and the individual in it (Stoetzel, 1968). Unhappily, as Stoetzel (1968: 84) notes in his biography:

It was by the most reckless, the most false, and the most harmful of his theories that Le Bon exerted his greatest influence, in France and even more so abroad. . . . Ironically, the fame of some men is based on their mistakes, and thereby confronts their critics with a painful dilemma: either to blame such a man for the very things that made him popular or to praise him for contributions that would not have existed were it not for his mistakes.*

In the next few decades, Bramson (1961) notes, several isolated books on the crowd appeared written by Europeans. Trotter, Freud, and Mc-Dougall, among others, appeared for the most part to echo in one way or another the themes of Le Bon: Trotter (1919) wrote of the "herd instincts" of crowds; Freud (1922) attempted to generalize the results of his study of individual psychopathology to mobs and crowds; McDougall (1927: 45) described the crowd as:

> . . . excessively emotional, impulsive, violent, fickle, inconsistent, ir-resolute and extreme in action, displaying only the coarser emotions and the less refined sentiments; extremely suggestible, careless in de-liberation, hasty in judgment, incapable of any but the simpler and imperfect forms of reasoning; easily swayed and led, lacking in self-consciousness, devoid of self-respect and of sense of responsibility, and apt to be carried away by the consciousness of its own force, so that it tends to produce all the manifestations we have learnt to expect of any irresponsible and absolute power. Hence its behavior is like that of an unruly child or an untutored passionate savage in a strange situation, rather than like that of its average member; and in the worst cases it is like that of a wild beast rather than like that of human beings.†

There had already begun in the early part of the century a transference from Europe to America of interest in what has come to be known as col-lective behavior (accompanying the rise of sociology in general in the latter country.) But the United States, lacking a feudal tradition and having from the beginning a liberal-democratic climate, offered barren ground for the development of an antidemocratic social psychology of the crowd. Al-though some of the traditions of Le Bon were perpetuated in the move, in general, the meanings of the European concepts were transformed or new concepts were developed more in keeping with the liberal tradition of America.[7]

---

* J. Stoetzel, "Le Bon: Gustave" in *International Encyclopedia of the Social Sci-ences*, D. L. Sills (ed.). (New York: Macmillan, 1968) 9; 84. Reprinted by permis-sion.

† W. McDougall, *The Group Mind* (New York: Cambridge University Press, 1927), p. 45. Reprinted by permission.

The American Perspective

The change ↑   distinctly American perspective on the crowd was not immediately a   ologist Edward A. Ross (1908), in the first textbook to be   hology, took up the Frenchmen's tone of
"melodrar   954: 31). Ross appeared to accept
the view   d the basis for social life,
thereby   liberalism.[8] At the
same ti   of the "bourgeois
virtue   ak with the European   on of research into
crow

na   rt E. Park coined the
te   n a pioneer sociology
                                studied at the turn of
                                erest in the crowd was
                                nctly American perspec-
                                discerned. Like his Euro-
                                er modernization of tradi-
tio   on of individual men.

   Park u   ew that isolated individuals,
in their gropings   led to form new associations
which had constructive po   he evolutionary concept of the
life-cycle of institutions: The   crowds, mobs, and masses[10]
represented to Park the beginnings of new institutions arising to meet
needs unsatisfied under the old (Bramson, 1961). Park's student at the University of Chicago, Herbert Blumer, developed this concept further in an
article first published in 1939 which "now seems destined to become a
classic" (Shibutani, 1970: vii). The appearance of what Blumer called "elementary collective groupings" (more specifically, the acting and the expressive crowd, the mass, and the public) signified a process of social change.
"They have the dual character of implying the disintegration of the old
and the appearance of the new. They play an important part in the development of new collective behavior and of new forms of social life"
(Blumer, 1939; 1951: 196).[11]
   A second shift in perspective took place in the period of American sociology between the World Wars: Whereas most European sociologists
were perenially concerned with the association of crowds and masses with
a specific group in a presumably fixed system of classes—"the social problem"—the field in the United States began to be viewed in terms of process
rather than structure. This, of course, was largely because Park, Blumer
and their students at the University of Chicago (the center for the diffusion

of most sociological ideas at the time) tended to perceive both self and society in processual terms. Blumer stated his predilection clearly:

> ... the likening of human group life to the operation of a mechanical structure, or to the functioning of an organism, or to a system seeking equilibrium, seems to me to face grave difficulties in view of the formative and explorative character of interaction as the participants judge each other and guide their own acts by that judgement.*

The study of collectivities in the United States, then, underwent two major changes prior to the 1960's: First, the sociopolitical climate of that country caused collective episodes to be viewed generally in a more rationalistic and positive way than was the case in Europe[12] (although Le Bon's imagery remained in the work of some). Second, Americans began to perceive collective behavior in terms of process not structure.

In the 1960's, new theoretical frameworks appeared emphasizing the importance of social structural "strains" as the root causes of all collective behavior (e.g., Smelser, 1962) and stressing its similarities, rather than its dissimilarities, to conventional behavior. The new frameworks, together with a spate of empirical data on the urban riots of the decade, did much to dispel the mystery which had always characterized the field. At the same time they prompted a research balance between the social structural determinants of crowd conduct and its dynamics.

Despite recent developments, the values which many present-day social scientists bring to their research continue, in the eyes of some critics, to color the former's images of crowd behavior. Currie and Skolnick (1972: 61–62) state that the "antidemocratic biases in 'crowd' theory were modified but not abolished" in the transference to American social science. They accuse Smelser (1962), in particular, of adopting an "official" or "managerial" bias toward collective behavior, one that "tends to discredit the claims and perspectives of the participants while uncritically accepting those of constituted authorities and agents of social control."

In a rejoinder, Smelser (1972) rejects this interpretation and takes Currie and Skolnick to task for uncritically accepting what people say they are doing as explanations of their own behavior, a methodological position apparent in their book, *The Politics of Protest* (1969). Marx (1972), in turn, notes the current sympathy of Currie and Skolnick—and American sociologists in general—for rioters who are seen uniformly as ideologically motivated. While basically agreeing with this interpretation of riot data,

---

* H. Blumer, "Psychological Import of the Human Groups," in *Group Relations at the Crossroads*, M. Sherif and M. D. Wilson (eds.). (New York: Harper & Row, 1953), p. 199. Reprinted by permission.

Marx suggests that the pendulum has swung too far away from Le Bon causing the neglect of "issueless riots" in which critiques of the existing order and beliefs that violence will bring needed social change are relatively unimportant as motivating factors.

Perspectives on the crowd, then, have been, and continue to be liberally flavored with ideological bias of one kind or another. The handful of scholarly investigations and "official reports" of riots involving sport crowds are not, by and large, exceptions; thus, these issues will again arise. Before turning to sport, however, the major theories of collective behavior are next examined.

MAINSTREAMS IN COLLECTIVE BEHAVIOR THEORY

There are at least four major orientations to the study of collective behavior: the contagion, convergence, emergent norm, and value-added approaches.[13] A brief overview and critique of each theory completes the underpinnings upon which a meaningful analysis of sport crowd behavior can be based.

Contagion Theories

Turner and Killian (1972: 12) note that most study of collective behavior "has emphasized some form of contagion whereby unanimous, intense feelings and behavior, at variance with usual predispositions, are induced among the members of a collectivity." The roots of this approach are found in Gustave Le Bon's (1960) nineteenth century work on the crowd. According to Le Bon's "law of mental unity," individuals in the crowd become possessed of a "collective mind" through a process of emotional "contagion" akin to hypnotism. The anonymity of large members, which leads to personal loss of responsibility, facilitates this process. In his (1960: 27) psychological crowd, he writes:

> Whoever be the individuals that compose it, however like or unlike be their mode of life, their occupations, their character, or their intelligence, the fact that they have been transformed into a crowd puts them in possession of a sort of collective mind which makes them feel, think, and act in a manner quite different from that in which each individual of them would feel, think, and act were he in a state of isolation. There are certain ideas and feelings which do not come into being, or do not transform themselves into acts except in the case of individuals forming a crowd.*

---

* G. Le Bon, *The Crowd* (New York: Viking Press, 1960), p. 27. Reprinted by permission.

Although Le Bon has been much maligned in recent literature for his anti-democratic, overly psychological view of the crowd, his work stimulated critical examination of the process whereby individuals in the crowd *apparently* come to "feel, think, and act" as if one. Many of the early great social psychologists, for whom the study of the crowd was a central concern (Brown, 1965), focused on psychological mechanisms such as imitation, suggestion, social facilitation, and identification in attempts to resolve the question of contagion. Tarde (1903) wrote that "imitation," enhanced by the physical contiguity of the crowd, is the basic process of contagion. McDougall (1927) argued that "suggestibility," springing from emotional excitement and the mob's feeling of power, creates a "primitive sympathy" among its members. "Social Facilitation" is the principal means of communication according to F. H. Allport (1924). Freud (1922) stated that "identification," whereby members of groups form intense attachments to common leaders and to their fellows in the crowd, is crucial in the mobilization for action. Le Bon (1960) held that leaders emerge from out of the crowd, whereas Tarde (1901) and Freud (1922) argued that the leader is prerequisite to the formation of the crowd. Much of the efforts of these early thinkers took place before the empiricism of the 1920's, and tended to concentrate on detecting irregularities and circularity in one another's reasoning (Brown, 1965).

The first major modern examination of contagion was that of Blumer (1939; 1951: 170–176) who stated that the nature of "elementary collective behavior" (that which arises "spontaneously" and is not due to "pre-established understandings or traditions") is revealed in the process of social interaction known as "circular" reaction:

> ... a type of interstimulation wherein the response of one individual reproduces the stimulation that has come from another individual and in being reflected back to this individual reinforces the stimulation. Thus the interstimulation assumes a circular form in which individuals reflect one another's states of feeling and in so doing intensify this feeling.*

Blumer contrasted this "circular" process with the "interpretive" reaction of normal groups in which responses follow the interpretation, not the stimulus behavior itself; responses are essentially "adjustments" to stimuli. Following Trotter (1919), he likened circular reaction to "herd behavior"

---

* H. Blumer, "Collective Behavior," in *Principles of Sociology*, A. M. Lee (ed.). (New York: Barnes & Noble Div. of Harper & Row, 1951), p. 170. Reprinted by permission.

in animals: "The expression of fear through bellowing, breathing, and movements of the body, induces the same feeling in the case of other cattle who, as they in turn express their alarm, intensify this emotional state in one another."

Blumer argued further that all instances of collective behavior proceed in three stages, each a more intense version of its forerunner. First, "milling" occurs: pure circular reaction in which individuals move amongst one another randomly and become increasingly sensitized and inclined to respond to one another "quickly, directly, and unwittingly." Second, "collective excitement"—essentially a speeding up of the "milling" process—increasingly "catches and rivets" the attention of others. Under the influence of "collective excitement" people become emotionally aroused and susceptible to being carried away by impulses and feelings. Finally, a stage of "social contagion" is reached in which there is "relatively rapid, unwitting, and nonrational dissemination of a mood, impulse, or form of conduct" and a lowering of "social resistance" resulting from "some loss of self-consciousness and . . . ability to interpret the activity of others."

A more recent extension of the idea of contagion has been suggested by Wheeler (1966). He uses the term "behavioral contagion" for the process whereby the action of a model lowers the internal or external restraints that keep his observers from engaging in the same activity. This occurs only in the absence of overt disapproval of the model's behavior by others in the group. "Behavioral contagion" becomes cumulative when the restraints are group derived and when a group member performs the initial act. Every member who then performs the act further reduces the restraints. Further elaborations of the concept of contagion can be found in the work of the Langs (1961), Klapp (1972), and in several papers of a collection in honor of Herbert Blumer (Shibutani, 1970).

Turner (1964: 386–387), while acknowledging the contributions of contagion theory to the understanding of the dynamics of collective behavior, cites several limitations in this approach. First, reports which support the theory best are reconstructions of rare and extreme occurrences by untrained and horrified observers. Even in the unlikely possibility that such accounts are reliable, it would be unwise to formulate a general model for collective behavior from aberrant cases. Second, the theory perpetuates the dubious view of man "as an animal with removable veneer of socialization." Third, only "suggestion," among the purported mechanisms of contagion, is well-verified. Psychological research, moreover, has led to a narrower and narrower set of circumstances under which suggestion occurs. Fourth, while contagion perhaps explains how shifts in behavior so often associated with the crowd take place, it is unhelpful in predicting the kinds of shifts that occur. Last, unless one accepts "the simplistic model of the crowd as an undifferentiated mass of persons accepting suggestions uniformly," the contagion approach is of little use in accounting for the organization of collective behavior.

Convergence Theories

Convergence theories account for collective behavior on the basis of the coming together of persons who share the same predispositions which are stimulated by some object or event. This approach formalizes the undercurrent of suspicion, which has always existed in the literature, that the crowd merely serves as an excuse for individuals to reveal their true natures. Three approaches in this tradition are distinguishable: The first rests on psychoanalytic notions about the latent pathology of crowds; the second on the assumption that there are "crowd-prone" categories of persons —usually marginal groups of some kind. The third is in the learning theory tradition of psychology (Turner, 1964).

The latent pathology view of the crowd, exemplified in the work of Martin (1920) and Meerloo (1950), is underpinned by age-old beliefs about man's inherently evil nature made respectable by the psychoanalytic concept of the unconscious (Turner, 1964). Crowds develop when persons with the same unconscious wishes gather; primitive impulses of hate and egotism are then released. The frustration-aggression hypothesis of Dollard et al. (1939) is an extension of the crowd pathology approach, but manages to avoid some of the extremes of the latter. In the Dollard et al. formulation, when aggression against a perceived source of frustration is blocked it will be redirected toward some other object perhaps only indirectly related to the original source. The claim that frustration always leads to aggression and aggression is always caused by frustration has been greatly modified since it first appeared, but continues to stimulate a great deal of research, not only in psychology, but at the macro level as well.

Feierabend, Feierabend and Nesvold (1969: 635), for example, apply the concept of "systematic frustration" to analysis of aggregate violent political behavior within social systems. They define systemic frustration as "frustration interfering with the attainment and maintenance of social goals, aspirations, and values . . . simultaneously experienced by members of social aggregates." Similarly, theories of "relative deprivation" and "rising expectations" usually have some notion of frustration at their root.

The belief that there are "crowd-prone" categories of persons seems first to have been elaborated by Le Bon (1960) in his odd catalogue of "inferior beings." More sophisticated, but not necessarily more credible, theories have since dwelt on the idea that riotous crowds are made up of recent migrants, criminal riffraff, teenage rebels, or a hard-core poor "underclass"; marginal peoples not fully committed to dominant norms. Sometimes accompanying these "folk theories" (Lupsha, 1969)[14] are beliefs that "crowd-prone" persons are mobilized by small numbers of individuals who promote civil disorder for their own ends. The conspiracy viewpoint, ever popular, especially among elites, has rarely been substantiated (Lupsha, 1969).

The recurring folk-belief that riotous crowds are composed mainly of "lower orders" of various sorts was perhaps first seriously questioned by George Rudé (1964) in his study of crowds in eighteenth and nineteenth century France and England. By studying police and judicial records, Rudé found that rioters were not primarily criminals and lumpenproletariat but rather shopkeepers, apprentices, craftsmen, laborers, and the like. They tended to be employed, of established residence, and without criminal record. Notions about "crowd-prone" groups have been laid to rest by recent research on black riot participants in United States cities during the 1960's revealing that the rioters were broadly representative of the ghetto population (Caplan, 1970; Fogelson and Hill, 1968; Kerner, 1968; Paige, 1971) and were motivated by a strong sense of indignation over the place of blacks in American society (Marx, 1972).

In the highly individualistic learning-theory version of collective behavior presented in the works of F. H. Allport (1924), Miller and Dollard (1941), and Turner and Killian (1972) crowd behavior is seen simply as the sum of the actions of individuals. "The individual in the crowd behaves just as he would alone, only more so" (Allport, 1924: 295). Persons in the crowd are predisposed to react in the same manner to a common object because they share the same human nature, quite apart from any social influence. "The crowd influences the behavior of the individual only by intensifying his behavior. This results from what Allport labeled 'social facilitation'; the reaction of each individual is intensified by seeing other people respond in the same way" (Turner and Killian, 1972: 60).

The major limitation of convergence approaches to collective behavior lies in the tendency to claim, after a particular mode of conduct has been observed in a crowd, that it was the result of a single predisposition; the shared predisposition then explains the crowd behavior. Although appealingly simple, this fails to recognize that men may have multiple latent tendencies that are appropriate to a given situation; thus, some other factor must be found to explain why one latency and not another is selected. Turner and Killian (1972: 21) note that a "convergence approach leads to formulations that take for granted that the crowd behavior is an automatic response to the nature of the situation which, in turn, is assumed to be self-evident to each individual." In fact, they state, a situation may be perceived as ambiguous by different individuals, in which case the collective definition of the situation, arrived at through some process of interaction, may be the main determining factor of the action.

The convergence approach, although overly simple and suffering from a lack of reliable empirical support, has performed a valuable task in deflating the exaggerated claims of some proponents of contagion by suggesting that the pre-existing attitudes of those who form a crowd are important; individuals are not uniformly amenable to the influence of the collectivity. At the same time, it must be conceded that contagion may absorb individuals without appropriate predispositions (Turner, 1964). In short, neither contagion nor convergence theory alone can fully explain the behavior of individuals in the crowd.

Emergent Norm Theory

Contagion and convergence theories have as their most salient feature the "oneness" of individuals in the crowd. The basis for the emergent norm approach, on the other hand, lies in the fact that although the crowd gives an overpowering impression of homogeneity—an observation shared by crowd members as well as onlookers—careful observation shows this to be an illusion. Rather, the crowd is characterized by "differential expression": Individuals feel and act differently; some are merely amused or interested bystanders; others are passive, even disapproving of the dominant orientation of the crowd. The tendency for untrained observers (upon whose reports the student of collective behavior often must rely) to be overwhelmed by dramatic happenings and to perceive in wholes rather than details likely has led to the myth of the unanimous crowd (Turner, 1969).

Ralph H. Turner (1964, 1969; Turner and Killian, 1972), the chief exponent of the emergent norm approach, argues that moods which create the impression of emotional homogeneity are imposed by the emergence of a norm peculiar to the situation. The shared understanding as to what kind of behavior is expected, which constitutes a norm, encourages conduct consistent with the norm, inhibits contrary actions, and justifies sanctions against those who dissent. Turner (1969: 556) provides an illustration: A private airplane carrying two well-known entertainers crashed in downtown Los Angeles a few years ago. A sociology student, hearing the crash, but not knowing what it was, ran to the scene. "An assemblage of persons had already congregated. As he ran, breathlessly asking, 'What happened?' he was quieted by the stony silence of those already present. His demeanor quickly took on the horror and silence of the assemblage."

In this example, the mood was imposed on the unsuspecting newcomer without the aid of excitement thought essential by contagion theorists. Further, his behavior was brought into conformity *prior* to any spontaneous feeling of the mood of the crowd. Turner (1969: 557) notes: "The impact of the group here resembles the operation of a social norm more than it does the impact of suggestion." The norm is "emergent" because it is necessarily specific to the situation to a large degree, there being no firmly established guidelines for the conduct of the crowd. Turner's contentions are supported by the experiments of Asch (1951) in which nonconforming group members acquiesce to the group because of the fear of disapproval (among other reasons). The general fear of crowds, especially hostile ones, probably facilitates the imposition of such a norm.

To summarize, emergent norm theory diverges from contagion theory in several important ways (Turner, 1969).

1. It is assumed that the unanimity of the crowd is an illusion.
2. Social pressure precedes the induction of emotion in crowd members.
3. A norm may emerge in a quiet as well as in the excited crowd.
4. As the collective behavior develops individuals both seek and supply justifications for the collectivity's course of action.
5. The emergent norm may include limits to the crowd behavior, unlike the spiraling of action implied by contagionists.
6. The possession of recognizable identities, rather than the loss of individuality assumed by contagion theories, facilitates the imposition of a norm.

Emergent norm theory represents a sharp break with previous approaches to collective behavior because it stresses the continuity between institutional and collective behavior. "Just as behavior in normal groups gives rise to, and is governed by, norms, so the crowd generates and is governed by normative control" (Turner, 1969: 392).

Value-Added Theory

Perhaps the most elaborate, comprehensive, and certainly the most sociological treatment of collective behavior is that of Neil Smelser (1962; 1968; 1969; 1972*a*) who, with Turner, maintains that collective behavior is analyzable by the same categories as conventional behavior. But while most of the foregoing approaches to collective behavior rest on assumptions about the individual, Smelser's analysis proceeds from assumptions and propositions about macrosocial systems. In addition, whereas the foregoing approaches are concerned mainly with the dynamics of collectivities,

Smelser's scheme combines the social structural roots and the processes of collective behavior within a single framework.

Smelser undertakes to answer the question: "Why do collective behavior episodes occur where they do, when they do, and in the ways they do?" (1962: 1). The key to the explanation of this skewing in time and space is the concept of "structural strain" under which a variety of conflicts, deprivations, and ambiguities in the social structure can be subsumed. One obvious example is interethnic conflict. Smelser's "master proposition" is that ". . . people under strain mobilize to reconstitute the social order in the name of a generalized belief" (1962: 385). Collective behavior then occurs by "short circuit": a jump from very general levels of blame to an attack on specific agents. Before "structural strain," however, can play a part in the buildup of a collective episode, there must be a condition of "structural conduciveness." That is, the ecological setting must permit the "strain" to occur; for example, the lack of institutionalized channels for expressing ethnic grievances is conducive to the buildup of "strain." Given the social structural conditions of "conduciveness" and "strain," the dynamics of a collective episode may occur: the growth and spread of a "generalized belief" giving meaning to the strain, attributing certain characteristics to the source, and sometimes specifying certain responses as possible or appropriate; the occurrence of "precipitating factors," dramatic, sometimes fortuitous, events that "touch off" the action; and the "mobilization of participants for action" having to do with leadership and communication in the organization of the action itself. Finally, the operation of social control arches over all, in effect, serving as a counterdeterminant which prevents or alters the accumulation of the other conditions.

The concept of "value-added," borrowed from economics, means that each determinant of collective behavior adds its value to the prior determinant, increasingly specifying the nature of the collective episode. Each of the determinants is said to be necessary for an incident of collective behavior; together, they are said to be sufficient.[15]

Although Smelser's theory is the most generally useful of all the approaches to collective behavior, its extreme breadth and resulting lack of precision creates problems. First, the breadth of many of the concepts makes disconfirmation difficult. A "generalized belief," for example, may be

> any common idea, simple or complex. It may or may not be normatively sanctioned. If it is normatively sanctioned, it may be either thoroughly socialized . . . or it may be primarily externally enforced.

... 'Generalized belief' may be an extemporaneous 'definition of the situation' ... or it may a highly institutionalized traditional ideology.*

Likewise, some sort of structural "strain" may be ferreted out in almost any social situation. Further, because value-added theory purports to be not only "a description of the reality of collective behavior situations," but "an abstract system of thought that will assist in the analysis of social situations, it would be highly unusual for any critique to be so broadly based as to call both aspects into question" (Manning, 1971: 102).

A second area of difficulty centers on the notion of "generalized belief," the central concept in the value-added scheme. Smelser's conception of "generalized belief" as exaggerated, distorted, and differing from ordinary beliefs links him, Currie and Skolnick (1972) argue, with earlier theorists who stressed the irrationality of collective behavior. Marx (1972: 50), on the other hand, suggests that emphasis on the "generalized belief" unduly restricts the study of collective violence, inasmuch as it causes an overlooking of episodes in which the "elements of protest, ideology, grievance, strain, lack of access to channels for redressing complaints, social change and social movements, are relatively insignificant factors, if not absent altogether." Marx presents several types of these "issueless riots."

Third, the emphasis on structural variables results in an overlooking of individual behavior; the question of "Who becomes involved and why?" (Hornbach, 1970: 61) cannot be easily addressed. It is noteworthy that Smelser (1972a: 98) has come to the conclusion that he "definitely underplayed the importance of psychological mechanisms in the dynamics of episodes of collective behavior."

Finally, Smelser (1962) explicitly denied, in assuming his first position on the subject, any temporal sequence of determinants in the development of collective episodes. The increasingly specific determinants have an analytical but not necessarily an empirical sequence; for instance, an isolated event of the past, on being recalled, may be activated as a "precipitating factor" in the genesis of the collective behavior. Despite this disclaimer, the sequential logic of the "life-cycle" or "natural-history" model is difficult to avoid (Turner, 1969). Here too, however, Smelser (1972a) has modified his initial position slightly.

In this section, the contagion, convergence, emergent norm, and value-added approaches to collective behavior have been examined, albeit briefly. Research on collective violence in sport has tended to borrow in eclectic fashion from these orientations.

---

* R. Manning, "A Critical Analysis of Contemporary Collective Behavior Theory," *Sociological Focus* **4** (1971: 99–106). Reprinted by permission.

COLLECTIVE VIOLENCE IN SPORT

Collective violence involving spectators, players—and sometimes both—seems to be increasingly plaguing sport; indeed, few spectator sports and few parts of the world have been immune in recent years. It is difficult to know whether the frequency of riotous outbursts has merely kept pace with the expansion of spectator-oriented sport or whether there has been a rise in incidence. It is hard to determine, also, if the apparent rise is, in part, a product of increased attention by the media.

A genuine increment in violence in other spheres (Graham and Gurr, 1969), however, bolsters the impression that collective violence in sport has intensified. Whatever the case, escalating social control attests to the fact that violent outbreaks associated with sport are *perceived* as a serious and growing problem. In the United States, the last ten years has witnessed the appearance of several official commissions to investigate specific sport "riots," the production of sport crowd control "manuals," prohibition of high school night contests in nearly every major city, and the presence at games of police in mounting force. In other countries, massive physical barriers—moats, barbed-wire topped fences, steel-doored dressing rooms, and the like—together with the usual phalanxes of control agents are increasingly in evidence (Smith, 1973a; Ingham and Smith, 1975).

In this last section of the chapter, the social structural conditions that undergird riotous outbursts in sport are examined. Attention is paid then to the dynamics of sport-related collective violence. Finally, the consequences of such violence are considered.

Social Structural Strains

Although many sociologists continue to insist that the proper study of collective behavior is the study of its "dynamics" or "processes" (Lang and Lang, 1970: 95) and delve no further into its sources than to assume they lie in "social unrest" of some kind,[16] most would concede that a comprehensive understanding of collective behavior cannot be achieved without at least some reference to the nature of the "unrest."[17] Similarly, although collective behavior implies a lack of pre-established understandings or traditions, its course is seldom totally inconsistent with the social and cultural contexts in which it runs (Kerckhoff, 1970). Hostile outbursts in Italian soccer take somewhat different forms than hockey riots in Canada. For these reasons, it is important to pay heed to the social structural strains (Smelser, 1962; Buckley, 1967) from which collective episodes in sport stem. Strain, in the following, is categorized as conflict or deprivation.

Conflicts. Perhaps the most obvious form of "strain" stems from inter-group conflict based on ethnic, political, economic, social class, or religious differences, or some interaction of these dimensions. It is not surprising that collective violence sometimes erupts when the representatives of groups already in conflict, owing to their location in the social structure, meet in sport in what amounts to a symbolic struggle for supremacy. As Carolyn Sherif (1972: 7) states: "The penetration of such small intergroup systems by the structural properties and cultural values of larger socio-cultural systems should be self-evident."

The notion of collective identity—a sense of "we"—is important in tracing crowd violence in sport to social structural strain; the greater the "we" feeling, the easier members of a collectivity can come to view an individual or team as representative of the collectivity, the struggle on the field then taking on the dimension of the wider intergroup conflict. The study of collective identity, then, ". . . provides a background for the study of collective behavior" (Klapp, 1972: 4). The idea of collective identity can perhaps be best illuminated by considering it in terms of two extremes: At one terminal, according to Klapp (1972: 6), is the transitory "we" feeling sometimes existing in anonymous crowds in which the only element appar-ently shared by members is allegiance to (in the case of sport) the team; at the other terminal lies the relatively permanent social system in which

> sufficient *system* exists [in member relationships] for them to continue to act jointly, share goals and rewards, recognize one another, keep in communication, build common memories, and maintain boundaries. . . . The minimum requirement seems to be a *closed feedback loop* of messages so that they can develop and maintain a collective identity over time. . . . When such a system exists, it is possible to build an identification with others that is more than transitory or merely a ref-erence. When a person has a well-developed "we," his personal identity is composed of two parts: the "I," "me" (ego, self-image) and the "we," or concepts of self-as-belonging, including one's place as mem-ber or memory of interactions with others (who have corresponding "we" feelings), and appropriate responses such as loyalty.*

When individuals share a common culture, then, there is greater potential for the establishment of a strong sense of "we."

Collective identity is both partly responsible for, and sharpened by, conflict with out-groups. Outsiders are stereotyped as evil; ingroup mem-

---

* O. E. Klapp, *Currents of Unrest* (New York: Holt, Rinehart, and Winston, 1972), p. 4. Reprinted by permission.

bers draw closer together in common cause (Sherif and Sherif, 1969; Sherif, 1972). Spicer (1971) argues that continuous opposition is *necessary* in sustaining cultural identity, a mechanism recognized in Hitler's Germany and deliberately fostered through mass festivals and other ritual as the 1936 Berlin Olympics approached (Mandell, 1971).[18] Promoters of commercial sport, of course, are only too aware of these processes and seek, where possible, to stage spectacles which not only feed off collective identities, but exacerbate (for future consideration) what euphemistically are termed "natural rivalries." Wrestling provides the most blatant examples: as when "Nazi" is pitted against "Rabbi" (Turowetz, 1973; Turowetz et al., 1973; see Chapter 12). Weinberg and Arond (1952) note, in their study of the occupational culture of the boxer:

> As the promoter is concerned primarily with attracting a large audience, he tries to select and develop fighters who will draw customers. Thus the fighter must have "crowd-pleasing" qualifications in addition to ability. In this connection, the race and ethnic group play a part. A good white fighter is preferred to a good Negro fighter; and in large cities, such as New York and Chicago, a Jewish fighter is considered highly desirable because the majority of fight fans are Jewish and Italian.*

The ethnic composition of fighters and fight fans has changed somewhat since Weinberg and Arond conducted their investigation, but crowd outbursts at Madison Square Garden and other New York City boxing centers have been commonplace since the mid-1960's. Today, spectators may riot when Puerto Rican confronts black or anglo (*Toronto Globe and Mail*, May 17, 1967; November 6, 1971).

Major sources of feedback for collective identity are what Klapp (1972: 7) calls "group superselves": individuals "who embody on a larger scale—through acts, style or personality traits—what the group believes and wishes itself to be." Numerous examples can be found: The Portuguese wrestler, Carlos Rocha, in 1971 mobilized the Portuguese community of Toronto in unprecedented fashion; the identification of black people with the boxer Joe Louis was legendary (Edwards, 1973). Indeed, there is a special pride felt by blacks when black athletes defeat white (Edwards, 1973). The notion of "group superself" calls into question Heinila's (1966: 33) hypothesis that international dual contests between *teams* supply the most favorable conditions for the formation of "distinct in and out group attitudes—and thus for inter-group conflicts as well. . . ."

---

* S. K. Weinberg and H. Arond, "The Occupational Character of the Boxer," *American Journal of Sociology* **57** (1952: 460–469). Reprinted by permission.

The outburst that erupted at the end of the 1962 Washington, D.C. high school championship football game provides a classic illustration of ethnic group strains crystallizing in sport. On this occasion, St. John's, a white, middle-class private school, met East High, a lower-class, predominantly black institution. An estimated 80 percent of the spectators at this game were blacks, roughly the same as black representation in the city's public schools. Race relations then, as now, were strained. At the conclusion of the rough game, won by St. John's, thousands of spectators brawled, and over 500 were reported injured (White, 1970: 101). Edwards (1973: 272) reasons that "fights after sporting events between fans from black and white schools are to be expected."

Ethnic group conflict invariably has economic and political dimensions; indeed, ethnic rifts usually stem from competition for scarce resources (Lang and Lang, 1968). The intertwining of the ethnic, economic, and political roots of collective violence can be seen clearly in the events leading to the 1969 Honduras–El Salvador "soccer war": In a several-year period prior to 1969, an estimated 30,000 people from relatively industrialized, rich, but overpopulated El Salvador immigrated illegally to rural, sparsely populated Honduras in search of jobs, deepening existing Honduran resentment of El Salvador's economic prosperity and domination of the Central American Common Market. This tension, together with frequent disputes over what constituted the border between the two countries and, consequently, who owned the land along it, provided the backdrop for the riots which accompanied all three World Cup soccer games between the two countries in June, 1969. Following the last game, diplomatic and commercial relations were severed, and the El Salvadorean army, prompted by rumors of "genocide" against their countrymen in Honduras, mobilized and moved across the border (*New York Times*, June 28, 1969; July 5, 1969; August 3, 1969).

Many other instances can be cited in which some combination of ethnic, political, economic—even religious—strains appear to have underlain sport-related riots. Soccer provides the most dramatic cases: The neighboring Italian cities of Bari and Taranto, for example, said to have a "long-standing rivalry from shipping to soccer," clashed after a 1957 game in the former city, supporters setting up roadblocks in the streets and causing widespread property damage (*New York Times*, March 11, 1957); similarly, federal troops had to quell rioting in the rival Turkish cities of Kaseri and Sivas following a 1967 game, as well as manning the border between the provinces in which each city is located. Forty-two were reported killed and six hundred injured during the street-fighting (*New York Times*, September 17, 1967). Catholic-Protestant antagonism is the source of the continuing disturbances associated with Glasgow Celtics versus Rangers contests (Harrington, 1968; *Toronto Globe and Mail*, August 20, 1973). Similar cases are reported in Smith (1973*a*; 1973*b*) and Ingham and Smith (1975).

Other kinds of intergroup conflict may be based on little more than the history of athletic encounters between the groups. The "vendetta" reportedly established in the National Hockey League between Philadelphia and St. Louis players (*Toronto Star*, December 5, 1973) presumably could widen its scale to encompass spectators. Many of the outbursts in college basketball in the United States seem to be of this type (Stump, 1973). Although in many of these cases there is no apparent basis for collective identification with a team other than a shared emotional attachment to it, this attachment, nevertheless, appears often to be intense[19] and contributes to existing strain.

Deprivations

A great deal of social research aimed at uncovering the causes of riots, revolutions, and other forms of turmoil has used the concept of deprivation in some sense. Sociologists have tended to use it in reference to "... the gap between the responsible performance in roles by individuals, groups, or organizations in society and the rewards which accrue to these roles" (Lupsha, 1969: 290). This deprivation gap can be real or threatened, absolute or relative. Although deprived groups may well be at odds with other specific groups—indeed usually owing their location in the social structure to exploiting or oppressing elites—deprivation is taken here to imply a conflict more with the contemporary social order itself than with any specific group within it.

It has already been suggested that minority or relatively powerless groups are prone to intense involvement in sport. The legendary commitment to their soccer teams of the "masses" in Latin America, where crowd outbursts have occurred regularly since at least 1932 (Glanville, 1968), provides an apt case-in-point. Hecht (1968: 743) describes the aftermath of winning and losing in World Cup competition:

> On 16 July 1950, in Rio's Maracana stadium, Uruguay beat Brazil 2–1 thus to become the winners of the fourth World Cup Competition. Unexpected as was this result in view of the Brazilians' excellence and previous form in the competition, for the 200,000 crowd present and to the millions of Brazilians following the match on radio, the event was considered nothing less than a national tragedy. Almost a hundred people fainted from shock, a large part of the stadium's attendance and all the players openly wept; a number of people both in Uruguay and Brazil died from heart attacks induced by the excitement and dis-

appointment. July 16 became a day of national mourning in Rio, whilst in Montevideo fervent celebrations in the streets went on all night. When in 1958 Brazilian national honour was restored by their team winning the Sixth World Cup in Sweden and thus becoming the first South American nation to win the trophy in Europe, and when in 1962 they went on to complete a unique double by becoming World Champions again in Chile, crowds in the hundreds of thousands turned out to hold a carnival of celebration in Rio, Sao Paulo and other main cities, though the games had been played in far distant lands.*

Other observers (Lever, 1972; Taylor, 1973) relate similar phenomena associated with football in Latin America. As Hecht (1968: 743) states: "Sport as a matter of patriotic pride is not uniquely a Latin American institution, but nowhere else perhaps is it so intensively identified by the people with their personal and national honour."

Taylor (1973) contends, further, that following the national team of Mexico's 1970 victory, in Mexico City, qualifying it to enter the quarter-final of the World Cup Tournament, the "authorities" (i.e., the ruling Revolutionary Institutional Party) deliberately condoned, as a means of social control, what one newspaper called the "wildest celebration in the history of Mexico." Thus, football celebrations in the streets may be a form of "state licensed relief" in the life of the masses, distracting the minds of the people from pressing social issues and other "problems." [20] Not only did the Mexican government in 1970 make little attempt to restore normality, Taylor notes, it used the occasion to demonstrate in several ways its solidarity with the revelrous crowds. Taylor presents evidence of the same kind of "repressive tolerance" exercised by Brazil's military junta after that country won the 1970 Cup.

The key to this collective identity through football would seem to lie in the absolute deprivation of much of the Latin American populace to whom the weekly football match is one of few sources of pleasure: ". . . it is the high spot of weekly life, to be savoured in person if possible, or vicariously through radio and television" (Hecht, 1968: 744).

Eighty percent of the professional players (football being virtually the only professional sport) come from the lowest socioeconomic positions (Hecht, 1968; Lever, 1972; Taylor, 1973); thus, although the number of players who can use the game as a social elevator is numerically small, "there is no boundary for the identification that millions of the poor can make with their soccer heroes . . ." (Hecht, 1968: 744).

---

* E. Hecht, "Football." In *Latin America and the Caribbean*, Claudio Velez (ed.). (New York: Praeger, 1968), pp. 743–748. Reprinted by permission of Praeger Publishers.

It is reasonable to suggest that defeats in important matches may be felt as intolerable deprivations by already deprived groups whose members have formed strong emotional attachments to teams. Given these circumstances (together with other conditions necessary for collective violence) a referee's call, say, nullifying a goal (as in the 1964 Lima riot and panic) or an act of violence on the field (Smith, 1973b) *is* a major affront which needs redress. What is usually referred to as the "revolution of rising expectations" (Davies, 1969) suggests that crowd outbreaks tend to occur late in important games when hopes for victory are high—then are abruptly dashed.

Ian Taylor's (1969; 1971a; 1971b) explanation of the "hooliganism" (Harrington et al., 1968; Lang et al., 1969) that has plagued British soccer for the past decade or so is amenable to discussion under the heading of deprivation. He proposes that the invasion of pitches by rioting spectators, the ransacking of soccer trains returning from games, and the destruction of property in and around stadia are responses by remnants of a working-class "soccer subculture" to hold onto a game which has become increasingly removed from its real or imagined control. Soccer "hooliganism," if Taylor's speculations are correct, is an example of what Rudé (1964) calls the "backward looking riot": an attempt to restore a prior state of affairs.

Central to this thesis are Taylor's notions of "soccer subculture" and "soccer consciousness":

> I will describe the groups of working men involved in the building and sustaining of these local teams as "sub-cultures" within which the values of the work-place found expression and a focus in the team itself. The "sub-culture" of soccer in a working-class community refers to the groups of working men bound together with a concern for the game in general (the soccer consciousness) and the local team in particular. ... During the last quarter of the nineteenth century and throughout the Depression, the evidence is that players were very much subject to control by such local soccer sub-cultures: expected to receive advice and "tips," expected to conform to certain standards of behavior (as the sub-cultures' "public representatives"), and (in return) given a wage for so long as they fulfilled these expectations.*

The rank-and-file supporter, in short, could see himself as having membership in a "collective and democratically structured enterprise" (Taylor, 1971b: 145).

---

* Ian R. Taylor, "Soccer Consciousness and Soccer Hooliganism," in *Images of Deviance*, Stanley Cohen (ed.). (Middlesex, England: Penguin Books Ltd., 1971), pp. 142–143. Reprinted by permission.

Professionalism and internationalism altered the relationship among management, players, and supporters. Under professionalism, subcultural relationships between club and players, and between players and supporters, were gradually replaced with contractual ones; internationalism caused changes in styles and strategies to the point where authentic local and national styles, with which supporters could identify, disappeared.

The "soccer conscious" did not defy all the changes which transformed British soccer in the last two decades; they supported some and were ambivalent about others. Taylor describes the reaction as a gradual and largely unconscious "drift" in the direction of attempts to reassert traditional control.

Whether the unrest in British soccer is characterized as "hooliganism" or as protest is both an ideological and an empirical question. The tendency of social scientists to find more political meaning in collective behavior than sometimes is warranted has been noted already. Marx (1972) suggests a number of criteria by which the investigator may begin to differentiate deviance from protest: To what degree is a generalized belief present? Has the disorder developed out of a prolonged community conflict or out of a focused context? Are conventional political activists present among participants in riotous crowds? Are there riot spokesmen and presentation of demands? Is there selectivity in attack? Is there a link between the source of the trouble, as identified in the generalized belief, and the target attacked? To what extent is rioting instrumental in collectively solving a group's problem?

These criteria suggest, to cite two examples, that the 1955 "Rocket" Richard hockey riot in Montreal (Katz, 1955; Lang and Lang, 1961) and the crowd outbursts associated with the movement to stop the South African rugby and cricket teams from touring Great Britain in 1969 and 1970 (Hain, 1971) were largely protest rather than deviance, but that conclusions regarding British soccer disorder must await more, and better, evidence.

Davies (1972: 98–114) provides a contrary view to Taylor in a vivid description of riding a "hooligan" train to a Tottenham Hotspur's away game in Coventry. About a thousand youths were on the police-jammed train. "Almost all of them had long hair and many could have passed for hippies, except for the big heavy boots. The average age was 15. They called themselves Smooths..." Most wore blue and white scarfs knotted at the waist. Deboarding, they were searched for weapons by a special "Task Force" of 50 Coventry police created especially for football crowds. Arriving in the stands about an hour before the game, they "charged for the middle of the West stand. The police had made out the demarcation lines, the Coventry fans one side, Spurs the other. Down the middle was a line of policemen, shoulder to shoulder, splitting the West stand in half."

About 30 minutes before kickoff, amidst ceaseless singing and chanting, the fights began in earnest.

> "Right, let's go," said one lad beside me. "Round the back and get them." He and a little party moved off through the singing sea of fans and approached Coventry from the other side, getting in amongst them and kicking, hoping other Spurs gangs would attack from the other side. But this time Coventry were strong enough to fight back. The supporters not involved swayed violently to one side. Immediately there was a human tidal wave as a great mass of bodies retreated from the action, or at least tried to, causing more damage and knocking down more people than the actual fighting. If you didn't see the wave coming and swayed with it, you got trodden on.*

Davies notes, further, that the "Smooths" hatred of opposing teams and their supporters bordered on the pathological, while at the same time they were fanatically and uncritically loyal to the "Spurs," and intimately acquainted with each player's background. They perceived themselves, moreover, as important to the team's welfare despite the fact they were officially disavowed by the club. These observations, together with Davies' statement that the supporters "... were all in rotten jobs, from rotten homes ..." and had "no other excitement or meaning in their lives," congeal with the Harrington et al. (1968) data on 497 convicted "hooligans." Both the Harrington group and Davies, although hinting vaguely at conditions of anomie as the source of the disturbances, appear to view them essentially as impelled by a quest for fun and excitement, and characterized by a general *expressiveness*. The divergent perspectives on crowd violence in British soccer are clearly, at the present time, more a conflict of faith than one based on fact.

Some of the spectator misbehavior in British soccer may be a close relative of "riots in victory and celebration" (Marx, 1972: 57) such as occurred in Vancouver in 1966 during the Canadian Football League's "Grey Cup Week" (*The Canadian Magazine*, November 25, 1972) or when the New York Mets won the 1973 National League Championship (*New York Times*, October 14, 1973). This kind of disorder has a ritualistic aspect and may even be institutionalized insofar as rioters and controllers expect it to occur. Strain and generalized belief appear to be relatively insignificant factors in its genesis.[21]

---

* H. Davies, *The Glory Game*. (London: Weidenfield and Nicolson, 1972), pp. 98–114. Reprinted by permission. This footnote also applies to passages quoted on pp. 311 and 316–317.

Crowd violence in sport, then, as in other spheres, appears to stem from social structural tensions. These have been categorized broadly as conflicts and deprivations with no claim made that such a classification exhausts the types of strain underlying sport crowd disorder. Having dealt with structural strain, crowd processes may now be examined.

Dynamics

Given the presence of a strain in the social structure, the stage is set for the collective outburst. These are examined under the headings of communication, precipitants, and mobilization for action.

Communication. Turner and Killian (1972) state that the characteristic mode of communication in collective behavior is rumor: the collective attempt to construct meaningful interpretations of events in ambiguous and sometimes critical situations. In these circumstances, official channels of communication often are inadequate; thus, individuals seek to confirm and supplement formal news by exchanging information with others in an atmosphere of contagion—a heightened responsiveness to cues provided by others. Gradually the network of communicators arrives at a collectively sanctioned definition of the situation. Smelser (1962) refers to this problem-solving process as the growth and spread of a "generalized belief." Hostile beliefs about Anglo-Italian soccer provide an illustration:

> In Italy it's assumed that all British footballers are brutes, concentrating more on the physical side of football than on ball skills, tackling from behind, going in hard, charging the goalkeeper and other nasty tricks. In Britain it's assumed by the man on the terraces that Italian footballers are a bunch of hysterical fairies who throw tantrums, pull shirts, body check and other nasty tricks (Davies, 1972: 268).

Such beliefs give meaning to strains by focusing on whatever is believed to be the source of the tension, attributing certain characteristics to it, and sometimes specifying courses of action as possible or appropriate.

In sport, conditions are usually conducive to communication of this kind. Mass media, which often devote a great deal of attention to sport, serve as generators or transmitters of rumor from which generalized beliefs emerge. Newspaper accounts of events associated with the 1969 Honduras–El Salvador soccer series suggest the probable role of the media in this process: There were reports of "alleged" mistreatment of Honduran fans, accusations of "brutality" directed at players on both teams, and stories that Honduran crowds were taking El Salvadorean property and lives (*New York Times*, June 28, 1969). The welter of vague and sometimes conflicting reports, in an already strained atmosphere, no doubt provided fertile ground for the development of hostile beliefs, which presumably played a part in the crowd violence at the games.

Conditions in the stadium itself are conducive to contagious communication. Here, "milling" may occur: physical and verbal activity that sensitizes individuals to each other. To illustrate: In boxing, both the physical contiguity and the expectations of the audience create a situation that eases verbal "milling" of a kind. Furst (1972: 12) describes the boxing arena as an "open region" where members of the audience expect accessibility to conversations between strangers:

> Brief verbal exchanges between strangers occur in a number of ways. One of the most common means of initiating verbal exchanges is when a member of the audience in a clearly audible voice declares his approval or disapproval of the ongoing boxing match. . . . Often after a declaration is made, the individual will seek eye contact with his neighbor to ascertain if his outburst has opened the way for a brief encounter. At one boxing show an unaccompanied middle-aged man shouted: "Did you see that guy? Did you ever see him look as bad as he does tonight?" After several seconds he quickly cast a glance toward his closest neighbor, a man accompanied by another male and sitting three seats away. As if on cue, one of the men turned toward him and said: "You know he doesn't look much like a fighter. Do you remember Willy Pep?" Before the first party could answer, another man, unaccompanied and sitting nearby, said: "Do you remember Billy Graham? What a helluva good fighter he was!" *

Verbal exchanges are closely tied to the action in the ring; they are precipitated sometimes by referees' announcements that are not heard or are misunderstood (Furst, 1972). The more ambiguous the situation, the faster the growth and spread of a belief. Ingham and Nixon (1970) speculate that one factor in the chain of determinants leading to hostile outbursts in soccer may be ambiguity caused by the high degree of reliance upon the official's interpretation of infractions; thus, in the 1964 Lima riot and panic, in which an estimated 400 were killed, the referee's nullification of a tying goal by Peru initially went unnoticed by a large segment of the crowd, creating a period of ambiguity following which the rioters stormed the field (White, 1970).

Several other conditions would appear to influence the contagious spread of hostile beliefs among crowd members at sport events. First,

---

* R. T. Furst, "The Boxer and His Audience: An Empirical Assessment." Paper presented at the Scientific Congress of the XX Olympic Games, Munich, 1972. Reprinted by permission.

French's (1944) experiment comparing organized athletic teams and un-organized groups under fear and frustration suggests that such communi-cation is freer in crowds characterized by pre-existing group ties—such as a common culture. Second, the laboratory research of Leonard Berkowitz (1972) indicates that loud noise, not weather, alcohol, and the sheer ex-citement of the event, among other things, generate emotional arousal in crowd members which, in turn, enhances interstimulation. Third, cheek-to-jowl congestion may facilitate communication, not only because the physi-cal contiguity of individuals sensitizes, but because status differences may be suspended (Wolff, 1964: 227). And fourth, the greater the mutual visibility of like-acting individuals, the greater the contagion; small arenas and stadia, then, may be more conducive than large ones to "perceptual contagion" (Furst, 1972: 20).

Precipitants.   The precipitating event, or series of events, "touches off" the action of the violent outburst by "crystallizing beliefs on specific events or objects" (Smelser, 1962: 247); a belief among spectators of sport, for example, about a player or team being "dirty" may be verified by an act of violence on the field. Because persons evolve meanings of a particular act in the light of their definitions of the situation in which the act occurs, the context of the precipitating incident is more important than its content; what appears to be a minor incident may in a time of tension be defined as an extreme provocation. The Kerner Report (1968: 117–118) is explicit on this point: "In this sense the entire chain—the grievances, the series of prior tension-heightening incidents, and the final incident—was the 'pre-cipitant' of disorder." The Report states, as well, that most of the "final incidents" in the 1967 urban riots were, objectively speaking, relatively minor, even trivial. The significance of the precipitating factor as a deter-minant can only be comprehended fully when viewed in the context of the historical forces that give it its meaning.

Although sometimes it is hard to distinguish empirically between pre-cipitant and prior or ensuing action, most reports of collective violence identify a single occurrence that triggered the larger episode. More often than not this occurrence was itself an act of violence. Leiberson and Silver-man (1965), in their examination of 72 United States race riots, 1913–1963, isolated precipitating factors in all but four of the cases. Most of the pre-cipitants were interracial violations of strongly held norms; of these, over 75 percent involved bodily assault of some sort. Similarly, the Kerner Com-mission (1968: 119) noted the "typical" case of the 1967 Newark riot in which a black cab driver was hurt during a confrontation with police fol-lowing a traffic accident.

The adage that "violence breeds violence" appears to hold frequently in the sport setting. In a study of 17 major soccer riots reported in the

New York Times, over half were preceded by assault (or the threat of it) by players, spectators, or police (Smith, 1973a). And some sort of assaultive behavior was said to precede 74 percent of 39 sport crowd outbursts reported in the *Toronto Globe and Mail* during the decade, 1963–1973 (Smith, 1973b). The most frequent type of assault was player attack on opposing players, ranging from individual acts to bench-emptying brawls. In the majority of cases, these were explicitly identified as precipitants of the collective action that followed. The report of an Ontario Junior A hockey game between Ottawa and London is typical: On this occasion, a "cross-checking incident sparked a fight" involving "most players from both teams, several hundred spectators, and 20 city policemen." In other accounts there was evidence merely that the games were particularly "rough" or "brutal," as when Toronto City met the Chicago Mustangs in a "rough and tough" soccer game in which a "player from each team was ejected." In several instances like the above, player violence and unpopular referee's calls appeared to be part of an escalating series of precipitating factors (Smith, 1973b: 10).

Numerous other reports buttress the claim that sport crowd riots are often "touched off" by individual or smaller-scale violence: A *Football Association News* editorial (Smits, 1968), in an analysis of 361 player offenses in English First Division soccer, associated widespread player violence with crowd outbreaks; likewise, the Harrington Report (1968) on British soccer notes a connection between spectator misbehavior and violence on the field. The Montreal hockey riot of 1955 (Lang and Lang, 1961), the 1962 Washington D.C. high school football riot (White, 1970), and the outburst following a South Africa–New Zealand rugby match in Kimberly (Hain, 1971) are but a few additional examples.

Unpopular referees' decisions comprise a second class of precipitants (Smith, 1973b). Disallowing a goal, ejecting a player from the game, and the like may be selectively defined by crowd members as discrimination against "their" team. It seems that "unwise" spectators misperceive much of the action on the field (Furst, 1972; Hasdorf and Cantril, 1954). Smits (1968) states that in soccer it is "almost always" the decision, or the lack of one, by the referee that ignites a crowd outbreak. Interestingly, in providing examples to bolster this statement, he reveals that player violence usually is the cause of the official's decision, a finding noted also by Smith (1973a). Player violence, then, if not always the "last straw," seems frequently to be part of the chain of precipitants. This is not surprising when one is reminded that bodily assault—when it is *perceived* as illegitimate—in almost all social contexts arouses the strongest sort of indignation. Indeed, as Leiberson and Silverman (1965) note, most societies reserve their

severest sanctions for illegitimate violence (while at the same time, paradoxically, rewarding the legitimate kind). An assaultive act on the sport
field, then, may be seen by spectators as a norm violation which must be
redressed.

Mobilization for action.   When a generalized belief has crystallized around
a precipitating incident, participants in the collectivity mobilize for action
(Smelser, 1962). Two factors shaping the course of the action are the nature of the crowd and the ecological setting. The latter provides conditions
conducive to some courses of action and not to others.

Most riotous crowds seem to be what Turner and Killian (1972: 87)
call "solidaristic"; that is, the common definition of the situation suggests
that the crowd's objective cannot be achieved without cooperation among
its members. This is in contrast to the "individualistic" crowd in which
individuals or groups pursue parallel goals, often competitively, as in
panics. The "solidaristic" crowd may be characterized further as either
"acting" or "expressive": The former has an objective external to itself,
say, to attack the referee; while the chief aim of the latter is the expression
of emotion (Blumer, 1951), as in riots in "victory and celebration." These
types, of course, are not mutually exclusive, as illustrated in the destruction
of the Soviet Airline offices in Prague during a frenzied celebration following Czechoslovakia's 4–3 victory over the Soviet Union in the 1969 World
Hockey Championships (Turner and Killian, 1972).

Although there is an illusion of unanimity and homogeneity in the
crowd, individuals, in fact, are differentially motivated and play varying
roles as the action unfolds. Turner and Killian (1972: 27–29) suggest the
following typology of collective behavior participants: First, there are the
"committed" who are ego-involved in the situation and define it as demanding immediate attention, although they may have only a vague idea
of what should be done. Second, the "concerned" share the ego-involve-
ment of the "committed" but are not as committed to immediate action;
they have less clearly defined attitudes regarding the situation. Third are
the individuals who get gratification out of participation in the collectivity,
no matter what the circumstances. They may find appealing the aura of
power and righteousness in the crowd, or they may see the collectivity,
simply, as providing an opportunity for excitement. Fourth are the "spectators" who, with others, form an audience to the nucleus. The "spectators" may be amused, curious, disinterested, even disapproving. The fifth
type is the "exploiter": the criminal, looter, drunk, or psychopath, ego-
detached rather than ego-involved and viewing others as merely means to
ends. From this mix, a division of labor emerges: leaders (probably drawn

from the "committed" or the "exploiters"); those who actively support in one way or another the leaders' suggestions; and the more or less passive "spectators" who typically constitute the largest segment.

The 1964 Lima riot provides an illustration of the emergence of a division of labor in a "solidaristic acting" crowd. Peru and Argentina met on May 24 in Lima's National Stadium in a soccer game which the former country had to win to stay in contention as South America's representative in the Tokyo Olympics. The violence that interrupted this match was precipitated by the Uruguayan referee's disallowance of a Peru goal, which would have tied the game with six minutes to play. Following this decision, Matias Rojas, known as "Bomba" (the Bomb) for his previous attacks on referees, was the first to scramble over the seven foot, barbed-wire topped fence. Rojas was stopped by several of the 173 police present before he could reach the referee but probably served as a model for several followers who gained access to the field in the same manner. Others sat down at the foot of the fence and pushing rhythmically with their feet tore three large holes in it. They then ran onto the field to battle the police. Still others set fires in the stands where three policemen were later found apparently murdered (White, 1970).

Crowd leaders may serve as behavioral models as Bomba seems to have done; in other instances, they may harangue the crowd to action. Harrington et al. (1968) state that "chant leaders" sometimes fill this latter role in soccer. Surrounded by mobs of partisan fans, they incite violence between groups of rival supporters by leading obscene and provocative chants.

Davies' (1972: 108) participant observation of the crowd at a Tottenham–Coventry match captures the mood of these events:

> The police let them stay where they were, but as the Coventry supporters slowly grew in number, the Coventry songs and shouts got louder, beginning to equal the volume of the Spurs songs. It became a dialogue, with each side of the thin blue line taking it in turns to sing insults at the other.
>
> "IF YOU ALL HATE CITY, CLAP YOUR HANDS," sang Spurs, and the claps that followed shook the ground.
>
> "MAN-CHESTER CITY, MAN-CHESTER CITY," shouted Coventry in reply, very nastily, getting in one below the belt. It had been Manchester City who'd hammered Spurs earlier in the season, 4–0.
>
> When they'd finished this chant, they continued with shouts CITY, CITY, this time meaning their own club. The Spurs boys punctuated it by shouting SHIT after each shout.

For an hour, they kept up the songs, solidly and without ceasing, one leading to another. I couldn't understand a lot of them. Many of the chants had actions with them, like "We hate Arsenal," where you punch one fist in the air in front of you, like a Nazi salute. My ears were numb, being right in amongst them. There was a definite feeling of power and excitement, but we were deafening ourselves more than anyone else.

The ecology of the stadium and surrounding area helps determine the form of the outburst governing, for instance, the accessibility of objects of attack. Basketball, owing to its proximity to the crowd, is constantly harassed by fans who run onto the floor to attack players or officials. Similarly, soccer spectators invade the pitch; while hockey fans, because of the boards and the slippery ice, tend to hurl missiles. Soccer referees have been vulnerable targets for crowd anger despite increasingly elaborate precautions. In 1948, in Buenos Aires, an official was beaten to death by players and fans who disagreed with his call. A nine-foot wide moat around the field was constructed in 1950 but failed to stop at least one fan from assaulting the referee a year later (*New York Times*, July 16, 1951). The referee of a 1954 Rio de Janeiro match was beaten unconscious by spectators who then set his dressing room afire (*New York Times*, April 19, 1954). When Angel Pazos, the referee of the 1964 Peru–Argentina game, was able to find safety in his steel-doored dressing room (*Time*, June 5, 1964), the crowd turned against the police, then against the scorekeeper who barricaded himself in his booth (White, 1970).

When human targets are inaccessible, other objects may be selected for attack. In the Montreal hockey riot, National Hockey League president, Clarence Campbell, the chief butt of the crowd's anger, managed to escape under a pall of tear gas to a basement room in the Forum. Spectators then spilled onto the streets assailing the exterior of the building with bricks and finally ransacking stores along St. Catherine Street (*Toronto Star*, March 18, 1955). Most targets, too, have symbolic meanings for the crowd; rioting racegoers at Montreal's Blue Bonnets Raceway, under the belief that the track had cheated them on a payoff, turned fire hoses on the sophisticated mutuel machines (*Toronto Telegram*, September 17, 1971). These observations are consistent with riot data in general indicating that crowd targets are not merely selected at random (Currie and Skolnick, 1972).

In summary, the literature on sport riots reveals several phases of crowd process: hostile beliefs which provide meaning to social structural strain by focusing on its source; precipitating factors which (by verifying beliefs) trigger the action; and finally the actual mobilization and organization of the rioters. It has been argued on several counts that the sport spectacle provides a medium especially conducive to these dynamics.

CONCLUSION: CONSEQUENCES OF COLLECTIVE VIOLENCE IN SPORT

One obvious consequence of sport crowd violence is escalating social control: some of it reform-oriented, some repressive. First, because of evidence regarding the connection between what transpires on the field and subsequent spectator disorder, attempts have been made to establish norms to govern potentially inflammatory conduct by players, coaches, and management. These attempts range from recommendations like those found in *Crowd Control For High School Athletics* (1970) to legislation such as the Toronto and District Soccer League's recent proposal that any player who assaults a referee be banned for life. Interestingly, several assaults in North American sport in recent years have been referred to courts of law; in 1972, for the first time in National Hockey League history, a fight between players and spectators was dealt with in court (*Toronto Globe and Mail*, December 21, 1973).

A second mode of control involves managing the physical environment. The Harrington Report (1968) urges construction of tracks around soccer pitches to form a space between crowd and players, especially near the goal areas. Where this is impossible, the Report recommends that steel barriers be built behind the goals to protect the goalkeeper from missile throwers. Bridged concrete ditches are also urged; whereas the Lang Report (1969) suggests "unclimbable" fences. Soccer grounds in some other countries are surrounded by moats, iron palings, and barbed-wire topped fences. In North America, in contrast, a United Press International nationwide survey discloses that although all major league parks, arenas, and stadiums take precautions against unruly fans, management is generally reluctant to take strong action for fear of offending supporters (*New York Times*, October 14, 1973).

Perhaps the most contentious crowd control device at sport events is the mounting presence of control agents: specially trained sport "mob squads," mounted constables, dogs, private and public police, state troopers, even soldiers, all carrying an ever more formidable array of weapons. In many European and Latin American countries police have a detention center within the soccer stadium. And sometimes a civil judge is on hand to mete out on-the-spot penalties to misbehavers (*New York Times*, October 14, 1973). A show of force often quells a developing riot but sometimes has the unintended consequence of inflaming those it seeks to subdue. This was frequently the case in the urban disorders of the 1960's (Marx, 1970) and appears to have occurred in several sport episodes. Whether or not control agents prevent or help cause a disturbance depends upon a number of factors (Marx, 1970), including tactics and the manner in which they are employed. Ingham and Smith (forthcoming) note several sport riots in which overzealous or panic-stricken police appeared to instigate the disorder. Police restraint, on the other hand, was instrumental in averting a potential riot at a 1965 Maryland motorcycle race (Shellow and Roemer, 1969).

Crowd control is clearly a short-term means of curbing collective violence. Alternatively, attempts ought to be made to alleviate the strains from which such disorder arises. Taylor (1971b) suggests (with respect to soccer in England) that structural changes be made in the relationship between club and supporter, and, more important, in the situation of the working class in society. Control by reform, however, "is a high goal not easily attained" (Turner and Killian, 1972: 176). In view of the argument presented in this chapter that sport not only provides a medium particularly conducive to the accumulation of conditions that culminate in collective violence but, more often than not, exacerbates the very conditions themselves, more realistic reform would bring about change in the *ways* spectator sport is conducted. Failing this, perhaps only the demise of sport spectatorship will provide a solution. Since elementary forms of collective behavior are said to contain the seeds of social movements and change (Blumer, 1951), this notion may not be altogether far-fetched.

NOTES

1. All, of course, would not agree with this definition of theory.

2. I am grateful to Alan G. Ingham for his critical comments on some of the ideas presented in this section.

3. Recent examples can be found in research conducted by Leiberson and Silverman (1965), Levy (1969), Taylor (1971a), and Smith (1973a; 1973b). Among others, Griffith (1949), Grusky (1963), and Tannenbaum and Noah (1959) have made imaginative use of the daily newspaper in research to do with other substantive issues in sport.

4. The information found in the "running record" is descriptive only, of course, but as Kahn (1972: 158) notes:

... descriptive statistics become tremendously more useful when they are collected repeatedly on a uniform and representative basis. Descriptive data collected once tells us the state of some system with respect to some characteristic at some point in time. If the descriptive process is repeated at regular intervals, it is still only descriptive, but the description becomes dynamic rather than static; we are told the direction and rate of change in the system with respect to the measured characteristics. (Robert L. Kahn, "The Justification of Violence: Social Problems and Social Solutions," *Journal of Social Issues*, Vol. 23, No. 1 (1972): p. 158. Reprinted by permission.)

5. Taine (1878), in his lurid descriptions of the mob during the Terror, provided many of the examples used by these writers. While Le Bon was unwilling to condemn democracy in all its ramifications, Sighele was clear in his denunciation. His work later became one of the cornerstones of fascist ideology (Allport, 1954).

6. In addition, Le Bon was a doctor of medicine, inventor, world traveler, and author of a half dozen books (Stoetzel, 1968).

7. For example, "the social problem" of European sociologists was the historical "question of the relationship between the social classes." To Americans, "social problems" meant delinquency, slums, divorce, and the like (Bramson, 1961: 48). An important reason for the upsurge in sociology and social psychology in the United States, following the First World War, lay in the pragmatic tradition of that country. "National emergencies and conditions of social disruption provided special incentive to invent new techniques, and to strike out boldly for solutions to practical social problems" (Allport, 1954: 4).

8. Allport (1954: 16–17) argues that most social psychologists, past and present, have favored irrationalist interpretations. It was the "gigantic impact of Darwin, McDougall, and Freud, with their varying conceptions of instinct, that assured the supremacy of irrationalism in present-day social psychology.... Only in recent years ... has there been any marked sign of reaction against irrationalism."

9. Although widely regarded as a definitive work, Bramson (1961: 60) describes the Park piece as a "masterpiece of ambiguity. He does not [for example] sufficiently distinguish between ordinary social behavior, which is by definition 'collective,' and the particular kind of behavior which occurs when ordinary social rules and usages break down or are absent from the situation."

10. Daniel Bell (1956) provides an illuminating discussion of various conceptions of "mass," the relationship of the "mass" to the "mob," and how these conceptions have been riddled with value judgments.

11. In general, however, the field was strangely static for several decades following the appearance of the Park-Burgess text. Until Turner and Killian's work in 1957 there was no book on the subject published in the United States. Since then, important texts on collective behavior have come from the Langs (1961), Smelser (1962), Klapp (1972), and recently, a revised edition from Turner and Killian (1972). In addition, there have appeared many readers and journal articles.

12. Some modern European depictions of the crowd retain the breathless quality of the early conservative theorists' prose and hint at the same kind of mysterious forces in operation:

Outside, facing the city, the arena displays a lifeless wall; inside is a wall of people. The spectators turn their backs to the city. They have been lifted out of its structure of walls and streets and, for the duration of their time in the arena, they do not care about anything which happens there; they have left behind all their associations, rules and habits. Their remaining together in large numbers for a stated period of time is secure and their excitement has been promised them. But only under one definite condition: the discharge must take place *inside the arena*.

The seats are arranged in tiers around the arena, so that everyone can see what is happening below. The consequence of this is that the crowd is seated opposite itself. Every spectator has a thousand in front of him, a thousand heads. As long as he is there, all the others are there too; whatever excites him, excites them; and he sees it. They are seated some distance away from him, so that the differing details which make individuals of them are blurred; they all look alike and they all behave in a similar manner and he notices in them only the things which he himself is full of. Their visible excitement increases his own. (Elias Canetti, *Crowds and Power*, translated by Carol Stewart. English translation copyright © 1962 by Victor Gallancz Ltd. All rights reserved. Reprinted by permission of The Viking Press, Inc.)

13. A fifth orientation is the "natural history" or "life-cycle" approaches of sociologists Carl A. Dawson and Warner E. Gettys (1929) and of historian Crane Brinton (1938). These seem to have gained only narrow currency in the sociological study of collective behavior, although Smelser's (1962) value-added theory is an offshoot of sorts.

    The main approaches to collection behavior are not always labeled and organized as presented here. For example, the chapter on collective behavior written by Neil Smelser in the text *Society Today* (1973) is organized around the psychological, social, interactionist, natural history, and value-added approaches to the subject. On the other hand, Turner (1969) suggests a theoretical framework organized around the concepts of "process-resolution versus infolding," "immanent versus interactive determination," and "emergent norm versus contagion."

14. Lupsha perhaps overstates his case. See Hornback (1970) for an argument that the socially marginal are predisposed to become involved in collective episodes.

15. Smelser first proposed six determinants of collective behavior: conduciveness, strain, generalized belief, precipitating factors, mobilization for action, and social control. Subsequently (1968), he revised his scheme making the precipitating factor a subcategory of the growth of a generalized belief. For specific tests of Smelser's model see Lewis's (1972) study of the Kent State shootings and Quarantelli and Hundley's (1969) investigation of a similar episode.

16. For example, the interactionist approaches to collective behavior typically begin at the point "... when people discover that they must do something together but do not know exactly what it is that they must do and are not

organized to do it" (Swanson, 1970: 126; and the entire series of papers presented in honor of Herbert Blumer in Shibutani, 1970).

17. Only Smelser (1962) has done this in detail, although the four United States Violence Commissions of the 1960's progressively noted the importance of social structural strain in the genesis of the urban disorder of that decade by pinpointing institutionalized racism and poverty as "root causes." Just how far back one must go to find the "roots," however, is problematic. Grimshaw (1972), for instance, notes that the violence commissions failed to come to grips with the "roots" of racism and poverty.

18. Mandell (1971) discusses, also, the dilemma of what was to be done with German Jewish athletes some of whom were potential medal winners for the Fatherland.

19. Indirect evidence of this is found in accounts of the lengths to which fans will go to obtain scarce tickets and riots and stampedes when they are unable to do so or are prevented for other reasons from getting into games. To cite several examples: Twenty-five people were taken to hospital after a struggle to gain access to the ticket windows prior to a 1967 Liverpool-Everton soccer match. Forty thousand had lined up for as long as thirty-six hours before the windows opened (*Toronto Globe and Mail*, March 8, 1967). Similarly, 9,000 fans lined up in hope of purchasing tickets for a New York Rangers playoff hockey game in 1967. Many were trampled and hurt when the windows opened, especially those caught napping in sleeping bags. Police finally sectioned off the fans into "bullpens" (*Toronto Globe and Mail*, March 28, 1967). In Italy, police resorted to tear gas grenades to fight back 4,000 soccer fans trying to get into a 1972 game between Internazionale and Juventus of Turin (*Toronto Globe and Mail*, January 3, 1972). And the Indian army was rushed to the scene of the 1967 India–West Indies cricket match in Calcutta when thousands of fans, not permitted to enter the park (already jammed with an estimated 100,000 people), fought with the police (*Toronto Globe and Mail*, January 3, 1967).

20. Tec (1964) examined gambling in soccer pools in Sweden and found the practice most prevalent in the lower classes. He speculates that the hopes provided by gambling tend to make a deprivational situation less acute and less urgent. Klapp (1972: 182–193) provides an extended discussion of the role of "safety-valve institutions," such as lotteries and horse-betting, in distracting the attention of the poor from their troubles.

21. Discussion of "riots in victory and celebration" in nonsport sectors are found in Lang and Lang (1970), Marx (1972), and Tilly (1972).

REFERENCES

AAHPER
1970 *Crowd Control for High School Athletics.* Washington, D.C.: American Association for Health, Physical Education, and Recreation.

Abel, T.
1970   *The Foundation of Sociological Theory.* New York: Random House.

Allport, F. H.
1924   *Social Psychology.* Boston: Houghton Mifflin.

Allport, G. W.
1954   "The Historical Background of Modern Social Psychology." In *Handbook of Social Psychology*, G. Lindzey (ed.). **1**. Cambridge, Mass.: Addison-Wesley. 3–56.

Asch, S. E.
1951   "Effects of Group Pressure Upon the Modification and Distortion of Judgment. In *Groups, Leadership, and Men*, H. Guetzkow (ed.). Pittsburgh: Carnegie Press. 177–190.

Bell, D.
1956   "America as Mass Society: A Critique." *Commentary*, **22**: 75–83.

Berger, P. L.
1963   *Invitation to Sociology.* New York: Anchor.

Berk, R. A.
1972   "The Controversy Surrounding Analyses of Collective Violence: Some Methodological Notes." In *Collective Violence*, J. F. Short, Jr. and M. E. Wolfgang (eds.). Chicago: Aldine-Atherton. 112–118.

Berkowitz, R.
1972   "Frustrations, Comparisons, and Other Sources of Emotion Arousal as Contributions to Social Unrest." *Journal of Social Issues*, **28**: 77–91.

Blumer, Herbert
1951   "Collective Behavior." In *Principles of Sociology*, A. M. Lee (ed.). New York: Barnes and Noble. 167–222. First published in 1939.
1953   "Psychological Import of the Human Group." In *Group Relations at the Crossroads*, M. Sherif and M. O. Wilson (eds.). New York: Harper and Row.
1957   "Collective Behavior." In *Review of Sociology: Analysis of a Decade*, J. B. Gittler (ed.). New York: Wiley.

Boring, E. G.
1963   *History, Psychology and Science.* New York: Wiley.

Bramson, L.
1961   *The Political Context of Sociology.* Princeton, N.J.: Princeton University Press.

Brinton, C.
1938   *An Anatomy of Revolution.* New York: Random House.

Brown, Roger
1965   *Social Psychology.* New York: Free Press.

Buckley, W.
1967   *Sociology and Modern Systems Theory.* Englewood Cliffs, N.J.: Prentice-Hall.

Canetti, E.
1962   *Crowds and Power.* New York: Viking.

Canadian Magazine
1972   November 25.

Caplan, N.
1970   "The New Ghetto Man: A Review of Recent Empirical Studies." *Journal of Social Issues,* **26**: 59–73.

Couch, C. J.
1968   "Collective Behavior: An Examination of Some Stereotypes." *Social Problems,* **15**: 310–322.

Currie, E., and J. H. Skolnick
1972   "A Critical Note on Conceptions of Collective Behavior." In *Collective Violence,* J. F. Short, Jr. and M. E. Wolfgang (eds.). Chicago: Aldine-Atherton. 61–71.

Davies, H.
1972   *The Glory Game.* London: Weidenfeld and Nicolson.

Davies, J. D.
1969   "The J-Curve of Rising and Declining Satisfactions as a Cause of Some Great Revolutions and a Contained Rebellion." In *The History of Violence in America,* H. D. Graham and T. R. Gurr (eds.). New York: Bantam. 690–730.

Dawson, C. A., and W. E. Gettys
1929   *An Introduction to Sociology.* New York: Ronald Press.

Dollard, J. et al.
1939   *Frustration and Aggression.* New Haven: Yale University Press.

Edwards, H.
1973   *Sociology of Sport.* Homewood, Ill.: Dorsey Press.

Feierabend, I. K., R. L. Feierabend, and B. A. Nesvold
1969   "Social Change and Political Violence: Cross-National Patterns." In *The History of Violence in America,* H. D. Graham and T. R. Gurr (eds.). New York: Bantam. 632–680.

Fogelson, R. M., and P. B. Hill
1968   "Who Riots? A Study of Participation in the 1967 Riots." *Supplemental Studies for the National Advisory Commission on Civil Disorders.* Washington, D.C.: U.S. Government Printing Office (July).

French, J. R. P., Jr.
1944   "Organized and Unorganized Groups Under Fear and Frustration." In *Authority and Frustration,* K. Lewin et al. (eds.). Iowa City: University of Iowa Press. 229–308.

Freud, S.
1922   *Group Psychology and the Analysis of the Ego.* London: Hogarth.

Furst, R. T.
1972   "The Boxer and His Audience: An Empirical Assessment." Paper presented at the Scientific Congress of the XX Olympic Games, Munich (August).

Glanville, B.
1968   *Soccer.* New York: Crown Publishers.

Graham, H. D., and T. R. Gurr
1969   *The History of Violence in America.* New York: Bantam Books.

Griffith, R. M.
1949   "Odds Adjustments by American Horse Bettors." *American Journal of Psychology,* **62**: 290–294.

Grimshaw, A. D.
1972   "Interpreting Collective Violence: An Argument for the Importance of Social Structure." In *Collective Violence,* J. F. Short, Jr. and M. E. Wolfgang (eds.). Chicago: Aldine-Atherton. 36–46.

Grusky, O.
1963   "Managerial Succession and Organizational Effectiveness." *American Journal of Sociology,* **69**: 21–31.

Hain, P.
1971   *Don't Play with Apartheid.* London: George Allen and Unwin.

Harrington, J. A.
1968   *Soccer Hooliganism: A Preliminary Report to Mr. Denis Howell, Minister of Sport.* Bristol: John Wright and Sons.

Hasdorf, A. H., and H. Cantril
1954   "They Saw a Game: A Case Study." *Journal of Abnormal and Social Psychology,* **49**: 129–134.

Hecht, E.
1968   "Football." In *Latin America and the Caribbean: A Handbook,* C. Véliz (ed.). New York: Praeger. 743–748.

Heinila, K.
1966   "Notes on the Inter-Groups Conflicts in International Sport." *International Review of Sport Sociology,* Vol. 1. Warsaw: Polish Scientific Publishers.

Hornback, K. E.
1970   "Toward a Theory of Involvement Propensity for Collective Behavior." *Sociological Focus,* **4**: 61–77.

Ingham, A. G., and H. Nixon
1970   "Riots on the Rails—An Axiomatic Approach to Collective Behavior." Paper presented at the 74th Annual Conference of the National College Physical Education Association for Men, Portland, Oregon (December).

Ingham, A. G., and M. D. Smith
1975 "The Social Implications of the Interaction Between Spectators and Athletes." In *Exercise and Sport Science Reviews*, J. Wilmore (ed.). Vol. 2. New York: Academic Press. 34.

Kahn, R. L.
1972 "The Justification of Violence: Social Problems and Social Solutions." *Journal of Social Issues*, **28**: 155–176.

Katz, S.
1955 "Strange Forces Behind the Rocket Richard Riot." *Maclean's Magazine*. September 17.

Kerckhoff, A. C.
1970 "A Theory of Hysterical Contagion." In *Human Nature and Collective Behavior*, T. Shibutani (ed.). Englewood Cliffs, N.J.: Prentice-Hall.

Kerner, O.
1968 *Report of the National Advisory Commission on Civil Disorders*. New York: Bantam.

Klapp, O. E.
1972 *Currents of Unrest: An Introduction to Collective Behavior*. New York: Holt, Rinehart and Winston.

Lang, J.
1969 *Report of the Working Party on Crowd Behavior at Football Matches*. London: Her Majesty's Stationery Office.

Lang, K., and G. E. Lang
1961 *Collective Dynamics*. New York: Crowell.
1968 "Collective Behavior." In *International Encyclopedia of the Social Sciences*, D. L. Sills (ed.). Vol. 2. New York: Macmillan and the Free Press. 556–564.
1970 "Collective Behavior Theory and the Escalated Riots of the Sixties." In *Human Nature and Collective Behavior*, T. Shibutani (ed.). Englewood Cliffs, N.J.: Prentice-Hall. 94–110.

Le Bon, G.
1960 *The Crowd*. New York: Viking. First published in 1895.

Leiberson, S., and A. R. Silverman
1965 "The Precipitants and Underlying Conditions of Race Riots." *American Sociological Review*, **30**: 887–898.

Lever, J.
1972 "Soccer as a Brazilian Way of Life." In *Games, Sport and Power*, G. P. Stone (ed.). New Brunswick, N.J.: Transaction Inc. 138–159.

Levy, S. G.
1969 "A 150-Year Study of Political Violence in the United States." In *The History of Violence in America*, H. D. Graham and T. R. Gurr (eds.). New York: Bantam.

Lewis, J. M.
1972   "A Study of the Kent State Incident Using Smelser's Theory of Collective Behavior." *Sociological Inquiry,* **42**: 87–96.

Loy, J. W., Jr.
1971   "The Nature of Sociological Theory and Its Import for the Explanation of Agônetic Behavior." In 74th Proceedings of the National College Physical Education Association for Men.

Lupsha, P. A.
1969   "On Theories of Urban Violence." *Urban Affairs Quarterly,* **4**: 273–296.

Mandell, R. D.
1971   *The Nazi Olympics.* New York: Macmillan.

Manning, R.
1971   "A Critical Analysis of Contemporary Collective Behavior Theory." *Sociological Focus,* **4**: 99–106.
1973   "Fifteen Years of Collective Behavior." *The Sociological Quarterly,* **14**: 279–286.

Martin, E. D.
1920   *The Behavior of Crowds.* New York: Harper.

Marx, G. T.
1970   "Civil Disorder and the Agents of Social Control." *Journal of Social Issues,* **26**: 19–57.

Marx, G.
1972   "Issueless Riots." In *Collective Violence,* J. F. Short, Jr. and M. E. Wolfgang (eds.). Chicago: Aldine-Atherton. 47–59.

Mazlish, B.
1970   "The French Revolution in Comparative Perspective." *Political Science Quarterly,* **85**: 255–264.

McDougall, W.
1927   *The Group Mind.* Cambridge: Cambridge University Press.

Meerloo, J. A. M.
1950   *Patterns of Panic.* New York: International Universities Press.

Miller, N. E., and J. Dollard
1941   *Social Learning and Imitation.* New Haven: Yale University Press.

Paige, J. M.
1971   "Political Orientation and Riot Participation." *American Sociological Review,* **36**: 810–820.

Park, R. E., and E. W. Burgess
1921   *Introduction to the Science of Sociology.* Chicago: University of Chicago Press.

Quarantelli, E., and J. R. Hundley, Jr.
1969   "A Test of Some Propositions About Crowd Formation and Behavior." In *Readings in Collective Behavior,* R. R. Evans (ed.). Chicago: Rand McNally. 538–554.

Ross, E. A.
1908   *Social Psychology.* New York: Macmillan.

Rudé, George
1964   *The Crowd in History.* New York: Wiley.

Shellow, R., and D. V. Roemer
1969   "The Riot that Didn't Happen." In *Readings in Collective Behavior*, R. R. Evans (ed.). Chicago: Rand McNally. 523–536.

Sherif, C. W.
1972   *Intergroup Conflict and Competition: Social-Psychological Analysis.* Paper presented at the Scientific Congress of the XX Olympic Games, Munich (August).

Sherif, M., and C. W. Sherif
1969   *Social Psychology.* New York: Harper and Row. Chapter 11.

Shibutani, T., ed.
1970   *Human Nature and Collective Behavior.* Englewood Cliffs, N.J.: Prentice-Hall.

Sighele, S.
1895   *Psychologie des Sectes.* Paris: Bailliere.

Skolnick, J. H.
1969   *The Politics of Protest.* New York: Simon and Schuster.

Smelser, N. J.
1962   *Theory of Collective Behavior.* New York: The Free Press.
1968   *Essays in Sociological Explanation*, Chapter 5. Englewood Cliffs, N.J.: Prentice-Hall.
1969   "Theoretical Issues of Scope and Problems." In *Readings in Collective Behavior*, R. R. Evans (ed.). Chicago: Rand McNally. 89–104.
1972a   "Some Additional Thoughts on Collective Behavior." *Sociological Inquiry*, **42**: 97–103.
1972b   "Two Critics in Search of a Bias: A Response to Currie and Skolnick." In *Collective Violence*, J. F. Short, Jr. and M. E. Wolfgang (eds.). Chicago: Aldine-Atherton. 73–81.
1973   "Collective Behavior." *Society Today*, Chapter 27. Del Mar, Calif.: CRM Books.

Smith, M. D.
1973a   "Hostile Outbursts in Sport." *Sport Sociology Bulletin*, **2**: 6–10.
1973b   "Precipitants of Crowd Violence in Sport." Paper presented at the First Canadian Congress for the Multi-Disciplinary Study of Sport and Physical Activity, Montreal (October).

Smits, T.
1968   *The Game of Soccer.* Englewood Cliffs, N.J.: Prentice-Hall.

Spicer, E.
1971   "Persistent Cultural Systems." *Science*, **174** (November): 795–800.

Stoetzel, J.
1968 "Le Bon, Gustave." In *International Encyclopedia of the Social Sciences*, D. L. Sills (ed.). Vol. 9. New York: Macmillan and the Free Press. 82–84.

Stump, A.
1973 "The Big Brawl Era of College Basketball." *T.V. Guide*, January 20–26: 30–34.

Swanson, G. E.
1970 "Toward Corporate Action: A Reconstruction of Elementary Collective Processes." In *Human Nature and Collective Behavior*, T. Shibutani (ed.). Englewood Cliffs, N.J.: Prentice-Hall. 124–144.

Taine, H.
1878 *Les Origines de la France Contemporaine. Le Révolution.* 3 volumes. Paris.

Tannenbaun, P. M., and J. E. Noah
1959 "Sportuguese: A Study of Sports Page Communication." *Journalism Quarterly*, **36**: 163–170.

Tarde, G.
1901 *L'Opinion et la Foule.* Paris: Librarie Félix Alcan.
1903 *The Laws of Imitation.* Translation by Elsie Parsons, New York: Holt.

Taylor, I. L.
1969 "Hooligans: Soccer's Resistance Movement." *New Society*, August 7: 204–206.

Taylor, I. R.
1971a " 'Football' Mad: A Speculative Sociology of Football Hooliganism." In *The Sociology of Sport*, E. Dunning (ed.). London: Frank Cass. 353–377.
1971b "Soccer Consciousness and Soccer Hooliganism." In *Images of Deviance*, S. Cohen (ed.). Middlesex, England: Pelican Books. 135–165.
"Social Control Through Sport: Football in Mexico." *Canadian Journal of Latin American Studies*, forthcoming.

Tec, N.
1964 *Gambling in Sweden.* Totowa, N.J.: Bedminster Press.

Tilly, C.
1969 "Collective Violence in European Perspective." In *The History of Violence in America*, H. D. Graham and T. R. Gurr (eds.). New York: Bantam. 4–45.

Time Magazine
1964 June 5.

Trotter, W.
1919 *Instincts of the Herd in Peace and War: 1916–1919.* London: Oxford University Press. First published in 1916.

Turner, R. H.
1964 "Collective Behavior." In *Handbook of Modern Sociology*, R. E. L. Faris (ed.). Chicago: Rand McNally. 382–425.

1969   "New Theoretical Frameworks: Collective Behavior and Conflicts." In *Social Psychology: Readings and Perspective*, E. F. Borgatta (ed.). Chicago: Rand McNally. 552–558.

Turner, R. H., and L. M. Killian
1972   *Collective Behavior.* Englewood Cliffs, N.J.: Prentice-Hall. First published in 1957.

Turowetz, A.
1973   "Wrestling: Rhetoric and Reality." Paper presented at the First Canadian Conference for the Multi-Disciplinary Study of Sport and Physical Activity, Montreal (October).

Turowetz, A., R. Fernandez, and L. Jacobs
1973   "Professional Sport and the Manipulation of Identities." Paper presented at the Northeastern Anthropological Association Annual Meeting, Burlington, Vermont (April).

Webb, E. et al.
1969   *Unobtrusive Measures: Nonreactive Research in the Social Sciences.* Chicago: Rand McNally.

Weinberg, S. K., and H. Arond
1952   "The Occupational Culture of Boxer." *American Journal of Sociology,* **57**: 460–469.

Weller, J. M., and E. L. Quarantelli
1973   "Neglected Characteristics of Collective Behavior." *American Journal of Sociology,* **79**: 665–685.

Wheeler, L.
1966   "Toward a Theory of Behavioral Contagion." *Psychological Review,* **73**: 179–192.

White, C.
1970   "An Analysis of Hostile Outbursts in Spectator Sports." Ph.D. Dissertation, University of Illinois, Champaign-Urbana.

Wolff, K. ed.
1954   *The Sociology of Georg Simmel.* Glencoe, Ill.: Free Press.

Zetterberg, H.
1965   *On Theory and Verification in Sociology.* New York: Bedminster Press.

Part III
The Occupational
Organization of Sport

Chapter 8
Occupational Subcultures in the Work World of Sport

Alan G. Ingham
School of Health and Physical Education
University of Washington
(Seattle, Washington)

Alan G. Ingham

Birth Place: Manchester, England

Age: 28

Birth Order: Only child

Formal Education:

City of Leeds College of Education and Carnegie College of Physical Education, Leeds, England	1967
B.Ed., Honors, University of Leeds, England	1968
M.S., Physical Education, Washington State University, Pullman	1969
Ph.D., Sociology, University of Massachusetts, Amherst, (now completing)	

Present Position:

Assistant Professor, School of Health and Physical Education, University of Washington

Professional Responsibilities:

Undergraduate: A Social Scientific Analysis of Sport: Social Psychological Perspectives Sport in the United States

Graduate: Sport: A Critical Appraisal

Scholarly Interests:

Research and analysis of:
the "rationalization" of organized sport; the effects of co-action upon individual performance in the learning and performance phases of motor skills; the effects of group size upon individual performance in a sport activity.

Sociology of sport, social psychology, collective behavior, sociological theory.

Professional Accomplishments:

Recent works appear in Rarick, *Physical Activity: Human Growth and Development;* Wilmore, *Exercise and Sport Sciences Review;* Landers, *Problems in Athletics: Essays in the Sociology of Sport* (in press).

Articles published in *Journal of Experimental and Social Psychology, International Review of Sport Sociology, Quest.*

Papers presented at meetings of the American Sociological Association, the Canadian Sociological and Anthropological Association, and at the International Symposium on the Sociology of Sport.

Sport Activities:

Participant: soccer (also coach), squash.

Spectator: soccer, tennis, and football.

Most Recent Books Read:

Crichton	*The Camerons*
Birnbaum	*The Crisis of Industrial Society*
Pruitt and Stone	*The Ruling Elites*

INTRODUCTION

Sport is a social institution and, as such, is characterized by regulation, formalization, ideological justification, and transmissibility.[1] Like other social institutions, sport appears to be a reified entity in our "taken-for-granted-life-world." That is, sport possesses ontological status and, as a result, is perceived as external to and independent of the athletes who participate in it. In a similar fashion to other social institutions, sport channels human actions so that they accord with predefined expectations. It is a regulatory agency having a variety of rewards and sanctions at its disposal.

Sport is also a part of the economic institutions of society in that it possesses a system of resource allocation and distribution. As a part of the labor market, sport's social structure contains those who control the resource allocation and those who sell their services for a salary (or if sport is viewed as manual labor, a wage). At the professional level, athletics has become work and the athletes provide services which have exchange value.

These characteristics of sport stimulate the sociological imagination. They direct our attention to an analysis of the relationships between the historical emergence of sport into its present forms, the social and economic structure of sport, and the biographies of athletes who participate in sport. To loosely paraphrase C. Wright Mills (1959), our curiosity becomes stimulated and can only be satisfied by searching for answers to questions such as:

1. How can we best describe the historical transformation of sport into its present forms?

2. What are the ideological premises which undergird the social institution of sport and are these premises hegemonic in society and throughout sport's social structure?

3. How can we best describe the relationships which exist in sport's social structures, i.e., between athletes, between the athletes and the

economic controllers of sport, between these producers and sport's consumers?

4. How are these relationships maintained and changed and how do such processes as socialization, social control, economic control, and ideological legitimation figure in maintenance and change?

These originating questions, while deserving more consideration than possibly can be given in this chapter, serve as frames of reference for the analysis which follows.

Sport in the last 100 years has not escaped the thrust of rationality, both technological and bureaucratic. Sport has increasingly mirrored the "formalized, hierarchical, rule-laden, and efficiency-seeking type of social organization the principal prototypes of which are big government, modern business enterprise, and the military establishment" (Page, 1973: 32). It has emerged as yet another productivity-oriented activity in social life and this coupled with the application of scientific and technological rationality has led us to debate whether such trends engender the suppression of personal autonomy. We are faced with the question of whether the rationalization of modern life has resulted in a new and more totalitarian form of domination. The historical emergence of rationality in professional sport provides the focus for a section of this chapter.

Modern professional sport has become a part of the labor market. As the athlete progresses to higher levels of competition the nature of his social role is transformed from recreational to occupational. Indeed the athletic role can be characterized as a service occupation in that the athlete is in "more or less direct personal contact with the ultimate consumer of the product of his work, the client for whom he performs the service" (Becker, 1951: 136). The transition from recreation to occupation requires that the athlete be socialized into the occupational subculture of sport.

The occupational role aspirant becomes a successful occupational role incumbent by learning the behaviors which are deemed appropriate by his fellow athletes, the professional sport establishment, and the consumers who pay for his services. Socialization enables the professional athlete to handle the expectations of the "wise" and the "unwise," those on the inside and those on the outside. Sometimes the expectations of the wise and the unwise are in congruence. Oftentimes they are not, and this feature of the service occupation places the athlete in role dilemmas—which expectations should be granted primacy in determining the role performance. An analysis of socialization into the occupational subculture will be provided. We will also confront the problems facing the athlete in the execution of his social role.

Sport, as previously stated, is also a social institution. As such, sport serves many different functions and, thus, contains inherent paradoxes. On the one hand, as an economic and social institution, sport has become instrumental. On the other hand, sport as a recreative activity is valued for its own sake: it retains the expressive component of games. Thus, one paradox inherent in sport is that while it possesses a degree of institutional autonomy, it is subsumed within the paramount reality of a social life-world which is steadily becoming rationalized.

A second paradox can also be identified: at the level of the performer, sport can be fun and provide for sociability—it possesses quasi-*Gemeinschaft* qualities. Yet, as a part of the labor market, sport can be used for pecuniary emulation, social mobility, and social status enhancement—it is part of the trend toward the meritocratic *Gesellschaft* society.[2] In its latter instrumental form, sport transforms the work role of the athlete from one of autonomy to one characterized by heteronomy. The professionalization of sport results in athletes working "for an apparatus which they do not control (and) which operates as an independent power to which individuals must submit" (Marcuse, 1955: 41). That is, the work role of the athlete, in a similar fashion to other work roles, might be envisaged as alienating. The rationalization of sport, facilitated by its professionalization, results in the athlete losing control over the products of his labor and the uses to which his labor is put. In the latter part of this chapter we shall attempt to briefly describe the relationship between rationalization and alienation in the occupational subculture of sport.

EXCURSUS: PROBLEMS OF EPISTEMOLOGY [3]

Before we proceed to develop the main arguments of the paper, which attempt to analyze the effects of rationality on the occupational subculture of sport, we would like to digress for a moment to consider the theoretical and methodological assumptions influencing the direction these arguments will take. There is much debate in sociological circles over which intellectual traditions should be adhered to if sociology is to make real contributions to the understanding of human behavior. Although written some years ago, the words of T. H. Marshall were both descriptive and prescient: sociology stands at the crossroads. It has its roots in the classical traditions of history and social philosophy and yet many sociologists have ignored these origins in their quest to emulate the methodology of the physical and biological sciences. Indeed, it might be claimed that much of what now passes for sociology has not simply ignored the historian's logic of inquiry but has rejected it. The concern with the analysis of here-and-now social structures is an attempt to freeze sociology in the knife-edged present: sociology becomes an analysis of social statics. However, the debates in sociology go beyond the now hackneyed question of whether sociology should be concerned with the analysis of social statics or social dynamics. For stemming from such debates are questions concerned with relativism and the search for invariant laws.

Since it might be claimed that history rarely repeats itself and no interaction between individuals occurs in exactly the same way on different occasions, some would claim that the search for scientific laws, subject to refutation and verifiability, cannot be the aim of sociology, or if it is the aim, would engage sociologists in a futile quest. The danger of such an interpretation is that it reduces sociology to the level of idealist subjectivism in which the value orientations of the sociologist, the ways in which he artificially structures his data, and the variability of milieu deny the possibility of validation. That is, it becomes difficult to ascertain how far a sociologist has stretched the facts to fit his preconceived theoretical or ideological notions. The alternative for many sociologists, then, has been to transform sociology into an experimental science which adheres to the doctrines of naturalism and objectivism. Yet such an alternative may not solve our problems. Although this approach is methodologically scientific it is limited: while pursuing internal validity facilitates objectivity and verifiability there is no guarantee that it obviates the imposition of an abstract and artificial order on the social world. There is no necessary relationship between internal and external validity; science remains on the level of assertion. Oftentimes the quest for generalization suffers from methodological inhibition (see C. W. Mills, 1959: 50–75), and the pursuit of precision does not guarantee congruence with empirical reality. Science is broader than scientific method.

But let us return to the question of statics and dynamics, social structure and social process, and resurrect the debate over the Marxian notion of *praxis*. "The concept of *praxis* in Marxism refers to the activity of Man which aims at transforming the world as well as aiding his own self-development" (Janousek, 1972: 279). Although the concept of praxis is not widely used in American sociology, the ideas enveloped by this concept have generated considerable polarization among theorists in the field. At the extremes, there are those sociologists of the Marxist tradition who see the concept of praxis as an integral part of their analysis of social process, and there are those, the structuralists, who have ignored or rejected this concept in their social theorizing. These extremes are characterized by Berger and Pullberg (1966: 56) as follows: "The first presents us with a view of society as a network of human meanings as embodiments of human activity. The second, on the other hand, presents us with society conceived of as a thing-like facticity, standing over its individual members with coercive controls and moulding them in its socialization processes." That is, one faction recognizes the dialectical relationship between reification and continual reconstruction whereas the other eristically emphasizes society and its social institutions as taken for granted, somewhat invariant over time, and independent of the volitions of its here-and-now members. These polar ideal-types have considerable import in the analysis of occupational socialization.

If we emphasize the dialectical nature of the relationship between the individual and his society, then, both individual "needs" and experiences and societal "needs" have to be juxtaposed. Individuals are to be viewed as constructing their social worlds in the light of their experiences rather than accepting the reified world, with its taken-for-granted definitions, which has been constructed by previous generations. Socialization, from this perspective, is person-centered.[4]

If, however, we emphasize the eristical argument that both the structural and normative components of society are taken for granted and that social change occurs independently of the individuals comprising that society, then socialization can be envisaged as a process whereby the individual succumbs to ever widening spheres of social influence. Socialization becomes a process through which the individual accommodates himself to and assimilates the contents of a predefined social reality. The individual appears passive, a spectator of, rather than a participant in, structural and normative change. In this sense, socialization is society-centered and can be judged as relatively successful if the individual conforms to and believes in the ideological and behavioral dictates necessary to preserve normative and structural order.

Before presenting some methodological debates, we would like to consider one final epistemological issue: the relationship between the sociologist and the moral questions raised by his theorizing and research. This epistemological issue focuses upon the idea of responsibility and its relationship to objectivity. Is the social scientist a "sardonic observer" (Berger, 1963) or a social reformer, a documentalist of social order and change, or an initiator of social change? Much has been written on this topic both by classical (e.g., Durkheim, Weber, Marx) and contemporary theorists (e.g., Bendix, Lynd, Mills). We have no intention to summarize these works but wish merely to point out that the issue is far from settled. We note, for example, that the crises which occurred in sociology during the sixties generated several major works in the area of the sociology of sociology (e.g., Aron, 1962; Bendix, 1960; Birnbaum, 1971; Gouldner, 1970).

Essentially, the epistemological issue focuses our attention on the ideologies of the sociologists themselves and the degree to which science has become alienated from its producers. Intrinsic in the issue is whether or not a specific mode of inquiry (i.e., the scientific method) has been reified to the extent that it dominates the scientist's labors either consciously or unconsciously. Also intrinsic to the issue is the question of "what the consequences are of political limitations on social inquiry" (Birnbaum, 1971: 183). In a sense the issue is a confrontation between sociologists from the "democratic left" and sociologists of the "conservative right" on the questions of involvement and commitment. In essence, the debate engenders a revitalization of and confrontation with Karl Marx's metaphysics. At the mundane level, the debate has often been translated into whether sociology should aim at solving the practical problems facing a society and engineering social reform or whether sociology should be concerned solely with the acquisition of knowledge for knowledge's sake. Oftentimes answers to this question result in an artificial separation of theory and empirical inquiry. At this juncture, we may return to the problems of method.

For the most part, science in recent years has become equated with scientific method, and a specific mode of inquiry has become conventionalized. This mode of inquiry, as it appears in sociology, generally involves the use of surveys, interviews, and questionnaires which, hopefully, contain information amenable to quantification and statistical analysis. The aim of such research is to observe changes occurring in a dependent variable assumed to be elicited by or associated with changes in the independent variable(s). Based upon the premises of epistemological realism, the scientific method emphasizes overt behavioral and situational stimuli and the behavioral responses they elicit rather than the covert processes of experience and interpretation which mediate between the stimuli and the response. If we view society and its social institutions as taken for granted, somewhat invariant over time, and independent of the volitions of the here-and-now individuals, then variable analysis is useful in our attempts to discover the underlying laws governing categoric relationships. Variable analysis enables us to predict general behavioral responses to generalized situational stimuli and tells us something about the range of those responses.

If, however, we view society as continually reproduced and ask how here-and-now individuals continually reinterpret and redefine the situations in which they are placed, then we may have to abandon our search for scientific laws. Instead, we may now have to ask how an individual's quasi theories[5] influence their behavioral responses. Conventional protocols of research, while yielding information about categoric relationships fails to yield information about how individuals mold their behaviors in the light of their interpretations and definitions of social situations. For example, employing conventional protocols of research in an analysis of a social role would yield information about the categories of responses available to the individual in a given social situation, but would be devoid of an analysis of why a given individual chooses to elect one set of responses over another, or elects to play the role tongue-in-cheek, or engages in a certain style of role performance. Variable analysis, therefore, is an appropriate technique for the study of role behavior in terms of its outcomes, but it leaves the question of process unexplored. Similarly, although conventional protocols of research can tell us much about the categoric relationships which exist in here-and-now social structures, they tend to fall short when we become concerned with how social structures have emerged into their present forms. That is, variable analysis and the analysis of categoric relationships have generally not tried "to study trends in an attempt to go behind events and make orderly sense of them" (Mills, 1959: 153).

One might well ask why we have engaged in this tortuous (and, perhaps, obscurantist) exercise of outlining the alternatives and issues in sociology. The major reason for this exercise is to allow us to state our value orientations so that they, as well as the arguments which follow, can be judged on their respective merits. Our sociological position is one of critical humanism. We use the word critical rather than radical since we believe that sociology, if it is to go behind the facades of everyday life, is both disenchanting and debunking but that this does not necessarily entail an attempt to replace existing institutions with ones developed according to some intellectual's blueprint. To say our sociology is critical is not to state that we value change for change's sake or that since our sociology points out deficiencies in existing institutions we see ourselves as social engineers capable of creating a new society devoid of such deficiencies. While we emphasize mutability we are not committed to it since mutability which is engineered is still susceptible to unintended consequences. This leads us to a discussion of the notion of praxis in social theory.

Our sociology is critical, therefore, there is no conservative celebration of status quo. Our sociology is humanistic and, hence, we do not intend to eliminate men from history nor to deny man's capacity to continually reconstruct the society in which he lives. Yet our sociology is not partisan or programmatic. How, then, should we view the notion of praxis as it applies to the sociological enterprise? Simply, we use the idea of praxis to suggest that we are prepared to examine "the moral and political implications of an assertion as to the organization of a society and its movement [and to explore] the possible consequences of a given historical situation ... in their relevance for the future direction of human activity" (Birnbaum, 1971: 126). Also we use the word, praxis, to acknowledge that the work of the scientist may have effects upon the future: social criticism and social research may influence the future course of events. That is, we recognize that the social scientist cannot completely disengage himself or his work from his views about the society which he seeks to describe and which affords him the opportunity to engage in the scientific enterprise.

Finally, we are prepared to identify our methodological premises. We concur with C. Wright Mills (1959: 6) that "no social study that does not come back to the problems of biography, of history and of their intersections within a society has completed its intellectual journal." Essentially this entails a broader conception of science than that of the scientific method per se. It entails a willingness to engage in historiography. It demands that we view social structure from a wider perspective than the one of empirico-analytic science. The description of categoric relationships, while valuable, should be enhanced by an analysis of experience and meaning. That is, we have no reason to submit the conventionalized variable analytic techniques to another public flogging but we do have reason to respect their limitations. In a sense, we are suggesting that there are other methods of gaining access to the social world than those which are emulative of the physical and biological sciences and that they ought to be granted scientific respectability. Although the preceding statement might indicate a shift from epistemological realism to epistemological idealism, we intend no such connotation. Rather we suggest that both positions have certain merits which would be denied to us should we adopt an unyielding addiction to one at the expense of the other.

THE RATIONALIZATION OF SPORT

Coauthored by Gurdeep Singh

Merely to state that sport has become rationalized and bureaucratized is inadequate. Description is only the first stage of the research adventure, the goals of which are understanding and explanation. Consequently, in this section of the chapter we shall attempt to outline the growth of rational-purposive action in modern industrial society in order to account for the infiltration of rationality into the social institution of sport. Essentially, we are adopting a Weberian approach to history. We are attempting to reconstruct historical reality according to an imaginary sequence in which we ask whether rationality would have occurred in sport if society had not undergone a scientific and industrial revolution. In creating this useful fiction (all theory is, in a sense, the imposition of a fictitious order upon the real world), we shall be forced to confront the question of

whether rational-purposive action has become methodologically hegemonic, the Weberian argument, or ideologically hegemonic, the Marcusean
argument, or whether institutions, since they are based upon value-orienta-
tions, inhibit the complete thrust of rationality, the Habermas synthesis.

A prevalent theme in many sociological commentaries which attempt
to explicate social change has been the idea that society has undergone a
transformation from *Gemeinschaft* to *Gesellschaft*. While not literally
translatable from the German, these ideal-typical concepts have been used
to describe the properties of the modern industrial state by comparing it
to the preindustrial agrarian forms of social life. Encompassed in the concepts, *Gemeinschaft* and *Gesellschaft*, are such ideas as Durkheim's mechanical and organic solidarity, Becker's sacred and secular forms of social
life, Redfield's folk-urban continuum, and MacIver's communal and associ-
ational relationships. Thus, *Gemeinschaft* is used to describe a form of
social organization which is backward looking (based upon tradition), intimate (blood-linked), communal (actions are performed for the collectivity), relatively homogeneous (little division of labor), and in which work
is viewed as life-activity. On the other hand, *Gesellschaft* is used to describe a form of social organization which is forward looking (suffers from
an illusion of progress, to use an idea of Sorel), loose (the most intimate
bonding being the nuclear family), personal (actions are performed for
one's own status or pecuniary enhancement), relatively heterogeneous
(specialization has engendered an increasing division of labor), and in
which work has become a means to an end (the acquisition of abstracted
commodities which have universal exchange value, e.g., money).

The transition from *Gemeinschaft* to *Gesellschaft* has been viewed in
many of the commentaries as directly attributable to the changes which
have taken place in the nature of the production process, that is, industrialization. The transition in social life might be viewed as an unintended
consequence of an accidental revolution. "This accidental revolution is the
sweeping and unprecedented technological transformation of the Western
environment which has been, and is being, carried out in a casual way"
(Harrington, 1965: 16). The changes taking place in industry, which involved the application of technological rationality to the production process, required a labor force that was liberated from communal obligations:
the laborer had to be free to enter into contractual relationships with an
employer. As a result, the home and the place of work became separated
from each other. As Tönnies pointed out, the major difference between the
Gemeinschaft and the *Gesellschaft* is that one lives one's total life within
the former whereas one enters into the latter only partially, with that part
of oneself which corresponds to the purposes of the organization or which
is involved in fulfilling the obligations of the contract. The transition from

Gemeinschaft to *Gesellschaft*, which occurred as a result of the rationalization of the means of production, has entailed the rationalization of social relationships in other spheres of life; individuals entering into social relationships on the basis of their perceived instrumentality. In terms of the Weberian perspective, rationality has become methodologically hegemonic; for knowing the ends and the alternative means to those ends, we select the most rational means-ends relationships. However, it should be noted that from the Weberian viewpoint "rationality" in the choice of means accompanies avowed irrationality in orientation to values, goals, and needs" (Habermas, 1970: 63). The rationalization of the means of production, government (in the form of bureaucracy), and of other forms of social relationships does not necessarily entail that the ends, which such rationalized means serve, are selected on a rational basis. For example, the rationalization of government which has resulted in a variety of bureaucratic forms does not necessarily entail a rational choice between ideologies or between various forms of domination. It is this claim that Marcuse seeks to elaborate by suggesting that rationality per se has emerged as ideologically hegemonic.

The Marcusean argument takes for granted the idea that from the rational revolution in the production process developed a belief that all areas of society could be submitted to rational organization. The question which Marcuse seeks to confront is whether science (in its practical form, technology) is being used in the service of democracy, the goal of which is an emancipated society, or whether science and technology have themselves constituted a new form of ideology which submits individuals to a new form of domination—namely, productive control. Habermas (1970: 85) summarizes the Marcusean position as follows: "Weber's 'rationalization' is not only a long term process of the transformation of social structures but simultaneously 'rationalization' in Freud's sense: the true motive, the perpetuation of objectively obsolete domination, is concealed through the invocation of purposive-rational imperatives."

Marcuse seeks to distinguish between authority and domination. The former, he contends (Marcuse, 1955: 33–34) "is inherent in any societal division of labor, is derived from knowledge and confined to the administration of functions and arrangements necessary for the advancement of the whole. In contrast, domination is exercised by a particular group or individual in order to sustain or enhance itself in a privileged position." This statement begs the question of how such domination is legitimated in a society which is capable of rational evaluation. To this question, Marcuse answers that such domination is veiled by the ideological hegemony of the "performance principle," the result of which is to envisage society as "an expanding system of useful performances" (Marcuse, 1955: 81).

The hegemonic nature of the meritocratic ideology results in the legitimation of a stratification system based upon competitive economic performance. Competing class interests are veiled through the implementation of a meritocratic status system in which "the interests of domination and the interests of the whole coincide" (Marcuse, 1955: 41). The individual believes that the system is rational and will deliver the goods, be they in terms of material reward or status enhancement, which are commensurate with his productivity. Thus, the class conflict postulated by Marx becomes flattened, and the benefits of rational organization appear to extend to everyone. As a result, Marcuse sees the rationalized society as ultimately more repressive than societies based upon class-linked ideologies. Indeed technology, now defined as mechanization—"the progressive transformation of human behavior according to one rule alone, that of efficacy of thought and computation" (Aron, 1968: xi)—cuts across various ideologies legitimating ownership (i.e., bureaucratic socialism or capitalism) as the theories of industrial society developed by Saint-Simon and Comte predicted.

The hegemony of the technological, meritocratic ideology results in a "new conformism which is a facet of technological rationality translated in social behavior" (Marcuse, 1964: 84). Individuals are reduced to "one-dimensional men" possessed by "happy consciousness." For Marcuse (1964: 166) the transition from ascriptive *Gemeinschaft* to meritocratic *Gesellschaft* has been accomplished as follows: "Nature scientifically comprehended and mastered, reappears in the technical apparatus of production and destruction which sustains and improves the life of the individuals while subordinating them to the masters of the apparatus. Thus, the rational hierarchy merges with the social one." As a result of this merger, the technological, meritocratic ideology is far more easily rationalized (in the Freudian sense) than those which legitimated social hierarchy alone. Why should an individual seek to debunk an ideology which he believes will produce an economic system that serves his own ends: the acquisition of greater pecuniary power and social status? Why should an individual seek alternatives to a system of reward, which on the surface, is fair since it is based upon universalistic rather than particularistic criteria? In the performance-principled *Gesellschaft*, technological rationality becomes a virtue: it is a source of individual and social salvation. Technology has become omniscient in the mind of the public—individual and social problems can be subjected to rational study so that they may eventually be mediated.

Having presented the Weberian argument and the Marcusean revision, the thrust of rationality into sport may now be analyzed. The Weberian

argument provides us with a theoretical basis for a discussion of technological innovation and bureaucratization in sport. The Marcusean argument will allow a theoretically grounded discussion of the economic and
social relationships existing in the occupational subculture of sport.

Rationality as a Means to an End: Increased Productivity

Sport has benefited (or suffered, depending upon one's viewpoint) from
the direct influence of technological changes taking place over the last 100
years. In a never ending quest for improved performance, the social institution of sport became enamoured with the technological process which
was successfully improving productivity in other areas of social life. And
since the effects of technology upon sport could be evaluated through the
use of performance "statistics," its relative success could be determined
and its innovations manipulated. Sport was, and is, amenable to rational
appraisal.

The impact of technological innovation upon sport from the middle of
the nineteenth century to early in the twentieth century has been discussed
by Betts (1953) in his paper, "The Technological Revolution and the Rise
of Sport." Although not primarily concerned with the concept of rationality, Betts' analysis has considerable import in our discussion if we define
technology in its narrow sense as the rational application of science to the
production process and the implements used in that process. In his paper,
Betts develops the argument that industrialization was a major antecedent
condition for the growth of modern sport. Implicit in his discussion is the
idea that technological innovations in communication and transportation
gave sport a more national flavor which suggests that sport like other
forms of industry was becoming divorced from the *Gemeinschaft*. As Betts
points out "industrialization and the urban movement were the basic
causes for the rise of organized sport. And the urban movement was, of
course, greatly enhanced by the revolutionary transformation in communication, transportation, agriculture, and industrialization" (1953: 255).
From this statement, we might conclude that while technological innovation allowed the mass production of equipment and so contributed to the
democratization of sport, it also firmly entrenched organized sport in the
Gesellschaft society.

A second concern of Betts's paper, which is more pertinent to present
arguments, is the effect which technological innovation had upon the implements used in sport and the rational appraisal of sport performances.
From the numerous examples provided by Betts we shall arbitrarily select
two. First, the technological innovations applied to sport equipment can be
exemplified by the changes taking place in the composition of the golf ball.

The emergence of the "rubber-wound gutta-percha ball" (gutta-percha being the gum substance of the Malayan *percha* tree) increased the length of golf drives and shots in general. This improvement necessitated a re-balancing of the game through the elongation of the golf course since performances outstripped existing facilities. Second, Muybridge's use and development of photography in sport allowed the study of sport performance to be placed on a more scientific footing. Cinematographic analysis became useful in technique and performance amelioration. Technological innovation became coupled to the "performance principles" of the modern industrial society. In the Weberian sense, technological rationality was entering into sport and providing critical standards through which the efficacy of existing implements of production and forces of production could be objectively assessed.

"The application of science in technology and the feedback of technical progress to research [became] the substance of the world of [sport]" (Habermas, 1970: 55). Many examples of this feedback process can be found in sport: baseball provides a case in point. Both Seymour (1960) and Voigt (1970) concur that the application of technological research to the implements used in baseball has considerably improved the performances of the athletes. For example, changes wrought in the construction of the baseball glove considerably improved defensive performances and, incidentally, reduced hand injury. In his analysis of glove changes, Voigt (1970: 73–77) points out that the glove has been transformed from the half-fingered palm protectors of the 1880's to the large webbed pocketed ones which emerged on the scene in the 1920's. "By 1919, the Rawlings Company offered three different types of glove including a big padded mitt for catchers, a shovel-shaped first baseman's glove, and an efficient five-fingered fielder's model. In all these, the big improvement was the multi-thonged web between the thumb and forefinger" (Voigt, 1970: 73). Implicit in this analysis is the idea that technological changes and the increased recognition of positionally specific needs went hand in hand (or dare we say in glove).

Technological changes did not only favor the defense. A change was made by the manufacturers (with the sanction of the National Commission) in the composition of the ball. In 1910, a cork centered ball covered with one eighth inch of rubber was introduced, the result of which was a sharp increase in hitting (cf. Seymour, 1971: 125–126). Despite official denials, changes in the composition of the ball were also made in 1920, and again in 1930 (officially acknowledged), which especially affected the production of home runs (cf., Cook, 1964: 26–36). "The catalyst of change . . . was George Herman Ruth. In 1919 he startled the baseball world by hitting 29 home runs . . . Ruth's bat was the medium. The club owners got its message and quickly translated it into a livelier ball" (Seymour, 1971: 426). Thus, the performance of "Babe" Ruth was rationally appraised in economic terms. Technology was put to use in the service of the articulated economic needs of the baseball oligarchy.

Baseball has not been the only sport to become infused with technological rationality. Football since its early days has made considerable changes in the uniform and equipment. "Professional football's advancement in technology has resulted in coming up with a battle dress as personalized as a scarf designed and autographed by Peter Max" (Myslenski, 1973: 190). The helmet in particular has advanced through technological innovation to its present pneumatic hydraulic form introduced by Riddell in 1968.

To continue the argument that many of the technological innovations have been developed at the request of the sporting oligarchy, we should especially take note of the transformation of playing surfaces from the products of nature to the products of technology. Despite players' complaints, "astroturf" and "tartan" surfaces are becoming the rule rather than the exception, since they are commercially more viable (reduced maintenance costs) and are necessary for the new enclosed stadia which prevent the photosynthetic process essential for grass. The development of the synthetic surface coupled with football's move indoors has greatly enhanced the game as a consumable product. Extraneous variables such as wind and weather no longer influence game plan and game outcome—the problem for the player is that he now has fewer excuses for a poor performance: he can be held directly responsible for his actions.

Rather than perpetuate the somewhat eristical argument that technology has simply benefited the sporting oligarchy we should note at this point that advances in technology have benefited the occupational subculture as a whole. Many refinements in apparatus have reduced the personal risks involved for the player in the pursuit of his career. However, it should be recognized that many of these refinements were initiated by the players themselves sometimes with the blessings of the management, other times despite managerial and coaching opposition. Roger Bresnahan provides a case in point. From firsthand experience he realized how "easily a tipped ball could collapse a flimsy wire mask. . . . Equally dangerous were the low foul tips that bruised legs and sometimes crushed genitals" (Voigt, 1970: 78). As a result of his experiences, Bresnahan persuaded "a sporting goods firm to build a stronger mask, while he himself devised padded shin guards and a batting helmet" (Voigt, 1970: 78). The threat to the genitals was also minimized by the production of the "cup" athletic supporter. Similarly, the use of the face mask in hockey was primarily instigated by Jaques Plante's decision to wear one of his own design (McFarlane, 1968: 134). Despite initial opposition from his coach, Toe Blake, and some initial dubiousness on the part of other goalkeepers, the mask has become an established feature of goalkeeping equipment (probably because of Plante's continued presentation with the Vezina Trophy which silenced the critics). Indeed, technological rationality has allowed some players to continue in a career which had been threatened by injury (e.g., Larry Csonka, for whom a special helmet was designed) or had been placed in question by personal defect (e.g., Larry Brown's hearing deficiency has been compensated through the use of a receiver wired into the helmet and various eye disorders of the players have been considerably alleviated through the production of the contact lens).

It is especially interesting that many technological innovations which improve performance have been conceived by the players themselves. As previously mentioned, the innovations in the baseball glove engineered by Doak improved fielding performances. Soccer shoes have been considerably modified by players acting in an advisory capacity to the shoe manufacturers. We can also cite examples from other professional sports such as golf and hockey (e.g., Nicklaus and MacGregor; Harper and Lang). While recognizing that these relationships have often allowed players to become sporting goods entrepreneurs, the paradox is that meritocratic technological rationality has diffused throughout sport's social and economic structure. That is, players' innovations increased their productivity within an apparatus over which they have no economic control. The ideological hegemony of the "performance principle" sustains the existing forms of hierarchy by flattening any inherent conflicts into a mutual search for productivity: "scientific-technical rationality and manipulation are welded together into new forms of social control" (Marcuse, 1964: 146).

Bureaucracy: The Rationalization of the Social Life-World

Weber recognized that the transformation of society from *Gemeinschaft* to *Gesellschaft* entailed more than the application of scientific rationality to the production process. It also required the application of rationality to the forms of social control. The rationalization of the forms of social control resulted in the growth of bureaucratic structures. As Wrong (1970: 32) makes clear, "the spread of hierarchical bureaucratic forms of social organization exemplifies the process of rationalization in the sphere of social structure. . . . Bureaucracy is the distinctly sociological manifestation of the process of rationalization." Weber used the concept of bureaucracy as an ideal type to describe organizations which: (1) are adapted to attaining a single functional goal, (2) are organized hierarchically with a strict chain of command, (3) have an elaborate division of labor, (4) have detailed general rules governing conduct, (5) have personnel selected on the basis of competence, and (6) tend to regard office-holding as a life-long vocation (cf. Wrong, 1970: 32). From Weber's viewpoint, the process of rationalization cut through existing and emerging ideologies such as capitalism and socialism. It was a feature of all societies undergoing transformation into *Gesellschaft*. Following Hegel, Weber argued that bureaucracy displayed a semblance of independence since it stood apart from class interests (cf. Ashcraft, 1972: 151): it was ideological and interest neutral.

A competing analysis of the role of bureaucracy in social control is provided by Marx. Marx did not believe that bureaucracy acted in a disinterested fashion since "it was dependent for its own existence primarily upon the ruling class" (Ashcraft, 1972: 151). From the Marxian perspective, bureaucracy serves existing forms of domination. A basic difference in the Weberian and Marxian viewpoints can be seen at the level of the individual. Despite Weber's recognition that bureaucracy results in a system of dependency, an "iron cage," rationality for Weber is the site of freedom (cf. Loewith, 1970: 110). For Marx, however, bureaucratization is another facet of man's self-alienation. That is, for Weber "rationality goes together with the freedom of action in that as a 'teleological rationality,' it is a freedom to pursue, with a free choice of the adequate means thereto, an end predesignated by ultimate values or life 'meanings'" (Loewith: 112). On the other hand, Marx saw bureaucracy as parasitic upon the various economic strata within the society with some strata having greater access to it than others, and believed that bureaucracy extended the power of domination, thus perpetrating in social life the alienation which had occurred in industrial life.

A second difference in the Weberian and Marxian analyses concerns the question of rationality as an inevitable trend. Weber suggested that rationalization is an inevitable trend for industrial *Gesellschaft* society. In a sense, he adopted the position that we must learn to live with it. On the other hand, Marx placed rationality firmly in prehistory which would come to an end (i.e., be transcended) in the final proletarian revolution. Since history seems to have favored the Weberian perspective we should ask what is left of the Marxian argument that is applicable to modern industrial society. Contemporary theorists such as Habermas (1970), Marcuse (1964), and Pappenheim (1959) have attempted to revise the Marxian argument. Recognizing the hegemony of rationalization, they confront the question of alienation in a way which acknowledges the transformation of society from one based on economic class conflict to one based upon technological meritocratic ideology. To use the Marcusean argument, rationality (specifically technological rationality) has become ideological in and of itself and, as a result, forms the basis of a new and more totalitarian system of domination. Thus, while accepting the Weberian argument that rationalization is inevitable they do not accept the idea that rationalization is the "site of freedom." Rather, rationalization, both technological and bureaucratic, results in "surplus repression"—the nonwork areas of social life are increasingly subjected to social control in the form of rational organization.[6]

Having presented the Marxian thesis, the Weberian antithesis, and the revisionist Marxian arguments, we now must confront the problem of how best to characterize the thrust of bureaucracy into the occupational subculture of sport.

The historical emergence of bureaucracy in sport has been dependent upon many of the same criteria which accounted for the expansion of bureaucracy into other areas of the social life-world: e.g., the development of a money economy, the increased size of the administrative units to be controlled, the growth of occupational specialization which created specialized administrative problems, the hegemony of the profit principle which required a disciplined work force subject to increased managerial control (cf., Blau, 1956: 36–43). Thus, the transformation of society from the folk *Gemeinschaft* into the money-economy *Gesellschaft* induced the continual expansion of rational will (*Kurwille*, Tönnies, 1957; or *Zweckrationalem*, Weber, 1947) into all areas of social life. And since the thrust of rationality undermined traditional legitimations, the bureaucratic structures of the industrial state became increasingly legalistic. This results in formal equality in its purest form because both the privileged and nonprivileged classes are subject to the same law (cf. Weber, 1947: 324–341). Although bureaucracy had been in evidence in preindustrial eras, it was essentially patrimonial not legalistic.[7]

Sport, as Charles Page (1973: 32) has noted, has been transformed during the last century from "player-controlled 'games' to the management-controlled 'big time.'" Although Page's comment applies equally to both amateur and professional, we shall concentrate upon the latter in the development of our argument. Recognizing that all sport has become imbued with the "performance principle" and, therefore, will adopt rationalized procedures in the quest for efficiency, we note that the rationalization of sport (both technological and bureaucratic) has been greatly facilitated by commercialization and professionalization. The rational pursuit of profit requires coordination both within and between organizations. "In other words, the combined effect of bureaucracy's characteristics is to create social conditions which constrain each member of the organization (and the organization per se) to act in ways that, whether they appear rational or otherwise from his individual standpoint, further the rational pursuit of organizational objectives" (Blau, 1956: 32).

An early example of the bureaucratization process, which was aimed at increasing economic efficiency, is provided in the sport of baseball. In 1903 the National Commission was inaugurated in an attempt to preserve the monopolistic practices of the owners of the National League. The commission was necessary to coordinate the merger of the National and American Leagues, the latter having been a threat to the monopolistic hold which the National League owners had over the sport. Obviously, the commission, since it was composed of two major league presidents and a third member of their choosing, was set up more for the benefit of the owners than for the athletes: "the relationship was at best paternalistic: the players standing as individuals, the owners in combination" (Seymour, 1971: 9). To use the Weberian concepts, baseball, while reflecting the thrust of bureaucracy which was occurring in all areas of social life, attempted to constrain the bureaucratic process within the framework of traditional patrimonialism. Indeed the owners of the major league franchises became quite resentful when Landis attempted to make the administrative arm of baseball into a power somewhat removed from owner control. Landis, who was appointed national commissioner following the problems which beset baseball, prior to and in 1920 (e.g., the congressional investigation which threatened baseball with antitrust legislation; the Federal League war which again raised the question of the reserve clause, and the Comiskey fixing scandal), became known as the "Czar of Baseball." Landis demanded, and received, absolute control over baseball matters. Thus, Landis could "fine, suspend, or remove wrongdoers, levy fines as high as $5,000 on clubs or leagues, and issue public rebukes, all in the interest of maintaining baseball's honor and morale" (Voigt, 1970: 139–141). The appointment of Landis facilitated the transformation of baseball's bureaucracy from one of patrimonialism to one based upon legalistic principles. However, "his death marked the end of the autocratic commission rule, an expedient born of guilt engendered by the scandals of 1919 and 1920" (Voigt, 1970: 149–150). While perpetrating the myth of legalistic bureaucracy, baseball returned to its previous patrimonialism, so much so that the present commissioner, Kuhn, is regarded by the players as an administrator who executes the owners whims (cf. Bouton, 1970; Flood, 1970: 49).

The use of the legalistic legitimation for authority as a facade which deflects attention from patrimonialism is evidenced also in professional football. The NFL in the last fifteen years or so has developed its bureaucracy from an administrative unit involving three people to one which employs over 40 administrative personnel under the leadership of Pete Rozelle. While presiding over the game's interests is the ostensible basis for the commission's authority, the game's interests are generally those which coincide with the interests of the owners rather than those of the players. Acting under the aegis of impartiality, Rozelle has consistently manipulated the press to provide distorted impressions of management-player relationships (Parrish, 1971: 115); turned a blind eye to the process of blacklisting, and the problems which the forfeiture clause created for the players (Parrish, 1971: 258). To rephrase the argument in theoretical terms, the difference between patrimonial bureaucracy and legalistic bureaucracy is that the former describes the case where the bureaucracy is dependent upon and shares the interests of the privileged minority which retains it, whereas the latter is free from the obligations which retainership engenders. Since the commissioner, Rozelle, is appointed by, paid by, and can be dismissed by the owners of the major league clubs, it would be naive to assume that legalistic impartiality prevails in the commission's execution of its duties.

The lack of player control over the game and their own fates has led the players to create bureaucratic structures which represent their own interests. The growth of the players' unions and associations has effectively produced a situation whereby combined players' interests can be represented. And since many of the players' challenges are of a legal nature, the growth of such associations may facilitate the transformation of patrimonial bureaucracy into legalistic bureaucracy. One outcome of the attempts to balance power through the development of player associations and unions has been the creation of arbitration boards. These boards are being used increasingly to break deadlocks between management and players over the question of contracts. Thus, the balance of power between management and player bureaucracies has proliferated the growth of an impartial bureaucracy which, of course, would have been unnecessary had the various league commissions adopted a legalistic rather than patrimonial frame of reference. Incidentally, the use of arbitration boards may result in an equalization of player salaries (by position) throughout each of the sport leagues (cf., *The Sporting News*, March 9, 1974: 32).

Bureaucratization has been facilitated by commercialism in terms of the propensity of the capitalistic system to concentrate assets by merger.[8] In the world of industry, the merger movement has caused considerable congressional concern as can be attested to by the hearings on antitrust and monopoly held in 1941, 1950 and 1968. The use of the merger to consolidate corporate control and decision-making among a relatively few vast companies is a direct result of the application of economic rationality in an attempt to reduce economic risk by regulating the competitive market. For example, in 1968, "the 200 largest industrial corporations controlled over 60 percent of the total assets held by all manufacturing corporations" (Economic Report on Corporate Mergers, 1969: 3). This principle of consolidating assets and, hence, reducing corporate competition has not been lost on sport. To summarize, "strange as it may seem, the free enterprise system fosters the development of bureaucracy in the government, in private companies, and in unions" (Blau, 1956: 38).

Finally, we should note that increased occupational specialization also encourages the expansion of bureaucracy. Sport, much like industry, has found that the pursuit of economic and organizational efficiency requires occupational specialization. In baseball, role specialization was starting to occur in all positions by the 1870's (cf., Seymour, 1960: 63–64). The recognition of position-specific attributes (e.g., intelligence in pitchers, strong throwing arms in outfielders) was a direct result of the organizational quest for efficiency. Role specialization is also in evidence in football which has been transformed from a relatively unstructured game to a highly differentiated sport. Strategic developments such as the forward pass, the double platoon system, and the increased use of speciality squads have necessitated increased division of labor. Role specialization, as is evidenced in baseball and football, creates special administrative problems. The positional specialization requires managerial specialization since experts must be brought in to handle the new administrative and coordinative problems. Baseball now has coaches for hitting, infielding, outfielding, pitching, relief pitching, base running, etc. Football now has quarterback coaches, backfield coaches, interior offensive linemen coaches, receiver coaches, etc. Recognizing the problems which player and coaching specialization may raise for organizational efficiency, football has employed coaches to coordinate the efforts of the specialists.

In summary, sport's increased quest for economic efficiency through the use of the merger and increased role specialization reflects Weber's conviction that the pursuit of profit inevitably entails rationalization. However, in the case of sport, traditional patrimonial authority has not entirely yielded to the thrust of the legalistic principle. Only in recent years due to the growth of players' associations has the possibility arisen that legalistic bureaucracy may replace the anachronistic patrimonial authority structures. Thus, while we would concur with Weber's argument that rationalization is inevitable we note that the Marxian premises have not been entirely refuted. Without the complete transformation of sports' authority structures into a legalistically legitimated bureaucracy the discussion of whether rationalization is a site of freedom or a site of alienation is premature. Until such things as the reserve clause, the option clause, and the forfeiture clause have been formally subjected to antitrust legislation, players will continue to be exploited by their owners since they lack the contractual freedom granted to workers in other areas of industrial and economic life.

SOCIALIZATION INTO THE OCCUPATIONAL SUBCULTURE [9]

We have, so far, suggested that the commercialization and professionalization of sport has rendered sport susceptible to the thrust of rationality (both bureaucratic and technological). In the presentation of this argument, we leaned heavily upon the Weberian position that rationalization was an inevitable trend exhibited by all societies undergoing transformation into modern industrial states. However, we tempered the Weberian argument by noting that Weber was essentially attempting to construct an ideal type which may not actually exist in the real life-world. In so doing, we raised the Marxian idea that the present forms of rationalization, rather than leading to democracy remained under the control of existing elites so preserving a form of class domination. Indeed, we alluded to the ideas of Marcuse who suggests that rationality, instead of leading to freedom, results in a new and more totalitarian form of domination since it subjects all members of society to a never ending quest for increased productivity. That is, we implied that rationality may have become a rationalization (in the Freudian sense) which deflects our attention from present forms of class conflict. Our discussion, then, reflects a pessimistic conviction—which Freud expressed years ago—that civilization's advance, rather than liberating the individual, subjects him to new and more varied forms of repression.

The process whereby societal needs are imposed upon individual needs —resulting in their repression—is termed socialization. Socialization "involves interaction and learning. On the one hand, it centers attention on the adaptation of individuals to their social situations; on the other hand, it centers attention on how individuals develop social identities as a result of their participation in various social situations" (Loy and Ingham, 1973: 258). While we recognize that socialization engenders repression, we also acknowledge that it would be nothing short of Utopianism to assume that social order could be maintained without it. All societies depend to a greater or lesser extent upon "bad faith" (cf., Berger, 1963: 142–145) for their continued existence. Without bad faith they could not assume their taken-for-granted nature. Similarly, without engaging in a degree of bad faith, individuals could not get on with the day-to-day business of life which presupposes shared definitions and meanings both with respect to ends and appropriate means. Yet to admit socialization is necessary is not to demand that socialization be totally successful in repressing individuality so as to deny the individual the opportunity to conceive of alternatives—demanding complete socialization is to admit to totalitarian sentiments.

Socialization is both a formal learning process, with specific agencies charged with the educative role, and an informal process in which continual interaction leads to some degree of conformity. Sport, as a taken-for-granted part of the social and economic life-world, requires that neophytes, seeking to gain admission, be exposed to both the formal and informal processes of socialization. On the one hand, sport has taken-for-granted values, social structures, regulations, and prescriptions for role performance which, if they are to be maintained, require that certain members of the sport organization be charged with their transmission. On the other hand, athletes engage in frequent and prolonged interaction out of which develops an informal system of shared values, norms, and attitudes. These shared definitions and meanings guide the athlete's behavior in interaction with his peers and often help to humanize the official organizational imperatives. To use an idea of Charles Page (1946), they are the components of "Bureaucracy's Other Face." Recognizing that both formal and informal processes of socialization are operating in the work-world of sport, we shall structure the discussion which follows around three basic problems:

1. How is the sport role transformed from a recreational pursuit into a service occupation?

2. What values are espoused by the sporting oligarchy and are these values hegemonic throughout sport's social structure?

3. Are these values ideological or rhetorical and what effects do they have upon occupational role performance?

The Sport Role: From Recreation to Occupation

The professional sport role is a rather unique occupational role in that large numbers of the population undergo a degree of anticipatory socialization as public education provides many with exposure to sport and establishes basic technical skills. For those who show special aptitude, induction into the professional role is presented as a conceivable possibility and formal socialization is provided at a relatively early age. Professional attitudes are inculcated in the gifted athlete which emphasize performance and the importance of victory (cf. Webb, 1969). Indeed, the commitment of the athlete to improving his performance and to winning is often a major factor in the gifted athlete's upward mobility. Thus, formal socialization agents such as the coach facilitate the internalization of the performance principle necessary for organizational efficiency. Woodley's (1973) observational study of a high school football team provides an example of the formal socialization process at work; using fictitious names he presents Coach Fowles's interpretation of the performance principle as follows: "What do I mean by 110 percent? I mean to push yourself beyond what *you* think you can do. . . . We will outwork other teams, we will be in better shape, we will hit harder, and we will have more pride." Woodley also provides evidence which lends validity to our claim that anticipatory socialization for the occupational role is initiated within the high school: again quoting from Coach Fowles, "We will go into details on all this later. But basically, on offense this year we will use pro splits. Both the flanker, on the 'pro' side, and the opposite end split 10 to 15 yards. We will use both the 'I' formation and the split backfield" (Woodley, 1973: 7). So at an early age, individuals seeking an athletic identity are required to learn the values and rules of sport and to identify with idealized stereotypes who exemplify preferred role performance. And since the identity of athlete has considerable prestige within the high school (cf. Coleman, 1961; Eitzen, 1973) the inducements to sustain one's athletic identity considerably facilitate the formal socialization process. One moral value which is necessary for organizational efficiency, whether it be in commercial industry or commercial sport, is discipline. As Blau notes, "Protestantism, therefore, has transplanted the ascetic devotion to disciplined hard work . . . from monastic life, to which it was largely confined earlier, to the mundane affairs of economic life" (Blau, 1956: 40). Throughout the formal socialization of the athlete the moral virtues of discipline are stressed and provide legitimation for the coaches' authority.

During the course of occupational socialization, the athlete learns the approved ways in which to present himself to a heterogeneous audience. Formal socialization processes aim at producing a properly demeaned athlete: "the well-demeaned individual possesses the attributes popularly associated with 'character training' or 'socialization,' these being implanted when a neophyte of any kind is housebroken" (Goffman, 1967: 77). Informal socialization enables the athlete to learn the range of behaviors which secure deference for him from his teammates. The formal socialization process, which is characterized by an asymmetrical power relationship (the agents of socialization have economic and social control over the athlete), acquaints the athlete with his obligations to the sport organization, whereas the informal socialization processes relate the expectations which teammates have for one another. The newcomer to the sport organization, therefore, has to learn how to handle both the formal authority structure and the informal or unofficial expectations of his teammates.

There is a third audience in sport comprised of the paying and viewing public. While the formal authority structure demands efficiency and the informal structure demands loyalty, the public demands a dramatic event.

Incorporated into both the formal and informal socialization process, then, is a more or less formal set of rules which guide the behavior of athletes in their interaction with the "external system." Athletes are taught to walk the fine line between play and display. Organizations, on the other hand, walk the fine line between sport and entertainment. Teammates will negatively sanction the athlete who goes commercial and indulges in "show boating." Similarly, the organization will negatively sanction the athlete whose entertainment antics reduce organizational efficiency. Yet both will applaud the spectacular play which furthers their goals. Thus, both the formal and informal processes of socialization attempt to acquaint athletes with the correct use of the spectacular.

We have previously stated that the sport role is a service occupation. In the early stages of role progression the performance of the service is pleasurable because it provides the athlete with relatively high rewards while incurring few personal costs. But as the athlete progresses from recreation to occupation, the pressures of pleasing the public become more problematical: the public begins to intrude. Often such intrusion breeds resentment in the athletes since they find it difficult to sustain "the emotional and dramatic level, expected by fans, over a full season's schedule" (Haerle, 1972: 18). The athlete often engages in impression management since he is expected to present an image which does not affront popular conceptions of the athletic role. As Gouldner (1970: 382) points out, "the management of impressions becomes problematic only under certain conditions: when men have to *work* at seeming to be what others expect them to be . . . . In short, the moral code shaping social relationships has become less internalized in them; while remaining a fact of social reality, it tends to become a set of instrumentally manageable 'rules of the game' rather than deeply felt moral obligations." The pressures of the fans, the absolute control of the sporting oligarchy, the self-conception of the player as simply a marketable commodity begin to undo the work of the socialization process. Instead of the athlete being irrationally committed he begins to engage in the rational strategies of impression management. Thus, the socialization process might be characterized as a cycle from commitment to cynicism—the latter being generated during the informal interactions of players exposed to similar conditions of existence. We would note, though, that the cynicism underlying the impression that management does not alter the hierarchical structure of sport, nor the obligation of the athlete to please the public. It allows the athlete to give the appearance of a properly demeaned individual while preserving a degree of autonomy. This Machiavellian behavior demonstrates the thrust of rationality into interpersonal relationships—one reaps the rewards by fulfilling one's obligations through an on-the-surface adherence to the "rules of the game."

The Value Components of the Organizational Charters

Having presented, albeit briefly, the role of the socialization process which transforms the athletic role into a service occupation, our second task is to ask what are the value components of the organizational charter, whose interests does the charter serve, and do the athletes internalize these value components so that they become hegemonic throughout sport's social structure? The sport organization is faced with the problem of justifying itself and its mission to the larger community. At the same time, it has to handle the practical reality of producing a winning team with which the community can identify. Therefore, the sport organization creates an organizational charter which, as Vaz (1972: 223–224) points out, is "a more or less formal statement or rhetoric of its objectives and ideals. This resembles an official version of meanings directed towards the representation of a specific image or impression of the group and what transpires within it. . . . It relates the group to the total values of the community." * Since the specified ideals and the practical realities are not necessarily congruent we should ask whether those espousing the values of the organizational charter are ideologues or rhetoricians. Both ideology and rhetoric may be distortions of practical reality which serve vested interests but, whereas the ideologue is sincere in his beliefs, the rhetorician may be engaging in a propagandist exercise or practicing utilitarian deceit.

What are the components of the organizational charter and what ideological premises do they reflect? Sport became professionalized and commercialized in the latter half of the nineteenth century. During the nineteenth century, America was undergoing a technological revolution and had entered into the spirit of laissez faire capitalism. In this period of rapid social and economic change the antebellum mood was rather conservative and "it was those who wished to defend the political status quo, above all the laissez faire conservatives, who were first to pick up the instruments of social argument that were forged out of Darwinian concepts" (Hofstadter, 1944: 5–6). The philosophy of social Darwinism, as applied to social and economic relationships, legitimated what Veblen has called the predatory temperament. During this era, which might be dubbed as capitalism's age of innocence, industrial entrepreneurs, uninhibited by the trade union movement, amassed large fortunes, often by exploiting the unpoliticized laborer created by the industrial revolution and the massive wave of immigration. If we take a Marxian interpretation, the laissez faire capitalistic

---

* From Edmund W. Vaz, "The Culture of Young Hockey Players: Some Initial Observations," in *Training: A Scientific Basis*, A. W. Taylor (ed.). (Springfield, Illinois: Charles E. Thomas, 1972), pp. 223–224. Reprinted by permission. This footnote also applies to passages quoted on pp. 363 and 366.

infrastructure adopted a social Darwinistic ideological superstructure to serve the vested interests of the new industrial entrepreneur. Social Darwinism was rational and secular. As Hofstadter (1944: 7) points out, it was "a body of belief whose chief conclusion was that the positive functions of the state should be kept to the barest minimum, it was almost anarchical, and it was devoid of that center of reverence and authority which the state provides in many conservative systems. Finally, and perhaps most important, it was a conservatism that tried to dispense with sentimental or emotional ties." Thus, it was a philosophy eminently suited to America's transformation into a *Gesellschaft* society.

Although social Darwinism was eventually tempered by the sentimental nature of Christian ethics, the socialist underpinnings of the trade union movement, and the thrust of bourgeois socialism in the form of the Welfare State, residuals remained. The notions of "survival of the fittest" and "struggle for existence" remained implanted for many years in the entreprenurial mind. Such values were particularly suited to serving the vested interests of the sporting oligarchy which remained relatively impregnable to such legislation as the Sherman Antitrust Act, which was supposed to hinder the monopolistic tendencies of anarchical capitalism. As Voigt (1971: 80) points out, "During the decade when Americans seemed to be fascinated by the deeds of businessmen and industrialists, baseball owners styled themselves as 'magnates.' Some, like Frank de Hass Robison, took their pretension so seriously as to promote a 'syndicate' of major league teams. As owner of a Cleveland team and a St. Louis team in the same league, Robison was in competition with himself which was carrying the robber baron bit rather far." Although such practices would be intolerable today, the social Darwinist values remain in residual form. They are incorporated into the organizational charter in the guise of the promotion of a competitive ethic; in the idea of sport being a test or a challenge whereby one can discover one's strengths and weaknesses; and in the idea of suffering pain and hardship as a test of durability and character. At the level of quasi-theories, these notions are given form in such locker room slogans as "when the going gets tough, the tough get going"; "winning isn't everything, it's the only thing"; and "nice guys finish last."

A second component in the organizational charter is encompassed by the idea of democratization. Since World War II, the claim that sport, once a pastime of the elite, has become available to all segments of society, has been somewhat hegemonic. As we have previously stated, sport is one of the few areas of social life to which large numbers of the population are afforded some anticipatory socialization. Capitalizing upon such notions, the sporting oligarchy has declared itself as an agency of assimilation and has emphasized its contributions to the ideal of "equality of opportunity." Pointing to the successes of hyphenated Americans, sport keeps alive the myth of the melting pot (cf., Voigt, 1971: 82). Similarly, pointing to the success of blacks, sport continually emphasizes its contributions to the upward social mobility of the disadvantaged.

Thus, sport contains in its organizational charter a reaffirmation of social values: the structural assimilation claimed to be present in sport is a reflection of the structural assimilation idealized in the American creed. Implicit in such notions, is the underlying assumptions of meritocracy. Sport is ideologically bolstered by the "performance principle," a principle which suggests that athletes are recruited and maintained on the basis of their merits. That is, sport presents itself as a rational organization which delivers the goods on the basis of the universalistic criterion of achievement. Indeed sport has gone so far as to use computers in player recruitment, a rational development which lends superficial credibility to the claim that sport values performance and devalues such particularistic criteria as race and ethnicity. Implicit in the organizational charter, then, is a reaffirmation of the meritocratic value that there should be equality of opportunity to be unequal: meritocracy legitimates structured inequality on a more rational basis.

The sport establishment has also emphasized that sport provides a unique and particularly appropriate medium for meeting the main objectives espoused by our educational institutions (cf., Loy and Ingham, 1973: 291). Claims have been made that participation in sport aids in the emotional, intellectual, and social development of the individual. Thus, explicit in the organizational charter is a view which suggests that sport is a major contributor to the socialization process in general. As Vaz (1972: 224) notes, "Minor League Hockey tends to emphasize the following objectives: to provide exercise, health and recreation for young people; to develop respect for the spirit and letter of the law, to develop sportsmanship and fair play; to develop qualities of self-discipline and loyalty, and also to develop emotional maturity, social competence and moral character in young boys." The sport establishment, then, has selected certain recreational games for commercial purposes and has legitimated such appropriation by incorporating into the organizational charter mainstream conceptions of the properly socialized individual.

The Organizational Charter: Ideology or Rhetoric?

Are the values of the organizational charter, outlined above, ideology or rhetoric? Do they reflect real intentions and beliefs or do they deflect attention from the practical realities of sport as a commercial enterprise? Social Darwinism as an ideology has been somewhat modified by the growth of scientific pragmatism. The current of pragmatism, which became the dominant American philosophy at the turn of the century, considerably modified the deterministic conceptions of social Darwinism by discrediting the natural law assumptions upon which it was based. The pragmatists emphasized human manipulation and control over gradualist fatalism. In this sense it was a much more rational philosophy since it viewed behavior with reference to teleological goals rather than the product of evolutionary causes. However, the metaphysical refutation of social Darwinism by pragmatism did not result in a reconstruction of social and economic infrastructure. Rather, it provided a more rational legitimation for structured inequality. The current of pragmatism neither undermined the secularized Protestant Ethic which social Darwinism espoused nor the belief that private profit and public good go hand in hand. Both in industry and sport, the change in metaphysics did not alter the belief that the competitive process allegedly results in the improvement of all. To use the idea of Pareto, the residuals remain but the derivations change.

The main reason for introducing the pragmatist refutation of social Darwinism was not to engage in an obscurantist metaphysical debate but to suggest that regardless of changes occurring in metaphysical assumption certain basic convictions remain. Thus, when the sport establishment incorporates such values as ascetic commitment to hard work, undiluted competition, discipline, endurance, and self-improvement into the organizational charter, it does so out of a sense of ideological conviction not out of a sense of rhetorical deflection. The sporting oligarchy has internalized such beliefs and are committed to their implementation. This does not change the fact that ideology can be a distortion which serves vested interests but it does elevate such beliefs from the level of rhetoric.

The question of whether the values espoused are hegemonic throughout sport's social structure depends ultimately upon how far the practical operations of sport remain in congruence with the espoused ideals. Essentially, we are asking whether the operating procedures of the sport organization foster and maintain a consensus of belief among management and players or whether they result in an antagonism between the players' individual needs and the organizational needs. We have previously suggested that the transformation of the athletic role from a recreation role into a service occupation results in increasing cynicism on the part of the athletes. Implicit in this suggestion, then, is the claim that during the athlete's socialization, the operational procedures reduce the consensus between the athletes and the management so as to result in a situation where the athletes pay lip service to the formal procedures while engaging in subversive activity. What operational procedures can be identified which reduce value consensus among players and management? Although numerous examples can be cited, suffice it here to mention one or two. The value of ascetic commitment to hard work is often procedurally translated as the separation of players from their families during preseason training and as the implementation of training rules and curfews. Similarly the value of endurance is operationalized as playing with injury or pain, the sanctioning of the use of novocaine, and the labeling of nonvisible injury as "faking." In these cases the formal requirements for organizational efficiency incur unnecessary hardships for the players which would not be tolerated by workers in other areas of commercial life.

The operational procedures of sport similarly reduce consensus on the question of democratization. While the organizational charter suggests that sport is a meritocratic organization, practices have remained which confirm the suspicion that the transformation from particularistic criteria to universalistic criteria has not yet been completely achieved. As Voigt (1971: 82) notes, "Baseball today still follows the myth of the tipping point; an assumption that more than a handful of blacks might destroy the balance of an integrated institution, and expose baseball to a black flood." The myth of the tipping point provides an example of organizational profit motives transcending the meritocratic notions of "equality of opportunity" contained within the organizational charter. Hence, while sport organizations claim credit for advancing the cause of structural assimilation, their operational procedures somewhat detract from their claims of being "repositories of democratic energy" (Voigt, 1971: 97). The myth of the tipping point has led to such procedures as stacking and the establishment of quotas (cf., Edwards, 1973: 202–216), which might lead us to conclude that the structural assimilationist claims are indeed rhetoric.

Some overzealous rhetoricians would like us to believe that sport is a leader in social change where structural assimilation is concerned. Such rhetoric, of course, conveniently ignores historical evidence to the contrary. A case can easily be made which would demonstrate the role of external legal pressure in the abolition of the color bar. The trials granted to blacks by the Red Sox and the Braves in the 40's were largely the result of Isadore Muchnick's threat to fight issuance of the annual permit for Sunday baseball unless these two clubs ended the ban on black players (cf. Peterson, 1970: 184). Similarly, La Guardia's inclusion of baseball in his antidiscrimination inquiry added to the squeeze being placed on owners (Peterson, 1970: 155). Such pressures were pragmatically assessed by the owners eventually when their Jim Crowism threatened their economic ventures. Owners were forced to pay lip service to antidiscrimination legislation by hiring a few token blacks while perpetuating discriminatory exclusion through the operational procedures of "stacking" and quotas—rationality did not exclude sentiment. This is especially true in the selection of field managers. Field managers are essentially company men selected by owners on the basis of cronyism (cf., Bouton, 1973: xv). Since few owners have black cronies, and since they doubt that blacks would be company men, the exclusion of blacks from field managerial roles is to be expected. In the case of managers, there has been insufficient threat to the organization's business venture to lead to antidiscriminatory measures being incorporated into operational procedure.

Finally, let us consider the organizational claims that sport provides a unique setting for the inculcation of desirable emotional and intellectual traits. Again we would note the discrepancies which exist between values and procedures so as to incur cynicism in the athlete. Perhaps, the most obvious example of procedure subverting proclaimed values is supplied by the organizational requirement that assaultive behavior be a part of selection criteria and role maintenance. Hockey provides a case in point. As Vaz (1972) notes in his study of the practices in Canadian Minor League Hockey, the use of controlled aggression often plays a major role in player evaluation and selection; in fact, the use of violence is a career contingency. Such findings tend to support the social Darwinistic premises which conceive of structured inequality in terms of the survival of the fittest. Occupational socialization concentrates on the technical aspects of "playing the man" and "taking him out"—the expedient use of aggression. Thus, despite the charter ideals of sportsmanship, fairness, and moral character development, the team is gradually "molded into a tough fighting unit prepared for violence whose primary objective is to win hockey games" (Vaz, 1972: 11). The ideals are simply rhetoric used to deflect attention from organizational procedures. In the case of aggression, the procedures do not necessarily induce cynicism in the players. Since aggressive tactics are linked to selection and recruitment, few players would reject such tactics at the expense of career goals. The use of controlled aggression becomes an instrumental means of achieving the teleological goals of the organization and the player —economic rationality transcends the legitimate rules of success.

Incorporated into the occupational charter are the values of honesty and self-discipline. Again, since spectator sport is a big business and the organizational goal is to produce a winning team with which fans can identify, such ideals are reduced to rhetoric. In order to secure the services of the best players expedient strategies are developed whereby legitimate norms are surreptitiously subverted. At the amateur level, "shamateurism" is commonplace. At the professional level, the age-old adage that "money is the root of all evil" is a source of constant consternation. The Chester Report (1968: 68), a British government-sponsored inquiry into the state of Association Football, summarized such concern as follows: "As 'the root of all evil' money is seen to produce bad sportsmanship, bribery, corruption, betting, excessive partisanship, indeed anything which is not thought to be 'sporting'. . . . Ammunition for such views is provided from time to time by the press and television accounts of the big league games, when some among the highest paid in the game are seen to lose their tempers with the referee or other players or commit serious fouls, and where the partisanship of the spectators can hardly be regarded as sporting."

Not only does the use of money as an incentive induce the players to use aggressive tactics, included in the occupational socialization process (both formal and informal) is an education into the use of the tactical foul. In some sports, specific players have become designated as "policemen," a role which demands either proactive or protective aggression. The tactical foul while being inimicable to the humanitarianism specified in the occupational charter nevertheless furthers the organizational goals. It demonstrates the diffusion of practical expediency throughout the organization and results not only in the sacrifice of the athlete's own human rights but also the rights of others against whom he is competing. An example of the brutal use of the tactical foul was supplied in the World Cup of 1966. In the game between Portugal and Brazil, Pelé was unmercifully hacked down whenever he carried the ball, a tactic which eventually resulted in his being forced to leave the game with an injury.

If we are to attempt to answer the question: "Are the values espoused by the organizational charter hegemonic throughout sport's social structures?" obviously a simple "yes" or "no" will not suffice. There is little doubt that some of the espoused ideals are rhetorical in that they deflect attention from the organizational operating procedures. Yet, to be characterized as rhetorical does not necessarily mean that they induce cynicism in the athlete. The use of expedient means to achieve organizational goals, although subverting professed values, appears to be hegemonic throughout sport. Athletes realize that the size of the pay check and the opportunity to continue their careers are dependent upon their contribution to organizational efficiency. While the inducement to use expedient or rational means invariably serves the business enterprise of the sporting oligarchy, it also is instrumental in providing greater pecuniary rewards for the athlete— organizational goals and individual goals are in congruence. As Dave Schultz has admitted, "I know that hitting got me to the NHL and hitting will have to keep me here" (*The Sporting News,* March 16, 1974: 3).

Cynicism appears to be generated when, in the name of organizational efficiency, management control extends beyond the sport arena per se, thus encroaching upon the athletes private lives. Operational procedures such as training rules seem to deny the validity of such claims as sport fosters self-discipline or sport makes men out of boys. Similarly, the claim that sport facilitates moral development seems to be refuted by the demands made upon the athlete to be "apolitical" (read "supportive of status quo"). Indeed the sporting oligarchy expects that its employees will contribute as opinion leaders to the ideological hegemony of attitudes which are already socially prevalent. Under such conditions we might assume that occupational social-ization could generate considerable conflict for the athlete in the perfor-mance of his occupational role.

THE SPORT ROLE AND ITS PARADOXES

Although the discussion which follows leans heavily upon the conceptual framework developed by Erving Goffman, our use of his concepts does not necessarily imply that we concur with the metaphysics implicit in his work. Goffman's sociology is mainly concerned with documenting the kinds of expressions which an individual gives off during the course of social inter-action and which allow his "audience" to infer meanings from his behavior. "In short, Goffman is concerned . . . with the techniques of impression man-agement—with the dramaturgical problems of presenting oneself and one's actions to others. He is interested in 'performances' or 'encounters,' or in the reciprocal influence of persons when in one another's presence" (Zeitlin, 1973: 192).

Implicit in Goffman's sociology is the idea that if we can infer meanings from the behavior of others, then, we can manipulate our own behavior to ensure that others attribute to our behavior the meanings which we desire —deception becomes a part and parcel of everyday life. In his book, *Stigma*, Goffman reveals this assumption since he suggests that we are all carriers of some form of stigma and are, therefore, compelled to engage in passing or covering so as to present an ideal image of ourselves. For those who are committed to their ideal image, impression management might be viewed as self-deception. For those who are manipulating their image as an instru-mental means of saving face or for reaping rewards, impression manage-ment might be viewed as other-deception; impression management is a hustle or gamesmanship. Goffman's sociology, then, presents us with a view of life characterized by alienation from ourselves and from others sharing our life-world. In a rational world, rationality diffuses into inter-personal relationships. In a meritocratic world, we obtain merits, perhaps not due to us, by instrumentally manipulating our impressions so that they conform to the expectations of others who are in a position to grant re-wards. Since Goffman is rarely critical of such instrumentality, his sociology demonstrates a lack of concern with the transcendence of alienated exist-ence.

During the course of occupational socialization, the athlete learns the approved ways in which to present himself to an heterogeneous audience comprised of his playing peers, the nonplaying persons exercising authority over him, and the vicarious participants of sport, the paying public. As a service occupation, it is not just the product of the service which is subject to evaluation; the production process and the producer are also placed under scrutiny. The athlete is often confronted with a fundamental dilemma, whether to conform to the expectations of his peers, the expectations of the management, or the expectations of the public. Since each of these audiences may use different criteria for evaluation, the athlete becomes adept at the art of impression management. He is "cool" for his peers, demeaned for the management, and dramatic for the fans. His teammates demand a demonstration of worth which entails conformity to their definitions of "occupational character" (Faulkner, 1971:2). They expect the athlete to show technical efficiency under pressure, gameness, and a knowledge of the appropriate use of aggression. The presentation of such attributes secures "deference" (Goffman, 1967: 77) for the athlete from his playing peers. While the management also views these attributes as essential for organizational efficiency, it makes further demands upon the athlete. Since the management controls a player's career mobility and salary, and its members have higher status in the hierarchical authority structure, then they are in a position to demand that the athlete demonstrate proper demeanor. Finally, the public expects to view a dramatic event and so requires the athlete to contribute to the drama. While demanding organizational efficiency, the public also expects the spectacular.

Front and Back Regions in the Work World of Professional Sport

Most athletes, because they share common conditions of existence and experience intrusions by the public and the nonplaying personnel in the sport organization, develop rationales and procedures for handling official demands which are made upon them. During their informal occupational socialization, athletes develop normative rules or standards which guide their behavior in the interaction with "outsiders." They learn which of the formal bureaucratic imperatives can be subverted without incurring punitive action from their superiors. Similarly, they learn the unofficial practices which are defined as being essential for membership within the athletic subculture. This informal organization admits new members on the basis of their willingness to adhere to the informal rules which it establishes. The athletic subculture, therefore, develops criteria for recognizing those who are in the know. That is, athletes recognize others who are prepared to share similar rationales for handling the asymmetrical power relationship to which they are subjected and for handling the intrusions of the unwise. Teammates, then, demand cooperation and loyalty because, in the presence of outsiders, they have to stage a performance which can be discredited by any one of them. Although "the work group does not have the power to remove one of its members from his job and deprive him of his income, it can ostracize him and thereby exclude him from genuine group membership" (Blau, 1965: 54–55) should he fail to perform in accordance with the unofficial norms. For example, an athlete who attempts to promote himself through ingratiation will incur negative sanctions from his athletic peers since fraternization with those holding managerial roles is not in keeping with the unofficial regulations of the work group. Similarly, those who seek to create favorable impressions of themselves by becoming "rate busters" usually are the recipients of satire and the cold shoulder. As Meggyesy (1970: 59) reports after being complimented for outstanding effort by Ben Schwartzwalder, "I was excited but felt ambivalent about Ben's remarks. On one hand I was tremendously happy over praise and approval. But on the other hand, those few words defined me, more clearly than before, as apart from the rest of the guys on the team. Ben had singled me out emphatically as one of the good boys, and I could feel the animosity of the veteran players."

The informal occupational socialization process establishes norms which, if violated, results in reducing the standing of the violator in the work group. Under such conditions of competing obligations (to the work group and to the management) it is understandable that athletes become adept at impression management and begin to draw a line between front and back regions. The front region is where the athletic work group actually presents their performance to the management and the paying public. The back region refers to any place which is off limits to the audience and those in the formal authority structure. While it is fairly easy to discern front and back regions in the performing arts, it is rather more difficult in sport. The problem revolves around one group of people having legitimate access to both front and back regions; namely the coaches. Thus while the dressing room provides security for the performing artist, the locker room offers no such guarantees for the athlete. And with the recent penchant of the mass media for "getting it while it's hot" or "telling it like it is," the intrusions of the public into the back regions are becoming increasingly irritating to athletes.

The establishment of front and back regions clearly demarcates when official or unofficial regulations are to be adhered to. In the front regions, the athlete, since he is exposed to the management and paying public, is constrained to follow the organizational procedures established by the management. Why does such adherence to the official regulations not result in work group denunciation? The answer is to be found in the work group's "defensive practices." Since all the athletes are engaged in putting on a performance to safeguard their careers, they mutually reinforce each other's performance and impression management—they avoid creating a scene which would embarrass their teammates or reduce their credibility. Thus, they enter into collusion: they uphold the occupational ethics of public role performance by engaging in their roles tongue-in-cheek. Overt cynicism is saved for the back regions.

What are the components of the occupational ethics established by the sport organization? Charnofsky (1972) has identified the following items of the baseball player's ethics when in the presence of the public: treat the fans with courtesy; do not fraternize with opponents since this may undermine the public's image of unadulterated competition; do not make the umpire appear foolish since it is his role to keep the show running smoothly and maintain the dignity of the game; do not make opponents appear inept as this incurs embarrassment so destroying another's popular image; and do not reveal cynicism in the presence of the unwise. In general, the public image presented in the front regions is in congruence with the ethics established by the organization.

However, in the back regions the athlete may feel free to criticise and even denigrate the authority figures of the organization, the umpire or referee, and the paying public. As Charnofsky (1972: 12) notes: "Interviews with players reveal that many of them (perhaps most, but some do not feel free to reveal their feelings for fear of violating occupational ethic) view adult fans in much the same way as Howard S. Becker reports jazz musicians perceive nonmusicians." In plain words, adult fans are 'squares,' people who lack understanding of the sport of baseball or the men who play it. They are seen as naive, uninformed, and fickle. With reference to the occupational ethic of not showing cynicism in front of the fans or the press, Curt Flood (1971: 48–49) explains: "On camera or within earshot of working reporters, the behaved player is an actor who projects blissful contentment, inexhaustible optimism, and abiding gratitude. 'I'll sweep out the clubhouse to stay here,' he says. 'I love the game. I owe everything to baseball. I am thankful to this grand organization for giving me my big chance. I'm in love with this town and its wonderful fans.' "

Since the sporting oligarchy has set up a patrimonial bureaucracy to watch over the "good" and "integrity" of the game, the commissioner and his staff usually come under fire in the back regions should they become overzealous in this respect. Players realize that the enforcement of pro-baseball, pro-fan, pro-organization sentiment constitutes an extension of domination serving the commercial interests of the owners. So while they realize that on-the-surface adherence to occupational ethics is career contingent (often, it is written into the contract), they suffer acute embarrassment during the delivery of "their ceremonial recitations" (Flood, 1971: 49).

Similarly, the players resent the public relations demands which owners make of them outside of the work place. The properly demeaned athlete adopts the approved posture of "tail-wagging thanks for the opportunities provided by the employer" while actually few feel "anything like such gratitude" due to the insecurity of their profession (Flood, 1971: 49).

Public relations and promotional activities provide an image of the player as follows: "the popular image suggests that baseball players love all children, gladly devote time and energy to signing autographs and making trips to hospitals, and are impervious to the ridicule but tolerant of the advice of adult fans, whom they also love" (Charnofsky, 1968: 51). Since such a posture is a career contingency, the players view such operational procedures with cynicism and discredit their own public performances in the back regions which is in accordance with the unofficial regulations established there. Impression management is an instrumental means of maintaining a career—it is a compromise of a player's actual sentiments and facilitates role distance. The players realize that their adherence to the occupational ethics is a necessary component of organizational efficiency yet they resent the repression which such adherence engenders. And since their adherence to the occupational ethics is rigidly enforced, sport as a patrimonial bureaucracy seems oblivious to the idea that strategic leniency can act as a compensatory device and increase the cohesion between management and players.

The Athlete and the Sport Role: Identity Work

Occupational socialization exhibits a cycle of belief-to-disbelief. Role progression follows a pattern of role-commitment to role distance. In the early stages of a player's career, we might claim that the public identity and the actual identity are in congruence—the player is taken in by his own routines. As Antonelli (1970: 34) points out, athletes may enter into the occupational subculture because sport is conceived of as a means of making easy sentimental conquests, achieving authority, or of attaining wealth, fame, social importance, and security. Thus, in the early stages of role progression the personal costs involved in the adoption of the sport role seem inconsequential when compared with the perceived gains. The athlete is "sincerely convinced that the impression of reality which he stages is the real reality" (Goffman, 1959: 17).

The transition from commitment to cynicism, we have suggested, is facilitated by the operational procedures of the sport organization which make increasing demands on the player so reducing his personal autonomy. Personal costs begin to outweigh perceived gains. The turning point in the cycle of commitment to cynicism may be at that phase of role progression during which the constraints and obligations of the role equal or exceed the anticipated or realized profits. When the athlete realizes that "he must continue to practise a sport which has become a difficult job and which has lost a large part of its previous pleasure" (Antonelli, 1970: 36) he becomes ambivalent and cynical in his feelings towards the organizational authority figures and the fans. A back region develops and the athletes are no longer taken in by their own routines; they engage in "identity work." Stone and Oldenberg (1967: 517) define identity work as the "building and husbanding (of) an identity that can mobilize the appreciations of the audience and maintain them over time." Identity work is similar in meaning to impression management: it implies that an athlete's image in front of the public and the management is a carefully constructed facade which allows the athlete to reap the rewards and stay in good grace since it conceals inner sentiment from the unwise. The public image or front, while expressing idealized or stereotypic standards, allows concealment of the actual identity which may be inconsistent with these standards.

As previously stated, identity work or impression management implies that defense mechanisms or identity shields are in operation. Since the back regions allow the athlete to drop his public image in favor of his actual image, those who have access to the back regions have to be either a part of the collusion or have to protect the public image by refusing to release for public consumption the dark secrets which are revealed there. For the athletes, the unofficial regulations of "bureaucracy's other face" protect their actual images. The demands of loyalty and cooperation effectively counteract public revelation. However, the unofficial regulations apply only while the athlete is part of the work group. The retired or released ("cut") athlete may no longer be constrained by unofficial imperatives and may commercialize his knowledge of the dark secrets. Revelations by retired or released athletes result in denials and anger by those who remain members of the work group or may result in the present members of the work group discrediting the revelations of the recalcitrant. As Jim Bouton (1971: 85–86) notes, the official and unofficial regulations which preserve the sanctity of the club house can be stated as follows: "What you see here, What you hear here, Let it stay here, When you leave here." Revelations by the recalcitrant draw official and unofficial recriminations—the recalcitrant is sometimes labeled a "flake" by here-and-now members of the organization. Recording the reactions to his book, *Ball Four*, Bouton lists the following: "Bob Gibson of the St. Louis Cardinals said I was stabbing people in the back. Lee Maye of the Washington Senators said I had a good chance to get my head busted. . . . Hank Soar, the umpire, said, 'If we all wrote about what we know about other people there'd be no baseball'. . . . Joe Cronin, president of the American League, said 'It's the most derogatory thing and the worst thing for baseball I've ever seen' " (1971: 111–112). For what we might assume to be different reasons, both the unofficial rules of the work group and the official code of occupational ethics prohibit the exposure of dark secrets to the public.

The mass media also act in the role of identity shields despite their claims of honest, no-holds-barred reporting. The media steadfastly portray the better qualities of the athlete and do not offer the dark secrets for public consumption. Since the sporting oligarchy controls the media representatives by threatening the loss of assignment or job transfer, the media representatives ask only conventional questions to which they receive conventional responses. As Shecter (1969: 20–21) has noted: "By and large, the people who work in sports departments are so droolingly grateful for the opportunity to make their living as nonpaying fans at sporting events that they devote much of their time and energy to stepping on no toes. This leads to an easily discernible genre of sportswriting, the kind we get in most of the sports sections around the country—consistently bland and hero-worshipful presented in pedestrian, cliché-ridden writing style." The mass media, then, potentially has the capacity to manipulate public opinion —limits are set by the sporting oligarchy which controls the media's access to sport and the content of reports arising from such access. The outcome of this oligarchical control is ideological hegemony—the public is presented with only one interpretation of sport and is denied exposure to alternatives.

In recent years, however, the public seems to have been demanding a more authentic picture and commercially supporting exposes of back region secrets. The public appears to be more tolerant of the "bad guy" and the "anti-hero" possibly because they add spice and color to sport which was becoming a bland reaffirmation of middle-class morality. Pro wrestling (if you can call it a sport), in particular, has deliberately played upon the public's demand for emotional identification and disidentification and has been aptly named a "passion play" (Stone and Oldenburg, 1967). That is, "with respect to morality, role types are set up dichotomously on the basis of good and evil. In native terminology, the roles of good and evil are referred to by such terms as 'Baby Face' and 'Heel' " (Turowetz et al., 1973: 1). Indeed, wrestling has capitalized upon racial and ethnic prejudice and other forms of intolerance. We might suggest that wherever structural strains exist in a society, wrestling can realize a profit by providing vicarious and cathartic exacerbation. Playing upon manifest and latent strains, wrestling keeps its followers "tingling pleasurably at the spectacle" (Goodhart and Chataway, 1968: 3). Wrestlers present public images which conform with the "sport's" desire to juxtapose a manufactured hero with a manufactured villain.

While the public seems to desire the confrontation of hero and villain, traditional spectator sports have generally attempted to provide the audience with the history book hero "... who epitomizes the best in cultural and moral values" (Smith, 1973: 59). Since the public vicariously participates through its heroes, the public image of the athlete again contributes to the ideological hegemony of prevalent social values. Maintaining that the athlete is a role model for the young, the management requires its athletes to embody all that is best in American values. With respect to the management's demand for historical heroes worthy of adulation, defensive practices and identity shields become important features of commercial sport. The hero's "slips" must be covered up; the dark secrets of the back region must not emerge into public view; actual images of the athletes must not discredit their public images. Yet, in recent years, mainstream American values have been challenged by the "New Left" and the "counter-culture." Some of the ideas espoused by such groups or movements have gained mainstream support. Especially important for the sport hero is the value of "just being yourself." If it is the case, as Smith (1973: 63) suggests, that "approximately every 20 years over the past century the type of sports hero in vogue has changed and these changes have roughly paralleled changes in societal values," then the discrepancy between an athlete's public image and actual image may be considerably reduced in the next few years. Less identity work may be necessary. However, while the management holds onto anachronistic conceptions of the sports hero, the athlete who provides the public with an anti-hero or bad guy will still suffer the official rebukes of sport's moral guardians. Perhaps the change in managerial attitude will come when the anti-hero or bad guy becomes necessary for the rational pursuit of profit.

THE SPORT ROLE: ALIENATION AND TRANSCENDENCE [10]

In the preceding sections we have suggested that several historical trends have influenced the nature of the athletic role and the occupational subculture. First, sport has become an institutionalized and reified part of the social life world. Second, sport has become increasingly susceptible to the process of rationalization. Not only has technological and bureaucratic rationality been applied to sport's organization and the athlete's performances, but also the tendency to compute an individual's worth on the basis of competitive economic performances has facilitated the diffusion of rationality into interpersonal social relationships. Third, the commercialization and professionalization of sport has placed sport within the larger entertainment industry and has transformed the athletic role into a service occupation so reducing the athlete to the level of a commodity. Finally, the growth of the "performance principle" has raised the idea of meritocracy to the level of ideology. Meritocracy has become somewhat hegemonic and has mitigated the idea that economic relationships can be characterized by class conflict. Class conflicts become flattened since meritocracy legitimates a more rational form of structured inequality. These historical trends, which reflect the transformation of society from *Gemeinschaft* to *Gesellschaft*, lead us to reconsider the question of alienation as it applies to social roles in general and athletic roles in particular.

The Preconditions of Alienation

As a social institution, sport is a taken-for-granted part of the sociocultural milieu. Sport as an institutionalized form of behavior requires that individuals participating in it accommodate themselves to pre-existing structures and predefined social roles. As we stated in the introductory paragraphs, sport seems to possess ontological status; we cannot wish it away since it possesses the quality of a thing. Sport as a reified entity, appears external to and independent of the here-and-now athletes participating in it. Formal occupational socialization, then, attempts to ensure that "individuals learn and internalize the frame of values legitimating sport, . . . learn and internalize the constitutive rules which guide interaction and give sport its form; and, . . . identify with idealized stereotypes exemplifying the necessary behavioral and attitudinal requirements for preferred role performance" (Ingham and Loy, 1973: 6). Occupational socialization attempts to ensure that the athlete accedes to structure and rules of form so that sport remains relatively unchanged in transmission.

What is it about institutionalization and reification which causes us to wonder whether they result in the de facto condition of alienation? The point is that when sport becomes institutionalized and reified, it tends to ignore the here-and-now athlete as an agent of reconstruction. Rather than the athlete being allowed to construct his sport world in the light of his experiences and in accordance with his individual needs, his attempts at reconstruction are repressed to ensure the preservation of status quo. The social structures man creates become external and coercive: they exercise constraint over the individuals who create them and limit the parameters of debate. It is in this sense that institutionalization and reification lead to alienation. Man becomes divorced from the products of his creativity. Man appears passive, a spectator of, rather than a participant in, structural and normative change. The athlete emerges, in C. Wright Mills's (1959: 175) terms, as a "cheerful robot" who, by virtue of occupational socialization, feels that his actions are based upon personal volition when, in reality, they are the result of a predefined external life-world being introjected into sub-jective consciousness. Whenever athletes act as "cheerful robots" they are engaging in bad faith: they pretend that "something is necessary that in fact is voluntary" (Berger, 1963: 143). While their careers lack security they feel that they cannot say "No!" to the reified sport world. Even though the oper-ational procedures of sport may engender cynicism in the athlete, for those who lack alternative careers, the presentation of behavior commensurate with the stereotypic public image appears obligatory. Athletes are forced to pay lip service to a reified entity over which they have no control. Those athletes, who in Mills's (1959: 175) terms become world constructing Renaissance men, suffer from official reprimands such as blacklisting. As Parrish (1971: 187) points out, "Walter Roberts, an outstanding flanker for the Washington Redskins in 1970, went from the Browns to New Orleans in their expansion pool. After one season Tom Fears suspected Walt of organizing the black players, so he made a deal with Detroit to take Roberts for a little while, then drop him and blackball him from the league. Roberts was out of pro football for a season." Similarly, as Hoch (1972: 108–110) has revealed, athletes who have been prominent in the formation of player associations have suffered various retributions (e.g., Joe Torre, Doug Harvey, Bert Olmstead, and Ted Lindsay). Reification results in athletes "con-stantly straining at their leashes, surrendering to the controlling authorities with gnashing teeth, constantly driven to obedience by fear of what may happen to them otherwise" (Berger, 1963: 93). Such alienation cannot be transcended unless athletes are allowed to construct their sport world rather than being required to accept the reified world of previous generations or the definitions handed down to them by those whose vested interests are served by the preservation of sport's status quo.

Sport, we have claimed, has become susceptible to the thrust of ra-tionality (both bureaucratic and technological). While rationality has had the manifest consequences of increasing sport's organizational efficiency and ameliorating the performances of the athletes, in recent years serious con-cern has been voiced about the latent consequences of rationality: namely, the trend toward depersonalization and dehumanization. Pappenheim (1959: 42) summarizes such concerns as follows: "This trend toward depersonal-ization . . . reflects the innermost tendency of the machine age, leading away from the vital and organic and turning to the mechanical and organized. Such a world of mechanization requires a matter-of-factness as the prevail-ing attitude of mind . . . Everything, including man, has to become predict-able and calculable." The argument can be continued: rationality once a means to an end has become an end in and of itself. If rationality was once positively envisaged as a way of creating a more humane existence, as a way of transforming class-linked domination into legalistic equality, as a way of creating a higher standard of living for all members of a society, then, we should also note that such positive achievements have not been gained without the negative trend toward the suppression of personal autonomy. Rationalization is a dialectical process which ameliorates the quantitative conditions of life while leaving the qualitative components relatively unchanged—rationality facilitates the domination of nature and also of man. "Nature, scientifically comprehended and mastered, reappears in the technical apparatus of production and destruction which sustains and improves the life of the individuals while subordinating them to the masters of the apparatus. Thus the rational hierarchy merges with the social one" (Marcuse, 1964: 166).

In sport, bureaucratic rationality has expanded the realm of social control. The transformation of sport from player-controlled games to management-controlled big time has resulted in sport moving from an arena of informal social relationships (a *Gemeinschaft* orientation) to an arena of formal bureaucratic domination. Sport has ceased to be undertaken for its own sake and the sociability of participation. Sport is now undertaken for the organization. The athlete's "onetime position as a more or less independent participant has largely been replaced by the status of skilled athletic worker under the strict discipline of coaches, managers and, in the case of the pro, the 'front office' " (Page, 1973: 33). While we recognize that sport has not completely succumbed to the process of rationalization—it still retains many of its playful elements—we note that the increasing emphasis upon organizational efficiency tends to set limits upon individual spontaneity and creativity. Bureaucratic control defines the parameters of acceptable behavior according to organizational rather than individual needs. "The modern coach, instead of being the man who encourages and guides others to struggle to do their thing, has instead become that person who manipulates and controls others and their environment so as to do his thing. Thus, the individual loses his chance to struggle with himself, to seek his own experience" (Morford, 1973: 86). In Marx's terms the athletic role as work role alienates the individual from the process of production. Sport ceases to be an embodiment of human subjectivity. It is characterized by the separation of labor from control. The athlete becomes an object of manipulation; he is reduced to the level of a marketable commodity and is evaluated in terms of his competitive economic worth.

Bureaucratic control has been aided and abetted by technological rationality. Control has been scientized. With the specialization of the athletic role, it has become increasingly possible to specify the kinds of positional attributes which facilitate organizational efficiency. Thus, individuals are rationally assessed prior to selection by the degree to which they possess these attributes. They are appraised on such characteristics as height, weight, speed, and performance statistics. In player selection "we do not relate to the other person as a whole . . . but we isolate the one part which is important to us and remain more or less remote observers of the rest" (Pappenheim, 1959: 12). Scientific appraisal of athletes has become very sophisticated through the use of computers and the development of farm league systems. Computers are used to store information on anybody resembling a likely candidate for the professional role. Some teams have gone so far as to use psychological and physiological tests in the screening of prospects, a practice which, although frowned upon by player associations, has resulted in the increased standardization of attributes deemed essential for organizational efficiency. These trends toward scientific appraisal reduce the athlete to a set of figures which can be conveniently stored upon a computer card. He loses his essential human qualities.

The farm system also exemplifies the scientization of bureaucracy. Initiated by Branch Rickey in 1919, the system was used to develop young players as prospects for the major leagues. As Seymour (1971: 413) notes: "This network made it possible to start youngsters at the bottom, sift out the best and move them up, repeating the process at each level until the most highly skilled were ready for the majors or high minors." Scientific appraisal coupled with meritocratic principles, while democratizing the base, ensures that only the fittest survive. Structured inequality in sport establishes itself on a rational footing since it appeals to an objective sense of fairness.

The objective nature of rationality and meritocracy has contributed to their ideological hegemony. Rationality has diffused throughout sport's social structure. As we have previously noted, technical efficiency while furthering organizational goals has also become a criterion for acceptability into the athletic work group. Not only does the management formally reward technical skill but so also do the members of the team. One reason for the diffusion of rational appraisal into the work group is that the instrumental goals of the athlete are closely tied to the technical efficiency of his team members. That is, "in order to assert ourselves as individuals, we relate only to those phases of reality which seem to promote the attainment of our objectives and we remain divorced from the rest of it" (Pappenheim, 1959: 12). Social relationships in the athletic work group become characterized by expediency: athletes relate to each other primarily on those attributes which further their economic goals. For example, in the early days of black involvement in professional sport, white athletes granted acceptability to blacks not on their essentially human qualities but on their ability to get the job done. Such a case might also hold for contemporary sport. As Charnofsky (1972: 11) reveals, while most players accept each other as part of the organizational unit, "white and black or brown players rarely spend leisure time with each other, and almost never room together on the road." In Marx's terminology, such instrumentality in social relationships alienates man from his "species being"—man ceases to relate to mankind in general; he relates only to fragmented attributes of another as they serve his instrumental goals.

"An immediate consequence of the fact that man is estranged from the product of his labour, from his life-activity, from his species being, is the estrangement of man from man" (Marx, cited in Mészáros, 1970: 15). In a competitive economic activity such as sport, athletes are engaged in intense competition not only with others who are challenging for their roles but also with opponents whose expressed aim is to facilitate their organization's efficiency by impeding the efficiency of others. As Robert K. Merton in his essay, "Social Structure and Anomie" (1957), has been anxious to explicate, the increasing emphasis upon victory and success through efficient means (can) only result in the primacy of expedience as a behavioral norm. Such criticisms do not apply only to professional athletics. The thrust of rationality reaches to the early stages of role progression: the increasing emphasis upon victory at the expense of fairness seems also to characterize high school athletics.[11] Concomitant with this diffusion of rationality into interpersonal relationships is the concern that the rational pursuit of victory might result in the athlete being prepared to sacrifice not only his own human rights but also the rights of others against whom he is competing. As we have previously noted, the ideas of "taking the man out" and "playing the man," the operational procedures which encourage the use of the tactical foul, confirm the suspicion that rational expediency results in the alienation of man from man. Instrumentality dissipates the agon ideal in sport. For as Morford (1973: 85) has acknowledged, "the performance of such acts by man does not elevate him to the humanistic level if they are performed merely for the benefits accrued by the outcome of the acts so as to achieve immediate gratification through materialistic rewards, paternalistic favor or public adulation."

The loss of the agon ideal in sport results not only from the thrust of rationality into interpersonal relationships. Professionalization and commercialization have enslaved the athlete into fulfilling the commercial and cathartic needs of others rather than those within himself. In a Marxian sense, professionalization and commercialization have transformed sport from the athletic pursuit of life-activity to a situation where the athlete works in order to live. The agonistic experience is transformed into a service occupation; sport ceases to be ennobling; the athlete is viewed as an entertainment commodity. At the professional level, athletes become envisioned as pawns "having utility in providing for successes that can be translated into some form of social or financial profit" (Petrie, 1971: 12). Alienation arises as a de facto condition of professionalization since man becomes viewed as an object with a commercial value.[12] Why is alienation a de facto and not an a priori condition for Marx? Marx accepted that an essential component of being human was to objectivate one's subjectivity through the products of one's activity. This objectivation, being a primary mediation of human existence, does not in and of itself produce alienation. Sport in its preprofessional days, then, was not alienating: it was an embodiment of human subjectivity. As Homer has said, "there is no greater glory for a man while yet he lives, than that which he achieves by hand and foot" (cited by Morford, 1973: 84). Alienation occurs when the products of man's activities are appropriated by others for their own commercial gain. Alienation is an historical concept related to appropriation. It arises through the secondary mediation of entrepreneurial capitalism which rationalizes value into monetary exchange and envisages labor as a commodity. Alienation arises as a de facto condition of the separation of labor from the control of the production process and product exchange. And, according to some Neo–Marxist scholars; it can only be transcended by transforming *Homo Faber* into *Homo Ludens* (cf., Marcuse, 1955: 170–171). Only when the athlete is freed from external constraint and compulsion will alienation cease to exist in sport. "Liberated from the pressure of painful purposes and performances necessitated by want, man will be restored into the 'freedom to be what he ought to be.' But what 'ought' to be will be freedom itself: the freedom to play" (Marcuse, 1955: 172). Only when sport is freed from the reality of the marketplace will the athlete be allowed to be himself rather than a manufactured public image. Then, and then only, will the athlete cease to sell his labor, to be treated as a commodity by those who appropriate it.

Transcendence: A Revolutionary Project?

Presenting the case that institutionalization, reification, rationalization, and commercialization inevitably produce the de facto condition of alienation is, of course, courting the dangers of determinism. Such an assertion fails to recognize the dialectical nature of the athletic role. The role is portrayed as a predefined entity having control over the volitions of the athlete who is engaging in 'bad faith.' Consequently, this assertion fails to adequately present the dialectical relationship between commitment and noncommitment or role distance. To quote Natanson (1972: 221), "the paradox of the role lies in the necessary distance between acceptance and performance, between affirmation and reflection," and it is precisely this paradox that we have ignored in our eristical reasoning. The athletic role is paradoxical: the athlete can be committed to athletics and at the same time be cynical about the ritualized ways in which he is required to perform. That is, not all athletes are "cheerful robots" possessed with a "happy consciousness." Not all athletes believe that the system is rational and will deliver the goods. Therefore, should we neglect the paradoxical nature of the social role, we shall fail to distinguish between the activity and the role which circumscribes it. And failing to distinguish between the activity and the role will rule out the possibility of transcendence. We confuse the activity as a primary mediation with appropriation, the secondary mediation. To transcend alienation we would not only abolish appropriation but the activity as well.

Similarly, to envisage the athlete as a "cheerful robot" possessed by "happy consciousness" suggests that the athlete's total self has been invaded by his athletic identity. But athletes do engage in role distance and are capable of separating actual from public identity. All athletes are not falsely conscious dupes who are unaware of their conditions of existence and the uses to which their labor is put. Athletes are beginning to reconstruct the social and economic structure of sport through their membership in players' unions, through their willingness to strike, through their attempts to transform sport from a patrimonial bureaucracy to a legalistic bureaucracy via their challenges of reserve, option and forfeiture clauses.

Yet it should be noted that while sport remains a part of commercial enterprise and athletes are dependent upon owners for their livelihoods, such attempts to transform the social and economic order of sport may not lead to the transcendence of alienation. Trade unionism in the form of player associations can be envisaged as an attempt to re-evaluate the worth of the athlete's labor which may not elevate it from the status of a commodity. Quantitative changes do not necessarily lead to the qualitative changes intrinsic in the notion of transcendence. To remain within the existing order of things without knowledge of alternatives is not the way to good consciousness. To perform the athletic role in a cynical fashion reduces such performance to a fraud. "Human freedom for Marx is not realized through 'radical improvements in the conditions under which men labour,' but requires free activity to be differentiated qualitatively from work" (Schoolman, 1973: 295–296).

Thus, if the athlete is to become an agent in the transcendence of his own alienation, he has to free himself from the ideological hegemony of rational, meritocratic capitalism. He has to see alternatives to the commodity structure in which he provides the public, in exchange for an admission fee, with artificial excitement, with thrills and sensationalism rather than confront them with the real questions and conflicts in human life (cf., Pappenheim, 1959: 107). To combat his alienation, the professional athlete has to work at reinstating and reaffirming the *Gemeinschaft* qualities which rationalism has endangered. The nonrational elements of compassion, tolerance, and the spirit of community need to be retained in an activity which has become somewhat instrumental and expedient. While we recognize that to dream of the ultimate transcendence of alienation is Utopian, to accept things as they are is to give up without a struggle. Athletes have to risk and strive for transcendence since opposition without praxis is at best an empty protest.

NOTES

1. I have discussed the process through which institutionalization takes place in a paper coauthored with John W. Loy, "The Social System of Sport: A Humanistic Perspective." *Quest*, 1973, **19**: 3–23.

2. The concepts, *Gemeinschaft* and *Gesellschaft*, while not originating in the work of Ferdinand Tönnies, were developed analytically by this man most adroitly. In essence, they are ideal types which facilitate a discussion of the historical transformation of society from that based upon tradition, communism (in its nonideological meaning), intimate family bonding, and relative stability to that based upon rational-purposive action, expedient association, contractual relationship, and the emphasis upon change (often interpreted as progress). See F. Tönnes, *Community and Society*, New York: Harper & Row, 1957.

3. I have deliberately entitled this section, an excursus, so that readers who wish to pass it over may do so without suffering from a loss in continuity.

4. To say that this view is person-centered is not to say that I am advocating that sociology become solipsistic, a position which would violate any form of intersubjective validation since it is both relativistic and subjectivistic. I am simply pointing out that one can analyze and view social reality through the eyes of the individuals comprising it.

5. John Hewitt and Peter Hall in their paper, "Social Problems, Problematic Situations, and Quasi-Theories" (*American Sociological Review*, 1973, **38**: 367–374) define quasi theories as "ad hoc explanations brought to problematic situations in order to introduce both order and hope into those situations." Ad hoc interpretations may be defined as commonsense notions which render situations meaningful.

6. Weber was not unaware of the possibility of uncontrolled (politically) bureaucratic domination. As Anthony Giddens (*Politics and Sociology in the Thought of Max Weber*. London: Macmillan, 1972: 18–19) has observed, "Weber saw the likelihood of 'uncontrolled bureaucratic domination' as the greatest threat of the hiatus in political leadership left by Bismarck's fall from power."

7. Patrimonial bureaucracy is used to describe the condition in which "the person exercising governing powers has personal control of the means of administration"—authority is decentralized but remains under the control of the privileged minority. The pure type of legalistic bureaucracy requires that the bureaucrat be freed from obligations to a privileged minority—the bureaucracy

becomes disinterested and executes authority on the basis of legal criteria to which both the privileged and nonprivileged are bound (cf., Max Weber, *The Theory of Social and Economic Organization*, translated by A. M. Henderson and T. Parsons, T. Parsons (ed.), New York: Oxford University Press, 1947: 324–341).

8. While not exactly a part of the merger movement, we should note that another example of the expansion of monopolistic and bureaucratic control is provided by the widespread use of the farm system. Although the farm system was ostensibly designed by Branch Rickey to secure better calibre recruits, it, in fact, enabled the major baseball league owners to expand their control over the whole of professional baseball. The major leagues thus came to control a part of the minors by 1928, and by 1939 the minors were largely under the economic and bureaucratic control of the majors (cf., David Q. Voigt, *American Baseball*, Vol. II. Norman, Oklahoma: University of Oklahoma Press, 1970). A similar case can be made for the sport of hockey where agreements have been reached between the NHL and the CHAA.

9. This section of the paper represents a condensed and somewhat revised version of sections of the paper "The Social Implications of the Interaction between Spectators and Athletes" written by Alan G. Ingham and Michael D. Smith (in *Exercise and Sport Sciences Review*, J. Wilmore (ed.). Vol. II. New York: Academic Press, 1974).

10. Parts of this section are taken from Alan G. Ingham, "The New Left and Sport: Some Reflections upon Opposition without Praxis" to be published in *Social Problems in Athletics: Essays in the Sociology of Sport*, D. Landers (ed.). University of Illinois Press.

11. See for example: H. Webb, "Professionalization of attitudes toward play among adolescents" (in *Sociology of Sport*, G. S. Kenyon (ed.). The Athletic Institute, Chicago, 1969); R. C. Mantel and L. VanderVelden, "The Relationship between the Professionalization toward Play of Pre-adolescent Boys and Participation in Organized Sport" (a paper presented at the International Symposium on the Sociology of Sport, Waterloo, Canada, 1971).

12. The purchase of a sport franchise provides a good example of players being viewed as a commercial object—they become depreciable assets. In short, the procedure is as follows: A nominal fee is paid for the actual franchise and most of the cost is in the buying of the players. Owners have selected this method because assets can be depreciated whereas stocks cannot (cf., P. Hoch, *Rip Off the Big Game*. Garden City, N.Y.: Anchor Doubleday, 1972: 51–52; B. Veeck, *Thirty Tons a Day*. New York: The Viking Press, 1972: 10–11).

REFERENCES

Antonelli, Ferrucio
1970   "Psychological Problems of Top-Level Athletes." *International Journal of Sport Psychology*, **1**: 34–39.

Aron, Raymond
1962   *The Opium of the Intellectuals.* New York: The Norton Library.
1968   *Progress and Disillusion: The Dialectics of Modern Society.* London: Pall Mall Press.

Aschcraft, Richard
1972   "Marx and Weber on Liberalism as Bourgeois Ideology." *Comparative Studies in Society and History,* **14**: 130–168.

Becker, Howard S.
1951   "The Professional Dance Musician and His Audience." *American Journal of Sociology,* **57**: 136–144.

Bendix, Reinhard
1970   "Sociology and the Distrust of Reason." *American Sociological Review,* **35**: 831–843.

Berger, Peter L.
1963   *Invitation to Sociology: A Humanistic Perspective.* Garden City, N.Y.: Anchor Doubleday.

Berger, Peter L., and Stanley Pullberg
1966   "Reification and the Sociological Critique of Consciousness." *New Left Review,* **35**: 56–71.

Betts, John R.
1953   "The Technological Revolution and the Rise of Sport." *Mississippi Valley Historical Review,* **40**: 231–256.

Birnbaum, Norman
1971   *Toward a Critical Sociology.* New York: Oxford University Press.

Blau, Peter M.
1956   *Bureaucracy in Modern Society.* New York: Random House.

Bouton, Jim
1970   *Ball Four.* New York: Dell Publishing Company.
1971   *I'm Glad You Didn't Take It Personally.* New York: Dell Publishing Company.
1973   *I Managed Good, But Boy Did They Play Bad.* Chicago: Playboy Press.

Charnofsky, Harold
1968   "The Major League Professional Baseball Player: Self-Conception Versus Popular Image." *International Review of Sport Sociology,* **3**: 39–53.
1972   "Ballplayers, Occupational Image, and the Maximization of Profit." Paper presented at the American Sociological Association Annual Meetings, New Orleans. August 28–31.

Chester, D. Norman (Chairman)
1968   *Report of the Committee on Football.* London: Her Majesty's Stationary Office.

Coleman, James S.
1961   *The Adolescent Society.* Glencoe, Ill.: The Free Press.

Cook, Earnshaw
1964   *Percentage Baseball*. Baltimore, Md.: The M.I.T. Press.

Economic Report on Corporate Mergers
1969   Hearings before the Subcommittee on Antitrust and Monopoly. Washing-
        ton: U.S. Government Printing Office.

Edwards, Harry
1973   *Sociology of Sport*. Homewood, Ill.: The Dorsey Press.

Eitzen, D. Stanley
1973   "Athletics in the Status System of Male Adolescents: A Replication of
        Coleman's, The Adolescent Society." Paper presented at Midwest Soci-
        ological Society Meetings, Milwaukee, Wisconsin. April 26–27.

Flood, Curt
1971   *The Way It Is*. New York: Trident Press.

Goffman, Erving
1959   *The Presentation of Self in Everyday Life*. Garden City, N.Y.: Anchor
        Doubleday.
1967   *Interaction Ritual: Essays on Face-to-Face Behavior*. Garden City, N.Y.:
        Anchor Doubleday.

Goodhart, Philip, and Christopher Chataway
1968   *War Without Weapons*. London: W. H. Allen.

Gouldner, Alvin W.
1970   *The Coming Crisis of Western Sociology*. New York: Basic Books.

Habermas, Jürgen
1970   *Toward a Rational Society*. Boston, Ma.: Beacon Press.

Haerle, Rudolf
1972   "Member of a Team—But Uniquely Alone: A Sociological Analysis of the
        Professional Baseball Player." Manuscript, Department of Sociology, Mid-
        dlebury College, Vermont.

Harrington, Michael
1965   *The Accidental Century*. Baltimore, Md.: Penguin Books.

Hoch, Paul
1972   *Rip Off the Big Game*. Garden City, N.Y.: Anchor Doubleday.

Hofstadter, Richard
1944   *Social Darwinism in American Thought*. Boston, Ma.: Beacon Press.

Ingham, Alan G., and John W. Loy
1973   "The Social System of Sport: A Humanistic Perspective." *Quest*, **19**: 3–23.

Janoušek, Jaromìr
1972   "On the Marxian Concept of Praxis." In *The Context of Social Psychol-
        ogy: A Critical Assessment*, J. Israel and H. Tajfel (eds.). New York: Aca-
        demic Press. 279–294.

Loewith, Karl
1970   "Weber's Interpretation of the Bourgeois-Capitalistic World in Terms of the Guiding Principle of Rationalization." In *Max Weber,* D. H. Wrong (ed.). Englewood Cliffs, N.J.: Prentice-Hall. 101–122.

Loy, John W., and Alan G. Ingham
1973   "Play, Games and Sport in the Psychological Development of Children and Youth." In *Physical Activity: Human Growth and Development,* G. L. Rarick (ed.). New York: Academic Press. 257–302.

Marcuse, Herbert
1955   *Eros and Civilization: A Philosophical Inquiry into Freud.* New York: Vintage Books.
1964   *One-Dimensional* Man. Boston, Ma.: Beacon Press.

McFarlane, Brian
1968   *The Lively World of Hockey.* New York: Signet Books.

Meggyesy, Dave
1970   *Out of Their League.* Berkeley, Cal.: Ramparts Press.

Merton, Robert K.
1957   "Social Structure and Anomie." In *Social Theory and Social Structure.* R. K. Merton (ed.). New York: Free Press.

Mészáros, István
1970   *Marx's Theory of Alienation.* London: Merlin Press.

Mills, C. Wright
1959   *The Sociological Imagination.* New York: Oxford University Press.

Morford, W. Robert
1973   "Is Sport the Struggle or the Triumph?" *Quest,* **19**: 83–87.

Myslenski, Skip
1973   "The Better Way." *The Gladiators.* Englewood Cliffs, N.J.: Prentice-Hall. 186–206.

Natanson, Maurice
1972   "Phenomenology and Social Role." *Journal of the British Society for Phenomenology,* **3**: 218–230.

Page, Charles H.
1946   "Bureaucracy's Other Face." *Social Forces,* **25**: 89–91.
1973   "Pervasive Sociological Themes in the Study of Sport." In *Sport and Society: An Anthology.* J. Talamini and C. H. Page (eds.). Boston: Little, Brown. 14–37.

Pappenheim, Fritz
1959   *The Alienation of Modern Man.* New York: Modern Reader Paperbacks.

Parrish, Bernie
1971   *They Call It A Game.* New York: The Dial Press.

Peterson, Robert W.
1970   *Only the Ball Was White.* Englewood Cliffs, N.J.: Prentice-Hall.

Petrie, Brian M.
1971   "The Athletic Group as an Emerging Deviant Subculture," Paper presented to the Conference on Sport and Social Deviancy, Brockport, New York. December 9–11.

Schoolman, Morton
1973   "Further Reflections on Work, Alienation, and Freedom in Marcuse and Marx." *Canadian Journal of Political Science*, 6: 295–302.

Seymour, Harold
1960   *Baseball: The Early Years.* New York: Oxford University Press.
1971   *Baseball: The Golden Age.* New York: Oxford University Press.

Shechter, Leonard
1969   *The Jocks.* New York: Paperback Library.

Smith, Garry
1973   "The Sport Hero: An Endangered Species." *Quest,* **19**: 59–70.

Stone, Gregory P., and Ramon A. Oldenburg
1967   "Wrestling." In *Motivations in Play, Games and Sports,* R. Slovenko and J. Knight (eds.). Springfield, Ill.: Charles C Thomas. 503–532.

Tönnies, Ferdinand
1957   *Community and Society* (Gemeinschaft und Gesellschaft), C. P. Loomis (trans.). New York: Harper & Row.

Turowetz, Allen, Ron Fernandez, and Leon Jacobs
1973   "Professional Sport and the Manipulation of Identities." Paper presented at the Northeastern Anthropological Association Annual Meeting, Burlington, Vermont. April 27–28.

Vaz, Edmund W.
1972   "The Culture of Young Hockey Players: Some Initial Observations." In *Training: A Scientific Basis.* E. A. Taylor (ed.). Springfield, Ill.: Charles C Thomas.

Voigt, David Q.
1970   *American Baseball,* Vol. 2. Norman, Okla.: University of Oklahoma Press.

Webb, Harry
1969   "Professionalization of Attitudes toward Play among Adolescents." In *Sociology of Sport,* G. S. Kenyon (ed.). Chicago: The Athletic Institute. 161–178.

Weber, Max
1947   *The Theory of Social and Economic Organization,* T. Parsons (ed.), A. M. Henderson and T. Parsons (trans.). New York: The Free Press.

Woodley, Richard
1973   *Team: A High School Odyssey.* New York: Holt, Rinehart and Winston.

Wrong, Dennis H.
1970   "Max Weber." In *Max Weber,* D. H. Wrong (ed.). Englewood Cliffs, N.J.:
          Prentice-Hall.

Zeitlin, Irving M.
1973   *Rethinking Sociology: A Critique of Contemporary Theory.* New York:
          Appleton-Century-Crofts.

Chapter 9
An Occupational Analysis of the College Coach

George H. Sage
Department of Physical Education
University of Northern Colorado
(Greeley, Colorado)

George H. Sage

Birth Place: Rifle, Colorado

Age: 44

Birth Order: Oldest, two sisters

Formal Education:

A.B., University of Northern Colorado	1955
M.A., University of Northern Colorado	1957
Ed.D., University of California, Los Angeles	1963

Present Position:

Professor, and Chairman, Department of Physical Education, University of Northern Colorado

Professional Responsibilities:

Currently teaching courses in Sociology of Sport, Sport Psychology, History of Sport.

Scholarly Interests: Research

Sociology of Sports occupation, socialization into and via sports, motivation and sports performances.

Professional Accomplishments:

Sport and American Society. Introduction to Motor Behavior: A Neuropsychological Approach.

Articles published in *Research Quarterly; Quest; Journal of Health, Physical Education and Recreation; Sportwissenschaft; International Journal of Health, Physical Education, and Recreation; Athletic Journal.*

Hobbies:

Reading and travel.

Sport Activities:

Participant: badminton, volleyball, golf.

Spectator: basketball.

Most Recent Books Read:

Jerry Izenberg	*How Many Miles to Camelot*
John F. Glass and John R. Staude (eds.)	*Humanistic Society*
Nicholas C. Mullins	*Theories and Theory Groups in Contemporary American Sociology*

INTRODUCTION

There are at the present over 20,000 men engaged in coaching intercollegiate athletics. These coaches are designated as "head" or "assistant" coaches, with the former having primary authority and responsibility for the direction of the team while the latter carry out various assigned tasks as stipulated by the head coach. Overall, there are probably as many assistant coaches as head coaches. Some major universities have as many as a dozen assistant football coaches but only one head football coach. In this paper the emphasis will be primarily directed to head coaching, since this position typifies this occupation, but career contingencies are similar for assistant coaches.

In higher education no group of persons is more visible than the athletic coaches. They are frequently the only persons at an institution whose names are known to the public. Moreover, most faculty and students on a campus typically know the names of the coaches while the names of other faculty are known to only a few. The collegiate athletic coach is visible because he must regularly place his students (athletes) on display, as it were, in competition against students (athletes) from other institutions. For many these contests are seen as a challenge to the reputation and prestige of the institution and a great deal of emotion is invested in the outcomes of the contests. For the coach, the outcomes serve as an evaluation of his effectiveness.

In American society, effectiveness in sports is synonymous with winning, and the coach whose teams win regularly is judged as "successful" while the coach whose teams amass a losing record is considered "unsuccessful" and, typically, steps are taken to replace this coach.

The college community and the public at large commonly equate the quality of an institution with the quality of its athletic teams, especially its football and basketball teams. Therefore, most major universities and a great many small colleges expend enormous funds to assure a viable athletic program. At the core of every intercollegiate athletic program is its coaches. They are expected to produce, i.e., win games. While the pressures vary from one institution to another, the prevailing norm is that the coach must produce winning teams to stay.

In the course of the past 70 years college coaching, as an occupation, has gradually grown to match both the increasing number of colleges and the increasing importance of intercollegiate athletics. No era has conferred as much popularity to sport as the present one, and certainly at no time in history has the athletic coach been awarded the power, prestige, and general status that exists today in the United States.

This analysis of collegiate coaching as an occupation begins with a review of the evolution of the occupation over the past century. The major concern is with the changes in the nature of intercollegiate athletics and the accompanying changes in the occupational role of coaching. Next, the personal-social characteristics of the role occupants is examined in the context, first, of personality traits, leadership styles, and value orientations and, second, from the standpoint of their social origins. Finally, career patterns such as recruitment, socialization, and other career contingencies are explored.

One thing that will be evident throughout the analysis: the limitation of empirical data on this occupation. Coaching as an occupational category has not interested many investigators. Of course, very few professions and occupations have been systematically studied; in general, the behavioral sciences have not included the study of work in the mainstream of their research.

THE EMERGENCE OF COLLEGE COACHING AS AN OCCUPATION

College physical education and intercollegiate athletic coaching are inexorably related because, with the exception of slightly over 100 of the major universities which employ fulltime, year-round coaches, most collegiate athletic coaches are employed in physical education departments, where coaching is only a part of their professional assignment. College physical education and intercollegiate athletics are also related in that both have developed as integral parts of higher education within the past century.

The Development of College Physical Education

Formal programs of physical education did not exist in American colleges prior to 1860. In that year, Amherst College trustees, concerned about the general health and welfare of their students, hired John W. Hooker, a physician, as professor of hygiene and physical education and gave him the responsibility of conducting physical exercise and recreation for all Amherst students. Dr. Hooker's health forced him to resign before the close of the school year, so in the fall of 1861 Amherst hired Edward Hitchcock, another professionally trained physician, and thus began a 50-year tenure for Dr. Hitchock as a physical educator at Amherst.

Amherst's employment of a physical education director set a precedent which was followed gradually by other colleges in the latter nineteenth century. Dr. Dudley Allen Sargent was employed by Harvard University in 1879 to serve as its director of physical education. Yale followed the trend by hiring William G. Anderson in 1887. Other colleges followed suit and by 1897 the "Society of College Gymnasium Directors" was organized. The object of the Society, according to the constitution, was "the advancement of physical education in institutions of higher learning, and to discuss the theoretical and practical questions pertaining to gymnastics in these institutions" (Scott, 1951: 56). From an original membership of about 25, the membership of the Society grew to 37 members by 1905, and today there are over 1,000 members.

With the exception of the University of Virginia, state universities did not adopt instruction in physical education before 1888. In that year, the University of California and the University of Wisconsin offered their first instruction in physical education. By 1900 many colleges had taken physical education programs as part of their curricula.

These early college physical education programs were primitive in that facilities were meager, professional instruction was rarely given, and the program was actually more or less a concession to the students, rather than a firm commitment by the faculty for physical education. With a few exceptions, instruction, when it was given, was either by an academic subject professor who engaged in physical training as an avocation, or by the athletic coach who taught the physical education classes as a means of supplementing his income from coaching (Babbit, 1908). For example, at Pomona College, the first physical education director (1895) was Byron Van Leuven who, as a member of the faculty recalled, "had no formal training in conducting a physical education program although he had played football and captained and coached the team" (Sage, 1963: 51).

College physical education programs in the latter nineteenth century were confined almost exclusively to gymnastics, derived from the apparatus exercises of the German system and the free exercises of the Swedish system. Games and sports were little used in departments of physical education. While there was a steady growth of intercollegiate contests and an increasing interest in sports, they were largely outside the scope of physical education. Physical education was promoted as the scientifically worked-out means of achieving and maintaining health. Athletics, on the other hand, served as a recreational outlet after class hours and on weekends (Van Wyck, 1942; Hartwell, 1905). The early physical educators who were hired specifically to direct programs of physical activity, such as Hitchcock, Sargent, Anderson, etc., did not think of themselves as coaches and indeed did not consider athletics as part of their programs of physical education. Perhaps Harvard's physical director best illustrates the attitudes of physical educators toward athletics. He said: "The system of athletics and heavy gymnastics carried on at the college [Harvard] during term time the authorities are in no way responsible for. These are managed by the students themselves through their different athletic organizations" (Sargent 1890: 67).

However, with the tremendous interest and popularity of intercollegiate sports in the latter nineteenth century, physical educators could not completely divorce themselves from athletics. In his 25th Annual Report to the board of trustees, Hitchcock (1886: 3) said: ". . . without discussing the evils which attend intercollegiate games, it must be said that the Department [Physical Education] encourages games of ball, tennis, and athletic sports for the few to whom they are suitable. . . ." Watson Savage (1899) had this to say about his position at Columbia:

> When I was appointed to take charge of the gymnasium at Columbia University, I found matters pertaining to the athletic or physical side of the University in a very unsettled state, and in talking the matter over with the President, he remarked: "We have had no gymnasium, and in consequence have had no one whose business it was to look after the athletics . . . of the University, and they were allowed to run themselves." I saw at once, in this remark, that I was expected not only to direct the gymnasium, but have much to say in the athletics of the University. . . [n.p.].

The earliest college appointment of a faculty member with specific responsibility for physical education and athletics appears to have occurred at Princeton. In 1869 Princeton appointed Mr. George Goldie as Director of Gymnastics and Athletics (Raycroft, 1941).

In the first two decades of the twentieth century, physical education programs became an integral part of most college curricula, and a great many colleges made this subject a requirement for graduation. In the years just prior to World War I, physical educators gradually rejected the foreign gymnastics systems, which had been so popular in the nineteenth century, and adopted the so-called "New Physical Education," which relied upon sports and games as a means of attaining educational objectives. This new approach proved to be popular with the students, so by 1920 sports and games had largely replaced formal gymnastics as the core of the curriculum in physical education. The "New Physical Education" provided a strong impetus to intercollegiate athletics, and from 1900 to 1930 there was an enormous expansion of intercollegiate sports programs, as dissatisfaction with the gymnastics programs declined and interest in sports rose.

In the past three decades, college physical education programs have grown along with the prodigious expansion in higher education throughout the nation. Surveys taken at different times during this period have rather consistently shown that over 80 percent of the colleges and universities have some form of required physical education. The curriculum has remained basically sports and games, but it has expanded to include a greater number of the so-called "lifetime" sports.

The Development of Intercollegiate Athletics

Although never sanctioned by the college authorities, sports of various kinds were played by college students in their free time throughout the colonial and early national periods. Most frequently competition was informally organized by dividing participants who happened to be on the field of play. For more formal organization, the practice of forming "class" teams gradually became popular, and regular freshman-sophomore or junior-senior sports competition was common. Another form of intraschool sports competition was organized around clubs on campus. Accounts of these class and club competitions regularly appear in the diaries of students who attended college in these periods.

By the mid-nineteenth century, as sports came to play a more prominent role in college life and as the number of colleges increased, the next logical step was for interschool competition to develop. The first intercollegiate sports competition was a boat race between boat clubs of Harvard and Yale in 1852. Rowing was a popular sport at this time, not only among college students but also among the general population.

Other intercollegiate sports followed. The first collegiate baseball game was played in 1859 between Amherst and Williams. Football, destined to become the most popular college sport, was first played by Rutgers and Princeton, in 1869. Other sports were taken up by college students and by 1900 at least ten sports were being played in colleges throughout the country. Thus, from small beginnings in a few eastern colleges, intercollegiate athletics grew to enormous proportions and spread to most of the colleges throughout the country by 1900.

The original emphasis on intercollegiate athletics came from the students, usually over faculty objection. As intercollegiate sports became commonplace the actual administrative management for them was vested in the students, usually through a student athletic association. The associations typically scheduled games, hired coaches, and managed the financial end of the athletic program. Any money lost on the athletic ventures had to be made up by the student association. Since the administration of the athletic program by the students almost invariably led to various kinds of mismanagement, by 1900 most colleges had formed a faculty athletic board to provide guidance and direction to the athletic program.

As the popularity of intercollegiate athletics grew, the need for money to maintain the programs increased. Since the colleges were not willing or able to financially support the programs, the student supporters of athletics realized that the existence of them depended upon marketing a sports program that would pay its way. It became immediately evident that financial support depended upon putting out winning teams. Athletic enthusiasts discovered that persons who were willing to support sports expected the teams to win the scheduled games and that if financial supporters were not rewarded with a winner their support ceased. As Bowen (1909) noted: "As soon as the promoters of athletics clearly grasped this principle, they at once set about making athletics pay. The qld idea of athletics for health and for discipline was discarded; that of athletics for revenue took its place. What had been sport became business, what had been friendly competition became war" (1909: 153).

When colleges began playing intercollegiate sports no one thought of them as having any serious importance; they were simply considered a form of amusement or recreation. No one could have predicted the dramatic impact that these "student amusements" would have on higher education. Educational and social forces combined to produce a dramatic increase in students attending college, an enormously expanded interest in spectator sports, and public interest in intercollegiate athletics. By the early years of the twentieth century, students, alumni, the public, and even a significant part of the college faculty and administrators considered the fielding of successful athletic teams as essential. At most of the larger colleges and universities athletics became a component of the alumni and public relations offices and a big business in its own right. Perhaps Bowen's (1909: 151–152) observation of the direction taken by intercollegiate sports best sums up the criticisms of these programs which are repeated year after year by writer after writer but with little impact on intercollegiate athletics. He noted:

> Along with the growing recognition of the hygienic and educational value of athletic practice has come the realization that high school and college sports, as now carried on, do not even remotely approach the accomplishment of what they can do along these lines. They are apparently conducted for the benefit of the few who least need such training, rather than for the good of the mass of students; their main purpose seems to be spectacular, rather than hygienic and educational;

they frequently lead to various forms of dishonesty and brutality and to all degrees of excess.

Intercollegiate sports rapidly caught the notice of the public in the first two decades of the twentieth century, culminating in the so-called "Golden Age" of intercollegiate sports in the 1920s. The professional college coach became recognized for his worth in creating winning teams and gained stature and achieved fame that was more than local. However, it was not until Knute Rockne at Notre Dame captivated the mass media with his dynamic personality while his teams were gaining national recognition for the Fighting Irish and collegiate football that college coaching struck it rich. It was Rockne and his teams which were largely responsible for building the national popularity of intercollegiate athletics (Danzig, 1956).

In the 1920s collegiate football became big business, with new and larger stadiums seating up to 100,000 people. This served as a stimulus to all college sports. Successful coaches now began commanding high salaries for their services. No other aspect of higher education is more visible than the intercollegiate sports programs. These programs, many of which manage budgets in excess of a million dollars per year, are controlled by two multimillion dollar associations, the National Collegiate Athletic Association and the National Association of Intercollegiate Athletics. The intercollegiate athletic programs have been expanded gradually to include competition in over 15 sports, with national championships in each held annually.

Organizational Relationship of College Physical Education and Athletics

College physical education and athletic programs were developed for different reasons by different persons and groups and generally retained separate purposes and functions from their origin until the early twentieth century. Responsibility for physical education was assumed by college faculty and administration whereas sports were governed by students and alumni through the athletic associations (Lowman, 1907; Sargent, 1890).

Two basic patterns of organization for intercollegiate athletics developed in the latter years of the nineteenth century and have been carried on to the present day. These patterns were: (1) athletics as an integral part of the physical education department, and (2) athletics as a completely autonomous department from the physical education department. The latter form of structure came first and was the most popular up to the first decade of this century. Gradually this form of organization lost its popularity except with the large universities which committed themselves to high-finance, high-pressure athletics. The integration of athletics under the administrative structure of physical education began near the turn of the century and has been the most common form of organization for the past half-century. Pritchard (1933) reported that more than 85 percent of the institutions of higher education he studied were organized with physical education and athletics in one department. Three years later De Groot (1936: 18) found "athletics and physical education assigned within one department in a majority of institutions."

More recently Marshall (1969) found that smaller colleges tend to subsume athletics within the department of physical education whereas in the large universities the athletic department is a separate and independent department. He found that in 69 percent of the NCAA College Division (small colleges) intercollegiate athletics were organized as a function of the physical education department, in 64 percent of the NAIA institutions (mostly small colleges) intercollegiate athletics were organized as a function of the physical education department, but in only 28 percent of the NCAA University Division (large universities) intercollegiate athletics were organized as a function of the physical education department.

Marshall (1969) indicated that there has been a trend in recent years toward the creation of autonomous departments of intercollegiate athletics, especially among the universities which play a "major" schedule. This trend is corroborated by Donnelly's (1963) study wherein he reported that of 255 colleges, 12 had separated intercollegiate athletics from the physical education program during the preceding five years.

The Growth of College Coaching as an Occupation

Harris, in his book, *Greek Athletes and Athletics*, indicated that athletic coaching has a rich heritage. He said: "Homer's Nestor is the precursor of every coach who ever admonished team, crew, or individual player" (1964: 10). He is referring to the first recorded evidence of giving advice to athletes. In the twenty-third book of the *Iliad*, Homer describes the funeral games held by Achilles in honor of his friend Patroclus. The first contest is a chariot race and the father of one of the contestants, Nestor, delivers a long speech of advice to his son, Antilocus, before the race, emphasizing the fact that skill is more important than fast horses. He directs his son on how to hug the turning post without actually touching it because that will help him cover the distance in the shortest time. Nestor coaches:

> ... as the mark round which the chariots shall turn; hug it as close as you can, but as you stand in your chariot lean over a little to the left; urge on your right-hand horse with voice and lash, and give him a loose rein, but let the left horse keep so close in that the nave of your wheel shall almost graze the post; but mind the stone, or you will wound your horses and break your chariot in pieces, which would be sport for others but confusion for yourself. Therefore, my dear son,

mind well what you are about, for if you can be first to round the post there is no chance of anyone giving you the go-by later . . .*

Forbes (1929) has noted that specialized coaching for young athletes was common in ancient Greece. The coaching was given by the *gymnastes* who was typically a retired athlete who had gained a reputation as an outstanding performer when he was younger. There were many famous coaches but one of the most notable was Melesias who trained and coached 30 wrestling and pankration champions. In the second century A.D., Philostratus wrote an elaborate handbook for athletic coaches in which he described how their duties differed from those of *paedotribai* (gymnastic teachers), the way to use psychology on the athletes, the type of examination they should give prospective athletes, the physical characteristics they should evaluate in athletes, and how each should be a specialist in speech and "physiognomy" (Robinson, 1955).

The gap between athletic coaching in ancient Greece and nineteenth century America is vast but the intervening centuries did not produce any notable examples of athletic coaching, other than that conducted by knights for their squires and pages. It is not until physical education and intercollegiate athletics began in American colleges that we see the development of careers in athletic coaching emerge.

Since physical education and athletic coaching are closely linked in American colleges, we shall first trace the development of professional careers in physical education and then discuss coaching developments.

The first American college physical educators were academically and professionally trained physicians. Medical training was considered essential for two reasons: (1) to secure academic and social position and (2) to have authority to conduct medical examinations and handle medical problems. But as the emphasis of physical education shifted from promotion of health and bodily maintenance to education through physical activities, especially sports and games, professional preparation for physical education moved away from medicine and toward an educational orientation.

In the latter nineteenth century many programs for teacher training in physical education emerged. Only a few can be mentioned here. In 1866 the North American Turnerbund, a German gymnastic and social organization, organized a school for preparing teachers of German gymnastics which became known as the Normal College of the American Gymnastic Union. Dudley Sargent began teaching professional preparation classes to the women at Radcliffe College in 1881 and this school became known as the

---

* L. R. Loomis (ed.), *The Iliad of Homer,* (Roslyn, New York: Walter J. Black, 1942), pp. 358–359. Reprinted by permission.

Sargent School of Physical Education. Up to 1920 one out of every three graduates of a teacher-education program in physical education was a product of Sargent's school (Bennett, 1948). The Y.M.C.A. movement began teaching classes for men in 1886 at the International Y.M.C.A. College in Springfield, Massachusetts to provide physical directors for the rapidly expanding Y.M.C.A.'s throughout the world. William G. Anderson organized the Brooklyn Normal School for Physical Education in 1886 while he was teaching at Adelphi College in Brooklyn, New York; and when he moved to Yale he transferred the school to New Haven where it became the Anderson Normal School of Gymnastics. In the period 1896–1898, four state universities—Washington, California, Indiana, and Nebraska—provided the first opportunities for teacher training in physical education by state universities. Other private and state supported colleges instituted programs of professional preparation for physical education and by the end of World War I some 20 institutions were offering undergraduate programs in physical education (Clarke, 1935; Berry, 1920; Zeigler, 1950).

Although the great majority of students who were enrolled in these professional preparation programs were women, and the vast majority taught in the elementary and secondary schools upon graduation from these schools, a large number of men who graduated from these programs became college physical educators and coaches. It is also true that many of the college physical educators employed by the rapidly growing number of colleges in the first three decades of the twentieth century did not have formal preparation in physical education but were employed primarily because they had been outstanding athletes and they were hired to direct the athletic teams as well as conduct physical education.

In the intercollegiate athletic programs of the nineteenth century coaches were not employed by the colleges with faculty status. Usually the coach was a student team captain, an alumnus who had played athletics while in college, or a professional itinerant athlete hired to coach on a seasonal basis. No thought was given to academic qualifications for the position of coach; usually the only necessary requirement was some technical knowledge of the sport to be coached.

From the late 1870s, graduates returned to help out the player-captains at their alma maters, but arrangements were informal and haphazard. Walter Camp is acknowledged as the "father" of American football and his coaching experience exemplifies the college coach's role prior to 1900. After completing his collegiate career at Yale in 1882, Camp returned each year to help out the player-captains, but beginning in 1888 and for much of the next 20 years Camp served as Yale's coach. He had no formal position on the faculty and he received no pay (Cohane, 1951). It was not until 1913 that Yale hired its first paid coach. At Harvard, organized coaching began in 1890 with the appointment of George Stewart, an alumnus from the class of 1884, and George Adams, another alumnus, but it was not until 1908 that Harvard employed a paid coach (Danzig, 1956). At Ohio State University football coaching was on a seasonal basis until 1911. None of the coaches up to this time had faculty status and only one of the coaches was employed on an all-year basis (Pollard, 1959). In 1912 a policy adopted by the board of trustees provided "that as soon as practicable and as far as possible all coaches of teams shall be employed for the regular academic year and when satisfactory, continued in their office from year to year . . . all coaches should be permanently identified with the life of the University" (Pollard, 1959: 108).

An example of the early years of coaching is provided by the career of Henry L. Williams, who played at Yale and graduated in 1891. After graduating, he took a teaching position at a prep school near West Point. The Cadet football teams were not doing well at the time, so they engaged Williams as coach. He coached by correspondence; that is, he would diagram plays and describe their execution and send them to West Point. On Saturdays he would attend practices and give further instructions on the fundamentals and plays. This form of coaching produced the first Army victory over Navy in 1892 (Danzig, 1956). Later, Williams did graduate study in medicine and earned an M.D. degree. Then in 1900 he was hired as football coach at the University of Minnesota at $2,500 a year, and he was granted permission to practice medicine. Under this arrangement he served as football coach at Minnesota for 22 years (Danzig, 1956).

Most of the early college coaches were employed on a seasonal basis. They spent most of their time pursuing careers in other fields. Some were lawyers, some physicians, and some were businessmen, but most of them did not make coaching their full-time occupation. Even in 1929 Savage (1929) reported that 35 percent of the college football coaches he surveyed had occupations other than football coaching.

The practice of employing seasonal coaches, which flourished in the two decades from 1890 to 1910, gradually came under increasing criticism from faculty and administration. There were a number of problems with this arrangement. The college administration had little or no control over the activities of the coach. The educational potential of sports was frequently sacrificed in the quest for victory. Many unscrupulous practices were employed by the coaches.

One solution to the seasonal coach was the employment of fulltime, year-round coaches. But only the large universities were able to afford this and it became common in these institutions. Although this arrangement had its advantages over seasonal employment, it had other consequences, as described by Savage (1915: 192).

The practice now quite common in the Middle West of hiring the football coach for the entire year is a step in the right direction, but in too many instances the presence of the coach serves only to increase the stress on football. He is constantly "sizing up" and working with his material for the next season; he has them practice boxing and wrestling through the winter, gives a number of talks on the fine points of the game, and in the spring calls them out for unseasonable and senseless "spring practice."

Another alternative to the seasonal coach was the employment of a physical educator. With the increased practice of requiring physical education classes for a degree, which had begun in the 1890s, the idea of employing a single person to serve as physical director and athletic coach grew. Thus, the roles of athletic coach and physical educator became vested in one person. Amos A. Stagg was the first college coach to receive faculty recognition. He was made an associate professor and Director of the Department of Physical Culture as a regular faculty member at the University of Chicago in 1892. In 1901 he was given a full professorship. Chicago's plan was copied by other schools (Danzig, 1956). Scott (1951: 96) noted: "Physical education which was educationally recognized, ... provided the avenue whereby qualified coaches of athletic teams eventually were recognized as members of the educational family and accorded academic rank."

Although this situation was generally supported by college and university faculties and administrators, it also had its problems. According to Scott (1951: 97); "Coaches ... owing greater allegiance to competitive athletics, tended to neglect their duties in the teaching of physical education. Hence, departments of physical education frequently carried on their payrolls coaches who did little to earn their salaries in so far as physical education instruction to all students was concerned." It seems that coaches as a group displayed little interest in the physical education program. Although they may have had course work, or even a degree, in physical education it was more a matter of expedience that they had an official connection with the department of physical education, and the relationship between physical education and coaching frequently was antagonistic because of basically different purposes (Scott, 1951).

Many colleges went through a series of different employment practices before settling upon one. An example in the pattern for employing coaches around the turn of the century is described by Sage (1963: 96–97):

Pomona's athletic teams were coached by different men, hired on a seasonal basis, with no faculty standing. In 1901 the football team was coached by a Pomona graduate ... Finally, in 1903 Pomona hired its first physical director, Walter Hempel. He not only coached all of the athletic teams, he also directed the physical education program which was required of all students ... Upon Hempel's resignation in 1905 Pomona decided to separate the positions of physical director and athletic coach, hiring separate men for the positions. This development came about because it was felt that a man hired to do both could not do justice to either. Therefore, Ernest Hastings was hired to teach physical education and Ralph Noble, a Pomona alumnus, was employed as the athletic coach. Hastings was given faculty status, Noble was not. In 1908, when William Stanton was employed as athletic coach and physical director, Pomona returned to the practice of having the physical director coach the athletic teams. Stanton was given faculty status. . . .

In 1929 two reports on physical education and intercollegiate athletics illuminated the coaching occupational status at that time. The first was a monumental study by Walter Savage (1929) and sponsored by The Carnegie Foundation entitled *American College Athletics,* and the second was a dissertation by Scott (1929) which was a personnel study of college physical education directors.

Savage (1929) identified various kinds of coaching positions which existed in the colleges. They were: (1) seasonal coaches, appointees who did not enjoy faculty status and who, after the close of their respective seasons of coaching, found their time practically unoccupied, (2) instructors or directors of physical education who coached in season and out of season delivered a few lectures on hygiene and many lectures on athletic coaching and spent the remainder of their time recruiting athletes, (3) coaching directors whose first concern was their football squads, but who were expected to direct the activities of a department of physical education and to coach or to supervise the coaching of all branches of athletics, (4) the teacher of academic subjects who coached in season and supervised athletic teams, and (5) alumni coaches who were paid for their work with or without appointment to a faculty.

Savage (1929) reported that at 63 (of 130) institutions he studied the head football coach held a full-time faculty appointment and had faculty status. Of those, 55 were members of the department of physical education, while eight were teachers of academic subjects. Savage (1929) found that of the head football coaches in his sample, only 18 were not college graduates, but only two had a degree in physical education. He noted: "None of the dozen outstanding football coaches in the United States today has been trained in a school of physical education" (1929: 163). He remarked: "Not every director of physical education should coach the football team, nor should every football coach be a professor of physical education" (1929: 167). He also noted that "of all the fields of higher education, physical education shows the largest number of members with the rank of professor who have only a bachelor's degree or no degree whatever" (1929: 167–168).

In his study of college physical education directors, Scott (1929) found that 78 percent were responsible for the intercollegiate athletic program, and 70 percent were coaching athletic teams. Only 13 percent of these directors, all of whom held faculty status in departments of physical education, had majored in physical education. Scott (1929) reported that the typical director was a former college athlete who taught theory courses in physical education and coaching in addition to coaching varsity teams. He said: "From the standpoint of hours per week [spent in work] . . . athletic coaching claims first place . . . Coaching plays a considerable part in the duties of the director of physical education" (1929: 14).

Savage (1929) made a strong plea for modification in intercollegiate athletic programs, recommending that the educational aspects be emphasized more and that coaches become truly educators rather than managers of entertainment for the campus and the public. While there was a brief outcry for reform, little meaningful change was affected in the direction of the programs, and their growth and popularity was only momentarily slowed by World War II. The post–World War II era witnessed an unprecedented expansion of intercollegiate sports.

In the 40 years since the Savage (1929) study, two primary college coaching positions have emerged. The first, and the most common, is the physical educator-coach. The coach in this pattern is employed as a professor of physical education, with faculty rank and status, and he divides his time between coaching and teaching classes. The second pattern of coaching is the full-time coach. This pattern exists at many of the major universities. The coach devotes his entire energies to coaching. He often becomes a national figure through the exploits of his teams. There are a few seasonal college coaches but the number constitutes a small portion of college coaches.

PERSONAL-SOCIAL CHARACTERISTICS OF COLLEGIATE COACHES

Personality and Coaches

The notion of occupational specific personality types is rather common. Thus we have the "Mr. Peepers" stereotype of the male teacher, the "absent-minded" professor, and many more. It may be true that certain personality traits are more compatible with successful conformity to certain norms and with certain pathways for satisfaction, but the extent to which the members of occupations actually conform to the stereotypes is largely undocumented.

There is a fairly clear stereotype of the athletic coach. Hendry (1972a: 36) said: "The mass media . . . tend to show the physical educationist or coach as a muscular, dominant, aggressive, social individual—a man of action rather than words." In recent years American collegiate athletic coaches have been characterized as being highly authoritarian, dogmatic, and manipulative. One of the most outspoken critics of American coaches is Jack Scott (1969, 1971). He has characterized the personality of coaches in this way:

> The typical . . . coach is a soulless, back slapping, meticulously groomed team oriented efficiency expert—a jock's Robert MacNamara . . . Most coaches have as much concern for the welfare of their athletes as a general has for the soldiers he sends into battle . . . For most college coaches, the athlete is significant only to the extent that he can contribute to a team victory . . . For every relaxed, understanding coach . . . there are one hundred rigid, authoritarian coaches who have so much . . . character armor that they rattle (1969: 7).

Another critic stated: "Traditionally you are going to find in the coaching professions men who are . . . more interested in power and manipulation and less interested in humanistic approaches. They prefer control organization, unquestioned commitment to their philosophy and so on" (Ogilvie, 1971: 33).

The allegations which have been made about the personality structure of coaches by Scott, Ogilvie, and others, and the "coaching stereotype" which has been promoted in the mass media, has undoubtedly led to a firm image of the personal-social characteristics of coaches by the general public.

While there have been numerous essays and impressionistic observations of what coaches are like, there have been few psychological studies concerned with coaches' personality structure. Of the few studies which have been done, the majority have used small, unrepresentative samples (such as a group of coaches that happened to be enrolled in the investigator's class), and in some cases the validity of the assessment instruments has not been fully confirmed. Furthermore, most of the studies have used physical educators, high school coaches, or amateur athletic coaches as subjects rather than college coaches. Only to the extent that college coaches may be considered a subset of these other groups are the findings generalizable to college coaches.

Several studies have shown that anywhere from 70 to 90 percent of high school and college coaches majored in physical education as undergraduate students (Arms, 1965; Maltozo, 1965; Wilcox, 1969; Loy and Sage,

1972). The profession of physical education has traditionally considered athletic coaching as one of the duties of a physical educator, and in American higher education athletic coaches are almost invariably assigned to the physical education department, if they have teaching duties and academic rank. Thus, there is some commonality between physical education and athletic coaching.

Locke (1962) compared the personality traits of 129 males who were teaching physical education or were coaching with a teacher group who were not physical educators. Subjects in both groups had previously indicated a common desire to move from teaching into some form of full-time public school administration. A comparison of Edwards Personal Preference Schedule scores of the total physical education group and the total teacher group showed that the physical educator group was significantly higher in succorance (need to obtain support and affection), affiliation (need to have many friends), and nurturance (need to give support and affection). The physical educator group also scored significantly higher on the Public Opinion Questionnaire, which represents a measure of prejudicial, absolutist, authoritarian attitudes (McGee, 1955).

When Locke (1962) restricted the physical educator sample to those which represent the most commonly accepted definition of what a physical educator is, it was found that there were no differences between physical educators and the secondary school personnel from other areas on succorance and nurturance but physical educators still were significantly higher in affiliation. Somewhat surprisingly, the teacher sample displayed significantly higher need for dominance than the physical educators. However, the physical educators were significantly higher on the Public Opinion Questionnaire.

Kenyon (1965) assessed several psychosocial and cultural characteristics of aspiring physical educators while they were students at the University of Wisconsin and compared them with students who were not majoring in physical education. He reported that the physical education majors were more dogmatic and rigid than other prospective teachers, as measured by Rokeach's Dogmatic Scale (Rokeach, 1960).

Although the linkage between physical education is close, one cannot assume that findings on aspiring physical educators or physical educators who are teaching in the public schools are generalizable to the collegiate coaching population. The investigators of the two studies cited above would probably be the first to warn about generalizing the findings to college coaches.

Andrud (1970) administered the Guilford–Zimmerman Temperament Survey inventory (which measures ten variables of personality) to 19 coaches who were enrolled in the 1970 University of North Dakota Football

Clinic. The investigator reported that general activity, emotional stability, and masculinity mean scores were at the seventieth percentile, based on a standard profile chart designed by Guilford–Zimmerman. These traits indicate that the coaches possessed a strong drive to succeed, and the energy and activity to follow up the drive. Three other variables—ascendance, sociability, and personal relations—represented scores in the upper fiftieth percentile range. These traits suggest that leadership and social activity habits were characteristic of the coaches. Restraint, objectivity, friendliness, and thoughtfulness represented scores which ranked at the fiftieth percentile.

In another study which used coaches who were enrolled in a coaching class, Gagen (1971) assessed the risk-taking and the need for achievement traits of "a random selection of coaches attending the 1971 coaching clinic held at Kent State University . . . who volunteered their services, and other coaches who were known to the author but did not attend the clinic" (1971: 5–6). Subjects (N = 35) were either high school or college football coaches. Gagen found that the coaches had a high level of need for achievement and were predisposed to achieving success; he concluded "that one personality disposition coaches have in common is high need achievement" (1971: 30). In addition, he found that the group of college football coaches exhibited higher need for achievement than high school coaches, thus suggesting the possibility that college coaches differ from high school coaches in some personal characteristics.

In one of the better designed studies of coaches' personality, Longmuir (1972) investigated the perceived and actual dogmatism of high school football and basketball coaches and their athletes, using the *Short Form Dogmatism Scale*. Rokeach (1960) developed the theory of dogmatism as an alternative to the concept of authoritarianism as measured by Adorno's (1950) F-scale because research has indicated the limitations of the F-scale, since the scale measures essentially fascistic authoritarianism of the right-wing variety but not of left-wing (Shils, 1954). Rokeach's scale is relatively free of the conservative bias. Dogmatism indicates the extent to which an individual has "an authoritarian outlook on life, an intolerance toward those with opposing beliefs, and a sufferance of those with similar beliefs" (Rokeach, 1960: 4). Persons who are high in Rokeach's dogmatism scale are more rigid in problem-solving behavior, more concrete in their thinking, and narrow in their grasp of a particular subject; they also tend toward premature closure in their perceptual processes and have a tendency to be intolerant of ambiguity (Rokeach, 1960).

Longmuir (1972) found that "coaches are not more dogmatic than others in a wide variety of other occupations" (1972: 86) established by Rokeach. He reached the following conclusion.

. . . the coach is not necessarily a dogmatic or authoritarian individual because (1) objectively (as measured by the *Short Form Dogmatism Scale*) he does not differ from others in the degree to which he is dogmatic and (2) subjectively (working with perceptions) the same coach may be perceived as high or low dogmatic, depending on whether the athletes themselves are high or low dogmatic (1972: 75).

L. B. Hendry, a Scottish sport psychologist, has been one of the most prolific researchers on the topic of the personality of coaches. He has been interested in the influence of coaches' personality traits on their interactions with athletes, and the outcome of these interactions on the competitive situation. The personality traits of 56 British amateur swimming coaches were assessed by Hendry (1968), using the Cattell 16PF inventory. He reported that his group of coaches were bright, driving, aggressive individuals, but also anxious and insecure, especially the older coaches (over 40 years of age). In a subsequent study, also with British coaches, Hendry (1969) found no significant personality differences between 30 "highly successful" swimming coaches and 26 other swimming coaches. In a more recent study, again with British subjects, Hendry (1972a) indicated that coaches were authoritarian types who apparently enjoy being the center of attention; he also suggested that they were aggressive.

Two psychologists at San Jose State University, Bruce Ogilvie and Thomas Tutko, are perhaps the most noted American investigators of personality of coaches. For the past few years these men have described their studies of coaches in various publications and conferences. Unfortunately, most of their actual data have not been published in scholarly journals where the findings could be carefully inspected. One fact that does seem clear, with regard to their collection of information on coaches, is that no systematic effort has been made to collect data on a representative basis. Subjects were clients or students of the investigators.

In their book *Problem Athletes and How to Handle Them*, Ogilvie and Tutko (1966) describe the personality profile of 64 coaches representing the four major sports in America—basketball, track, football, and baseball. They reported that the coaches were highly success-driven, sociable, highly organized, dominant, conscientious, emotionally stable, open and trusting, could freely express aggression, had very high psychological endurance, were inflexible and had a low interest in the dependency needs of others. In regard to the last two traits, Ogilvie and Tutko (1966: 23–24) state:

. . . we found two traits that we felt . . . would be detrimental in handling effectively young men in athletics. The first was the very low tendency to be interested in the dependency needs of others . . . in other words, to give a great deal of emotional support to others. The coaches in this study, as a group, were extremely low in their interest and willingness to perform in this role . . . The second characteristic which was lacking in this group was related to inflexibility or rigidity in terms of utilization of new learning.

The investigators do warn that the sample of coaches is not a representative sample of coaches throughout the United States nor representative of any particular coaching specialty.

In a second study by the same investigators (Ogilvie and Tutko, 1970), they assessed the personalities of 132 students, all of whom were high school coaches, enrolled in a class of theirs. They found that the coaches were high in needs for achievement, order, dominance, deference, endurance, abasement, and aggression, and low in needs of intraception, exhibition, nurturance, and change. They suggest that this study supports their previous generalization that coaches are high in those traits that promote "getting ahead" and succeeding and which do not require personal involvement, but coaches score low on those personality traits which contribute most to being sensitive and support close interpersonal relationships. It should be noted that in this study, as well as in the previous one, the sample of coaches was small and not representative of any group of coaches.

In one of the few studies done specifically with college coaches, Albaugh (1972) assessed ressentiment among college basketball coaches. Ressentiment is an attitudinal characteristic which negatively affects learning as a result of a leader's covert and subtle attitude toward learning. One high in ressentiment demands obedience, denies individual rights, demands that inflexible rules be kept, is high in distrust, and commands docile, conforming, and spiritless individuals as subjects.

Albaugh (1972) administered a revised form of the Parsons–Kreuter Ressentiment Index (Kreuter, 1971) to 24 coaches and a revised form of the Friedenberg–Nordstrom Ressentiment Index (Friedenberg et al., 1961) to 175 collegiate basketball players from 17 teams. He found that, as a total group, coaches and players did not differ in their perceptions of ressentience, but when comparisons of coaches and players were made by athletic classifications, university division varsity and freshmen showed wider mean differences between coaches and players in their assessments of ressentiment. The university division players assessed their athletic environments as more ressentient than did players in the other groups. Black athletes were significantly higher in their perception of ressentience than were white players. There were no differences between starters and substitutes.

The extent to which college basketball coaches are ressentient compared to other groups cannot be ascertained from Albaugh's study, since the instrument which he used was a revision of the Parsons–Kreuter Ressentiment

Index, but Albaugh did find that the coaches' (N = 24) mean score was approximately one standard deviation higher than teachers (N = 900), as reported by Kreuter and Parsons (1971).

LaGrand (1970) elicited responses of collegiate athletes (N = 304) about behavioral characteristics of coaches for whom they had played in high school and college. Athletes from four different sports (basketball, soccer, wrestling, and tennis) responded to a semantic differential scale which the investigator developed to measure fourteen behavioral characteristics of athletic coaches. LaGrand found no significant differences between individual and team sport coaches in giving personal attention to their athletes. In a hierarchy of behavioral characteristics, he reported that "knowledge of sport" received the highest ratings by all groups, followed closely by "enthusiasm." His findings also indicated that coaches are somewhat weak in sensitivity and understanding of the individual attitudes and needs of athletes.

Meyer (1972) studied the interpersonal perceptions of collegiate basketball coaches and players, using a semantic differential technique. He developed scales for six behavioral factors (general evaluative, potency, oriented activity, stability, receptivity, and aggressiveness) and reported that the players perceived head coaches as being more stable than assistant coaches and assistant coaches perceived themselves as being more stable than did either players or head coaches. The findings did not indicate any major discrepancies in interpersonal perceptions between athletes and coaches.

One of the few studies which has attempted to obtain a national sampling of collegiate athletic coaches is Sage's (1972a) study of Machiavellianism among college football and basketball coaches. Statements made about coaches in recent years suggest that they tend to be highly manipulative and have a tough-minded, relatively affectless view of other persons. Christie and his colleagues (Christie and Geis, 1970) have developed an instrument which is specifically designed to measure this dimension of personality. Using the writings of Machiavelli (*The Prince* and *The Discourses*) as an example of the manipulatory tactics, Christie and his associates have developed an instrument to evaluate opportunism, guile, and duplicity in interpersonal relations, and their laboratory research with this instrument indicates that the tendency to respond in certain ways to the instrument is reliably related to interpersonal behaviors. That is, subjects who endorse guile, the use of illegal power, opportunism, and duplicity in interpersonal relations tend to engage more often and more readily in exploitive behaviors, presumably in an effort to implement their own desired ends.

Christie (Christie and Geis, 1970) calls his instrument the Machiavellian (Mach) Scale. Basically, a score on the Mach Scale may be interpreted as representing the degree to which a respondent believes that people in general are manipulatable, that is, that interpersonal manipulation is possible. Machiavellianism reflects a tough-minded and relatively affectless view of other persons. Christie suggests that a high Machiavellian view might be, "People are no damn good. So what? Take advantage of it." He reports the statement of one high-Mach: "Win by any means." One of Christie's associates stated: "Machiavellianism is associated with emotional detachment in interpersonal relations, a tendency to exploit situations and others for self-gain, and a tendency to take over control in small groups" (Geis, 1968: 407). A series of laboratory studies have confirmed the validity of the Mach Scale for successfully predicting interpersonal manipulative behavior in a variety of situations. High-Machs manipulate more, win more, are persuaded less, persuade others more, and differ significantly from low-Machs. The experimental evidence indicates that high-Machs are markedly less likely to become emotionally involved with other people; they are cold, amoral, and possess a detached personal unresponsiveness and a covertly aggressive willingness and ability to manipulate others. From their research, Christie and Geis (1970) suggest that high-Machs will be found in situational conditions in which there is: (1) face-to-face interaction, (2) latitude for improvisation, (3) irrelevant affect. In applying the three conditions to athletic coaching, it would appear that this occupation would attract persons who are high in Machiavellianism, since the situational conditions of coaching resemble the experimental conditions in which high-Machs are more successful.

Sage (1972a) selected a sample of college football (N = 150) and basketball (N = 150) coaches from coaching directories published by the National Collegiate Athletic Bureau to complete the Mach Scale. He found no differences in Machiavellianism between the athletic coaches and male college students, no differences among coaches with regard to years of age or head coaching experience, and no differences among coaches with winning records (over 60%) and coaches with won-lost records under 60%.

In a recent paper Hendry (1972b) suggested "the possibility of a closed conceptual system where successful athletes become coaches and perpetuate sporting 'types.' " In other words, he is suggesting that coaches possess sport-specific personalities. This notion is based on Hendry's premise, which, in his words, is: "It is well documented that athletes following different kinds of sporting pursuits possess different personality characteristics" (1972b: 442). As a matter of fact, about the only thing that is well documented with regard to athletes' personality structure is that the overall findings are patently equivocal (See Sage, 1973b; Rushall, 1970; Kroll, 1970). So the notion that coaches of certain sports possess the same personality of the athletes in that sport rests on an unsubstantiated assumption.

It is evident from this brief review of the personality and personal behaviors of coaches that the present research evidence is meager and that which has been done suffers from small and unrepresentative sampling. As if these limitations were not enough, the findings are equivocal. It does appear, however, that characteristics such as need for achievement, enthusiasm, energetic, and persistence toward goals are common among coaches. They do tend to be, or are perceived to be, somewhat insensitive to certain interpersonal relations, but there is wide variability here; there are coaches who are seen as supportive and humanistically orientated.

Leadership Styles of Coaches

The coach is the authority figure for an athletic team; thus he serves as the appointed leader. While it really is not known to what extent the success or failure of a team is due to the leadership competence of the coach, there is little doubt that it is an important factor in team performance and the coach, as the leader, is held responsible for the team's performance.

In recent years, coaches have come under a barrage of criticism for their leadership practices (Scott, 1969, 1971; Ogilvie and Tutko, 1971). Tutko and Richards (1971) suggest that as leaders most coaches believe in strong discipline, rigidity of rules, extrinsic motivation, and an impersonal attitude towards their athletes, and they characterize most coaches as being hard-nosed or authoritarian. Sage (1973a) noted that this leadership strategy bears a strong resemblance to that employed by the Scientific Management movement which emerged from the studies and writing of Frederick W. Taylor (1911). Thus, many coaches have tended to view team members as objects in a machine-like environment where emphasis is on instrumental rather than consummatory behaviors. The players become another man's (the coach's) instrument, and are used to reach the objectives and goals of the organizational collectivity; they are reduced to cogs in the organization's machinery.

Undoubtedly, each coach has a unique leadership style of his own and generalizations concerning coaches' leadership behaviors do not capture the individual patterns which exist. Empirical study of coaching leadership style is scarce.

Mudra (1965) attempted to ascertain the leadership behaviors of collegiate football coaches through an assessment of the applications which coaches make of certain learning principles. Learning principles were conceptualized as being gestalt-field or stimulus-response (S-R) and a list of practices in the coaching of football based upon these two learning approaches was developed by the investigator. Mudra indicated that leaders who use the gestalt-field approach to learning view man as purposive and interacting with his environment, see learning as an acquisition of cognitive structures rather than an acquisition of habits, and favor insight and problem solving to trial and error learning, whereas the S-R approach sees man as passive and the victim of his environment, views learning as the acquisition of habits rather than as a process of differentiating, generalizing, and restructuring the psychological field, and favors trial and error learning explanations.

Mudra found that small college coaches, as a group, were more gestalt-field oriented and had more individual coaches with a strong gestalt leaning than the major university coaches who were more S-R oriented and had more individuals with a strong S-R leaning. He noted that there may be several reasons for the differences that occurred between the two coaching groups:

> Since the athletic programs at major universities are not closely related to the academic programs as they are in small colleges, the philosophy undergirding the administration of these programs reflects this difference. The major college programs are generally financially independent of the general college program and the athletic director relates to the president directly. The small college program exists primarily for the values that are accrued to the participant with secondary emphasis on winning . . . The major college program traditionally has existed primarily as a means of publicizing the university, with secondary emphasis on the development of the individuals in the program.
>
> Since the S-R position is one of authority and control, it might have been anticipated that the major college coaches would find it easier to play the role of the authoritarian, or would find it easier to justify their use of control. . . .*

In a study specifically designed to assess leadership styles, Swartz (1973) compared four types of leadership—laissez-faire, democratic-cooperative, autocratic-submissive, and autocratic-aggressive—of 72 collegiate coaches in five midwestern states classified as "successful" (won-lost record over 50 percent) or "unsuccessful" (won-lost record under 50 percent). He found that successful and unsuccessful coaches employ essentially the same leadership style.

There is not enough evidence at the present time to make any definite statements about the effectiveness of the leadership styles which are em-

---

* D. E. Mudra, "A Critical Analysis of Football Coaching Practices in Light of a Selected Group of Learning Principles," doctoral dissertation, University of Northern Colorado, 1965. Reprinted by permission.

ployed by coaches. If coaches' practices follow trends in industrial management, we might expect to see leadership in sport become more player centered and more emphasis given to player input to the decision-making functions of team organization.

Social Attitudes and Value Orientations of Coaches

Kenyon (1968: 30) defines an attitude as "a complex, but relatively stable behavioral disposition reflecting both direction and intensity of feeling toward a particular psychological object, whether it be concrete or abstract." Although attitudes and values are closely related, values are usually viewed from a slightly different perspective. A value is considered as one's concept of an ideal relationship (or state of affairs), which is used to assess the "goodness" or "badness," the "rightness" or "wrongness" of actual relationships which one observes or contemplates (Scott, 1965). Furthermore, values refer to personal and social ideals, beliefs, or standards which may be used to evaluate and regulate one's own or others' behavior. These involve ideals or beliefs about what is good, right, desirable, or true (Kluckhohn, 1951). It is assumed that attitudes and values form the basis for behavior, but the possibility of inconsistency between the attitudes and values held by an individual and the behavior of that individual is also recognized.

Social attitudes and value orientations are learned; they are not instinctive. Thus the kind and extent of these characteristics possessed by athletic coaches reflect their background of social experiences and they, in turn, may transmit them to the athletes who come under their tutelage. Jeffreys (1962) has suggested that the promotion of attitudes and values is the business of education and that education is not only concerned with communication of knowledge and the acquisition of skill, but also with the formation of attitudes and values. Assuming that the athletic setting is an educational setting—as most coaches do—the coaches have the potential for making a marked impact of some sort upon the attitudes and values of intercollegiate athletes. Snyder (1971) has convincingly shown how coaches deliberately impose their attitudes and value system upon their athletes through the use of locker-room slogans.

The extent to which athletes actually internalize coaches' attitudes and values is unknown. But social learning theory and research indicate that models which are perceived as prestigeful (as most coaches are) and are rewarded for their behavior (as most coaches are) may play a very important role in influencing the behavior of those with whom they come in contact. Socialization theory suggests that youth tend to internalize personal-social characteristics of adults whom they admire and respect. Thus, coaches have the potential for powerfully influencing attitudes and values of their athletes, and this influence will be in terms of transmitting their own attitudes and values. But what are coaches' attitudes and values?

There are few comprehensive studies of the social attitudes and value orientations of the college coaching community. As with personality studies, several of the related studies which have been done include physical educators or high school coaches as subjects, and these persons, although they are in the same general occupational field, may or may not reflect accurately college coaches' characteristics.

The social attitudinal disposition of coaches which has attracted the most research interest is sportsmanship. The development of positive sportsmanship is perhaps the most frequently cited social attitudinal objective of school athletic programs. Athletic codes invariably refer to this as an objective and coaches give support to this objective in their speeches and writings. One important question is: What are coaches' sportsmanship attitudes? If coaches are indeed interested in transmitting good sportsmanship attitudes, it is likely that the most effective means for accomplishing this objective is through their own attitudes and behaviors.

Lauffer (1970) compared the sportsmanship attitudes of collegiate coaches and faculty members in mid-Eastern institutions, using the Haskins–Hartman Action-Choice Test for Competitive Situations. He found that the sportsmanship attitudes of small college coaches do not differ from coaches at major universities, sportsmanship attitudes of coaches of one sport classification (contact) do not differ from those of coaches of another sport classification (noncontact) and that the sportsmanship attitudes of coaches do not differ from those of faculty members in various disciplines. The investigator noted that the mean scores of both faculty (12.31) and the coaching groups (12.20) showed that neither group displayed a high degree of sportsmanship qualities, since during the original validation of the instrument mean scores of 13.67, 14.53, and 15.15 (higher score indicates better sportsmanship) were recorded for freshman, sophomore, and junior physical education majors.

Richardson (1967) assessed the sportsmanship attitudes of a national sample of NCAA college division and university division coaches. He found that university division coaches scored lower on the sportsmanship test than the college division coaches. Since Richardson found that university division coaches perceive greater expectations of pressure from poor won-lost records than college division coaches and that university division presidents and athletic directors report that they would receive pressure to replace their coaches as a result of poor won-lost records to a much greater extent than college division administrative officials, the investigator suggested that this increased pressure to win probably produces less regard for sportsmanship.

In a uniquely designed study, Harvey (1963) assessed the extent to which collegiate coaches in baseball, football, basketball, and track practiced various "ethically questionable" actions. The analysis was based upon the extent to which the coaches were reported by lettermen as having practiced the questionable actions. The evaluations of the coaches were based upon the opinions of former college varsity lettermen. The lettermen had participated in athletics during an eight-year period, extending from the fall of 1950 to the spring of 1958 inclusive.

The responses by the lettermen indicate that collegiate coaches do practice ethically questionable actions while carrying out their athletic duties. According to the lettermen of the four sports, the basketball and football coaches practiced the ethically questionable actions more than did the coaches of the other two sports, and baseball coaches had more questionable practices than did track coaches. The investigator commented: "There is some relationship between the amount of pressure under which athletic coaches work and the extent to which coaches practice questionable actions" (Harvey, 1963: 368). It appears, then, that Harvey's findings provide behavioral support for Richardson's findings of attitude.

Social change in American society has been dramatic in the past decade and traditional values based upon the Protestant Ethic have been challenged by a "counter-culture" ideology based upon a different moral and ethical system. The stimulus of the new movement is a strong disillusionment with traditional values and interpersonal relations as manifested in corporate organizational values and behavior and the Protestant Ethic (c.f., Slater, 1970; Reich, 1970, for a fuller discussion). While the "counter-culture" ideology has certainly had an impact on value orientations, older values have not been completely abandoned by the majority of persons, and indeed coaches have been accused of being the bastions for the retention of traditional values.

Scott (1969, 1971), one of the most outspoken critics of athletic coaches, has suggested that the value orientations of coaches are so conservative as to be almost aberrant. Ogilvie (1971), another frequent critic of athletic coaches, also believes that coaches are conservative in value orientation. He stated: "Traditionally you are going to find in the coaching profession men who are socially and politically conservative" (1971: 137). John Underwood (1969), in a series appearing in *Sports Illustrated* entitled "The Desperate Coach," said "... the student activists ... regard the coach as a neofascistic racist" (1969: 66). Even some coaches view their colleagues as possessing extremely conservative values. Dr. David Nelson, athletic director at the University of Delaware and formerly the head football coach there, said: "Having been a coach ... I know that most of us are almost Harding

Republicans and three degrees to the right of Genghis Khan" (1969:1). Unfortunately, there is little research to support these impressionistic observations about coaches.

Kenyon (1965) administered the Allport-Vernon-Lindzey Study of Values to undergraduate students at the University of Wisconsin who were enrolled in various majors. He found that physical education majors were significantly lower than liberal arts students on the theoretical and aesthetic scales but were higher on the political and religious scales. This indicates that the physical education students held intellectual and artistic values in lower regard but held personal power and spiritual values in higher regard. Physical education majors scored higher on the economic scale and lower on the aesthetic scale than students enrolled in other teacher-preparation majors. Thus, when compared to persons going into the same general profession, physical educators care less for artistic values and more for the "practical" values of accumulation of material things. Finally, Kenyon found that prospective male physical education teachers, in contrast to other prospective teachers, have a somewhat traditionalist philosophy of education.

Nelson (1970) used the Allport-Vernon-Lindzey Study of Values with college men and women physical educators and undergraduate students majoring in physical education. She reported that male physical education faculty placed greater value on social and religious choices and less value on theoretical, economic, and aesthetic values than did a national sample of college men, as reported by Allport et al., (1960). Thus, the physical educators held higher regard for love of people and spiritual concerns and less regard for intellectual, material, and artistic values than other educated males. Another interesting finding was that the physical education undergraduate students held similar value orientations to those faculty who teach physical education. Nelson noted: "Senior men in professional preparation programs in physical education hold basic life value patterns similar to those of the male faculty who teach and administer those programs" (1970: 70).

In a 1969 survey by the Carnegie Commission on Higher Education (Lipset, Trow, and Ladd, n.d.) on the political opinions of over 60,000 full-time college faculty members, physical education faculty (N = 1208) ranked second out of 30 fields in percentage of respondents who characterized themselves as strongly conservative, and also second in percentage of those who characterized themselves as moderately conservative. Only agriculture faculty were more conservative. In response to the question: "What do you think of the emergence of radical student activism in recent years?" physical educators were second in "disapprove with reservations" and fourth in "unreserved disapproval."

In apparently the only study specifically concerned with the comprehensive value orientations of collegiate coaches, Sage (1972b) assessed value orientations of football, basketball, and track coaches and compared them with those of college students and with businessmen. One hundred ten coaches from each of the three sports were randomly selected from the National Collegiate Athletic Bureau Guides as subjects. The Polyphasic Values Inventory (PVI) (Roscoe, 1965) which measures values on a liberal-conservative continuum was administered to the subjects. The investigator reported that on 14 of the 20 items of the PVI the combined coaching groups expressed a significantly more conservative orientation than college students, the coaches expressed greater liberalism on three of the items, and there were no differences on three of the items. In summarizing the differences between college coaches and college students Sage said:

> The total response profile of the college coaches showed them to possess moderate-conservative values ... Although conservatism is not extreme among coaches, it is more pronounced than it is among college students. ... The findings of this study support the notion that coaches possess a greater conservatism than college students. But an item by item analysis of the response choices certainly does not support the assertions which have been made recently that coaches are extremely conservative —even reactionary—in value orientation (1972b: 184).

In comparing the value orientation of collegiate coaches and businessmen, Sage found that in 12 of the 20 items coaches expressed a more liberal perspective, while coaches were more conservative on two items, and there were no differences on six of the items. Sage concluded: "Overall, this study showed that coaches hold more liberal value orientation than businessmen from ten occupational categories" (1972b: 186).

Using data from the same sample of college coaches, Sage (1973c) compared the value orientations of the three coaches groups. On the basis of socialization theory and previous research in occupational sociology, it was hypothesized that college coaches in the three sports possess similar value orientations. The findings supported the hypothesis.

It seems that the social attitudes and value orientations of collegiate coaches are not much different from those which are termed "middle-class–middle-America." Sport is only one aspect of coaches' lives and the attitudes and values of the larger society undoubtedly play as important a role in influencing coaches as their experiences in sport. It has been said that sport is a microcosm of the society, which suggests that attitude and value formation is only minimally affected by sport. But it is also true that organized sports programs support and reinforce almost every norm of American industrial organization.

SOCIAL ORIGINS OF COLLEGE COACHES

College coaches can properly be regarded as being members of the general occupational category of educators, since their place of work is in educational institutions. They view themselves and are viewed by most of the public as educators, and they have met the same general educational achievement requirements of other educators, i.e., a college degree.

There is a widely held generalization that educators originate in the lower income and occupational strata of society. As Pavalko (1968: 515) said: "To describe teachers as coming from 'lower-middle class' backgrounds has become a popular generalization among social scientists and laymen alike." The notion that educators come primarily from the lower social classes is based largely on a stratification system which presumed that farming was a lower class occupation (Coffman, 1911; Whitney, 1927; Moffett, 1929). More recent studies on the social origins of teachers suggest that the composition of the profession has been undergoing considerable change (Richey and Fox, 1948; Carlson, 1951; Wattenberg et al., 1957). Nevertheless, although most of the research on the social origins of educators lacks conclusiveness as a result of the utilization of small and unrepresentative samples and weaknesses in the research design, the various studies over the past 60 years do indicate that the overall majority of elementary and secondary teachers come from lower-middle and upper-lower classes, with a decreasing number coming from farm backgrounds. Of course, there is wide variability and teachers do come from wealthy as well as poverty backgrounds.

College coaches should perhaps be classified with college faculty rather than with elementary and secondary teachers, although not all of the coaches actually hold academic rank. The social origins of college faculty seem to be from slightly higher strata than elementary and secondary educators. In 1938 the American Association of University Professors reported that a sample of 4667 members revealed that 26.6 percent of the professors' fathers were businessmen and 12.1 percent were manual laborers (Kunkel, 1938). Coffman's (1911) study done in 1911 showed that only 6 percent of the fathers of public school teachers were businessmen and Richey and Fox (1948) reported that only 22 percent of their group of teachers came from business-employed fathers. However, 14 percent of Coffman's group and 26 percent of Richey and Fox's group came from households where the father was a manual laborer. Furthermore, where Kunkel found 24.7 percent of college professors from farm backgrounds, Coffman found 66 percent of his group having farm social origins (of course the urbanization of population between 1911 and 1938 should be taken into consideration).

Recent research with college faculties suggest that a classification of social class origins is difficult, since regional tendencies exist. Stecklein and Eckert (1958) reported that professors at the University of Minnesota came from predominantly middle and lower-middle class origins; on the other hand, Lazarsfeld and Thielens (1958) indicated that in eastern universities college faculties have predominantly upper-middle class origins. Ignoring discrete distinctions, it appears that middle class backgrounds is the norm for college professors (cf., Lipset and Ladd, 1972).

Until recently no systematic study had been done on the social class backgrounds of collegiate athletic coaches. Biographical data on prominent collegiate coaches suggest that while there is certainly varability in social backgrounds, they tend to have been drawn primarily from the lower and middle class social strata. Since a good many college coaches originally aspired to a career in secondary school teaching and coaching, and indeed many have spent time in this level of teaching and coaching, one might guess that they would possess social origins similar to secondary school teachers.

The social background of college football and basketball coaches has recently been analyzed by Loy and Sage (1972). A twofold assessment was made of fathers' occupational status for the two groups of coaches. First a score from the Duncan Socioeconomic Index (cf., Blau and Duncan, 1967; Reiss, 1961) was assigned to the job each father held at the time his son entered college. Second, each father's job was classified according to Turner's ninefold occupational typology (cf., Turner, 1964; Pavalko, 1971) with the added category of "farmers."

A comparison of the occupational status of the coaches' fathers, as measured by the Duncan scale, indicated that over 50 percent of the two groups of college coaches came from occupational backgrounds wherein

Table 1

Parental occupational status of college coaches as defined by Duncan's Socio-economic Index*

Status categories	Very Low	Low	Middle	High	Very High
Status scores	1–19	20–39	40–59	60–79	80–99
Basketball (n = 349)	101	101	82	48	17
Football (n = 253)	63	74	59	42	17
Basketball (%)	28.94	28.94	23.50	13.75	4.87
Football (%)	24.71	29.02	23.14	16.47	6.67

* From Loy and Sage, 1972.

their fathers held low prestige occupational positions (Table 1) if a status score of 40 is taken as the upper limit for low status occupations.

A more descriptive analysis of the occupational status of the coaches' fathers emerges when Turner's typology is employed (Table 2). This analysis shows that although approximately 20 percent of the coaches' fathers were small-business owners and managers or retail salesmen, the majority of fathers worked at manual jobs.

The same study showed that over one-half of the fathers of football coaches and some 60 percent of the fathers of basketball coaches did not complete high school. Less than 14 percent of the football coaches' fathers and less than 12 percent of the basketball coaches' fathers earned college degrees.

Using a modification of the Morris and Murphy conceptualization of occupational situs (see Morris and Murphy, 1959), Sage and Loy (1973) classified college football and basketball coaches' fathers' occupations. Situs refers to a category of individuals or positions placed on a level with other categories, all of which are given the same evaluation. The basic assumptions behind situs classification are that the occupations in each situs contribute to the performance of an essential societal function and that each function is equally necessary to the maintenance of society. Each situs includes all occupations that contribute to the performance of that function.

That college football and basketball coaches tend to come from similar social backgrounds is evident from the situs classification (Table 3). Both football and basketball coaches' fathers tend to work in occupations classified as manufacturing, building and maintenance, and commerce. Based upon the Duncan and the Turner analyses discussed above, this analysis suggests that the coaches' fathers hold the lower echelon jobs in the various situses.

It appears that college coaches come from markedly lower socioeconomic backgrounds in relation to college and university faculty. Lipset and Ladd (1972), working with the Duncan occupational scale, classified occupations as high status, middle status, and low status, and they found that about 22 percent of fathers of college professors in general held high status jobs; Loy and Sage (1972) found that only 6 percent of the fathers of college football and basketball coaches worked in high status occupations (Table 4).

It may be seen that a large proportion of college coaches are upwardly mobile persons, with many having moved from upper-lower and lower-middle status. If college coaching is assumed to carry the same occupational status as college professors, then by Duncan's scale over 90 percent of college coaches have experienced some upward social mobility.

Table 2

Parental occupational status of college coaches as defined by Turner's typology*

Occupational classification	Fathers of basketball coaches (n = 324)		Fathers of football coaches (n = 254)	
	n	%	n	%
1. Large-business owners and officials	7	2.16	9	3.54
2. Professionals	31	9.57	21	8.27
3. Business agents and managers	12	3.70	22	8.66
4. Semiprofessionals	16	4.94	7	2.76
5. Small-business owners and managers and retail salesmen	70	21.60	45	17.72
6. Clerical workers and sales clerks	24	7.41	18	7.09
7. Skilled workers and foremen	72	22.22	49	19.29
8. Semiskilled laborers	30	9.26	46	18.11
9. Unskilled laborers and unemployed	44	13.58	25	9.84
10. Farmers	18	5.55	12	4.72

* From Loy and Sage, 1972.

Table 3

Parental occupational situs of college coaches as defined by a modification of Morris and Murphy's topology

Situs categories	Basketball coaches (n = 315)		Football coaches (n = 250)	
	n	%	n	%
Political authority	0	0.0	1	0.4
Legal authority	11	3.2	7	2.5
Finance and records	20	5.7	14	5.1
Manufacturing	60	17.2	48	17.4
Transportation	27	7.8	13	4.7
Extraction	12	3.4	11	4.0
Agriculture	23	6.6	15	5.4
Building and maintenance	48	13.8	46	16.7
Commerce	68	19.5	59	21.4
Communications	6	1.7	4	1.4
Arts and aesthetics	4	1.1	2	0.7
Recreation and entertainment	3	0.9	3	1.1
Education and research	21	6.0	15	5.4
Health and welfare	10	2.9	11	4.0
Military authority	2	0.6	1	0.4

CAREER PATTERNS OF COLLEGE COACHES

The term "career pattern" does not have a single precise meaning, but it typically reflects a developmentally oriented characterization of the work histories and role relationships of individuals within an occupational category over some period of time (Morris, 1957). Occupational careers can be thought of as movement over time between positions at the same status level or between positions at different levels of a status hierarchy. Thus the patterned series of adjustments made by the individual to the network of informal and formal relationships in which the role tasks of the occupation are performed constitute career patterns. This series of adjustments is typically considered in terms of recruitment and socialization into career roles, mobility between positions in the hierarchy of the occupation, status and prestige, and role conflict.

Table 4

A comparison of social background of college coaches with other faculty, by field*

Academic discipline (or profession)	Father's education (% attending college)	Father's occupation (% manual workers)	Father's occupation (% high status jobs)†
Medicine	57	10	39
Law	50	14	32
Anthropology	53	16	30
Political science	48	22	26
Humanities	43	21	24
Economics	43	18	21
Biological sciences	42	23	22
Physical sciences	41	25	21
Psychology	41	22	20
All Fields	40	23	22
Engineering	39	26	19
Sociology	34	25	18
Social work	34	26	23
Business	32	27	13
Education	30	32	14
Agriculture	25	21	9
Athletics	23	51.5	6
Basketball	22	51	5
Football	24	52	7

* Data adapted from Lipset and Ladd (1972), Table 7, page. 89, in Loy and Sage, 1972.
† Based on Duncan Occupational Prestige Scale, scores greater than 80.

General Characteristics of a College Coaching Career

Before examining the career patterns of college coaches, we will describe college coaching in broad outline and in terms of salient features which distinguish it from other occupations and professions. The majority of college coaches are professors as well as coaches (Woodbury, 1966; Wilcox, 1969) but we will focus primarily upon the coaching role relationships and contingencies.

The coach's clients are his athletes and the sports team as a whole is built around this coach-athlete relationship. The college coach also has secondary groups of clients—the student body, faculty-administration, and, in varying degrees, alumni and public spectators. The occupation, then, is in a sense described by the coach's relationship with these various groups of people.

The college coach functions within an organization that is relatively formalized, highly structured, and bureaucratic. Nevertheless, he has a great deal of autonomy; for example, many coaches speak of "my program" when referring to the sport which they coach at an institution. There is typically no direct or continuous supervision over the day-to-day methods which the coach uses to minister to his athletes, although there is a great deal of bureaucratic structure and routine in terms of the organizational system. The performance of the collegiate coach is evaluated almost exclusively by the won-lost records of his teams. Many highly competent and ethical coaches have lost their jobs because their teams have failed to win consistently while unscrupulous coaches with favorable won-lost records have been retained.

In comparison to many occupations, college coaching involves a relatively long period of formal education. Several studies indicate that almost all college head coaches have a bachelor's degree and over 70 percent have earned a master's degree (Harvey, 1963; Sage, 1973c; Loy and Sage, 1972). In terms of traditional professions such as medicine and law, the formal educational requirements are less but if experience in high school coaching or assisting as a college coach are considered as internship training, becoming a head college coach typically requires longer preparation than the other professions. The average head coach is approximately 40 years old (Sage, 1972a; Loy and Sage, 1973; Harvey, 1963) and approximately 55 percent of the football and basketball coaches have been head college coaches for less than seven years (Sage and Loy, 1973).

College coaching is characterized by movement from one level to another in the educational hierarchy. The majority of college head coaches began their careers in secondary schools (Sage and Loy, 1973). From secondary schools the coaches typically entered the college ranks as assistant coaches and finally achieved a head coaching position. This pattern differs from sport to sport, of course, and is most characteristic of football, basketball, track, and baseball. It is also true that many college coaches never achieve head coaching positions, so progress up the coaching hierarchy may end with assistant coaching roles.

Recruitment to College Coaching

One requirement of any social system is that persons must be recruited to occupy the various positions within the system and perform social roles associated with these positions. Sociologists have long been concerned with the process whereby persons select, and are at the same time selected, for particular roles (Pavalko, 1968); but, as Caplow (1954: 214) noted, "surprisingly little is known about occupational choice in our own or any mobile society." What was true in the mid-1950s is still true 20 years later.

Occupational recruitment is typically thought of as occurring only at the beginning of a career as the recruit obtains his initial entry into the occupation. But recruitment also involves filling vacancies within an occupation which occur as a result of death, retirement, promotion, and demotion. In the former, recruitment is drawing occupants into the system whereas in the latter recruits may be drawn from within the system.

Recruitment which is concerned with attracting persons into an occupation may be viewed from two standpoints: (1) the individual choosing an occupation, (2) the deliberate effort on the part of the occupational group to draw recruits to the occupation. An analysis of occupational choice can be made from either of these two vantage points, but in practice they are integrally related for career decision-making.

The process by which a person selects an occupational career and prepares for it is a rather complex mixture of personal characteristics, social background, selective procedures of the occupational gatekeepers, chance, and the actual acquisition of skills and normative orientations of the occupation. The process is by no means the same for any two persons.

Persons who become college coaches do so for a variety of reasons, some of which they recognize and some of which they probably do not. For some, coaching may be a way to prolong, or recapture, the satisfactions and "glories" which they experienced as youthful athletes. For others, those who never had great athletic ability, coaching may be a way of vicariously experiencing sports competition. For still others, coaching may be viewed as a way of securing recognition and prestige, since sports have such high visibility in American society. Finally, persons may go into coaching because they enjoy social relations with young people and they see coaching as an opportunity to lead a life of service to the youth of the nation. In this regard, Pooley (1970) reported that 42 percent of male physical education majors (the undergraduate major of most college coaches) indicated that "profession was useful to society" was the most important reason for choosing physical education as a major course of study. Surely, few persons go into coaching because it offers short hours and long-term security. On the contrary, most coaches put in extremely long hours and they frequently find that they are fired for arbitrary or capricious reasons.

Pavalko (1971) has described three theoretical approaches for the study of occupational choice: Rational Decision-Making approach, Fortuitous approach, and the Socio-Cultural approach. It appears that each one of these approaches is operative to some extent in coaches' career selection.

In Rational Decision-Making, there is assumed to be a large measure of rational planning on the part of the individual and there is a compromise between one's abilities, interests, opportunities, and values (Ginzberg et al., 1951). In this regard Holland (1959) suggested that occupational choice is primarily a function of trying to maximize the congruence between personal traits and social experiences and the characteristics of occupations. For coaches, undoubtedly the inclination to become a coach is related to sports experiences in childhood and adolescence. Several studies (Sage, 1973c; Loy and Sage, 1973) indicate that collegiate coaches were excellent athletes in their youth. Presumably these experiences were satisfying and served to make the young man wish to continue to be a part of these experiences. Pooley (1970), in a study concerned with the process by which students are socialized into professional preparation programs in physical education, found that 35 percent of his respondents indicated that "athletic skill" was the most important reason for choosing physical education as a major course of study. Furthermore, over 70 percent of the physical education majors had become interested in taking this as a major course of study before the age of 17.

Apparently playing certain positions on a sports team has a differential effect in recruiting persons into coaching. Grusky (1963) examined the effects of formal structure on managerial recruitment and found that major league baseball managers were more likely to come from the central positions, where there was high interaction potential. Loy (1970) extended this work and found that this differential attraction to coaching held for collegiate baseball coaches; over 50 percent of all college baseball coaches had played in the battery while they were players, a percentage more than twice as high as predicted by chance. Other central positions contributed more than their proportion of collegiate baseball coaches, too. Bolton (1956) found that high school football coaches were overrepresented as former players in the central positions of center, quarterback, and fullback.

Another personal attribute that is related to sports performance and to career choice is somatotype. Among other variables, it has been found that there are characteristic somatotype distributions for persons selecting certain occupations (Carter et al., 1965; Damon and McFarland, 1955). Several studies indicate that there is a characteristic somatotype for male physical education majors, with patterns of dominant and moderately high mesomorphy (Carter et al., 1973).

Several social scientists have suggested that the image of an occupation is an important factor in recruitment to it (Caplow, 1954; Super, 1957). Thus, potential recruits may match their personal characteristics and interests against those of the image and may be attracted or repelled by it. Identification with the image may, then, be a strong motive in occupational self recruitment. O'Dowd and Beardslee noted:

An occupational sterotype provides the student with a model of the average member of the occupation against which he can measure his present traits and his ambitions about the kind of person he would like to become . . . Students will seek an occupational image that fits with their present conception of themselves and their beliefs about what they might become . . . From the point of view of the occupation, this means that the properties of the image will exercise a selective effect upon students. It will appeal to those who believe they fit the image and will repel others who find the image unacceptable.*

Since coaches are such a ubiquitous part of organized sports in the United States, the coaches under whom young athletes play serve as powerful models for occupational choice. That coaches serve as career models has been clearly documented by several recent studies. Snyder (1972) found that for a group of high school coaches, their own coaches had been the most prominent reference persons in career selection. Pooley (1970) reported that 58 percent of his sample of physical education majors selected "coach" as the most important socialization agent in the choice of physical education as a major field.

In the second approach to occupational selection—the Fortuitous approach—suggested by Pavalko (1971: 48), choice is regarded as less purposive and rational and persons are seen "as drifting into occupations through a process of elimination rather than explicitly choosing them." Persons are seen as choosing in a spontaneous, nonrational way, influenced frequently by situational conditions. Although the extent to which this avenue has been used by college coaches has not been specifically studied, there are indications that it might apply to a good many of them. Several investigators (Stecklein and Eckert, 1958; Gustad, 1959) have found that college professors entered college teaching more by accident than by planned design; the majority did not plan to teach at the college level. Pooley (1970) reported that only 12 percent of his physical education major respondents viewed college teaching-coaching as an ultimate career aspiration. Thus, since most young coaches look forward to a coaching career in secondary schools from a "realistic" standpoint, many college coaches probably "drifted" into their positions due to a combination of fortuitous circumstances.

Pavalko's (1971) third approach to occupational choice—Socio-Cultural approach—hypothesized that various social characteristics are related to career choice. These characteristics are such things as social class background, urban-rural residence, race, and sex, and they are seen as factors which limit the kinds of occupational choices which individuals may make.

---

* D. D. O'Dowd and D. O. Beardslee, "The Image of the College Professor." *AAUP Bulletin,* Vol. 47, No. 3 (September, 1961): pp. 220–221. Reprinted by permission.

As with the previously discussed approaches, the exact extent to which social characteristic factors affect the choice of coaching as a career are unknown and certainly vary with each individual. Social class background characteristics of coaches were discussed in a previous section of this paper and it is evident that coaching, like positions throughout the field of education, has served as an attractive occupation for lower and middle class youth. With regard to hometown residence, Sage and Loy (1973) found a strong tendency for college coaches to have come from a rural background. College football and basketball coaches came from very small communities, with over one-third of both samples of coaches from hometowns of less than 10,000 population.

In light of the countless contributions which have been made to collegiate sports by black athletes, it is curious that the coaching field has lagged behind in bringing greater numbers of blacks into the profession. It is rather obvious that racial considerations have produced differential recruitment patterns into college coaching. Racial discrimination has clouded the pretensions of equalitarianism in college coaching just as it has in other aspects of college athletics. Blacks who have aspired to college coaching positions have faced discrimination from the formal and informal hierarchy of college athletics. Until very recently, the only college coaching positions open to blacks were in the black colleges. Although black athletes have played on collegiate athletic teams since before the turn of the century, and although a great many blacks undoubtedly aspired to college coaching, this occupation has tended to exclude blacks in the same ways that have been employed by many other occupations in American society. Today, the number of black collegiate coaches is negligible, and there is still no black head football coach at a major university. Only in the past three or four years, with the aid of considerable "outside" pressure, have blacks been appointed as head coaches in basketball, track, and a few other sports at predominantly white institutions.

Regardless of the factors which have been operative in the choice of an occupation, once a commitment to an occupation has been made, the individual must secure the prerequisite skills, competencies, and certification for appointment into the occupation. For some occupations this entails a period of apprenticeship training, for others it requires in-service experiences, and for many it involves a period of formal education.

For collegiate coaching, formal education leading to a bachelor's degree is the most conspicuous prerequisite to employment (Loy and Sage, 1972). Indeed, a high percentage of college coaches have earned advanced degrees; Sage (1973c) reported that over 75 percent of college football, basketball, and track coaches have an earned master's degree. Seventy-one percent of Harvey's (1963) sample of collegiate coaches reported an earned master's degree. Sage and Loy (1973) reported that most football and basketball coaches attended small colleges (less than 5000 enrollment); however, football coaches tended to have gone to large public colleges to a greater extent than basketball coaches. This probably reflects the extent to which the two sports are emphasized at the two types of institutions. Many small colleges do not even field a football team while placing great emphasis on basketball, e.g., Providence College, Creighton University, Marquette University, etc.

While an aspiring coach need not major in physical education as a college student, the majority of high school and college coaches do select this major (Arms, 1965; Maltozo, 1965; Wilcox, 1969; Loy and Sage, 1972). Thus departments of physical education serve as the academic "home" for aspiring coaches and it is in this department where they receive a major part of their formal indoctrination into the coaching role prescriptions.

An additional source of occupational preparation for coaches is in actual participation in collegiate sports in which they expect to coach. Sage and Loy (1973) found that over 40 percent of collegiate basketball coaches and about 38 percent of collegiate football coaches lettered at least once in the sport which they are coaching. Wilcox (1969) reported a much higher percent, 93 percent, of his college football coach respondents had "playing experience" in football at the college varsity level. These sport experiences may be viewed as assisting the aspiring coach to develop competencies in skill, strategy and tactics, leadership style, and organizational ability which will be useful upon securing a coaching position.

No systematic program for the recruitment of collegiate coaches is carried out by institutions of higher education, presumably because there are far fewer jobs than there are persons seeking these jobs. Coaching is a part of the labor market, and as such is subject to the variations in the supply and demand of that market. The demand for college coaches is a function of the number of institutions and the number of intercollegiate sports at each institution. The number of college coaches has been steadily increasing for the past 80 years. With the enormous expansion of intercollegiate athletics in the first three decades of the twentieth century, a shortage of coaches existed, but by the beginning of World War II the supply had just about caught up with the demand. After the war, many of the millions of ex-servicemen who returned to college prepared for a career in coaching, and a general oversupply of coaches has existed for the past 25 years. It is common for a college to have as many as 50 applicants for a coaching vacancy. It appears that, at least in the near future, there will continue to be an oversupply of coaches. College enrollments are leveling off and therefore there will probably be very few new institutions to start athletic programs but the trend toward a wider variety of sports may partially offset enrollment stability.

Securing a college coaching position is occasionally done through college placement bureaus, but personal letters of recommendation and phone calls are more commonly used. The smaller the college and the greater the emphasis on the employment of a professor-coach, the greater the reliance upon college placement bureaus. The larger the university and the greater the emphasis on full-time coaching, the more frequently the personal recommendation and phone call approach is used.

Most professor-coaches are selected through a faculty committee process. Full-time coaches are usually selected by an athletic board, which may include alumni and booster club representatives. A recent trend is to include athletes in the selection process. The national coaching association conventions are frequently used by coaches and potential employers for holding interviewing conferences.

Occupational Socialization and College Coaches

Socialization is the process by which an individual learns the behaviors, the values, and the expectations of others that enable him to assume effectively particular roles in society. Although the foundation for cultural behaviors and values are laid in childhood and adolescence, socialization is a continuous process throughout the life cycle since the individual is constantly taking on new roles. To be effective in these new roles, he has to be socialized through training and interpersonal experiences.

There are two basic aims of socialization which are paramount in preparing individuals to perform roles in a social system. First, persons must learn the knowledge and skills which constitute proper role performance; second, persons must be led to internalize certain attitudes and values which are consistent with the roles. The aims are accomplished in a variety of formal and informal ways, and, for occupational socialization, the process may begin before the individual becomes a full-fledged member of an occupation.

In American society the majority of adult males and a growing portion of females are engaged in occupational roles, and the occupational milieu plays a central function in adult socialization. Most research into the process of socialization has been concerned with infancy and childhood, but there is a considerable amount of socialization involved in learning and performing occupational roles. Occupations are performed in a social context which is characterized by norms, values, and behaviors which are distinct to occupational categories. Unfortunately, there are relatively few studies of adult socialization which are concerned with the process by which organizations and occupational groups socialize a person into a specific role. Moore (1969: 861) stated: "Occupational socialization appears not to have excited scholarly interest proportional to its importance." A few prototypical studies on occupational socialization were conducted by Becker and his colleagues (Becker et al., 1961) and Merton and his colleagues (Merton, 1957) and more recently other scholars have begun to build on previous work (Western and Anderson, 1968; Pooley, 1970).

According to Moore (1970: 71), occupational "socialization involves acquiring the requisite knowledge and skills and also the sense of occupational identity and internalization of occupational norms typical of the fully qualified practitioner." It is clear that for an individual to function in an occupation he must learn a variety of behaviors, attitudes, and value orientations. The formal socialization of individuals to perform institutionalized occupational roles is managed in a variety of ways such as in-service training, apprenticeship, professional education, etc. The informal socializing agents are diverse and consist of fellow workers, role models, and significant others who induce normative compliance, and, typically, an actual sharing of attitudes and values.

There are actually three time periods over which occupational socialization occurs: (1) the period prior to the onset of formal training, (2) the period of formal training and, (3) the period of actual occupational role enactment.

Merton (1957) claimed that occupational socialization begins before students enroll in training programs. He labeled this phenomenon "anticipatory socialization" and defined it as a process that occurs in fantasy as students anticipate their acceptance in actual training programs. The function of anticipating socialization lies in the fact that persons begin to acquire the behaviors, attitudes, and values of groups in which membership is desired or anticipated.

Once an occupation has been chosen the individual is likely to incorporate into his present self-image certain aspects of his future occupational status and he develops the values, attitudes, and behaviors which are appropriate for a member of this occupation. Most persons enter an occupation (especially a profession) only after they have had time to think about and develop a general understanding of its role requirements. Since a good deal of time and preparation may occur between the decision to enter an occupation and actual participation in it, it is likely that a considerable amount of socialization effect is achieved before the person enters. Rosenberg (1957: 24) stated: "The occupational status still to be occupied influences the current attitudes, values, and behavior of the individual. Thus, in addition to people choosing an occupation in order to satisfy a value, they may choose a value because they consider it appropriate for the occupational status they expect to fill in the future."

The initial occupational socialization for most coaches was probably carried out in sports settings. Most coaches were active participants in inter-school athletics (Havel, 1951; Healy, 1953; Arms, 1965; Wilcox, 1969; Loy and Sage, 1972). Healy (1953) reported that earning letters as a player is a prerequisite for appointment to a head college coaching position in that sport. Havel (1951: 17) noted: "A successful record of undergraduate participation in intercollegiate sports is to be considered a most vital and necessary qualification for men in this field, especially in the activity one is to coach." The athletic experiences and the opportunity to observe their own coaches' behavior undoubtedly serve to socialize aspiring coaches to the role prescriptions. In several studies, coaches have acknowledged that their own coaches were powerful models for them in their youth (Pooley, 1970; Snyder, 1972; Sage, n.d.).

A good many aspiring coaches serve as coaches of youth teams in football, basketball, baseball, etc. These experiences, too, provide opportunities for learning about coaching role behaviors (Pooley, 1970).

It appears that most aspiring coaches make a firm choice of occupation in early adolescence (Pooley, 1970) but in order to become a fully certified coach formal education is a necessity. The formal college professional preparation program imparts knowledge and skills which will be useful in the occupational role enactment, but the communication of attitudes and values is equally important. In the college program the less advanced students derive role behaviors and value cues from the more advanced students as well as from instructors (Merton et al., 1957; Becker et al., 1961). In this respect, Nelson (1970) found that senior class physical education majors held basic life value patterns similar to those of the male faculty who teach in those programs (many of whom are coaches).

Formal educational programs designed to prepare an aspirant for an occupation convey with varying degrees of accuracy the formal requirements and the norms of behavior appropriate for that particular occupation. Verbal prescriptions and admonitions are usually accompanied by an apprenticeship or on-the-job internship. In the case of coaching this may begin with coaching preadolescents in a "little league" program or with student teaching, which is usually part of the college degree requirement in physical education major programs.

Burlingame (1972: 41) has aptly observed: "The professional training that occurs in colleges of education explains only a part of how teachers teach—and, at that, an insignificant part of teachers' behavior. That part of teaching experience which really counts begins when the freshman teacher faces his or her classroom for the first time." Playing experiences, part-time coaching experiences, and the college preparation program provide small opportunity for the aspiring coach to learn the varieties and subtleties of coaching role behaviors, and though they are helpful, the recruit enters the coaching field with minimal knowledge of the procedures of the occupation.

For about two-thirds of college football and basketball coaches, the first "real" coaching position was in junior and senior high schools (Loy and Sage, 1972) as an assistant coach or head coach. In this job the coach's final phase of occupational socialization begins.

Occupational roles establish functional links between the individual and most parts of the social structure. Individuals with similar occupations tend to develop their closest friendships with colleagues; an individual is thus likely to find that most of his friends are fellow workers. The individual learns the norms and values appropriate to his occupation through interaction with others who hold normative beliefs about what his role should be. Moore (1968: 879) suggests that "if we add the probability that peers and . . . role models constitute significant others, and thus that relations with them are marked by some degree of affectivity, we are well on the way to comprehending how an occupational identity gets formed." Furthermore, Goode (1957: 196) stated: "Characteristic of each of the established professions, and a goal of each aspiring occupation, is the community of profession. Each profession is a community without locus [but it] . . . may nevertheless be called a community by virtue of these characteristics . . . Its members share values in common." Appropriate role models appear to be an important source of occupational socialization too because they provide the symbolic and concrete reference point for values and behavior in a social situation.

The person who learns the norms, values, and behaviors will emerge not only with an internalized occupational commitment, but also with an identification with the collectivity, the brotherhood. Thus, the main consequence of the various occupational socializing agents and agencies is that there is a relative homogeneity in the employee group—all persons having behaviors and values which are compatible with the demands of the occupation. As Burlingame (1972: 44) said, "the intent of socialization is to obviate personalistic, idiosyncratic differences in freshmen [persons new to an occupation] and replace them with the universalistic, norm-governed behaviors of seniors." The literature indicates that the existence of common dispositional traits among professionals is well recognized (Caplow, 1954; Wallace, 1966).

The actual processes by which employers, colleagues, and clients socialize coaches has not been systematically studied. But the control over powerful rewards and punishment in the hands of these persons suggests that they are probably very effective agents for occupational socialization of coaches. Sage (1973c) found that the outcome of the various agents and agencies for socialization of coaches is a homogeneity of value orientations among collegiate football, basketball, and track coaches.

As the aspiring coach passes through the various phases from anticipation of becoming a coach to actually becoming an established college coach, an occupational identity is formed which is creditable to the individual and to others with whom he interacts in the performance of his job. Undoubtedly, the process is slightly different for each coach but the general pattern for occupational socialization of coaches is probably similar to that which has been described in this paper.

Mobility Patterns of College Coaches

In college coaching, just as in most occupations in American society, there is a considerable amount of job position changes. Career mobility may be viewed from two perspectives: mobility within various levels in an occupational hierarchy and mobility from one spatial location to another, or geographical mobility. We shall examine both aspects of mobility for collegiate coaches.

Movement within various levels of an occupation's hierarchy may be conceptualized as horizontal (changes to similar positions) or vertical (changes to positions with higher or lower status, prestige, or responsibility). Vertical and horizontal mobility of personnel through the various positions within an occupation functions, at least theoretically, to make certain that competent persons get in the right positions at the right time.

Although athletic coaches move from one coaching position to another for a variety of reasons, the typical pattern of mobility is from lower educational levels to higher ones—junior high school to high school and high school to college—and from smaller to larger schools. This movement is generally accompanied by additional coaching experience and added academic qualifications. The major incentives are increased salary, higher prestige, and increased security. Although only a small proportion of the total coaches in American education ascend to the collegiate level, a premium is placed upon "moving up" from one educational level to another because it symbolizes success in the coaching world.

In general, coaches whose career patterns have led to collegiate coaching seem to have been circumstantial rather than planned. Most young men wishing to become coaches set their occupational sights on high school coaching. College coaching seems to be a "dream," an aspiration, which is too unlikely to occur. It is well known that there are only a few college coaching positions for all those who would like to be college coaches, and it is believed that a college coaching position comes as a reward for being an outstanding high school coach. For the young, aspiring coach who has not proven himself as a high school coach there are just too many factors which might prevent his being a winning high school coach. Thus, most aspiring coaches do not view collegiate coaching as a realistic occupational goal (Pooley, 1970).

Two major career patterns of mobility appear to have existed for those who have become head college coaches. The first may be called the "working your way up," or contest mobility, pattern and the second may be called "starting near the top," or sponsored mobility, pattern (Turner, 1960).

In the first path, that of "working your way up," the young coach begins as an assistant coach at a junior high or senior high school and then, by successful achievement, he is elevated to a head coaching position in a high school. At this point, if the high school is small it becomes necessary to advance to a large high school. After achieving a favorable won-lost record over a period of years at the high school level, he is employed as an assistant or a head coach at a college. If the first college position is as an assistant, the coach may become a head coach after serving the apprenticeship as an assistant. While this exact career pattern is an idealized one, Loy and Sage (1972) found that a majority of collegiate head football and basketball coaches have traveled a similar career path. It is important to make two points with regard to this mobility pattern: (1) many coaches' mobility stops prior to achieving a head college coaching position, and (2) a key contingency in this pathway of coaching mobility is the production of championship teams at each step; this avenue is blocked if the coach is unable to develop "a winner" at any one of the levels.

The second major pattern for coaching career mobility is "starting near the top," or sponsored mobility. In this pattern a fortuitous set of circumstances enable the young coach to obtain desirable coaching positions without having to start at the bottom of the occupational ladder; he is sponsored into positions high in the occupational hierarchy. The existence of systems of sponsorship has been well documented in the histories of large companies (See Bennett, 1951, for an example in the Ford Motor Company). Caplow and McGee (1958) and more recent investigators (Hargens and Hagstrom, 1967; Kinloch, 1969; Kinloch and Perrucci, 1969) have shown that university professors' career patterns reveal a strong element of sponsorship. The place where a professor obtained his Ph.D. will usually determine the prestige of the institution at which the first job is acquired, and the higher the prestige of the university where the doctorate was received the greater the probability that the first job will be in another university with essentially the same prestige.

Applying the phenomenon of career sponsorship which has been found to be prevalent in business and university departments to coaching suggests that persons who become coaches at the prestigious universities probably were products of those institutions and developed acquaintances with key personnel in these institutions who were able to "sponsor" them into desirable coaching positions.

Loy and Sage (1973) examined sponsored mobility patterns of collegiate coaches. The investigators sought to determine the degree to which universities having high athletic prestige recruit their football and basketball coaches from other collegiate institutions possessing similar status. It was hypothesized that: (1) coaches who participated as varsity athletes at high prestige institutions were more likely to have served as assistant coaches at high prestige institutions than coaches who participated at low prestige institutions, (2) coaches who served as assistant coaches at high prestige institutions were more likely to have obtained their first head coaching position at high prestige institutions than coaches who served their apprenticeships at low prestige institutions, (3) coaches who held their first head job at high prestige institutions were more likely to presently hold head jobs at high prestige institutions than coaches whose first head jobs were at low prestige institutions. All three hypotheses were found to be statistically significant beyond the 0.001 level. The authors concluded: "The empirical conformation of the three hypotheses underlying the investigation indicates a process of 'sponsored mobility' with respect to the career patterns of college coaches" (1973: 11). Of course, only collegiate football and basketball coaches were studied. The extent to which the findings generalize to other coaching groups is unknown. However, Harvey (1963: 103) reported: "Administrators of institutions included in this study tended strongly to employ coaches who were graduates from colleges and universities of their own type." The coaches were head varsity coaches of baseball, track, basketball, and football.

A second general aspect of occupational movement is geographical mobility, that is, changing spatial location of jobs. Since the competencies and role expectations for a coach are approximately the same throughout the country, there is a great deal of movement from one coaching position to another, which has given rise to the image of the coach as an itinerant.

The only study to date which was specifically concerned with the geographical mobility of college coaches was done by Sage and Loy (1973), who focused on the geographical mobility patterns of collegiate football and basketball coaches, tracing their movement from hometown origin through their collegiate education and coaching careers. They found that the majority of both football and basketball coaches entered the coaching occupation at the secondary school level, but over one-third of the coaches of both sports entered coaching at the collegiate level, which probably enabled many of them to remain at that level of coaching. The mobility pattern of college coaches suggests that they have been more occupationally mobile than the general labor force. About 70 percent of the college coaches in both groups held four or more coaching jobs, and over 25 percent held more than five coaching positions. Job switching is the rule. Because loyalty to coaching transcends loyalty to a school and because coaching skills are readily transferable among schools, mobility is accepted and approved by the coaching profession just as it is for other educational personnel.

Sage and Loy reported that collegiate football and basketball coaches tended to remain near their undergraduate college when taking their first coaching position. Indeed 80 percent of the basketball coaches and 84 percent of the football coaches remained in the same NCAA District (The NCAA Districts divide the United States into eight regions, each of which is made up of five to ten states within a geographical region of the U.S.) as their undergraduate institution for their first coaching job. The tendency for coaches to remain in a fairly small geographical region persisted when mobility patterns were examined for movement from first coaching job to present one, since over 68 percent of the two coaching groups did not move from one NCAA District to another. When migration occurred across NCAA District boundaries, it tended to be between contiguous districts. College football coaches tended to be more geographically mobile than their basketball coaching colleagues; districts in the eastern one-half of the United States experienced the most frequent movement of coaches between districts.

Status and Prestige Contingencies

The social status and prestige of collegiate coaches varies and is dependent upon a number of factors such as the institution at which one coaches, the community in which one coaches, the salary which one obtains from coaching, the visibility of one's teams in terms of mass media coverage, and, of course, one's won-lost record. There are enormous extremes in status and prestige among college coaches. The majority coach in institutions which receive little publicity outside the community or region. They are hired as physical educators as well as coaches and they receive the same financial remuneration as other faculty. By and large, these coaches interact with middle-class persons and they fit into the social structure of their communities as middle-class people. On the other hand, coaches who coach the "spectator" sports at major universities, such as Notre Dame, Ohio State, Alabama, Southern California, etc., draw large salaries, in some cases in excess of the president of the university, and they become "public" persons —they get wide coverage by the mass media, and are even treated to locker room telephone calls from the President of the United States. These coaches possess the social and financial accoutrements of the upper social class.

The ways that prestige among collegiate coaches is symbolized and displayed range from very obvious things to subtle things. The specific accomplishments which are appropriate to prestige building are related to size of the collegiate institution and to the success of a coach's teams. "Small college" and "major university" are the two main categories of collegiate stratification. Of course, there are strata within these categories but movement within the categories is more subtle. Basically, coaching positions in major universities carry a great deal more prestige than coaching positions in small colleges.

Accompanying and supporting the prestige of major university coaching positions are a number of benefits. The major university coach typically is given the authority to select his assistants, and the actual number of assistants is frequently negotiable. He is often given an expensive paid-up life insurance policy, a new car each year for personal use, and faculty status, for job security just in case he is fired as a coach. Promises to build or enlarge stadiums, athletic dormitories, and to make improvements in other facilities have come to be used as "fringe" items when a large university is bargaining for a new coach.

For success, and thus prestige, one needs the good opinion of peers and significant others. The coach, like persons in any occupational field, is expected to meet certain established criteria of competence and performance, and he is rarely isolated from reinforcements. Each time he places his team in competition he is subject to the rewards and punishments of his peers and the public. In American society about the only criterion applied to a coach's competence is the performance of his teams—if they are winners, he is a success, if they are losers, he is a failure. Thus, the coach demonstrates his ability most reliably by producing winning teams and less reliably by his reputation as a teacher of motor skills. A winning coach is rewarded with a coaching position at a more prestigious institution or, if he is already at a top university, he may be given various material rewards, from a more lucrative contract to a new house.

Although the highest status and prestige reside in the major university positions, the coaches who hold these positions have little job security. Job security is almost entirely dependent upon winning teams. Very few university coaches of the major (or revenue) sports are able to retain their jobs unless they keep a favorable balance of wins and losses. The extent to which the coach's job is dependent upon winning depends primarily upon the public's interest in the sport. In most major institutions, football and basketball are the only sports where the public is concerned about won-lost records, but there are universities where track, baseball, or one of the other sports has managed to attract enough public interest for a real concern to be expressed about the team's wins or losses.

Success criteria applied to coaches at the university level are the same as those applied at the small colleges. While some small college coaches whose teams lose consistently may be beloved by students, alumni, and the public for their gentle, sympathetic, and patient methods, those coaches are a rarity. The small college coach may not be blatantly fired because his teams are not winners; instead various groups (students, alumni, etc.) frequently conspire to put subtle pressures on the coach to force his resignation.

Role Conflict in College Coaching

One important career contingency with which the collegiate coach is inevitably confronted is role expectations, which are, or seem to be, incompatible; that is, he experiences role conflict. On the one hand, he is expected to be an educator, primarily concerned with the personal-social growth of his athletes; on the other hand, his professional success, as judged by his peers and others, and indeed his job security are dependent upon the production of winning teams. There is no admiration for losing coaches in collegiate sports, even if they are excellent educators.

For most of the history of intercollegiate athletics the programs have been justified on the basis that they are educational. College authorities, coaches, alumni, and even public figures have extolled the educational virtues of intercollegiate sports (Scott, 1951; Lewis, 1969). The notion that intercollegiate athletics is educational implies that the participants learn valuable lessons in character development and such traits as honesty, sportsmanship, leadership, self-discipline, courage, etc., are developed for use in diffuse roles which they play now and will play in the future. It also implies that the athletic program is an integral part of the college or university, and that its goals are compatible with the mission and functions of the institution.

While the publicly expressed function of athletic coaches is one of educators who use sport as a means for developing favorable personal-social characteristics in the athletes, coaches have rarely been rewarded for this function. Instead collegiate coaches have almost universally been rewarded for a single accomplishment: winning. Actual teaching ability or ability to transmit character values through coaching has not been systematically rewarded by career advancement. Career advancement has depended entirely upon the production of winning teams; coaches are regularly dismissed if their teams are losers. Duthie (1971: 9–10) put it nicely as follows.

Society quickly ensures that a coach is programmed to win for he is rewarded for winning and receives the negative reinforcement of criticism when the team loses. If the latter occurs too frequently, the process demands a new coach.

It is clear that unlike workers in other fields in which prestige is a mixture of various overt and informal criteria, the collegiate coach has a rather clearly defined criterion applied for career success—winning. Although collegiate athletics are invariably justified for their contribution to education, they nevertheless quite clearly are more easily judged by won-lost results. Such hard to operationalize and measure objectives as "character development" are just not given much consideration in evaluating coaches. As a former coach at Southern Methodist University said: "In pro football, it's obvious that you must win. In college football there's sometimes talk of other goals, but when you get right down to it that's what really matters there, too" (Bridges, 1969: 8).

The approval of others is desired by coaches, just as it is by most people, so coaches seek to maintain self-approval and gain the approval of others by striving to increase the visible signs of success. Moore (1969: 881) noted: "Indifference to the opinions of peers is exceptional and plainly pathological." Thorstein Veblen put it this way: "Only individuals with an aberrant temperament can in the long run retain their self-esteem in the face of the disesteem of their fellows . . ." (1953: 38–39). We should not be surprised, then, when we read that coaches frequently violate ethical codes and conference and national intercollegiate association policies in their quest to develop winning teams.

The employment of college athletic coaches with faculty status has rarely afforded the same job security protections which are granted to other faculty. Academic status and appointment to membership in a faculty have not protected a coach's tenure when his teams ceased to win. Probably in no other aspect of American academic life is the choosing and firing of faculty so often affected by the decisions of persons not intimately connected with the administration of the institution. Although higher education has insisted upon the educational outcome of intercollegiate athletics for the past 70 years, the practice of hiring and firing coaches on the basis of won-lost records has been accepted with little question, and an annual rite in college sports is the firing of coaches whose teams lost more games than they won.

It is evident that role conflict is abundantly present in collegiate coaching. Social expectations justify the sports programs on one basis but the directors of these programs, the coaches, are clearly evaluated upon an entirely different basis. Perhaps no other aspect of higher education is more hypocritical.

REFERENCES

Adorno, T. W., E. Frenkel-Brunswik, D. J. Levenson, and R. N. Sanford
1950   *The Authoritarian Personality*. New York: Harper and Brothers.

Albaugh, G. R.
1972   "The Influence of Ressentience as Identified in College Basketball Coaches." *75th Proceedings of the National College Physical Education Association for Men*. 60–68.

Allport, G. W., P. E. Vernon, and G. Lindzey
1960   *Manual: Study of Values*. Boston: Houghton Mifflin.

Andrud, W. E.
1970   "The Personality of High School, College, and Professional Football Coaches as Measured by the Guilford-Zimmerman Temperament Survey." Master's thesis, University of North Dakota.

Arms, O. R.
1965   "The Professional Status of the High School Coach in Arkansas." Master's thesis, University of Arkansas.

Babbit, J.
1908   "Present Condition of Gymnastics and Athletics in American Colleges," *American Physical Education Review*, **8**: 280–283.

Becker, H. S., B. Geer, E. C. Hughes, and A. Strauss
1961   *Boys in White: Student Culture in Medical School*. Chicago: University of Chicago Press.

Bennett, B. L.
1948   "Contributions of Dr. Sargent to Physical Education," *Research Quarterly*, **19**: 77–92.

Bennett, H.
1951   *We Never Called Him Harry*. New York: Gold Medal Books, Fawcett Publications.

Berry, E.
1920   "Problems in the Recruiting of Teachers in Physical Education," *American Physical Education Review*, **25**: 233–239.

Blau, P. M., and O. D. Duncan
1967   *The American Occupational Structure*. New York: John Wiley.

Bolton, W. R.
1956   "The Personal, Educational, and Professional Background and Experiences Which Characterize Head Football Coaches in Selected High Schools of Pennsylvania." Doctoral dissertation, Pennsylvania State University.

Bowen, W. P.
1909   "The Evolution of Athletic Evils." *American Physical Education Review*, **14**: 151–156.

Bridges, J.
1969   Quoted in scorecard section of *Sports Illustrated*, **30**: 8, January, 6.

Burlingame, M.
1972   "Socialization Constructs and the Teaching of Teachers." *Quest,* **18**: 41–56.

Caplow, T.
1954   *Sociology of Work.* Minneapolis: University of Minneapolis Press.

Caplow, T., and R. J. McGee
1958   *The Academic Marketplace.* New York: Basic Books.

Carlson, R. O.
1951   "Variations and Myth in the Social Status of Teachers." *The Journal of Educational Sociology,* **35**: 104–18.

Carter, J. E. L., and M. L. Rendle
1965   *The Physiques of Royal New Zealand Air Force Men.* Report to the Royal New Zealand Air Force, Air Department, Wellington, New Zealand.

Carter, J. E. L., J. Stepnicka, and J. P. Clarys
1973   "Somatotypes of Male Physical Education Majors in Four Countries." *Research Quarterly,* **44**: 361–371.

Christie, R., and F. L. Geis
1970   *Studies in Machiavellianism.* New York: Academic Press.

Clarke, H. H.
1935   "A Survey of the Requirements for the Master's Degrees in Physical Education." In *A Report from Professional Preparation,* Jay B. Nash (ed.). New York: A. S. Barnes.

Coffman, L.
1911   *The Social Composition of the Teaching Population.* Contributions to Education No. 41, Teachers College, Columbia University.

Cohane, T.
1951   *The Yale Football Story.* New York: G. P. Putnam's Sons.

Damon, A., and R. A. McFarland
1955   "The Physique of Bus and Truck Drivers; With a Review of Occupational Anthropology." *American Journal of Physical Anthropology,* **13**: 711–42.

Danzig, A.
1956   *The History of American Football.* Englewood Cliffs: Prentice-Hall.

DeGroat, H. S.
1936   "A Study Pertaining to the Athletic Directorship of Intercollegiate Athletics." *Research Quarterly,* **7** (October): 14–35.

Donnelly, R.
1963   "Summary of Recent Trends in Organizational Structure of College Physical Education Programs for Men." Minneapolis, Minnesota: The University of Minnesota (mimeographed).

Duthie, J. H.
1971   "Sport: A Component of the Counter-Culture." Paper presented at the 66th annual convention of the American Sociological Association, Denver, Colorado.

Forbes, C. A.
1929   *Greek Physical Education.* New York: The Century Company.

Friedenberg, E., C. Nordstrom, and H. Gold
1961   *Society's Children: A Study of Ressentiment in Secondary Schools.* New York: Random House.

Gagen, J. J.
1971   "Risk-taking within Football Situations of Selected Football Coaches." Master's thesis, Kent State University.

Geis, F. L.
1968   "Machiavellianism in a Semi-real World," *Proceedings of the 76th Annual Convention of the American Psychological Association,* **3**: 407–408.

Ginzberg, E., S. Ginzberg, S. Axelrad, and J. L. Herma
1951   *Occupational Choice: An Approach to a General Theory.* New York: Columbia University Press.

Goode, W. J.
1957   "Community Within a Community: The Professions." *American Sociological Review,* **22**: 194–200.

Grusky, O.
1963   "The Effects of Formal Structure on Managerial Recruitment: A Study of Baseball Organization." *Sociometry,* **26**: 345–353.

Gustad, J. W.
1959   "They March to a Different Drummer: Another Look at College Teachers." *The Educational Record,* **40**: 204–211.

Hargens, L. L., and W. O. Hagstrom
1967   "Sponsored and Contest Mobility of American Academic Scientists." *Sociology of Education,* **4**: 24–38.

Harris, H. A.
1964   *Greek Athletes and Athletics.* London: Hutchinson Company.

Hartwell, E.
1905   "On Physical Training." Report of the Commissioner of Education for 1903, Washington, D.C.: Government Printing Office. 721–757.

Havel, R. C.
1951   "The Professional Status of Head Coaches of Athletics in Colleges and Universities." Doctoral dissertation, Teachers College, Columbia University.

Harvey, R. R.
1963   "An Evaluation of the Practices of Selected Ethically Questionable Actions by College Athletic Coaches." Doctoral dissertation, Indiana University.

Healy, W. A.
1953   "Administrative Practices in Competitive Athletics in Midwestern Colleges." *Research Quarterly,* **24**: 295–303.

Hendry, L. B.
1968   "The Assessment of Personality Traits in the Coach-Swimmer Relation-
         ship, and a Preliminary examination of the 'Father-Figure' Stereotype."
         Research Quarterly, **39**: 543–551.
1969   "A Personality Study of Highly Successful and 'Ideal' Swimming Coaches."
         Research Quarterly, **40**: 299–305.
1972*a* "The Coaching Stereotype." In *Readings in Sports Psychology*, H. T. A.
         Whiting (ed.). London: Kimpton.
1972*b* "Coaches Personality and Social Orientation." *Proceedings of the Fourth
         Canadian Psycho-Motor Learning and Sport Psychology Symposium*, Ot-
         tawa, Canada.

Hitchcock, E. W.
1886   *Twenty-Fifth Annual Report of the Professor of Hygiene to the Board of
         Trustees of Amherst College.* June 29.

Holland, J. L.
1959   "A Theory of Vocational Choice." *Journal of Counseling Psychology*, **6**:
         35–45.

Jeffreys, N. V. C.
1962   *Personal Values in the Modern World.* New York: Pelican Books.

Kenyon, G. S.
1965   "Certain Psychosocial and Cultural Characteristics Unique to Prospective
         Teachers of Physical Education." *Research Quarterly*, **36**: 105–112.
1968   *Values Held for Physical Activity by Selected Urban Secondary School
         Students in Canada, Australia, England, and the United States.* Washing-
         ton, D.C.: United States Office of Education.

Kinloch, G. C.
1969   "Sponsored and Contest Mobility among College Graduates: Measure-
         ment of Relative Openness of a Social Structure." *Sociology of Education*,
         42: 350–367.

Kinloch, G. C., and R. Perrucci
1969   "Social Origins, Academic Achievement and Mobility Patterns: Sponsored
         and Contest Mobility among College Graduates." *Social Forces*, **48**: 36–45.

Kluckhohn, C.
1951   "Values and Value Orientations in the Theory of Action." In *Toward a
         General Theory of Action*, T. Parsons and E. A. Shils (eds.). Cambridge:
         Harvard University Press.

Kreuter, M.
1971   "Study of Ressentient Attitudes as Measured in Selected Sixth Grade
         Teachers." Doctoral dissertation, University of Utah.

Kreuter, M., and M. Parsons
1971   "Continued Research on Ressentient Attitudes." Faculty Research Grant,
         University of Utah.

Kroll, W.
1970   "Personality Assessment of Athletes." In *Psychology of Motor Learning*, L. E. Smith (ed.). Chicago: The Athletic Institute.

Kunkel, B. W.
1938   "A Survey of College Faculties." *AAUP Bulletin*, **24**: 249–262.

LaGrand, L. E.
1970   "A Semantic Differential Analysis of the Behavioral Characteristics of Athletic Coaches as Reported by Athletes." Doctoral dissertation, Florida State University.

Lauffer, R. A.
1970   "Stated Sportsmanship Attitudes of Selected College and University Coaches and Faculty Members." Doctoral dissertation, University of Maryland.

Lazarsfeld, P. F., and W. Thielens, Jr.
1958   *The Academic Mind.* Glencoe, Ill.: The Free Press.

Lewis, G. M.
1969   "Adoption of the Sports Program, 1906–39: The Role of Accommodation in the Transformation of Physical Education." *Quest*, **12**: 34–36.

Lipset, S. M., and E. C. Ladd
1972   "The Politics of American Sociologists." *American Journal of Sociology*, **78**: 67–104.

Lipset, S. M., M. A. Trow, and E. C. Ladd
(n.d.)   *Faculty Opinion Survey.* Carnegie Commission on Higher Education.

Locke, L.
1962   "Performance of Administration Oriented Educators on Selected Psychological Tests." *Research Quarterly*, **33**: 418–429.

Longmuir, G. E.
1972   "Perceived and Actual Dogmatism in High School Athletes and Coaches: Relationships and Some Consequences." Doctoral dissertation, University of New Mexico.

Loomis, L. R. (ed.)
1942   *The Illiad of Homer*, Roslyn, New York: Walter J. Black, Inc.

Lowman, G.
1907   "The Regulation and Control of Competitive Sports in Secondary Schools of the United States." *American Physical Education Review*, **12**: 307–323.

Loy, J. W.
1907   "Where the Action Is! A Consideration of Centrality in Sport Situations." In *Proceedings, 2nd Canadian Psychomotor Learning and Sports Psychology Symposium*, R. H. Wilberg (ed.). University of Windsor.

Loy, J. W., and G. H. Sage
1972   "Social Origins, Academic Achievement, Athletic Achievement, and Career Mobility Patterns of College Coaches." Paper presented at the 67th annual meeting of the American Sociological Association, New Orleans, Louisiana.

1973 "Organizational Prestige and Coaching Career Patterns." Paper presented at the 36th annual meeting of the Southern Sociological Society, Atlanta, Georgia.

Maltozo, M. G., Jr.
1965 "An Analysis of the Professional Preparation of Interscholastic Coaches in Selected Sports." Doctoral Dissertation, Springfield College.

Marshall, S. J.
1969 "The Organizational Relationship between Physical Education and Intercollegiate Athletics in American Colleges and Universities." Doctoral dissertation, Springfield College.

McGee, H.
1955 "Measurement of Authoritarianism and Its Relation to Teacher's Classroom Behavior." *Genet. Psychol. Monogr.*, **52**: 89–146.

Merton, R. K.
1957a *Social Theory and Social Structure*. Glencoe, Ill.: The Free Press.

Merton, R. K., G. Reader, and P. L. Kendall (eds.)
1957 *The Student Physician*. Cambridge: Harvard Univerity Press.

Meyer, D. W.
1972 "A Comparison of Perceptions of University Basketball Coaches." Doctoral dissertation. University of Utah.

Moffett, M.
1929 *The Social Background and Activities of Teachers College Students*. New York: Bureau of Publications. Teachers College, Columbia University.

Moore, W. E.
1969 "Occupational Socialization." In *Handbook of Socialization Theory and Research*, D. A. Goslin (ed.). Chicago: Rand McNally Company.
1970 *The Professions: Roles and Rules*. New York: Russell Sage Foundation.

Morris, C. N.
1957 "Career Patterns of Teachers." In *The Teacher's Role in American Society*, L. J. Stiles (ed.). New York: Harper.

Morris, R. T., and R. J. Murphy
1959 "The Situs Dimension in Occupational Structure." *American Sociological Review*, **24**: 231–239.

Mudra, D. E.
1965 "A Critical Analysis of Football Coaching Practices in Light of a Selected Group of Learning Principles." Doctoral dissertation, University of Northern Colorado.

Nelson, D.
1970 Quoted in *The Oregonian*. Sports Section. December 28.

Nelson, E. A.
1970 "Value Patterns of Physical Educators in Colleges and Universities of the United States." Doctoral dissertation, University of Minnesota.

O'Dowd, D. D., and D. O. Beardslee
1961 "The Image of the College Professor." *AAUP Bulletin*, **41**: 216–221.

Ogilvie, B.
1971   Quoted from J. Jares. "We Have a Neurotic in the Backfield, Doctor."
        Sports Illustrated, **34**: 30–34.

Ogilvie, B. C., and T. A. Tutko
1966   *Problem Athletes and How to Handle Them*. London: Pelham Books.
1970   "Self-perception as Compared with Measured Personality of Selected Male
        Physical Educators." In *Contemporary Psychology of Sport*, G. S. Kenyon
        (ed.). Chicago: The Athletic Institute.

Pavalko, R. M. (ed.)
1968   *Sociology of Education*. Itasca, Illinois: F. E. Peacock.

Pavalko, R. M.
1971   *Sociology of Occupations and Professions*. Itasca, Illinois: F. E. Peacock.

Pollard, J. E.
1959   *Ohio State Athletics 1879–1959*. Ohio State University Athletic Depart-
        ment.

Pooley, J. C.
1970   "The Professional Socialization of Physical Education Students in the
        United States and England." Doctoral dissertation, University of Wiscon-
        sin.

Pritchard, G. M.
1933   *The Administration of Physical Education and Athletics in Institutions of
        Higher Education*. Cape Girardeau, Missouri: State Teachers College.

Raycroft, J. E.
1941   "History and Development of Student Health Programs in Colleges and
        Universities." *The Journal-Lancet* (September).

Reich, C. A.
1970   *The Greening of America*. New York: Bantam Books.

Reiss, A. J., Jr.
1961   *Occupation and Social Status*. New York: The Free Press.

Richardson, H. D.
1967   "Coaching Tenure and Its Relationship to Sportsmanship." Doctoral dis-
        sertation, University of Utah.

Richey, R., and W. Fox
1948   "An Analysis of Various Factors Associated with the Selection of Teach-
        ing as a Vocation." *Bulletin of the School of Education*, Indiana Univer-
        sity, Division of Research and Field Services (May).

Robinson, R. S.
1955   *Sources for the History of Greek Athletics*. Cincinnati, Ohio: Author.

Rokeach, M.
1960   *The Open and Closed Mind*. New York: Basic Books.

Roscoe, J. T.
1965   "The Construction and Application of the Polyphasic Values Inventory."
        Doctoral dissertation, University of Northern Colorado.

Rosenberg, M.
1957   *Occupations and Values.* Glencoe, Ill.: The Free Press.

Rushall, B. S.
1970   "An Evaluation of the Relationship between Personality and Physical Performance Categories." In *Contemporary Psychology of Sport,* G. S. Kenyon (ed.). Chicago: The Athletic Institute.

Sage, G. H.
1963   "A History of Physical Education at Pomona College (1880–1960)." Doctoral dissertation, University of California, Los Angeles.

1972a   "Machiavellianism among College and High School Coaches." *75th Proceedings of the National College Physical Education Association for Men.* 45–60.

1972b   "Value Orientations of American College Coaches Compared to Male College Students and Businessmen." *75th Proceedings, National College Physical Education Association for Men.* 174–186.

1973a   "The Coach as Management: Organizational Leadership in American Sport." *Quest,* **19**: 35–40.

1973b   "An Assessment of Personality Profiles between and within Intercollegiate Athletes from Eight Different Sports." *Sportwissenschaft,* **2** (Jahrgang): 408–415.

1973c   "Occupational Socialization and Value Orientation of Athletic Coaches." *Research Quarterly,* **44**: 269–277.

(n.d.) "Most Admired Person in American Life by College Coaches." Unpublished material, University of Northern Colorado.

Sage, G. H., and J. W. Loy
1973   "Career Mobility Patterns of College Coaches: Geographical Implications of Coaching." Paper presented at the 69th annual convention of the Association of American Geographers, Atlanta, Georgia.

Sargent, D. A.
1890   "The System of Physical Training at the Hemenway Gymnasium." *Physical Training: A Full Report of the Papers of the Conference Held in Boston in November 1889.* Boston: Press of George H. Ellis.

Savage, C. W.
1915   "The Professional Versus the Educational in College Athletics." *American Physical Education Review,* **20**: 187–194.

Savage, H. J.
1929   *American College Athletics.* New York: Carnegie Foundation, Bulletin 23.

Savage, W. L.
1899   "What Should be Physical Standards to Guide the Physical Director in Passing Candidates for Athletic Teams?" Paper presented at the annual meeting of the Society of College Gymnasium Directors. December 30.

Scott, H. A.
1929   *A Personnel Study of Directors of Physical Education for Men in College and Universities.* New York: Teachers College, Columbia University.

1951   *Competitive Sports in Schools and Colleges.* New York: Harper.

Scott, J.
1969   *Athletics for Athletes.* Hayward, California: Quality Printing Service.
1971   *The Athletic Revolution.* New York: The Free Press.

Scott, W. A.
1965   *Values and Organizations.* Chicago: Rand McNally.

Shils, E. A.
1954   "Authoritarianism 'Right' and 'Left'." In *Studies in the Scope and Method of the Authoritarian Personality,* R. Christie and M. Jahoda (eds.). New York: The Free Press.

Slater, P.
1970   *The Pursuit of Loneliness.* Boston: Beacon Press.

Snyder, E. E.
1971   "Athletic Dressing Room Slogans as Folklore: A Means of Socialization." Paper presented at the 66th annual meeting of the American Sociological Association, Denver, Colorado.
1972   "High School Athletes and Their Coaches: Educational Plans and Advice." *Sociology of Education,* **45**: 313–325.

Stecklein, J. S., and R. E. Eckert
1958   *An Exploratory Study of Factors Influencing the Choice of College Teaching as a Career.* Cooperative research program, United States Office of Education, Washington, D.C.

Super, D. E.
1957   *The Psychology of Careers.* New York: Harper.

Swartz, J. L.
1973   "Analysis of Leadership Styles of College Level Head Football Coaches from Five Midwestern States." Doctoral dissertation, University of Northern Colorado.

Taylor, F. W.
1911   *The Principles of Scientific Management.* New York: Harper.

Turner, R. H.
1960   "Sponsored and Contest Mobility in the School System." *American Sociological Review,* **25**: 855–867.
1964   *The Social Context of Ambition.* San Francisco: Chandler.

Tutko, T. A., and J. W. Richards
1971   *Psychology of Coaching.* Boston: Allyn and Bacon.

Underwood, J.
1969   "The Desperate Coach." *Sports Illustrated,* **31**: 66–76. August 25.

Van Wyck, C. B.
1942   "The Harvard Summer School of Physical Education 1887–1932." *Research Quarterly,* **13**: 403–431.

Veblen, T.
1953   *The Theory of the Leisure Class.* New York: Mentor Books.

Wallace, S. E.
1966 "Reference Group Behavior in Occupational Role Socialization." *Sociological Quarterly*, **7**: 366–372.

Wattenberg, W. et al.
1957 "Social Origins of Teachers—A Northern Industrial City." In *The Teacher's Role in American Society*, L. J. Stiles (ed.). New York: Harper.

Western, J. S., and D. S. Anderson
1968 "Education and Professional Socialization." *The Australian and New Zealand Journal of Sociology*, **4**: 91–106.

Whitney, F. L.
1927 "The Social and Economic Background of Teachers College and University Students." *Education*, **47**: 449–456.

Wilcox, G. W.
1969 "An Analysis of the Professional Preparation of College Head Football Coaches in the Northeast." Master's thesis, Springfield College.

Woodbury, D. S.
1966 "The Administrative Relationships between Athletics and Physical Education in Selected American Universities." Doctoral dissertation, University of Utah.

Zeigler, E. F.
1950 "A History of Professional Preparation for Physical Education in the United States (1861–1948)." Doctoral dissertation, Yale University.

Chapter 10
Career Patterns and Career Contingencies of Professional Baseball Players: An Occupational Analysis

Rudolf K. Haerle, Jr.
Department of Sociology
Middlebury College
(Middlebury, Vermont)

Rudolf K. Haerle, Jr.

Birth Place: Indianapolis, Indiana

Age: 43

Birth Order: One older brother

Formal Education:

A.B., Dartmouth College, New Hampshire	1953
M.A., University of Chicago	1962
Ph.D., University of Chicago	1965

Present Position:

Associate Professor of Sociology, Department of Sociology-Anthropology, Middlebury College, Vermont. (Former Chairman of the Department at Middlebury, 1967–74.)

Professional Responsibilities:

Teaching courses in Introductory Sociology; Sociological Theory; Research Methods; Work, Leisure, and Sport; American Community Studies. Limited involvement in the American Studies Program.

Scholarly Interests:

Sociology of sports, sociology of work (occupations and professions, work careers), interfaith marriages.

Professional Accomplishments:

"Church Attendance Patterns Among Intermarried Catholics: A Panel Study." *Sociological Analysis* 30 (Winter, 1969).

"The Athlete as Moral Leader: Heroes, Success Themes and Basic Cultural Values in Selected Baseball Autobiographies, 1900–1970." *Journal of Popular Culture* (forthcoming).

Hobbies:

Reading (especially political novels and novels about the professions); rabid baseball fan and collector of baseball memorabilia (gum and cigarette cards, autographs, record guides, and assorted "junk").

Sport Activities:

Participant: skiing, tennis, squash.

Spectator: basketball, baseball.

Able member of the faculty basketball team in the students' intramural league at the age of 40!

Recent Books Read:

Studs Terkel	*Working*
New York Times	*White House Transcripts*
Tom Wicker	*Facing the Lions*
Edward Shorter (ed.)	*Work and Community in the West*
Robert A. Nisbet	*The Sociology of Emile Durkheim*

INTRODUCTION

Professional sports, although representing a very small segment of the labor force,[1] have traditionally had a disproportionately strong impact on the general population. Mass media coverage alone runs into several "prime time" hours each week. More specifically, professional baseball is said to mirror and reinforce some basic American values like individualism and competition (Voigt, 1971); to provide folk heroes and teams for vicarious, yet meaningful, identification (Klapp, 1969; Andreano, 1965); and, as a microcosm of the economy, illustrating all the key features of supply and demand, labor-management problems, cartel behavior, and the like (Gregory, 1956; Andreano, 1965; Weistart, 1973). In short, an analysis of professional sport as an occupation can be highly instructive.

The occupation of professional baseball player shares much in common with other occupations. There are recruitment patterns and socialization to work expectations, technical and social skills, rules of appropriate conduct, authority and colleague relationships and the like. At the same time, the baseball player's job exhibits some features which, when taken in combination, result in a rather unique set of organizational values and demands in conflict with personal motivations and economic desires. By comparative contrast, then, an analysis of the work situation of the baseball player will tell us much about the meaning of work in our society, the effect of specific

I wish to acknowledge the helpful suggestions of Everett C. Hughes, Charles H. Page, David Q. Voigt, Cliff Kachline, and the editors of this book, Donald Ball and John Loy. I did not accept all of their advice, thus I am totally responsible for whatever shortcomings are contained in this paper. Middlebury College supported this research through a faculty leave and a grant from the Faculty Research Fund. My wife, Helen G. Haerle, provided invaluable computer assistance, and Mrs. Susan Ross Seward helped with earlier drafts. A special thanks goes to Mrs. JoAnne Lessard, who showed considerable patience while completing several drafts of this manuscript.

461

contextual features on work performance, and the factors involved in career contingencies.

A suitable subtitle for this chapter could be "Member of the team, yet uniquely alone," [2] for it conveys some of the basic features of professional baseball which make it an exceptional occupation. The player, as a member of a team, finds great emphasis placed on teamwork and all that this implies in terms of subordinating himself to the larger unit. At the same time, his individual achievement is a very public event and his performance records are individually calculated and also open to public scrutiny as in almost no other type of occupation. In the specific moment of the game where a special activity is required—a smooth, successful double play or a base hit to break up a tie game—the player is "uniquely alone," with all eyes glued on him to see how he, as an individual, performs under pressure. The close juxtaposition of team responsibilities and individualistic performance illustrates one dominant theme in this chapter. The player, while attempting to resolve this dilemma of conflicting expectations, is not operating in a social vacuum. He is enmeshed in a set of structural relationships, both internal and external, which further complicate his attempts to perform his occupation at maximum efficiency.

Yet there are other aspects of the professional athlete's career which are equally interesting and sociologically informative. For example, consideration must be given to the process by which an individual is recruited into playing major league baseball and the predispositional factors that lead to success in this endeavor. Additionally, since the average athlete is "forced" to retire at a relatively young age, we must investigate what happens to him at the other end of the active playing career. The question of whether an athletic career facilitates later occupational mobility is an important one.

It is the purpose of this chapter to describe and evaluate some of the organizational or structural constraints or alternatives which operate in the occupational environment of the professional major league baseball player. Essentially we shall attempt to give general answers to the following kinds of questions which have served as guides in this analysis. What background factors are associated with recruitment and baseball success? What is the nature of the work situation of the professional baseball player? What kinds of conflicting pressures and expectations are brought to bear? To what degree and in what manner does the organizational structure of professional baseball inhibit or facilitate successful role performance? What types of work does the former player find available upon retirement? What problems of adjustment, if any, does he experience? Does an active career in professional baseball serve as a stepping-stone to later occupational mobility?

CONCEPTUAL FOCUS [3] AND THE NATURE OF AVAILABLE DATA

For the social scientist, all social phenomena are viewed as complex and multi-faceted. Faced with an overwhelming quantity of potential data, the sociologist must make choices concerning the themes and topics upon which he will focus. In doing so, he will rely on some basic concepts as sensitizing tools for bringing some order, focus, and clarity to the mass of information available for analysis. It is our purpose in this section to introduce some of the key concepts to be employed throughout the remaining sections of the chapter.

Essentially, the sociologist is interested in the *structure* and *process* of social life. By the concept of "social structure," we mean to refer to those recurrent patterns of interaction between people that result in an emergent social organization, such that human behavior becomes reasonably predictable. Individuals become located in social space as they occupy such "status positions" as father, husband, machinist, baseball player, and the like. Their contacts with others are mediated through the learning and playing out of the "roles" which are associated with the various status positions occupied.

In this context, the notion of "process" is meant to convey the fact that social organization is never static and unchanging—that structured patterns of interaction are in a constant state of change and modification. As a consequence, since one's social identity is conceived as the cumulative result of myriads of personal interactions, the individual actor's conception of "self" will tend to be in a constant state of flux, a constant process of becoming.

Fortunately, for the study of an occupation, these important dimensions of structure and process are captured in the concepts of "career" and "career contingencies." Everett C. Hughes (1971: 295) sketches some of the key elements of "the career":

> Career, in the most generic sense, refers to the fate of a man running his life cycle in a particular society at a particular time. . . .

> Occupations vary in their strength as named reference-groups, as the basis for full and lasting self-identification and firm status. They also vary in their demand for full and lasting commitment and the age and life-phase at which one must decide to enter training for them. Some occupations are more visible to young people than are others, and effective visibility varies also by class and other social circumstances. The inner workings of the best known cannot be seen by outsiders. . . . The career includes not only the processes and sequences of learning the techniques of the occupation but also the progressive perception of the

whole system and of possible places in it and the accompanying changes in conceptions of the work and of one's self in relation to it.*

Generally, occupational career patterns are seen as rather orderly, with the individual progressing in a predictable manner through a sequence of steps or stages. Some (Wilensky, 1960) have challenged the degree of orderliness for individual careers. Nonetheless, it is clear that each individual must make crucial decisions, at what Hughes (1971: 124) calls "turning points"—important decisions about one's occupational future with both known and unknown implications. The existence of these "career contingencies" as process elements will allow us to focus on the significance of specific structural consequences.

Thus, the concepts of career and career contingency are particularly pertinent to our analysis of the baseball player's occupational history. For purposes of clarity and simplicity, we shall divide the player's career into three major phases: (1) the prebaseball period, where one considers the importance of background factors, the learning of skills, and the recruitment process; (2) the period of active play, during which greater attention will be given to the structural and interpersonal characteristics of the job; and finally (3) the postbaseball, second-career stage, where we shall consider the types and success of postplaying adjustment to the world of work. The transition from one phase to the next generally involves momentous contingency-type decisions which we shall attempt to assess.

Before moving on to our discussion and analysis, a brief word should be said about the nature of the data available in this study. Ball (1975) has summarized the state of the field of the sociology of sport with respect to methods and sources. Drawing on a variety of sources and a personal history as a lifetime baseball fan, we shall present our discussion as a combination of qualitative and quantitative approaches.

The data and information on professional sports are in large supply. With regard to qualitative types of information, use can be made of the rich sociological potential of such works as sports histories by sports writers and personal autobiographies of the players themselves. Several social scientists (Gregory, 1956; Andreano, 1965; Rottenberg, 1960; Voigt, 1966, 1970; Seymour, 1960, 1971; Charnofsky, 1968; Grusky, 1963a, 1963b; Blalock, 1962; Rosenblatt, 1967; and Loy and McElvogue, 1970) have also made significant and useful contributions. The insights from these sources will be utilized.

In a more quantitative vein, professional sports are noted for their plethora of figures and statistics which are amenable to various kinds of

---

* Everett C. Hughes, *The Sociological Eye: Selected Papers.* (Chicago: Aldine-Atherton, 1971), p. 295. Reprinted by permission.

analyses. We intend to take advantage of the accessibility of basic performance records. In addition, we are fortunate to have available survey data from a study of 335 retired baseball players.[4] Data were gathered on several phases of the occupational career. Because career data of this type fall neatly into a causal model, we shall use a statistical technique known as path analysis.[5] Recently, Kenyon (1970) has called for its application in the sociology of sport. In the simplest of terms, this approach enables us to deal with matters of cause and effect by specifying a set of causal relationships among a number of variables in a system. The fact that the results of this procedure can be clearly represented graphically in the creation of a "path diagram" (illustrated below) is a strong aid in communicating the underlying theory involved as well as the results of the investigation.

In short, our analysis will attempt a blend of both quantitative and qualitative approaches.

CAREER STAGES AND CONTINGENCIES

The First Phase of Career: Background Factors in the Prebaseball Period

The process by which one gets into a particular line of work and becomes a success or failure at it is not a random thing. All sorts of background characteristics of the individual enter into the selection of jobs and influence the final outcome (Taylor, 1968; Hall, 1969; Gross, 1958). For example, age, sex, social class, education, geographic location, and family background are often instrumental in initial occupational choices. Individuals located at different points in the social structure will find that they have before them a dissimilar set of opportunities. For example, the son of a physician will have more options available than the son of a garbage collector.

Another critical factor has to do with the amount and type of training required for the job. Some occupations are clearly defined and have definite training programs, while other jobs entail a less-structured entry procedure. The preprofessional training which is necessary to become a lawyer is highly organized and structured. By contrast, the aspirant to professional athletics faces a series of ill-defined problems and contingencies. Officially, there are no schools or special programs that are designed to train the future professional athlete in the same way that law school prepares the future lawyer.

In baseball, there is a series of age-graded, recreational leagues that provide rudimentary instruction and an opportunity for competitive play. For example, the Babe Ruth League operates two divisions: 13 to 15 and 16 to 18 years of age. These divisions are in turn fed by programs that service boys the age of 12 and younger. The uneasy relationship between these leagues and professional baseball was recently illustrated when a report indicated that there was a rather substantial "dropout rate" between the "12 and under" leagues and those run by the Babe Ruth organization (Spink, 1974: 10). In the past, four out of five boys would move from the 12-year-old ranks to the 13 to 15 years of age Babe Ruth Leagues. Today, only half that number continue in these amateur baseball programs.

> That should alarm any baseball man—that half the baseball-playing youngsters quit the game at this formative stage of their lives. . . .

> The major leagues occupy the top floor of the baseball structure. But if the foundation, as represented by boys' baseball, continues to show signs of deterioration, then every level from high school to college to professional baseball will begin to feel it.*

Throughout one's school career, participation in athletics is considered a part of the overall educational program. Learning the game, character development, fun, and recreation are among the intended purposes of the athletic program. But training for a professional career in athletics is not an explicit part of interscholastic and intercollegiate competition.[6] Essentially, it is a matter of "amateur standing" and playing for the pure love of the game. No thought or expectation of financial gain is supposed to enter the mind of the participant. The problem faced by the potential professional athlete is to overcome the "amateur orientation" which seeks to prevent him from receiving the necessary grounding in his chosen profession and which may make it difficult for him to develop a conception of himself as an aspirant to a legitimate occupation. These dilemmas point up the seriousness and difficulty faced by the young man who desires a career in professional sports.

Potential insight into the importance of personality formation at this stage is offered by the work of La Place (1954). In a study of success in baseball, La Place compared 49 major league players with those ($N = 64$) who never progressed beyond the lowest minor league teams—thus, essentially the "successes" and "failures" within professional baseball. He found no significant differences between these two groups in terms of physical potential or skill possession. Rather, the crucial differences were located in the psychological makeup of the two groups of athletes, as measured by the MMPI. Those who were successful were characterized by more dedication, initiative and self-discipline and the ability to get along well with other people. Apparently those with a strong sense of self and

---

* C. C. Johnson Spink, "Baseball Depends on Boys." *The Sporting News*, 1974, **177**: 10. Reprinted by permission.

purpose were better equipped to the move up the competitive ladder of the professional baseball structure.

Moving beyond these general observations to our empirical data on 335 former major leaguers, it is interesting and instructive to focus on the facts about their prebaseball occupational experience and the role played by formal education. Of the 312 respondents for whom we have information, about 22 percent did not have any sort of part-time work while in school and these men also were least likely to obtain a high degree of fame in baseball.[7] Of those who did have part-time work while in school, the ones who were engaged in farming or sports-related jobs had the greatest success in their later baseball careers. The significance of postschool, full-time work (characteristic of roughly one-third of our respondents) was negligible.

In an earlier exploratory study of our sample (Haerle, 1971), it was found that almost no influence on future baseball performance was exerted by such traditional variables as region of origin, size of the city of birth or father's status (as measured by both father's occupation and education).

However, the level of education which one received and the importance of educational achievement probably constituted one of the most, if not the most, important contingency during the prework phase of one's career. For example, the ages at which our respondents signed their professional contracts bore little relation to their future performance level as major leaguers. Yet the level of education achieved by our respondents was negatively associated with their level of baseball performance. Those with more education were significantly less apt to have outstanding baseball records ($r = -0.15$, $p = <0.01$).[8] Interestingly, the level of education had a very strong effect on the age at which these future players signed their professional contracts ($r = 0.26$, $p = <0.01$). Among those with only an elementary education, almost two-thirds signed their contracts between the ages of 19 through 22. Presumably they were employed in some other line of work and were perhaps playing baseball in semipro or industrial leagues. About half of the men who ended their education at the high school level signed on at the age of 18 or younger. Obviously, these men were moving directly into professional baseball upon completion of their formal education. Most of the others made their professional commitment from 19 to 22 years of age. Among those who went on to higher education, slightly over 7 out of 10 signed during the college ages of 19 to 22, while an additional 12 percent were 23 or older.

It is the role of higher education in general, and athletic scholarships in particular, that illuminate the aforementioned negative correlation between education and baseball success in the major leagues. Apparently attendance at a college or university opens up a different set of options for the young man who had earlier expressed an interest in an athletic career.

It is entirely possible that what was originally defined as a goal or end—a career in professional athletics—has been redefined as a means to other ends.

Let us attempt to sketch out the career pattern that seems to emerge for our sample of former major leaguers. In a previous analytic study (Haerle, 1974), the not-too-surprising finding came to light that the father's years of education were highly predictive of his son's level of education. The 177 respondents who attended college and for whom we had data were predominantly from higher occupational origins. Beyond this fact, however, we were interested in the extent to which athletic scholarships might enable those from lower-class backgrounds to overcome these inhibiting influences. It was discovered that those who came from lower-class backgrounds were significantly more likely to be attending college with the aid of an athletic scholarship. Thus, the scholarship based on athletic skill provided another opportunity route to future success for those from less fortunate socio-economic backgrounds.

A related and controversial issue has to do with the degree to which the athletic abilities of the scholarship student are exploited—that is, his sports skills are utilized until his athletic eligibility has expired and then he does not receive the academic support that would enable him to complete his college work and receive his degree. Although we did not find strict statistical support for this phenomenon, when compared to those college athletes without such aid, there was a strong tendency for those with athletic scholarships to have a lower rate of completion and graduation.

Within the college-attending group, those with athletic scholarships did not differ significantly from those without such financial aid in terms of the age at which they signed their professional contracts, the league classification of their first or last professional team, or the age at which retirement from baseball took place. However, several important and significant differences were discovered in various measures of baseball skill. Surprisingly, those with athletic scholarships gave evidence of less skill in professional baseball when compared with those college-attending athletes who did not have athletic scholarships. The former spent fewer total years in professional baseball, had a smaller proportion of their active years in the major leagues, compiled lower total "baseball fame index" (BFI) scores and had lower average yearly BFI scores. In short, those who attended college with athletic scholarships were found to have less successful professional baseball careers than their college peers who did not have any such scholarships.

It is also possible, as mentioned earlier, that the commitment to professional baseball declined somewhat as these men began to see what benefits might accrue to them as a result of a college education. Thus the factor of education and the decisions surrounding its acquisition are seen to constitute a critical phase in the career of the professional baseball player.

The Second Phase of Career: Structural and Interpersonal Aspects of the Active Baseball Career

Once an individual has signed a professional baseball contract, he has officially left the "amateur ranks" and embarked on an important phase of his new career. The point at which he enters the league structure and the speed with which he advances to the major leagues are crucial to his developing career pattern and eventual success or failure. We shall also be interested in the day-to-day features of the occupation as shapers of his orientation to work. But first, we must consider the pattern of movement toward fame and fortune in the major leagues.

1. Career Patterns and Correlates of Success. Professional sports are among the few occupations which have a clear-cut, public set of career lines neatly laid out in advance. Those who have signed a professional contract but lack the necessary skill and training to handle the major league level are generally relegated to one of the minor league baseball clubs, anywhere from the higher ranking open classification or AAA down to the lower ranking Class D leagues.

The essence of this movement and its relationship to baseball performance (as measured by the BFI) is clearly illustrated in the path diagram presented in Fig. 1. Keeping in mind that the path coefficients are a measure of the strength of the causal-like[9] relationship between the two variables (while all the other variables are held constant), we find some rather interesting results from our analysis of the factors associated with achieved baseball fame (BFI).

The path diagram seems to represent the following account. Those players with more education tended to sign their contracts at a later age, thereby retaining their amateur status so that they might continue to participate in interscholastic and intercollegiate competition. There was a strong tendency for these individuals to enter the baseball league structure at the higher levels (major leagues or upper minor leagues), rather than with the lower-ranking minor leagues. Thus, staying in school longer resulted in greater physical maturity and the development of a degree of baseball skill that was translated into a more competitive and advanced league entry point. Those who were young and less experienced were more apt to start in a Class C or D league.

Once the baseball career started, the pattern among variables 3, 4, 5, and 6 spell out the movement profile for these players. If one started out in

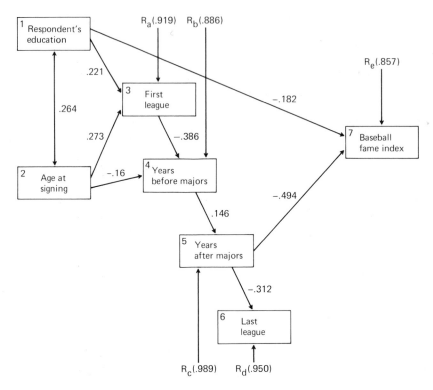

Fig. 1 *Path diagram of background and baseball career factors influencing baseball fame. (The correlation matrix for this path diagram is shown in Table 1.)*

the lower minor leagues (variable 3), it would take more years of playing before he reached the major leagues (variable 4), although the number of years played before reaching the majors was partially influenced by the age at which the initial professional contract was signed (variable 2). Thus the first league of entry was somewhat predictive of how long it would take to make it to the major leagues. But interestingly, these two variables had little or no influence on overall major league success as measured by the BFI (variable 7).

Apparently, the crucial question seems to be, not whether one can reach the major leagues, but rather whether the player has the ability and dedication to remain competitive and perform at a superior level, reminiscent of the earlier observations by La Place (1954). Thus we find that the years spent in professional baseball after leaving the major leagues (variable 5) were most predictive of the BFI. Those who spent a great deal of time in the minor leagues *after* playing in the majors simply did not have

Table 1

Zero-Order Correlation Coefficients for Background and Baseball Career Variables Influencing Baseball Fame. (Number of cases for each correlation is noted in parentheses.)

Variables	1	2	3	4	5	6	7
1 (Respondent's Education)	...						
2 (Age at signing contract)	.264 † (332)	...					
3 (First league classification)	.293 † (321)	.331 † (324)	...				
4 (Number of years before majors)	−.222 † (332)	−.287 † (335)	−.439 † (324)	...			
5 (Number of years after majors)	−.089 (332)	−.058 (335)	−.129 * (324)	.146 † (335)	...		
6 (Last league classification)	.122 * (326)	.082 (329)	.045 (319)	.057 (339)	−.312 † (329)	...	
7 (Baseball fame index, BFI)	−.152 † (332)	−.074 (335)	.031 (324)	−.214 † (325)	−.475 † (335)	.165 † (329)	...

* Significant at the .05 level.
† Significant at the .01 level.

the opportunity or the ability to achieve stardom. This relationship was certainly not unexpected, but it conjures up an image of the former major leaguer who "hangs on" in the minor leagues, attempting to make a comeback. As one of our interviewees remarked,

> Was a sad day in St. Petersburg, Florida. I was of the opinion that I could still do a good job in the major leagues as a player but if I couldn't I would either manage or become a baseball scout.

As another retired player put it:

> I have always felt that baseball was a most jealous mistress. Too many fail to reach the top and fail to provide for professional work thereafter.

Although a longer amount of time spent in the minors after playing in the majors results in a player's dropping to a lower ranking league, the level of the last league in which he played apparently had little influence on the BFI score.

In short, each of the players in our sample made it to the major leagues. However, the route of each individual was somewhat different and one could begin to predict, in terms of predisposing factors, who might be successful. The essential factor seemed to be the ability to remain in the major leagues once that top level had been reached. In passing, one should be reminded of the negative association of education with the BFI score, a finding consistent with our earlier discussion.

In an attempt to understand the day-to-day stresses and strains that accompany these career movements, it is instructive to turn to a more qualitative analysis of the key characteristics of the occupation of professional baseball.

2. Role Analysis of the Baseball Player's Daily Occupational World. Because his occupational performance is so public, the professional baseball player is subject to pressures and expectations from diverse sources in his social environment on a daily basis. Some of these social groups might be thought of as located in the player's *external system* (Homans, 1950: 90–94), that is, groups which are parts of the larger environment in which a baseball team may function. In contrast, the *internal system* (Homans, 1950: Chapter 5) refers to those groups and individuals who are an integral part of the daily role performance of the individual player. This internal system denotes the group behavior that is the expression of the sentiments the members feel toward one another as they carry out their daily tasks and the differentiation and ranking that takes place in the group (Homans, 1950: Chapter 6).

Together these two, the internal and the external, make up the total social system or meaningful social world of the professional baseball player. Each of these social groups in the role set (Merton, 1957: 368–384) applies normative expectations of behavior to the status occupant—and these expectations, in turn, can be thought of as the *role requirements* of the specific position. But what is important for our consideration here is the fact that different normative expectations, emanating from diverse sources, could conceivably converge on a single individual and amount to conflicting demands, i.e., *role conflict* (Sarbin and Allen, 1968: 540–544). The nature of these role conflicts and their resolution become our primary focus at this point.

Essentially we shall deal with five selected and significant segments in the total system of the individual baseball player. Each of these groupings makes specific demands on his energy and his attention, often resulting in conflicting role expectations. Three of these belong to the system external to the more immediate team activities and thus are involved in the survival of the ball club in its (primarily economic) environment: the fans, the umpire-scorer, and the club ownership group.

From this external system, the player may be faced with incompatible demands: baseball as a dramatic event (fans) and baseball as a business (owners) versus the player's enjoyment of the game and his awareness of job routine. One of his adjustment problems is to resolve this dilemma.

Besides outside pressures from the external system, there are two constituencies internal to the immediate operation of the team in an actual game: the field manager and coaches, and fellow players. The focal point of the potential dilemma in the internal system would appear to be the demands of the team versus the ego-needs of the individual player. The player must satisfy the needs of his own ego for public acclaim and the necessity of high performance statistics for later salary bargaining. At times these run counter to the interests of the team as a whole and thus he may incur the displeasure of his manager and teammates.

These conflicting expectations of the "significant others" of the baseball player are presented in Fig. 2. It now remains to analyze the manner in which the expectations of each of these system-segments impinges on the occupational performance of the professional baseball player. It is our contention that certain dilemmas are produced out of the conflicting expectations emanating from the different locations in the total social system which makes up the player's work environment.

a. The External System: The Conflict Between Baseball as a Dramatic Event and a Business versus Baseball as Game Enjoyment and Job Routine. The contacts that the player has with the fans, the umpires, and front-office

Career patterns and career contingencies of professional baseball players

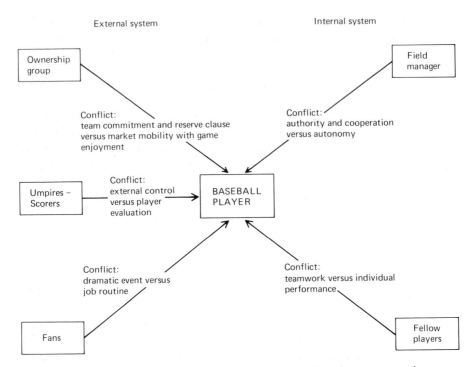

Fig. 2 *Conceptual scheme for analysis of structural and interpersonal aspects of the work environment of the major league baseball player.*

management are socially distant. Nevertheless, the expectations of these three important groups place severe limitations on his behavior and require that he resolve the inherent conflict between their demands and his own individual needs.

Fan Interest and Umpire-Scorer Evaluation: Public View of the Game. The average fan wants to see a *game* of baseball, meaning that he expects uncertainty of outcome, excitement, and drama. To some extent, attendance at the game is a means of escape from the daily pressures and competition of his job. Yet, he is drawn to the competition and pressure of the game, and he can identify with the players on the field. The fan may be looking for a hero or he may want to identify with the underdog.

But the fan's expectations are strongly felt and of high intensity. Although winning is not the only thing, it certainly is to be strongly emphasized. The fan expects the player to do his absolute best, to fight hard to win, and not to fold under pressure. Even though he is capable of identifying with the difficulties and pressures faced by the player, the average fan somehow expects effort and performance beyond that normally expected of other humans. The athlete must be superhuman. And somehow, although fan-player contacts are socially distant, these audience demands are made known to and felt by the player.

Yet the player knows that he must go out onto the field 162 times during the baseball season. He must play hard to win but he must not permit a single loss—even a particularly difficult loss caused by avoidable errors—to get him "down" in succeeding days. However, the fans may be very upset by such a loss and make their feelings known with constant jeering and booing. Somehow the player must maintain a psychological balance akin to hospital personnel who see the patient's emergency as their own routine (Hughes, 1958: 54, 88). The baseball player must evaluate the fans' outraged reaction on a given day in terms of the season-long requirements of his job. The fans' sense of urgency cannot be matched on a daily basis by the players. Obviously, there are times (during the World Series or a close pennant race) when players and fans may share the same sense of urgency but these tend to be the exceptions.

Thus, one crucial aspect of the work situation of the professional athlete is the public nature of the performance. Few occupations are subjected to such close scrutiny by the client or the audience. Much of the work of the lawyer is carried on behind the scenes and outside the direct viewing of the client. Even the surgeon anesthetizes his patient with the unintended consequence that only the end result will be known (if the patient lives) but never all the activity leading up to it.

True, entertainers share this public display with professional athletes and they, too, feel the external pressures which come with audience response. But professional athletes, especially the baseball player, have one distinct characteristic which sets them apart from all other occupations whether on public display or not: statistical records and regularly published summary reports. No doctor finds his yearly average of "hits and misses" printed in full view for the perusal of the lay public. Nor does the clergyman see his name listed with a tally of souls gained or lost. Even the entertainer, whose work is performed publicly, does not have an official and published tally of all the "bloopers" committed or lines missed (although attendance records could be compiled by any hard-working researcher as a kind of measure of success).

The baseball player is truly a member of the team, yet uniquely alone. When the ball comes his way, he must act—quickly and accurately. If not, he is charged with an error or strikes out. At that moment, he is uniquely alone, with all eyes riveted on his actions—to judge and then to approve or disapprove in a manner immediately evident to the player.

The importance of this aspect of the professional ball player's work situation is highlighted by Everett C. Hughes. In a thought-provoking essay entitled "Mistakes at Work" (Hughes, 1958b), he explores the meaning of the inevitable slip-ups which occur in every line of work. In his usual style, he is urging us to adopt a comparative approach to the study of occupations, especially in the search for common themes that link all occupations at some level of abstraction. One of these common problems, Hughes argues, is the problem of "mistakes or failures" in work and what they mean to both outsiders and participants.

> One may speak of a calculus of the probability of making mistakes, in which the variables are skill and frequency of performance. It is obvious that there are many possibilities. One who never performs a given action will never do it wrong. . . . Some skills require more repetition than others for the original learning and for maintenance. . . . Occupations, considered as bundles of skills, are subject to the contingencies contained in all combinations of these factors of learning and maintaining skill, and, correlatively, subject to variations in the probability that one will sometimes make mistakes (Hughes, 1958b: 89).*

To illustrate his ideas, Hughes draws heavily on the professions, particularly medicine. In addition, he emphasizes more the recipient of the mistake rather than the one who commits the error. In so doing, he stresses the importance, for the practitioner group, of maintaining control over the definition of failure in competition with the critical judgment of the layman.

Hughes' discussion provides an interesting contrast to the professional baseball player, thereby pinpointing some of the most important meanings of the public display of his performance. For example, Hughes says

> . . . there are psychological, physical, social and economic risks in learning and doing one's work. And since the theoretical probability of making an error some day is increased by the very frequency of the operations by which one makes one's living, it becomes natural to build up some rationale to carry one through. It is also to be expected that those who are subject to the same work risks will compose a collective rationale which they whistle to one another to keep up their courage, and that they will build up collective defenses against the lay world. These rationales and defenses contain a logic that is somewhat like that of insurance, in that they tend to spread the risk psychologically

---

* E. C. Hughes, "Mistakes at Work." *Men and Their Work.* Glencoe, Illinois: Free Press, 1958. Reprinted by permission. This footnote also applies to those passages quoted on pp. 476, 477, 478.

(by saying that it might happen to anyone), morally, and financially. A study of these risk-spreading devices is an essential part of comparative study of occupations (Hughes, 1958b: 90).

But how is the baseball player to withstand the judgment of the fans, when the majority of those in attendance have either played the game themselves and/or are thoroughly conversant with the rules? Few surgeons face this problem, while an occasional plumber may find a knowledgeable client looking over his shoulder. Of course, the meaning of the "error" for the ball player depends on a number of conditions. If the team is far ahead or if the runner who got on base does not score, then no real harm has been done to the team effort—although the ego of the player has had to suffer through the moment when he was the focus of attention and, of course, the error will become part of the official record of the game (and of his personal statistics). If the player is not so fortunate and the error figures in the scoring, the athlete still may have the opportunity to redeem himself during the same game with a spectacular play. In addition, fellow players will shout encouragement and try to minimize the blame for mistakes, knowing full well they might be the next unfortunate individual.

Negative fan reaction, however, may not always have a crushing effect on the errant player. Those who *really know* the difficulty of a play, that is, one's fellow players, are often able to counteract the negative response from the stands and thus provide the kind of defense about which Hughes speaks.

As can be noted, this particular dilemma raises the question of the standards by which the "worker" shall be judged and who shall make the judgment. On this subject, Hughes is again most pertinent.

> . . . we are faced with another [problem]: that of defining what a failure or mistake is in any given line of work or in a given work operation. This leads to still another, which turns out to be the significant one for the social drama of work: Who has the right to say what a mistake or a failure is? The findings on this point are fairly clear; a colleague-group (the people who consider themselves subject to the same work risks) will stubbornly defend its own right to define mistakes, and to say in the given case whether one has been made.[1] (Hughes's footnote follows: [1] The colleague-group does not in all cases succeed in getting and keeping this right. Perhaps they do not always want the full responsibility of convicting one another of error and of applying sanctions. It would be more correct to say that a kind of jurisprudence of mistakes is an essential part of the study of any occupation. Professor Norman Ward has suggested that a study of the official *error* in baseball would throw light on the processes involved.) (Hughes, 1958b: 93)

When one starts comparing occupations in this regard one finds that in most of them it is very difficult to establish criteria of success or failure, and of mistakes as against proper execution of work. The cases where all parties to the work drama would agree are few indeed.

. . . the people who work and those who receive the product as goods or services will have quite different degrees and kinds of knowledge of the probabilities and contingencies involved. The colleague-group will consider that it alone fully understands the technical contingencies, and that it would therefore be given the sole right to say when a mistake has been made. The layman, they may contend, cannot even at best fully understand the contingencies. This attitude may be extended to complete silence concerning mistakes of a member of the colleague-group, because the very discussion before a larger audience may imply the right of the layman to make a judgment; and it is the *right* to make the judgment that is most jealously guarded (Hughes, 1958*b*: 93–94).

All of this does not apply very adequately to professional baseball and thus the player is left correspondingly vulnerable. The audience has a degree of expertise rarely found in most practitioner-client relationships and, in one sense, the client has paid for the privilege of voicing his opinion in the form of cheering or booing. And those who make the official judgments, the umpire and especially the official scorer, are not part of the player's colleague-group. So "mistakes at work" are closely watched by the fans, judged by an outsider and computed and published regularly in the mass media and official record books. In sum, baseball players as a group have lost the battle to retain control over the setting of standards of judgment, a feature rather uncharacteristic of most occupational groups.

Hughes speaks of the difficulty of arriving at agreed-upon standards of success or failure in most occupations. But in professional baseball, there is much greater certainty. A hit is a hit and an out is an out.[10] The judgment of an error by the official scorer, generally a local newspaper man, is not quite so clear-cut but in most cases there is a high degree of consensus among the participants and the fans. Nevertheless, periodic disagreements do arise.[11]

So the team loses the game and the loss will be charged against the pitcher who was in the game when the winning runs were scored against him. But what if the winning run was the result of an error by the shortstop? The loss must still be recorded as such but, in the official statistics of the game, an important distinction is made between "earned" and "unearned" runs. In turn, although the pitcher is charged with the loss, the "unearned" run will not be charged against him. This is reflected in one of the pitcher's most important statistics, the ERA (earned run average, based on the number of "earned" runs he allows per each nine innings pitched). Thus, a pitcher with a poor fielding team may have a bad won-lost record and still maintain professional stature with a respectable ERA. The morality of the game dictates that he should not be held totally responsible for that over which he has limited control. A kind of distinction is made between team responsibility and individual responsibility which is carried into the official statistical records for evaluation by the knowledgeable.

The possibility of being successful under crucial game conditions places considerable pressure on the individual performer. Although a member of a team with an expected and clearly called for set of activities, the ball player, at the crack of the bat, stands uniquely alone—will he be the hero or the goat? With thousands of eyes (millions on television) glued to his actions, the experience of pressure must be immense. Physical ability to perform the required actions is one thing, but the psychological "cool" to meet the challenge of the moment is an equally necessary, yet difficult-to-measure, quality.

In sum, occupational performance is a very public event. Fans form a significant portion of the impinging external environment. In interaction terms, they are socially distant and have virtually no face-to-face contact or influence. But in their role as fans, they express their sentiments, both positive and negative, rather clearly and strongly. They demand an exciting, dramatic event each time they go to the ball park. The players, on the other hand, cannot possibly sustain the emotional and dramatic level, expected by the fans, over a full season's schedule. They view much of their work as rather routine and only periodically reach the fever pitch of the fans. But fan expectation is a recognized aspect of the game and the player must deal with its incompatibility alongside his view of the routine nature of his occupation. Added to this is the fact that the umpire or official scorer is the final arbiter of "mistakes" at work.

The Economic Complex: Ownership and Business Policy as Part of the Occupational Environment. For the player, baseball is a job, a livelihood. The fact that the fan is unconcerned with this aspect does not mean the player can afford to overlook the impact of market conditions and prevailing business practices within the occupation. The player also experiences intrinsic enjoyment in playing the game. At the center of contention, so to speak, is the player's personal fulfillment and economic autonomy, his right to move in the labor market in an effort to maximize his position.

In the matter of the ownership and control of the "means of production," professional baseball is among the unusual occupations in the U.S. economy. Up until an individual signs his first playing contract, he is subject to the so-called "free agent" draft. When this draft system went into effect in 1965, it virtually eliminated the player's freedom to choose the team for which he would like to play. Rather the various teams vie for the "right" to draft him. Once a "uniform player contract" has been signed, the labor market is no longer free in any sense. The player can no longer exercise any control over who his employer will be.

> An elaborate system of rules has been devised to govern contractual relationships between players and teams and among teams in the disposition of player's services. This system of rules structures the labor market and imposes constraints upon freedom in the market.*

The crux of the restricted market is the so-called "reserve clause," [12] a part of the uniform contract which all players must sign. In essence, this gives the employer, the baseball club, the right to renew the contract at the end of each year (most contracts run for only one year, although in recent years some players have been successfully negotiating multi-year contracts) but the player does *not* have the option of selling his services to another club.

The reasoning behind the reserve rule is simply stated. Since there are rich clubs and poor clubs, the fear is that the wealthy owner would gradually buy up all the best players by outbidding his poorer opponents, eventually creating an imbalance in team quality. Thus, true competition would be lost, uncertainty of outcome would cease to exist, and attendance would gradually fall off. The reserve clause was instituted to protect the poorer clubs from the raiding of their roster and to ensure the equal distribution of talent in the whole league.

Does the reserve clause prevent the unequal distribution of talent? Rottenberg (1960: 8–13) argues that it does not; instead it is used to depress the salary of the individual player, since he is not free to sell his abilities to the highest bidder. There have been periodic attempts by individual players to bring suit against professional baseball for "illegal restraint of trade" and "illegal monopoly" in violation of antitrust laws. One recent attempt (in 1971) was that by outfielder Curt Flood, then of the St. Louis Cardinals, who signed with the Washington Senators, played a few games and wrote a book (Flood, 1971) and then left the club because of some "very serious personal problems." Flood was contesting (with his attorney, Arthur Goldberg) the 1922 Supreme Court decision which exempted baseball from existing antitrust legislation. The court had said baseball was not an interstate commerce. Since 1922, other cases have resulted in the same conclusion: "... baseball is still a sport rather than an interstate business and is therefore not subject to the federal antitrust laws" (Gregory, 1956: 162).

---

* Simon Rottenberg, "Squeeze Plays in Baseball's Labor Market," *Midway* **2** (1960), 5–6. Chicago: University of Chicago Press. Reprinted by permission.

The approach of plaintiffs has always been to attack the "reasonable-ness" of the reserve arrangement, arguing that ". . . the present set of rules is not reasonable but too restrictive, and that the industry could still operate without so rigidly monopolistic a framework" (Koppett, 1971). But Koppett mentions a recent decision in a federal district court where the judge ruled an agreement to be a violation per se, thus clearly illegal. This casts doubt on the viability of many sports operations and agreements, even if they are considered reasonable. However, in the Flood case, the Supreme Court once again ruled in favor of retaining baseball's immunity to federal anti-trust laws (by a 5 to 3 vote). The decision did not deal directly with the issues raised about the reserve clause; rather the court stressed its unwilling-ness to overturn previous rulings. The court pointedly said it should be up to the congress to handle the "anomalous" exemption for baseball. The im-plications of all this have yet to be fully developed and scholars have begun the task (Morris, 1973).

In the face of the reserve clause restriction, what alternatives are open to the player who is dissatisfied with his contract offer? His basic approach in the past has been to refuse to sign his contract, not show up for spring training and thus be considered a "holdout." Both the player and the owner realize that he is not free to negotiate with another team. All the player can do is hope that his services are valuable enough to force the ball club to reopen negotiations and consider raising his salary. Obviously, the su-perior player, who is a gate attraction, has a distinct advantage over the player who rides the bench as a substitute. The latter's bargaining power is almost nonexistent. For the more established star, some sort of com-promise is generally worked out. Rarely has a player missed all of spring training, let alone remain out of action the entire season.

In more recent years, the players have banded together into a kind of union, The Players' Association. Since 1967, operating with attorney Mar-vin Miller as a full-time director, the Players' Association has conducted collective bargaining-like discussions with owners on a series of issues which affect all those in major league baseball: minimum salary levels, ex-pense allowances, pension plans, collective endorsement arrangements, the players' cut of the lucrative television contracts and the like. The legal im-plications of collective bargaining for the entire professional team sport in-dustry are wide-ranging (Lowell, 1973). Generally, however, the individual player still conducts his own contract and salary negotiations with the owners, although often now with the aid of his private attorney or financial advisor.

In order to ensure that the owners pay attention to the players' needs, the Players' Association threatened to strike in the past and in the spring of 1971 actually carried out a reasonably successful strike during the early days of spring training. A similar strike has been threatened by professional football players for the 1974 season.

Prior to the 1974 baseball season a new wrinkle was added.

> Twenty-nine players, about 6 percent of the approximately 500 major leaguers eligible, chose to have their salary disputes handled by professional arbitrators .... In 16 cases, the arbitrators found in the clubs [sic] favor; the players [sic] salary figures were selected in the other 13 (Chass, 1974: 1).

With the introduction of more formalized negotiation, the balance of power between owner and player has been significantly altered. The reserve clause is still in effect, but the players have improved their position overall.

In sum, the owner, concerned with team success and club profits, seeks to enjoin the player for his entire work career. He expects a total commitment to the team from the player, in return for a salary that the owner considers equitable. The owner and the player experience little interaction with each other and thus the owner's demands are communicated in more subtle ways.

For his part, the player desires two things: economic success and personal fulfillment in the game. It should never be forgotten that most men play the game because they love it (at least at the beginning of their careers) and they crave and derive intrinsic satisfaction from the competition. But the average player is also concerned with his economic potential. Both of these normative desires of the player group may be infringed upon by certain business and management policies in baseball. The athlete cannot ignore the demands of the owner, yet he must try to satisfy his own need for accomplishment. The resolution of these conflicting expectations requires considerable social and economic skill.

The External System: A Summary. In the external occupational environment, we find three important constituencies making demands on the players, with the three often being incompatible. The fan says, "Don't bother me with your business troubles and don't let business principles force you into changing the game I love so well. You owe it to your teammates to play your very best and you owe it to the fans to provide them with escape, release, and a dramatic and cathartic event." On the other hand, club owners and general managers stress the need for instituting current business practices and keeping the player under tight control so as to restrict his labor mobility and his ability to bargain for the best employment opportunity. If the player expresses his dissatisfaction openly, he incurs the wrath of both sectors for different reasons. Management doesn't want a public malcontent—it is bad publicity and gives the game and the specific club a bad name. The fan begins to wonder about his hero, spending all his time and energy with such crass considerations as salary increases, outside business interests, and the like. He wonders whether this won't affect the morale and cohesion of the team. And for someone playing "the game," these don't seem to be legitimate concerns.

The role of the umpire-scorer has a direct effect on the player's performance. Certain of his decisions, if negative, will appear in the official statistics of the individual player. In turn, this could influence the player's bargaining position for next year's salary.

In short, we have the values inherent in viewing "baseball as a game" coming into rather open conflict with viewing "baseball as a business." The individual player is the focal point of these incompatible pressures. Somehow he must attempt to resolve this dilemma without lessening his bargaining power or letting his daily performance be affected.

b. The Internal System: Teamwork Demands versus Individual Performance in the Immediate Work Environment. In his daily work setting, the professional baseball player must contend with two major constituencies: fellow team members and the field manager (with his coaches). Bonded by common activity and goal, high rates of interaction yield strong sentiments and result in the gradual development of equally strong normative expectations. However, once again these seem to result in role conflict for the individual player.

Interaction with Fellow Players: Teamwork as a Normative Standard. Interaction with fellow players is extremely intense and close. This is especially true when the team is traveling on the road and members must share hotel accommodations. Even when the schedule calls for a series of home games, there is still considerable contact among ball players' families away from the ball park. Their common activities, both at practice and in the game, require sustained interaction. If positive sentiments result, the team is said to have good morale, and this should be an added factor in the achievement of their goal, i.e., winning games. However, if there is jealousy or rivalry on the team, the intense interaction would only exacerbate it and presumably lower morale.

It should also be remembered that there is a high degree of division of labor and specialization on the team. In fact, the entire game is played by men occupying nine distinct positions, each with its own special skill requirements. For example, many "outsiders" are unaware of the different running-speed and throwing-strength requirements of the three outfield positions. Beyond the nine men who play first string, the flexibility required for bench strength means that others must be good pinch hitters,[13] relief pitchers and the like. Each man on the 25-man roster has a special role to play.

But the successful completion of the task is clearly a group responsibility. There are several jobs to be done and they must be highly coordinated to ensure successful performance. To achieve the necessary coordination of these several specialized positions requires considerable effort and motivation. All of this is captured in the normative theme of teamwork.

In professional sports coordinated teamwork is not like the teamwork of the automobile assembly line with its preplanned work schedule and timed processes. Rather the teamwork of the athletic squad has a strong element of spontaneity and the need for instantaneous adjustment. In baseball, with a runner on first base and one out, a ball hit to the shortstop calls for a series of coordinated movements resulting in a double play. Under the same conditions, a grounder to the first baseman would require a different set of coordinated activities to achieve the same, desired double play. Given the speed of the ball and the runner, these responses must be instantaneous.

In this connection, it is both interesting and instructive to turn to the writings of social psychologist George Herbert Mead for insight into the almost unconscious nature of this "spontaneous teamwork." In his discussion of the genesis and development of "the self," Mead makes a crucial distinction between play and the game and often employs the ball game to illustrate his point.

The development of the self involves the progressive ability to "take the role of the other" and to see oneself through the other's eyes, to essentially view oneself, self-consciously, as an object. The development necessarily goes through several stages, of which play and the game are revealing. Mead says:

> Of course, this playing with an imaginary companion is only a peculiarly interesting phase of ordinary play. Play in this sense, especially the stage which precedes the organized games, is a play at something . . . taking different roles . . . He has a set of stimuli which call out in himself the sort of responses they call out in others. He takes this group of responses and organizes them into a certain whole. Such is the simplest form of being another to one's self. . . .

> If we contrast play with the situation in an organized game, we note the essential difference that the child who plays in a game must be ready to take the attitude of everyone else involved in that game, and that these different roles must have a definite relationship to each other. . . . In that early [play] stage he passes from one role to another just as a whim takes him. But in a game where a number of individuals are

involved, then the child taking one role must be ready to take the role of everyone else.*

At this point, Mead employs the game of baseball for illustrative purposes. Our point in dwelling on Mead's ideas are twofold: first, to indicate the unconscious nature of teamwork in professional sports, and, second, to emphasize, as Mead does, the importance of this feedback process to the basic dimensions of the self-concept and even the larger social order.

> The fundamental difference between play and the game is that in the latter the child must have the attitude of all the others involved in that game. The attitudes of the other players which the participant assumes organize into a sort of unit, and it is that organization which controls the response of the individual. The illustration used was of a person playing baseball. Each one of his acts is determined by his assumption of the action of the others who are playing the game. What he does is controlled by his being everyone else on that team. . . . We then get an "other" which is an organization of the attitudes of those involved in the same process.

> The organized community or social group which gives to the individual his unity or self may be called "the generalized other." The attitude of the generalized other is the attitude of the whole community. Thus, for example, in the case of such a social group as a ball team, the team is the generalized other in so far as it enters—as an organized process or social activity—into the experience of any one of the individual members of it (Mead, 1934: 153–154).

> If he gets in a ball nine he must have the responses of each position involved in his own position. He must know what everyone else is going to do in order to carry out his own play. He has to take all of these roles. They do not all have to be present in consciousness at the same time, but at some moments he has to have three or four individuals present in his own attitude, such as the one who is going to throw the ball, the one who is going to catch it, and so on. These responses must be, in some degree, present in his own make-up (Mead, 1934: 151).

> The game has a logic, so that such an organization of the self is rendered possible: there is a definite end to be obtained; the actions of the different individuals are all related to each other with reference to that end so they do not conflict; one is not in conflict with himself in the

---

* G. H. Mead, *Mind, Self and Society*, Charles W. Morris (ed.). (Chicago: University of Chicago Press, 1934.) Reprinted by permission. This footnote also applies to passages quoted on pp. 485–486.

attitude of another man on the team. If one has the attitude of the person throwing the ball he can also have the response of catching the ball. The two are related so that they further the purpose of the game itself. . . .

The game is then an illustration of the situation out of which an organized personality arises. In so far as the child does take the attitude of the other and allows that attitude of the other to determine the thing he is going to do with reference to a common end, he is becoming an organic member of society. He is taking over the morale of that society and is becoming an essential member of it (Mead, 1934: 159).

Thus, playing the game and learning the rules is much like participating in the larger society. In essence, the game acts as a microcosm of the larger society. The high degree of division of labor and specialization is made effective through a rather complex and spontaneous teamwork. In this context it raises the old conflict between the freedom of the individual and the demands of the society (Freud, 1961).

One consequence of these traits for the baseball player is the inevitable conflict between individual performance and team requirements. The individual player must balance the team's need for his special services (perhaps calling for him to "sacrifice" under certain game conditions) and his own desire to augment his personal statistics, thereby receiving the adulation of the fans. Organizational demands often interfere with individual desires.

In sum, the normative expectation of teamwork demands that the individual player subordinate his actions to the requirements of the group as a whole entity. Out of intense team interaction, he is expected to develop positive sentiments for the group goal of winning such that he will perform his specialized role without thought of personal gain.

The Manager and Coaches: Coordination and Cooperation as Normative Themes. It is the job of the manager to provide team leadership on the field. It is he who must deal directly with the teamwork-induced dilemmas faced by the individual players as he attempts to mold them into a winning combination. Often in doing so, he will unavoidably create another dilemma for the professional player. In his desire to achieve success through demands for cooperation, the manager may place requirements on the player which the athlete is unwilling to accept.

In fulfilling his job, the manager must play a great variety of roles and have several, sometimes rare, qualities: good "baseball man" (i.e., knowledge of the game); astute strategist; public relations expert; team "psychiatrist"; inspirational or charismatic leadership ability; sensitive to team morale and aware of contributing factors; ability to implement policies while maintaining the loyalty of 25 different men, etc. The list is almost endless and the complexity of the job makes it enormously difficult. The man who combines all of these qualities is rare in mathematical probability terms. Where do they come from?

Grusky (1963a) has looked at the possible impact of formal structure on the pattern of selection of baseball managers. He was especially interested in the degree to which certain interactional constraints associated with different positions (spatial location, nature of the task and rate of interaction) influenced one's chances of becoming a team manager. In considering these factors, Grusky defined two types of positions in the formal team structure: high interactors (infielders and catchers) and low interactors (pitchers and outfielders). Given the high involvement, dependent tasks, and central location of the former, Grusky hypothesized that field managers would more likely be recruited from former catchers and infielders. The data he reviewed confirmed this thesis. Further, among high interactors, catchers were the more likely source of managerial talent. Grusky argues that occupants of these higher interaction positions have the opportunity to develop role skills appropriate to a managerial future and also the chance to gain the players' respect as they coordinate team effort and identify closely with total welfare of the team.

Once a manager has been chosen, we are faced with the question of his job security and the degree of his effectiveness. In a strange twist of Weber's (Gerth and Mills, 1946) expected pattern of hierarchy of authority, we find that manager to be hierarchically vulnerable. True, he is in a position of dominance and he is the field leader. Nevertheless, there are certain aspects of the game of baseball which tend to undermine his position as the unquestioned authority figure. It is widely known that the star player often receives a yearly salary far in excess of what his own manager may earn. Then, too, there have been instances where members of the team have voted "no confidence" in their field leader or in other ways tried to influence the front office to change managers.

In a companion article, Grusky (1963b) again has provided us with some pertinent data. There is a kind of tradition in baseball that, if a team is doing poorly, the manager will become the "scapegoat" and be relieved of his job. Although he was not trying to impute causality, the question Grusky attacked was the extent to which high rates of managerial turnover (succession) were related to the record of team wins (organizational effectiveness). With the data he presented, the researcher found a negative correlation between rates of managerial succession and organizational effectiveness. In addition, over time, those teams which increased their rate of manager turnover had significantly poorer team performance than those teams which tried to increase team stability by increasing the length of tenure of the team managers.

But the direction of causation is a difficult and dangerous one (Grusky, 1963: 25ff).

> A common sense explanation of our results might suggest that effectiveness alone is the cause. The manager is fired because the team performs badly. Not only is the simplicity of this explanation appealing, but the negative correlation between the succession and effectiveness is fully consistent with it. However, if taken by itself, this approach possesses all the deficiencies properly attributed to orientations that rest only on common knowledge. . . .

> If we assume that effectiveness and succession influence each other by contributing to managerial role strain, it is possible to formulate an alternative explanation for the major findings, one that ties in with a growing body of theory and research. . . . Succession, because it represents a universal organizational process, and effectiveness, because all formal organizations tend to strive toward the attainment of their official objectives, are strategic concepts for studying organizations within a comparative framework. . . . Accordingly, the relationship between rates of succession and organizational effectiveness was analyzed within the context of a conceptual scheme that focused on their interrelationships with a number of other variables: managerial (or executive) role strain, expectation of replacement, style of supervision, subgroup stability, morale, clientele support, degree of discrepancy between managerial authority and responsibility, and availability of objective assessment of organizational performance.*

The interplay among these variables is rather complex and little empirical work has been done to discover the actual direction and magnitude of the several relationships. Grusky did report a positive correlation between rates of succession and effectiveness and also clientele support (game attendance) and effectiveness. Beyond this, he summarized

> Our orientation focused on a set of ten variables. Analysis of the situation of the ineffective team may be used illustratively. If a team in [sic] ineffective, clientele support and profitability decline. Accordingly, strong external pressures for managerial change are set in motion and, concomitantly, the magnitude of managerial role strain increases. A managerial change may be viewed in some quarters as attractive in that it can function to demonstrate publicly that the owners are taking con-

---

* O. Grusky, "Managerial Succession and Organizational Effectiveness." *American Journal of Sociology.* (Chicago: University of Chicago Press, 1963.) Reprinted by permission. This footnote also applies to passages quoted on pp. 488–489.

crete action to remedy an undesirable situation. The public nature of team performance and the close identification of community pride with team behavior combine to establish a strong basis for clientele control over the functioning of the team. These external influences tend to increase the felt discrepancy between managerial responsibility and actual authority. Since the rewards of popularity are controlled externally, individual rather than team performance may be encouraged. Similarly, the availability of objective performance standards decreases managerial control and thereby contributes to role strain. The greater the managerial role strain, the higher the rates of succession, the stronger the expectations of replacement when team performance declines. Frequent managerial change can produce important dysfunctional consequences within the team by affecting style of supervision and disturbing the informal network of interpersonal relationships. The resulting low primary-group stability produces low morale and may thereby contribute to team ineffectiveness. Declining clientele support may encourage a greater decline in team morale and performance. The consequent continued drop in profitability induces pressures for further managerial changes. Such changes, in turn, produce additional disruptive effects on the organization, and the vicious cycle continues (Grusky, 1963b: 30).

Thus, we find the manager charged with the basic responsibility of coordinating the activities of the team members and motivating them to achieve their full potential. In carrying out these tasks, the manager must demand full cooperation and this may run counter to the individualistic desires of a particular player. The fact that the manager's authority position is vulnerable adds another dimension to manager-player interaction. Yet, presumably, the manager has been recruited from among those individuals best equipped with the necessary social skills to handle these sensitive interpersonal situations.

The normal "table of organization" for a baseball team is illustrated in Fig. 3. One must keep in mind that the "ideal-typical" expectations of hierarchy of authority (from Weber) are not totally achieved in this instance. The player can influence the tenure of the manager and can also resist the pressures of front-office management to some degree.

The Rotating Coaches System: A Brief Case Study.[14]   The above discussion provides an interesting backdrop for a brief case study to follow. In 1961, the Chicago Cubs, under the ownership of Philip K. Wrigley, Jr., embarked on an experiment that caused considerable controversy and raised eyebrows. The experiment was popularly known as the "rotating-coaches" sys-

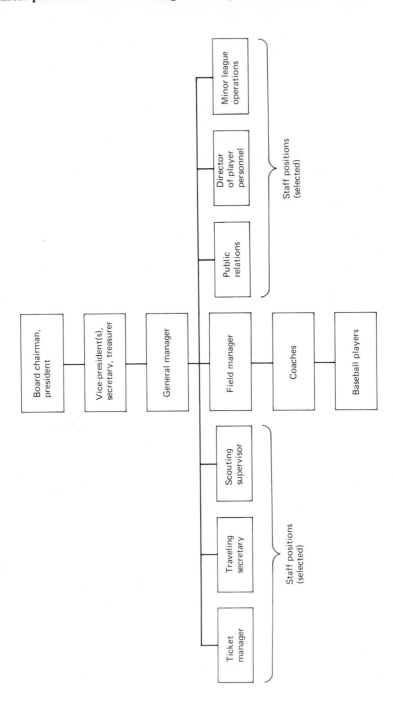

Fig. 3 *Model organization chart for typical major league team.*

tem of management, designed to replace the traditional "team manager" form. It was to embody some new structural features in administration and organization.

Some comments by Herbert Simon (1948) on evaluating administrative organization are especially pertinent here.

> The question is an empirical one. . . . What is needed is empirical research and experimentation to determine the relative desirability of alternative administrative arrangements. The methodological framework for this research is already at hand in the principle of efficiency. If an administrative organization whose activities are susceptible to objective evaluation be studied, then the actual change in accomplishment that results from modifying administrative arrangements in these organizations can be observed and analyzed.
>
> There are two indispensable conditions to successful research along these lines. First, it is necessary that the objectives of the administrative organization under study be defined in concrete terms so that results expressed in terms of these objectives, may be accurately measured. Second, it is necessary that sufficient experimental control be exercised to make possible the isolation of the particular effect under study from other disturbing factors that might be operating on the organization at the same time (Simon, 1948: 42).*

The first condition is easily met in professional baseball. The objective of each team is to win the most games and secure the championship. Comparative team performance is a matter of public record. The second criterion mentioned by Simon is not so easily attained because there are just too many variables to be controlled. Yet this is the closest example we have to a controlled experiment, since available information will allow us to reconstruct the events as accurately as possible.

The Chicago Cubs baseball team of the National League had just come off another bad season in 1960, ending up in seventh place in an eight-team league and adding a fourteenth straight year to their string of second division finishes. Clearly the executives needed to do something to produce a winner. Owner Philip K. Wrigley, Jr., successful chewing gum executive and well-known unpredictable innovator, finally devised a new management idea for the operation of his ball club. He decided to do away with the title and position of "field manager." In its place, he would hire a group of

---

* Herbert A. Simon, *Administrative Behavior*. (New York: Macmillan, 1948.) Reprinted by permission.

coaches, from 8 to 12 in number, from whom a "head coach" would be appointed. This might look like the old manager system but it was not intended to operate that way. At least in the beginning of the new experiment, different coaches were to be periodically rotated into the position of "head coach." At other times, coaches would be rotated into the minor leagues to serve as head coaches or instructors, since only four or five coaches were to be with the parent club at any one time. Wrigley also acknowledged that this would eliminate the necessity of "firing" a manager when the club was doing poorly. It seems clear that no one man could ever establish himself as the sole field leader since he was apt to be moved from the head coach's position and rotated into the minor leagues. But what would be the consequences of this divided authority?

During spring training in 1961, the new coaching concept was greeted with enthusiasm and seemed to be reasonably successful. Wrigley was trying to apply business efficiency to baseball. The coaches stressed the values of efficiency, providing advice and encouragement to the players, the use of specialists, the creation of congeniality and harmony and the more effective use of the teaching skills of the coaches.

But once the regular season started, several problems emerged. How was the head coach to be chosen? How long would he stay in the position before being rotated? What were the limits to his authority, if any, when he occupied the top leadership position? What if all the coaches could not agree on personnel (i.e., lineup) or strategy decisions? What would happen if a "strong man" were to emerge from the panel of coaches? As these issues were raised, the ownership group tried to clarify them or resolve them. However, all too often policies were announced, only to be contradicted in the days that followed.

In the first weeks of the season, there was considerable shifting into and out of the position of "head coach." Since each man had his own preferences, there was a corresponding degree of shifting in player personnel. Then, with one-third of the season gone, one man was rotated into the position of "head coach" and he remained in that capacity until the end of the season. In all, four different men had served as head coach during the 1961 season.

During the second year of the experiment, the 1962 season, the general plan continued, this time with only three different men occupying the position of "head coach." The first two operated in that capacity only a short time (20 to 30 games) and then an apparent "strong man" was assigned the head coach's job for the remainder of the season. There were reports of friction among the coaches. The team had a poor finish and at the end of the season the "strong man" coach was fired.

During the next three seasons, 1963–65, one man played a prominent role as head coach. He was in complete command in 1963 and 1964 (when the team showed some improvement) and he began the 1965 season in charge. However, he was "kicked upstairs" to an administrative post and replaced as head coach by another of the rotating coaches for the rest of the 1965 season. By the 1966 season, owner Wrigley had returned to the manager system and hired a man known to be tough, demanding and knowledgeable.

What can be said, by way of evaluation, about this experimental plan? In particular, what effect did it have on the individual player? The effect of this situation is difficult to evaluate, particularly in the brief space allotted here. The most immediate evidence available would be in the form of statistical records for the Chicago team and scattered comments by players and coaches, most of whom had been traded to other teams or had been released.

An intensive study of Table 2 proves informative. Here the reader can find a series of yearly resumes of several measures of team performance, including the team won-lost record, final position of team finish, number of managers or head coaches, and finally team batting, fielding and pitching records (each with a comparative ranking against all other teams during that season). The table also contains years both before and after the coaching experiment to allow for more accurate evaluation.

As Table 2 reveals, there was little improvement in league standing during the 5-year experiment. However, the team's won and lost record did show some improvement, significantly during the years (1963–64) when there was only one "head coach." On most of the other measures of overall team performance (batting, fielding, and pitching), the Cubs generally ranked seventh or eighth. The only exception here was an improvement in team fielding in the middle years of the experiment.

Why was the team less successful than anticipated by the ownership group? A basic problem emerged as a result of the several roles required of the traditional manager and his coaching staff. In the hierarchy of authority on the field, the manager is at the apex. He is charged with the task of coordinating the activity and learning sequences of the players, often through his coaches. The coaches are the teaching arm of the manager, thus allowing the manager the time for other responsibilities and the social distance necessary to deal with hard-nosed personnel decisions. Under the "rotating coaches" system, each head coach was (or had been) both teacher and leader on the field. He was being asked to carry out two sets of role expectations which, in fact, did not complement each other. The teaching role brought him into close contact with the player, while the more "managerial"

Table 2

Team statistics of the Chicago Cubs, 1956–1970

Year	Won–loss record	Total percent	Team finish	Number of managers or head coaches	Team batting average (ranked)	Team fielding average (ranked)	Team pitching ERA (ranked)
1956	60–94	.390	8th	1	.244 (7th T)[a]	.975 (6th T)[a]	3.96 (6th)
1957	62–92	.403	7th	1	.244 (8th)	.975 (6th)	4.13 (7th)
1958	72–82	.468	5th	1	.265 (3rd)	.974 (6th T)[a]	4.22 (6th)
1959	74–80	.481	5th	1	.249 (7th)	.976 (4th)	4.01 (5th)
1960	60–94	.390	7th	2	.243 (7th)	.976 (4th T)[a]	4.35 (8th)
1961[c]	64–90	.416	7th	4	.255 (7th)	.970 (8th)	4.48 (7th)
1962[c]	59–103	.364	9th[b]	3	.253 (7th)	.977 (3rd T)[a]	4.54 (9th)
1963[c]	82–80	.506	7th[b]	1	.238 (8th)	.976 (4th T)[a]	3.08 (2nd)
1964[c]	76–86	.469	8th[b]	1	.251 (5th)	.975 (4th)	4.08 (8th)
1965[c]	72–90	.444	8th[b]	2	.238 (8th)	.974 (8th)	3.78 (7th)
1966	59–103	.364	10th[b]	1	.254 (7th)	.974 (8th)	4.33 (10th)
1967	87–74	.540	3rd[b]	1	.251 (3rd)	.980 (1st)	3.48 (7th)
1968	84–78	.519	3rd[b]	1	.242 (5th)	.981 (1st)	3.41 (9th)
1969	92–70	.568	3rd[d]	1	.253 (5th T)[a]	.979 (4th)	3.34 (5th)
1970	84–78	.519	5th[d]	1	.259 (7th T)[a]	.978 (4th T)[a]	3.76 (4th)

[a] "T" means that the team average was tied at that rank with one or more other teams.

[b] From 1962–1968, the National League had 10 teams due to expansion with the New York Mets and the Houston Astros.

[c] From 1961–65, the Chicago Cubs were under the "rotating head coach" experiment.

[d] In 1969, the National League added two new teams, the San Diego Padres and the Montreal Expos, and broke the 12 teams into two six-team divisions. The team finishes and rankings noted for 1969 and 1970 are based on the 12 teams. Actually the Chicago Cubs finished second in the Eastern Division both years.

role required a certain social distance and demanded a more submissive respect from the player. Without the latter, his authority was questionable. Then, too, the possibility that he might be rotated out of the head coaching position tomorrow minimized the legitimacy of his demands on the player and also reduced the certitude of knowing what to expect.

These two key roles of the field leader, teacher and decision-maker, had mixed success during the five-year experiment, according to reports by former players and released coaches. During spring training, when each coach was engaged in teaching his specialty to both veteran and rookie players, the instructor role was carried out very successfully. In addition, during the regular season, those coaches who rotated into the minor league farm system to continue teaching apparently upgraded the ability of many players. This resulted in several young players moving up rapidly to the parent club.

However, the "head coach," in his position as field leader and authority figure, was less than successful. His position was compromised by division of authority and uncertainty of tenure. There was reported conflict among several of the coaches and their inability to present a united front reduced the effectiveness of the plan.

What about the effect of this experiment on the players? It seemed apparent that the players were often left either confused or uncertain about their role on the team. Sometimes they got conflicting advice from the coaches and in some situations there was no clearcut authority to resolve the conflict. It soon became apparent that when Coach A was acting as head coach, a certain player would be used regularly. But when Coach B took over, that same player knew he was temporarily out of a regular assignment. In short, changing head coaches meant changing policies, changing expectations, changing assignments, and the like. In an atmosphere of constant change and frequent uncertainty, it was not possible for the team to develop the necessary cohesion and teamwork to win consistently. The player was also unable to receive sustained confidence from one team leader and, in return, grant that man his respect.

The evidence for this interpretation, although not impeccable, is found in the improved record of the team under a single head coach (1963 and 1964) and in the years since the end of the experiment (notably 1967, 1968, and 1969). What, then, does this "deviant case" tell us about the more traditional manager form and the resulting manager-player contacts? The player seems to function most effectively when he is operating in a situation where the manager has a reasonably stable position and where the manager's expectations are clearly known. As instability in any form is introduced into this system, it detracts from the player's sense of certainty and self-confidence. Obviously, this interpretation is based on the premise that the player has accepted the normative themes of teamwork and cooperation with the manager. To the extent that he stressed his own individual accomplishments, the player is expressing his independence from the normative expectations in the internal system.

In sum, the field manager plays many roles in his attempt to coordinate effectively the activities of the team. His background may equip him to accomplish his goal but he must use his skills with careful balance as he makes demands on a player who has his own individualistic ambitions. The conflict between authority and autonomy can be volatile.

The Internal System: A Summary. The elements of behavior (interaction, activity, and sentiments, in Homans, 1950) are considerably more intense in the internal system. This is where the player performs his basic tasks; this is the focus of his motives and aspirations. The strong normative expectations of teamwork and cooperation with authority are compelling. Yet they may run counter to the individual player's aims. Role conflict under these conditions is potentially quite severe.

c. The Player's Solution: Different Role Performances. In the foregoing analysis, we have found the player at the intersection of two major sources of role expectations, resulting in severe role conflict. The first, from the external system, consisted of the fans' demands for an exciting, drama-packed game and the owner's more sober concern for business practices and club profits. The second conflict, within the internal system, was the fellow players' expectation of teamwork and the manager's demand for cooperation and submission. But these are potentially incompatible with the individual athlete's self-conception and his desire for personal autonomy and personal acclaim. At this point, it is even possible to see how, as Homans suggested, the elements in the external system have influence on behavior in the internal system. The fans' cry for heroics during a game appeals to the player's need for individualistic recognition, while the owner's demand for commitment to team success meshes well with expectations of coordination and teamwork.

How does one resolve these role dilemmas? What possible solutions are there to the role conflicts we have outlined?

In his attempt to reduce the cognitive strain experienced, the player may do one of several things (Sarbin and Allen, 1968: 540–544 and Lindesmith and Strauss, 1968: 378–380). Regardless of his choice, the player is making a decision to respond to different "audiences." Although not an exhaustive list, we can note certain types of responses available to the player: team-oriented, fan-oriented, individualistic rationalizer, legitimate star, dropout, and transient. Clearly each is not as simple a solution as may appear in its description and an individual player in reality may give evidence of dimensions of several response patterns.

The first two types of solution result from the decision to respond to one set of conflicting expectations rather than another, or what has been called "attention deployment." The two subtypes are the "fan-oriented" and the "team-oriented" player. The fan-oriented player performs for the crowd in the stands. He tries to provide the audience with the heroic play, regardless of the game situation. This is the player who makes the easy play look difficult. The other players, as "insiders," know what is going on and they often refer to this behavior as "showboating."

By contrast, the team-oriented player would be regarded by his fellow players as the more professional. He would do what is required by the game situation and he would give the team's welfare and the manager's orders top priority. Because his behavior is more quietly professional, his contribution to the team is largely overlooked by the fans. But these men gain the respect of their colleagues, who understand that the complex division of labor on the team necessitates everyone performing his unique function.

A third technique would involve a "change in beliefs" relevant to these incompatible expectations from different structural sources. The conflicting dilemma is still there but the player may convince himself that "what is good for me is also good for the team." This may be nothing more than a re-evaluation of priorities and this style might be termed the "individualistic rationalizer." This player is primarily concerned with the success of his own performance. He is constantly aware that he must compile a standout record in order to negotiate more effectively with the front office for next year's contract. If his level of play benefits the team, so much the better. If challenged, he would argue that his individual contributions could not help but aid the team's overall record.

There is another type of response, although probably not so self-conscious a technique as those cited above. This might be labeled the "legitimate star." He is essentially a team man. But because of superior natural talent and a strong drive to succeed, this type of player, in conforming to the team's needs, may provide the fan with his dramatic moment and thus further his own individualistic aims as far as fan adulation and economic bargaining power are concerned. Striking examples might be players such as Ernie Banks, Brooks Robinson, Willie Mays, Al Kaline and the like—men known as both offensive and defensive standouts who consider the team's performance to be of vital importance.

An interesting illustration of the different emphasis of the team player versus the individualist comes to mind. There are several players who are known to keep "little black books" on player performance. In the one case, the player will make notes of the habits and characteristics of opposing players in order to use this information against them in future games. The player is trying to educate himself so that he might improve the team performance in a later meeting. By contrast, we hear of players who jot down a daily record of their own individual performance so that they might refer to this information during future salary negotiations with management.

Apparently, there are several players who never live up to their potential. They "have all the tools" but their physical abilities are often neutralized by social or psychological shortcomings. These are the players whose baseball careers are marked by periodic trades to other teams in the major leagues. This fifth technique of conflict resolution we have labeled the "transient." His inability to adjust to the social demands of the occupation only serves to increase the problem. Because he does not remain with a single team for any meaningful duration of time, he is rarely able to enjoy an important role in the network of team relationships. Always the "outsider," this type of player experiences little sense of achievement and therefore receives minimal recognition. Perhaps he is never able to make a commitment to any one constituency in his occupational environment.

Finally, some players periodically find their solution to these pressures by "leaving the (psychological) field" or escaping from the conflict. We would label this, a sixth and final technique, as the "dropout." Both Curt Flood of the Washington Senators and Alex Johnson of the California Angels were under extreme social, financial, and psychological pressure during the 1971 season. Although for different reasons, both were unable to finish out the season as active players, yet their athletic prowess was unquestioned. These men must perceive themselves at the center of a barrage of conflicting expectations coming from all directions at once. Obviously, their response is the most extreme reaction to role conflict and is not really a very satisfactory solution.

Thus, some players are able to develop a successful mode of adjustment, while others are incapable of achieving a satisfactory role performance. Some athletes gain the respect of the manager and their fellow players, others receive fan adulation, while some men find their careers to be nothing more than a series of manager-player or player-player conflict, followed by movement to another team via the trade route. The specific mode of adjustment adopted by a particular baseball player would depend on several factors.

The Third Phase of Career: Adjustment to the Post-Baseball, Second Career

Perhaps the most interesting and theoretically important career contingency occurs when the major league player is forced to retire from active playing. At a relatively young age, when most of his age peers in other occupations are reaching maturity and stability on the job, the retired player must embark on an entirely new career. In short, this is a crucial "turning point" in the lifelong occupational career of the professional athlete.

1. The Socio-Psychological Dimension.   The trauma of this moment can best be seen as a natural outgrowth of the desire to remain in the game and the lack of planning for a second career. Without going into great detail, the following information on our sample of former baseball players is illustrative. On the questionnaire the players were asked to estimate when they first had begun to think about retirement from active playing. About 75 percent of the 312 respondents reported that they did not even begin to consider retirement until they were in the last quarter of their active career in baseball (thus, in their early to mid-30s). Among their first thoughts, remaining in baseball in some capacity or obtaining a sports-related position (e.g., teaching and coaching) was mentioned approximately one-third of the time: the most common set of expressed hopes.

The impact of this harsh reality raises somewhat unique problems of adjustment:

> Fairly self-evident are the maladjusting consequences of loss of economic security. Not so apparent, but quite as vital to the individual involved, are the psychological consequences of being displaced from one occupation and forced to seek employment in another one. A man has more than an economic interest in his occupation. He has presumably spent some years learning the skills required by the occupation; . . . but he has also adjusted himself to the occupational way of life. To shift to another occupation, then, means more than learning the necessary manual and intellectual skills. It means adjusting to another occupational way of life (LaPiere and Farnsworth, 1943: 246).*

When queried about their feelings at the time of leaving the playing career, slightly over half of the 360 codable responses (some gave more than one classifiable answer) were oriented rather nostalgically toward the past. Interview and questionnaire disclosures included regret, sadness and shock with the aging process that brought on the forced decision.

> It scared hell out of me. I wanted to stay in baseball in some capacity for the rest of my life.
>
> I thought it was the end of the world. My first year out I almost went out of my mind. In fact, my wife made me go to spring training on my own, alone in 1952 as a vacation, and at that time while working out I

---

* R. T. LaPiere and P. R. Farnsworth, *Social Psychology.* (New York: McGraw-Hill, 1943.) Reprinted by permission.

realized it was all over, I was an old man as far as baseball was concerned.

Leaving something that seemed to be part of my life.

I did not realize that time had gone that fast and was almost remorseful.

At the other extreme were those retirees who were future-oriented. About one-quarter of the answers fell into this grouping (with the remaining responses characterized as a mixture between past and future orientation). The comments of the future-oriented indicated a strong sense of self-confidence and acceptance of the inevitable.

I didn't mind as I was one of the very few who had something to go to. Had business from 1941.

I knew I was out of baseball so didn't worry to [sic] much. I had my mind made up that I could do about anything I selected by hard work.

Confident of the future. Had money and an education.

I had always intended to use baseball to get something better since I was not good enough at the game to make it an end in itself. I decided to quit in the middle of the year when traded to a place I didn't think would further my purpose and never regretted it.

The respondents were asked to comment about the most difficult adjustment they had to make upon retirement. One-third of their answers were concerned with aspects of their post-baseball lives which they found lacking in their current activities.

I missed very much the fine associations I made in baseball, the personal contact, the activity of the ball field, these things I missed most.

I naturally missed the game itself which I loved very much. The contacts and friends I made I very much appreciated and the opportunity for travel. I missed them all.

One respondent virtually poured out his "guts" in response to this question:

But adjusting yourself, that's what bothered me. (How do you mean?) It was a great sensation, being on the field of play facing a lot of people. It's like a person who drinks or has some sort of habit. It was always a relief for me, getting in front of the public. As long as I could perform before them I could feel strong and good. . . . It bothered me. I craved that. I really craved that part of it. It seemed like life—I was lost to the world. There wasn't enough going on. There wasn't enough excitement.

But in spite of all the socio-psychological trauma connected with retirement, the vast majority of our respondents reported that they had little or no difficulty in obtaining their first post-baseball job (about 90 percent) and that they were situated either immediately or within a three-month period (75 percent).

In sum, these men, very often with little or no definite planning for the future, suddenly had retirement forced upon them, due primarily to the physical processes of aging. This career contingency created a major socio-psychological strain that necessitated a corresponding adjustment. Many of these men truly missed important aspects of the baseball occupation— especially the associations with teammates. Yet the majority expressed the view that the necessary adjustments had been made.

2. The Occupational Dimension. The problem of the second career has recently received more sustained attention (Hiestand, 1971; Levinson, 1968; Haug and Sussman, 1970; Brim, 1973; *Vocational Guidance Quarterly*, 1971). Although primarily concerned with professional education in the middle years, Hiestand's (1971: 1) general premise is instructive:

> By popular consensus, the middle years of life are expected to be a stable period of fulfillment. From an occupational vantage, we tend to view the middle years as a plateau, on the supposition that most people have attained their ambitions or have settled for less success than they had anticipated.*

It is into this kind of setting that our "retired" baseball player begins to seek work, a relative newcomer to the job market in competition with many peers who have reached that stable occupational plateau. In short, it is a reversal of the normal progression from an early trial period of jumping around in the process of finding suitable work which characterizes the new teenage or early-20s applicant to the more stable period of job security (Miller and Form, 1964).

In order to clarify the issues involved in the second career for retired athletes, it is useful to borrow from the visual imagery of Becker and Strauss (1956). In discussing patterns of occupational placement and adjustment, these authors refer to the concepts of "multiple routes" and "switching." Picture, if you will, a number of escalators on which individuals engaged in the business of making a living are actively riding up and down, and constantly switching back and forth, in an attempt to find the escalator which supplies the occupational role best suited to their abilities.

---

* Dale L. Hiestand, *Changing Careers after Thirty-Five: New Horizons Through Professional Graduate Study.* (New York: Columbia University Press, 1971.) Reprinted by permission.

More specifically, let us follow those individuals on the escalator marked "professional baseball." As they ride to the top, in this case the major leagues, they find themselves forced to switch over at retirement to another escalator, in an attempt to maintain or better that position, via a "second career." This is oversimplified, of course, because some players will have started a downward course within the baseball hierarchy (i.e., playing in the minor leagues) before actual retirement, not unlike Cressey's (1972) dance hall girls who come to realize the decline of their popularity with the onset of aging. The changing structural factors in "failure" in sport have been discussed by Ball (1971). Other retired players will be able to remain on a baseball-related escalator in the inactive capacities of manager, scout, coach, and so on. And others will make the switch away from baseball and immediately begin a downward trip for any number of reasons.

It is the situation encountered at the point of "switching" escalators, or in adjusting to a nonactive role on the "baseball-related escalator," that concerns us here. Just what are the dynamics of this situation? Our first task is to get an overview of the level of post-baseball occupational attainment. We chose to measure the ranking of occupations in two ways: (1) a simple distinction between the census breakdown of white-collar and blue-collar jobs, with nonactive, but baseball-related occupations (i.e., manager, coach, scout, etc.) retained as a separate category, and (2) a numerical rating based on the North–Hatt study (1947) of 90 occupations.[15] Baseball-related jobs were integrated directly into the ratings in the latter approach. In both of these measurement strategies, attention was given to the first job obtained by the former player and also his "main" (i.e., longest-held) job. Overall, there was a high degree of consistency between the "first" job and the "main" occupation.[16]

Based on the analysis of occupational rank according to the two measurement approaches, former players exhibited the following distribution for "main" occupations:

Census categories	Percent	North-Hatt scale	Percent
White-collar	64.9	High (1–29)	17.5
Blue-collar	10.8	Medium (30–40)	63.3
Baseball-related	24.1	Low (50+)	19.3

As can be noted, the majority of these former major leaguers were working in some nonbaseball capacity. Yet those retired athletes who "switched" to the baseball-related escalator are of special interest, given the strong desire of most players to remain in the baseball industry. Their active-baseball career patterns were significantly different from those men who had caught onto one of the more "normal" occupational escalators. For example, our data indicate that those men who remained in baseball in some sort of inactive position (for main occupations) had the following characteristics (when compared with those who severed all ties with baseball in their post-playing careers): they retired from baseball at a much older age ($x^2 = 14.97$; $p = 0.005$); their last league affiliation was more apt to be in the lower-level minor leagues ($x^2 = 20.13$; $p = 0.0007$); and they had spent a far smaller proportion of their active careers in the major leagues ($x^2 = 16.08$; $p = 0.003$). There is also strong evidence ($x^2 = 24.38$; $p = 0.0002$) that those who remained in baseball as a manager, coach, or scout had much less stable job patterns.

It is traditional in professional sports that managers and coaches are highly expendable when a team is not winning—the scapegoat phenomenon. Our data would appear to support this notion for there was considerable job movement among those who remained in a baseball-related field.

The overall picture seems clear. Some men (those with relatively less athletic ability and perhaps with fewer options available in the "outside" occupational world) found that opportunities in the sports field held the greatest promise for them. During their playing days, they continued to participate and sought to achieve stardom. But as the inevitable aging process reduced their effectiveness and they began to slip down to lower and lower minor league clubs, many would take on coaching duties as a means of hanging on. In this way, their "commitment" to the game as a lifelong career was gradually reinforced. Thus, the "switch" to the non-active baseball escalator seemed natural.

By contrast, most of the men were either unable to catch on to baseball-related jobs or desired to move into the wider business world. Their ties to baseball often appeared to be rather loose. These men retired at an earlier age and often after completing play for a major league club (rather than allowing themselves to slip to the lower minor leagues). For many, the baseball career was seen more as a means to other ends. The notoriety obtained in baseball was to be translated into a white-collar occupation.

This observation raises one of the critical issues that prompted our original research—the relative impact of education and baseball fame on post-baseball occupational achievement. Once we have ascertained the occupational adjustment of these former players, it is natural to question the factors in their past which have "caused" them to end up where they have. Once again, path analysis provides us with relevant insights, as illustrated in Fig. 4.

Our theoretical perspective and the existing research literature called attention to certain background factors as influences on occupational achievement. For example, Blau and Duncan (1967) were concerned with the interplay between ascriptive circumstances at birth and problematic and

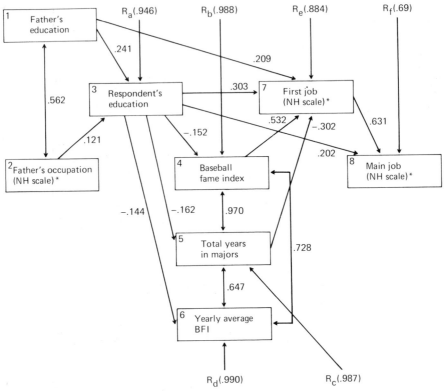

Fig. 4 *Path diagram of background and baseball career factors influencing the post-playing main job. (The correlation matrix for this path diagram is shown in Table 3.)*

contingent factors during the individual's lifetime as factors influencing occupational achievement.

The governing conceptual scheme in the analysis is quite a commonplace one. We think of the individual's life cycle as a sequence in time that can be described, however partially and crudely, by a set of classificatory or quantitative measurements taken at successive stages. . . .

Given this scheme, the questions we are continually raising in one form or another are: how and to what degree do the circumstances of birth condition subsequent status? and, how does status attained (whether

Table 3

Zero-Order Correlation Coefficients for Background and Baseball Career Variables Influencing Post-Career Occupational Level. (Number of cases for each correlation is noted in parentheses.)

Variables	1	2	3	4	5	6	7	8
1 (Father's Education)	⋯							
2 (Father's Occupation)	.562 † (230)	⋯						
3 (Respondent's Education)	.309 † (240)	.256 † (281)	⋯					
4 (Baseball fame index, BFI)	.026 (241)	.029 (282)	−.152 † (332)	⋯				
5 (Total years in major leagues)	.034 (241)	.049 (282)	−.162 † (332)	.971 † (335)	⋯			
6 (Yearly average for BFI)	.026 (241)	.024 (282)	−.144 † (332)	.728 † (335)	.647 † (335)	⋯		
7 (First nonbaseball job, North–Hatt Scale)	.306 † (238)	.233 † (275)	.335 † (321)	.198 † (324)	.173 † (324)	.151 † (324)	⋯	
8 (Main nonbaseball job, North–Hatt Scale)	.309 † (239)	.282 † (279)	.413 † (329)	.113 * (332)	.103 (332)	.054 (332)	.699 † (323)	⋯

* Significant at the .05 level.
† Significant at the .01 level.

by ascription or achievement) at one stage of the life cycle affect the prospect for a subsequent stage?*

To implement these ideas, Blau and Duncan employed a simple, but causal path analysis model with only five variables: father's education, father's occupation, respondent's education, status of respondent's first job and status of the respondent's 1962 occupation. Based on the statistical test, the respondent's education exerted the strongest influence on his first job, followed by the impact of the father's occupation and then father's education (Blau and Duncan, 1967: 169–170). Interestingly, the 1962 job was more strongly influenced by the respondent's education than his first job (although the authors cautioned that this difference was not large enough to be overemphasized). They concluded:

> The model suggests that factors salient at an early stage of a man's career may continue to play a *direct* role as he grows older. But the direct effects of education and father's status are attenuated drastically with the passage of time. A compensatory effect is the increasing relevance of the accumulation of occupational experience as time passes (Blau and Duncan, 1967: 186–187).*

In the final analysis, however, education "... exerts the strongest direct effect on occupational achievements (the path coefficient is 0.39), with the level on which a man starts his career being second ($p = 0.28$)" (Blau and Duncan, 1967: 403). In a follow-up and slightly expanded analysis, Duncan, Featherman and Duncan (1972) reached essentially the same conclusion.

In our diagram in Fig. 4, we used the same factors as Blau and Duncan, with the important addition of three measures of baseball career performance: the BFI (baseball fame index), the total number of years spent in the major leagues, and the yearly BFI average.[17]

Contrary to the Blau–Duncan findings, our respondent's "main" job (based on the North–Hatt scale) was highly dependent upon the level of the "first" job held (path coefficient, 0.63). The only other factor, respondent's education, trailed far behind (path coefficient, 0.20). The role of the father's status appeared to have only an indirect effect. No measure of baseball fame or skill had a direct, measurable impact on "main job" occupational achievement.

However, when we consider the factors that influenced the achievement level of the "first" job (based on the North–Hatt scale), the situation

---

* P. M. Blau and O. D. Duncan, *The American Occupational Structure*. (New York: John Wiley and Sons, 1967), p. 164. Reprinted by permission.

is more complex. The father's education showed some impact (path coefficient, 0.20), but not as strong as the effect of the respondent's own education (path coefficient, 0.30). An interesting, but puzzling finding was the negative influence of "number of years in the majors" on the respondent's first job. We can only speculate that spending too long a period of time playing baseball may begin to limit the number of opportunities available upon retirement.

But of greater significance was the effect of BFI (baseball fame index) on the first job held (path coefficient, 0.53). The baseball player apparently found that the rank of his initial post-playing job was highly dependent upon the degree of success he had achieved in baseball. Being a well-known player does open doors to all sorts of business opportunities and he was able to translate his fame into improved occupational achievement. However, in the long run, the BFI exerted no direct influence on the occupational attainment level of the longest-held or main job.

Previous research had shown that education was the basic causal factor in occupational achievement. Our concern with the relative impact of baseball fame and education can now be evaluated. With regard to the first nonplaying job, baseball fame was the most important predictor of occupational achievement, with the respondent's education running second at a moderate distance. But over the long haul, the player's level of achievement is more dependent on the traditional factor of education, while the impact of the BFI has dropped out of sight.

In short, employers may be initially dazzled by having a well-known athlete connected with their organization, but the ability to produce on the job, associated strongly with years of education, gradually assumes priority.

CONCLUSION

The professional baseball player's occupation is viewed by many in the general public as a near-perfect job, with highly romantic overtones. He is a hero who makes a great deal of money and yet works only part of the year.

In this chapter, we have tried to dispel this unrealistic picture of the work environment of the professional athlete. As with any occupation, there are several sets of relationships with which the status occupant must contend. The structurally based sources of incompatible expectations that impinge on his occupational performance are indeed diverse and obligatory. Each constituency can make a legitimate claim to his energy and attention. The baseball player's desire for autonomy, ego satisfaction, sense of economic worth and independent performance was constantly curtailed or questioned by significant audiences in the social structure of his work environment. Role conflict was inevitable and he was faced with choosing from among a set of alternative adjustments.

Thus, the occupational life of the baseball player shares many problems of structurally induced role conflict with other pursuits. But several characteristics of the athlete's job make occupational life rather unique: public performance, restricted economic mobility, "outsider" control by fans and umpires, insecurity of tenure, and uncertainty about the authority structure.

And these occupational traits become especially critical when considered in the context of the short-term athletic career and the necessity of a second career. More than several other types of work, athletic careers are characterized by periodic contingencies which often involve radical shifts in orientation and activity. Throughout our analysis, the crucial role played by education at each major turning point has been carefully noted and discussed. Although not unexpected, the documentation of the educational impact on athletic careers is especially significant. The only qualification is introduced when we view the role of sports fame in the acquisition of the first post-playing job.

The primary focus of this paper was on the professional baseball player. But a major task remains. Employing some of the same conceptual tools, attention should be directed toward other professional sports in an effort to test the comparative validity of our findings and analysis. For example, professional football and basketball players are known to have obtained greater educational experience than baseball players. We need to study the implications of this fact for career patterns and career contingencies. Then we might begin to explore the extent to which other nonsport, short-term occupations differ from, or share similarities with, professional sports as work.

In this manner, additional insights into the meaning of work could be obtained. To the average spectator, sports are viewed as fun, play, and recreation. However, we have seen that the professional athlete takes his work very seriously since it is his means of livelihood. Thus, one man's work may be another individual's leisure. Most professional athletes give evidence of strong commitment to their jobs and they derive all-important self-esteem and self-conception from these activities. Why do men seek a livelihood through the medium of professional sports? Clearly it involves something beyond money, prestige and the like, although these are definitely important considerations. The satisfaction in personal accomplishment, especially when one is being tested in the public arena, must have a special appeal. The chance to face the competitive challenge from others, under conditions of nonviolence (or controlled violence) and clear-cut regulations, would seem to tell us something about the motivations and ego needs that man tries to satisfy in the variety of his work experiences in professional sports.

Finally, brief mention should be made of the impact of the institution of sport on the larger society and its value system. Sports, and the men who make them their career, act as reinforcers of some very basic cultural values in American society: teamwork, success through dedication, controlled competition, universalistic criteria of judgment, to note a few. In addition, sports often serve an important integrative function for the larger society by bringing together people of diverse backgrounds at major events. No better example of this phenomenon could be presented than the recent festivities surrounding the successful assault by Hank Aaron on Babe Ruth's career record of 714 home runs. When Aaron hit number 715 on the evening of April 8, 1974, millions of fans were watching on national television. It had all the makings of a major cultural and ritual event. The game of baseball can serve as a morality play (Levine, 1972) for the larger society, acting as the game of life in miniature.

NOTES

1. In the 1960 Census, professional athletes were reported as .01 percent of the total experienced civilian labor force with 4,579 persons (U.S. Bureau of Census, 1964). In a 1967 report (Fountain and Parker, 1967), it was stated that an estimated 31,900 professional athletes participated in competition in 1966, 8 of 10 in individual as opposed to team sports. By the 1970 Census (U.S. Bureau of Census, 1973), there were a reported 50,116 "athletes and kindred workers," comprising only .065 percent of the total of employed persons 16 years old and over. Of the total number of athletes, 72 percent were male and 28 percent female.

2. This phrase was taken from an opening line in a baseball movie viewed at the Baseball Hall of Fame Library, Cooperstown, New York, July 27, 1971.

3. Anyone familiar with the work of Everett C. Hughes will note immediately the extent to which several ideas and concepts in this paper have their origin or development with him. Several of the foci of this analysis and discussion derive from his course in the Sociology of Occupations and Professions given at the University of Chicago. Professor Hughes is well-known for his insights and interests in the area of occupations and professions (Hughes, 1958a, 1971) and for the impact he has had on innumerable sociologists (Becker, Geer, Riesman, and Weiss, 1968). I must also acknowledge his personal support and encouragement, offered above and beyond the constant intellectual stimulation which he always provided. I owe him a great personal and intellectual debt.

4. Over a period of about two months, some 876 mail questionnaires were sent out to former major league baseball players in the spring of 1958. We received 335 useable forms, for a 38 percent return rate. The five-page questionnaire requested background data, facts about the playing career, and questions designed to elicit information about the postbaseball career. In addition, 20 former players were interviewed. The sample was not random, but by contrasting it with a random sample drawn from a list of known, living former major leaguers, it was possible to ascertain the degree and direction of sample bias. Thus, our sample of respondents was highly skewed in the direction of players of more recent birth, longer major league tenure, greater fame, and better yearly quality of performance.

5. There are several excellent sources on the technique of path analysis (Duncan, 1966; Land, 1968; Heise, 1968). Nygreen (1971) describes the computer application of path analysis closely paralleling that used in this study, while Kenyon (1970) illustrates its use with a sport example.

   Path analysis is based on a simple zero-order correlation matrix for a given number of variables. Essentially partial regression coefficients (which measure the relationship between two variables while all the other variables in the system are held constant or controlled) are computed and these become the path coefficients in the path diagram. As Kenyon (1970: 192) says, "thus the path coefficient is the proportion of the standard deviation in the dependent variable for which the antecedent variable is directly responsible, with all other variables, including residuals, held constant." It should be pointed out that there are several assumptions which are basic to the employment of the path model (Land, 1968). For example, there should be interval scale measurements on all variables, the effect between variables should be linear and additive, clearcut causal priorities, a recursive set of equations, etc. But Nygreen is quick to point out that it is a rare case where all these assumptions are met. Yet most projects proceed, after realizing what decisions have been made. Our work is no exception to this observation.

6. Obviously this statement must be realistically qualified in light of the recruitment schemes and "professional" training which take place at some of the larger universities known as "football factories" and the like. Frequent sanctions by the NCAA against its member schools and periodic exposés about recruiting violations pinpoint the dilemma of the aspiring professional athlete. (Time, 1974: 62–63 and Durso, 1974: 1, 52) The Durso article is one of a series of articles in the New York Times. For a more complete treatment of these and related issues, see Cross (1973) and Koch (1973).

7. A word should be said about the measure of baseball fame or success used in this research. We computed a "baseball fame index" (BFI) for each player. It consisted of a weighted scoring of three performance items: batting or pitching record, number of games played, and the level of team performance (whether first or second division finish). Thus, two out of the three items used were measures of individual skill and performance and these two were also

weighted more heavily in the overall index. Due to the limited availability of minor league records in a single, easily accessible source, the BFI is based *solely* on major league records. Further information on this index can be obtained by writing to the author.

8. All the correlations mentioned in the text can be found in the correlation matrices in the Appendix. These matrices serve as supplemental information to the path diagrams presented in this paper. The correlations presented were computed by using the Pearson product moment coefficient (Young and Veldman, 1965) and the significance levels were determined with reference to Appendix E from Young and Veldman.

9. The path diagram is designed to show the nature of causation among a set of time-sequenced variables, hence the connecting lines with the arrow indicating the causal direction (with the exception of the curved, two-headed arrow connecting the first two variables, indicating a simple zero-order correlation). For each of the later variables in the diagram, you will note the R value or residual is given, indicating the influence of all possible unspecified determinants of the variable in question which have been left unexplained. In Fig. 1, we have retained only those path coefficients which were .10 or more, on the assumption that those which were smaller were of relatively little influence.

10. The home TV viewer, privy to the "instant replay," is able to observe the rare "mistakes" of the umpire as he judges a close play at first base. Imagine the reaction of the fans at the game, if they were allowed to see such replays.

11. This is illustrated by a rather strong editorial from the June 20, 1961, issue of *The Sporting News.*

    Clearing Up a Mistaken Notion. One of the most popular misconceptions in baseball is that a defensive player cannot be charged with an error if he doesn't touch the ball.

    Some fans who have been going to games for years have clung to this theory. Even more surprisingly, many players have the same idea. Their feelings are hurt when they are charged with an error under the circumstances. "I didn't even touch the ball," they will say in aggrieved tones to the official scorer.

    An error is to be charged when, in the judgment of a scorer, a ball could have been handled by a fielder. If the "no touch, no error" theory were allowed to stand, you would have the ridiculous situation of calling a hit on a ball which went right through a fielder's legs.

    Ball players should understand and appreciate this situation, especially in the major leagues. They are expected to make the major league play in the Big Time.

    They are also expected to accept the judgment with major league good sportsmanship. (From a 1961 editorial in *The Sporting News*, **151**: 10. Reprinted by permission.)

This quote clearly contains an implicit morality, but so, too, does the whole notion of the "error" and its full meaning to the baseball world. Somehow victory should go only to those who deserve to win, those with superior ability.

12. In concise terms, Rottenberg describes the essential features of the clause:

> The team with which the player is contracted has exclusive right to the use of his playing services; he may not play baseball elsewhere without its consent. His contract may be assigned by this team to another team, and he is bound to report for play with the assignee team. No other team in organized baseball may employ him.
>
> Once a player has signed his first contract in organized baseball, therefore, he is no longer free to dispose of his services. He may withdraw from organized baseball and follow some other calling, but he may not choose freely among bidders for him within baseball.
>
> Some attempts have been made to enforce in the courts the exclusive right to contracted players' services which is conveyed by the uniform contract. On the principle that involuntary servitude is contrary to public policy, the courts have been reluctant to compel players to fulfill their contracts, to restrain them from performing for others, or to restrain others from employing them, and these attempts have met with little success.
>
> Baseball has therefore resorted to extralegal sanctions to enforce exclusive rights. A player who refuses to play for a team by which he is contracted, or refuses to play for a team to which his contract has been assigned, is suspended; he may not be employed by another team in organized baseball. A team in organized baseball that employs a suspended player will find that other teams will refuse to meet it on the field. (From Simon Rottenberg, "Squeeze Plays in Baseball's Labor Market," *Midway* **2** (1960), 5–6. Chicago: University of Chicago Press. Reprinted by permission.)

A brief discussion of the origin and early history of the reserve clause can be obtained in any one of several baseball histories (Voigt, 1966; Seymour, 1960). Gregory's discussion (1956) is particularly helpful since it is presented from the point of view of the economist. First instituted by club owners to reduce raiding and the "revolving" players which lessened team morale and cohesion, the reserve clause has had a checkered and revealing career. In 1879, five players on each team were reserved. This grew to 11 in 1883, to 14 in 1887 and by 1921, all players under major league contract were considered "reserved." Several owners abused the rule by suspending dissident or deviant players and periodically entire rival leagues were organized to "war against" the reserve clause idea. At times, compromises between warring leagues were worked out, so that they respected each other's reserve lists. This meant that club owners could use the clause to keep salaries down as well.

13. During the 1973 season, the American League experimented with a 10th starter, the "designated hitter." He was inserted in the regular lineup to bat for the pitcher, thus freeing the latter from the need to be lifted from the

game. There are several implications of this change. Managers must now re-order their strategies to accommodate this new element. Even more important for this paper are the "career consequences" of this innovation. Outstanding hitters who are on the decline and cannot play the field position may prolong their major league careers, since the batting eye and hitting power generally outlast running ability. On the other hand, there may be need for fewer pitch-ers and the speciality of "relief pitcher" may be increasingly threatened. The long-term future of the DH rule is uncertain.

14. A more complete analysis of this case is currently under way with the tenta-tive title, "The Team Without a Manager: An Organizational Analysis of a Professional Baseball Team." The bulk of the material for this analysis was taken from *The Sporting News*, 1960–1967. In addition, special thanks are due to Mr. Wrigley for supplying the author with copies of basic documents.

    The value of this type of "deviant case analysis" has been described else-where (Lipset, Trow, and Coleman, 1956: 12–13). A detailed investigation of this unusual form of leadership will provide great insight into the reasons for, and meaning of, the more traditional managerial structure. This should allow us to understand more fully the effect of the manager on the performance of the individual player.

15. Each occupation was given the score of its ranking on the North–Hatt list, from 1 to 90 (with the lower number indicating a higher rank). Because not all the occupations reported by the players were included, some scoring prob-lems arose. Each occupation which did not appear on the original list was as-signed a number corresponding to the listed occupation judged to be most comparable. When analyzing these data, we generally used three categories (with companion North–Hatt ratings): high (1–29), medium (30–49) and low (50+). Thus, the "high" group would include such occupations as physician, banker, civil engineer, and accountant for a large business; the "medium" category would have such jobs as captain in the regular Army, public school teacher, radio announcer, and trained machinist; and the "low" group would involve such jobs as bookkeeper, policeman, clerk in a store, truck driver, and janitor.

16. In those cases where an individual reported only one post-baseball job, these two obviously coincided.

17. The yearly BFI average was used as an indicator of the *average* level of skill/performance, especially for short careers. This contrasts sharply with the total BFI, which is cumulative and highly dependent on the total number of years played.

REFERENCES

Andreano, Ralph
1965   *No Joy In Mudville: The Dilemma of Major League Baseball.* Cambridge, Mass.: Schenkman Publishing Company, Inc.

Ball, Donald W.
1971   "Failure and Sport." Unpublished paper.
1975   "Methods and Sources in the Study of Sport." In *Sport and Social Order: Contributions to the Sociology of Sport*, Donald W. Ball and John W. Loy (eds.). Reading, Mass.: Addison-Wesley.

Becker, Howard S., and Anselm L. Strauss
1956   "Careers, Personality, and Adult Socialization." *American Journal of Sociology*, **62** (November): 253–263.

Becker, Howard S., Blanche Geer, David Riesman, and Robert S. Weiss (eds.)
1968   *Institutions and The Person*. Chicago: Aldine Publishing Company.

Blalock, H. M., Jr.
1962   "Occupational Discrimination: Some Theoretical Propositions." *Social Problems*, **9** (Winter, No. 3): 240–247.

Blau, Peter M., and Otis Dudley Duncan
1967   *The American Occupational Structure*. New York: John Wiley and Sons, Inc.

Bouton, James
1970   *Ball Four*. New York: Dell Publishing Company, Inc. (Edited by Leonard Shecter.)

Brim, Orville J. et al.
1973   "Committee on Work and Personality in the Middle Years: Description of Proposed Activities." Mimeographed by Social Science Research Council (June).

Brosman, Jim
1960   *The Long Season*. New York: Harper and Brothers.
1962   *Pennant Race*. New York: Harper and Brothers.

Charnofsky, Harold
1968   "The Major League Professional Baseball Player: Self-Conception Versus the Popular Image." *International Review of Sport Sociology*, **3**: 39–55.

Chass, Murray
1974   "Even Some Losers Emerge as Winners in Baseball's New Arbitration Procedure." *New York Times* (Sunday, March 3, Section 5): 1–2.

Cressey, Paul G.
1972   *The Taxi-Dance Hall: A Sociological Study in Commercialized Recreation and City Life*. Montclair, New Jersey: Patterson Smith. (Reprint of 1932 edition.)

Cross, Harry M.
1973   "The College Athlete and the Institution." *Law and Contemporary Problems*, **38** (Winter–Spring): 151–171.

Duncan, Otis D.
1966   "Path Analysis: Sociological Examples." *American Journal of Sociology*, **72** (July): 1–16.

Duncan, Otis D., David L. Featherman, and Beverly Duncan
1972   *Socioeconomic Background and Achievement.* New York: Seminar Press.

Durso, Joseph et al.
1974   "Sports Recruiting: A College Crisis." *New York Times,* CXXIII (March 10): 1, 52. (This article was the first of a series that ran for about a week on consecutive days.)

Flood, Curt (with Richard Carter)
1971   *The Way It Is.* New York: Trident Press.

Fountain, Melvin C., and Judson Parker
1967   "They Play For Money." *Occupational Outlook Quarterly* (December). Washington, D.C.: U.S. Department of Labor, Bureau of Labor Statistics.

Freud, Sigmund
1961   *Civilization and Its Discontents,* translated and edited by James Strachey. New York: W. W. Norton.

Gerth, Hans H., and C. Wright Mills (trans. and eds.)
1946   *From Max Weber: Essays in Sociology.* New York: Oxford University Press.

Gregory, Paul M.
1956   *The Baseball Player: An Economic Study.* Washington, D.C.: Public Affairs Press.

Gross, Edward
1958   *Work and Society.* New York: Thomas Y. Crowell.

Grusky, Oscar
1963a   "The Effects of Formal Structure on Managerial Recruitment: A Study of Baseball Organization." *Sociometry,* **26**: 345–353.
1963b   "Managerial Succession and Organizational Effectiveness." *American Journal of Sociology,* LXIX (July, No. 1): 21–31.

Haerle, Rudolf K., Jr.
1971   "Social Background Factors for Success in Major League Baseball in the United States." Paper delivered before the Third International Symposium on the Sociology of Sport, University of Waterloo, Waterloo, Ontario, Canada.
1974   "Education, Athletic Scholarships and the Occupational Career of the Professional Athlete." Paper presented to the Occupations and Organizations Section Roundtable, American Sociological Association, August.

Hall, Richard
1969   *Occupations and the Social Structure.* Englewood Cliffs, N.J.: Prentice-Hall.

Haug, Marie R., and Marvin B. Sussman
1970   "The Second Career—Variant of a Sociological Concept." In *Toward An Industrial Gerontology,* Harold L. Sheppard (ed.). Cambridge, Mass.: Schenkman. 121–131.

Heise, David R.
1969   "Problems in Path Analysis and Causal Inference." In *Sociological Methodology: 1969*, Edgar F. Borgatta (ed.). San Francisco: Jossey-Bass.

Hiestand, Dale L.
1971   *Changing Careers after Thirty-Five: New Horizons Through Professional and Graduate Study.* New York: Columbia University Press.

Homans, George C.
1950   *The Human Group.* New York: Harcourt, Brace and Company.

Hughes, Everett C.
1958a   *Men and Their Work.* Glencoe, Illinois: Free Press.
1958b   "Mistakes at Work." *Men and Their Work*, Chapter 7. Glencoe, Illinois: Free Press.
1971   *The Sociological Eye: Selected Papers.* Chicago: Aldine-Atherton.

Information Concepts Incorporated
1969   *The Baseball Encyclopedia.* Toronto: The Macmillan Company.

Kenyon, Gerald S.
1970   "The Use of Path Analysis in Sport Sociology with Special Reference to Involvement Socialization." *International Review of Sport Sociology*, **5**: 191–203.

Klapp, Orrin E.
1969   *Collective Search for Identity.* New York: Holt, Rinehart and Winston.

Koch, James V.
1973   "A Troubled Cartel: The NCAA." *Law and Contemporary Problems*, **38** (Winter-Spring): 135–150.

Koppett, Leonard
1971   "A Job For Congress?: Muddled Legal Status of Athletes May Require a Full Investigation." *New York Times*, April 4.

Land, Kenneth C.
1968   "Principles of Path Analysis." In *Sociological Methodology: 1969*, Edgar F. Borgatta (ed.). San Francisco: Jossey-Bass. 3–37.

LaPiere, R. T., and P. R. Farnsworth
1943   *Social Psychology.* New York: McGraw-Hill.

LaPlace, John P.
1954   "Personality and its Relationship to Success in Professional Baseball." *Research Quarterly*, **25**: 313–319.

Levine, Stuart
1972   "Art, Values, Institutions and Culture: An Essay in American Studies Methodology and Relevance." *American Quarterly*, XXIV (May): 131–165.

Levinson, Daniel J.
1968   "A Psycho Social Study of the Male Mid-Life Decade." Mimeographed research proposal.

Lindesmith, Alfred R., and Anselm L. Strauss
1968   *Social Psychology.* New York: Holt, Rinehart and Winston.

Lipset, Seymour M., Martin A. Trow, and James S. Coleman
1956   *Union Democracy.* Glencoe, Illinois: The Free Press.

Lowell, Cym H.
1973   "Collective Bargaining and the Professional Team Sport Industry." *Law and Contemporary Problems,* **38** (Winter-Spring): 3–41.

Loy, John W., and Joseph F. McElvogue
1970   "Racial Segregation in American Sport." *International Review of Sport Sociology,* **5**: 5–24.

Mead, George Herbert
1934   *Mind, Self and Society.* Chicago: The University of Chicago Press. (Edited by Charles W. Morris.)

Merton, Robert K.
1957   *Social Theory and Social Structure.* Glencoe, Illinois: The Free Press.

Miller, Delbert E., and William H. Form
1964   *Industrial Sociology.* (2nd ed.) New York: Harper and Row.

Morris, John P.
1973   "In the Wake of the *Flood.*" *Law and Contemporary Problems,* **38** (Winter-Spring): 85–98.

North, C. C., and Paul K. Hatt
1947   "Jobs and Occupations: A Popular Evaluation." *Opinion News,* IX (September): 3–13.

Nygreen, G. T.
1971   "Interactive Path Analysis." *The American Sociologist,* **6** (February): 37–43.

Parsons, Talcott
1951   *The Social System.* Glencoe, Illinois: The Free Press.

Ritter, Lawrence S.
1966   *The Glory of Their Times.* Toronto: Macmillan.

Robinson, Jackie (as told to Wendell Smith)
1948   *Jackie Robinson: My Own Story.* New York: Greenberg Publisher.

Rosenblatt, Simon
1967   "Negroes in Baseball: The Failure of Success." *Transaction Magazine,* **4** (September): 51–53.

Rottenberg, Simon
1960   "Squeeze Plays in Baseball's Labor Market." *Midway* **2**: 3–13. (Reprinted with adaptation from "The Baseball Players' Labor Market." *The Journal of Political Economy,* **64** (June, 1956): 242–258.)

Sarbin, Theodore R., and Vernon L. Allen
1968   "Role Theory." In *The Handbook of Social Psychology,* Gardner Lindzey and Elliot Aronson (eds.). Vol. 1, Second Edition. Reading, Mass.: Addison-Wesley Publishing Company.

Seymour, Harold
1960   *Baseball, The Early Years.* New York: Oxford University Press.
1971   *Baseball: The Golden Age.* New York: Oxford University Press.

Simon, Herbert A.
1948   *Administrative Behavior.* New York: Macmillan Company.

Spink, C. C. Johnson
1974   "Baseball Depends on Boys." *The Sporting News,* **177** (January 26): 10.

Sporting News, editorial
1961   "Clearing Up Mistaken Notion." *The Sporting News,* **151** (June 20, No. 22): 10.

Taylor, Lee
1968   *Occupational Sociology.* New York: Oxford University Press.

Time Magazine
1974   "Recruiting: The Athlete Hunting Season Is On." *Time* (January 21): 62–63.

Turkin, Hy, and S. C. Thompson
1956   *The Official Encyclopedia of Baseball* (rev. ed.). New York: A. S. Barnes and Company.

U.S. Bureau of the Census
1964   *U.S. Census of Population: 1960, Volume I, Characteristics of the Popula-
        tion.* Part 1, United States Summary. Washington, D.C.: U.S. Government
        Printing Office.
1973   *Census of Population: 1970. Subject Reports: Occupational Characteris-
        tics.* Final Report PC (2)-7A. Washington, D.C.: U.S. Government Print-
        ing Office.

U.S. Congressional House. Committee on the Judiciary
1951   "Study of Monopoly Power," hearings before the Subcommittee on the
        Study of Monopoly Power. 82nd Congress, 1st session. Serial No. 1, part
        6, "Organized Baseball," July, August, October.
1957   "Organized Professional Team Sports, hearings before the Anti-Trust
        Subcommittee." Pts. 1–3, Y 4.J89/1:85/8/pts. 1–3.

U.S. Congressional Senate. Committee on the Judiciary
1958   "Organized Professional Team Sports, before Subcommittee on Anti-
        Trust and Monopoly," Y 4.J.89/2:Sp 6.
1959   "Organized Professional Team Sports, Subcommittee on Anti-Trust and
        Monopoly." Y 4.J.89/2:Sp 6/959.
1960   "Organized Professional Team Sports, 1960, before Subcommittee on
        Anti-Trust and Monopoly." Y 4.J89/2:Sp 6/960.
1960   "Professional Sports Anti-Trust Act of 1960," 86th Congress, 2nd session,
        Report No. 1620, June 20.
1964   "Professional Sports Anti-Trust Bill, 1964, before Subcommittee on Anti-
        Trust and Monopoly." Y 4.J89/2:Sp 6/964.
1965   "Professional Sports Anti-Trust Bill, 1965, before Subcommittee on Anti-
        Trust and Monopoly." Y 4.J89/2:Sp 6/965.

Vocational Guidance Quarterly
1971   "Second Careers as a Way of Life: A Symposium." *Vocational Guidance Quarterly*, **20** (December): 88–118.

Voigt, David Q.
1966   *American Baseball: From Gentleman's Sport to the Commissioner System.* Norman, Oklahoma: University of Oklahoma Press.
1970   *American Baseball: From the Commissioners to Continental Expansion.* Norman, Oklahoma: University of Oklahoma Press.
1971   "America Through Baseball." *America's Leisure Revolution.* Reading, Pennsylvania: Albright College Book Store. 74–94.

Weistart, John C. (ed.)
1973   "Athletics." *Law and Contemporary Problems*, **38** (Winter-Spring). (Entire issue devoted to economic and legal aspects of athletics.)

Wilensky, Harold
1960   "Work, Careers, and Social Integration." *International Social Science Journal*, **12** (Fall): 543–560.

Young, Robert K., and Donald J. Veldman
1965   *Introductory Statistics for the Behavioral Sciences.* New York: Holt, Rinehart and Winston.

Chapter 11
Coming of Age in Organizations: A Comparative Study of Career Contingencies of Musicians and Hockey Players

Robert R. Faulkner
Department of Sociology
University of Massachusetts
(Amherst, Massachusetts)

Robert R. Faulkner

Birth Place: Boston, Massachusetts

Age: 35

Birth Order: Only child

Formal Education:

        B.A., University of California, Los Angeles 1963
        M.A., Sociology, University of California,
        Los Angeles 1965
        Ph.D., Sociology, University of California,
        Los Angeles 1968

Present Position:

        Associate Professor of Sociology, University of Massachusetts, Amherst

Professional Responsibilities:

        Teaching courses in Research–Qualitative Methods; Deviance; Occupations and Professions.

Scholarly Interests:

        Analysis of occupational careers and the comparative study of work socialization; present research on the social organization of artistic labor, career precariousness, and the work of Hollywood freelance film composers.

Professional Accomplishments:

        Hollywood Studio Musicians

Hobbies:

        Motion pictures, film music, and jazz.

Sport Activities:

        Participant: golf.
        Spectator: hockey.
        Also interview professional hockey players.

Most Recent Books Read:

Lenny Bruce	*Zen and the Art of Motorcycle Maintenance*
Lenny Bruce	*Ladies and Gentlemen*
Rudy Behlmer (ed.)	*Memo from David O. Selznick*

INTRODUCTION

The processes of promotion and demotion in organizations are of major sociological relevance because the contingencies of status passage (Glaser and Strauss, 1971) are linked to the beliefs and the social organization of success and failure. It is no small irony that work organizations characterized by universalistic-achievement orientations often use ascriptive attributes to determine their members' eligibility for both placement and advancement. The impact of attributes such as age and sex upon occupational inclusion or exclusion is not self-evident, however, for as Strauss (1959), Berger (1960), Cain (1964), and Ryder (1965) have suggested, age is a socially constructed and sustained category which may either facilitate or impede access to valued positions and processes. A number of empirical studies (Weinberg and Arond, 1952; Chinoy, 1955; Martin and Stauss, 1956; Wager, 1959; Westby, 1960; Roth, 1964; Reif and Strauss, 1965; Sofer, 1970; see Glaser, 1968) have shown that age is a major ascribed attribute by which occupational populations are selected and distributed into career lines. Age can be viewed as a fundamental career contingency, a factor upon which mobility within occupations and work organizations depends. It defines certain roles as available or unavailable and affects individual members' commitments to appropriate lines of collective action. Despite the theoretical importance of age-grading[1] in nonfamilial settings such as occupations, sociological investigations have paid only passing attention to age as a component of selective recruitment policies.

This paper draws on comparative materials to demonstrate the applica-

A number of people supplied valuable suggestions and needed encouragement in generous amounts. I wish to thank, and absolve from any responsibility, Howard S. Becker, Anselm L. Strauss, Charles H. Page, Anthony R. Harris, and especially Gerald M. Platt. I am deeply indebted to the orchestra musicians and hockey players who freely shared with me their personal reflections and concerns.

From *Sociology of Work and Occupations* Vol. 1, No. 2 (May 1974) pp. 131–173. Reprinted by permission of the publisher, Sage Publications, Inc.

bility of one specific approach to career mobility and adult socialization.
an approach which emphasizes age as a critical variable for understanding
both the objective features of career status passage and subjective changes
in the mobility motivations and occupational outlooks of individual members. The paper focuses on the meanings the participants in two occupations
impute to their mobility experiences in the context of age-grading and what
this *kind* of change in adult life implies about their attitudes toward their
work worlds. Moreover, the relationships between the objective and
subjective contingencies of career mobility (Becker and Strauss, 1956;
Becker, 1963) take us to some core organizational and practical problems: the schedules for the development and advancement of talent, the
management of aging and immobility, and the processes for generating individuals' commitment in the face of possible disappointment and failure
(Merton, 1957). Thus, in such diverse contexts as professional sports and
the performing arts, and in general where the quick demonstration of performance excellence is required, we can hypothesize that conceptions of age
influence the selection of career occupants for mobility. This makes more
crucial the organizational problem of maintaining standards of behavior
without alienating the demoted, or destroying the motivation of middle-level
"rookies" and "veterans."

This approach explains some thus far implicit assumptions in the sociological study of organizational careers. Five sections are presented. The first
develops an overview of current approaches to mobility in work settings and
the mechanisms for sustaining the involvement of members. The second
describes the study's methods and the settings at issue. The third examines
the relation between the structural features of interorganizational careers
and the direct impact of ascriptive features on the differential availability
and selection of personnel. The personal consequences of these contingencies are discussed in a fourth section, particularly the turning points at
which members' expectancies of access to top strata positions undergo
transformation. A fifth and concluding section discusses career contingencies in light of the adaptations made by individuals and organizations
to these problems. It should be apparent that this paper is an attempt to
apply an important, but neglected, sociological perspective to one aspect of
organizational structure; it is not to deny the substantive relevance of other
aspects of these institutions.

ORGANIZATIONAL CAREERS

The progressive differentiation of work in the direction of age-graded standardization, technical expertise, and ideologies of equal access to valued
processes often lead to an *inconsistency between the promise of success
through upward mobility and the reality of failure through immobility.*

These inconsistencies underlie various expressions of discontent, the most prevalent, perhaps, being the sense of disaffection that arises from the enforced separation of individuals from valued ongoing courses of action, situations, and objects (including the self) within a given structure. Organizations in which careers unfold thus confront the problem of motivating achievement and mobility aspirations of members toward top level positions while, at the same time, sustaining the involvement of subordinates to whom access has been denied. The study of these processes has been pursued from two theoretical vantage points.

One approach employs the familiar means-ends theorizing and locates the problem of demotion, immobility, and discharge in terms of hierarchical settings which encourage career occupants to move onward and upward but which simultaneously permit fewer participants to do so at more exclusive and prestigious status levels. This viewpoint offers the distinct advantage of focusing on the functions of stratification in motivating incumbents to fill differentiated positions in a bureaucratic, achievement-oriented social system. Empirical research focuses on the organizational arrangements through which disjunctions can arise between aspirations and avenues as well as the subsequent structural adaptations for promoting the commitment of the stranded, the less able, or the demoted in complex organizations (Levenson, 1961; More, 1962; Smigel, 1964; Goldner, 1965; Goldner and Ritti, 1967; Maniha, 1972). Unless organizations can legitimize failure and promote the identification of the less successful with their work roles, they run the risk of resentment and disengagement among their labor force. Procedures and collective actions for "cooling out" failures become essential for the continuity and integrity of existing social arrangements (Goffman, 1952; Clark, 1960).

A second approach emphasizes that the proper analysis of organizational mobility must include changes in the mobility motivations, purposes, and expectations of the individual. This approach focuses not only on the mobility routes and sequences of personnel circulation through positions, but also on the personal adjustments and shared experiential concerns of actors (Hall, 1948; Becker, 1952; Solomon, 1953; Wilensky, 1956; Wager, 1959; Goffman, 1961; Carlin, 1962; Glaser, 1964; Wood, 1967; Friedman, 1967; Stebbins, 1970; Faulkner, 1973, 1971; Spector, 1973, 1972). In focusing on definitions of success and failure, the term "career" here applies to the sequence of passage through objective statuses and "the moving perspective in which the person sees his life as a whole and interprets the meanings of his various attributes, actions, and the things which happen to him" (Hughes, 1958: 63).

In view of the theoretical importance of careers to the analysis of social psychology, one would expect sociologists to have contributed at both the theoretical and hypothesis testing levels. Such has not been the case. Despite Chinoy's (1955) study of automobile workers, which examined the process by which workers adapted to limited opportunity in a society that stresses advancement, we have few detailed studies of the chronological demise of mobility aspirations in early adulthood or the impact of age on the lowering of career sights. That a kind of "coming to terms" does take place has been noted in studies of the meaning of work and work alienation (Morse and Weiss, 1955; Seeman, 1967) as well as in Howard S. Becker's essays on personal change (1954; 1970). But the empirical issue—the meanings of such transition phases in the life-cycle and how they are managed by personnel in occupations—has been left in question.

Adaptations to blocked mobility are usually assumed to have a stable meaning, invariant to the practical exigencies of aging in the work settings under investigation. Although contrasts between "idealistic dreams for success" and "realistic" outlooks are commonplace in the literature, the meanings of the personal mollification of success aspirations appear to be assumed rather than documented. Brim (1968: 204) laments this state of affairs when, in a review of the literature on occupational socialization, he states, "It is indeed puzzling that there are so few sociological studies (there are, of course, many plays and novels) of male efforts to adjust aspirations with achievement in their careers." Most efforts beg the sociological question: how do people in highly competitive work structures define and organize their careers so as to handle issues of denial and failure?

In this overview, I must also note the relevance of career socialization for the study of organizational processes. A predominant theme in the literature on socialization presents life as movement from youthful idealism to more or less realistic mobility motivations, more or less contented adjustments which progressively confine behavioral potentialities and imputed identities within an acceptable range and to which an individual becomes committed (Miller and Form, 1951; Becker, 1964; Banton, 1965; Geer, 1966; Faulkner, 1973). Nevertheless, most efforts have been concerned with adaptations to immobility or "coming to terms" as individual processes, and only marginally with the organizational contexts which *facilitate the acquisition of these career outlooks* (for an exception see Goldner, 1965). Insofar as "nothing succeeds like success," selection procedures are effected by the way an organization arranges its career lines and personnel circulation, cushions the blows of failure, and structures the temporal processes by which young neophytes become committed to on-going lines of action. Such contingencies are recognized as fundamental in the allocation of talent. What is less acknowledged is that *inasmuch as youth intensive organizations are required to structure their career selection procedures around a perishable resource, an aging labor force creates certain specific problems for organizations of high competence.*

METHODS AND SETTING

The material for this paper is drawn from a three-year comparative study of career socialization and mobility patterns of personnel in the occupational worlds of the performing arts and professional sports. Although several work settings are being investigated and several kinds of data gathered (fieldwork observations, analysis of personnel records, informant interrogation, and longitudinal respondent interviewing), the ones I shall report on here derive mainly from long unstructured interviews with 60 symphony players in two organizations ranked in the middle strata of the orchestral hierarchy, and from 38 hockey players on two teams in the highest minor league level of professional hockey. The documentation offered is drawn from those sections of the taped interviews which deal with the conditions of interorganizational mobility, definitions of success, and career concerns.

Comparative analysis of orchestra and hockey teams suggests that these two settings have reached a stage of organizational development which seemingly anticipates the growth of other complex, purposely created systems. These formal structures are of theoretical interest because the career lines and allocation of rewards for members are divisible into organizational positions of higher or lower rank in comparison with other such units. In both settings, the network of institutions in which mobility takes place consists of a top-ranking group of distinguished or elite organizations, a number of second-rank but solidly established organizations below the top, and a third level of marginal quality. The top and middle levels of symphony work and professional hockey can be conceptualized as *organizational sets* (Caplow, 1964: 201–216): stratification systems composed of two or more settings. The higher a given system's prestige and power, (a) the more influence it has on the standards of achievement and excellence for the entire array of organizations, (b) the more status and other rewards enjoyed by career incumbents experiencing mobility from the middle levels into the elite ranks, and (c) the more complex the mechanisms for sorting out the promising from the unpromising.

As the terms "major" and "minor" league suggest, organizational arrangements of this type (1) offer the presence of minor league *pipeline organizations* which produce candidates with the requisite skills to meet performance demands in the major leagues, (2) develop a supply of available personnel for whom vertical, interorganizational mobility is a strong career motivation, and (3) generate expectancies of access among colleague competitors throughout the set. A foremost sign of achievement is promotion into the major leagues, and incumbents are encouraged to look forward to reaching the top according to a more or less temporally specific schedule.

The symphony orchestra world is one of the most complex, competitive, and stratified organizational sets in existence. It is comprised of five major symphonies employing a total of about 450 players. In musical excellence, calibre of musicianship, total contract weeks, basic salary, length of season, pension plans, recording guarantees, and paid vacations, the elite set in this country consists of the Boston, Chicago, Cleveland, New York Philharmonic, and Philadelphia orchestras. Below this top rank are 24 established organizations employing about 2,250 total employees; roughly 75 percent of symphony musicians are situated at the middle echelon level. The sample of performing musicians interviewed is drawn from two orchestras in this middle stratum.[2] One organization is located in the eastern part of the country, the other on the West Coast. During the years of the study, the number of retirements and voluntary departures ranged from 5 to 8 percent in each organization. The age of those interviewed ranged from 21 to 61; 11 were between the ages of 21 and 27, 22 were between 28 and 34, and 27 musicians were 35 or older. Interviews were also conducted with players in early career in two major league orchestras. Since the concern here is with interorganizational mobility from the middle levels and the problematic features of immobility, unless otherwise noted my observations shall deal primarily with minor league personnel.

As of the 1970–72 seasons, the period of my interviewing and fieldwork, the organizational set of hockey was stratified into 14 teams in the National Hockey League (NHL) with a total of approximately 270 players, and 23 teams in the middle-level American, Central and Western minor leagues totaling around 460 players.[3] Over sixty percent of the players are situated in this latter strata in the set. The two organizations studied are in the highest minor league system, the American League (AHL), from which the NHL recruits over 70 percent of its talent, and to which it sends its fringe players, those in need of experience, or veterans in the twilight of their playing years. The turnover between seasons on these teams ranged from 40 to 80 percent, for trades, promotions, retirements, and dismissals produce an active system of personnel circulation. The ages of these men ranged from 20 to 33 years; 24 were between the ages of 20 and 24, and 14 interviewed were 25 years of age or older.

CONTINGENCIES OF INTERORGANIZATIONAL CAREERS

The development of a modern organizational structure that facilitates the training and distribution of high level talent is contingent upon some indispensable mechanisms for the maintenance of interlinking relationships between pipeline and elite strata and for the regulation of the exigencies of aging. While elite or major league organizations may develop their own talent from within, few organizations studied are willing or able to do so.

The National Hockey League and top five orchestras must rely on the output of their respective "farm systems" for the socialization and training of aspirants into the occupational culture and its work roles. *The processes by which a population is distributed in these sets stem, at least in part, from institutional arrangements that make certain categories of career incumbents more readily available at certain points of selection for mobility and immobility.* The organizational problem of role placement demands that elite strata select wisely among young aspirants who are in competition for scarce positions at the top and that middle echelon recruits be prepared and motivated to meet high level performance demands at these standardized selection points in their careers. Players in the minor leagues are a mixed lot, some needing a few years "seasoning" to "be ready," as it is put in hockey, or a necessary period of "routinization" to orchestral playing, as one personnel committee member phrased it. Other players and performers may indeed be motivated and prepared, but must wait for a vacancy in the major leagues. Also career occupants are at different stages of their careers; some are rookies and others are veterans, and the effective functioning of these organizational sets requires the balancing of the young and older members, keeping the former in anticipation of promotion and the latter motivated in the face of denial.

Professional Hockey

There are several conditions inherent in the structure of hockey which necessitate the efficient selection of talent by management as well as the quick demonstration of excellence by players. First, recent expansion from six NHL teams of 20 players each to twelve teams (about 240 players) in 1967, and then to fourteen teams (about 280 players) in 1970, has given rise to a personnel market characterized by a scarcity of high-quality performers to fill the number of new positions. Expansion clubs must be stocked with players, and all the organizations compete for promising recruits who are likely to develop rapidly into exemplary performers with several seasons of productive playing ahead of them.[4] All teams must select wisely if they are to build a balanced NHL lineup of first-rate men in the early stages of their careers as well as a core of seasoned veterans. In addition, their continuity and competitive advantage can only be ensured if they develop a backlog of promotable and aspiring minor leaguers for possible future assignment to the parent NHL team.

Second, the paths of movement of personnel through the system of positions in this set are structured by the fact that organizations placing a premium on physical skills can be expected to develop timetables or age-situated schedules for recognition-producing performances. Since it is felt that most athletes in professional hockey are at their peak only for about four or five years, the pace at which players move through this career line becomes shaped by shared conceptions of physiological attrition. Thus, the meaningfulness of age as a basic status shares an elective affinity with the organizational methods for detecting, processing, and otherwise handling aging in this occupation. The spirit of youth predominates and aging is looked on as a process of steady decline. The gradual "fall from grace" builds upon these socially-constructed features of occupational age that render "growing older" meaningful in the first place. Decision-makers in the front office are circumspect about discussing the link between age and role placement, but players are candid about their own timetables for promotion, shaping them against what they define as managerial agendas for advancement. The players view getting a chance for promotion and an opportunity to shape and strengthen their capacities through use in the NHL as major career problems which are contained in a series of *running adjustments with time*. The players interviewed feel that, unless they have been promoted into the NHL parent organization to play a continuous set of games before the age of 25, the occupancy of minor league status for the duration of their careers is heavily ruled in by existing social arrangements. Given a developmental cycle of relatively short duration, superiors prefer to turn to younger, and potentially more qualified recruits. As a result, the probability of access to the major leagues declines in the late twenties.

Third, and related, interorganizational mobility from the minors to the majors is precarious by virtue of the power which decision-makers (managers, coaches, and scouts) exercise over these players. The term "career precariousness" would seem appropriate where incumbents face the continuous prospect of being displaced by newcomers throughout their work life as well as subject to quick shifts in fortune which are not totally foreseen. Additionally, because these players are the property of the club, they can be moved both vertically and horizontally within this organizational set as management dictates. Not surprisingly, the structure of control over the paths and rates of mobility leads to rather large doses of player anxiety and concern about the impermanence and possible reversibility of status passage.

Critical trial periods are initiated early in the career cycle and involve formidable tests of expertise, patience, and occupational character. Beginning with his early performances in amateur Canadian hockey, or in the college ranks, the player is placed in the midst of a short and fateful testing period. Swift ascent is normatively prescribed as organizations' attempt to manage the timing and pacing of their personnel. Starting with the entrance into the professional ranks, it usually takes only two to five years to determine the level of career achievement likely to be attained by the young hockey professional.

Several mobility patterns are generated from these demands for efficient role placement. Thirty-two percent (86) of those on the active rosters in 1971–1972 were promoted into the elite strata in their first or second year of hockey.[5] At the other extreme, 14 percent spent seven or more years in the minor leagues before "getting a good shot at the National" or before being promoted for a continued stay that lasted longer than half a season. A handful had been in the minors from 10 to 14 years before becoming aged but eager NHL rookies; the importance of such anomalous cases will be discussed shortly. Despite these variations in entry times into the major league, 60 percent (163) had arrived in the top strata from the minor leagues before they were 24 years of age. The American Hockey League is the major pipeline for this interleague mobility; three-fourths of the minor leaguers called up by their NHL teams during this season were from the AHL affiliate.[6]

Being called up is a crucial point for getting a leg up on the career ladder but this foothold is a precarious one indeed. From three to five of the players on each team studied had been promoted but were sent back down to the minors during the course of the season. Only about one or two in twenty stayed in the NHL to become a regular. About one-quarter of the men on the clubs studied were former elite regulars. This indicates that even players who have been promoted for two or more seasons are faced with the prospect of demotion to the farm team. Aggregate data for players in the NHL show that only 22 veterans have sustained a career at the top for 15 or more years and only 30 percent have been there for six or more seasons. Metaphorically, players step onto a quickly moving career escalator with a prospective ride of short duration ahead of them.

Orchestra World

The processes of personnel succession in orchestras stand in distinct contrast, both in route and timing, to what happens in pro hockey. While a certain structural similarity of interstrata mobility avenues has been noted, the complexes differ in other fundamental aspects. First, orchestras have experienced nothing as remarkable as the organizational expansion of professional hockey in the United States during the last decade (see Hart, 1973; Mueller, 1951). Second, professional hockey much like baseball, tends to be institutionalized around a closely integrated linkage between the minor affiliate and major league organizations. Hockey players are the property of these organizations or clubs. In the symphony world, the individual's possible control over his/her status is much greater because musicians are not formally under contract to a single management at both levels of the set. There are no reserve clauses in orchestra contracts, prohibiting the musician from voluntarily moving in order to better one's career situation in another organization. Each performing artist is in effect potentially recruitable; consequently, musicians have more opportunities to establish their availability in the labor market through auditions for openings, thereby lessening the exclusive power of any particular employing unit over their career chances.

Third, and related, the range of positions by which a musician can improve his or her standing in the profession is much more diversified than in hockey. Orchestral performers and professional hockey players agree that the elite strata are desirable—it is viewed by most as "the only place to be." Ninety-five percent of the hockey players and about 75 percent of the musicians acknowledge that their early career aspirations were to play in their respective "major leagues." The actual pattern of mobility, however, is more complex in the orchestral world. Musicians can increase their prestige by moving downward, into a middle level organization from a major orchestra (from the Chicago Symphony Orchestra to the Los Angeles Philharmonic, for example) while simultaneously increasing their *positional status* in a particular instrumental section within the orchestra. Fifteen of the musicians interviewed had gone from the major to the minor leagues in order to play principal chair to be co-principal of a section (for a similar mechanism in the academic world see Caplow and McGee, 1958; Caplow, 1964: 210–223, develops this concept of organizational exchange). Moreover, career routes can be either horizontal, as in a move between minor league organizations, or vertical, such as in a move from the middle to top level positions. Musicians recognize that patterns such as these are part of a career strategy, for it is important to be on the right terrain at the right promotion time.

The outcome of this diversity of movement and greater degree of control is not so individualistic as the entrepreneurial ethos might suggest. Personnel mobility in this organizational set is an *aggregate phenomenon dependent on the availability of positions into which members seek entry,* as well as on the number of potential recruits for those positions. In the top stratum of the orchestral world, yearly vacancies ranged from about 4 to 35 positions out of the total of about 540. In one of the "big five" orchestras investigated, the number of vacancies due to retirements and career moves to other work settings ranged from two to eight players per season over a seven-year period. The average was three vacancies per season in each orchestra. As many as 100 applicants—minor-league performers, players fresh out of music conservatories, and others working free-lance in the music world—may apply for one of these openings.[7]

The vacancy rate, per se, at the top stratum is only one characteristic by which an organizational set is differentiated from its neighbors. The tempo and circulation of movement into the elite level is heavily influenced by how long any one incumbent stays at the top. Duration of occupancy is fundamental to organizational regeneration and change. It is a basis for role allocation and thereby a key indicator of a set's flow chart. Comparisons between professional hockey teams and symphony orchestras at the top strata are instructive in this regard. Table 1 indicates that more than three-fourths of the top level musicians have been in a major orchestra for six or more years, while only slightly more than 30 percent of the NHL players have been situated in that stratum for the same length of time. While one out of every three NHL regulars is a newcomer, in his first or second season, only one "top five" musician in ten has a similar length of service. More-over, the average stay in the "top five" organizations for musicians is around 18 years (a range from 1 to 53 years). In the NHL it is five years. Thus, the incorporation of new members and loss of older veterans is exceedingly rapid in hockey but much less so in the orchestral elite.

Table 1 also suggests that hockey players are distributed in a bimodal fashion, indicating a differential recruitment or "weeding out" process whereby the "superstars" and "near greats" remain at the top for tem-porally longer career spans when compared to the modal career pattern. When musicians, however, move into the top stratum, they receive tenure after a one- or two-year probationary period, and are then likely to remain at the elite level (if they so choose) for the remainder of their careers. Hockey players, who face the continuous possibility of being displaced by

Table 1

Length of time in elite organizational strata, 1971–1972 (in percent)

Number of years in top strata of organizational set	National Hockey League * (n = 270)	Elite orchestra † (n = 540)
1 year or less	15	6
2 years	19	3
3 years	10	2
4 years	9	4
5 years	15	4
6 years or more	32	81
Total	100%	100%

* 1972–1973 Hockey register (St. Louis: *The Sporting News*, 1972).
† Personnel files of The Boston Symphony Orchestra, Chicago Symphony Orches-tra, Philadelphia Orchestra, New York Philharmonic, and Cleveland Orchestra.

newcomers throughout their careers are unable to generate such an organizational commitment.

The differentiation of activities gives a distinctive pattern to the recruitment of performing artists seeking entry into top strata positions from pipeline organizations. In two of the "top five" orchestras studied, the average age of all members is about 45; the average age of new members in their first or second orchestral season is 24 years old (a range of 22 to 44). This suggests that the time of selections is skewed toward younger persons, in their mid-to-late twenties who have been seasoned in minor league organizations. While personnel committees typically cite universalistic selection procedures in which the "best player" is always chosen regardless of age and other circumstances, the long-run advantages of hiring youthful but modestly experienced players are not disregarded. Not surprisingly, of those who left the minor league orchestras studied for other orchestras during the period of investigation, nearly 90 percent were 35 years of age or younger.

As the development of talent and differentiation of recruits by ability and performance comes to be demanded in organizations of high competence, so too *there exist well defined normative expectations as to the level of excellence deemed appropriate at various age levels.* Starting from the players' entrance into the business of orchestra music, it may take five to eight years to determine where he or she will be situated for the rest of his/her career. The musician, like the hockey player, runs the risk of remaining in a second-rate organization too long and thereby diminishing the chances for selection into the elite stratum. Major league orchestras are by and large reluctant to hire people in their forties and even late thirties, and because the supply of talent always exceeds the number of top jobs available per season, incumbents can miss opportunities at crucial contingency points. These organizationally shaped agendas for selection may vary because of different local arrangements and rates of personnel circulation; nevertheless, the launching of a successful career appears to be contained by processes that extend over brief spans of career time and that are experienced in different ways by those affected.

SUBJECTIVE CAREERS AND PERSONAL ADAPTATIONS

The theory of occupational socialization suggested here posits that objective and subjective careers develop concurrently in a process of interdependence and mutual transformation. In this framework, rewards are not inherent in the statuses or organizational arrangements themselves. They must be interpreted and defined as such if they are to motivate behavior toward top level positions. Since actors need symbols for purposes of interaction, and symbols cannot be shared except in an interactional context, status passage can be conceptualized as a mutually adjusted program of joint behavior that facilitates the acquisition of cognitive beliefs and norms about age. There exists some communication structure by means of which participants acquire the shared meanings of career turning points, signs of promotion, and rules concerning how old candidates for certain positions should be.

Actors view length of time in certain locations as guidelines by which they actively construct benchmarks and understandings about the possibilities and probabilities of receiving major recognition, becoming a "star" performer or "first among equals," and gaining access to processes or situations which are important to them. The import here is that these organizational careers have a prospective contour. Musicians and hockey players can estimate the probabilities of their own mobility into the major leagues by consulting (1) the progress of others, and (2) what is taken to be the typical career escalator. In attempting to construct and enact their careers, they assess their own age against the standardized schedules for selection, and then subjectively calculate their personal chances of success—a process which presupposes, of course, determinate and patterned selection points.

The coming of age contains a double viewpoint. Not only do changes take place in the objective chances of interorganizational mobility, but changes also begin to take place within the individual as well. This section examines some of the career concerns expressed, the ways in which performers and players sustain their self-regard in the face of immobility and demotion, and the ways in which they continue as productive members of their respective organizations. I hypothesize *that much of the "coming to terms" that is activated by the perception of mobility opportunities has to do with the impingement of age-graded criteria for interorganizational advancement.*

Career Problems

The initiation of neophytes into organizational careers involves the transmission of basic sentiments and norms concerning status passage—specifically, the inculcation of attitudes toward time. In characterizing the subjective outlooks of those interviewed, the elements discussed below are, or have been, present in most respondents' definitions of their career situation.

First, there is general agreement that one is constrained to do something on his or her own to improve one's position. One's place in the division of labor stands for where one is situated socially and professionally. Careers are consequential; frequent expressions of frustration and annoyance over blocked mobility and about getting into the right occupational terrain point to the effects of this hierarchical system. Since positions are assessed in terms of the extent to which they condition the establishment of footholds or "stepping stones" toward the major leagues, a personal problem centers around being kept waiting at some step in the career process.

Second, and closely related, the ethos of improvement, the more or less continuous competition between colleagues, status rivalry, and subjectiye effects of this appraisive drama in sports and music, generates a concern over whether a particular position in the set enlarges a person's expertise. Here the concern centers around the conditions for personal development in a given direction and for the chance to be or become a more skilled practitioner.

The following quotations from the interviews suggest that the problem of access to organizational opportunities is in essence the same sort of problem as that of success. These definitions of the situation are an activating and unifying force, precursors of subjective concerns, and forerunners of subsequent adaptations to immobility. These themes are well put by the following respondent:

> Hockey is a race with time. You feel you have to move up a level a year in the minors and make it into the National by 24 or 25, maybe 26 at the latest. This axe is always hanging over your head, you've got around four or five years they say to show yourself, to show what you can do. You have to get the ice time to play, you have to get a good shot at it, play steady, get to know the guys on your line, then you can do it. This is a now sport, you can't waste any years. I think I'm ready now, this is my third season, I can play with the guys up there now [in the NHL].

Demands for recognition-producing work, for quick demonstration of talent, and awareness of rapid deterioration of chances, all tend to aggravate personal aging. In both organizational sets, it is clear that one cannot afford to waste any years. Thus, many were concerned that the possibility of getting "boxed into" attitudes and skills would decrease their chances of improving their situation. One musician offered: "I think you can destroy your chances of going to a top place if you play in a section for too long. It's not a disgrace, but people stereotype you just the same; no one's going to be interested in a player who is too old or has lost that shine in his playing by being buried in a poor orchestra." A 30-year-old colleague summed up a more general feeling:

> Some places will not look at you if you're over a certain age, like 35 or 36, so you have to move fast, audition, and you cannot settle for a lesser job, you have to improve your position with each move. Who wants to get stuck at 40 in some situation you can't stand in some nowhere orchestra? This is why I moved here as principal (from a major

league setting). My ambition now is to get into one of the big orchestras as a principal, the solos and responsibility I think are important. This is sort of a stepping stone on my way of thinking. I can't spend my life here . . . A lot of first-rate players are looking for much the same thing I am.

A harder line is taken by hockey players who have been promoted and are under heavy pressure to produce while playing in the major league. They realize that the testing period is of short duration and make invidious comparisons about the career fates of colleague competitors whose own success may, in effect, rule out their own occupancy of desired places. Some become dissatisfied with what they see as low rates of demotion for others and the feeling of denial becomes painfully obvious very rapidly. Related to this is the observation that hockey professionals are exceedingly critical of the chances they are given and the promotion practices of management. This pattern is not as pronounced in the orchestra world. Nearly 80 percent of the pros interviewed noted some sort of dissatisfaction with the politicking, favoritism, and injustice of selection procedures. Following Stouffer and his colleagues (1949), dissatisfaction with the management of mobility by decision-makers can be viewed as the outcome of a system in which opportunities are viewed as relatively plentiful. Specifically, under the conditions of league expansions over the past few seasons, players see a number of their competitors being promoted into the NHL. To be sure, some stay, others are taken up for only a short "look-see" and then demoted. Nevertheless, being denied access to these positions—often seen as one's due for dedicated work in the minor league salt mines—comes to be defined as unfair just because so many others throughout the set have received this opportunity. By way of contrast, in the orchestra world where promotion into the "top five" is comparatively rarer, those who have climbed to the elite strata feel they have done very well while the nonpromoted are less bitter towards their fate because fewer of their competitors have surpassed them.

My main complaint is that many of the guys up there shouldn't be in the National at all, and guys who are down here ought to be up there. The management's to blame for that. Politics. Many of us don't even get the chance to go up, they've made up their minds already. I was up but didn't get a chance to really play . . . I'd say my only shot this year, or maybe next year too, would be if someone gets injured or traded, maybe I'll be traded. I don't think D. or E. [players in his team position on the NHL parent club] will be sent down, so you can't figure it out. I think some guys don't pull their weight, eh? But I have only so many years, you can't play forever. I'd like to get a good shot at it to see if I'm going to play there or not, if I can do it. This is what you look towards, this is it. The problem with hockey is that you don't play long enough to call it a career, a future, you either make it or spend it in the minors and then it's over in, what, ten years? Is that a career? Unless you're a superstar you can't really count on anything.

Q.: You never know if you'll go up to stay?

There's one hell of a difference between playing yourself *off* the team and playing yourself *on* the team. If you're on it they will stick with you, give you a chance. If you just go up, if you don't play steady you won't improve, then there's no way. . . .

Any of these events may affect the career, then, in any of several ways, depending on what is happening to the progress of others and the extent to which personal chances of mobility diminish because of the state of a career line at the time the event occurs.

Given the contingencies expressed above, one can hypothesize that mobility assessments will vary according to how long the person has been on the career time track. One concrete aspect of the consequences of age-grading and selection procedures might be seen in the data linking length of service in the organizational set and perceived chances of being promoted. As the phrase "coming of age" indicates, we might predict collisions of expectations with occupational realities to occur at some of the selection points discussed previously. Although the small number of cases compels caution in the use and interpretation of this index, an important feature of adult socialization is nevertheless reflected by a decline with age in the subjective estimates for achieving a position at the top of these organizational sets. Five response alternatives used in the lengthy interviews were subsequently collapsed into three for presentation here: "Very likely" and "possible" are termed as indicating "high expectations" and "very unlikely" and "not likely" as "low expectations." The "undecided" responses are classified as "undecided."

Table 2 indicates that a substantial proportion of those minor leaguers interviewed start their careers in orchestras and hockey organizations with high expectations and that their present positions are for many viewed as a stepping-stone on the way to the top. Almost three-fourths of the musicians under 27 years of age and nearly 60 percent of the hockey professionals 24 years and younger start with high expectations for making it into the majors. They see a promotion in the prospective future. Many regard it as a strong likelihood or reasonable possibility that they will be among the chosen sooner or later, if indeed they are not already close to the realization of their desired career move.

Table 2

Expectations for achieving top strata position in organizational set, by age and occupation of minor league respondents (in percent)

Expectations	Hockey players		Orchestra musicians			Total
	20–24 yrs. (n = 24)	More than 24 yrs. (n = 14)	21–27 yrs. (n = 11)	28–34 yrs. (n = 22)	More than 34 yrs. (n = 27)	N (n = 98)
High	58	43	72	46	22	41
Undecided	25	36	10	13	19	23
Low	17	21	18	41	59	34
Total	100%	100%	100%	100%	100%	

Few, however, retain these expectations and hopes for achievement throughout their careers. The erosion of subjective assessments is most dramatic among the minor league orchestra players; after about eight to twelve years in the career, more than 50 percent either have low expectations or are undecided about mobility into the top five. Even though this kind of status passage is still viewed as desirable, the responses strongly suggest that after their mid-thirties it is no longer treated as a very serious prospect. Principal players in the minor leagues may in fact get the chance they look for, and several did experience this mobility during the brief years of this study, but most performers find themselves stranded in the middle levels of the orchestral structure. Such experiences change the musicians' attitudes about themselves, and about how far they have progressed towards the dream they had hoped to achieve. This personal change leads many, such as the 37-year-old musician quoted, to redirect their career sights away from their original ambition of being in a major symphony towards their current work reality.

> My chances of successfully auditioning as a principal in a major orchestra might not be as great as they should be. I've been asked to play second in C. ["top five" orchestra], but I prefer first here. There are just not that many openings, a few years ago . . . Now my aspiration, as I said, isn't as great as it was when I took the job here, not quite as great. I wouldn't turn down something like I had in mind when I came here at first (chair in the section), but my hope isn't as great as it was. My hope isn't any less, it would be nice, but it is just that my goals are now slightly different than they were then.

A string playing colleague was more direct:

> Look, let's not kid ourselves, I'm nearly 40 years old. I make a good living here, I do some recording work on the side, I'm not going to be first in The New York Philharmonic anyway, not at my age. Maybe at some time we feel this, but face the facts, we've done very well in music, we've done well out here (on the West Coast). The orchestra has really improved, it's now one of the best in the country, and like they say, things could be worse, like being stuck in some bush league place with little money and no musical satisfaction.

Among the professional hockey players interviewed, the sharp dampening of expectancies for inclusion into the elite strata is not as dramatic as among orchestra musicians. Promotion is for these men almost automatically accepted as desirable, for a career at the top represents what they have wanted throughout their lives. In assessing their promotion chances as well as the amount of difficulty to be encountered in becoming an elite regular, they recognize that those who stay too long in the middle strata may be penalized. During their first few seasons the young pros are developing their skills and many at this stage do not consider themselves equipped or "ready" to be promoted. Then there is a period of perhaps three years, starting when the pro is around 23 or 24, after he has had experience in the minors, after some of his colleagues have been promoted, and after he has survived the rituals of status passage accompanying initial entry into the professional ranks. A turning point of immense personal change begins to set in around the age of 25 or 26, when there is a greater degree of uncertainty over success. Table 2 indicates that almost one-half (43 percent) have high expectations for promotion into the major league, while some 36 percent can be described as undecided. This latter figure indicates that these players too are not entirely without hope for mobility and getting access to valued activities. Compared to the patterns of mobility and concerns in the orchestral world, the perception of high-level social locations being ruled out it is not as clearcut. The following 28-year-old player was asked a question directed toward each respondent:

Q: What are your chances for being promoted or getting a shot this year?

It can happen I suppose, injuries, or the line might get hot, someone might be sent down, you might get the right break at the right time, and luck and chance are part of this.

A colleague in mid-career was more direct about the gradual erosion of mobility chances and the points of no return in which management and coaches "give up on you." He said:

My chances this year are . . . well, this is a business and they go with youth. I'd say that after 28 the odds are against you. The longer you wait the harder it is, you know? The earlier you get there, the more money you're going to make while you're in the National League. You take a look at what others are doing and you see where you are and with guys who have had as much experience as you've had, the guys in the same position as you are. My wife and I say we'll give it till 26 or 27 maybe, then I'll know if I'll be in the NHL. After that they give up on you. Some have gone up after 30, look at E. [an older player who just became a NHL rookie during the season]. He is 34 I think, a 34-year-old rookie—he got a shot and then played in the playoffs. It can happen.

Q: Your chances for going up are harder with age? What about your chances next year of getting a promotion?

If I have a good season, we'll get a shot, it's going good. You see the thing is after a while you realize that you're not a big star anymore like maybe you were in Junior A [amateur Canadian hockey]. Now you're just one of the boys, you've got to work, it will pay off I think. But it's a tough transition to make, and each year you don't get any younger, you know?

Players and performers change a great deal from the time they initially enter the career until they reach turning points such as these. We might term the first five or six years of hockey and the first ten or twelve years of an orchestral career as periods of "illusionment" where the person's career is being launched though not securely fulfilled. At this time footholds are being established, occupational ambitions for "arrival" are high, and while access to top organizations is recognized as difficult, such mobility is viewed as a real possibility. What occurs during these early- and mid-career years of adult socialization is not so much a stark collision of success dreams with the realities of recruitment and differential promotion by age as much as a construction of new mobility outlooks and motivations.

MAKING DO IN THE MINORS: FACILITATING CONDITIONS

As these performers and players remain in the middle levels, dramatic changes take place in the meanings imputed to mobility. This kind of personal adaptation is rarely consummated in one dramatic moment or turning point. Rather it is contained in a process of self-redefinition that extends over a period of time and is subjectively experienced in different ways by those affected. Throughout the interviews a number of themes describing coming to terms with immobility in the minors appear.

1. Members stress the personal benefits of their present position.
2. They comment on the prices to be paid in moving up the career ladder.
3. They strive for average recognition or esteem rather than for outstanding prestige in the set.
4. They shift their life interest away from work to other areas of life, specifically the familial sphere.
5. They often stress a calculative orientation towards their organizational involvement.

These are the components of their emerging "realism," and they make it easier to accept a lack of mobility or demotion (compare with Chinoy, 1955; Goldner, 1965; Faulkner, 1973). A 33-year-old minor leaguer with two seasons in the NHL outlined some of these personal changes in a blunt style; when asked if he had once aspired to superstar status, he said:

> Sure, you want to be best, you want to come close to the best; if you don't have any ambition then you're not going to get anywhere, right? I enjoyed playing in the National, I enjoyed the stay very much. I was sent down towards the end of the '68 season. If you got so many that are advanced ahead of you, where's the *room* for *you*? I'd be kidding myself if I'd say I didn't want to be the best but come on, stop daydreaming. This stuff is fine when you're young, but not now, come on. I'm not going to be a superstar, those days are over. Now I'm doing it for the money, for my personal bonus, my own pride. You have qualifications for a certain job, fine, work hard and put yourself in a position where people will need you. You can make a very good living here (in the minors).

A colleague noted that lack of success in the NHL need not be seen as failure but rather as *relative success* (Glaser, 1964). The following suggests that players revise their expectations about the desirability of promotion itself while acquiring a new perspective leading to satisfaction with a smaller accomplishment.

> The National League is *not* the only league to play in. Believe me, I've given it a good shot but the going up and down like a yo-yo, the moving of the family, and all that. We've paid the price, but it's a good life here. Even right here in (the minors) where else can you make this kind of money and meet the people you do? I enjoy my friends here, I have no complaints because not everyone gets the chance to have the life we've had. I want to play a few more years, and like I say, it's been good to us.

On this more restricted scale, journeymen players can thus attain a fair measure of recognition, view themselves relative successes because of their material rewards, and prolong their playing careers in the minors where the years of peak productivity are extended. The potential dysfunctions of immobility and demotion for hockey organizations are further minimized by arrangements which facilitate the accumulation of rewards such as esteem and income—rewards which would have to be relinquished if the player chose to start another career at this point in the life cycle. Moreover, in coming to terms with age and occupancy of minor league status, the player often finds that involvements are being deepened for him in other areas as well. During the mid-twenties the process of acquiring familial involvements heightens the attractions of economic rewards which develop as unanticipated offshoots of his work and career involvement. These crescive commitments are not easily turned aside or undone as players approach the age of 30 and begin facing the possibility of only a few remaining playing years. Taken together, income, personal attachment to the sport itself, and psychic benefits from shared camaraderie sustain the player's affiliation to the middle ranks of the hockey world.

At the same time, the precariousness of the career line still holds out the prospect of interorganizational mobility. Quite consistently, those interviewed display a skepticism towards "not facing the facts" of aging while discussing the problem of "hanging on" past one's playing prime: "I'll give it a few more years, I'll steal a few seasons from the younger kids, but I sure as hell won't hang on. The point is you want to go out with good memories, not bad ones." Somewhat paradoxically the *anomalous case* itself is a recurrent and integral part of player's mobility motivations. The older rookie, the promoted veteran who goes up to stay (and there are typically one or two cases every playing season) affects the organizational commitment of other players because they are given hope that the same thing may happen to them. This feature of age-status asynchronization (Cain, 1964) tends to promote staff continuity and individual contribution to the team by providing available recruits in the pipeline strata who never fully give up on the chance of having an exemplary season and then being tapped for the major leagues. The sentiments surrounding this motivation, and the impact of recent league expansion on these, were summed up by a 28-year-old goalie. He said: "Maybe you'll go up, maybe not. You take it a year at a time. With expansion we all have a shot at it. If the legs hold out, who knows? You're as good as your last season, that's what they remember. I still might get a shot." While several older men dismiss the most blatant exhortations for success with "be serious, those days are long gone," they nevertheless do not casually dismiss the potent, but statistically remote, possibility of becoming an elite regular. These outlooks suggest that personal adaptations to careers characterized by peak earnings for incumbents, structured uncertainty, and the potential for "windfalls" or reversals in career fortune actually enlarge the individual's contribution to collective goals by making it possible for the incumbent to entertain simultaneously the possibility of future success as well as immobility. *The integration of these complex features not only ties the player to a particular minor league situation but sustains as well the illusion and pleasure of viewing oneself if not forever young, then at least forever promising.*

The changing expectancies for inclusion and personal adjustments to immobility appear to be no more stable than the ongoing arrangements to which members adapt. In a comparative sense, professional hockey has the ambience of a series of precarious situations while the orchestra world has the structure of a long ladder with secure rungs or mobility plateaus. For minor league hockey players, their career footholds are shifting and uncertain. Their occupational world is one of contingency, the stay in the minors a provisional one. Ideally, their present place is merely one of transit. It is as if they are all at a railroad station. Yet they are constrained to adjust to a highly active structure of personnel circulation and colleague competition. They come to face the prospect of their own eventual demise as players.

Musicians, by way of contrast, remain in an orchestra until they retire. The situation is one of stability. Their stay has a prospective future. They have arrived at their destination. Hockey players are in an occupation which sustains the hope of being among the select; orchestra musicians relinquish career dreams of this sort, scale down their expectations for inclusion, and adjust to what is probable in the long run rather than possible over the short run. *Making a successful personal adaptation lies in the process of personal change and reevaluation of such organizational locations.*

Very often the relinquishing of mobility motivations occurs in conjunction with efforts to disavow invidious comparisons among organizations at the middle level. It would appear that emphasizing the unstratified features of the organizational set makes it easier to accept one's own lack of mobility. A 38-year-old string player had this to say:

> It's not where you are but how well you're doing. I always felt that the career will take care of itself. Music cannot be thought of as something you can put in some economic formula, how do you know that this place is better than that place, this string section is better than that one? Are we two or three notches better than D. [minor league symphony]. You can play here or there, the important thing is your own progress.

Comments like this suggest that to the extent a ranking of minor league organizations is loosely defined, the larger the number of incumbents who can (1) be satisfied with playing in what they consider to be either a top minor league orchestra or one just below the top, (2) remain preoccupied with their chances of moving within the minor leagues rather than into the majors, and (3) move to orchestras at roughly the same level and consider the move a step upward. The interface of positional and organizational mobility noted earlier further facilitates this tradeoff. Unlike the world of professional hockey, the mobility paths in the orchestra are more diversified and the definitions of success decidedly more complex. This very complexity allows for redefinition or modification of career aspirations—an adapatation that may occur in *anticipation of immobility.*

A related condition of organizational socialization occurs with the development of essential changes in the nature of musician's minor league involvement. Following Becker (1952; 1960) and Geer (1966), career incumbents become committed whenever they realize that it will cost them more to change their organizational position than it will to remain where they are. The following are some of the valuables whose accumulation restrains career mobility and increases the likelihood of staying at this orchestral level: contributions to pension plan, adjustment to one's way of doing things, rewarding relations with colleagues, a clientele of students, and a measure of local eminence. At about the age of 35, players begin exhibiting intense identification with their particular institutional position and a particular set of predictable and knowable customs; they become increasingly reluctant to face the prospects of, in the words of several, "starting all over again" in another organization. A concern centers around losing the accumulated perquisites and privileges of their present work role:

> I suppose part of my situation here is that I've developed a nice reputation for myself, I hope so ... and going to a major orchestra now would be nice but this is hard to give up. There's a lot of pressure in a big orchestra, take F. ["big five" symphony], the place is divided into two factions, the one centering around the oboe player, the other around the flute player—you're in one camp or the other. Now we don't have that kind of thing here, it's great here, sort of like a family. The people in my section are my friends, my students have done well, there's not that continual fighting. You see, I'm aware of my ability and I hope I have an understanding of my liabilities, and I just would feel a certain amount of fear about moving someplace else.... I admire the players with that confidence and drive to get into the top orchestras, that's great. But for me, at this point, things might not work out and then ... then were would you be?

Despite the small number of cases, my impression is that comments on difficulties and personal price to be paid for "making it" in the major leagues function as "cooling-out" mechanisms for these players. Moreover, they facilitate those conditions which allow the abandoning of further aspirations without bitterness while still making it possible for musicians to admire the striver while being perfectly happy not to be one themselves.[8] To repeat, such personal outlooks have concrete consequences for pipeline organizations because they dampen motivations to move onward and upward while calling forth the individual's contribution to institutional efforts.

One of the most potentially important aspects of these careers comes about through the development of unintended involvement deepened for the musician in other areas of life. Unanticipated side-benefits of organizational participation, such as community localization tied to the family, household, and schools are of sufficient value that their loss is subjectively defined as a constraint by the performing artist. The development of investments in the *private sphere* become linked to a more or less permanently given line of occupation action (see Wilensky, 1960; Berger and Kellner, 1964; Friedman, 1967). "Sinking roots" and related familial obligations during the late twenties to mid-thirties are in turn made conditional on the musician's continuing to remain in the minor league setting. The prospect of staying in the minor leagues becomes commonplace and even expected, whether they approve or disapprove of it, for these families can produce for themselves a private world in which they can feel secure and at home. Performers may in this way eradicate a sense of inadequacy surrounding their career progress. Asked about his future plans a 32-year-old brass player had this to say:

> We want to stay here for a bit, I like the teaching and all that goes with this job. We still have plenty of time for the kids. The guys in the brass section . . . we all go skiing, so this is important to me. You asked about my chances for auditioning and getting into a big orchestra like Chicago or Boston, and I don't think I really want that now, not anymore, it's too much work . . . Maybe at one time, but the family and the leisure, I don't want to lose that, I don't want to be away from them that much.

The solidarity-affirming nature of role reorientation coupled with supportive relationships in other spheres of the life-career can now be briefly enumerated. First, it should be observed that musicians are encouraged to adopt these standpoints, discovering and emphasizing the admirable features of current organizational roles while discounting other possible career lines; they come to reaffirm a multiplicity of collective affiliations, thereby enhancing their current organizational and familial involvement. These arrangements also enhance the shared views of like-situated colleagues who have preceded the person along this adaptive line of action. Second, by eliminating himself or by being eliminated through the operation of occupational expectations and bureaucratic arrangements, any one career fate within a minor league orchestra tends to confirm the views of other immobile colleagues concerning the hazards, injustices, difficulties, and politics of going higher in the organizational ranks. The individual can find, for example, a sympathetic audience of others who have considerable interest in avoiding excessive talk about bootstrap betterment. They will spare him the censure for not having climbed fast or far enough. Finally, in lowering career sights and shifting mobility expectations away from the illustrious slopes toward more probable terrain, many confess relief that their major career speculations and fears are now put to rest. The burning of bridges in this fashion dampens the poignancy of negative self-judgment and allows for appropriate disengagement from intense colleague competition for top strata positions. Considering the length of career time left and the high degree to which the present situation provides valuables out of which commitment grows, a "cooling-out" process is facilitated in which life in the minors constitutes available alternative achievements. This alleviates the potentially disruptive consequences of striving for success at the top of the organizational set. Personnel circulation is thus achieved, current selection procedures are maintained, and the mollification of the immobile prevents disturbances that can arise from the gap between mobility promises and structured exclusion.

CONCLUSIONS AND IMPLICATIONS

The analysis of career socialization has cogency, insofar as it deals directly with the interplay between member's perspectives and the structural context within which they operate. Referring as it does to directly observable actor-oriented (sometimes called "subjective") constructs and to discernable patterns of personnel turnover and age-grading, "career contingency" is seen as a fundamental concept. I have argued that the way in which a person views himself and colleague competitors in the process of occupational aging affects how one experiences a world of work. Career incumbents develop collective and distinctive ways of looking at the world. The focus and scope of the lenses may be different depending on certain conditions, but the problems of success and access appear to be critical features of this symbolic screen. I have also emphasized that within work organizations persons move through temporally situated opportunities. A comparative approach has been utilized to reveal the arrangements by which certain categories of incumbents are more readily available at certain career points than others for selection into the elite strata. The interdependency between organizational context and career outlook is, so I would argue, a general phenomenon, even if its particular form differs in various occupations.

Research studies of work careers have had no difficulty enumerating the ways in which formal organizations are people processing institutions. Investigators typically point to the impact of mobility patterns on career concerns. To date, however, emphasis has been placed on one or the other, but rarely on both. Moreover, sociologists often produce their understanding of structural conditions from either the generation of ideal types or by directly consulting the accounts given by various personnel within the organization in question—usually those in positions of command authority. As a partial remedy for this state of affairs, I have blended available organizational records and interview interrogations. Some fundamental mobility patterns have thereby been revealed. First, commitment appears to be essentially a segregation, boundary-maintaining mechanism; it promotes the internal cohesion of the pipeline organization and ensures its continuity as a distinctive unit. This is facilitated at the personal level by both "cooling-out" those who do not reach top strata positions as well as by making alternative goals viable. Second, situational adjustment to the exigencies of youth-intensive recruitment can be viewed as an essential feature of the interlinking, associative relations which connect major and minor league units. Thus, where age-grading is more intensive, as in professional sports, personal adaptations have their structural consequences in providing the ready availability of recruits. Third, and related, the similarity between these and Goldner's (1965) findings is instructive. Both suggest the importance of managerial control over mobility. The amount of direct and displayed discretion available to top strata managers is much greater in professional hockey than in the orchestra world. This discretion is reinforced by the fact that superiors control the major rewards meaningful to subordinates. High rates of success among colleague competitors should be associated with relatively lower expectancies of anticipatory immobility. Conversely, where managerial decision-making at the elite level is more diffuse and overall organizational metabolism is relatively slower (as in the low turnover patterns per season in the "top five" orchestras), we should observe increased expectancies of future immobility. Finally, to speculate somewhat, it may well be that both systems are more productive because they utilize their middle-level members efficiently than because they give greater opportunity to the more able. It appears that some proper balance between the mobile and immobile is necessary. As Everett C. Hughes pointed out years ago, it is essential that occupations ". . . have a breed known as the 'Thank God' people . . . who can be counted on to stay where they are, and who keep things running while others are busy climbing the mobility ladder from one job to another" (Hughes, 1949: 219).

These data also suggest that occupational culture develops to the degree that members identify, assemble, recognize, and act on the problem of success and failure. In effective interaction with one another, both players and performers turn their concerted attention to discovering what they take to be the "objective facts" of their personal mobility. In so doing, they acquire a practiced grasp in discriminating between age-related and "nonage-related" problems while learning to act differentially with respect to them. If an occupational culture can be said to be a distinctive set of understandings and ways of acting that arise in response to the problems faced by a group, there is to be found in the materials a dialectic suggesting that age and mobility are to be seen in terms of one another. In both the world of hockey players and that of orchestra musicians time has its moments and age its crucial objectivity. I have pointed out how age shapes members' conceptions of work reality itself; it defines what is and how to deal with it. Thus the tracking and formulating of career aspirations constitutes an important feature of social organization as well as the very reality in which musicians and athletes are obliged to live.

To follow out the implications of this observation, the making of careers becomes a basic activity through which knowledge of an occupation is detected and displayed. The various practices members employ in sustaining and reporting on their chances for "making it" develop in tandem with their understanding of the recalcitrant features of mobility. The social construction of meaning can be viewed as centering around the conditions of occupational age. Thus fashion models (see Becker and Strauss, 1956), professional fighters (Weinberg and Arond, 1952), lawyers (Smigel, 1964; Spector, 1973), scientists (Reif and Strauss, 1965), industrial executives (Martin and Strauss, 1956), strippers, dancers, actors and actresses, teachers (Becker, 1952; Friedman, 1967), engineers and technical specialists (Sofer, 1970), and astronauts are urged to recognize and face up to the career dilemmas of becoming occupationally and biologically older. All have much in common: looked at in the proper light, their very differences connect them. It is what might be called age-consciousness: an aspect of occupational and organizational life whose centrality has, to borrow a phrase from Alfred Schultz, a paramount reality in experience.

In contrast to some sociological versions of work careers as passage through consensually validated positional structures, the approach advanced here suggests that we view *careers as constructions and concerted accomplishments through and by which occupational actors apprehend the objective arrangements in their work lives.* I have been concerned principally with analyzing the ways in which coming to terms—as a temporally situated achievement—consists of a set of practical maxims and reigning attitudes for coping with immobility and failure. I have also been concerned with documenting the ways in which these performers and players conceive of their own biographies as subject to, influenced by, and known in terms of the intelligible features of aging and career success. More than a crude set of retrospective reconstruction of the past, coming of occupational age by coming to terms with the work world consists of learning a set of assumptions. These assumptions are known, used, and taken for granted by organizational incumbents. They direct attention to the practical ways in which careers are to be interpreted as well as to the facticity of their design. More than a method of modifying career expectations, the coming of age in adult work life is a way of conceiving what is possible and what is not, what is real and what is not.

It is a sociological commonplace to assert that man actively conceptualizes his work biography and thereby comes to know the working constitution of the setting in which his career is located. Yet the problem of how this is temporally achieved is seldom posed. It seems an obvious matter that personal change occurs during crucial marking points in occupational lives. It seems equally obvious that the selection and sorting processes within organizational sets will affect the manner and degree to which incumbents align success aspirations with actual accomplishments. But the very obviousness of these phenomena should motivate close inspection of them. It is the very special characteristic of occupational socialization that it is the result of a process of social production designed to show the exigencies of age and erosion of mobility chances.

To see the social character of occupational aging, therefore, one must see how contingencies unfold. What characterizes organizational membership is not that individuals are merely concerned about their chances of success and access, but that they share these concerns in effective interaction, and produce lines of mutual adjustment under the auspices of their conceptions of occupational reality itself. I have argued that such conceptions of membership are articulated on those occasions when middle-level incumbents review and contemplate the features upon which their personal success depend. Coming up adult in the socially produced world of work is, then, an occasion for us to document the ways in which players and performers display a hard-headed commitment to "becoming realistic" —a stance that is the mark of occupational adulthood. An effort should be made to determine whether these formulations (and modifications thereof) apply in a wider variety of organizational sets and occupational worlds.

NOTES

1. This term has a very technical meaning in the sociological and anthropological literature (Eisenstadt 1956); I use it here to refer to socially recognized age-positions or categories defined by work organizations. As such, it is one of the social phenomena about which everyone knows, as in the ratified assumptions about "how old" candidates for certain positions should be. Relying on participants' knowledge or intuitive understanding of just what occupational age is, the professional social-scientific literature provides little in the way of analytical unity or comparative development of the normative definitions and structural consequences of allocation by age in organizations.

2. The orchestral leagues are composed of organizations in the following urban areas: Atlanta, Baltimore, Buffalo, Cincinnati, Dallas, Denver, Detroit, Houston, Indianapolis, Kansas City, Los Angeles, Milwaukee, Minneapolis, Montreal, New Jersey, New Orleans, Pittsburgh, Rochester, St. Louis, San Antonio, San Francisco, Seattle, Toronto, and The Washington National Symphony. Below these are the bush leagues comprised of semi-pro and amateur symphonies. (See Hart, 1973 and Caplow, 1964).

3. Over these two seasons the teams were distributed in the following way. *American Hockey League:* Baltimore, Boston, Cincinnati, Cleveland, Hershey, New Haven, Nova Scotia, Providence, Richmond, Rochester, Springfield, Tidewater. *Central Hockey League:* Dallas, Fort Worth, Kansas City, Oklahoma City, Omaha, Tulsa. *Western Hockey League:* Denver, Phoenix, Portland, Salt Lake, San Diego, Seattle.

4. The amateur draft is comprised of Canadian and college performers who are at least 20 years old by December 31. In 1971 the 14 clubs drafted 115 players. Fewer than 15 percent went directly into the NHL, most were sent to the minor league affiliate. The expansion draft is the next organizational mechanism by which new clubs acquire the bulk of their players. Here the new teams have to be stocked with 18 to 20 players; they get these men from the already established clubs. The latter want to retain their finest talent so they make out a "protected list," a roster of from 13 to 15 men whom the new teams cannot select. The remaining players are available. Whether one is protected or not, therefore, becomes an important sign of one's standing with managers and coaches. This concern is further intensified as in the 1971–1972 season where each club could dress 17 skaters and two goalies for each game. The active roster of 19 is typically comprised of three forward lines and five defensemen, or 14 skaters. In selecting lines some choices are automatic and coaches turn to their proven players, superstars, and talented rookies. Filling out the roster is a managerial procedure of some consequence for the remaining players–those on the low end of the status hierarchy—for it determines how much, or even whether, one is going to have access to the most important activity of all, namely, playing time or "ice time."

5. This data is drawn from the *1971–1972 Pro and Senior Hockey Guide* (St. Louis: *The Sporting News,* 1971).

6. Of the 379 players who played one or more games in the NHL during the 1971–1972 season, 125 experienced some form of *interleague mobility.* Of the latter, 92 (or around 75 percent) were from the American Hockey League, 17 (or 14 percent) were from the Central Hockey League, 12 (or 10 percent) from the Western Hockey League, and a handful from the International Hockey League. The remaining 254, of course, played every game at the NHL level.

7. Viewed in an a priori fashion, the probability of any musician in the minor orchestral set being hired by a big league orchestra is less than 2 percent (30/2250) The attractive simplicity of this ratio conceals the processes by which minor league orchestra players remain immobile and unavailable for auditions for any one opening at the level of the "big five." Still, in any one year the active players in the musical marketplace may be as large as 30 percent (675) raising the chances of any person securing a position at the top to around 4 percent. This will vary depending upon the status of the opening, orchestral policies concerning hiring from within, etc. By way of contrast, in professional hockey over the past seasons around 45 jobs have been available in any one year; there are 460 players in the minors, their chances of being promoted are about one in ten.

8. This insight was suggested by Ralph H. Turner in a personal communication.

REFERENCES

Banton, M.
1965   *Roles: An Introduction to the Study of Social Relations.* London: Tavistock.

Becker, H. S.
1970   "The Self and Adult Socialization." In *Sociological Work: Method and Substance.* Chicago: Aldine. 289–303.
1964   "Personal Change in Adult Life." *Sociometry,* **27** (March): 40–53.
1963   *Outsiders.* New York: The Free Press.
1952   "The Career of the Chicago Public School Teacher." *American Journal of Sociology,* **57** (March): 470–477.

Becker, H. S., and A. L. Strauss
1956   "Careers, Personality, and Adult Socialization." *American Journal of Sociology,* **62** (November): 253–263.

Berger, B. M.
1960   "How Long Is a Generation?" *British Journal of Sociology,* **11**: 557–568.

Berger, P. L., and Hansfried Kellner
1964   "Marriage and the Construction of Reality." *Diogenes,* **4** (Summer): 1–24.

Brim, O. G., Jr.
1966   "Socialization through the Life Cycle." *Socialization After Childhood: Two Essays.* New York: John Wiley. 3–49.
1968   "Adult Socialization." In *Socialization and Society,* John A. Clausen (ed.). Boston: Little, Brown. 183–226.

Cain, L. D., Jr.
1964   "Life Course and Social Structure." In *Handbook of Modern Sociology,* R. E. L. Faris (ed.). Chicago: Rand McNally. 272–309.

Caplow, T.
1964   *Principles of Organization.* New York: Harcourt, Brace and World.

Caplow, T., and R. J. McGee
1958   *The Academic Marketplace.* New York: Basic Books.

Carlin, J. E.
1962   *Lawyers on Their Own: A Study of Individual Practitioners in Chicago.* New Jersey: Rutgers University Press.

Chinoy, E.
1955   *Automobile Workers and The American Dream.* New York: Random House.

Clark, B. R.
1960   "The 'Cooling Out' Function in Higher Education." *American Journal of Sociology,* **65** (May): 569–576.

Eisenstadt, S. N.
1956   *From Generation to Generation.* New York: Free Press.

Faulkner, R. R.
1973   "Career Concerns and Mobility Motivations of Orchestra Musicians." *Sociological Quarterly,* **14** (Summer): 334–349.
1971   *Hollywood Studio Musicians: Their Work and Careers in The Recording Industry.* Chicago: Aldine-Atherton.

Friedman, N. L.
1967   "Career Stages and Organizational Role Decisions of Teachers in Two Public Junior Colleges." *Sociology of Education,* **40** (Summer): 231–245.

Geer, B.
1966   "Occupational Commitment and the Teaching Profession." *The School Review,* **74** (Spring): 31–47.

Glaser, B. G.
1964   *Organizational Scientists.* Indianapolis: Bobbs-Merrill.

Glaser, B. G., and A. L. Strauss
1971   *Status Passages: A Formal Theory.* Chicago: Aldine-Atherton.

Goffman, E.
1961   *Asylums: Essays on the Social Situation of Mental Patients and Other Inmates.* Garden City, N.Y.: Doubleday.
1952   "On Cooling the Mark Out: Some Aspects of Adaptation to Failure." *Psychiatry,* **15** (November): 451–463.

Goldner, E.
1965   "Demotion in Industrial Management." *American Sociological Review,* **30** (October): 714–724.

Goldner, E., and R. R. Ritti
1967   "Professionalization as Career Immobility." *American Journal of Sociology,* **72** (March): 489–502.

Hall, O.
1948   "The Stages of a Medical Career." *American Journal of Sociology,* **53** (March): 327–336.

Hart, P.
1973   *Orpheus in The New World: The Symphony Orchestra as an American Cultural Institution.* New York: W. W. Norton.

Hughes, E. C.
1958   *Men and Their Work.* New York: The Free Press.
1949   "Queries Concerning Industry and Society Growing out of Study of Ethnic Relations in Industry." *American Sociological Review,* **14** (April): 211–220.

Levenson, B.
1961   "Bureaucratic Succession." In *Complex Organizations,* A. Etzioni (ed.). New York: Holt, Rinehart and Winston. 362–395.

Maniha, J. K.
1972   "Organizational Demotion and the Process of Bureaucratization." *Social Problems,* **20** (Fall): 161–173.

Martin, N. H., and A. L. Strauss
1956   "Patterns of Mobility within Industrial Organizations." *Journal of Business,* **29** (April): 101–110.

Merton, R. K.
1957   *Social Theory and Social Structure.* Glencoe: Free Press.

Miller, D. C., and W. H. Form
1951   *Industrial Sociology.* New York: Harper and Brothers.

More, D. M.
1962   "Demotion." *Social Problems,* **9** (Winter): 213–221.

Morse, N. C., and R. S. Weiss
1955   "The Function and Meaning of Work and the Job." *American Sociological Review,* **20** (April): 191–198.

Mueller, J.
1951   *The American Symphony Orchestra: A Social History of Musical Taste.* Bloomington, Indiana: Indiana University Press.

Reif, F., and A. L. Strauss
1965   "The Impact of Rapid Discovery upon the Scientist's Career." *Social Problems,* **12:** 297–311.

Roth, J. A.
1963   *Timetables.* Indianapolis: Bobbs-Merrill.

Ryder, N. B.
1965   "The Cohort as a Concept in the Study of Social Change." *American Sociological Review,* **30** (December): 834–861.

Seeman, M.
1967   "On the Personal Consequences of Alienation in Work." *American Sociological Review,* **32** (April): 273–285.

Smigel, E.
1964   *The Wall Street Lawyer.* New York: The Free Press.

Sofer, C.
1970   *Men in Mid-Career: A Study of British Managers and Technical Specialists.* London: Cambridge University Press.

Solomon, D. N.
1953   "Career Contingencies of Chicago Physicians." Ph.D. Dissertation. Chicago: University of Chicago.

Spector, M.
1973   "Secrecy in Job Seeking among Government Attorneys: Two Contingencies in the Theory of Subcultures." *Urban Life and Culture,* **2** (July): 211–229.

1972   "The Rise and Fall of a Mobility Route." *Social Problems,* **20** (Fall): 173–185.

Stebbins, R. A.
1970   "Career: The Subjective Approach." *Sociological Quarterly,* **11** (Winter): 32–49.

Stouffer, S. A., E. A. Suchman, L. C. Devinney, S. A. Star, and R. M. Williams, Jr.
1949   *The American Soldier: Adjustment During Army Life.* Princeton, N.J.: Princeton University Press.

Strauss, A. L.
1959   *Mirrors and Masks: The Search for Identity.* New York: Free Press.

Wager, L. W.
1959   "Career Patterns and Role Problems of Airline Pilots in a Major Airline Company. Ph.D. Dissertation. Chicago: University of Chicago.

Weinberg, S. K., and H. Arond
1952   "The Occupational Culture of the Boxer." *American Journal of Sociology,* **57**: 460–469.

Westby, D. L.
1960   "The Career Experience of the Symphony Musician." *Social Forces,* **38** (March): 223–230.

Wilensky, H. L.
1960   "Work, Careers, and Social Integration." *International Social Science Journal,* **12**: 543–560.
1956   *Intellectuals in Labor Unions: Orgnaziational Pressures on Professional Roles.* Glencoe: Free Press.

Wood, A. L.
1967   *Criminal Lawyer.* New Haven: College and University Press.

Chapter 12
The Wrestler
and the Physician:
Identity Work-up and
Organizational Arrangements

M. Michael Rosenberg and Allen Turowetz
Departments of Sociology
Rutgers University and Dawson College
(New Brunswick, New Jersey and Montreal, Canada)

M. Michael Rosenberg

Birth Place.   Jaffa, Israel

Age: 24

Birth Order: One older sister

Formal Education:

B.A., Sir George Williams University, Montreal	**1971**
M.A., Rutgers University, New Jersey	**1974**
Currently Ph.D. student at Rutgers	

Present Position:

Lecturer, Department of Sociology, Dawson College, Westmount, Quebec

Scholarly Interests:

Sociology of death

Professional Accomplishments:

Book on Sociology of Sport in preparation with Gregory Stone and Allan Turowetz.

Hobbies:

Guitar

Sport Activities:

Basketball

Most Recent Books Read:

Jane Van Lawick-Goodall	*In the Shadow of Man*
Jean Piaget	*Judgement and Reasoning in the Child*
Arthur C. Clarke	*The Nine Billion Names of God*

Allen Turowetz

Birth Place: Montreal, Canada

Age: 26

Birth Order: Two older brothers

Formal Education:

B.A., Honors (with distinction), Sir George Williams
University, Montreal   1971

M.A., McGill University, Montreal   1974

Present Position:

Lecturer (full-time), Department of Sociology, Dawson College, Westmount, Quebec

Lecturer (part-time), Department of Sociology, Concordia
University, Quebec

Professional Responsibilities:

Teaching courses in Systematic Sociology, Methodology, Leisure and Sport, Social Psychology.

Scholarly Interests:

Sociology of sport; occupations and professions; symbolic
interaction.

Professional Accomplishments:

Presented papers; forthcoming paper and book publications.

Hobbies:

Classical music appreciation, folk music appreciation.

Sports Activities:

Participant: football and basketball.

Spectator: all sports, notably hockey and football.

Most Recent Books Read:

Maas	*Serpico*
Mannheim	*Ideology and Utopia*
Gouldner	*The Coming Crisis in Western Sociology*

INTRODUCTION

As they learn the staging of contests, professional wrestlers must learn to match their subjective experience with the objective reality which is presented to them by the promotional organizational arrangement of their particular occupation. Central to this is the wrestlers' appropriation of those identities in which the organization places them. This appropriation process is problematic in any occupation, but becomes even more so when, as in wrestling, there are multiple identities and multiple roles to learn and perform. In this chapter, we examine the problematic elements of identity work-up in professional wrestling. This is done in part by comparing the wrestler with the physician, a comparison illustrating the interrelationships between role and identity as varying in different organizational, communicative, and experiental contexts.

While sociologists in general have emphasized the pregiven or normative aspects of role performance and identity, it has been the merit of such sociologists as symbolic interactionists, ethnomethodologists, and "phenomenological" sociologists to examine as well the problematic nature of social interaction. These "interpretive" sociologists (Dreitzel, 1970) have well shown that role performances do not merely follow a set script (Cicourel, 1970), nor are identities automatically—or even necessarily—internalized with role performance (Goffman, 1961). Neither do people respond to situations like robots acting out an identity. They must often appraise, assess, and evaluate themselves and others in any social encounter, modifying their definitions of the situation as new circumstances arise (Blumer, 1969).

It would not do, however, to overstate the case. Much of our activity remains taken for granted, predefined by shared meanings and relevances

This is a revised version of a paper presented at Midwest Sociological Society meetings 1973. We would like to thank Gregory Stone, Norman Denzin, Anton Zigderveld and Ralph Selinger for their comments on earlier versions of this paper.

(Berger and Luckmann, 1966). But the contexts appropriate to those meanings have often become dissociated from those meanings. Simultaneous and conflicting systems of relevance often decrease the pre-predicative character of social reality in terms of all but the most fundamental relevances basic to the modern structures of consciousness (Berger, 1966; Zijderveld, 1970; Mills, 1940).

Despite this inherently problematic possibility, social order continues to be experienced as real, as Glaser and Strauss note (1965), because the individual is continually "working at" the bases of this order and thus managing their problematic experiences. To the extent that this is true, interpretive sociologists are viewing interaction in a manner consistent with our common experience, at least in contemporary everyday life. This experience is one that goes beyond merely "working at" social reality. The individual participates in the construction of that reality (Berger and Luckmann 1966), he actively "works up" its various aspects.

The concept of identity work-up when used as a heuristic device permits us to examine the experience, internalization, and acting out of an identity. That these three aspects of identity can be differentiated and not merely subsumed under internalization is the peculiarly and typically modern aspect of identity. Such internalization cannot be taken for granted as an adequate role performance does not necessarily imply that one experiences the role as part of one's identity.

Under what set of social conditions, then, will identity be experienced as problematic and under what set taken for granted? In our view one can begin to answer by examining the communicative and institutional contexts of structural and interpersonal relations in which identities are forged. The assumption is that the context of interaction with others becomes important in determining the nature of the social self and of social action. An institution as a set of structural relations generates both a social self (especially in its most social aspect: identity) and social action (especially in its most social aspect: role performance).

A communicative context is a set of interpersonal relations capable of making institutional roles as identity plausible or problematic. One condition which we might assume to be inherently problematic is a communicative context which typically deals with outsiders as part of the organizational structure. Such institutionalized outsiders provide the context with which each organization must come to terms in a manner that greatly affects maintaining any identity. As an example, the physician must typically interact with patients. Yet, the physician has been popularly characterized by sociologists as one for whom identity is definite and unproblematic. The professional wrestler must also deal with outsiders, the audience, but our research has indicated that in this case, identity often does become problematic.

Comparing then, the acting out and experience of identity for both the physician and the wrestler, it is our intention here to examine the physician and the wrestler in terms of how the identity work-up of each indicates either a fit between institutional and communicative contexts or lack of fit.

PERFORMANCE AND IDENTITY WORK-UP

In modern society, role performances are situationally developed and experienced, and, as such, both role performance and identity are often experienced as problematic. It is this problematic quality which has made the sociologist and the everyday man conscious of roles, scripts, performances, and identities. This awareness emerges because neither the role-performance "models," as labeled by social scientists, nor predefined behavioral expectations, as understood by ordinary men, can satisfactorily deal with all the varied situations encountered in the course of everyday life activities. People *are* given a script, but they must work up that script—fill in the gaps and add all of the nuances—as they act. It is in this typically modern situation of "performance work-up" that consciousness of and thinking about our actions occurs.

This is perhaps even more the case with identity. Identities are no longer necessarily congruent with institutionalized roles nor need they be consistent with any overarching order, institutional or otherwise. While such orders, as for example kinship, once provided the individual with a basic and "real" identity, all identities today tend to be equally "real"—a condition that prevents any of them from being completely real—and they are so experienced. Thus, we can develop a concept of "identity work-up" equivalent to performance work-up.

Since Nelson Foote's seminal article on identification two decades ago (1950), the concept of identity has come to be intimately linked to that of role. Although Foote used identity as a necessary concept for the further development of a theory of motivation, the concept of identity has itself come under scrutiny by contemporary social psychologists. Here we shall follow Gregory Stone's notion of identity:

> When one has identity, he is *situated*—that is, cast in the shape of a social object by the acknowledgement of his participation or membership in social relations. One's identity is established when others *place* him as a social object by assigning to him the same words of identity that he appropriates for himself or *announces* (Stone, 1970: 399).

Such placement and announcement should not be viewed as a static condition but as a dynamic process. They are ever subject to changing circumstances. Such changing circumstances can do more than merely change definitions of identity. They may change as well the ways in which identities are experienced. As Peter Berger points out:

Inasmuch as identity is always part of a comprehensive world, and a humanly *constructed* world at that, there are far reaching consequences in the ways in which identity is conceived and, consequently, experienced. Definitions of identity vary with overall definitions of reality. Each such definition, however, has reality-generating power. Men not only define themselves, but they actualize these definitions in real experience—*they live them* (Berger, 1970: 344).

Two common contexts of experience in which identity is forged have been characterized by Stone (1970) as those identities generated in *interpersonal relations* and those identities generated in *structural relations*. Structural relations can be seen as providing identities in terms of institutional roles. These roles can be viewed as typified responses to typified expectations. While not all roles are salient in placing an individual (Kuhn & McPartland, 1954), they do constitute those consensual terms by which expectations can be mobilized in a specific situation.

Mobilization occurs not only in structural but also in interpersonal relations. Interpersonal relations can be seen as providing the experience of identity in those consensual and subconsensual terms developed in interpersonal interaction both within and outside of institutional roles. Thus the announcements and placement of one's identity establishes that one is a doctor, a parent and/or a citizen. Yet, one may be a "good" parent either to oneself or to others when one's performance of the collectively defined behavioral expectations are seen by oneself or by others as in accordance with those expectations.

Roles, of course, refer to more than just behavioral expectations. They imply the acceptance of certain sets of attitudes, beliefs, and motives. Typically, we understand the behavior of others because we understand the attitudes, beliefs and motives underlying their behavior. We take the role of the other. As such, we are aware of and understand far more roles than we consider either a part of or consistent with our identity. In a sense, roles are often resources brought into a situation, for while the role performance within the situation is usually appropriate to it, the understanding of the role precedes its performance.

This generalized notion of the role must be modified in actual performance. Role performance work-up involves developing role-appropriate behavior and experience. Some roles come with more explicitly detailed behaviorial expectations than others, as for example, "professionalized" occupations. Their role performance involves less work-up. More formal learning may actually be required in attaining a certain role, such as that of medical doctor, but their role performances are usually limited to specific spatio-temporal contexts where entailed role performances are relatively clear and rarely experienced as problematic.

PHASES OF IDENTITY WORK-UP

The initial experience of any individual performing his role is an experience of role distance. It takes a while to become convinced. Ordinarily there is a sequence in role performance and its concomitant internalization of the role, its experience as part of one's identity. This sequence involves qualifying for the role performance, training, certification, and performance. The completion of medical school and internship of the doctor, for example, are phases of the process of learning role performance. In the same way, the novice wrestler engages in a two-year apprenticeship to prepare for certification and role performance.

The sequential arrangement involves two distinct phases; entrance phases: qualification, recruitment, and training; and performance phases: certification, announcement, and placement. As we shall show, physicians and wrestlers each differ greatly in the degree and form of identity work-up necessitated by each phase of performance work-up.

Entrance Phases

Qualification need not be consciously undertaken by any individual. People create identities and confer them. Through recruitment, one may be labeled as qualified for particular role performances. The recruit must then appropriate those identities and learn to perform roles linked to them.

In medicine, any individual must establish qualifications for performance. Formal qualification requirements are very rigorous and consequently there is a high failure rate in the qualification phase. Even before being recruited, one must prove one's potential through a better than average undergraduate record in hard science.

Recruitment usually comes in the form of application. This implies that the applicant has some vague notion of what a medical doctor is and what the role performance will entail. While initial doubts may exist about ability to perform (Preiss, 1968: 207), this vague notion will serve to guide the applicant through the initial learning process making experiences (to the degree that it matches or fails to sharply contradict those notions) less problematic and decreasing the extent of identity work-up.

Upon acceptance to candidacy, one must master both the technical skills and the technical vocabulary to complete medical school and qualify for further training (internship and possible residency, etc.). As Hughes observed:

> Medical education is the whole series of processes by which the medical culture is kept alive (which means more than merely imparted) through time and generations . . . the education of the members of the medical profession is a set of planned and unplanned experiences by which laymen, usually young and acquainted with the prevailing lay medical culture, become possessed of some part of the technical and scientific medical culture of the professionals . . . Initiation into a new role is as much a part of medical training as is the learning of techniques; indeed, part of it is to learn the techniques of playing the role well (Hughes, 1958: 118–119).

That is not to say that the technical aspects of becoming a physician are not rigorous, but that the training also involves the internalization of the assumptions, attitudes and beliefs generated by the formal organizational structure of the medical community. This organizational structure channels not only one's actions but also one's perceptions of those actions and of the social reality of which they are a part.

When this rigorous training is satisfactorily completed, candidates are certified by the appropriate professional bodies and presented with diplomas or state-approved licenses which establish for themselves and for others that they are indeed "Doctors." In other words, the person's professional role claims are objectively validated by an officially established audience. This objective nature of the audience's validation of the person's role announcement makes such claims more internally credible to that person. As Priess discovered, only 30 percent of fourth-year medical students retained "some doubt" about occupational choice as opposed to 59 percent of the students upon first acceptance. We should expect doubt to be much lower among practicing physicians beyond internship. In this particular organizational arrangement, then, others validate one's newly formed identity in most objective terms and this fact makes individual identity work-up during entrance phases only minimally necessary.

For professional wrestlers, there are no formal qualification requirements. The potential wrestler is usually labeled as qualified by the promotional office. Active recruitment on the part of the promoter consists of contacting friends and relatives of wrestlers, scouting free-style matches in Europe, and checking carnivals, circuses, and "freaks" (the obese, the giant, and the midget). To be admitted to candidacy, a wrestler undergoes no pre-requirement of a preliminary passage through a training institution comparable to undergraduate school for premedical students. The potential wrestler must, however, demonstrate agility and a high degree of physical fitness and be perceived as one with a "natural touch."

Upon acceptance to candidacy, the potential wrestler must learn to master the technical skills and strategies, and must be able to competently dramatize the symbolic identity given him by the promotional offices: the Nazi, the Japanese, the Russian, etc. If the candidate's training is completely successful, he will have learned not only the prerequisite number of holds, but also the cues and theatrical displays necessary for a proper presentation in his role as wrestler.

The wrestling community has not created a definite culture of intense commitment to a wrestling "world," in the sense that the medical community has. Obviously, the effectiveness of the wrestler's physical training is not designed to involve the life and death of many others, although it must certainly be competent enough to prevent any bodily harm during physical exertion in the arena. Timing and precision become all important in the execution of holds and the reading of cues. Errors in athletic performance can be catastrophic, and while examples are legion, one incident which quickly became legendary in wrestling lore is the losing of an ear by "Yukon" Eric Humbolt in a match with Wladek "Killer" Kowalski more than a decade ago. Such an incident in no sense compares, however, with the degree of commitment with which the doctor confronts the everyday realities of illness and death. This activity can be maintained only by the creation of an extensive and convincing objective reality which sustains the role of the physician and his experience of it.

The case is reversed in terms of symbolic presentation. Inadequate symbolic performance can as quickly end the wrestler's career as any physical mishap. The physician's "bedside manner" is precisely that, a "manner." In contrast, the wrestler's symbolic "identity" determines the nature of his role performance in so far as and when he acts as "the wrestler." While the organizational structure of the medical community is organized around and by the person of the physician, it is fundamental to an understanding of the organizational structure of professional wrestling that the promotional office and not the wrestler himself organizes role performances—the wrestling culture is a promotor's culture.

In comparison with medicine, then, we see that while the training process is much less rigorous, there is an element of working-up a self-definition which is more problematic for the would-be wrestler than the fledging physician. That is to say, learning the technical aspects of medicine is more a part of the physician's training; learning the technical aspects of wrestling is a relatively smaller part of the wrestler's training. Instead, the presentation of a symbolic identity must also be mastered. While the doctor may believe in his "manner," the French-Canadian farm boy cannot believe in his "Russianness" when billed as the "Mad Russian" in the ring. Nor does the would-be wrestler come equipped with predefined general notions which can guide him. And, finally, in order to become a full-fledged wrestler one must indicate the ability to do more than physical feats; one must be able to generate a response from a paying audience.

Performance Phases

Upon certification the candidate is perceived as qualified to act out what he has learned. In action he must now face problematic and unexpected situations. In action he must make variations in, and additions to, his earlier training.

For the physician, performance after formal certification generally becomes more or less automatic (Hughes, 1958). The tasks of the physician are extensively defined. The physician's obligations are determined by the requirements of medical science and medical culture. That is to say, the behavioral obligations of the physician are predefined by training—they are mapped out in advance by professional education. Role performance, we might say, is very well "scripted."

While there may be many reasons for this, one obvious one is the fact that the physician deals daily with the marginal realities of disease and death. The physician must be technically competent to achieve this task. But he must also be attitudinally competent if he is to deal coherently and objectively while in a situation of intense attention to the realities of death and disease whose awareness places them at the very center of our structures of relevance. To this end the individual's efforts in becoming a physician are almost exclusively expended in fulfilling the entrance and training requirements: once having done so, there is little chance of his not going along with the behavioral expectations of being a physician—there is little chance of his rejecting the script (Preiss, 1963). This is because the institutional context of the role implies whole sets of attitudes, beliefs, and motives which have been internalized during the entrance phases. The successful completion of medical training implies such internalization.

Fundamental to an understanding of the physician's role is the realization that its performance occurs only within specific spatio-temporal contexts. Only in those structural relations in which the physician defines the situation as relevant to his medical identity does he engage in appropriate role behavior. The announcement and placement of the medical identity precludes the need for extensive identity work-up.

For the wrestler the role performance is much more problematic when compared with that of the physician. Upon certification by the promotional office (the billing) each wrestler must simultaneously act out two sets of scripts: one as an athlete, the other as a performer. As an athlete, he must satisfactorily perform the technical skills of the trade as well as be a part of an institutional context in which he seeks to be both respected and active. As a performer, the identity of the wrestler is dependent upon his ability to portray the role predefined for him by the promotional offices—such as "hero" or "villain" (Stone, 1970); nor is that predefinition very clear.

In the course of his identity work-up, then, the wrestler must generate a self-concept consistent both with the behavioral expectations of his audience as determined by the promotional office, and with his conception of self as a professional merely playing a role. Despite his role distance from the promotionally assigned role the wrestler must engage in a convincing role presentation to his audience. The inability on the part of others to distinguish the professional wrestler from the professional "bad guy" subverts his ability to maintain role distance. The wrestler who is assigned the "bad guy" role may begin to wonder, "Why me?" The wrestler who comes home from a hard day at the ring, which he perceives to be no different from a hard day at the office, is beaten by his children because he is the "bad guy." The placements of the performer identities become distorted when they are transferred to the interpersonal setting from the structural setting in which they are appropriate. Such distortions weaken the credibility of *any* announcement. In effect, the identity "athlete" becomes short-circuited.

CONCLUSION

Identity work-up, as we have continually stressed, is not static but rather a process. When looking at identity, one must first examine the communicative and institutional context, such as the structural or interpersonal, in which that identity is forged. While acting out the role script, an individual must determine—in action—what that script is. As we have tried to show, this is different for the physician than for the professional wrestler.

In one sense, however, the scripting process is the same: the particular identities which are being worked up are assigned by the organizational structure. Identification becomes a process of qualifying for and accepting other's placements. Identity work-up does not refer to freedom but to individuals constructing the social order and locating themselves within it.

Thus, identity as a concept cannot stand alone as a motive, but must be understood in a relational context. The identification of the wrestler as a "bad guy" does not permit him to act on stage in terms of any identification of self as "good." It also precludes him from acting in any manner that the audience would identify as good. This particular announcement of self as "good" is in danger of becoming subconsensual and losing its objectivity, even, as we have seen, in the wrestler's own immediate circle.

The criterion by which identity is understood in any social reality is situationally defined. In his interpersonal relations with other wrestlers, each wrestler is identified in interpersonal terms. One wrestler is honest, another a thief. For the audiences, identities are structural relations manipulated by the promotional offices. Assigned the role of the evil Nazi, he is perceived by audiences only in that context. Indeed, he may be a responsible husband and a kind father. This the audience neither knows nor cares. Each definition of reality has its own definition of, and experience of, identity.

Wrestlers, actors, or anyone who actually "plays" at roles are good indications of how many of us experience our identity. At the same time, however, they must be poor indications. Few of us are ever really allowed to play at our roles. The scripts have been written and usually need only minimal work-up. Should we change too much, the right to play at all may be taken away. This last observation indicates some of the inadequacies of a purely symbolic interactionist approach. Power, for instance, is rarely an intruder in such an analysis. Yet, an analysis in terms of power, while it would tell us some things which this paper has ignored, would miss the differences in the ways in which we experience identities within structural relations as opposed to interpersonal relations. One is a doctor, but one is also a parent, and the experience of identity in each instance is different. That being the case, we can see that our examples are typical of a vast number of identities which are perhaps not as divergent as those of the physician as a physician and the wrestler as a wrestler. We are often many things at once. The wrestler merely gets paid to be so.

What is needed now is a much more systematic analysis of the interrelationships between roles and identity in various organizational, communicative, and experimental contexts. This paper makes no pretense to having presented a systematic analysis of the interrelationship between identity work-up and organizational arrangements. It does, however, discern some of the elements necessary to such an analysis. Obviously, other kinds of organizational arrangements exist which may necessitate other degrees, and different forms, of identity work-up. But such an approach must be further researched to determine both the structure and the experience of the relationship between role and identity.

REFERENCES

Backman, Carl W., and Paul F. Secord
1968 "The Self And Role Selection." Chapter 28 in *The Self in Social Interaction*, Vol. 1, Chad Gordon and Kenneth Gergen (eds.). New York: John Wiley and Sons.

Becker, Howard S. et al.
1961 *Boys In White.* Chicago: University of Chicago Press.

Berger, Peter
1961 *Invitation to Sociology.* Garden City, N.Y.: Doubleday Anchor.
1966 "Identity as a Problem in the Sociology of Knowledge." *European Journal of Sociology.* Vol. 7 (December) pp. 105–119.
1970 "On the Obsolesence of the Concept of Honour." *European Journal of Sociology.* Vol. 11 (December) pp. 339–347.

Berger, Peter, and Thomas Luckmann
1967 *The Social Construction of Reality.* Garden City, N.Y.: Doubleday Anchor.

Blumer, Herbert
1969 *Symbolic Interactionism.* Englewood Cliffs, N.J.: Prentice-Hall.

Cicourel, Aaron
1970 "Basic and Normative Rules in the Negotiation of Status and Roles." *Recent Sociology No. 2,* Hans Drietzel. New York: Macmillan.

Denzin, Norman K.
1970 *The Research Act.* Chicago: Aldine.

Drietzel, Hans
1970 *Recent Sociology No. 2.* New York: Macmillan.

Dunning, Eric
1972 *Sport: Readings from a Sociological Perspective. Toronto:* University of Toronto Press.

Foote, Nelson N.
1951 "Identification as the Basis for a Theory of Motivation." *American Sociological Review,* XVI (February) pp. 14–21.

Garfinkel, Harold
1967 *Studies in Ethnomethodology.* Englewood Cliffs, N.J.: Prentice-Hall.

Goffman, Erving
1959 *The Presentation of Self in Everyday Life.* Garden City, N.Y.: Doubleday Anchor.
1963 *Encounters.* New York: Bobbs-Merrill.

Gordon, Chad, and Kenneth Gergen
1968 *The Self In Social Interaction,* Vol. 1. New York: John Wiley and Sons.

Hughes, Everett C.
1958 *Men And Their Work.* Glencoe; Ill.: Free Press.

Kuhn, Manford, and Thomas McPartland
1954 "An Empirical Investigation of Self-Attitudes." *American Sociological Review*, Vol. 19 (February) pp. 68–76.

Manis, Jerome G., and Bernard N. Meltzer
1972 *Symbolic Interaction: A Reader in Social Psychology*. Boston: Allyn and Bacon.

Mills, C. W.
1940 "Situated Actions and Vocabularies of Motive." *American Sociological Review*. Vol. V (December) pp. 904–913.

Preiss, Jack
1968 "Self and Role in Medical Education." Chapter 19 in *The Self in Social Interaction*, Vol. 1, Chad Gordon and Kenneth Gergen (eds.). New York: John Wiley and Sons.

Stone, Gregory P.
1970 "Wrestling—The Great American Passion Play." In *Sport: Readings from a Sociological Perspective*, Eric Dunning. Toronto: University of Toronto Press (1972) pp. 301–335.
1970 "Appearance and the Self." In *Social Psychology Through Interaction*, Gregory P. Stone and Harvey A Faberman (eds.). Waltham, Mass.: Ginn-Blaisdell, pp. 394–414.

Strauss, Anselm
1959 *Mirrors and Masks*. Glencoe, Ill.: The Free Press.

Zijderveld, Anton
1970 *The Abstract Society*. Garden City, New York: Doubleday Anchor.